WINDOWS SYSTEM PROGRAMMING

Peter Wilken and Dirk Honekamp

Abacus
A Data Becker Book

First Printing

Printed in U.S.A.

Edited by: Gene Traas, Louise Benzer, Robbin Markley

ISBN 0-55755-116-2

Table of Contents

1 Windows 3 - The New Standard

Microsoft Windows 3 provides many new visual and interface capabilities for the PC user. Windows 3 is more than just a flashy graphics-based release of a product that has been on the market for several years. Windows 3 represents an entirely new programming environment for the MS-DOS programmer - even the 640K limit may be broken.

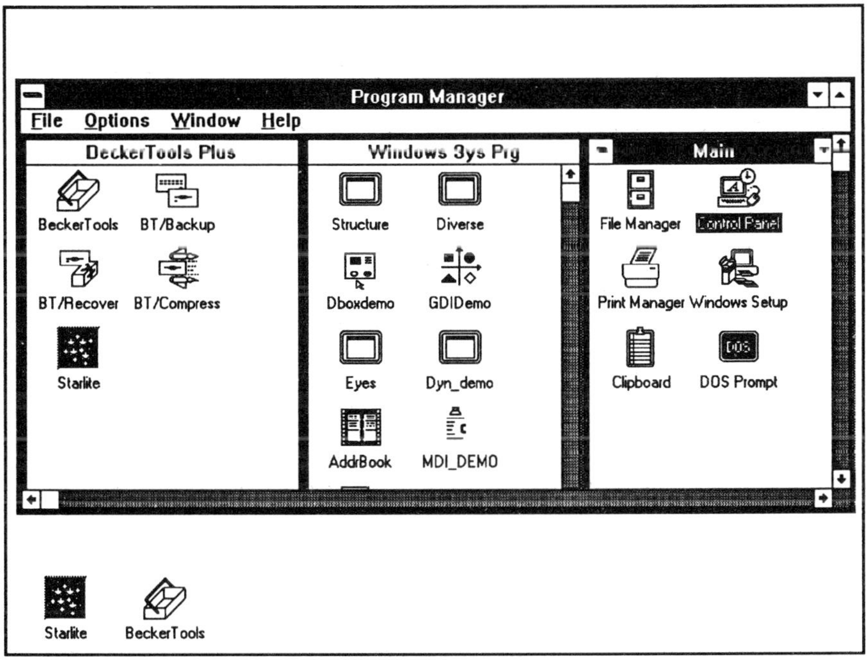

Below is a brief description of the important features that are available in this new environment:

True multitasking

Windows 3 finally offers true multitasking. This means that the operating system divides available CPU time between all applications running on the system. The user can easily select which application he/she wants in the foreground by clicking a mouse button.

Virtual DOS machines

By using Protected Mode, several standard MS-DOS applications can be run in parallel. Protected Mode places each application in its own virtual 8086 environment, with 600K or more RAM available to each application. These MS-DOS applications can run either in full screen mode or in their own windows. The Windows virtual DOS machines compare quite favorably to even the compatibility boxes of OS/2. Only Version 2.0 of OS/2, which will support the 80386 processor, can offer comparable capabilities.

Cut & Paste

You are probably already familiar with the cut and paste capabilities of most Windows applications. Now it's also possible to use Windows to transfer data between many "older" MS-DOS applications.

Windows 3 looks and feels a lot like OS/2's Presentation Manager (PM). An object-oriented File Manager and Program Manager, the ability to handle multiple documents and three-dimensional control icons simplify using a computer. This graphic user interface can also be used on PCs that have been installed as LAN workstations. In these instances, the File Manager would support network drives, network printers and even network print queues.

Three-in-one

Windows 3 works with all 80x86 processors, unlike its predecessor Windows 2.xx. When you start Windows 3, you can use a switch to set the desired operating mode. The supported modes are Real Mode (/R), Standard Mode (80286 Protected Mode, /2 or /S) and 80386 Enhanced Mode (/3). Windows 3 is intended to be run on a machine that has an 80286 or more powerful processor.

Virtual memory management with demand paging

When in 80386 Enhanced Mode, the memory manager uses *demand paging*. This allows you to run applications that require more memory than is physically available on your system. This is accomplished by removing parts of the program, that are not being used, from memory and writing them to *swap files* on hard disk in 4K blocks. When part of the program that was written to disk is needed, it is swapped back into memory.

Other performance features, such as dynamic data exchange (DDE) between applications, indicate the direction in which software development under Windows is heading. Multifunction packages seem to be losing popularity. It seems that future demand will be for powerful specialized packages that can make their capabilities and data available to other packages.

For example, you could use Microsoft Word for word processing and Microsoft Excel for creating spreadsheets, and then combine data from both packages into a single document. Both packages have flexible DDE capabilities.

This book will focus on the problems that programmers of Windows applications may encounter. We start with an introduction to the basic philosophy of Windows. You'll read about terms such as *object oriented programming*. Programmers that have never worked with a graphic user interface before should feel comfortable with the many C examples.

After you have finished reading this book, you should be able to develop your own compatible Windows applications that utilize the many special features offered by this unique environment. This will be extremely important in the future, because only those applications that are fully compatible and make the best use of the Windows environment will survive.

Development tools

In order to develop a Windows application, you will need:

- A Microsoft C compiler. We use Microsoft C Version 6.0 and the Professional Development System (PDS).
- The Microsoft Software Development Kit (SDK). We use SDK Version 3.0.

Microsoft C

The C compiler comes with several files:

- Executable files: The CL.EXE compiler, the LINK.EXE linker.
- The standard library files, which handle the different memory models: ?LIBCE.LIB (? is S, L or M, depending on the memory model). We use the SLIBCE.LIB file.
- The include (.H) files such as DOS.H and CONIO.H.

SDK

The Microsoft Software Development Kit (SDK) adds new files for Windows programming. Among these files, you will find:

- The executable files: A linker (LINK.EXE or LINK4.EXE), a resource compiler (RC.EXE), the CodeView debugger (CVW.EXE), FONTEDIT.EXE and SDKPAINT.EXE.

Installation

To insure an optimal configuration, we recommend that you first install Microsoft C, then install the SDK in a separate directory. We have installed Microsoft C Version 6.0 in the D:\C600 directory, and the SDK Version 3.0 in the D:\WINDEV directory. We then configured the system as follows using the AUTOEXEC.BAT file:

```
PATH C:\DOS;C:\WINDOWS;D:\C600;D:\C600\BIN;D:\C600\BINB;D:\WINDEV;
     D:\WINDEV\INCLUDE;D:\WINDEV\INCLUDE\SYS
SET LIB=D:\WINDEV\LIB;D:\C600\LIB
SET INCLUDE=D:\WINDEV\INCLUDE;D:\C600\INCLUDE
SET HELPFILES=D:\C600\HELP\*.HLP
SET INIT=D:\C600\INIT
```

Program layout

The program lines are printed in this book flush with the left margin so that we could show single program lines as single printed lines as much as possible. Here's an example of program code, the way you will see it in this book:

```
/*******************************************************************************
 E X A M P L E

 This is an example of left flush program code as it appears in the Abacus book

 WINDOWS SYSTEM PROGRAMMING.
*******************************************************************************/
```

Please note

This book is not a tutorial on using Microsoft Windows, the Windows Software Development Kit (SDK) or Microsoft C. Before attempting to compile or edit the programs in this book, make sure that your environment variables and path are configured for proper program compilation (see your SDK and Microsoft C documentation for details).

2 Windows Application Basics

What are the differences between Microsoft Windows and MS-DOS, or between Windows and other typical PC operating systems? One important feature offered under Windows is *multitasking*.

2.1 Windows and the Operating System

Multitasking terms

First let's discuss some elements of multitasking and the terms describing them. A *multitasking environment* is an environment that allows several programs (also called *applications*) to run at the same time on the same system. Each program is called a *task*. Tasks can be different applications or a single application running more than once on the same system. When the same program is running more than once on a multitasking system, each occurrence of the program is called an *instance*.

It may seem strange to run the same application more than once on the same system, but this allows you to have the same program process different sets of data simultaneously. For example, you may be working with a C listing in your text editor when you encounter an Include file that you would like to view while you work on the C listing. With multitasking, you can start a second instance of the text editor program to view the Include file while keeping the C listing on screen with the other instance. By switching between the two tasks, you can work with both files without having to close one file and open the other.

Scheduling

Operating systems handle multitasking in different ways. In most cases, one process called the *scheduler* controls how the processor time is divided among the other tasks that are currently running. Remember that, even with a multitasking operating system, the processor can still only execute a single machine language command at any given time. The scheduler gives each task a slice of processor time for the execution of its program code, and then control passes to the next task (assuming another is waiting). Only one task can be processed at any given time, while the other tasks remain in a waiting state.

UNIX and multitasking

Different operating systems have different ways of implementing a multitasking scheduler. UNIX uses an algorithm that gives each *process* (UNIX's word for task) a certain amount of processor time. This means that the operating system (or more specifically, the *kernel*) is responsible for task switching.

Windows and multitasking

Windows uses a different principle to control multitasking: The individual applications themselves determine when the processor is free for the next task. If an application does not give up the processor, the other tasks cannot be processed and the system locks up. This method of task switching (called *non-preemptive* multitasking) is controlled with *messages* and the *message loop* that underlies the heart of Windows. The term message is very important for understanding the way Windows works. We'll discuss messages in more detail later in this chapter.

Graphic Device Interface (GDI)

Another characteristic of Windows is the use of a special graphic interface. Windows does not use a text-based screen, which is normally used on a PC. All output is done in graphics mode. A special part of the Windows system, called the Graphics Device Interface (GDI), handles this output. The GDI contains a library of routines that are used by Windows and by other applications for graphics and text output. These routines operate using device context (also called display context or DC), which is a Windows mechanism for controlling (driving) physical output devices such as printers, screens, plotters, etc. This allows the developer to create applications independent of the output devices controlled by the system. From the programmer's point of view, the use of graphics routines such as these is fairly common.

The primary differences between developing programs for MS-DOS and developing programs for Windows are in the *message concept* and *resource management*. Let's first examine how *resources* are managed under Windows.

Resources

Handle is a term used in object-oriented programming in general, as well as in Windows programming. A handle enables you to access an object in the system even if you don't know very much about it. You may think that it's easier to call objects directly (e.g., using the addresses of the objects). However, there's a reason for calls using handles. Windows views objects as resources, which can be windows, device contexts, graphic objects, etc. These resources are stored in the computer's memory. To make the most effective use of the computer's memory, the Windows memory manager will sometimes move objects to other memory locations, or even delete them. But, if an application accessed a resource by its address, the application would have trouble finding a resource that had been moved by the memory manager.

To avoid this, the application uses special Windows routines to retrieve a handle for the desired resource. Internal to Windows, handles are represented as 16 bit numbers. Windows then ensures that a given handle always points to the proper object, even if the memory manager shifts that object around in memory. The memory manager keeps track of the current memory address. Using handles is very different from the traditional methods of PC memory management and memory addressing.

Sharing, defining and linking resources

Let's take a look at *resource sharing* and *code sharing*. Windows views the following objects as resources: Strings, bitmaps, icons, cursors, menus, fonts, dialog boxes, and other special data. These are managed by separate program codes under Windows. The programmer must define these objects in the resource file, which is identified by an .RC file extension. The alternative is to directly embed character strings in the program code. The resource file can then be compiled using the resource compiler RC.EXE, and the resulting .RES file can then be added to the .EXE executable file using the linker.

By separating the program code from the resources, you don't have to re-link files if the resources need changing. All you have to do is recompile the resource file and insert it in the .EXE file.

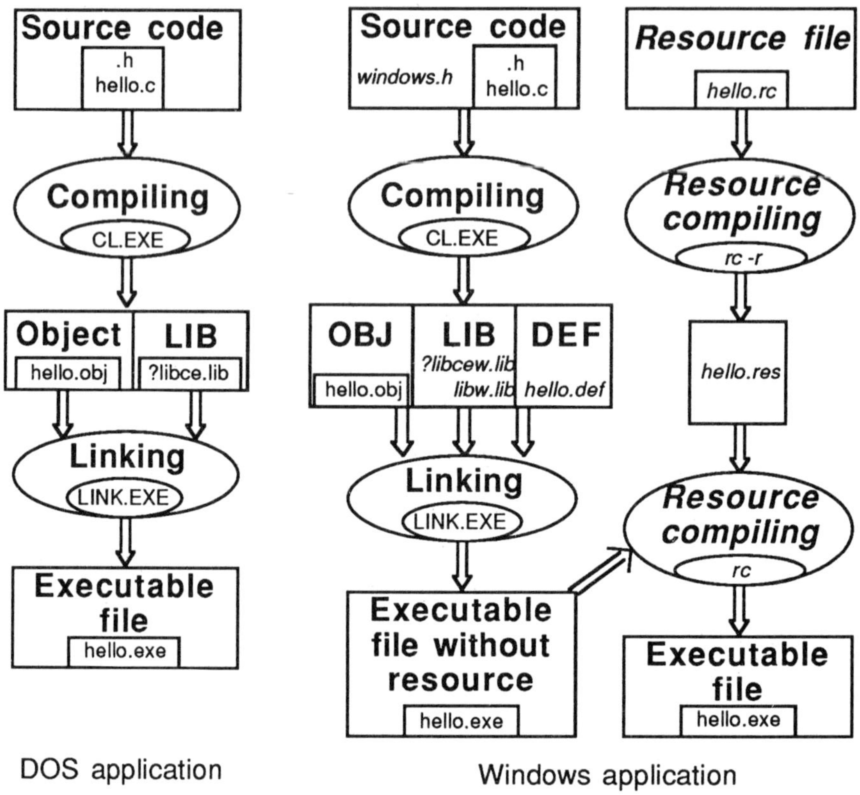

Generating DOS and Windows applications

Sharing and memory use

From the beginning, the entire Windows system was designed to use the system's main memory economically. This is why applications will usually load resources as needed (the *load on demand* or *demand-load* principle). In general, the term *sharing* refers to the use of the same object by more than one user. With resource sharing, several applications can use the same resource without having to load that resource more than once. This can save much memory—a precious commodity when running more than one application at a time. In general, any object defined as read-only can be shared.

Code sharing means that more than one task uses a given program code segment. This is particularly useful when running multiple instances of the same program. In that case, all instances can share the same code segment to access the program code, while still using individual data segments to access different data files.

The module definition file, identified by a .DEF file extension, provides a way to define Windows' use of its sharing features. This file allows you to set a number of options that define how the code sharing and data sharing for a particular application will work. We will discuss the exact structure of this file in detail later.

Hardware independence

Another advantage of Windows is hardware independence. Windows was developed in such a way that the application programmer doesn't need to worry about the hardware configurations of the systems that will run the application. For example, the programmer does not need to know if the user's system will have a CGA, EGA or VGA video adapter, or whether the user's printer is a 9-pin dot matrix or a PostScript laser printer. Windows acts as an interpreter between the application and the hardware connected to the system, thus achieving hardware independence. However, the programmer must follow certain rules to maintain hardware independence:

1) He or she must never try to "bypass" Windows and address hardware directly. The Windows 3.0 Software Development Kit (SDK) contains a number of routines for things such as screen output or addressing the serial port. These SDK routines should always be used when developing Windows applications.

2) Direct hardware addressing could cause synchronization problems in the multitasking environment. Think of the hardware as a collection of resources.

Elements of Windows

The idea of a full graphic user interface is something quite new for those users who are used to the command line interface of MS-DOS. As the name indicates, all output under Windows is done in various windows on the screen. You can have one large window that occupies the entire screen, or a number of smaller windows. This allows you to take full advantage of the multitasking environment by having several applications or instances running at once. You can use the Windows interface to link a wide variety of applications and perform data transfers that would be impossible under other user interfaces.

Menus and mouse

Along with windows, there are menus that make it easier to work with your programs. Menus and windows can be controlled with a mouse. Although you can also use the keyboard, the mouse is the quickest and most convenient way to communicate in Windows.

2.2 Windows Application Structure

A programmer writing a Windows-compatible C program for the first time will often be surprised at how much overhead is required. The "overhead" refers to the amount of code involved. The source listing at the end of this chapter contains over 200 lines. If you deleted all the commentary we've included, the amount of coding needed is overwhelming, even for a simple task like displaying a line of text on the screen. Make no assumptions about program size when developing—most likely the source code will be considerably larger than you might expect.

Another surprise in coding a Windows program is the order of functions and statements in the program. This order is quite different from the strictly sequential order you may have learned in other languages. Sequence is important in Windows programming.

Before we create our first C program, let's look at the basic requirements for programming under Windows. There are certain conventions, including standards for types, variables and functions in your C source code.

2.3 Standard Notation

Many programmers will use a prefix with a variable to make the name meaningful. Variables usually begin with lowercase letters which denote the data type of the variable. Here's a list of the most frequently used prefixes:

Prefixes

Prefix	Meaning
b	Boolean Variable (only two states are possible: 0 or 1, FALSE or TRUE etc.).
c	Character Variable (1 byte).
dw	Long Unsigned Integer (32 bit value).
f	Flag Variable (16 bit value).
h	General Handle (16 bit value).
n	Short Integer (16 bit value).
l	Long Integer (32 bit value).
lp	Long Pointer (32 bit value).
lpsz	Long Pointer to a character string ending in '\0' (32 bit value). The abbreviation stands for "long pointer string zero(-terminated)".
p	Short Pointer (16 bit value).
pt	Two-Dimensional Coordinates with x and y values stored in a long integer (32 bit value).
rgb	RGB Color Values (32 bit value).
sz	Short Pointer to a character string ending in '\0' (16 bit value). The abbreviation stands for "string zero(-terminated)".
w	Short Unsigned Integer (16 bit value).

In addition to the usual C types such as int, short, etc, there is a number of Windows-specific types that are intended to make the program code easier to read and to help make applications programmed for Windows more compatible. These additional types are defined in the include file WINDOWS.H, which we will examine in detail later. The following table lists the most commonly used Windows types:

Windows types

Type identifier	Meaning
BOOL	Boolean 16 bit value.
BYTE	Unsigned 8 bit value.
char	Signed 8 bit value (also ASCII characters).
DWORD	Unsigned 32 bit value.
far or FAR	Tells the compiler to use a long pointer (32 bit address).
HANDLE	General Handle (16 bit value).
HDC	Handle for a device context (16 bit value).
HWND	Handle to a window (16 bit value).
int	Signed 16 bit value.
long or LONG	Signed 32 bit value.
LPINT	Long pointer to type int.
LPSTR	Long pointer to a character string.
near or NEAR	Tells the compiler to use a short pointer.
PINT	Short pointer to type int.
PSTR	Short pointer to a character string.
short	Signed 16 bit value.
WORD	Unsigned 16 bit value.
void or VOID	Indicates that a function does not return a value.

Another point to remember when creating variable and function names is that each word or word fragment in the name should start with a capital letter. This makes it much easier to determine the meaning of the name at a glance. For example, the following would stand for an integer variable that defines the maximum width of a character string:

```
int nMaxCharWidth
```

Or the following would represent an SDK function for sending messages:

```
SendMessage
```

Although this syntax may take time to learn, after you use it for a while you'll see that it makes the program code for your Windows applications easier to read. This is helpful for both yourself and anyone else who may have to work with your code.

2.4 Application: STRUCTUR.EXE

For the rest of this chapter, we'll take you step by step through the development of a simple Windows C program. This program, STRUCTUR.C, will be the basis for most of the more complex programs that are used as examples in this book.

When compiled, STRUCTUR.C simply displays the line "Hello there, Windows" in the main window on your screen, followed by the number of the current instance of the program. As already mentioned, this simple program has a lot of overhead. Some of this overhead includes extensive commentary, which will help you understand the program.

As you read through STRUCTUR.C, we'll explain a number of new concepts used in the source code.

2.4.1 Basic structure of the main program

First, let's take a look at the overall structure of our simple program. Then we can analyze it piece by piece. The first levels of the program can be described graphically, using the following box:

Main program structur.c
Include files
Variables
Function prototypes
Main function WinMain()
Initialization function InitFirstInstance()
Window function MainWndProc()
Paint function PaintStructur()

2.4.2 Include files

We mentioned include files earlier. The file WINDOWS.H is always included in a Windows program.

The include file WINDOWS.H is part of the SDK. This file is very large (over 100K) and contains Windows-specific type definitions, declarations, macros, etc. You can use #define statements to exclude certain parts of this file, which decreases your compile time. As a general rule, the first line of your program should be:

```
#include <windows.h>
```

The second line includes a string handling file:

```
#include <string.h>
```

After this, you can specify the program-specific include files. For our example program STRUCTUR.C, we will need the corresponding include file STRUCTUR.H. So our third line of program code will be:

```
#include "structur.h"
```

This program-specific include file contains only one line:

```
#define IDS_APPLNAME 1
```

2.4.3 Variables

This part of a Windows program is similar to variable declarations found in many other C programs. The global program variables are declared. This section of STRUCTUR.C will look like the following:

```
HANDLE hInst;                                  // Instance of application
HWND   hwMain;                                 // Main window
char   szApplName[20];                         // Application name
char   szMessage[] = "Hello there, Windows"; // Message to be displayed
int    nInstanceCount;                         // Marker for current
                                               // instance
```

hInst acts as a global counter for the instance of the application. hwMain is assigned as the handle for the main window. The name of the application is stored in the STRINGTABLE section of the resource file STRUCTUR.RC. This is the usual place for storing the character strings used by a Windows program. The program then invokes the LoadString function whenever a string is needed.

2.4.4 The resource file STRUCTUR.RC

```
#include "structur.h"
STRINGTABLE
BEGIN
  IDS_APPLNAME, "Structure" ; Application name
END
```

IDS_APPLNAME is defined in the include file STRUCTUR.H.

The LoadString function has the following structure:

```
int LoadString (HANDLE   hInstance, // Instance of application
                unsigned StringID,  // ID of string in the RC file
                LPSTR    lpszBuffer // Buffer to which the string is copied
                int      nLength);  // Maximum number of characters to copy
```

The returned value gives the number of characters actually copied. In our program, this function loads the string from the resource file into the szApplName variable:

```
LoadString(hInstance, IDS_APPLNAME, (LPSTR)szApplName, 20);
```

To show that character strings can also be defined directly within Windows programs, we use the variable szMessage. We assigned the string "Hello there, Windows" to szMessage. The last variable in this section is nInstanceCount, which counts the current instance of the application.

This program can be run in multiple concurrent instances under Windows. Each time the program is started, the value of nInstanceCount is assigned using the GetInstanceData function. GetInstanceData is a useful function for obtaining information, about the current instance, from the data segment.

The GetInstanceData function has the following format:

```
int GetInstanceData (HANDLE hInstance, // instance number from which the data
                                       // will be copied
                     NPSTR  pData,     // pointer to the destination variable
                     int    nCount);   // maximum number of bytes to copy
```

The value returned provides the actual number of bytes copied. In our program, we will use this function as follows:

```
GetInstanceData(hPrevInstance, (PSTR) &nInstanceCount, sizeof(int));
```

2.4.5 Function prototypes

Prototyping a function means declaring only the return value type(s), name(s) and the parameter(s) passed in the function header. The compiler supports prototyping by checking for errors in the function call.

The compiler can even correct certain errors in the prototyped function call with an automatic casting. You must include a function prototype in your program in the following cases:

- The function is used or is called by another function before it is defined in the main function WinMain().
- A C library function is used but the corresponding include file was not linked.

You should always declare all the functions used in your programs, with the exception of WinMain(), as prototypes. Here is the prototyping section of our program STRUCTUR.C:

```
/* ----------------------< Function prototypes >----------------------- */

int  InitFirstInstance (HANDLE ,HANDLE, int);
LONG FAR PASCAL MainWndProc (HWND, unsigned, WORD, LONG);
void PaintStructure (HWND);

int  sprintf (char *, const char *, ...);
```

2.4.6 The Windows main function WinMain()

The WinMain() function, which serves as the main function of a Windows program, is similar to the main() function of a normal C program. Windows uses WinMain() function as its entry point into a Windows program. The WinMain() function has the following basic structure:

Main function WinMain()
Local variables
Initialization of the first instance
Initialization of additional instances
Initialization of all instances
Message loop
WM_QUIT Message received: End of program

Like any other function, WinMain() can use local variables. The STRUCTUR.EXE application uses the variable msg, which stores messages. We will discuss msg in more detail later in this chapter.

The first instance of the application is initialized in WinMain() by calling the InitFirstInstance function. This is where we load the name of the application from the resource file as described above and initialize the instance counter with a value of 1. The main window type for the STRUCTUR.EXE application is also recorded. The following statement in the WinMain() function prevents further instances of the program from repeating this initialization:

```
{
  if (!InitFirstInstance(hInstance, hPrevInstance, nCmdShow))
    ...
}
else                              // Initialization of multiple instances
{
    ...
}
```

If a value other than 0 is returned for the handle of the previous instance, then the "else" clause is executed. Since we use the GetInstanceData function to get information on additional instances, it is not necessary to repeat this initialization. All other actions will be carried out for all instances of the program.

In our example, the hInstance parameter of the WinMain() function is copied to the global variable hInst. The CreateWindow function opens a new window on the screen for each new instance of the program.

Next, the message loop of the WinMain() function will be processed until a WM_QUIT message is received to end the program. Since the message concept used by Windows is very important, we will explain it in detail in the next subsection.

2.4.7 The Windows message concept

MSG data structure format

Windows uses messages to manage and synchronize multiple applications. External events, such as mouse movements, keyboard input, etc., can also be converted to messages by the Windows event handlers. The format for a message as defined in the include file WINDOWS.H is as follows:

```
typedef struct tagMSG {
   HWND  hwnd;     // window that will receive the message
   WORD  message;  // message type
   WORD  wParam;   // 16 bit parameter
   LONG  lParam;   // 32 bit parameter
   DWORD time;     // time in ms
   POINT pt;       // mouse position
} MSG;
```

MSG is defined as a structure with six *fields*. The fields that are of importance to us are hwnd, message, wParam and lParam. These are special because they are passed, in this order, as parameters to window functions.

A message does not exist on its own—it is always associated with a window. The hwnd field in the MSG data structure is the handle for this window. The message field defines the message types, which are declared in the include file WINDOWS.H. They all start with WM_ (for Windows Message). wParam is a message-dependent 16 bit parameter and lParam is a message-dependent 32 bit parameter. The time field shows when the message was entered in the queue (expressed in milliseconds from system start). The pt field gives the current position, in screen coordinates, of the mouse cursor.

Storing messages

Windows has an internal *system queue* that stores all I/O messages in the order in which they are received (first in first out, the FIFO principle). These messages are used to communicate between windows or between a certain window and Windows itself. Windows stores the messages in buffers and then directs them to the proper window. An *application queue* is also used to store messages for each specific application. The system queue can store a maximum of 30 messages and an application queue can store up to 8 messages. If necessary, an SDK routine can increase the maximum number of messages accepted by an application queue.

Message dispatcher

The message dispatcher manages messages under Windows. This dispatcher takes messages from the system queue and passes them to the appropriate application queue depending upon the value of the hwnd parameter. The application must then process any messages that arrive in its application queue. The following is the structure of a message loop:

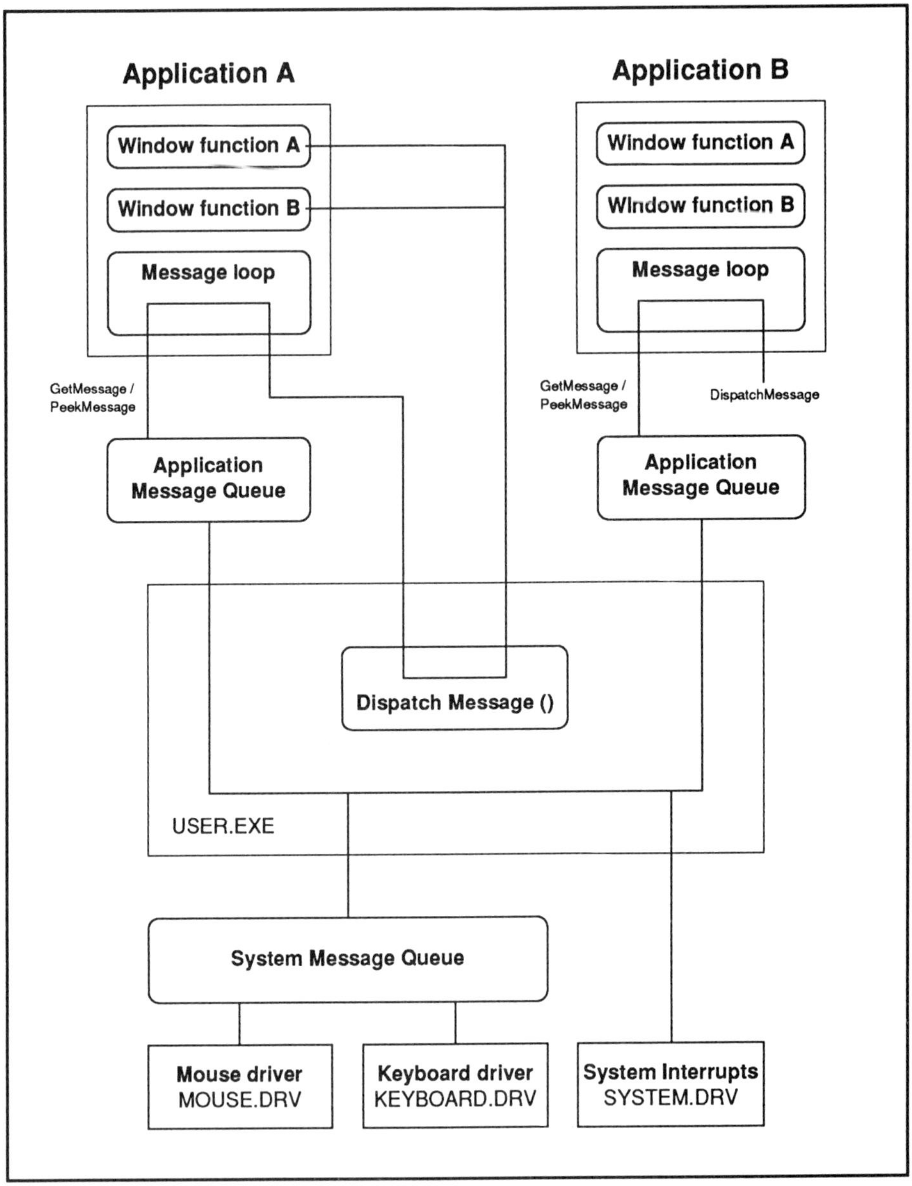

Processing mouse and keyboard inputs

Let's look at the structure of a typical message loop:

```
while (GetMessage(&msg, NULL, 0, 0)) // Message reading
{
   TranslateMessage(&msg);           // Message translation
   DispatchMessage(&msg);            // Send message to Windows
}
```

The GetMessage function checks the application message queue for messages. If a message exists, it is stored in the MSG data structure indicated by the first parameter. If no messages are found or if there are messages for other applications that have a higher priority, Windows passes control to the other application. This ensures that multitasking will continue. The second parameter indicates which window should receive the message. If this value is NULL, the message pertains to all windows. Parameters 3 and 4 can be used to limit the message to a certain type, such as keyboard or mouse messages. If these parameters are both 0, then all messages are processed. The while loop will continue to run until the GetMessage function returns a value of 0. This happens when the loop reads a WM_QUIT message from the queue. WM_QUIT tells the application to end. The application will complete any outstanding processing. The next program line passes the value msg.wParam to Windows and ends the application:

```
return (msg.wParam)
```

After the GetMessage function has retrieved a message from the queue, the first line of the while loop executes. The TranslateMessage function is called with the new message as the parameter. This function is required if you want to control the application's window with the keyboard so that it will also work without the mouse. Windows translates input from the keyboard into virtual keyboard codes. When a key is pressed, Windows sends a message containing the number of the virtual code for this key to the window that currently has the "input focus". The TranslateMessage function recognizes this type of message, converts it to the ASCII key codes and inserts the message in the application queue. Messages that do not contain any keyboard information are unaffected by the TranslateMessage function. We recommend that you always include the TranslateMessage function in the message loop of a program.

After TranslateMessage has done its job, the message is passed to the DispatchMessage function. This function is used by the message dispatcher, which was described above. The message dispatcher recognizes the window for which the message is intended and directs the message to that window.

Every window belongs to a certain window type, which defines certain characteristics that are common to all windows of this type. This principle is common in object-oriented programming. The window function is set once the window type is known. The window function processes all messages sent to windows of its type. Messages that cannot be processed by this window function are usually sent to the Windows default window function DefWindowProc.

This function examines each message it receives and then decides what action to take based on the message type. Often a message will cause DefWindowProc to generate several new messages, which create new actions.

A typical window function has the following structure:

```
LONG FAR PASCAL WindowProc (HWND hWnd, WORD message, WORD wParam, LONG lParam)
{

// variables and initialization


  switch (message)       // message processing
  {
    case NOTE_1:         // processes NOTE_1
      break;
    case NOTE_2:         // processes NOTE_2
      break;
    case NOTE_n:         // processes NOTE_n
      break;
    default:             // other messages are sent to the default window function
      return DefWindowProc(hWnd, message, wParam, lParam);
      break;
  }
  return (0L);
} // WindowProc
```

The type declaration of the window function as LONG FAR PASCAL is necessary for the following reasons:

1) All window functions are callback functions. This means that instead of a function of the application itself, Windows will call the function directly. This call is performed from a different code segment than the code segment where the application is located. For this reason, the full 32 bit address (segment and offset) must be used, as indicated by the word FAR.

   When using the Microsoft C compiler, the Gw compile option automatically inserts new pieces of code before and after the FAR function. These are called the prolog and epilog, and are required for initializing the data segment. There is more information about this subject in the chapter on Windows memory management (Chapter 16).

2) Windows uses the Pascal calling sequence when calling a callback function. This sequence differs from the C calling sequence in the way the function parameters are put on the stack. The C calling sequence places function parameters on the stack from right to left, which means the first on is the last off. The reason for this is that many C functions can receive a variable number of parameters. A disadvantage of this method is that the calling function must know the distance of each parameter from the stack. So, this code overhead is duplicated with each function call. The Pascal calling sequence puts the parameters on the stack from left to right. The function being called knows the distance of each parameter from the stack. Since the routine for cleaning up the stack doesn't have to be repeated, you can save some code overhead with multiple function calls. During the development of the Windows system, using the Pascal calling sequence resulted in decreasing the code overhead by 10 percent.

3) Window callback functions must return LONG values (32 bit values) as the result of message processing. The returned value is dependent upon the message type.

The four parameters passed to a window function correspond to the first four fields of the MSG data structure. Think of a window function as a filter that permits only the most important messages from the constant stream of messages and sends all other messages to DefWindowProc.

It is also important to mention that a window function (as well as all callback functions in the module definition file of the application) must be exported. This is done by listing the functions in the EXPORTS section of the .DEF file. Here's the EXPORTS section of a typical .DEF file:

```
EXPORTS                 WindowProc1 1
                        WindowProc2 2
                           ...
                        WindowProcN N
```

The EXPORTS section of the STRUCTUR.DEF file looks like this:

```
EXPORTS
            MainWndProc
```

If exporting is omitted, serious errors in the Windows system, such as a system crash with no warnings or error messages, may occur.

2.4.8 Registering window classes

After our discussion of window functions, we need to look at registering window classes. This is only necessary for windows that don't belong to any previously defined Windows window class. The predefined classes include edit boxes, buttons, list boxes, etc. These windows are classified as controls. The SDK function RegisterClass registers a window class. This function has the following format:

```
BOOL RegisterClass (LPWNDCLASS lpWndClass)
```

lpWndClass is a long pointer to a WNDCLASS data structure. This data structure contains all the information needed to characterize a window class.

Here's the format of the WNDCLASS data structure as it appears in WINDOWS.H:

```
typedef struct tagWNDCLASS
{
   WORD     style;                          // window class style
   LONG     (FAR PASCAL * lpfnWndProc) (); // pointer to window function
   int      cbClsExtra;                     // extra bytes - end of structure
   int      cbWndExtra;                     // extra bytes - end of window instance
```

```
    HANDLE    hInstance;                  // window class instance
    HICON     hIcon;                      // window class icon
    HCURSOR   hCursor;                    // window class cursor
    HBRUSH    hbrBackground;              // background color
    LPSTR     lpszMenuName;               // menu associated with window class
    LPSTR     lpszClassName;              // window class name
} WNDCLASS;
```

The style word determines the style of a window in this window class. The different styles all start with CS_ (for Class Style). Styles can be combined with an OR operator. Let's look at each of the values in this structure separately.

lpfnWndProc is a pointer to the window function assigned to the window class. The cbClsExtra value defines a certain number of extra bytes that can be appended to the end of the window class structure and reserved for special purposes. The "cb" prefix stands for "count of bytes." cbWndExtra is the number of extra bytes added to the end of each newly created window structure. hInstance is the handle for the instance of the application for which the window class is being registered. hIcon defines the icon assigned to the window class. hCursor is the handle for a cursor type. hbrBackground is a handle for a background brush. A brush is a certain bit pattern used by the GDI to paint the background of your screen. lpszMenuName is a long pointer to a character string ending with "\0". This character string assigns a menu resource for the window class. lpszClassName is a long pointer to a character string ending in "\0", that contains the name of the window class. The RegisterClass function will return a non-zero value if the window class is successfully registered. Otherwise, zero is returned.

Here are the steps required for registering a window class:

1) Define a variable of type WNDCLASS.

2) Fill in the variable fields with the desired values.

3) Call the RegisterClass function using the variable's address as a parameter.

2.4.9 Displaying windows

Now that we've learned about window classes and window functions, let's see how a window is actually created and displayed on screen. The following steps describe the procedure for creating and displaying a window:

1) Register the window class and set the window function.

2) Create the window with the CreateWindow function.

3) Use the ShowWindow function to make the window visible on screen.

4) Update the client area of the window with the UpdateWindow function.

CreateWindow sets the characteristics that determine how a window will appear on screen. You can also modify individual characteristics so that windows of the same class can differ. Here's the format of the CreateWindow function:

```
HWND CreateWindow    (lpClassName,   // window class
                      lpWindowName,  // window title
                      dwStyle,       // window style
                      X,             // x coordinate of upper left corner
                      Y,             // y coordinate of upper left corner
                      nWidth,        // window width
                      nHeight,       // window height
                      hWndParent,    // parent window of this window
                      hMenu,         // menu assigned to this window
                      hInstance,     // window instance
                      lpParam);      // parameter for WM_CREATE message
```

Here's the CreateWindow function as it appears in STRUCTUR.C:

```
hwMain = CreateWindow(szApplName,            // Window class name
                      szApplName,            // Window caption
                      WS_OVERLAPPEDWINDOW,   // window style (overlapped)
                      CW_USEDEFAULT,         // X-position (default)
                      CW_USEDEFAULT,         // Y-position (default)
                      CW_USEDEFAULT,         // Initial X-size (default)
                      CW_USEDEFAULT,         // Initial Y-size (default)
                      NULL,                  // No parent window
```

```
NULL,                          // Window menu used
hInstance,                     // Application instance
NULL);                         // No creation parameters
```

After the window has been successfully created with the desired characteristics, the CreateWindow function returns a handle for the window. This handle can then be used in other function calls.

CreateWindow creates the window, but the ShowWindow function displays the window on the screen. This function receives two parameters. The first parameter is the window handle and the second parameter determines how the window should appear. In our program, the function call looks like this:

```
ShowWindow (hwMain, nCmdShow);
```

hwMain is the main window we created with CreateWindow and nCmdShow is the fourth parameter of the main program function WinMain(). This parameter indicates whether the main window should appear full size or as an icon when the program is started.

RUN and LOAD modes

The actual value of nCmdShow depends on how the program is started from the Windows interface. If it is started from RUN mode (with a double-click, pressing the <Enter> key or by an automatic start using a RUN entry for the program in WIN.INI), nCmdShow will have the value SW_SHOWNORMAL (SW_ stands for Show Window). If it is started from LOAD mode (by pressing <Shift>+<Enter> or by using a LOAD entry for the program in WIN.INI), nCmdShow will have the value SW_SHOWMINNOACTIVE and the application's main window will be displayed as an icon. If the ShowWindow function is called again later, the previously defined SW_ value will be used instead of the nCmdShow value passed from Windows.

Updating windows

To ensure that the contents of the main window will be correct, we must receive a WM_PAINT message, which updates the contents of the client area of the window. This type of message is sent to a window whenever the contents of the client area change and must be redrawn. These messages are placed at the end of the application queue and processed only when no other messages are available. This can sometimes result in a noticeable gap between the time a certain action is performed and the time the screen is actually updated. The UpdateWindow function actually generates the WM_PAINT message and places it at the start of the queue, where it is passed immediately to the appropriate window (this process is called asynchronous message handling). UpdateWindow is called with the window handle as the only parameter.

The paint function

The paint function is required in order to process the WM_PAINT message received by the main window. In our application, the MainWndProc window function calls the PaintStructure paint function. The window handle hWnd is passed as a parameter. The paint function's first responsibility is to retrieve a display context for the client area of the window. This is done as follows:

```
hDC = BeginPaint(hWnd, &ps); // Get display context of main window
```

ps is a variable of type PAINTSTRUCT. This data structure contains various information about the current status of the client area of the window indicated by hDC (such as which regions need to be redrawn or whether the background needs to be cleared). For the moment, we are only interested in ensuring that the BeginPaint function returns a valid display context that can be used by the GDI functions that create window output.

One such GDI function is the TextOut function. This function passes text output to a display context. It will be used in our program to display the words "Hello there, Windows", followed by the current instance number. The TextOut function has the following structure:

```
BOOL TextOut (HDC   hDC,         // Handle for a display context
              int   X,           // X coordinate
              int   Y,           // Y coordinate
              LPSTR lpszString,  // Long pointer to the output character string
              int   nLength);    // number of characters to output
```

The TextOut function writes nLength characters, from the character string indicated by lpszString, at the X and Y coordinates indicated (0,0 is the upper left corner). This position is expressed in logical units instead of characters. In the standard GDI display mode, one logical unit corresponds to one screen pixel. The value returned by this function will be non-zero if the string was output successfully. Otherwise, the result is zero.

Our program writes the character string to the upper left corner of the window with:

```
TextOut(hDC, 0, 0, (LPSTR)szBuffer, strlen(szBuffer));
```

Next, the WM_PAINT message is processed by the EndPaint function. EndPaint ensures that the client area is valid and that the display context that was used is free again. It is very important to free display contexts after they are used, because only five display contexts are available in the entire Windows system. These five contexts can be used up quickly by applications running in parallel. BeginPaint and EndPaint function calls must always be paired. So, if you include a BeginPaint in a program, be sure that you also include an EndPaint function, and vice versa.

Using WM_PAINT messages to output data to a window ensures that our application is always prepared for a change in the screen contents (opening a new window or menu, changing the size of a window, etc.). Windows recognizes these changes and immediately sends a WM_PAINT message to the appropriate window. This message can be read by the window function and then sent to the paint function for processing.

2.4.10 Other files in STRUCTUR.EXE

The module definition file STRUCTUR.DEF

Earlier in this chapter we briefly described the purpose of the module definition file. This file is required by the linker LINK4 or LINK to determine certain characteristics of the application. The module definition file for our application looks like this:

```
NAME         STRUCTUR
DESCRIPTION  'Program showing the basic structure of a Windows program'
EXETYPE      WINDOWS
STUB         'WINSTUB.EXE'
```

```
CODE          PRELOAD MOVEABLE DISCARDABLE
DATA          PRELOAD MOVEABLE MULTIPLE
HEAPSIZE      4096
STACKSIZE     4096
EXPORTS
              MainWndProc
```

NAME specifies the name of the application. This value is used by Windows when the application is loaded. Other applications also use this as an identifier for the application. The name entered here should always coincide with that of the main program file assigned to the application.

DESCRIPTION is a brief comment about the application. The character string stored here is copied to the .EXE file for the application. This field is especially useful for storing copyright information.

EXETYPE Windows means that this application is intended to run under the Windows system. This tells the linker which header to use for the .EXE file. It is especially important to have the correct entry in this field when using the new LINK.EXE compiler instead of LINK4.EXE. The LINK.EXE compiler uses OS/2 mode as a default.

The value of STUB tells what code, in the .EXE file, to use when an attempt is made to load and run a Windows application under MS-DOS. Normally this field refers to the file WINSTUB.EXE, which displays the message "This program requires Microsoft Windows."

Code reading

The CODE field tells how to handle the code segments of the application. PRELOAD means that the specified code segments will already be loaded when the application is started. LOADONCALL means that the segments will be loaded as they are needed. MOVEABLE will allow the Window memory manager to move the segments around in memory if necessary. FIXED indicates that the code segments must remain in the same memory location once they're loaded. DISCARDABLE tells the memory manager that the code segments can be removed from memory if necessary.

The DATA field determines how the data segments of the application will be handled. PRELOAD and MOVEABLE have the same meaning as described above for the CODE field. MULTIPLE creates separate data segments for each instance of the application. SINGLE means that only one data segment is allowed for the application. NONE means that the application has no data segment.

HEAPSIZE determines the size of the local heap for the application. The number represents the minimum number of bytes to reserve. If available, Windows will allocate additional bytes above and beyond this minimum value.

STACKSIZE sets the size of the local stack for the application. The stack is used for such things as storing parameter values for function calls. Recursive function calls also use the stack for temporarily storing local variables. A minimum stack size of 5K is recommended. You can also use the 5K value for HEAPSIZE.

EXPORTS determines which functions can be called directly by the Windows kernel (callback functions). This includes window functions, among others. You should include an ordinal number ("@" followed by an integer) after the name of each export function. When many export functions are used, this can save storage space, because only two bytes are required to identify each function instead of the complete function name. This also accelerates access to export functions.

The MAKE file

The MAKE file STRUCTUR.MAK is required for correctly generating the Windows executable file STRUCTUR.EXE from the source codes. It contains the rules that tell NMAKE.EXE (or some other MAKE program) how to compile and link the program files. Our MAKE file has the following structure:

```
Model  = S
Warn   = 2

ALL: structur.exe

structur.res: structur.h structur.rc
  rc -r structur.rc

structur.obj: structur.h structur.c
  cl -c -A$(Model) -W$(Warn) -Gsw -Zpe -Os structur.c

structur.exe: structur.obj structur.def structur.res
```

```
  link /NOD /al:16 structur,structur.exe,,libw+$(Model)libcew,structur.def
  rc structur.res
```

Two variables are defined at the start of the MAKE file. Model, which is the memory model being used, is set to SMALL in this case. Warn is for the warning level of the Microsoft C compiler. Here Warn contains a value of 2. The value of a MAKE variable is accessed with $(variable).

The MAKE file consists of a target file, rules and actions. The target file is listed at the start of a line followed by a colon and then the names of the files upon which it "depends". The MAKE program compares the date and time of the files after the colon with those of the file before the colon. If one or more of these files have a date newer than that of the target file, then the actions that follow are executed up to the next empty line. This ensures that the compiler/linker does only the work that is necessary. This can save a significant amount of time, especially with large programs. Notice the following line:

```
all: structur.exe
```

This is intended for the Microsoft Professional Development System 6.0 NMAKE.EXE program. This new MAKE program is not completely compatible with the older MAKE.EXE program. The main difference is that NMAKE will process only those target files that are passed to it when it is called. Otherwise, it will only process the rules for the first target file in the MAKE file and then quit. The simplest way to change a MAKE file that was intended for MAKE.EXE so that NMAKE.EXE can use it is to enter a pseudo target file in the first line of the MAKE file. The name of the executable file for the application is given after the colon. NMAKE must then process all target files in the MAKE file in order to create the executable file.

The STRUCTUR.RES file, which is created by the resource compiler, is dependent on the files STRUCTUR.H and STRUCTUR.RC. The resource compiler is started with the -r option to create the target file. This option prevents the compiled resource file from being linked to the .EXE application file. The STRUCTUR.OBJ object file depends on the include file STRUCTUR.H and the program file STRUCTUR.C. If one of these two files is processed by

STRUCTUR.OBJ after it has been created, then the following line in the compilation procedure is executed:

```
cl -c -A$(Model) -W$(Warn) -Gsw -Zpe -Os structur.c
```

The following is a brief explanation of Microsoft C compiler options:

Microsoft C compiler options

-AS Selects the SMALL memory model. This model stores the application code in a 64K segment. This is the recommended memory model for small applications that use NEAR pointers for quick access to code and data.

-AC Selects the COMPACT memory model. This model divides the code into several 64K segments. It is usually used for programs that are relatively small but use a lot of data. The compiler uses NEAR pointers for the code and FAR pointers for access to data. This is the most common memory model among Windows applications. Even though it is not as compact as the SMALL model, it still allows the memory manager to handle the code in a single code segment, easing the division of available memory between several active programs. Using this model also requires the DATA FIXED statement in the module definition file for the application.

-AM Selects the MEDIUM memory model. This model uses several code segments and a single data segment. Each segment is 64K. It is typically used for programs that have a lot of program code but not much data. The compiler uses FAR pointers for the code and NEAR pointers for data access.

-AL Selects the LARGE memory model. This model allows multiple 64K segments for both code and data. It is used with programs that have a lot of code and require large amounts of data. The use of FAR pointers for both code and data access means that the use of this model will result in a slightly slower application. Using this model requires a DATA FIXED statement in the module definition file for the application.

-FPi Specifies the use of a coprocessor/emulator for floating point arithmetic. This option is set by default. In this mode, the coprocessor will automatically be located and used for floating point arithmetic. If no coprocessor is found, then the coprocessor commands are emulated by the software. When using this option under Windows, you should also link the library WIN87EM.LIB. When you execute the program, the file WIN87EM.EXE must also be available in the search path or the current directory.

-FPa Specifies the use of alternative floating point arithmetic. Even if they're available, coprocessors are ignored in this mode. Although the floating point arithmetic will be less exact than with the -FPi option, the application will run a little faster.

-c Creates the .OBJ file without using the link procedure.

-Gw Creates the prolog and epilog code sequences, required by Windows, before and after functions that are exported.

-Gs Turns off stack checking. Without this option, the C compiler generates code that calls a stack checking routine for every function call. If this routine encounters a stack overrun at run time, it calls the Window FatalExit debugging function. This uses a little extra storage space and the execution is somewhat slower. After your application has been fully developed and debugged, you should turn off the stack check option.

-Zp Turns on the option for the use of packed structures, which saves storage space.

-Ze Allows the recognition of keywords such as _near, _far, _pascal, etc., which in turn enables the corresponding #defines NEAR, FAR, PASCAL (default: ON).

-Zi Creates symbolic information for the Microsoft CodeView debugger.

-Os Optimizes the program according to the available storage space. By default, the C compiler will optimize for execution speed. For Windows applications, it is more important to optimize storage space and memory use.

-Od Turns off all optimization (for debugging).

The executable file for the application STRUCTUR.EXE is created with the Microsoft linker LINK4.EXE or LINK.EXE from the object files and the information in the module definition file.

The linker call to LINK(4).EXE can use direct parameters as follows:

```
link(4) <Options> object file(s),         // separated by "+" (plus sign)
                  <EXE file>,             // name of executable file
                  <MAP file>,             // debugging information
                  <Library files>,        // separated by "+"
                  Module definition file
```

Alternatively, you can specify a filename with LINK(4) @FILENAME. Any parameters are then specified on the same line. The most important linker options are:

Microsoft Linker options for LINK.EXE and LINK4.EXE:

/al(ign):nBytes
: Aligns the data segments of the EXE file in groups of nBytes. nBytes must be a multiple of two. For Windows, it is recommended to use 16 byte segments (/al:16). The default value is 512 bytes.

/co
: Tells the linker to insert symbolic information to prepare the application for debugging with the Microsoft CodeView debugger.

/map
: Creates a MAP file (file extension .MAP). This file can be transformed into a symbol file (file extension .SYM) with the MAPSYM program. The symbol file is primarily used by debuggers.

/NOE
: Stands for NO Extended Dictionary Search, which stops the linker from searching the extended dictionary. This dictionary contains a list of symbols used by the linker for internal management. The /NOE option should be used if the linker returns multiple symbol definitions as error messages.

/NOD
: Stands for NO Default Library Search, which tells the linker not to use the standard C runtime libraries for external references. This prevents functions from libraries, which aren't Windows-compatible, from being compiled. When you

use this option, you must specify the desired library names under <Library files>.

/NOI Stands for NO Ignore Case, which tells the linker to distinguish between upper and lowercase letters.

The following line compiles using the Windows Version 3.0 SDK:

```
link /NOD /al:16 structur,structur.exe,,libw+$(Model)libcew,structur.def
```

The following line compiles using the Windows Version 2.0 SDK (notice the differences from the above line because of library management):

```
link4 /NOE /al:16 structur,structur.exe,,$(Model)libw+$(Model)libcew,structur.def
```

Let's take a closer look at how Windows manages libraries.

Library management under Windows

There is a basic difference between libraries for Windows SDK functions and C runtime functions. The floating point arithmetic mode used by the application also makes a difference. The libraries for C runtime functions that are compatible with Windows have the following syntax:

```
mLIBCfW.LIB.
```

The "m" represents the corresponding memory model ("S", "M", "C", "L" for Small, Medium, Compact and Large) and the "f" represents the floating point arithmetic mode ("E" for coprocessor/emulation and "A" for alternative floating point arithmetic). The "W" after the floating point arithmetic letter identifies the corresponding library as Windows-compatible.

IMPORTANT:

Although omitting the "W" was allowed when developing applications for Windows 2.x, do not omit it from this line. Also, don't forget the /NOD option, which prevents the linker from searching runtime libraries that are not Windows-compatible.

Import libraries

The libraries for Windows SDK functions are also called Windows import libraries. Under Windows 2.x, each memory model had its own import library. These libraries used the syntax mLIBW.LIB, where "m" stood for the memory model. Under Windows 3, the functions that depend upon the memory model are stored in the C runtime libraries as previously mentioned. There is only one import library, which is called LIBW.LIB.

To complete our discussion of libraries, we must mention the dynamic link libraries (or DLLs). This subject is covered in its own chapter later in the book. Under Windows 2.x, the DLLs were identified with mWINLIBC.LIB, where the "m" stood for the memory model. Under Windows 3, DLLs are named mDLLCfW.LIB. The "m", "f" and "W" have the same meanings as they do with the C runtime libraries.

Now let's look at the last line of our MAKE file. The line:

```
rc structur.res
```

calls the resource compiler again but without the -r option. This links the resource file STRUCTUR.RES with STRUCTUR.EXE, which completes the application. The only thing left to do is start STRUCTUR.EXE under Windows. Once this is done, we've successfully created our first Windows application. The remainder of this chapter contains a listing of the source code for the STRUCTUR application.

2.5 Source Code: STRUCTUR.EXE

We've listed excerpts of the STRUCTUR.C source code throughout this chapter. Here's the complete listing of the source codes, which are required to make STRUCTUR.EXE, as they appear on the companion diskette for this book.

STRUCTUR.H include file

```
#define IDS_APPLNAME        1
```

STRUCTUR.RC resource file

```
#include "structur.h"

STRINGTABLE
BEGIN
  IDS_APPLNAME, "Structure" ; Application name
END
```

STRUCTUR.MAK MAKE file

```
Model  = S
Warn   = 2

ALL: structur.exe

structur.res: structur.h structur.rc
  rc -r structur.rc

structur.obj: structur.h structur.c
  cl -c -A$(Model) -W$(Warn) -Gsw -Zpe -Os structur.c

structur.exe: structur.obj structur.def structur.res
  link /NOD /al:16 structur,structur.exe,,libw+$(Model)libcew,structur.def
  rc structur.res
```

STRUCTUR.DEF module definition file

```
NAME         STRUCTUR

DESCRIPTION  'Program showing the basic structure of a Windows program'
```

```
EXETYPE     WINDOWS

STUB        'WINSTUB.EXE'

CODE        PRELOAD MOVEABLE DISCARDABLE
DATA        PRELOAD MOVEABLE MULTIPLE

HEAPSIZE    4096
STACKSIZE   4096

EXPORTS
           MainWndProc
```

STRUCTUR.C source code

```
/************************************************************************
STRUCTUR.C
==========

 This program demonstrates the basic structure of Windows applications. It
 displays "Hello there, Windows" and the current instance in a window.

 ************************************************************************/

/* -------------------------< Include files >---------------------------- */

#include <windows.h>
#include <string.h>

#include "structur.h"

/* -----------------------< Global variables >-------------------------- */

HANDLE hInst;                              // Instance of application
HWND   hwMain;                             // Main window
char   szApplName[20];                     // Application name
char   szMessage[] = "Hello there, Windows";  // Message to be displayed
int    nInstanceCount;                     // Marker for current
                                           // instance

/* ---------------------< Function prototypes >------------------------- */

int  InitFirstInstance (HANDLE ,HANDLE, int);
LONG FAR PASCAL MainWndProc (HWND, unsigned, WORD, LONG);
void PaintStructure (HWND);
```

```
int  sprintf (char *, const char *, ...);

/**************************************************************************
 W i n M a i n ()
 ================

 The WinMain function is the main function for every Windows program. WinMain
 is the equivalent of the main() function found in standard C programs, and
 represents the application's "point of entry" for execution.

 Parameters:

   HANDLE hInstance:     Current instance handle of the application.
   HANDLE hPrevInstance: Previous instance handle of the application. NULL
                         if the current instance is the first instance.
   LPSTR  lpszCmdLine:   Long pointer to the string placed after the program
                         name during program execution.
   int    nCmdShow:      Parameter which specifies the application window's
                         appearance when the program starts.

 Return values

   int:                  The wParam parameter for the last message received.

 **************************************************************************/

int PASCAL WinMain (HANDLE hInstance,  HANDLE hPrevInstance,
                    LPSTR lpszCmdLine, int nCmdShow)
{
  MSG   msg;                         // Message variable

  if (!hPrevInstance)                // Initialization of first instance
  {
    if (!InitFirstInstance(hInstance, hPrevInstance, nCmdShow))
      return NULL;

  }
  else                               // Initialization of multiple instances
  {

    // This is where multiple instance data would usually be listed.
    // We have added the name of the application, which is taken from
    // the resource file. In addition, the instance counter is incremented
    // by 1 for each additional instance.

    GetInstanceData(hPrevInstance, szApplName, 20);
    GetInstanceData(hPrevInstance, (PSTR) &nInstanceCount, sizeof(int));
    nInstanceCount++;
```

```
  }

  // The following section lists all executing instances. This section
  // usually specifies the appearance of the application's main window.

  hInst   = hInstance;                          // Declaration of global
                                                // instance variable

  hwMain = CreateWindow(szApplName,             // Window class name
                        szApplName,             // Window caption
                        WS_OVERLAPPEDWINDOW,    // window style (overlapped)
                        CW_USEDEFAULT,          // X-position (default)
                        CW_USEDEFAULT,          // Y-position (default)
                        CW_USEDEFAULT,          // Initial X-size (default)
                        CW_USEDEFAULT,          // Initial Y-size (default)
                        NULL,                   // No parent window
                        NULL,                   // Window menu used
                        hInstance,              // Application instance
                        NULL);                  // No creation parameters

   if (!hwMain)
     return NULL;

   ShowWindow(hwMain, nCmdShow);                // Make window visible
   UpdateWindow(hwMain);                        // Update window

  /* -------------------------< Message  loop >--------------------------- */

  while (GetMessage((LPMSG)&msg, NULL, 0, 0))   // Message reading
  {
    TranslateMessage((LPMSG)&msg);              // Message translation
    DispatchMessage((LPMSG)&msg);               // Message -> Windows
  }

  /* -------------------- < End of application > ----------------------- */

  return (msg.wParam);                          // wParam of last message
                                                // as return value
} // WinMain

/*************************************************************************
 I n i t F i r s t I n s t a n c e ()
 ====================================

 This function initializes the first instance of the "Structur" application.

 Parameters:
```

```
   HANDLE hInstance:     Current instance handle of the application.
   HANDLE hPrevInstance: Previous instance handle of the application. NULL
                         if the current instance is the first instance.
   int    nCmdShow:      Parameter which specifies the application window's
                         appearance when the program starts.
 Return values:

   int:                  NULL if the "Structur" window class registers.
                         Otherwise, a value other than NULL.

 ****************************************************************************/

int InitFirstInstance (HANDLE hInstance, HANDLE hPrevInstance, int nCmdShow)
{
  WNDCLASS MainWndClass;                    // Main window class

  /* ----------< Load application name from the resource file >----------- */

    LoadString(hInstance, IDS_APPLNAME, (LPSTR)szApplName, 20);

    nInstanceCount = 1; // Initialize instance counter with 1

  /* ---------------< Specify window class information >------------------ */

  MainWndClass.lpszClassName = szApplName;              // Window class
  MainWndClass.hInstance     = hInstance;               // Instance
  MainWndClass.lpfnWndProc   = MainWndProc;             // Window function
  MainWndClass.style         = CS_HREDRAW | CS_VREDRAW; // Horizontal and
                                                        // vertical redraw
                                                        // of client area
  MainWndClass.lpszMenuName  = (LPSTR) NULL;            // No menu
  MainWndClass.hCursor       = LoadCursor(NULL, IDC_ARROW);      // Mouse cursor
  MainWndClass.hIcon         = LoadIcon(NULL, IDI_APPLICATION); // Default icon
  MainWndClass.hbrBackground = GetStockObject(WHITE_BRUSH);
                                                        // White background
  MainWndClass.cbClsExtra    = 0;                       // No extra bytes
  MainWndClass.cbWndExtra    = 0;                       // No extra bytes

  /* --------------< Registering "Structur" window class >---------------- */

  return (RegisterClass(&MainWndClass));

} // InitFirstInstance


/****************************************************************************
 M a i n W n d P r o c ()
 ========================
```

```
 This function acts as the main window function. All messages are sent to
 this window.

 Parameters:

   HWND      hWnd:     Window handle.
   unsigned msg:       Message type.
   WORD      wParam:   Message-dependent 16 bit value
   LONG      lParam:   Message-dependent 32 bit value

 Return values:

   LONG                0L if the window function has sent the message.
                       Otherwise, the return value from the DefWindowProc
                       default window function.

 ***************************************************************************/

LONG FAR PASCAL MainWndProc (HWND      hWnd,
                             unsigned msg,
                             WORD      wParam,
                             LONG      lParam)
{
   switch (msg)
   {
     case WM_DESTROY:
       PostQuitMessage(0);                 // Send WM_QUIT if window
                                           // is destroyed
       break;

     case WM_PAINT:                        // Client area redraw needed
     PaintStructure(hWnd);
       break;

     default: // Pass other messages to the default window function

       return (DefWindowProc(hWnd, msg, wParam, lParam));
       break;
   }
   return 0L;
} // MainWndProc

/***************************************************************************
 P a i n t S t r u c t u r e ()
 ==============================

 This function redraws the client area of the main window.
```

```
Parameter:

  HWND    Wnd:      Window handle.

Return values:      None.

****************************************************************************/

void PaintStructure (HWND hWnd)
{
  PAINTSTRUCT ps;
  HDC         hDC;
  char        szBuffer[80];

  hDC = BeginPaint(hWnd, &ps); // Get display context of main window

  sprintf(szBuffer, "%s, Instance %d", szMessage, nInstanceCount);

  // Display the message "Hello there, Windows" and the current instance

  TextOut(hDC, 0, 0, (LPSTR)szBuffer, strlen(szBuffer));

  EndPaint(hWnd, &ps);
} // PaintStructure
```

3 Text Output

In the previous chapter, we learned about the basic structure of an executable Windows program. Although the application STRUCTUR.C is a complete program, its only purpose is to display a line of text and the instance number on the screen. In this chapter, we'll add to the framework created in Chapter 2.

This chapter examines the more extensive capabilities that Windows provides. Specifically, we'll see how several lines of text are formatted and sent to the client area of a window. This isn't as easy as it sounds because Windows uses a different screen layout from the usual PC screen configuration of 25 lines by 80 columns. If you were using the C screen, you'd simply send the text to the screen using the printf function.

Client area

The client area is the part of the window where output appears. This area has the following characteristics, which you must keep in mind when developing programs:

- The client area is divided into pixels.
- The client area has no "standard" size. Windows can change in size at any time.
- Standard C I/O library functions (printf, puts, etc.) do not apply to the client area.

Formatted text display in a client area requires some logical structure.

Text lines that must be scrolled either vertically or horizontally (i.e., no longer fit completely in the client area) require special handling. Windows provides two ways to control this—the mouse and the keyboard.

Scrolling with the keyboard and mouse

Scrolling with the keyboard (one page up, one page down, etc.) is similar to other text editors and word processors. You can also use the mouse to activate the *scroll bars* on the right and bottom borders of the window to scroll the window contents.

A good application will always allow the user to scroll text with both the keyboard and the mouse. In this chapter, we'll create an application that demonstrates the output of multiple text lines and the use of the scrolling functions. This application is called DIVERSE.C, for the diverse features it includes.

Before taking a closer look at this program, we need to discuss some other areas of Windows in detail.

ANSI and OEM fonts

In this chapter you'll learn how to select a certain font in a display context. The application will allow you to choose between the ANSI (Windows default) and OEM (DOS) fonts. These two fonts display special characters differently.

Menus

Windows provides menus to help users execute commands and other actions that are available within an application. The menu bar, which appears at the very top of a window, lists the top level items or menu titles. The top level menu is usually divided into several submenus or popup menus. Each submenu can contain simple menu items used to execute certain actions or they can contain items which open up additional popup menus.

Menu items

Each popup menu can then contain simple menu items or additional popup menus. The latter feature, which is new to Windows 3, allows you to create cascading or nested menus. A nested menu is activated by clicking on the small right arrow next to the name of the menu item. The new menu will then open next to the corresponding menu item.

3.1 Application: DIVERSE.EXE

Now that you have some background information, we can discuss the source code for the application DIVERSE.C. As you'll see, we've taken the basic functions from STRUCTUR.C and expanded them. Also, several new functions have been added to perform additional tasks.

The basic objective of this program is to display multiple lines of text in a window. We will use the source code DIVERSE.C as the text. This file will be loaded from the current directory and displayed in the client area of the main window.

To do this, we need a function that loads a file from the hard drive:

```
int ReadFile (PSTR szFileName);
```

The parameter szFileName is a char pointer to the name of the file that is to be loaded. The result of the ReadFile function is the number of lines that were read. ReadFile reads text files that end each line with the character combination CR (Carriage Return, 0x0D) and LF (Line Feed, 0x0A). Here is the statement that opens the file for access in text mode:

```
FilePointer = fopen(szFileName, "rt");
```

In this mode, the CR/LF combination is translated to a single line feed as the file is read. This procedure is reversed for write operations.

3.1.1 Using a message box

If the specified file cannot be opened, a message box notifies the user of the problem:

```
if (!FilePointer)                              // No file opening
{
  MessageBox(GetFocus(), "File could not be opened", szApplName,
             MB_OK | MB_ICONEXCLAMATION);
  return 0;
}
```

A message box is a type of popup window. The easiest way to display a message box is with the MessageBox function:

```
int MessageBox (HWND hWnd, LPSTR lpszText, LPSTR lpszCaption, WORD wType);
```

Handles to windows and input focus

hWnd is the window assigned the *input focus* after the message box closes. Windows uses the input focus mechanism to indicate which window will receive input from the mouse and keyboard. We have set the window handle equal to the result of the GetFocus function. This function provides an easy way to determine which window currently has the input focus.

lpszText is a long pointer to the text that is to be displayed within the message box. lpszCaption is a long pointer to the character string used for the message box title. If this parameter is NULL, a default title is displayed. wType is an OR combination of several values.

These values determine which buttons and bitmaps will be used within the message box. The most important values are:

MB_OK	Displays an "OK" button
MB_YESNO	Displays a "Yes/No" button
MB_ICONEXCLAMATION	Displays an exclamation point
MB_ICONQUESTION	Displays a question mark
MB_ICONHAND	Displays a hand

By using an OR operator these values can be combined with either of the following flags:

MB_APPLMODAL	Application modal message box No additional input is allowed for the application until this message box is closed
MB_SYSTEMMODAL	The entire Windows system will not accept any input until this message box is processed

The result of the MessageBox function is one of the following values, which is determined by the button the user selects to exit the message box:

IDOK	"OK" button was selected
IDCANCEL	"Cancel" button was selected
IDYES	"Yes" button was selected
IDNO	"No" button was selected
IDABORT	"Abort" button was selected
IDIGNORE	"Ignore" button was selected

If the result is null, then there is no memory available to the message box.

Message boxes can be used to notify the user of errors or to ask the user for confirmation before executing a certain action.

3.1.2 The mouse cursor

Before we actually read the text from the file, we will create a cursor that informs the user that Windows is performing an action that will require some time and that the user should wait before attempting any other input:

```
SetCursor(LoadCursor(NULL, IDC_WAIT));          // Hourglass cursor
```

The LoadCursor function expects two parameters. The first is type HANDLE, which gives the instance of the application whose .exe file contains the cursor resource to be loaded. The second parameter is a long pointer to the character string that contains the cursor name. If the instance handle parameter is NULL, then a default value for the Windows cursor type can be used. Common cursor types include:

IDC_ARROW	Arrow cursor (the default cursor)
IDC_BEAM	Vertical line for text input
IDC_CROSS	Cross-hair cursor
IDC_WAIT	Hourglass (timer) cursor

The SetCursor function uses the cursor handle, that's returned by the LoadCursor function, to set the system cursor. After all of our text lines have been loaded, we reset the system cursor to the standard arrow cursor:

```
SetCursor(LoadCursor(NULL, IDC_ARROW));         // Restore arrow
```

The lines read by the fgets function are stored in the global field TextArray. The line number serves as the index to this field. Each line can contain up to MAXLINELENGHT characters. Unfortunately, this static method of storing text isn't the most effective.

Line lengths

Since each line is given a fixed length, the field will require a predetermined amount of memory regardless of how much text is actually in each line. This kind of text field can reach the 64K limit (the maximum size of a data object without using a HUGE declaration) very quickly. You can avoid wasting storage space with this type of data structure by using one of Window's dynamic memory allocation functions. However, we won't discuss this now; a later chapter will cover Windows memory management in detail.

When the ReadFile function encounters a file that is longer than MAXLINES, the additional lines are not read.

This function is called in the following section of the MainWndProc function:

```
case WM_COMMAND:                    // Messages from menu bar
  switch (wP)
  {
    case MI_LOADFILE:               // Load file
      nTextLines = ReadFile("diverses.c");
      if (nTextLines)
      {
        // Set scroll range
        SetScrollRange(hWnd, SB_VERT, 0, nTextLines - 1, TRUE);
        ...
        ...
```

3.1.3 Menu basics

A file is loaded by selecting the **Load File** item from the **File** popup menu. Here is the complete listing of the DIVERSE.RC resource file:

Resource file DIVERSE.RC

```
#include <windows.h>
#include "diverse.h"
STRINGTABLE
BEGIN
  IDS_APPLNAME, "Diverse" ; Application name
END
```

```
MainMenu MENU
BEGIN
  POPUP "&File"
  BEGIN
    MENUITEM "&Load File",      MI_LOADFILE
    MENUITEM SEPARATOR
    MENUITEM "E&xit", MI_QUIT
  END
  POPUP "&Options"
  BEGIN
    MENUITEM "&Display Line Numbers", MI_LINENUMBERS
    MENUITEM "&ANSI Display",       MI_ANSI
  END
END ; MainMenu
```

We read about the STRINGTABLE section in the previous chapter. Next comes the definition of the main menu:

```
MainMenu MENU
BEGIN
 ...
END
```

The POPUP "&File" statement defines the **File** menu. The name given after POPUP will appear as the menu title in the menu bar. The "&" symbol indicates that the "F" in the menu title will be underlined. By pressing the <Alt> key and the underlined letter, the user can activate the menu item from the keyboard. The lines between the BEGIN and END statements contain the individual menu items. This section has the following structure:

```
MENUITEM "Character String", MI_ITEMIDENTIFIER
```

Letters from the "Character String" can also be underlined with the "&" character. MI_ITEMIDENTIFIER is an integer value normally defined in an include file. Our menu item identifiers are defined in the file DIVERSE.H:

Include file DIVERSE.H

```
#define IDS_APPLNAME    1
/* File menu    */
#define MI_LOADFILE     100
#define MI_QUIT         101
/* Options menu */
#define MI_LINENUMBERS  110
```

```
#define MI_ANSI          111
```

Under Windows 3, a popup menu can contain other popup menu definitions in place of or in addition to the MENUITEMS. This nesting of popup menus results in the cascading menu systems described above.

By defining a menu in the resource file of an application, the structure is set and the compiled menu is contained in the .EXE file. The menu is not automatically used by the application, however. To do this, you must also explicitly load a menu resource:

```
hMenu = LoadMenu(hInstance, "MainMenu");
```

This statement loads a menu resource from the .EXE file of the instance using the instance handle hInstance and returns a handle for the menu. If the menu is already loaded, the handle is returned directly to the already available menu. In case of an error, NULL is returned.

In our program, we use the result of the LoadMenu as a parameter for the CreateWindow function, which creates the main window for the application. After the "MainMenu" menu is assigned to the main window hwMain, all messages for the "MainMenu" menu are directed to the window function for this window, MainWndProc. When the user clicks on a menu item, Windows generates a WM_COMMAND message. The wParameter parameter of this message will contain the menu item identifier for the selected menu item. The window function is then able to evaluate which menu item was selected in the switch (wP) branch:

```
switch (wP)
{
  case MI_LOADFILE:               // Load file
    nTextLines = ReadFile("diverse.c");
         ...
```

At this point, the filename is "hard coded" into the application. When we learn about edit boxes, we will see how we can allow the user to enter the filename. After the file is successfully loaded, the next step is to display the text on screen. In the next section we'll describe some of the basics we will need to know before we can accomplish this.

3.1.4 Scroll bars

The value returned by the ReadFile function - the number of text lines read—is used to set the scroll region:

```
// Set scroll range
SetScrollRange(hWnd, SB_VERT, 0, nTextLines - 1, TRUE);
```

To understand the scroll region, you must first know a little about scrolling under Windows. In Windows you can assign horizontal and vertical scroll bars with the WS_VSCROLL and WS_HSCROLL flags in the window style parameter of the CreateWindow function. The vertical scroll bar, which is displayed on the right edge of the window, is used for scrolling up and down. The horizontal scroll bar, which is located on the bottom edge of the screen, is used for scrolling right and left.

Scroll bars and thumbs

Using a mouse is often the only way a user can scroll the window contents. The current position in the document is indicated by the location of the thumb (sometimes called the scroll box) in the scroll bar. You can click on this thumb and drag it anywhere within the scroll bar to move to a new location within the document. You can also click either above or below the thumb to move a fixed distance through the document (usually one screen page). The horizontal scroll bar works the same way for scrolling to the right and left. You can also move the thumb by clicking on the arrows at either end of one of the scroll bars.

Windows generates a corresponding message for each of the actions executed above. These messages are sent to the window function for the window. A WM_VSCROLL message is generated for vertical scrolling and a WM_HSCROLL message is generated for horizontal scrolling. As is often the case with Windows messages, the message type is encoded in the wParameter parameter. The information in parentheses in the following table refers to the horizontal scroll bar.

Scroll messages

Contents of wParam	Meaning
SB_TOP	Thumb is in upper (left) end
SB_BOTTOM	Thumb is in lower (right) end
SB_LINEUP	Generated when up (left) arrow is clicked
SB_LINEDOWN	Generated when down (right) arrow is clicked
SB_PAGEUP	Generated when scroll bar is clicked above (left of) the thumb
SB_PAGEDOWN	Generated when scroll bar is clicked below (right of) the thumb
SB_THUMBPOSITION	Generated when thumb is moved. Current position is in the low Word of lParam
SB_THUMBTRACK	Generated as thumb is being moved Current position is in the low Word of lParam
SB_ENDSCROLL	Generated when mouse button is released

SB_TOP and SB_BOTTOM are not generated by the scroll bars of normal windows. These messages are generated when using dialog boxes (more on this later).

These messages are read by the WM_SCROLL branch of the MainWndProc function without considering SB_THUMBTRACK and SB_ENDSCROLL. Since this program is intended for demonstration purposes only, WM_SCROLL messages weren't used. However, you should try adding this option yourself as an exercise.

```
case WM_VSCROLL:
  switch (wP)
  {
...
    case SB_LINEUP:
    {
      if (nTopLine > 0)
         --nTopLine;
      break;
    }
    case SB_LINEDOWN:
    {
      if (nTopLine > nTextLines - 1)
         ++nTopLine;
      break;
    }
    ...
```

The processing continues by taking the TopLine variable, which determines where the first line of text will be output, and incrementing or decrementing it by a certain value.

For scrolling actions that involve an entire page (SB_PAGEUP, SB_PAGEDOWN), the logical line counter is incremented or decremented by the number of lines in the window minus 1. The screen contents are then updated with a WM_PAINT message at the end of the WM_SCROLL branch:

```
// Create WM_PAINT message after clearing client area.
InvalidateRect(hWnd, NULL, TRUE);
```

The paint function PaintDiverse is described later in this chapter (see Section 3.1.5).

It is important to know that Windows only generates messages and creates the graphic display of the scroll bars on screen. All other actions must be programmed; the programmer must also determine how the messages are to be evaluated.

More about scroll range

Let's return to setting the scroll range, which is a logical representation of the actual size of the document using the length of the scroll bars (from top to bottom, SB_TOP to SB_BOTTOM). In our program, we use the following to set the upper end of the scroll bar equal to the first line of the text in the file and the lower end of the scroll bar equal to the last line of text:

```
SetScrollRange(hWnd, SB_VERT, 0, nTextLines - 1, TRUE);
```

The index for the first line is 0.

If the upper and lower scroll limits (the third and fourth parameters) of the SetScrollRange function are set to the same value, then the scroll bar won't be visible.

The last parameter of the SetScrollRange function indicates whether the scroll bars should be redrawn after the scroll range is set (TRUE or FALSE).

3.1.5 The WM_PAINT message

Once Windows knows the size of our document, it must be displayed in the client area. To do this, we will use the same mechanism we used to process the WM_VSCROLL message—we will create a WM_PAINT message by calling the InvalidateRect function.

```
// Redraw client area
InvalidateRect(hWnd, NULL, TRUE);
```

The hWnd parameter provides the window handle used in the function call. The second parameter is of type LPRECT. It represents a long pointer to a rectangular region of the client area that has been declared invalid. An invalid region of the client area is one that requires complete or partial repainting. Windows internally maintains a list of all invalid rectangular regions.

Processing a WM_PAINT message

When a WM_PAINT message is processed, the update region is taken to be the sum of all of the invalid regions in the client area. This allows Windows to identify only those regions that absolutely need to be repainted. This can save a lot of time because repainting a complex graphics display can be complicated. If the second parameter in this function call is NULL, then the entire client area is considered invalid. The third parameter tells Windows whether to clear the update region (TRUE) or not (FALSE) before repainting.

When a WM_PAINT message is processed, we can access the update region and other information about the client area using the fields in a variable of type PAINTSTRUCT. This structure is filled by calling the BeginPaint function. The definition of the PAINTSTRUCT data type from the file WINDOWS.H is given below:

```
typedef struct tagPAINTSTRUCT
{
  HDC   hdc;
  BOOL  fErase;
  RECT  rcPaint;
  BOOL  fRestore;
  BOOL  fIncUpdate;
  BYTE  rgbReserved[16];
} PAINTSTRUCT;
```

Handle to display context

hdc is a handle to the display context of the window that needs complete or partial repainting. This is the same handle that is returned by the BeginPaint function. fErase indicates whether the background of the update region should be cleared (TRUE) or not (FALSE). rcPaint is the rectangle that contains the update region. Under Windows, a rectangle of type RECT consists of the upper left corner (rcPaint.left, rcPaint.top) and the lower right corner (rcPaint.right, rcPaint.bottom). The other three parameters (fRestore, fIncUpdate, and rgbReserved) are required by Windows for internal management functions.

The WM_PAINT message created by InvalidateRect is processed with the PaintDiverses function. Here, we use the same procedure we have seen before to get the handle to the display context of the main window and to fill the variable ps (type PAINTSTRUCT):

```
hDC = BeginPaint(hWnd, &ps);
```

Next, the font is set according to the value of the Boolean variable bANSIFont:

```
// set desired font
if (bANSIFont)
  hOldFont = SelectObject(hDC, GetStockObject(ANSI_FIXED_FONT));
else
  hOldFont = SelectObject(hDC, GetStockObject(OEM_FIXED_FONT));
```

3.1.6 Selecting character tools

Under Windows, fonts are selected in a display context using the SelectObject function. This function has two parameters:

- The first parameter for this function call is the handle to the display context, from which an object is selected. Objects selectable within a display context are bitmaps, brushes, fonts, pens and regions.

- The second parameter is a handle to the object that is to be selected. We use the GetStockObject function to retrieve a handle to a font or some other Windows standard defined resource. The parameters for the GetStockObject function are short integer index values that are defined in the WINDOWS.H include file.

OEM and ANSI

If ANSI_FIXED_FONT is used as the index value, GetStockObject will return a non-proportional ANSI font. If you wanted to display special characters or foreign language letters, you can pass the OEM_FIXED_FONT index value to the GetStockObject function to return a handle to the OEM non-proportional font.

Let's return to our discussion of the SelectObject function. The new object selected replaces the object previously contained in the display context. The "old" object is not lost, however, since SelectObject returns a handle to it as a result. Since we will want to re-select the original font within the display context after the text output to the client area is complete, this handle is stored in the hOldFont variable. This is accomplished with the following excerpt from the code:

```
// Select original font in display context
SelectObject(hDC, hOldFont);
```

The following excerpt from MainWndProc sets bANSIFont:

```
case MI_ANSI:
  hMenu = GetMenu(hWnd);
  if (bANSIFont)
  {
    bANSIFont = FALSE;
    CheckMenuItem(hMenu, MI_ANSI, MF_UNCHECKED | MF_BYCOMMAND);
  }
  else
  {
    bANSIFont = TRUE;
    CheckMenuItem(hMenu, MI_ANSI, MF_CHECKED | MF_BYCOMMAND);
  }
  InvalidateRect(hWnd, NULL, TRUE);
  break;
```

3.1.7 More on menus

When you select the menu item "ANSI Display" from the popup menu "Options", the window function MainWndProc receives a message, of type WM_COMMAND, with the value MI_ANSI in the wParam parameter. First you must get a handle to the menu associated with the main window. To do this, the window handle is passed to the GetMenu function and the handle to the window's menu is returned as the result.

Next, we will check the current value of the bANSIFont variable and change it.

We will want to indicate the new contents of the font variable in the popup menu. To do this, Windows allows us to use checkmarks to indicate which menu items are currently active. A checkmark next to a menu item indicates that it is currently "on", or active. Items without checkmarks are not currently active. The application itself is responsible for ensuring that the checkmarks are properly set and updated. This is done with the help of the CheckMenuItem function:

```
BOOL CheckMenuItem (HMENU hMenu, WORD wCheckItem, WORD wMode);
```

hMenu is a handle to the menu that contains the items to be checked. wCheckItem is either the menu item ID (if wMode == MF_BYCOMMAND) or an index that starts with 0 and indicates the position of the menu item of interest within the menu (if wMode == MF_BYPOSITION). wMode is an OR combination of the bits in two of the four flags MF_BYCOMMAND, MF_BYPOSITION, MF_CHECKED and MF_UNCHECKED. MF_CHECKED means that the menu item has been assigned a checkmark and MF_UNCHECKED indicates that the checkmark has been removed. The function result returns the previous state of the menu.

Checkmarks

So that Windows knows how to display the menus, the checkmarks for the menu items must be explicitly set before the main window is first drawn. Windows uses a WM_CREATE message to do this. This message is sent to the window shortly before it appears on screen to initialize the checkmarks. This part of our program looks like this:

```
switch (msg)
{
  case WM_CREATE:                         // For creating window
    hMenu = GetMenu(hWnd);
    bLineNumbers = FALSE;
    bANSIFont = FALSE;

    // Store Options menu items
    EnableMenuItem(hMenu, MI_LINENUMBERS, MF_GRAYED | MF_BYCOMMAND);
    EnableMenuItem(hMenu, MI_ANSI, MF_GRAYED | MF_BYCOMMAND);
    break;
```

We start by getting a handle to the main menu. Then, the variables bLineNumbers and bANSIFont are set to FALSE. We have already seen bANSIFont. The bLineNumbers variable indicates whether or not line numbers should be displayed with the text output. Then, the EnableMenuItem function displays the **Display Line Numbers** and **ANSI Display** menu items in gray.

Although menu items cannot be selected when they're displayed in gray, they are still listed so that the user can see which items the menu contains. These menu items will become available again after the user has loaded a file in the TextArray field. The EnableMenuItem function, which performs this task, is called as follows:

```
BOOL EnableMenuItem (HMENU hMenu, WORD wCheckItem, WORD wMode);
```

This function is similar to the CheckMenuItem function. hMenu is again a handle to the menu that contains the menu item of interest. wCheckItem is either a menu item ID (if wMode == MF_BYCOMMAND) or an index value (if wMode == MF_BYPOSITION). wMode can be an OR combination of the following values:

MF_ENABLED	Menu item enabled
MF_DISABLED	Menu item disabled
MF_GRAYED	Menu item grayed (and disabled)
MF_BYCOMMAND	wCheckItem represents a menu item ID
MF_BYPOSITION	wCheckItem represents a menu item index

The result of this function gives the previous status of the menu. After a file has been loaded, the two menu items we mentioned above can be selected again:

```
EnableMenuItem(hMenu, MI_LINENUMBERS, MF_ENABLED | MF_BYCOMMAND);
EnableMenuItem(hMenu, MI_ANSI, MF_ENABLED | MF_BYCOMMAND);
```

3.1.8 TEXTMETRIC: Font information

Now that we have learned something about how to handle menu items, let's return to our discussion of WM_PAINT. The last thing we did was to select a new font in the display context of the main window. In order to output text using different fonts, we will need certain information about the size of each character. This information is obtained with the GetTextMetrics function.

```
// get information about current text font
GetTextMetrics(hDC, &tm);
```

As its first parameter, GetTextMetrics requires a handle to the display context whose font will be used to output the text. The second parameter is of type LPTEXTMETRIC. This is a long pointer to a TEXTMETRIC data structure. We pass the address of the TEXTMETRIC variable tm to the function, which stores the desired information in the fields of this structure. The TEXTMETRIC data structure is defined in the include file WINDOWS.H. Although it contains 20 fields, only a few of these are important to our work with fonts:

tm.tmHeight	Height of the tallest character in the font
tm.tmAveCharWidth	Average character width
tm.tmMaxCharWidth	Width of the widest character in the font
tm.tmExternalLeading	Recommended spacing between lines
tm.tmInternalLeading	Spacing used for accents or other special symbols within a character

Each of the fields listed above is of type short integer.

The height of a text line is taken as tm.tmHeight plus the recommended line spacing for the font (tm.tmExternalLeading).

```
// Compute height of one line of text
nLineHeight = tm.tmHeight + tm.tmExternalLeading;
```

3.1.9 Setting window dimensions

After we have established the height of a line of text for the current font, we can calculate how many text lines will fit in the client area. However, first we must call a function that will provide the information we need about the size of the client area:

```
// Get client area dimensions
GetClientRect(hWnd, &rRect);
```

The first parameter is a handle to the window that owns the display context. As a second parameter, the function expects a variable of type LPRECT, which is a long pointer to a RECT variable. All we need to do is pass the address of the RECT variable rRect and then rely on the automatic casting of the C compiler, which knows the prototypes of the SDK API (Applications Interface) functions contained in the WINDOWS.H include file. This saves us the work of doing the casting ourselves and helps cut down on errors.

If the address of a bad structure is given, the compiler returns a warning message. There are no warnings given when explicit castings are in error. The GetClientRect function returns the dimensions of the client area in client area coordinates. These are given relative to the upper left corner of the window that contains the client area. The upper left corner of the RECT structure (rRect.left, rRect.top) is (0,0) in this case. rRect.right is the width and rRect.bottom is the height of the client area in pixels:

```
// Compute number of screen lines
nScreenRows = rRect.bottom / nLineHeight;
```

Next, we check to determine whether the scroll bars need to be displayed or if all of the text will fit in the space available within the client area:

```
// Do we really need scroll bar display?
if (nScreenRows >= nTextLines)
  ShowScrollBar(hWnd, SB_VERT, FALSE); //No
else
  ShowScrollBar(hWnd, SB_VERT, TRUE);  // Yes
```

The SetScrollBar function either displays (TRUE) or suppresses (FALSE) the scroll bars.

After this, the actual output of the text lines begins. The vertical position of the beginning of each line is the product of the line index and the line height:

```
nYPos = i * nLineHeight;
```

If the variable bLineNumbers is TRUE, then the line numbers are displayed at the beginning of each line with one empty space between them and the start of the text. To do this, we must also calculate the length of the line number string:

```
// Compute line number length plus a space in pixels
nOffset = LOWORD(GetTextExtent(hDC, (LPSTR)szLineNr,strlen(szLineNr)));
```

The GetTextExtent function returns information on the height and width of a character string:

```
DWORD GetTextExtent (HDC hDC, LPSTR szLineNr, int szLineNr);
```

hDC is the display context that contains the font that is to be used in the calculations. lpText points to the character string and nLength gives its length. The result of this function is formatted so that the low word contains the length and the high word contains the width of the string. We can easily access either word in a DWORD variable using the LOWORD or HIWORD macros of the API:

```
nLowWord  = LOWORD(dwVariable); // access the low word
nHighWord = HIWORD(dwVariable); // access the high word
```

3.1.10 Text output: TextOut & DrawText

After the string's length has been calculated, the line number is displayed with the TextOut function:

```
// Line number display
TextOut(hDC, nXPos, nYPos, szLineNr, strlen(szLineNr));
```

Now we must display the contents of the text line itself. We use the DrawText function for this rather than TextOut. DrawText, which is somewhat more complex than TextOut, has the following format:

```
int DrawText (HDC hDC, LPSTR lpText, int nLength, LPRECT lpRect, WORD wFormat);
```

hDC is a handle to the display context. lpText is a long pointer to a character string that must end with "\0" if the following nLength parameter is -1. Otherwise, nLength gives the length of the lpText string. lpRect is a long pointer to a RECT variable. This variable describes the rectangle within which the function will format and output the text line. wFormat is an OR combination of the bits from various flags that determine the format of the character string. The most important formats for wFormat are:

DT_CENTER	Centered string
DT_EXPANDTABS	Expanded tab stops (replaced by specified number of spaces (default=8)
DT_LEFT	Left-justified string
DT_NOCLIP	Text clipping disabled
DT_NOPREFIX	Disables prefix function that uses an "&" character to underline the following character
DT_RIGHT	Right-justified string
DT_SINGLELINE	Carriage returns and line feeds ignored
DT_WORDBREAK	Enables word break function so that words which cannot be completely displayed within the output rectangle are carried over to the next line

The DrawText function interprets the carriage return and line feed characters as line break symbols if the DT_SINGLELINE option is not selected.

The next step is to calculate the output rectangle for the line of text:

```
// Compute output rectangle for the text line
SetRect(&rLineRect, nXPos + nOffset, nYPos, rRect.right,
        nYPos + nLineHeight);
```

Setting rectangle coordinates

The SetRect function turns four coordinate values into a rectangle. The left side of the rectangle is the sum of the starting x coordinate nXPos and the line number length nOffset. The top side is the vertical output position nYPos, which we have already calculated. The right side is the same as the right side of the client area and the bottom side is calculated by adding the starting vertical position and the line height.

The text line is output to the rLineRect rectangle using DrawText as follows:

```
// Display text line, expand tabs
DrawText(hDC, TextArray[nTopLine + i], -1, &rLineRect,
         DT_EXPANDTABS | DT_NOPREFIX);
```

With longer lines (especially when the line number option is used), the text may be cut off at the right edge of the window. This is called clipping. The window contents are clipped so that complex graphics displays do not get wrapped around themselves. DrawText will normally clip the text within the limits of the output rectangle. If the DT_NOCLIP option is selected, the clipping function is shut off and the text output will be slightly faster.

3.1.11 Scrolling with mouse or keyboard

Finally, we must reposition the thumb in the scroll bar to reflect the new position within the file:

```
// New thumb position
SetScrollPos(hWnd, SB_VERT, nTopLine, TRUE);
```

The SetScrollPos function moves the thumb to the position specified with nTopLine. The fourth function parameter indicates whether the scroll bar should be redrawn (TRUE) or not (FALSE) after a change. The value returned by the function gives the previous position of the thumb.

The EndPaint function declares the update region of the client area as valid again and the display context is freed.

Next, we will look at the keyboard interface that allows us to control scrolling from the keyboard. Windows sends a WM_KEYDOWN message to tell us when a key has been pressed. These messages are evaluated in the window function MainWndProc as follows:

```
// The following routines allow scrolling with the keyboard.
case WM_KEYDOWN:                      // Key pressed

  // Pass virtual keycodes
  switch (wP)
  {
    case VK_UP:                       // Cursor up
      PostMessage(hWnd, WM_VSCROLL, SB_LINEUP, 0L);
      break;
    case VK_DOWN:                     // Cursor down
      PostMessage(hWnd, WM_VSCROLL, SB_LINEDOWN, 0L);
      break;
    case VK_PRIOR:                    // Page up
      PostMessage(hWnd, WM_VSCROLL, SB_PAGEUP, 0L);
      break;
    case VK_NEXT:                     // Page down
      PostMessage(hWnd, WM_VSCROLL, SB_PAGEDOWN, 0L);
      break;
    case VK_HOME:                     // HOME key
      PostMessage(hWnd, WM_VSCROLL, SB_TOP, 0L);
      break;
    case VK_END:                      // END key
      PostMessage(hWnd, WM_VSCROLL, SB_BOTTOM, 0L);
```

```
            break;
        default:
            return (DefWindowProc(hWnd, msg, wP, lP));
            break;
    }
```

When a WM_KEYDOWN message is received, the wParam parameter will contain the value that identifies the virtual keyboard code for the key that was pressed. These values always begin with VK_ (for Virtual Key). For example, VK_UP stands for the <PageUp> key on a PC. When we have captured the keyboard codes that are used for scrolling, we generate a message that we send to ourselves (the MainWndProc function). This is done with the help of the PostMessage function, which has the following format:

```
BOOL PostMessage (HWND hWnd, unsigned msg, WORD wParam, LONG lParam);
```

hWnd is the window that will receive the message. msg, wParam and lParam are identical to the normal window function parameters with the same names. The result of the function indicates whether the message could be sent (TRUE) or not (FALSE). The PostMessage function places the message at the end of the window's message queue. SendMessage is another function for sending messages. It has the same parameters as PostMessage. However, instead of placing the message in the queue, SendMessage calls the window function directly as a subprogram.

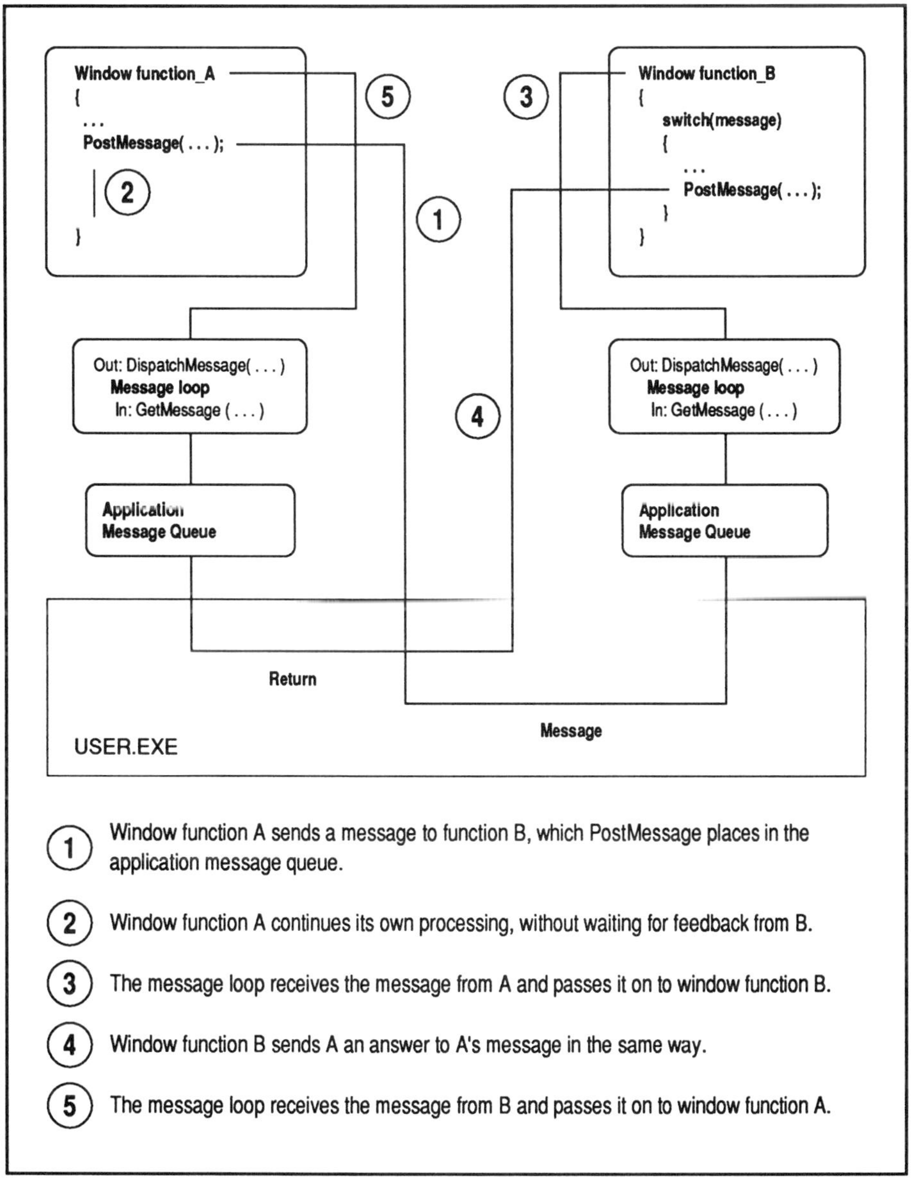

Sending a message with PostMessage()

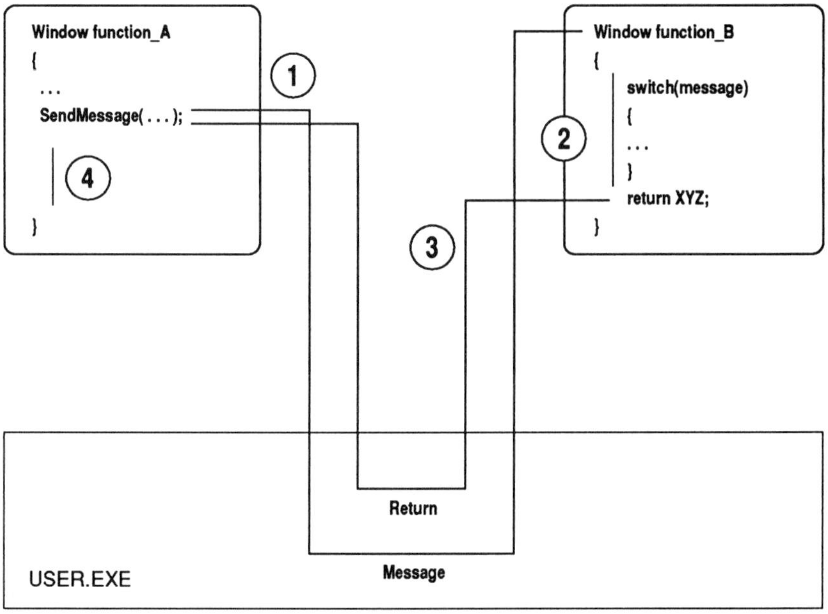

(1) Window function A sends a message to function B.

(2) Window function B receives the message from A and processes it.

(3) Window function B finishes processing and returns XYZ to A.

(4) Window function A has received a return from B and continues its own cycle.

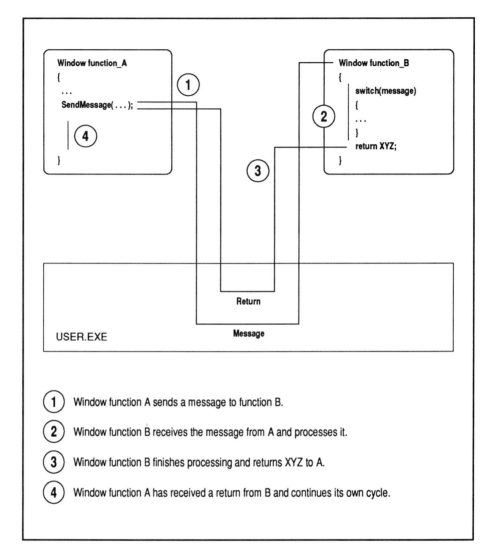

Sending a message with SendMessage()

The MainWndProc function receives the scrolling message, which will be identical to one generated by scrolling with the mouse.

Now we will look at how the menu item "End program" is handled. The code for this is in the following excerpt from the MainWndProc function:

```
case MI_QUIT:                           // end program
   PostMessage(hwMain, WM_SYSCOMMAND, SC_CLOSE, 0L);
   break;
```

The PostMessage function is also used here. First, we generate a WM_SYSCOMMAND message, which is usually sent from Windows to an application when the system menu is addressed in some way. If the wParam parameter is SC_CLOSE, this indicates that the user double-clicked on the system menu field, selected the "Close" item or pressed <Alt> + <F4>. By sending this message to the main window, we can simulate these actions and exit the application.

3.2 Source Code: DIVERSE.EXE

We'll end this chapter with listings of the module definition file, the MAKE file and the source code needed to compile the DIVERSE.EXE application.

DIVERSE.DEF module definition file

```
NAME          DIVERSE

DESCRIPTION   'Program showing miscellaneous Windows features'

EXETYPE       WINDOWS

CODE          PRELOAD MOVEABLE DISCARDABLE
DATA          PRELOAD MOVEABLE MULTIPLE

HEAPSIZE      4096
STACKSIZE     4096

EXPORTS
              MainWndProc @1
```

DIVERSE.MAK MAKE file

```
Model = S
Warn   = 2
Linker = link

all: diverse.exe                    ; pseudo-target for NMAKE.EXE

diverse.res: diverse.h diverse.rc
  rc -r diverse.rc

diverse.obj: diverse.h diverse.c
  cl -c -A$(Model) -W$(Warn) -Gsw -Zpe -Os diverse.c

diverse.exe: diverse.obj diverse.def diverse.res
  $(Linker) /NOD /al:16 diverse,diverse.exe,,libw+$(Model)libcew,diverse.def
  rc diverse.res
```

DIVERSE.C source code

```
/***************************************************************************
 DIVERSE.C
 =========

 This program expands upon the basic principles outlined in the "structur.c"
 application, and describes some new subjects:

 1) Simple menus
 2) Displaying multiple-line texts
 3) Screen scrolling
 4) Font specification
 5) Message boxes
 6) Simple file operations
 7) Interpreting keyboard input

 ***************************************************************************/

/* --------------------------< Include files >--------------------------- */

#include <windows.h>
#include <stdio.h>                              // FILE definition
#include <string.h>
#include <stdlib.h>
#include <io.h>

#include "diverse.h"

/* -----------------------------< Defines >------------------------------ */

#define MAXLINES        550                     // Max. number of text lines
#define MAXLINELENGTH   90                      // Max. line length

/* ------------------------< Global variables >-------------------------- */

HANDLE hInst;                                   // Instance of application
HWND   hwMain;                                  // Main window
char   szApplName[20];                          // Application name
char   TextArray[MAXLINES][MAXLINELENGTH];      // Text line array
char   szFileName[MAXLINELENGTH];               // Filename
int    nTopLine = 0,                            // Top screen row
       nTextLines,                              // Number of lines read
       nScreenRows;                             // Max. number of screen rows
BOOL   bLineNumbers,                            // Line number flag
       bANSIFont;                               // ANSI or OEM font flag
```

```
/* ----------------------< Function prototypes >------------------------ */

int  InitFirstInstance (HANDLE ,HANDLE, int);
int  ReadFile (PSTR);
LONG FAR PASCAL MainWndProc (HWND, unsigned, WORD, LONG);
void PaintDiverse (HWND);
int  sprintf (char *, const char *, ...);

/***********************************************************************
 W i n M a i n ()
 ================

 The WinMain function is the main function for every Windows program. WinMain
 is the equivalent of the main() function found in standard C programs, and
 represents the "point of entry" for program execution.

 Parameters:

   HANDLE hInstance:     Current instance handle of the application.
   HANDLE hPrevInstance: Previous instance handle of the application. NULL
                         if the current instance is the first instance.
   LPSTR  lpszCmdLine:   Long pointer to the string placed after the program
                         name during program execution.
   int    nCmdShow:      Parameter which specifies the application window's
                         appearance when the program starts.

 Return values:

   int:   The wParam parameter for the last message received.
 ***********************************************************************/

int PASCAL WinMain (HANDLE hInstance,  HANDLE hPrevInstance,
                    LPSTR lpszCmdLine, int nCmdShow)
{
  MSG msg;                          // Message variable

  if (!hPrevInstance)               // Initialization of first instance
  {
    if (!InitFirstInstance(hInstance, hPrevInstance, nCmdShow))
      return NULL;

  }
  else                              // Initialization of multiple instances
  {
    // Placement of application names from previous instances
    GetInstanceData(hPrevInstance, szApplName, 20);
  }
```

```
  hInst  = hInstance;             // Declaration of global
                                  // instance variable

  hwMain = CreateWindow(szApplName,               // Window class name
                        szApplName,               // Window caption
                        WS_OVERLAPPEDWINDOW |
                        WS_VSCROLL,               // Window style (overlapped)
                        CW_USEDEFAULT,            // X-position (default)
                        CW_USEDEFAULT,            // Y-position (default)
                        CW_USEDEFAULT,            // Initial X-size (default)
                        CW_USEDEFAULT,            // Initial Y-size (default)
                        NULL,                     // No parent window
                        LoadMenu(hInstance, "MainMenu"),
                        hInstance,                // Instance of application
                        NULL);                    // No creation parameters

   if (!hwMain)
     return NULL;

   ShowWindow(hwMain, nCmdShow);                  // Make window visible
   UpdateWindow(hwMain);                          // Update window

  /* ------------------------< Message loop >---------------------------- */

  while (GetMessage((LPMSG)&msg, NULL, 0, 0))    // Message reading
  {
    TranslateMessage((LPMSG)&msg);                // Message translation
    DispatchMessage((LPMSG)&msg);                 // Message -> Windows
  }

  /* -------------------- < End of application > ---------------------- */

  return (msg.wParam);                            // wParam of last message
                                                  // as return value
} // WinMain

/****************************************************************************
 I n i t F i r s t I n s t a n c e ()
 ====================================

 This function initializes the first instance of the "Diverse" application.

 Parameters:

   HANDLE hInstance:     Current instance handle of the application.
   HANDLE hPrevInstance: Previous instance handle of the application. NULL
                         if the current instance is the first instance.
   int    nCmdShow:      Parameter which specifies the application window's
```

```
                         appearance when the program starts.

 Return values:

   int                   NULL if the "Diverse" window class registers.
                         Otherwise, a value other than NULL.

 ************************************************************************/

int InitFirstInstance (HANDLE hInstance, HANDLE hPrevInstance, int nCmdShow)
{
  WNDCLASS MainWndClass;                         // Main window class

  // Load application name from resource file
  LoadString(hInstance, IDS_APPLNAME, (LPSTR)szApplName, 20);

  // Specify window class information
  MainWndClass.lpszClassName = szApplName;       // Window class
  MainWndClass.hInstance     = hInstance;        // Instance
  MainWndClass.lpfnWndProc   = MainWndProc;      // Window function
  MainWndClass.style         = CS_HREDRAW | CS_VREDRAW;  // Horizontal and
                                                         // vertical redraw
  MainWndClass.lpszMenuName  = (LPSTR) NULL;     // No menu
  MainWndClass.hCursor       = LoadCursor(NULL, IDC_ARROW);      // Mouse cursor
  MainWndClass.hIcon         = LoadIcon(NULL, IDI_APPLICATION); // Default icon
  MainWndClass.hbrBackground = GetStockObject(WHITE_BRUSH);
                                                  // White background
  MainWndClass.cbClsExtra    = 0;                 // No extra bytes
  MainWndClass.cbWndExtra    = 0;                 // No extra bytes

  // Registering "Diverse" window class
  return (RegisterClass(&MainWndClass));
} // InitFirstInstance

/************************************************************************
 M a i n W n d P r o c ()
 ========================

 This function acts as the main window function. All messages are sent to
 this window.

 Parameters:

   HWND     hWnd:     Window handle.
   unsigned msg:      Message type.
   WORD     wP:       Message-dependent 16 bit value
   LONG     lP:       Message-dependent 32 bit value
```

```
 Return values:

   LONG          0L if the window function has sent the message.
                 Otherwise, the return value from the DefWindowProc
                 default window function.
 **************************************************************************/

LONG FAR PASCAL MainWndProc (HWND     hWnd,
                        unsigned msg,
                        WORD     wP,
                        LONG     lP)
{
   HMENU hMenu;                 // Menu handle variable

   switch (msg)
   {
     case WM_CREATE:                // For creating window
       hMenu = GetMenu(hWnd);
       bLineNumbers = FALSE;
       bANSIFont = FALSE;

       // Store Options menu items
       EnableMenuItem(hMenu, MI_LINENUMBERS, MF_GRAYED | MF_BYCOMMAND);
       EnableMenuItem(hMenu, MI_ANSI, MF_GRAYED | MF_BYCOMMAND);
       break;

     case WM_DESTROY:
       PostQuitMessage(0);            // Send WM_QUIT if window
                                      // is destroyed
       break;

     case WM_COMMAND:                 // Messages from menu bar
       switch (wP)
       {
        case MI_LOADFILE:              // Load file
          nTextLines = ReadFile("diverse.c");

          if (nTextLines)
          {
            // Set scroll area
            SetScrollRange(hWnd, SB_VERT, 0, nTextLines - 1, TRUE);

            // Release Options menu title
            hMenu = GetMenu(hWnd);
            EnableMenuItem(hMenu, MI_LINENUMBERS, MF_ENABLED | MF_BYCOMMAND);
            EnableMenuItem(hMenu, MI_ANSI, MF_ENABLED | MF_BYCOMMAND);

            // Redraw client area
```

```
          InvalidateRect(hWnd, NULL, TRUE);
        }
        break;

      case MI_QUIT:                    // End program
        PostMessage(hwMain, WM_SYSCOMMAND, SC_CLOSE, 0L);
        break;

      case MI_LINENUMBERS:             // Line numbers Option
        hMenu = GetMenu(hWnd);         // Get menu handle
        if (bLineNumbers)
        {
          bLineNumbers = FALSE;
          CheckMenuItem(hMenu, MI_LINENUMBERS, MF_UNCHECKED | MF_BYCOMMAND);
        }
        else
        {
          bLineNumbers = TRUE;
          CheckMenuItem(hMenu, MI_LINENUMBERS, MF_CHECKED | MF_BYCOMMAND);
        }
        InvalidateRect(hWnd, NULL, TRUE); // Update client area
        break;

      case MI_ANSI:
        hMenu = GetMenu(hWnd);
        if (bANSIFont)
        {
          bANSIFont = FALSE;
          CheckMenuItem(hMenu, MI_ANSI, MF_UNCHECKED | MF_BYCOMMAND);
        }
        else
        {
          bANSIFont = TRUE;
          CheckMenuItem(hMenu, MI_ANSI, MF_CHECKED | MF_BYCOMMAND);
        }
        InvalidateRect(hWnd, NULL, TRUE);
        break;

      default:
        break;
    }
    break;

  case WM_PAINT:                       // Client area redraw needed
    PaintDiverse(hWnd);
    break;

  case WM_VSCROLL:                     // Message from vertical
```

```
                                    // scroll bar
   switch (wP)
   {
    case SB_TOP:                    // Thumb at top end
    {
      nTopLine = 0;
      break;
    }
    case SB_BOTTOM:                 // Thumb at bottom end
    {
      nTopLine = nTextLines - 1;
      break;
    }
    case SB_LINEUP:                 // One line up
    {
      if (nTopLine)
        nTopLine -= 1;
      break;
    }
    case SB_LINEDOWN:               // One line down
    {
      if (nTopLine < (nTextLines - 1))
        nTopLine += 1;
      break;
    }
    case SB_PAGEUP:             // One page up
    {
      if (nTopLine >= nScreenRows - 1)
        nTopLine -= nScreenRows - 1;
      else
        nTopLine = 0;
      break;
    }
    case SB_PAGEDOWN:           // One page down
    {
      if (nTopLine <= nTextLines - (nScreenRows - 1))
        nTopLine += nScreenRows - 1;
      else
        nTopLine = nTextLines - 1;
      break;
    }
    case SB_THUMBPOSITION:      // Thumb position
    {
      nTopLine = LOWORD(lP);
      break;
    }
    default:
      return (DefWindowProc(hWnd, msg, wP, lP));
```

```
            break;
        }

        // Create WM_PAINT message after clearing client area.
        InvalidateRect(hWnd, NULL, TRUE);
        break;

      // The following routines allow scrolling from the keyboard.

      case WM_KEYDOWN:                      // Key pressed

        // Pass virtual keycodes
        switch (wP)
        {
          case VK_UP:                       // Cursor up
            PostMessage(hWnd, WM_VSCROLL, SB_LINEUP, 0L);
            break;
          case VK_DOWN:                     // Cursor down
            PostMessage(hWnd, WM_VSCROLL, SB_LINEDOWN, 0L);
            break;
          case VK_PRIOR:                    // Page up
            PostMessage(hWnd, WM_VSCROLL, SB_PAGEUP, 0L);
            break;
          case VK_NEXT:                     // Page down
            PostMessage(hWnd, WM_VSCROLL, SB_PAGEDOWN, 0L);
            break;
          case VK_HOME:                     // HOME key
            PostMessage(hWnd, WM_VSCROLL, SB_TOP, 0L);
            break;
          case VK_END:                      // END key
            PostMessage(hWnd, WM_VSCROLL, SB_BOTTOM, 0L);
            break;
          default:
            return (DefWindowProc(hWnd, msg, wP, lP));
            break;
        }
        break;

      default: // Pass other messages to the default window function

        return (DefWindowProc(hWnd, msg, wP, lP));
        break;
    }
    return 0L;
} // MainWndProc

/*****************************************************************************
 P a i n t D i v e r s e ()
```

```
========================

This function performs redrawing of the main window's client area. When
redrawing all screen lines, some video cards may take longer to redraw
than others.

Parameters:

  HWND    hWnd:    Window handle.

Return values:     None.
*************************************************************************/

void PaintDiverse (HWND hWnd)
{
  PAINTSTRUCT ps;              // Client area information
  TEXTMETRIC  tm;              // Text font information
  RECT        rRect,           // Rectangle structure
              rLineRect;       // Rectangle for draw text
  HDC         hDC;             // Display context handle
  int         nXPos = 0,       // Horizontal position in pixels
              nYPos = 0,       // Vertical position in pixels
              nLineHeight,     // Single text line height in pixels
              nOffset,         // Line number offset
              i;               // Counter variable
  char        szLineNr[5];     // Line number buffer
  HFONT       hOldFont;        // Handle for a font

  hDC = BeginPaint(hWnd, &ps); // Get main window's display context

  // Set desired font
  if (bANSIFont)
    hOldFont = SelectObject(hDC, GetStockObject(ANSI_FIXED_FONT));
  else
    hOldFont = SelectObject(hDC, GetStockObject(OEM_FIXED_FONT));

  // Get information about current text font
  GetTextMetrics(hDC, &tm);

  // Compute height of one line of text
  nLineHeight = tm.tmHeight + tm.tmExternalLeading;

  // Get client area dimensions
  GetClientRect(hWnd, &rRect);

  // Compute number of screen lines
  nScreenRows = rRect.bottom / nLineHeight;
```

```
  // Do we really need scroll bar display?
  if (nScreenRows >= nTextLines)
    ShowScrollBar(hWnd, SB_VERT, FALSE);  // No
  else
    ShowScrollBar(hWnd, SB_VERT, TRUE);   // Yes

  // Text line output
  for (i=0; i<nScreenRows; i++)
  {
    if ((nTopLine + i) > nTextLines)
      break;

    nYPos = i * nLineHeight;

    if (bLineNumbers) // Include line numbers with output?
    {
      sprintf(szLineNr, "%3d ", nTopLine + i + 1);

      // Compute line number length plus a space in pixels
      nOffset = LOWORD(GetTextExtent(hDC, (LPSTR)szLineNr, strlen(szLineNr)));
      // line number display
      TextOut(hDC, nXPos, nYPos, szLineNr, strlen(szLineNr));
    }
    else
      nOffset = 0;

      // Compute a line for the rectangle
      SetRect(&rLineRect, nXPos + nOffset, nYPos, rRect.right,
              nYPos + nLineHeight);
      // Display text line, expand tabs
      DrawText(hDC, TextArray[nTopLine + i], -1, &rLineRect,
               DT_EXPANDTABS | DT_NOPREFIX);
  }

  // New thumb position
  SetScrollPos(hWnd, SB_VERT, nTopLine, TRUE);
  // Select original font in display context
  SelectObject(hDC, hOldFont);

  EndPaint(hWnd, &ps);          // Release display context
} // PaintDiverse

/***************************************************************************
 R e a d F i l e ()
 ==================

 This function reads a text file specified in the global array TextArray.
```

```
 Parameters:

   PSTR szFileName:  Name of the file to be read.

 Return values:       Number of lines read.
 ***************************************************************************/

int ReadFile (PSTR szFileName)
{
  FILE     *FilePointer;                        // File pointer
  int      nLineNr = 0;                         // Line counter
  char     szLineBuffer[MAXLINELENGTH];         // Line buffer
  unsigned char ch;                             // Character buffer

  FilePointer = fopen(szFileName, "rt");        // Open text file for reading

  if (!FilePointer)                             // No file opening
  {
    MessageBox(GetFocus(), "File could not be opened", szApplName,
               MB_OK | MB_ICONEXCLAMATION);
    return 0;
  }
  SetCursor(LoadCursor(NULL, IDC_WAIT));        // Hourglass cursor

  // Read file
  do
  {
    if (fgets(szLineBuffer, MAXLINELENGTH, FilePointer) == NULL)
      break;
    szLineBuffer[strlen(szLineBuffer)-1] = '\0'; // Remove linefeed
    strcpy(TextArray[nLineNr++], szLineBuffer);
  } while (nLineNr < MAXLINES-1);

  fclose(FilePointer);                          // Close file
  SetCursor(LoadCursor(NULL, IDC_ARROW));       // Restore arrow cursor
  return (nLineNr);                             // Number of lines read
} // ReadFile
```

4 Dialog Boxes

In the preceding chapter we spent a lot of time coding text display under Windows. This chapter discusses an area where Windows saves us a lot of work in programming—dialog boxes and controls.

User interaction

When developing an application to run under MS-DOS, the programmer eventually encounters the problem of handling user interaction with the program. Earlier MS-DOS compatible programs tended to be "user-obnoxious." A prompt (and little else) would appear on the screen and, if the user was lucky, the screen might offer some help. Fortunately, now developers strive for user-friendly applications.

As you write your own applications, you should ask yourself two important questions about user interaction:

1) How is input from the keyboard or mouse handled?

2) How are errors trapped?

Dialog boxes are the friendliest method of user-system communication and a standard in Microsoft Windows.

You can avoid a lot of frustration by using predefined dialog boxes and controls. Under Windows, dialog boxes are window types that provide standard ways of dealing with the most common user inputs. This chapter discusses dialog box programming in detail, and features a simple database using dialog boxes.

4.1 Window Classes

As we know from the CreateWindow function, you must specify the window class when creating a window. The window class can be one of the predefined Windows classes or it can be one you create yourself with the RegisterClass function. Dialog boxes with controls are usually predefined.

Classes and functions

You can also create your own controls. Since each window class must have a window function assigned to it, the programmer usually must provide a window function for any new window classes that are created. For controls, however, Windows has standard window functions available. Here is a list of the window classes supported by Windows:

STATIC — This is a static control, which means that text or graphics contained in it remains constant. This type of control is commonly used to put titles or comments on other controls or to emphasize a certain point.

SCROLLBAR — Scroll bar controls were described in Chapter 3. These are displayed as horizontal or vertical scroll bars, which scroll the contents of the client area, or as sliders, which set numerical values in an analog fashion.

BUTTON — This window class creates buttons. We've already seen how buttons work in message boxes. Clicking on a button executes the action associated with that button. Buttons usually have standard meanings under Windows, such as [OK] or [EXIT]. The buttons under Windows 3 have a 3-D appearance, so you can actually see when a button is "pushed".

EDIT — This window class produces a rectangular field called an edit box. This box allows the user to enter text (as with a simple text editor). You can also load existing text (e.g., from a file) into the edit box and use the mouse to mark and edit it. Also, edit boxes can be given scroll bars to scroll through longer texts that won't fit completely in the box and can have one or more lines.

LISTBOX — Controls of this class create a rectangular list box for displaying a collection of character strings. Unlike the edit box, the user cannot modify the text in the list box. However, list boxes may use scroll bars.

COMBOBOX — A combo box, which is a new structure under Windows 3, represents a combination of an edit box and a list box. In most cases, a combo box is displayed as a one-line edit box with a down arrow symbol next to the title.

Only one item is displayed in the list unless the user clicks on the arrow icon (the pop box) or presses <Alt> + <Down Arrow>. The one-line edit box then opens up into a complete list box. When an item from the list is selected, the list box closes and the selected item appears in the one-line edit box. Depending on the style of combo box you use, the list box can also be displayed at all times.

Remember that you can use these standard window styles or you can define your own. In addition to the window class, the window style also plays an important role in determining how the control window will look and operate. The next section is devoted to this subject.

4.2 Window Styles

We used the "WS_OVERLAPPEDWINDOW" window style for the main window in both the STRUCTUR and the DIVERSE applications. The window style is assigned when the CreateWindow function is called. In DIVERSE.C, we also assigned the WS_VSCROLL flag so that vertical scroll bars would be added.

*WS_ and CS_*

The window styles that begin with "WS_" can be different for every window of the same class that is created with the CreateWindow function. On the other hand, the "CS_" style (for Class Style), which is set in the style field of the WNDCLASS variable when the window class is registered, will apply to all windows of that class which are created. We have used the class styles CS_HREDRAW and CS_VREDRAW in the previous examples. These styles generate a WM_PAINT message when the horizontal or vertical window size is changed so that the client area can be repainted.

Windows recognizes three basic window classes:

WS_OVERLAPPED
: Creates windows that overlap. This window class is normally used for the main window of an application.

WS_POPUP
: A window of this class can appear anywhere on screen. These windows are not restricted to the client area of a certain window. Dialog boxes are examples of popup windows. A popup window can also be associated with another window (in the form of a window handle in the eighth parameter of the CreateWindow function). Then, if this window is closed, the associated popup window will also close.

WS_CHILD
: This window class creates a child window, which is stored below the associated parent window in a hierarchical relationship. According to this relationship, the child window can only be displayed within the client area of the parent window. So you cannot move a child window outside of the parent window. If you try to do this, the part of the window that would appear outside of the parent window is

clipped. Child windows are also automatically closed if the parent window is closed.

To create a parent-child relationship, the window handle for the parent window is given as the eighth parameter of the CreateWindow function. The third to last parameter of the CreatcWindow function would normally contain a menu handle for the WS_OVERPLAPPED or WS_POPUP window classes. For a child window, however, this parameter contains a unique integer value, known as the child ID, that is assigned by the application.

Window styles

In addition to the three basic window classes, there are window styles which further define a window's characteristics:

WS_BORDER Assigned to windows that have a simple border.

WS_CAPTION Creates a title line for the window. This style automatically includes the WS_BORDER style.

WS_CHILDWINDOW
Same as WS_CHILD.

WS_CLIPCHILDREN
The child window is clipped when drawn within the client area of the parent window.

WS_CLIPSIBLINGS
Clips multiple child windows that overlap within the parent window.

WS_DISABLED
Creates a window that starts out disabled.

WS_DLGFRAME
Creates a double border with no title line.

WS_GROUP This is a style for dialog boxes. It defines the start of a series of controls through which the user can move forwards and backwards with the help of the cursor keys. The end of the group (and the start of the next group, if present) is defined by re-entering the WS_GROUP style.

WS_HSCROLL Creates a horizontal scroll bar for the window. This scroll bar will only be displayed if the entire horizontal contents of the window cannot be displayed within the client area simultaneously.

WS_ICONIC This style displays a window as an icon. It can only be used together with WS_OVERLAPPED.

WS_MAXIMIZE
Displays the window at its maximum size.

WS_MAXIMIZEBOX
In the upper right corner, the window will contain a button that, when clicked, enlarges the window to its maximum size.

WS_MINIMIZE
The window will initially be displayed in its minimum size.

WS_MINIMIZEBOX
In the upper right corner, the window will contain a button that, when clicked, reduces the window to its minimum size.

WS_OVERLAPPEDWINDOW
A combination of the WS_OVERLAPPED, WS_CAPTION, WS_SYSMENU and WS_THICKFRAME styles. The main windows in the programs listed in earlier chapters of this book use this style.

WS_POPUPWINDOW
A combination of the WS_POPUP, WS_BORDER and WS_SYSMENU styles.

WS_SYSMENU The window adds a system menu in the upper left corner. This will only work for windows that have a title bar. For a child window, this style will create a button for closing the window.

WS_TABSTOP A control created with this window style can be operated with the <Tab> key.

WS_THICKFRAME
Assigns a frame, to the window, that can be used to change the window size.

WS_VISIBLE The window will be visible on screen from the beginning.

WS_VSCROLL This style gives the window a vertical scroll bar. The scroll bar will only be displayed if the vertical contents of the window will not fit completely within the client area.

As you can see from the descriptions provided for each window style, not all window styles can be combined at will. For example, a window with the WS_CHILD style cannot also be assigned the WS_POPUP style. Also, there are certain styles that must be combined with other styles (for example WS_ICONIC and WS_OVERLAPPED).

More about controls

Now let's return to our discussion of controls. Controls are special types of windows that can be created with the CreateWindow function. Controls are always child windows.

In the preceding chapter, we limited the DIVERSE application to displaying its own C source code on the screen with the help of the ReadFile function. If you added an edit box, the user could then enter any text filename from the keyboard. Once entered, the system could then display that file.

Here's an example of an EDIT window definition:

```
#define ID_EDIT 10                          // Unique child ID
hEditWnd = CreateWindow ("EDIT",            // Window class for edit box
                   "",                      // No title
                   ES_LEFT |                // Left-justified text
                   WS_HSCROLL |             // Horizontal scroll bar
                   ES_AUTOHSCROLL |         // Automatic horizontal scrolling
                   WS_CHILD |               // Child window
                   WS_VISIBLE,              // Make window visible from the start
                   100,                     // X-position
                   100,                     // Y-position
                   200,                     // Width
                    12,                     // Height
                   hwMain,                  // Parent window
                   ID_EDIT,                 // Child ID
                   hInst,                   // Instance number of the application
                   NULL);                   // No lParam value
```

This function call creates an edit box at position (100, 100) within the client area of the main window. The width of the edit box will be 200 pixels and the height will be 12 pixels. Coordinate values are relative to the upper left corner of the main window's client area, since the child window cannot be displayed outside of the parent window.

Classes and styles used

The function call uses the window class ("EDIT") in combination with the (ES_LEFT, WS_HSCROLL, ES_AUTOHSCROLL, WS_CHILD, and WS_VISIBLE) window styles to create the edit box.

Let's take a closer look at the window styles for controls that do not begin with WS_. The abbreviation used at the start of each style indicates the type:

SS_ "Static Style"

SBS_ "Scroll Bar Style"

BS_ "Button Style"

LBS_ "List Box Style"

CBS_ "Combo Box Style"

These special styles can be used to change the appearance of the control and the way it works. Here is a list of the most important styles for each type.

Styles for STATIC controls

SS_LEFT Text is left justified.

SS_RIGHT Text is right justified.

SS_CENTER Text is centered.

SS_ICON Displays an icon.

SS_BLACKFRAME
Displays a rectangle with a black frame.

SS_BLACKRECT
Displays a rectangle filled with black.

SS_WHITEFRAME
Displays a rectangle with a white frame.

SS_WHITERECT
Displays a rectangle filled with white.

SS_GRAYFRAME
Displays a rectangle with a gray frame.

SS_GRAYRECT
Displays a rectangle filled with gray.

SS_USERITEM Displays an item defined by the user.

Styles for SCROLLBAR controls

SBS_HORZ Displays a horizontal scroll bar using the position, width and height given in CreateWindow.

SBS_VERT — Displays a vertical scroll bar using the position, width and height given in CreateWindow.

SBS_BOTTOMALIGN
Aligns the scroll bar with the bottom of the window rectangle defined by CreateWindow.

SBS_TOPALIGN
Aligns the scroll bar with the top of the window rectangle as defined by CreateWindow.

SBS_LEFTALIGN
Aligns the scroll bar with the left edge of the defined window rectangle.

SBS_RIGHTALIGN
Aligns the scroll bar with the right edge of the defined window rectangle.

SS_NOPREFIX — The "&" character will not underline the following character.

Styles for BUTTON controls

BS_PUSHBUTTON
This type of button contains the text string given in the second parameter of the CreateWindow function. Push buttons are normally used to take some direct action (for example leaving a dialog box by clicking [OK]).

BS_DEFPUSHBUTTON
This button is given a double frame to indicate to the user that it is the default response.

BS_CHECKBOX — A check box is a rectangular area used to indicate whether a feature or option is "on" or "off". An "X" in the check box indicates the "on" condition. The text associated with the check box is displayed to the right.

BS_AUTOCHECKBOX
: This is the same as BS_CHECKBOX except that the user can toggle it on and off by clicking on it.

BS_3STATE
: This is a check box with three possible states. The third condition is indicated when the check box is displayed in gray.

BS_AUTO3STATE
: Same as BS_3STATE, but Windows allows the user to select the state by clicking on the box.

BS_RADIOBUTTON
: A radio button is a small circle that indicates an "on" (the circle is filled in) or "off" (the circle is empty) condition. Radio buttons are typically used to select one item from a list of several. In a group of items with radio buttons, only one can be "on" at a given time.

BS_AUTORADIOBUTTON
: Same as BS_RADIOBUTTON except that clicking on one radio button will turn off the marking of any other radio button in the group.

BS_GROUPBOX
: Displays a group box, which is used to arrange a collection of controls into a logical group. A group box is represented simply as a rectangle around all of the included controls. Any text is displayed in the upper left corner.

BS_OWNERDRAW
: This style will display a button designed by the user. It replaces the BS_USERBUTTON style from Windows 2.x.

Styles for EDIT controls

ES_LEFT
: An edit box with left-justified text.

ES_RIGHT
: An edit box with right-justified text.

ES_CENTER An edit box with centered text.

ES_MULTILINE Displays an edit box with multiple lines. To move from one line to the next in a multi-line edit box, you cannot use the <CR> key. This key is reserved for executing the default action in a dialog box. Instead, you must press <Ctrl> + <CR>.

ES_AUTOHSCROLL
If you enter text beyond the right edge of the edit box, it will automatically scroll 10 characters further.

ES_AUTOVSCROLL
When you reach the last line of the edit box and press the <Enter> key, the text will scroll one line up to create a new blank line.

ES_PASSWORD Any text entered in the edit box will be displayed as asterisks ("*") or any other character you select.

ES_LOWERCASE
All letters entered in the edit box will be displayed in lowercase.

ES_UPPERCASE All letters entered in the edit box will be displayed in uppercase.

ES_NOHIDESEL Displays selected text in the edit box in reverse video, even if the input focus is not on this box.

Styles for LISTBOX controls

LBS_SORT The entries in the list box are automatically sorted alphabetically.

LBS_NOTIFY The parent window of the list box is notified using messages when the user clicks on a list entry.

LBS_STANDARD
This creates a list box with vertical scroll bars and

the styles LBS_SORT, LBS_NOTIFY and WS_BORDER.

LBS_MULTIPLESEL
Multiple items from the list box can be selected simultaneously.

LBS_EXTENDEDSEL
New in Version 3. This style is similar to LBS_MULTIPLESEL, but it uses the CUA (Common User Access) recommended keyboard interface.

LBS_MULTICOLUMN
Displays a multiple-column list.

LBS_USETABSTOPS
Recognizes and expands tab characters in a list box.

Styles for COMBOBOX controls

CBS_SIMPLE The list box will always be displayed.

CBS_DROPDOWN
The list box will be displayed when the user clicks on the pop box icon to the right of the selection box.

CBS_DROPDOWNLIST
Similar to CBS_DROPDOWN, except that the selection box is replaced with a text string that cannot be changed.

CBS_SORT The list box entries are sorted alphabetically.

Until now, we have discussed the use of controls created with the CreateWindow function. However, controls are actually more commonly created using dialog boxes under Windows.

4.3 Modal and Modeless Dialog Boxes

Dialog boxes are popup windows that act primarily as parent windows for controls. As the name suggests, a dialog box establishes communication with the user. This communication could consist of entering text, selecting an option or confirming a question asked by the application. Dialog boxes help create a consistent user interface—one that is familiar to the user across all Windows applications.

Modal dialog boxes

Different types of dialog boxes serve different purposes. Modal dialog boxes limit user input to the controls within the dialog box itself. This means that the parent window becomes inactive as soon as the dialog box opens. Also, modal dialog boxes have their own message loop that is not processed by the WinMain function. This means that while a modal dialog box is active, the main window cannot process any messages sent to it.

Application modal boxes

There is a distinction between *application modal* and *system modal* dialog boxes. With an application modal dialog box, the user must first complete any actions in the dialog box and then close it before any other windows in the application created by this dialog box can be used. However, it is still possible to work with windows from other applications.

System modal boxes

With system modal dialog boxes, all windows in other applications are also locked until the dialog box has been closed. This type of dialog box should only be used when the application needs immediate input from the user (e.g., disk errors or insufficient memory).

Modal dialog box styles

There are certain styles recommended for creating modal dialog boxes; the most common are WS_POPUP, WS_CAPTION, WS_SYSMENU and DS_MODALFRAME. The WS_POPUP style assures that the dialog box can be displayed regardless of the current state of the parent window's client area. The WS_SYSMENU will assure that the dialog box contains the system menu, which will allow the user to close the dialog box or move it with the keyboard. WS_CAPTION allows you to enter a title line. DS_MODALFRAME creates the proper frame for the dialog box.

However, a modal dialog box must not use the WS_CHILD style under any circumstances. As we mentioned earlier, whatever happens to the parent window is carried over to the child. A modal dialog box deactivates its parent window. So the dialog box itself would also be deactivated if it were a child window. This means that you could not make any entries in either the parent window or the dialog box.

As you may have already determined, we used a type of modal dialog box in the DIVERSE application—the message box. Message boxes are typically application modal dialog boxes. By setting the MB_SYSTEMMODAL flag, you can create a system modal message box.

Modeless dialog boxes

Now let's discuss modeless dialog boxes. These differ from their modal cousins because they can be active at the same time as other windows in the application. This means that the parent window remains active and the dialog box can remain open while you work with other windows. Modeless dialog boxes are more like a "normal" window. They usually have a system menu, a title bar and a simple frame. Modeless dialog boxes usually use the WS_POPUP window style, but not WS_DLGFRAME.

Another difference is that modeless dialog boxes use the message loop from the WinMain function, rather than their own message loops. This message loop must be modified if the keyboard port is to be used within the dialog box. We'll discuss this in detail later.

4.4 Defining a Dialog Box

How do you create a dialog box? First you must define its structure. There are two ways to do this:

1) By describing the dialog box in the resource file for the application.

2) By dynamically creating a dialog box template (a special kind of data structure) at runtime.

The first method is used more often than dynamic creation. Describing a dialog box resource in the resource file is done with the DIALOG statement:

```
DialognameID DIALOG [Load_Options] [Memory_Options] XPos, YPos, Width, Height
[STYLE styles]
[CAPTION text_for_title_bar]
[MENU menu_name_ID]
[CLASS dialog_box_class]
[FONT point_size, font_name]
BEGIN
  LTEXT         "Text", ID, XPos, YPos, Width, Height [, Styles]
  RTEXT         "Text", ID, XPos, YPos, Width, Height [, Styles]
  CTEXT         "Text", ID. XPos, YPos, Width, Height [, Styles]
  PUSHBUTTON    "Text", ID, XPos, YPos, Width, Height [, Styles]
  DEFPUSHBUTTON "Text", ID, XPos, YPos, Width, Height [, Styles]
  RADIOBUTTON   "Text", ID, XPos, YPos, Width, Height [, Styles]
  CHECKBOX      "Text", ID, XPos, YPos, Width, Height [, Styles]
  GROUPBOX      "Text", ID, XPos, YPos, Width, Height [, Styles]
  LISTBOX               ID, XPos, YPos, Width, Height [, Styles]
  EDITTEXT              ID, XPos, YPos, Width, Height [, Styles]
  COMBOBOX              ID, XPos, YPos, Width, Height [, Styles]
  ICON           Text,  ID, XPos, YPos, Width, Height [, Styles]
  CONTROL       "Text", ID, Class, Styles, XPos, YPos, Width, Height
END
```

In the following descriptions, the information in square brackets is optional.

DialognameID A name or integer ID that uniquely identifies the dialog box resource.

DIALOG	The keyword that identifies this as a dialog box resource.

[Load_Options] can use the following values:

PRELOAD	The dialog box resource is loaded as soon as the program is started.
LOADONCALL	The dialog box resource is loaded only when it is needed.

[Memory_Options] can be:

FIXED	The dialog box resource cannot be moved to a new memory location by the memory manager.
MOVEABLE	The memory manager can move the dialog resource to a new memory location as needed.
DISCARDABLE	The memory manager may delete the dialog box resource from memory if needed.
XPos, YPos	These coordinates define the upper left corner of the dialog box resource when it is displayed on screen. With dialog boxes of type WS_POPUP, these coordinates are measured relative to the upper left corner of the screen. If the dialog box is type WS_CHILD, the coordinates will be relative to the upper left corner of the parent window.
Width	Gives the width of the dialog box in units equal to 1/4 of the width of the system font.
Height	Gives the height of the dialog box in units equal to 1/8 of the height of the system font.

System font dimensions

The units of measurement "1/4 of the width" and "1/8 of the height" of the system font are used for a special reason. By using this relative measurement, it is possible to define the dimensions of dialog boxes independently of the type of graphics adapter card used (CGA, EGA, VGA, etc.). If the dimensions were given in pixels, then many dialog boxes could appear too large on lower resolution screens. By using the system font, the pixel size isn't needed and dialog boxes will be displayed properly regardless of the screen resolution.

[STYLE styles] Used to specify the window styles for the dialog box. If this option is not used, then the default styles WS_POPUP | WS_SYSMENU | WS_BORDER are used. A system modal dialog box will also use the DS_SYSTEMMODAL style.

[CAPTION text_for_title_bar]
The text string used for the title bar of the dialog box.

[MENU menu_name_ID]
Allows you to assign a menu to the dialog box. In practice, dialog boxes rarely contain menus.

[CLASS dialog_box_class]
Specifies an integer ID or a character string that uniquely identifies the dialog box class. This entry is important when using your own dialog box classes.

[FONT point_size, font_name]
Selects a font for the dialog box. The point size is an integer value that gives the size of the font in points. The font name is the character string that identifies the font. It must be entered in quotes.

Here is a description of the control statements:

LTEXT control of type SS_LEFT for window class "static"

RTEXT control of type SS_RIGHT for window class "static"

CTEXT control of type SS_CENTER for window class "static"

PUSHBUTTON control of type BS_PUSHBUTTON for window class "button"

DEFPUSHBUTTON
control of type BS_DEFPUSHBUTTON for window class "button"

RADIOBUTTON
control of type BS_RADIOBUTTON for window class "button"

CHECKBOX control of type BS_CHECKBOX for window class "button"

GROUPBOX control of type BS_GROUPBOX for window class "button"

LISTBOX control for window class "listbox"

EDITTEXT control for window class "edit"

ICON control of type SS_ICON for window type "static"

CONTROL general statement for all controls

CONTROL parameters

Here is a description of the parameters that follow the control statements:

Text The text string (enclosed in quotes) that will be displayed next to the control. Preceding a letter with the "&" character underlines that character. Pressing <Alt> + the underlined letter then executes the action represented by the control. If you wish to display the "&" character itself, then you must enter the character twice. With the ICON control, "Text" will be the name of an icon resource in the .RC file.

ID This is an integer ID which is normally given in the include file with a #define statement. This ID is the same as the child ID parameter of the CreateWindow function. It identifies the controls in a dialog box. You should enter -1 here for controls that do not allow interaction with the user.

XPos, YPos	These values define the upper left corner of the control relative to the dialog box. XPos is given in units 1/4 the width of the system font and YPos is given in units 1/8 the height of the system font.
Width	Sets the width of the control (in units 1/4 of the width of the system font).
Height	Sets the height of the control (in units 1/8 of the height of the system font).
[Styles]	This is where you assign the allowed window styles to the control.

Imitation with "class"

The CONTROL statement has a special feature in the "class" parameter. This statement can imitate any other control (including those you define yourself). The dialog editor DIALOG.EXE takes advantage of this feature. The resource files created by the dialog editor (file extension .DLG) describe dialog boxes using only the CONTROL statement.

The "class" parameter is used in these statements to assign a class to each control—"static", "scrollbar", "button", "listbox", "edit", "combobox" or "user-defined class". The other characteristics of the control are defined with window styles and dimensions.

Setting the dimensions of the dialog box and its controls in units equal to 1/4 of the width and 1/8 of the height of the system font is a relatively time-consuming process. Because of this many programmers prefer to use the dialog editor to create new dialog boxes and to modify existing ones.

4.5 The Dialog Editor

The dialog editor allows you to change all parameters, associated with the creation of a control, interactively on the screen. It also offers a test mode, which allows you to test the functions executed by the controls. In addition, the dialog editor provides a convenient way to edit include files. In short, the dialog editor is a convenient environment for creating and modifying dialog boxes and controls, thus saving you the work of manually coding the definitions.

For simple modifications, it may be faster to take the .DLG file created by the dialog editor and edit the CONTROL statements with a simple text editor.

Using DIALOG.EXE

Let's look at the creation of a simple dialog box as an example. The dialog box we want to create will contain an edit box in which the user can enter a filename. The static text string "Filename:" will appear above the edit box. The dialog box will also contain two buttons: [OK] and [Cancel].

To create this dialog box with the dialog editor, we must first start the dialog editor program under Windows. Run Windows, then find the SDK Tools window. Double-click the Dialog Editor icon to run the application.

When the main window of the dialog editor appears, select the **File** menu and the **New** item. This tells the dialog editor that you want to create a new dialog box, rather than edit an existing dialog box resource. The dialog editor will then ask if you want a new include file created for this dialog box resource. You can select either [Yes] or [No] here, since this does not affect the result generated by the dialog box.

Next, select the **Dialog** menu and the **New...** item to create a new resource. A dialog box appears on screen for you to enter the name of the new dialog box you want to create. Enter "TESTDLG" and click [OK].

After this, an empty rectangle with sizing controls in the corners and in the middle of the edges will appear on screen. This rectangle represents the empty dialog box. You can use the sizing controls to change the size of the box and move it to the desired position on the screen. You can now select the **Static Text**, **Edit** and **Push Button** items from the **Control** menu to add the desired controls to the empty dialog box. After you select each item, a cross-hair cursor will appear on screen so you can set the position of the control within the dialog box. When the cursor is in the desired position, press the left mouse button and the control will appear on the screen in a pre-determined size. You can also change the size of the control within the dialog box.

Setting controls

The **Styles...** item from the **Edit** menu sets the parameters that determine the control characteristics. Here you can enter the window styles, child IDs and control text. If no include file is used, the IDs for the controls must be entered as numbers. Otherwise, the #define values from the include file can be used. Getting the appearance of the dialog box just right can be a truly artistic endeavor. When you are satisfied, select the **Save** item from the **File** menu. The dialog editor will then create a corresponding ASCII .DLG file and a binary .RES file. Here is a listing of the .DLG file we created for this dialog box (yours may look different depending upon the graphics card you use, and the exact locations and sizes you chose for the controls):

```
TESTDLG DIALOG LOADONCALL MOVEABLE DISCARDABLE 39, 34, 99, 63
STYLE WS_DLGFRAME | WS_POPUP
BEGIN
    CONTROL "Filename:", -1, "static", SS_LEFT | WS_CHILD, 7, 8, 40, 10
    CONTROL "", 100, "edit", ES_LEFT | ES_AUTOHSCROLL | WS_BORDER | WS_TABSTOP |
WS_CHILD, 7, 21, 83, 12
    CONTROL "&Ok", 1, "button", BS_DEFPUSHBUTTON | WS_TABSTOP | WS_CHILD, 8, 43,
28, 14
    CONTROL "&Cancel", 2, "button", BS_PUSHBUTTON | WS_TABSTOP | WS_CHILD, 46,
43, 44, 14
END
```

Without the CONTROL statement, the definition for this dialog box would look like this:

```
TESTDLG DIALOG LOADONCALL MOVEABLE DISCARDABLE 39, 34, 99, 63
STYLE WS_DLGFRAME | WS_POPUP
BEGIN
    LTEXT "Filename:", -1, 7, 8, 40, 10, SS_LEFT | WS_CHILD
    EDIT "", 100, 7, 21, 83, 12, ES_LEFT | ES_AUTOHSCROLL | WS_BORDER |
WS_TABSTOP | WS_CHILD
```

```
    PUSHBUTTON "&Ok", 1, 8, 43, 28, 14, BS_DEFPUSHBUTTON | WS_TABSTOP | WS_CHILD
    PUSHBUTTON "&Cancel", 2, 46, 43, 44, 14, BS_PUSHBUTTON | WS_TABSTOP |
WS_CHILD
END
```

Notice that ID -1 is used for the static text control "Filename:". It is generally recommended to assign the ID value of -1 to controls that cannot be directly changed by the user. We arbitrarily assigned the value of 100 for the ID of the edit box. You can use any values for control IDs, except the numbers 1 through 7. These are reserved by Windows for the standard controls defined in the WINDOWS.H file:

```
/* Dialog Box Command IDs */
#define IDOK          1
#define IDCANCEL      2
#define IDABORT       3
#define IDRETRY       4
#define IDIGNORE      5
#define IDYES         6
#define IDNO          7
```

The most frequently used IDs are 1 or IDOK for an OK button and 2 or IDCANCEL for a Cancel button. We have used these values in our dialog box definition. These are especially useful because Windows automatically sends a WM_COMMAND message for IDOK and IDCANCEL when you press <Enter> or <Esc>. This saves you the work of having to define these keyboard shortcuts yourself.

4.6 Dialog Functions

Until now, we have limited our discussion of programming dialog boxes to the definition of their structure. Another important aspect is the creation of dialog functions. Although dialog functions are similar to normal window functions, they differ in several important ways.

Basically, a dialog function is responsible for managing and processing messages for a dialog box.

Here is the basic structure of a dialog function for a modal dialog box:

```
BOOL FAR PASCAL SampleDlgProc (HWND hDlg, unsigned msg, WORD wP, LONG lP)
{
  // Local variables (if used)

  switch (msg)
  {
    case WM_INITDIALOG: // Sent before dialog box is displayed
      // Initialization

      return TRUE;
      break;

    case WM_COMMAND:              // Messages from menu bar
      switch (wP)                 // wP gives additional info
      {
        case IDOK:                // "OK" button pressed
          // Section for storing values in global variables (if applicable)

          EndDialog(hDlg, TRUE);  // Close dialog box
          return TRUE;            // Message successfully processed
          break;

        case IDCANCEL:            // "Cancel" button pressed
          EndDialog(hDlg, FALSE); // Close dialog box
          return TRUE;            // Message successfully processed
          break;

        default:                  // Other messages
          return FALSE;           // Messages not processed
          break;
      }
      break;
```

```
    default:                          // Other messages
      return FALSE;                   // Messages not processed
      break;
  }
} // SampleDlgProc
```

Dialog functions and window functions are both callback functions, which means they must be exported to the module definition file. Forgetting to do this is one of the most common Windows programming errors.

Type declaration, dialog functions and window functions

The first difference between a dialog function and a window function is the type declaration. A window function is type LONG FAR PASCAL, but a dialog function is type BOOL FAR PASCAL, which means that it returns either a TRUE or FALSE value as its result. A dialog function will return a result of TRUE when it has successfully received and processed a message. The value FALSE will be returned if the message was not processed. With a window function, the message would then be directed to the default window function DefWindowProc, but this function cannot be used with dialog boxes. A value of FALSE from a dialog function means that Windows must process the message itself. Windows sends the message to DlgWndProc, the default function for dialog boxes. The DlgWndProc function cannot be called directly from the application.

4.7 Message Processing

This section explains the art of processing messages within dialog boxes. The WM_INITDIALOG message is a special message for dialog boxes. Windows sends this message to a dialog box just before the dialog box is displayed on the screen. This gives the programmer a chance to do some initialization work with the dialog box before it is displayed. For example, an edit box may be filled in with a default text string or the input focus may be given to a certain control within the box.

WM_PAINT messages are not usually processed in dialog functions. This is because applications are not supposed to paint the screen within dialog boxes and the controls are painted using predefined dialog functions.

WM_COMMAND

We've already seen the WM_COMMAND message. WM_COMMAND was included in the window function of the main window in the DIVERSE application, where it selected commands from the menu. This message has a new meaning with dialog boxes. It is sent to a dialog box each time a change is made, to a control, that the dialog box must know about. The dialog box can determine which control sent the message because the control ID is passed to the dialog function by the wP parameter. The lP parameter is also important. The window handle of the control is usually stored in LOWORD(lP) and the notification code, which indicates why the message was sent, is stored in HIWORD(lP).

The following naming conventions are used with notification codes that are sent from controls to dialog boxes:

BN_	Button Notification Code
LBN_	List Box Notification Code
EN_	Edit Box Notification Code
CBN_	Combo Box Notification Code

Static controls and scroll bar controls are not really included in this case. Scroll bar controls send the same messages to dialog boxes as normal scroll bars (WM_VSCROLL and WM_HSCROLL with the corresponding SB_ values in the lP parameter). Static controls do not send any notification codes to dialog boxes because they cannot be changed by the user.

Here is a brief description of the various notification codes sent by controls:

BN_CLICKED — Indicates that a button was clicked.

BN_DOUBLECLICKED — Indicates that a button was double-clicked.

BN_PAINT — Indicates that the button should be repainted. This message is sent only by buttons of type BS_OWNERDRAW, since the programmer is responsible for redrawing this type. This is also true for the notification codes BN_DISABLE, BN_HILITE and BN_UNHILITE.

BN_DISABLE — A deactivated button should be repainted.

BN_HILITE — Used to highlight a button.

BN_UNHILITE — Removes the highlighting from a button.

LBN_SELCHANGE — Indicates that the list box selection has changed.

LBN_DBLCLK — A character string in the list box was double-clicked.

LBN_ERRSPACE — No more memory is available for the list box.

EN_CHANGE — The user has changed the text in an edit box.

EN_SETFOCUS — Indicates the edit box that has the input focus.

EN_KILLFOCUS — Indicates lost input focus for an edit box.

EN_UPDATE — Updates the edit box contents to display the new text.

EN_VSCROLL	The horizontal scroll bar of an edit box was clicked.
EN_HSCROLL	The vertical scroll bar of an edit box was clicked.
EN_ERRSPACE	No more memory available for the edit box.
CBN_DBLCLK	A character string in the list box of a combo box was double-clicked.
CBN_DROPDOWN	The list box of a combo box was opened.
CBN_EDITCHANGE	The user has changed the text in the edit box of a combo box.
CBN_EDITUPDATE	Displays the changed text in the edit box of a combo box.
CBN_ERRSPACE	There is no more memory available for the list box of a combo box.
CBN_KILLFOCUS	Indicates that a combo box has lost the input focus.
CBN_SETFOCUS	Indicates that a combo box now has the input focus.
CBN_SELCHANGE	The list box selection of a combo box has changed.

Let's return to our discussion of the WM_COMMAND message and our SampleDlgProc dialog function. In this function, a switch statement checks to see whether the [OK] or the [Cancel] button was pressed. Both actions will close the dialog box, but under different circumstances.

When the user clicks the [OK] button, the following program code is executed:

```
case IDOK:                    // "OK" button was pressed
  // store values in global variables here (if applicable)

  EndDialog(hDlg, TRUE);  // close dialog box
  return TRUE;            // message was processed
  break;
```

Before the dialog box is closed, any important input or values from the user must be saved. Then, the EndDialog function is called. This function closes a modal dialog box. It has the following format:

```
void EndDialog (HWND hDlg, int nResult);
```

hDlg is the window handle for the dialog box that is to be closed. nResult is a value returned from the dialog box function used to create the dialog box.

More about EndDialog

The way the EndDialog function works is interesting. Instead of closing the dialog box as soon as it is called, EndDialog merely sets a flag. The dialog box is actually closed only after the return statement in the next line. If the dialog box was exited by pressing the Cancel button, usually any values changed or input made by the user doesn't have to be stored. The dialog box function will return the value FALSE to nResult in this case.

4.8 Displaying a Dialog Box

So far we've been examining the code of an example dialog function. Now we will discuss the other preparations that must be made before a dialog box can actually be displayed on the screen. A typical code sequence would look like this:

```
// Creating a modal dialog box

FARPROC lpfnProc; // long pointer to a function
int     nResult;  // result of the dialog box function
HANDLE  hInst;    // instance handle for the application
HWND    hwMain;   // main window handle
...
...
case MI_LOADFILE: // load new file
   lpfnProc = MakeProcInstance(SampleDlgProc, hInst);
   nResult = DialogBox(hInst, "TESTDLG", hwMain, lpfnProc);
   FreeProcInstance(lpfnProc);
   break;
...
```

Under Windows, a dialog function is a callback function that can handle multiple instances. This means that more than one instance of the application can use the same code in the dialog function. It does not have to exist separately for each instance. However, since each instance has only one data segment, there must be a way to link a function to a certain data segment so that the function variables can be accessed.

The function itself does not have this information. The MakeProcInstance function exists for this purpose. This function has the following structure:

```
FARPROC MakeProcInstance (FARPROC lpfnProc, HANDLE hInstance);
```

lpfnProc is a long pointer to a callback function. hInstance is the instance handle for the application whose data segment needs to be linked to the function. The result does not point directly to the function code. Instead, a long pointer to a code sequence called the Thunk is returned. This value is also known as the procedure instance address. The Thunk is responsible for linking the function and the data segment of the application instance. We will discuss Thunks in more detail later when we cover dynamic link libraries. For now, all you need to know is that the MakeProcInstance function returns a long pointer that can be used as a parameter in other function calls that require the procedure instance address.

One such function is the DialogBox function, which you can use to create a modal dialog box:

```
int DialogBox (HANDLE hInstance, LPSTR lpTemplateName, HWND hWndParent, FARPROC
lpfnDialogFunc);
```

hInstance is the handle for the current instance of the application. lpTemplateName is either a text string enclosed in quotes that gives the name of the dialog box from the resource file or an integer ID that has been converted with the help of the MAKEINTRESOURCE macro (corresponds to the DialognameID parameter). hWndParent is the handle to the parent window of the dialog box. lpfnDialogFunc, which is returned by the MakeProcInstance function, is the procedure instance address of a dialog function. The result of this function is the nResult parameter for the EndDialog function.

Now all that remains is the FreeProcInstance function:

```
void FreeProcInstance (FARPROC lpfnProc);
```

This function removes the Thunk connection between a callback function and the data segment of an application. The parameter for this function call is a procedure instance address generated by the MakeProcInstance function. Similar to BeginPaint and EndPaint, MakeProcInstance and FreeProcInstance must always be paired in your programs.

4.9 Handling Modeless Dialog Boxes

Let's discuss modeless dialog boxes in the opposite order. This means that we will see how the dialog function is called and then we will look at how it is created. Calling a modeless dialog box is done as follows:

```
// Creation of a modeless dialog box

BOOL    bDlgModeless; // variable that stores the status of the dialog box
FARPROC lpfnProc;     // long pointer to a function
HANDLE  hInst;        // instance handle of the application
HWND    hwMain;       // main window handle
HWND    hDlgModeless; // modeless dialog box handle
HMENU   hMainMenu;    // main menu handle
...
...
case MI_DLGMODELESS:        // fictitious menu item
   if (!bDlgModeless)       // dialog box must be displayed
   {
     lpfnProc = MakeProcInstance(SampleDlgProc, hInst);
     hDlgModeless = CreateDialog(hInst, "TESTDLG", hwMain, lpfnProc);
     bDlgModeless = TRUE; // save new status
     // status of dialog box also stored by menu item
     CheckMenuItem(hMainMenu, MI_DLGMODELESS, MF_CHECKED);
   }
   else                     // dialog box must be closed
   {
     DestroyWindow(hDlgModeless);
     FreeProcInstance(lpfnProc);
     bDlgModeless = FALSE;
     hDlgModeless = NULL; // for the modified message loop
     // remove checkmark
     CheckMenuItem(hMainMenu, MI_DLGMODELESS, MF_UNCHECKED);
   }
   break;
...
```

Dots and items

Modeless dialog boxes are usually called and closed by a menu item. Including three dots (...) after menu items that open and close dialog boxes is a Windows practice. A boolean variable keeps track of the status of the modeless dialog box while the program is running (bDlgModeless in our example). At the same time, the status of the menu item (checked or unchecked) will indicate the status of the dialog box (open or closed).

Once again, we will use the MakeProcInstance function to get a procedure instance address. In this case, we pass it to the CreateDialog function rather than the DialogBox function.

```
HWND CreateDialog (HANDLE hInstance, LPSTR lpTemplateName, HWND hWndParent,
FARPROC lpfnDialogFunc);
```

The CreateDialog function displays a modeless dialog box. Remember that you must always use the WS_VISIBLE window style with modeless dialog boxes; otherwise the dialog box would not be visible on the screen unless you called the ShowWindow function. The four parameters have the same meanings as with the DialogBox function. The function result is different, however. The CreateDialog function returns the window handle to the modeless dialog box.

This window handle closes the dialog box. Modal dialog boxes are generally closed by using a button within the box itself, whereas modeless dialog boxes are usually closed using menu items. The DestroyWindow function closes modeless dialog boxes and all windows in general:

```
BOOL DestroyWindow (HWND hWnd);
```

hWnd is the handle for the window or modeless dialog box that you want to close. The function returns a non-zero value if the window was successfully closed.

After the dialog box is closed, the connection to the data segment must be freed with the FreeProcInstance function. Also, you will want to indicate the new status of the dialog box in the menu by removing the checkmark.

4.10 Modifying the Message Loop

Unlike a modal dialog box, a modeless dialog box does not have its own message loop. Instead, it uses the application's message loop. However, this can lead to problems, when interpreting keyboard input. For example, the <Tab> key moves the input focus from one WS_TABSTOP control to another within a dialog box. But this action will not be executed by the TranslateMessage function. The message loop must therefore be modified to interpret keyboard entries in modeless dialog boxes.

```
// example of a message loop for use with modeless dialog boxes

while (GetMessage((LPMSG)&msg, NULL, 0, 0)
{
  if (!(hDlgModeless != NULL &&                          // dialog box active?
        IsDialogMessage(hDlgModeless, (LPMSG)&msg))) // dialog box message?
  {
    TranslateMessage((LPMSG)&msg);
    DispatchMessage((LPMSG)&msg);
  }
}
```

Modeless or modal?

Before a message is sent to the TranslateMessage and DispatchMessage functions, you must check whether it is intended for a modeless dialog box. The IsDialogMessage function will return a value of TRUE if such a message is encountered in the message loop. When this happens, the IsDialogMessage function will take over processing the message, including evaluating keyboard entries (such as tabs or cursor key movements). These messages will not be passed to the TranslateMessage and DispatchMessage functions. The IsDialogMessage function should only be called when the modeless dialog box is actually open. This is checked by querying the window handle hDlgModeless, since the application is supposed to set the value of a closed modeless dialog box to zero.

4.11 Modeless Dialog Functions

There aren't many differences in the code for modal and modeless dialog functions. Let's take a look at SampleDlgProc as a modeless dialog function:

```
BOOL FAR PASCAL SampleDlgProc (HWND hDlg, unsigned msg, WORD wP, LONG lP)
{
  // local variables (if used)

  switch (msg)
  {
    case WM_INITDIALOG: // sent prior to initialization of dialog box
      // execute initialization

      return TRUE;
      break;

    case WM_COMMAND:              // message from a control
      switch (wP)                 // wP gives additional information
      {
        // messages from the dialog box's controls are processed here

        default:                  // other messages
          return FALSE;           // don't process message
          break;
      }
      break;

    case WM_SYSCOMMAND:           // message from system menu
      switch (wP)
      {
        case SC_CLOSE:            // close dialog box
          DestroyWindow(hDlgModeless);
          FreeProcInstance(lpfnProc);
          bDlgModeless = FALSE;
          hDlgModeless = NULL;
          // remove checkmark
          CheckMenuItem(hMainMenu, MI_DLGMODELESS, MF_UNCHECKED);
          return TRUE;
          break;

        default:
          return FALSE;
          break;
      }
```

```
    default:                          // other messages
      return FALSE;                   // don't process message
      break;
  }
} // SampleDlgProc
```

Buttons and modeless dialog boxes

As you can see, we don't have to include the code for handling the OK and Cancel buttons since modeless dialog boxes are controlled with menu items. However, this doesn't mean that you cannot include these buttons in a modeless dialog box along with the corresponding code. The code used in this example was used when we processed the WM_SYSCOMMAND message. This message is sent when the user selects a menu item. In a dialog box, the menu will only contain items labeled **Move** and **Close**. If **Close** is selected, the wParam parameter will contain the value SC_CLOSE. This is the same as if the user closed the window with the MI_DLGMODELESS menu item.

4.12 Control Direction in Applications

So far we have concentrated on the formal structure of dialog boxes, dialog functions and the message codes associated with controls. Now, we will take a look at how the application itself can influence controls, for example by entering text in an edit box or placing a number of strings in a list box. There are two basic ways to accomplish this:

1) By sending messages to the control.

2) By calling a function to influence the control in a certain way.

Internally, there isn't much difference between these two options because the functions that affect controls also do this through messages. To keep our discussion concise, we will only include some of the most important functions. Many of the other messages and functions used for programming dialog boxes will be discussed, within the context of specific applications, in later chapters.

4.13 Control Functions

The following function sends messages to a control within a dialog box:

```
LONG SendDlgItemMessage (HWND hDlg, int nControlID, unsigned msg, WORD wP, LONG
lP);
```

hDlg is the window handle for the dialog box that contains the control with child ID nControlID. The other parameters and the result are the same as with the SendMessage function. An alternative to the SendDlgItemMessage function is the following code sequence:

```
hControl = GetDlgItem(hDlg, nControlID);
SendMessage(hControl, msg, wP, lP);
```

The GetDlgItem function retrieves the window handle for a dialog box control. This can then be passed to the SendMessage function as a parameter.

The following function writes text to a control (usually an edit box):

```
void SetDlgItemText (HWND hDlg, int nControlID, LPSTR lpszText);
```

hDlg is the window handle for the dialog box that contains the control. nControlID is the child ID of the control. lpszText is a long pointer to a character string, ending in "\0", which contains the text to be used.

The following function copies text from a control to a buffer:

```
int GetDlgItemText (HWND hDlg, int nControlID, LPSTR lpBuffer, int nMaxCount);
```

hDlg and nControlID have the same meanings as with SetDlgItemText. lpBuffer is a long pointer to the buffer used to store the character string. A maximum number of nMaxCount characters is copied. The function result gives the number of characters actually copied.

This function places the value wNumber (which has been converted to a character string) in a control in a dialog box:

```
void SetDlgItemInt (HWND hDlg, int nControlID, unsigned wNumber, BOOL bSigned);
```

bSigned indicates whether or not wNumber has a sign. The minus sign is automatically generated for negative numbers. hDlg and nControlID are used the same as above.

The following function attempts to convert a character string from a control to a signed (bSigned == TRUE) or unsigned (bSigned == FALSE) numerical value:

```
unsigned GetDlgItemInt (HWND hDlg, int nControlID, BOOL FAR * lpbSuccess, BOOL
bSigned);
```

hDlg and nControlID are the same as before. *lpbSuccess is TRUE if the conversion is successful; otherwise it is FALSE. The function result is the converted numerical value.

4.14 Application: DBOXDEMO.EXE

Now that we've covered a lot of information on programming dialog boxes, it's time to look at an application that utilizes these ideas. We have written a program that uses both a modal and a modeless dialog box, as well as all of the most commonly used controls. This application is called DBOXDEMO. In addition to demonstrating the use of dialog boxes, this program should prove helpful for music lovers who are beginning to lose track of all the titles in their record, cassette or CD collections.

4.14.1 The structure of DBOXDEMO.EXE

With the DBOXDEMO application you can manage a music library consisting of LPs, cassettes or CDs. In addition to using dialog boxes to enter each title, the program also offers search capabilities so that you can find the titles again.

Data entry

The heart of the application is a modal dialog box called "Enter Data". This dialog box will allow you to enter new titles into the database and to modify or delete existing titles. This modal dialog box is supported by a modeless dialog box that allows you to search for data records by using the criteria "Performer" and "Title". When a data record is found, it is displayed in the "Enter Data" dialog box.

Menus

After the application is started under Windows, the menu bar offers two pull-down menus: **File** and **Dialog Boxes**. The **File** menu contains the menu items **Exit** and **About DBoxDemo...**. The **About DBoxDemo...** menu item displays an about box for the application. An about box is a modal dialog box that contains information about the program, such as the copyright and version number, etc. About boxes (including the one we will use) usually have only an OK button to close them.

The **Dialog Boxes** menu has two items: **Enter Data...** and **Search for Data...**. The **Enter Data...** menu item will open the modal dialog box described above. This dialog box contains edit boxes for entering the performer, title, label and index for each data record. The index is simply a unique number that is assigned sequentially and is used to identify each data record.

Categories and recorded media

This dialog box also contains a combo field from which you can select the style of music for each title in your collection. Either click the pop box next to the edit box and select one of the descriptions from the list box that will open or type character string directly into the edit box. The group box entitled "Recorded Medium" contains three radio buttons used to indicate the format of the recording (LP, cassette or CD).

The "Enter Data" dialog box contains several other controls. The Add button creates a new entry in your database. Clicking this button will open a message box that asks you to confirm the creation of a new entry. By clicking Yes, all of the information entered is stored in a new data record. The new record is not written to the database on disk until you exit the dialog box by clicking the OK button.

The Edit button allows you to change the information that is stored with an existing data record. After confirmation, the new information will overwrite the existing information for the selected data record. The Delete button deletes the current data record after confirmation from the user. The next data record from the database will then be displayed as the current record. The Forward and Back buttons move to the next or the previous record in the database.

The "Search for Data" dialog box contains two edit boxes for entering a title and/or performer. The "Search Criteria" group box contains the check boxes "Upper/Lower" and "Whole Word". These options can be set independent of one another. When "Upper/Lower" is selected, the upper- and lowercase letters given in the search string must match exactly in order to find a data record. The "Whole Word" option means that the entire word, instead of the first few characters, must match the search string.

The Search button starts the search according to the specified search string(s). The records found by the search are ordered by index, performer and title and displayed in the "Records Found" list box. To select any data record from this list and make it the current data record, simply double-click it. If the "Enter Data" dialog box is open at this time, the information for the selected data record will be displayed immediately. Otherwise, this dialog box will be automatically opened and the selected data record will be displayed.

4.14.2 Important routines

Let's begin with the database structure. We won't need a complex indexing scheme for this application. Each data record is defined in the DataArray field with a MAXDATAENTRIES entry of type DataRecord_t:

```
DataRecord_t DataArray[MAXDATAENTRIES];
```

DataRecord_t is simply a structure that contains all of the important attributes of a data record:

```
// Type definition of data records used
typedef struct tagDataRecord_t
{
  char      szPerformer[MAXFIELDLENGTH];      // Performer
  char      szTitle[MAXFIELDLENGTH];          // Music title
  char      szLabel[MAXFIELDLENGTH];          // Music label
  char      szKindOfMusic[MAXFIELDLENGTH];    // Music category
  short     nMedium;                          // RECORD, CASSETTE or CD
  unsigned  wIndex;                           // Index arrangement
  BOOL      bUsed;                            // Used marker
} DataRecord_t;
```

The current data record is stored in the DataRecord variable of type DataRecord_t. The ReadData and WriteData functions are used to load and store the DataArray field. The C runtime function fwrite does most of the work for the WriteData function:

```
// Save data records
nItems = fwrite(DataArray, sizeof(DataRecord), MAXDATAENTRIES, FilePointer);
```

This function writes MAXDATAENTRIES blocks of size sizeof(DataRecord) starting at the position of the DataArray field in the file that is linked with the FilePointer. All elements of the DataArray field are written in one operation to the "MUSIC.DAT" file that was previously opened with fopen. The ReadData function can then use the C runtime function fread to load a data record:

```
// Read file
```

```
nItems = fread(DataArray, sizeof(DataRecord), MAXDATAENTRIES, FilePointer);
```

A disadvantage of this simple method is that the entire field is stored or read each time, even if only a minor change is made to one element. However, this isn't really important considering the small amount of data managed by this application.

Dialog box management

Two global variables are used to manage the modal and modeless dialog boxes (hDlgModal and hDlgModeless). These variables contain the current dialog box handle and they will be set to zero if the dialog box is not active. The flag bDlgModeless also exists for the modeless "Search for Data" dialog box to indicate the dialog box status in the menu.

The dialog functions for the about dialog box, the modal "Enter Data" dialog box and the modeless "Search for Data" dialog box are MdfAboutProc, MdfMusicProc and NdfSearchProc, respectively. These are exported to the module definition file for the application as callback functions.

Calling dialog boxes

Each dialog box is called from within MainWinProc, the window function for the main window. When the user selects a menu item, a corresponding MI_ABOUT, MI_ENTERDATA or MI_SEARCHDATA message is sent and processed by MainWinProc function. In addition, the "Search for Data" dialog box can call the "Enter Data" dialog box directly by sending an MI_ENTERDATA message to the main window. We have already discussed the function call to the DialogBox or CreateDialog function and the use of the MakeProcInstance and FreeProcInstance procedures in this situation.

The MdfAboutProc dialog function for the about dialog box is quite simple. It simply processes the OK button and the messages of the system menu. It has the same basic structure we have seen with other modal dialog functions. The details of the MdgMusicProc dialog function are more interesting. WM_INITDIALOG is the first message processed after a dialog box is opened. This message allows us to assign selected values to the controls or perform other initialization tasks within a dialog box before it appears on the screen.

The MdfMusicProc function stores the handle for the dialog box in the variable hDlgModal. This will be used later by the "Search for Data" dialog box to send a user-defined message.

Next, the list box from the "Categories" combo box is loaded with the predefined strings from the string table of the resource file:

```
// Fill "Categories" combo field with entries
for (i=0; i<MAXCOMBOITEMS; i++)
{
  // Read entry from STRINGTABLE resource
  LoadString(hInst, IDS_KINDOFMUSIC+i, (LPSTR)szBuffer, MAXFIELDLENGTH);
  // Insert in list fields of combo field
  SendDlgItemMessage(hDlg, CO_KINDOFMUSIC, CB_ADDSTRING, 0,
                     (LONG)(LPSTR)szBuffer);
}
```

We use the SendDlgItemMessage function to do this. This function sends a CB_ADDSTRING message to the combo box for each string it reads. This message adds the character string, indicated by lParam, to the end of the list box or to the appropriate location if it is a sorted combo box. The wParam parameter is not evaluated for this message. The value returned by the message is not evaluated. This value could be CB_ERR in the case of a general error or CB_ERRSPACE if there is not enough storage space.

After this, the program checks to see if the variable nRecNr, which represents the field index of the current data record, shows a valid data record in the DataArray field. If it doesn't the next data record is copied to the DataRecord variable and the corresponding value is assigned to nRecNr. Finally, the DisplayData function displays the fields of the data record, in the appropriate controls of the dialog box, using the SetDlgItemText and SetDlgItemInt functions, which we have already seen. Also notice how the CheckRadioButton function is used:

```
// Initialize radio buttons
CheckRadioButton(hDlg, RB_RECORD, RB_CD, RB_RECORD+DataRecord->nMedium);
```

The CheckRadioButton function has the following syntax:

```
void CheckRadioButton (HWND hDlg, int nIDFirstButton, int nIDLastButton,
int nIDCheckButton);
```

hDlg is the handle for the dialog box that contains the radio buttons. nIDFirstButton is the ID for the first radio button in the group and nIDLastButton is the ID for the last button in the group. A group of radio buttons should always be assigned sequential numerical IDs. Otherwise, CheckRadioButton may not be able to find the radio button that you want to deselect. nIDCheckButton gives the ID of the radio button that is selected.

Finally, the input focus is set to the "Performer" edit box using the SetFocus function:

```
// Set input focus to first edit field
SetFocus(GetDlgItem(hDlg, EB_PERFORMER));
return FALSE;                    // Return value FALSE unless SetFocus
break;
```

For a SetFocus call, the result of the dialog function must be FALSE even though the WM_INITDIALOG message is processed by the application; otherwise the text within the edit box will be selected when it is displayed. In this case, Windows would then assign the input focus to the first control with its WS_TABSTOP flag set (and whose handle was passed to the WM_INITDIALOG message as a word parameter).

Next, we come to the processing of messages in the "Enter Data" dialog box. When the Add button is clicked, the ReadMusicData function reads the current contents of the control after a message box is displayed. This is done with the help of the GetDlgItemText and GetDlgItemInt functions. The IsDlgButtonChecked function determines which radio button is checked:

```
  // Determine which radio button is checked
  for (i=0; i<3; i++)
  {
    if (IsDlgButtonChecked(hDlg, RB_RECORD+i))
    {
      DataRecord->nMedium = i;
      break;
    }
  }
} // ReadMusicData
```

The IsDlgButtonChecked function has the following syntax:

```
WORD IsDlgButtonChecked (HWND hDlg, int nControlID);
```

hDlg is the handle for the dialog box. nControlID is the ID of the radio button being checked. The function returns 0 if the radio button is not checked, 1 if it is checked and 2 for a three-way radio button that is gray.

After the ReadMusicData function is called, the next free data record is found and the contents of the DataRecord structure are stored there.

The [Edit] button is processed in much the same way but, instead of finding a new data record, the current record in the DataArray field is overwritten. Pressing the [Delete] button will set the bUsed flag for the current data record to FALSE. Then the next valid data record is found with the help of the PostMessage function, which sends a WM_COMMAND message and the wP parameter, which contains the value PB_FORWARD, to the dialog box. The field index is incremented until a valid record is found or all records have been checked. PB_FORWARD is also used when the [Forward] button is pressed. Similarly, PB_BACKWARD is processed when the [Back] button is pressed. In this case, the search for a valid data record goes through the DataArray field in the opposite direction.

SEARCH_DATA is one message that is not processed in the WM_COMMAND branch of the MdfMusicProc function. This is a user-defined message:

```
#define SEARCH_DATA      WM_USER+1          // Your own messages
```

Windows provides message values, starting with WM_USER (which is defined in the include file WINDOWS.H), for creating your own message within an application. You can use these in the message loops of windows and dialog boxes just as you would any other messages.

In our case, the modal dialog box "Enter Data" receives this type of message when the user double-clicks a list box entry, from the "Data Records Found" box, in order to make this data record current:

```
case SEARCH_DATA:                  // Msg from "Search for Data" dialog box
  nRecNr = (short)wP;              // Record number
  DataRecord = DataArray[nRecNr];  // Select data record
```

```
DisplayData(hDlg, &DataRecord); // Display data record
return TRUE;
break;
```

When the OK button is pressed, the entire DataArray field is saved in the "MUSIC.DAT" file and the dialog box is closed with the EndDialog function. The hDlgModal window handle is also set to NULL.

Now let's look at the dialog function NdfSearchProc, which belongs to the modeless "Search for Data" dialog box. The first thing that happens when the WM_INITDIALOG message is processed is that the "Search Criteria" check boxes are initialized. This is done with the CheckDlgButton function:

```
case WM_INITDIALOG:        // Dialog box display message

  // Check "Title" check box with CheckDlgButton function
  CheckDlgButton(hDlg, CB_NOIGNORECASE, TRUE);
  bCBNoIgnoreCase = TRUE;

  // Alternate: Send a control message
  SendDlgItemMessage(hDlg, CB_WHOLEWORD, BM_SETCHECK, FALSE, 0L);
  bCBWholeWord = FALSE;
  return TRUE;
  break;
```

The CheckDlgButton function is used as follows:

```
void CheckDlgButton (HWND hDlg, int nControlID, WORD wCheck);
```

hDlg is the dialog box handle. nControlID is the check box ID. wCheck determines how the check box is handled by the function. If it is 0, the mark is removed from the check box. If this parameter is 1, the mark is set. If the value is 2 and the check box can have three conditions, then it will be displayed in gray.

The CheckDlgButton function sends a BM_SETCHECK message to the corresponding check box control. We have already seen this mechanism for checking the CB_WHOLEWORD check box. In this case, the check mode is passed with the wParam parameter. The boolean variable bCBWholeWord indicates the status of the checks:

```
case CB_NOIGNORECASE:  // "Upper/Lower" check box
  bCBNoIgnoreCase = !bCBNoIgnoreCase;
  CheckDlgButton(hDlg, CB_NOIGNORECASE, bCBNoIgnoreCase);
  return TRUE;
  break;

case CB_WHOLEWORD:      // "Whole Word" check box
  bCBWholeWord = !bCBWholeWord;
  CheckDlgButton(hDlg, CB_WHOLEWORD, bCBWholeWord);
  return TRUE;
  break;
```

The [Search] button plays a major role within the "Search for Data" dialog box. When this button is pressed, the contents of the "Performer" and "Title" edit boxes are read. Any entries that may already be in the "Records Found" box are removed by sending an LB_RESETCONTENT message. Then the data records in the DataArray field are compared with the character strings in the edit boxes by using the CompareStrings function.

In addition to the two character strings being compared, this function receives the parameters bNoIgnoreCase and bWholeWord. These boolean variables determine whether the search should be case sensitive and if entire words must match the search string. A value of TRUE means that the additional search attribute is activated.

When a data record that matches the search string is found, the most important fields are combined with the wsprintf function to create a character string that is then displayed in the "Records Found" box:

```
if ((bPerformer && (szTitle[0] == 0)) ||
    (bTitle && (szPerformer[0] == 0)) ||
    (bPerformer && bTitle))     // Similar data record found?
{
     // Format list field entry
    wsprintf(szListboxString, "%-3d %-25.25s %-25.25s %25d",
            DataArray[i].wIndex,
             (LPSTR)DataArray[i].szPerformer,
             (LPSTR)DataArray[i].szTitle,
              i);
     // Append entry to list field
     SendDlgItemMessage(hDlg, LB_FOUND, LB_ADDSTRING, 0,
                         (LONG)(LPSTR) szListboxString);
}
```

The wspintf function is a Windows API function that is used the same way as the sprintf C runtime function. As a rule, the wsprintf function should be used in Windows 3.0 applications, since this reduces the size of the .exe file by several kilobytes. Also, this function has been specially optimized for Windows applications. There is one thing to watch out for when using this function: If you use a % symbol in the format character string, the corresponding variable must be cast after LPSTR. Otherwise you will receive an "application error" and the application will crash. This happens because the wsprintf function contains variable parameters and will not work with the automatic prototyping of the compiler.

Index

In addition to the index, the performer and the title, the list box character string also contains the index value DataArray. This is given as the last entry in the character string. This value is not displayed in the list box because it has no meaning to the user. However, the program uses it later to retrieve the entire data record when a list entry is selected with a double-click.

With this in mind, let's discuss how list box messages are handled within the "Search for Data" dialog box. The only thing we are interested in is a double-click on one of the list box entries. This is how a user selects a specific data record after a search locates several. A double-click is distinguished by the value LDN_DBLCLK in the high word of the lparam parameter:

```
case LB_FOUND:        // Message from "Record Found" list field
  if (HIWORD(lP) == LBN_DBLCLK)        // Double-click an entry
  {
```

Next, we retrieve the index of the double-clicked entry by sending an LB_GETCURSEL message:

```
// Get index for currently selected entry
i = (int) SendDlgItemMessage(hDlg, LB_FOUND, LB_GETCURSEL, 0, 0L);
```

We can then select the corresponding list box entry with the help of this index:

```
// Insert in list fields of combo field
SendDlgItemMessage(hDlg, CO_KINDOFMUSIC, CB_ADDSTRING, 0,
                    (LONG)(LPSTR)szBuffer);
```

Now we can use the sscanf C runtime function to read the index value from the character string:

```
// Specify field index
sscanf(&szListboxString[57], "%d", &nSearchRecNr);
```

This value is then used by the variable nRecNr, which indicates the current data records. It is also used to send a message, to the main window, to open the "Enter Data" dialog box if it isn't already on the screen. Otherwise, the main window is sent the user-defined SEARCH_DATA message and the wParam parameter passes the index value of the data record found, by the search, so that the information in the record can be displayed in the "Enter Data" dialog box:

```
// Adapt current data record
  if (DataArray[nSearchRecNr].bUsed)
  {
    // Open "File Entry" dialog box if record doesn't exist
    if (!hDlgModal)
    {
      nRecNr = nSearchRecNr;
      SendMessage(hwMain, WM_COMMAND, MI_ENTERDATA, 0L);
    }
    else              // Post found records
      PostMessage(hDlgModal, SEARCH_DATA, nSearchRecNr, 0L);
  }
  return TRUE;
}
break;
```

4.15 Source Code: DBOXDEMO.EXE

DBOXDEMO.H include file

```
/* Stringtable defines */

#define IDS_APPLNAME        1
#define IDS_KINDOFMUSIC  2

/* Application icon */

#define IDDIALOGICON    50

/* File menu */

#define MI_QUIT         100
#define MI_ABOUT        101

/* Dialog menu */

#define MI_ENTERDATA    110
#define MI_SEARCHDATA   111

/* Dialog box control IDs */

#define EB_PERFORMER    200 /* Edit fields    */
#define EB_TITLE        201
#define EB_LABEL        202
#define EB_INDEX        203

#define LB_FOUND        210 /* List fields    */

#define CO_KINDOFMUSIC  220 /* Combo fields    */

#define RB_RECORD       230 /* Radio buttons   */
#define RB_CASSETTE     231
#define RB_CD           232

#define CB_NOIGNORECASE 240 /* Check boxes    */
#define CB_WHOLEWORD    241

#define PB_NEW          250 /* Buttons */
#define PB_DELETE       251
#define PB_FORWARD      252
#define PB_BACKWARD     253
#define PB_SEARCH       254
```

```
#define PB_CHANGE       255

/* Other defines */

#define MAXCOMBOITEMS     5 /* Number or entries in type of music combofield */
```

DBOXDEMO.RC resource file

```
#include <windows.h>

#include "dboxdemo.h"

IDDIALOGICON ICON dboxdemo.ico    ; Icon

rcinclude dboxdemo.dlg            ; Contains dialog box definitions

STRINGTABLE
BEGIN
  IDS_APPLNAME,      "DboxDemo" ; Application name
  IDS_KINDOFMUSIC,   "Pop"      ; Category of music
  IDS_KINDOFMUSIC+1, "Rock"
  IDS_KINDOFMUSIC+2, "Jazz"
  IDS_KINDOFMUSIC+3, "Instrumental"
  IDS_KINDOFMUSIC+4, "Classical"
END

MainMenu MENU
BEGIN
  POPUP "&File"
  BEGIN
    MENUITEM "E&xit",     MI_QUIT
    MENUITEM SEPARATOR
    MENUITEM "A&bout DBoxDemo...", MI_ABOUT
  END
  POPUP "&Dialog Boxes"
  BEGIN
    MENUITEM "&Enter Data...",  MI_ENTERDATA
    MENUITEM "&Search for Data...",           MI_SEARCHDATA
  END
END ; MainMenu
```

DBOXDEMO.DLG dialog box file

```
SEARCHDLG DIALOG LOADONCALL MOVEABLE DISCARDABLE 53, 15, 189, 128
CAPTION "Data Search"
STYLE WS_BORDER | WS_CAPTION | WS_DLGFRAME | WS_SYSMENU | WS_VISIBLE | WS_POPUP
```

```
BEGIN
    CONTROL "Performer:", -1, "static", SS_LEFT | WS_CHILD, 6, 5, 51, 10
    CONTROL "", 200, "edit", ES_LEFT | ES_AUTOHSCROLL | WS_BORDER | WS_TABSTOP |
WS_CHILD, 6, 16, 104, 12
    CONTROL "Title:", -1, "static", SS_LEFT | WS_CHILD, 6, 34, 46, 10
    CONTROL "", 201, "edit", ES_LEFT | WS_BORDER | WS_TABSTOP | WS_CHILD, 7, 45,
103, 12
    CONTROL "Search Criteria", -1, "button", BS_GROUPBOX | WS_TABSTOP | WS_CHILD,
119, 4, 64, 53
    CONTROL "Upper/Lower", 240, "button", BS_CHECKBOX | WS_GROUP | WS_TABSTOP |
WS_CHILD, 125, 18, 53, 12
    CONTROL "Whole Word", 241, "button", BS_CHECKBOX | WS_TABSTOP | WS_CHILD,
125, 36, 54, 12
    CONTROL "Records Found:", -1, "static", SS_LEFT | WS_GROUP | WS_CHILD, 6, 68,
99, 11
    CONTROL "", 210, "listbox", LBS_NOTIFY | LBS_SORT | LBS_STANDARD | WS_BORDER
| WS_VSCROLL | WS_CHILD, 6, 82, 178, 41
    CONTROL "Search", 254, "button", BS_PUSHBUTTON | WS_TABSTOP | WS_CHILD, 119,
63, 65, 12
END

MUSICDLG DIALOG LOADONCALL MOVEABLE DISCARDABLE 22, 23, 257, 124
CAPTION "Data Entry"
STYLE WS_BORDER | WS_CAPTION | WS_DLGFRAME | WS_SYSMENU | WS_POPUP
BEGIN
    CONTROL "Performer:", -1, "static", SS_LEFT | WS_CHILD, 7, 9, 35, 12
    CONTROL "", 200, "edit", ES_LEFT | ES_AUTOHSCROLL | WS_BORDER | WS_TABSTOP |
WS_CHILD, 47, 6, 92, 12
    CONTROL "Title:", -1, "static", SS_LEFT | WS_CHILD, 7, 30, 31, 12
    CONTROL "", 201, "edit", ES_LEFT | ES_AUTOHSCROLL | WS_BORDER | WS_TABSTOP |
WS_CHILD, 47, 27, 92, 12
    CONTROL "Label:", -1, "static", SS_LEFT | WS_CHILD, 7, 51, 32, 12
    CONTROL "", 202, "edit", ES_LEFT | ES_AUTOHSCROLL | WS_BORDER | WS_TABSTOP |
WS_CHILD, 47, 49, 92, 12
    CONTROL "Index:", -1, "static", SS_LEFT | WS_CHILD, 7, 73, 34, 12
    CONTROL "", 203, "edit", ES_LEFT | WS_BORDER | WS_TABSTOP | WS_CHILD, 47, 72,
24, 11
    CONTROL "Category:", 106, "static", SS_LEFT | WS_CHILD, 167, 9, 66, 11
    CONTROL "", 220, "combobox", CBS_DROPDOWN | WS_VSCROLL | WS_CHILD, 167, 27,
81, 55
    CONTROL "Recorded Medium", -1, "button", BS_GROUPBOX | WS_TABSTOP | WS_CHILD,
167, 47, 81, 69
    CONTROL "LP", 230, "button", BS_AUTORADIOBUTTON | WS_GROUP | WS_TABSTOP |
WS_CHILD, 175, 63, 68, 12
    CONTROL "Cassette", 231, "button", BS_AUTORADIOBUTTON | WS_TABSTOP |
WS_CHILD, 175, 81, 55, 12
    CONTROL "CD", 232, "button", BS_AUTORADIOBUTTON | WS_TABSTOP | WS_CHILD, 175,
99, 28, 12
```

```
    CONTROL "OK", 1, "button", BS_DEFPUSHBUTTON | WS_GROUP | WS_TABSTOP |
WS_CHILD, 8, 104, 33, 13
    CONTROL "Add", 250, "button", BS_PUSHBUTTON | WS_TABSTOP | WS_CHILD, 46, 104,
34, 13
    CONTROL "Edit", 255, "button", BS_PUSHBUTTON | WS_TABSTOP | WS_CHILD, 85,
104, 34, 13
    CONTROL "Delete", 251, "button", BS_PUSHBUTTON | WS_TABSTOP | WS_CHILD, 124,
104, 35, 13
    CONTROL "Back", 253, "button", BS_PUSHBUTTON | WS_TABSTOP | WS_CHILD, 85, 86,
34, 13
    CONTROL "Forward", 252, "button", BS_PUSHBUTTON | WS_TABSTOP | WS_CHILD, 124,
86, 35, 13
END

ABOUTDLG DIALOG LOADONCALL MOVEABLE DISCARDABLE 72, 15, 157, 89
CAPTION "About DBoxDemo"
STYLE WS_BORDER | WS_CAPTION | WS_DLGFRAME | WS_SYSMENU | DS_MODALFRAME |
WS_POPUP
BEGIN
    CONTROL "DboxDemo", -1, "static", SS_CENTER | WS_CHILD, 58, 5, 37, 10
    CONTROL "Version 1.00", -1, "static", SS_CENTER | WS_CHILD, 46, 20, 62, 10
    CONTROL "Copyright  1991", -1, "static", SS_CENTER | WS_CHILD, 36, 35, 86, 11
    CONTROL "Abacus", -1, "static", SS_CENTER | WS_CHILD, 40, 51, 79, 11
    CONTROL "OK", 1, "button", BS_DEFPUSHBUTTON | WS_TABSTOP | WS_CHILD, 66, 70,
24, 12
    CONTROL "", -1, "static", SS_ICON | WS_CHILD, 13, 25, 16, 27
END
```

DBOXDEMO.DEF module definition file

```
NAME        DBOXDEMO

DESCRIPTION  'Program demonstrating simple dialog boxes'

EXETYPE      WINDOWS

CODE        PRELOAD MOVEABLE DISCARDABLE
DATA        PRELOAD MOVEABLE MULTIPLE

HEAPSIZE     8000
STACKSIZE    8000

EXPORTS
             MainWndProc   @1
             MdfAboutProc  @2
             MdfMusicProc  @3
             NdfSearchProc @4
```

DBOXDEMO.MAK MAKE file

```
Model = S
Warn   = 2
Linker = link

all: dboxdemo.exe

dboxdemo.res: dboxdemo.h dboxdemo.rc dboxdemo.dlg
  rc -r dboxdemo.rc

dboxdemo.obj: dboxdemo.h dboxdemo.c
  cl -c -A$(Model) -W$(Warn) -Gsw -Zpe -Os dboxdemo.c

dboxdemo.exe: dboxdemo.obj dboxdemo.def dboxdemo.res
  $(Linker) /NOD /al:16 dboxdemo,dboxdemo.exe,,libw+$(Model)libcew,dboxdemo.def
  rc dboxdemo.res
```

DBOXDEMO.C source code

```
/***************************************************************************
 DBOXDEMO.C
 ==========

 This program demonstrates basic techniques for programming dialog boxes
 (modal and modeless) under Windows. This application is a simple database,
 with which the user can keep track of records, cassettes and CDs.
 ***************************************************************************/

/* ---------------------------< Include files >--------------------------- */

#include <windows.h>
#include <stdio.h>
#include <string.h>
#include <stdlib.h>
#include <io.h>

#include "dboxdemo.h"

/* -----------------------------< Defines >------------------------------- */

#define MAXFIELDLENGTH 25                    // Maximum data field length
#define MAXDATAENTRIES 200                   // Maximum number of records
#define RECORD          0                    // Records
#define CASSETTE        1                    // Cassettes
#define CD              2                    // CD
```

```
#define SEARCH_DATA     WM_USER+1           // Your own messages

/* ------------------------< Type definitions >------------------------- */

// Type definition of data records used
typedef struct tagDataRecord_t
{
  char     szPerformer[MAXFIELDLENGTH];     // Performer
  char     szTitle[MAXFIELDLENGTH];         // Music title
  char     szLabel[MAXFIELDLENGTH];         // Music label
  char     szKindOfMusic[MAXFIELDLENGTH];   // Music category
  short    nMedium;                         // RECORD, CASSETTE or CD
  unsigned wIndex;                          // Index arrangement
  BOOL     bUsed;                           // Used marker
} DataRecord_t;

/* ------------------------< Global variables >-------------------------- */

HANDLE        hInst;                        // Instance of application
HWND          hwMain,                       // Main window
              hDlgModeless = NULL,          // Modeless dialog box handle
              hDlgModal = NULL;             // Modal dialog box handle
HMENU         hMainMenu;                    // Main menu handle
char          szApplName[MAXFIELDLENGTH];   // Application name
BOOL          bDlgModeless = FALSE;         // Marker for a modeless
                                            // dialog box
FILE          *FilePointer;                 // File pointer
DataRecord_t DataArray[MAXDATAENTRIES];     // Data record field
DataRecord_t DataRecord;                    // Current data record
short         nRecNr = 0,                   // Current data record number
              nSearchRecNr;                 // Used for searching
FARPROC       lpfnModal,                    // Used by modal dialog boxes
              lpfnModeless;                 // Used by modeless dialog boxes

/* ----------------------< Function prototypes >------------------------ */

LONG FAR PASCAL MainWndProc   (HWND, unsigned, WORD, LONG);
BOOL FAR PASCAL MdfAboutProc  (HWND, unsigned, WORD, LONG);
BOOL FAR PASCAL MdfMusicProc  (HWND, unsigned, WORD, LONG);
BOOL FAR PASCAL NdfSearchProc (HWND, unsigned, WORD, LONG);
BOOL CompareStrings (char *, char *, BOOL, BOOL);
BOOL ReadData (void);
BOOL WriteData (void);
int  InitFirstInstance (HANDLE ,HANDLE, int);
void ReadMusicData (HWND, DataRecord_t *);
void DisplayData (HWND, DataRecord_t *);
void PaintDialog (HWND);
```

```
/*****************************************************************************
 W i n M a i n ()
 ================

 The WinMain function is the main function for every Windows program. WinMain
 is the equivalent of the main() function found in standard C programs, and
 represents the "point of entry" for program execution.

 Parameters:

   HANDLE hInstance:     Current instance handle of the application.
   HANDLE hPrevInstance: Previous instance handle of the application. NULL
                         if the current instance is the first instance.
   LPSTR  lpszCmdLine:   Long pointer to the string placed after the program
                         name during program execution.
   int    nCmdShow:      Parameter which specifies the application window's
                         appearance when the program starts.

 Return values:

   int:                  The wParam parameter for the last message received.
 *****************************************************************************/

int PASCAL WinMain (HANDLE hInstance,  HANDLE hPrevInstance,
                    LPSTR lpszCmdLine, int nCmdShow)
{
  MSG   msg;                          // Message variable

  if (!hPrevInstance)                 // Initialization of first instance
  {
    if (!InitFirstInstance(hInstance, hPrevInstance, nCmdShow))
      return NULL;

  }
  else                                // No additional instances allowed
  {
    return NULL;
  }

  hInst  = hInstance;                           // Declaration of global
                                                // instance variable

  hwMain = CreateWindow(szApplName,             // Window class name
                        szApplName,             // Window title
                        WS_OVERLAPPEDWINDOW |   // Window style
                        WS_VSCROLL,             // (overlapped)
                        CW_USEDEFAULT,          // X-position (default)
                        CW_USEDEFAULT,          // Y-position (default)
```

```
                    CW_USEDEFAULT,          // Initial X-size (default)
                    CW_USEDEFAULT,          // Initial Y-size (default)
                    NULL,                   // No parent window
                    LoadMenu(hInstance, "MainMenu"),
                    hInstance,              // Instance of application
                    NULL);                  // No creation parameters

  if (!hwMain)
    return NULL;

/* -------------------< Execute initialization tasks >------------------ */

  FilePointer = fopen("MUSIC.DAT", "rb");      // Open file
  if (FilePointer == NULL)                     // File not found?
  {
      fclose(FilePointer);                     // Close file
      memset(DataArray, 0, sizeof(DataArray)); // Initialize data array
      WriteData();                             // Save data array
  }
  else
    fclose(FilePointer);                       // Close file

 // Get handle to main menu
 hMainMenu = GetMenu(hwMain);
 // Initialize "Search for Data" item
 CheckMenuItem(hMainMenu, MI_SEARCHDATA, MF_UNCHECKED);
 // Read data records
 ReadData();

/* ---------------------< Display main window >----------------------- */

  ShowWindow(hwMain, nCmdShow);                // Make window visible
  UpdateWindow(hwMain);                        // Update window

/* -------------------------< Message  loop >--------------------------- */

 while (GetMessage(&msg, NULL, 0, 0))          // Message reading
 {
   if (!(hDlgModeless != NULL &&               // Dialog box active?
        IsDialogMessage(hDlgModeless, &msg)))  // Dialog box message?
   {
     TranslateMessage(&msg);                   // Message translation
     DispatchMessage(&msg);                    // Message -> Windows
   }
 }
 return (msg.wParam);                          // End application
} // WinMain
```

```
/******************************************************************************
 I n i t F i r s t I n s t a n c e ()
 ====================================

 This function initializes the first instance of the "DboxDemo" application.

 Parameters:

   HANDLE hInstance:     Current instance handle of the application.
   HANDLE hPrevInstance: Previous instance handle of the application. NULL
                         if the current instance is the first instance.
   int    nCmdShow:      Parameter which specifies the application window's
                         appearance when the program starts.

 Return values:

   int                         NULL if the "DboxDemo" window class registers.
                         Otherwise, a value other than NULL.
******************************************************************************/

int InitFirstInstance (HANDLE hInstance, HANDLE hPrevInstance, int nCmdShow)
{
  WNDCLASS MainWndClass;                    // Main window class

  // Load application name from resource file
  LoadString(hInstance, IDS_APPLNAME, (LPSTR)szApplName, 20);

  // Specify window class information
  MainWndClass.lpszClassName = szApplName;                  // Window class
  MainWndClass.hInstance     = hInstance;                   // Instance
  MainWndClass.lpfnWndProc   = MainWndProc;                 // Window function
  MainWndClass.style         = CS_HREDRAW | CS_VREDRAW;
  MainWndClass.lpszMenuName  = (LPSTR) NULL;                // No menu
  MainWndClass.hCursor       = LoadCursor(NULL, IDC_ARROW); // Mouse cursor
  MainWndClass.hIcon         = LoadIcon(hInstance,
MAKEINTRESOURCE(IDDIALOGICON));
  MainWndClass.hbrBackground = GetStockObject(WHITE_BRUSH); // White background
  MainWndClass.cbClsExtra    = 0;                           // No extra bytes
  MainWndClass.cbWndExtra    = 0;                           // No extra bytes

  // Registering "DboxDemo" window class
  return (RegisterClass(&MainWndClass));
} // InitFirstInstance

/******************************************************************************
 M a i n W n d P r o c ()
 ========================
```

```
This function acts as the main window function. All messages are sent to
this window.

Parameters:

  HWND      hWnd:      Window handle.
  unsigned  msg:       Message type.
  WORD      wP:        Message-dependent 16 bit value
  LONG      lP:        Message-dependent 32 bit value

Return values:

  LONG                 0L if the window function has sent the message.
                       Otherwise, the return value from the DefWindowProc
                       default window function.
***************************************************************************/

LONG FAR PASCAL MainWndProc (HWND hWnd, unsigned msg, WORD wP, LONG lP)
{
   HMENU   hMenu;                 // Menu handle variable
   int     nResult;               // Return value for DialogBox function

   switch (msg)
   {
     case WM_CREATE:              // For creating window

       // Initialization of global data record variable
       memset(&DataRecord, 0, sizeof(DataRecord));
       break;

     case WM_DESTROY:
       PostQuitMessage(0);        // Send WM_QUIT if window
                                  // is destroyed
       break;

     case WM_COMMAND:             // Messages from menu bar
       switch (wP)
       {
         case MI_QUIT:            // End program
            PostMessage(hwMain, WM_SYSCOMMAND, SC_CLOSE, 0L);
            break;

         case MI_ABOUT:           // Call "About DBoxDemo" dialog box
           lpfnModal = MakeProcInstance(MdfAboutProc, hInst);
           nResult = DialogBox(hInst, "ABOUTDLG", hwMain, lpfnModal);
           FreeProcInstance(lpfnModal);
           break;
```

```
        case MI_ENTERDATA:       // Call "Enter Data" dialog box
          lpfnModal = MakeProcInstance(MdfMusicProc, hInst);
          nResult = DialogBox(hInst, "MUSICDLG", hwMain, lpfnModal);
          FreeProcInstance(lpfnModal);
          break;

        case MI_SEARCHDATA:      // Call "Search for Data" dialog box
          if (!bDlgModeless)     // Dialog box must be displayed
          {
            lpfnModeless = MakeProcInstance(NdfSearchProc, hInst);
            hDlgModeless = CreateDialog(hInst, "SEARCHDLG", hwMain,
lpfnModeless);
            bDlgModeless = TRUE;
            // Check menu entry
            CheckMenuItem(hMainMenu, MI_SEARCHDATA, MF_CHECKED);
          }
          else                   // Dialog box must be disturbed
          {
            DestroyWindow(hDlgModeless);
            FreeProcInstance(lpfnModeless);
            bDlgModeless = FALSE;
            hDlgModeless = NULL;
            // Remove checkmarks
            CheckMenuItem(hMainMenu, MI_SEARCHDATA, MF_UNCHECKED);
          }
          break;

         default:
           break;
      }
      break;

    case WM_PAINT:               // Client area update needed
      PaintDialog(hWnd);
      break;

    default: // Pass other messages to default window function
      return (DefWindowProc(hWnd, msg, wP, lP));
      break;
  }
  return 0L;
} // MainWndProc

/***********************************************************************
 M d f A b o u t P r o c ()
 ==========================

 This function processes messages for the "About DBoxDemo" dialog box.
```

```
 Parameters:

   HWND     hDlg:     Dialog box handle.
   unsigned msg:      Message type.
   WORD     wP:       Message-dependent 16 bit value
   LONG     lP:       Message-dependent 32 bit value

 Return values:

   BOOL               TRUE if the dialog function contains the given message.
                      Otherwise, FALSE.
 ***************************************************************************/

BOOL FAR PASCAL MdfAboutProc (HWND hDlg, unsigned msg, WORD wP, LONG lP)
{
  switch (msg)
  {
    case WM_INITDIALOG:         // Dialog box display message
      return TRUE;              // Do not execute initialization
      break;

    case WM_COMMAND:            // Dialog box control message
      switch (wP)
      {
        case IDOK:              // Click on OK button
          EndDialog(hDlg, TRUE);
          return TRUE;
          break;

        default:                // Other messages
          return FALSE;
          break;
      }
      break;

    case WM_SYSCOMMAND:         // Message from dialog box system menu
      switch (wP)
      {
        // ALT+F4, double-click system menu or select "Close" from system
        // menu

        case SC_CLOSE:
          EndDialog(hDlg, TRUE);
          return TRUE;
          break;

        default:                // Other system menu messages
```

```
          return FALSE;
          break;
      }
      break;

    default:                        // Other messages
        return FALSE;
        break;
  }
} // MdfAboutProc

/***************************************************************************
 M d f M u s i c P r o c ()
 ==========================

 This function processes messages for the "Data Entry" dialog box.

 Parameter:

   HWND     hDlg:     Dialog box handle.
   unsigned msg:      Message type.
   WORD     wP:       Message-dependent 16 bit value
   LONG     lP:       Message-dependent 32 bit value

 Return values:

   BOOL               TRUE if the dialog function contains the given message.
                      Otherwise, FALSE.
 ***************************************************************************/

BOOL FAR PASCAL MdfMusicProc (HWND hDlg, unsigned msg, WORD wP, LONG lP)
{
  int  i;
  BOOL bFound;
  char szBuffer[MAXFIELDLENGTH];

  switch (msg)
  {
    case WM_INITDIALOG:          // Dialog box display message
      hDlgModal = hDlg;          // Mark dialog box handle

      // Fill "Categories" combo field with entries
      for (i=0; i<MAXCOMBOITEMS; i++)
      {
        // Read entry from STRINGTABLE resource
        LoadString(hInst, IDS_KINDOFMUSIC+i, (LPSTR)szBuffer, MAXFIELDLENGTH);
        // Insert in list fields of combo field
        SendDlgItemMessage(hDlg, CO_KINDOFMUSIC, CB_ADDSTRING, 0,
```

```
                        (LONG)(LPSTR)szBuffer);
    }
    // Does nRecNr point to a valid data record?
    if (!DataArray[nRecNr].bUsed)
    {
      // If not, display first record found in data field
      for (i=0; i<MAXDATAENTRIES; i++)
      {
        if (DataArray[i].bUsed)
        {
          nRecNr = i;
          break;
        }
      }
    }
    DataRecord = DataArray[nRecNr]; // Select data record
    DisplayData(hDlg, &DataRecord); // Display data record
    // Set input focus to first edit field
    SetFocus(GetDlgItem(hDlg, EB_PERFORMER));
    return FALSE;                   // Return value FALSE unless SetFocus
    break;

  case SEARCH_DATA:                 // Msg from "Search for Data" dialog box
    nRecNr = (short)wP;             // Record number
    DataRecord = DataArray[nRecNr]; // Select data record
    DisplayData(hDlg, &DataRecord); // Display data record
    return TRUE;
    break;

  case WM_COMMAND:             // Message from dialog box controls
    switch (wP)
    {
      case IDOK:               // Click on OK button
        WriteData();           // Write entered records
        EndDialog(hDlg, TRUE); // Close dialog box
        hDlgModal = NULL;
        return TRUE;
        break;

      case PB_NEW:              // Save a new data record
        if (MessageBox(hDlg, "Add record - are you sure?", "Add Record",
                       MB_ICONQUESTION | MB_YESNO) == IDYES)
        {
          ReadMusicData(hDlg, &DataRecord); // Read values

          // Search for a free data record in DataArray
          bFound = FALSE;
          for (i=0; i<MAXDATAENTRIES; i++)
```

```
      {
        if (!DataArray[i].bUsed)         // Free entry
        {
          DataArray[i] = DataRecord;     // Copy structure data
          DataArray[i].bUsed = TRUE;     // Entry marked as USED
          bFound = TRUE;
          nRecNr = i;                    // Current data record number
          break;
        }
      }
      if (!bFound)
        MessageBox(hDlg, "No more fields available", szApplName,
                   MB_OK | MB_ICONEXCLAMATION);
    }
    return TRUE;
    break;

  case PB_CHANGE:          // Change an existing data record
    if (MessageBox(hDlg, "Edit record - are you sure?", "Edit Record",
                   MB_ICONQUESTION | MB_YESNO) == IDYES)
    {
      ReadMusicData(hDlg, &DataRecord); // Read values
      DataArray[nRecNr] = DataRecord;   // Move to data records - fields
    }
    return TRUE;
    break;

  case PB_DELETE:          // Delete a data record
    if (MessageBox(hDlg, "Delete record - are you sure?", "Delete Record",
                   MB_ICONQUESTION | MB_YESNO) == IDYES)
      DataArray[nRecNr].bUsed = FALSE;

    // Go to next data record
    PostMessage(hDlg, WM_COMMAND, PB_FORWARD, 0L);
    return TRUE;
    break;

  case PB_FORWARD:         // Next data record
    i = nRecNr+1;
    if (i >= MAXDATAENTRIES)
      i = 0;
    while (!DataArray[i].bUsed)
    {
      i++;
      if (i >= MAXDATAENTRIES)
        i=0;
      if (i == nRecNr)    // One complete loop
        break;
```

```
        }
        if (DataArray[i].bUsed)
        {
          nRecNr = i;
          DataRecord = DataArray[i];
          DisplayData(hDlg, &DataRecord);
        }
        else
          MessageBox(GetFocus(), "No records found", szApplName,
                     MB_ICONEXCLAMATION | MB_OK);
        return TRUE;
        break;

      case PB_BACKWARD:      // Previous data record
        i = nRecNr-1;
        if (i < 0)
          i = MAXDATAENTRIES-1;
        while (!DataArray[i].bUsed)
        {
          i--;
          if (i < 0)
            i=MAXDATAENTRIES-1;
          if (i == nRecNr)   // One complete loop
            break;
        }
        if (DataArray[i].bUsed)
        {
          nRecNr = i;
          DataRecord = DataArray[i];
          DisplayData(hDlg, &DataRecord);
        }
        else
          MessageBox(GetFocus(), "No records found", szApplName,
                     MB_ICONEXCLAMATION | MB_OK);
        return TRUE;
        break;

      default:
        return FALSE;
        break;
    }
    break;

  case WM_SYSCOMMAND:        // Message from dialog box system menu
    switch (wP)
    {
      // ALT+F4, double-click system menu or select "Close" from system
      // menu to select
```

```
        case SC_CLOSE:
          EndDialog(hDlg, TRUE);
          hDlgModal = NULL;
          return TRUE;
          break;

        default:                    // Other system menu messages
          return FALSE;
          break;
      }
      break;

    default:                        // Other messages
        return FALSE;
        break;
  }
} // MdfMusicProc

/****************************************************************************
 N d f S e a r c h P r o c ()
 ============================

 This function processes messages for the modeless "Search for Data"
 dialog box.

 Parameters:

   HWND      hDlg:      Dialog box handle.
   unsigned  msg:       Message type.
   WORD      wP:        Message-dependent 16 bit value
   LONG      lP:        Message-dependent 32 bit value

 Return values:

   BOOL                 TRUE if the dialog function contains the given message.
                        Otherwise, FALSE.
 ***************************************************************************/

BOOL FAR PASCAL NdfSearchProc (HWND hDlg, unsigned msg, WORD wP, LONG lP)
{
  int         i;                          // General counter
  static BOOL bCBNoIgnoreCase;            // Marker-"Upper/Lower" check box
  static BOOL bCBWholeWord;               // Marker-"Whole Word" check box
  BOOL        bPerformer,                 // "Performer Found" marker
              bTitle,                     // "Title Found" marker
              bEntryFound;                // "Record Found" marker
  char        szTitle[MAXFIELDLENGTH],    // Title
```

```
            szPerformer[MAXFIELDLENGTH], // Performer
            szSearch[MAXFIELDLENGTH],    // Search string
            szListboxString[255];        // Formatted list field entries

  switch (msg)
  {
    case WM_INITDIALOG:       // Dialog box display message

      // Check "Title" check box with CheckDlgButton function
      CheckDlgButton(hDlg, CB_NOIGNORECASE, TRUE);
      bCBNoIgnoreCase = TRUE;

      // Alternate: Send a control message
      SendDlgItemMessage(hDlg, CB_WHOLEWORD, BM_SETCHECK, FALSE, 0L);
      bCBWholeWord = FALSE;
      return TRUE;
      break;

    case WM_COMMAND:            // Dialog box control message
      switch (wP)
      {
        case PB_SEARCH:         // Select Search button
          // Read search fields
          GetDlgItemText(hDlg, EB_PERFORMER, szPerformer, MAXFIELDLENGTH);
          GetDlgItemText(hDlg, EB_TITLE, szTitle, MAXFIELDLENGTH);

          // Delete preceding list field entries
          SendDlgItemMessage(hDlg, LB_FOUND, LB_RESETCONTENT, 0, 0L);

          // Search data record fields
          for (i=0; i<MAXDATAENTRIES; i++)
          {
            if (DataArray[i].bUsed)  // Data record used?
            {
              bPerformer = bTitle = FALSE;
              // Compare strings
              if (CompareStrings(DataArray[i].szPerformer, szPerformer,
                      bCBNoIgnoreCase, bCBWholeWord) && (szPerformer[0] != 0))
                bPerformer = TRUE;
              if (CompareStrings(DataArray[i].szTitle, szTitle,
                      bCBNoIgnoreCase, bCBWholeWord) && (szTitle[0] != 0))
                bTitle = TRUE;

              if ((bPerformer && (szTitle[0] == 0)) ||
                  (bTitle && (szPerformer[0] == 0)) ||
                  (bPerformer && bTitle))    // Similar data record found?
              {
                // Format list field entry
```

```
        wsprintf(szListboxString, "%-3d %-25.25s %-25.25s %25d",
                 DataArray[i].wIndex,
                 (LPSTR)DataArray[i].szPerformer,
                 (LPSTR)DataArray[i].szTitle,
                 i);
        // Append entry to list field
        SendDlgItemMessage(hDlg, LB_FOUND, LB_ADDSTRING, 0,
                    (LONG)(LPSTR) szListboxString);
      }
    }
  }
  return TRUE;
  break;

case LB_FOUND:       // Message from "Record Found" list field
  if (HIWORD(lP) == LBN_DBLCLK)       // Double-click an entry
  {
    // Get index for currently selected entry
    i = (int) SendDlgItemMessage(hDlg, LB_FOUND, LB_GETCURSEL, 0, 0L);
    // Read entry
    SendDlgItemMessage(hDlg, LB_FOUND, LB_GETTEXT, i,
                    (LONG)(LPSTR)szListboxString);
    // Specify field index
    sscanf(&szListboxString[57], "%d", &nSearchRecNr);
    // Adapt current data record
    if (DataArray[nSearchRecNr].bUsed)
    {
      // Open "File Entry" dialog box if record doesn't exist
      if (!hDlgModal)
      {
        nRecNr = nSearchRecNr;
        SendMessage(hwMain, WM_COMMAND, MI_ENTERDATA, 0L);
      }
      else              // Post found records
        PostMessage(hDlgModal, SEARCH_DATA, nSearchRecNr, 0L);
    }
    return TRUE;
  }
  break;

case CB_NOIGNORECASE:  // "Upper/Lower" check box
  bCBNoIgnoreCase = !bCBNoIgnoreCase;
  CheckDlgButton(hDlg, CB_NOIGNORECASE, bCBNoIgnoreCase);
  return TRUE;
  break;

case CB_WHOLEWORD:     // "Whole Word" check box
  bCBWholeWord = !bCBWholeWord;
```

```
          CheckDlgButton(hDlg, CB_WHOLEWORD, bCBWholeWord);
          return TRUE;
          break;

        default:                // Other messages
          return FALSE;
          break;
      }
      break;

    case WM_SYSCOMMAND:         // Messages from dialog box system menu
      switch (wP)
      {
        // ALT+F4, double-click system menu or select "Close" from system
        // menu to select

        case SC_CLOSE:          // Close dialog box
          // Send message to main window
          PostMessage(hwMain, WM_COMMAND, MI_SEARCHDATA, 0L);
          return TRUE;
          break;

        default:                // Other system menu messages
          return FALSE;
          break;
      }
      break;

    default:                    // Other messages
        return FALSE;
        break;
  }
} // NdfSearchProc

/*****************************************************************************
 P a i n t D i a l o g ()
 ========================

 This function is needed for redrawing the client area of the main window.

 Parameters:

   HWND    hWnd:    Window handle.

 Return values:     None.
 ****************************************************************************/

 void PaintDialog (HWND hWnd)
```

```
 {
   PAINTSTRUCT ps;                // Client area information
   HDC         hDC;               // Display context handle

   hDC = BeginPaint(hWnd, &ps); // Get main window display context

   // Client area output eventually appears in main window from here

   EndPaint(hWnd, &ps);           // Release display context
 } // PaintDialog

/*****************************************************************************
 R e a d M u s i c D a t a ()
 ============================

 This function reads the contents of the "Enter Data" dialog box.

 Parameters:

   HWND           hDlg           Window handle for dialog box.
   DataRecord_t *DataRecord   Pointer to record structure to be filled.

 Return values:                  None
*****************************************************************************/

void ReadMusicData (HWND hDlg, DataRecord_t *DataRecord)
{
  int i;

  GetDlgItemText(hDlg, EB_PERFORMER, DataRecord->szPerformer, MAXFIELDLENGTH);
  GetDlgItemText(hDlg, EB_TITLE, DataRecord->szTitle, MAXFIELDLENGTH);
  GetDlgItemText(hDlg, EB_LABEL, DataRecord->szLabel, MAXFIELDLENGTH);
  GetDlgItemText(hDlg, CO_KINDOFMUSIC, DataRecord->szKindOfMusic,
                 MAXFIELDLENGTH);
  DataRecord->wIndex = GetDlgItemInt(hDlg, EB_INDEX, NULL, FALSE);

  // Determine which radio button is checked
  for (i=0; i<3; i++)
  {
    if (IsDlgButtonChecked(hDlg, RB_RECORD+i))
    {
      DataRecord->nMedium = i;
      break;
    }
  }
} // ReadMusicData

/*****************************************************************************
```

```
C o m p a r e S t r i n g s ()
==============================

This function compares two strings.

Parameters:

  char *       szString1      First string.
  char *       szString2      Second string.
  BOOL         bNoIgnoreCase  TRUE if upper/lowercase should be considered.
                              FALSE if upper/lowercase should be ignored.
  BOOL         bWholeWord     TRUE if both strings should be considered in
                              their entirety. FALSE if only the shortest
                              string should be considered.

Return values:BOOL            TRUE if both strings match. Otherwise, FALSE.
***********************************************************************/

BOOL CompareStrings (char *szString1, char *szString2, BOOL bNoIgnoreCase,
                     BOOL bWholeWord)
{
  char szPattern1[MAXFIELDLENGTH], // Search pattern
       szPattern2[MAXFIELDLENGTH];
  WORD nLength1,                   // String lengths
       nLength2;

  nLength1 = strlen(szString1);
  nLength2 = strlen(szString2);

  strcpy(szPattern1, szString1);
  strcpy(szPattern2, szString2);
  if (!bWholeWord)     // Compare strings as whole words only
  {
    szPattern1[min(nLength1, nLength2)] = '\0';
    szPattern2[min(nLength1, nLength2)] = '\0';
  }
  if (!bNoIgnoreCase)  // Ignore upper/lowercase
  {
    // Convert both strings to uppercase
    AnsiUpper((LPSTR)szPattern1);
    AnsiUpper((LPSTR)szPattern2);
  }
  // Compare
  if (lstrcmp((LPSTR)szPattern1, (LPSTR)szPattern2) == 0)
    return TRUE;
  else
    return FALSE;
} // CompareStrings
```

```
/**************************************************************************
 D i s p l a y D a t a ()
 ========================

 This function displays the current record stored in DataArray in the
 "Enter Data" dialog box.

 Parameters:

   HWND          hDlg          Dialog box window handle.
   DataRecord_t *DataRecord  Pointer to record structure to be displayed.

 Return values:                None
**************************************************************************/

void DisplayData (HWND hDlg, DataRecord_t *DataRecord)
{
   // Initialize edit fields with current data record contents
   SetDlgItemText(hDlg, EB_PERFORMER, DataRecord->szPerformer);
   SetDlgItemText(hDlg, EB_TITLE, DataRecord->szTitle);
   SetDlgItemText(hDlg, EB_LABEL, DataRecord->szLabel);
   SetDlgItemText(hDlg, CO_KINDOFMUSIC, DataRecord->szKindOfMusic);
   SetDlgItemInt(hDlg,  EB_INDEX, DataRecord->wIndex, FALSE);

   // Initialize radio buttons
   CheckRadioButton(hDlg, RB_RECORD, RB_CD, RB_RECORD+DataRecord->nMedium);
} // DisplayData

/**************************************************************************
 W r i t e D a t a ()
 ====================

 This function stores DataArray and current records in the MUSIC.DAT file.

 Parameters:         None.

 Return values:

   BOOL              TRUE if records saved successfully. Otherwise, FALSE.
**************************************************************************/

BOOL WriteData (void)
{
  int nItems;                                 // Number of data records
                                              // to be written
  FilePointer = fopen("MUSIC.DAT", "wb");     // Open binary file for writing
```

```
  if (!FilePointer)                            // No file opening
  {
    MessageBox(GetFocus(), "File could not be opened", szApplName,
               MB_OK | MB_ICONEXCLAMATION);
    return FALSE;
  }
  SetCursor(LoadCursor(NULL, IDC_WAIT));       // Hourglass cursor

  // Save data records
  nItems = fwrite(DataArray, sizeof(DataRecord), MAXDATAENTRIES, FilePointer);

  fclose(FilePointer);                         // Close file
  SetCursor(LoadCursor(NULL, IDC_ARROW));      // Restore arrow cursor

  // All data records written?
  if (nItems == MAXDATAENTRIES)
    return TRUE;
  else
    return FALSE;
} // WriteData

/*****************************************************************************
 R e a d D a t a ()
 ==================

 This function puts data records from the MUSIC.DAT file in DataArray.

 Parameters:         None.

 Return values:

   BOOL              TRUE if data read is successful. Otherwise, FALSE.
 *****************************************************************************/

BOOL ReadData (void)
{
  int       nItems;                            // Number of data records read

  FilePointer = fopen("MUSIC.DAT", "rb");      // Open binary file for reading

  if (!FilePointer)                            // No file opening
  {
    MessageBox(GetFocus(), "File could not be opened", szApplName,
               MB_OK | MB_ICONEXCLAMATION);
    return FALSE;
  }
  SetCursor(LoadCursor(NULL, IDC_WAIT));       // Hourglass cursor
```

```
  // Read file
  nItems = fread(DataArray, sizeof(DataRecord), MAXDATAENTRIES, FilePointer);

  fclose(FilePointer);                        // Close file
  SetCursor(LoadCursor(NULL, IDC_ARROW));     // Restore arrow cursor

  // All data records read?
  if (nItems == MAXDATAENTRIES)
    return TRUE;
  else
    return FALSE;
} // ReadData
```

4.16 Dynamic Dialog Boxes

In the preceding pages, we saw how dialog boxes are created and linked into the executable code of the .exe file. Now we will see how to create and modify dialog boxes at runtime.

Remember that there are basically two kinds of dialog boxes. If the DialogBox function creates a modal dialog box, Windows executes an EnableWindow call, which locks the parent window for as long as the dialog box is open. When a modeless dialog box is created with the CreateDialogBox function, this extra function call is not made. So the user is still able to select menu items or work with other elements outside the dialog box. Dialog boxes created in this way are referred to as static dialog boxes.

The format and contents of a static dialog box is determined with a dialog box template. A dialog box template can be created either manually or with the dialog box editor DIALOG.EXE, which is part of the Windows SDK. The template is interpreted by the resource compiler and linked with the executable code for the application. The second parameter of the dialog box creation functions CreateDialogBox and DialogBox is lpTemplateName. This parameter represents a long pointer to the name of the template, which is stored in the .RC file for the application.

If we look through the Windows documentation, we'll find that there are two additional functions for the creation of dialog boxes: CreateDialogIndirect and DialogBoxIndirect. These functions differ from the static dialog box creation functions only in the second parameter.

Instead of the name of a dialog box template, these functions use a long pointer (CreateDialogIndirect) or a handle (DialogBoxIndirect) for a data structure of type DLGTEMPLATE. This structure defines the form and contents of the dialog box to be created. Unlike static functions, this data structure is stored in the global memory instead of a file. Since this structure can be changed at runtime, the appearance of the dialog box itself can be changed dynamically without having to relink the application.

4.16.1 The DLGTEMPLATE structure

In the following section we will examine the DLGTEMPLATE structure to see how it can be used to create dynamic dialog boxes.

The DLGTEMPLATE structure consists of two components:

- The dialog box header defines the height and width of the dialog box, its style and the type of frame. The header also keeps track of how many control elements (also called items) are in the dialog box. In addition to this information, which has a fixed length in the header, there are three variable length character strings that contain the name of the menu bar, the window class name and the window title for the dialog box.
- An item structure must be created for each control element that our dialog box will use. This structure defines the style and class of each item, its position in the dialog box, its width and its ID number. You can also store text here (such as a description of a radio button) and reserve room for additional information (comparable to the cbClsExtra and cbWndExtra elements in the WNDCLASS structure).

A look at the header file DYNDLG.H will show us an example of this structure:

```
/*-----------------------< DialogHeader >--------------------------*/

typedef struct
{
   long lStyle;          // Dialog box style
   BYTE nItemNumber;     // Number of controls in the dialog box
   int  X;               // X-coordinate of upper left corner of box
   int  Y;               // Y-coordinate of upper left corner of box
   int  Cx;              // Box width
   int  Cy;              // Box height

   /*-------------------------------------------------------------

     Variable portion of DialogHeader structure

     char pzMenuName[]; //  Resource identifier of menu bar
     char pzClass[];    //  Class name
     char pzCaption[];  //  Caption
```

```
   ------------------------------------------------------------*/
} DialogHeader_t;


/*------------------------< DialogItem >-------------------------*/

typedef struct
{
   int  X;              // Control element X-coordinate
   int  Y;              // Control element Y-coordinate
   int  Cx;             // Control element width
   int  Cy;             // Control element height
   int  CtrlId;         // Control identifier
   long lStyle;         // Control element style
   BYTE nCtrlClass;     // Control element class

   /*----------------------------------------------------------

     Variable portion of DialogItem structure

     char pzText[]        Control text
     BYTE nExtraBytes[]   ExtraBytes for additional information

   ------------------------------------------------------------*/
} DialogItem_t;
```

Now that we have defined the DLGTEMPLATE structure used for dynamic dialog boxes, we will show you how to create one.

4.16.2 Creating the dialog box header

The first step in creating a dynamic dialog box is to create the header structure. The CreateDlgHeader function is used for this purpose. You will need the following information:

- Style specification for the dialog box. This is done by specifying previously defined style elements such as WS_BORDER, WS_CHILD or WS_VISIBLE. These can be combined with the OR operator (|). The keyword STYLE is used indicate a style definition in the .DLG file.

- Location of the upper left corner of the dialog box. Remember that the size information for the dialog box template is always relative to the height and width of the system font. The units for the x coordinate are 1/4 the width of the system font and the units for the y coordinate are 1/8 the height of the system font. The corner coordinates are given relative to the point of origin of the parent window's client area.

- The height and width of the dialog box. If you are used to the old text-based way of calculating using x*character width and y*character height, the following formula can be used to make conversions:

```
Dialog box height   =  number_of_lines   * 8 + 10 (for the frame)
Dialog box width    =  character_width * 4 + 10 (for the frame)
```

Example: The dialog box will be 50 characters wide and 12 lines high.

```
Cx = 50 * 4 + 10 = 210;
Cy = 12 * 8 + 10 = 106;
```

- Resource name of the menu bar for the dialog box (if applicable). The name will be a character string ending in "\0".
- Class name of the dialog box.
- Dialog box title.

The following demonstrates how the CreateDlgHeader function works in the source code:

```
/*********************************************************************
 C r e a t e D l g H e a d e r ()
 ================================

 This function allocates a range in global memory and inserts the dialog
 header structure.

 Parameters:
      lStyle           Style of new dialog box
      X,Y              Upper left corner coordinates of box
      Cx,Cy            Height and width of dialog box
      pzMenuName       Name of menu resources in application's .RC file
      pzClass          Class name of dialog box
      pzCaption        Caption of dialog box
```

```
Return values:
       HANDLE   Returns handle to the global memory range. This range
                must be locked before access. Handle is still NULL if not
                enough memory can be allocated.

*********************************************************************/

BOOL FAR PASCAL CreateDlgHeader(LONG lStyle,
                      int X, int Y, int Cx, int Cy,
                      LPSTR pzMenuName,
                      LPSTR pzClass,
                      LPSTR pzCaption)
{
  LPSTR             pMem;
  DialogHeader_t   *pDlg;
  int               StatSize, AktSize, lenS1, lenS2, lenS3;

  StatSize = sizeof(DialogHeader_t);    // Size of static portion
  lenS1    = lstrlen(pzMenuName)+1;
  lenS2    = lstrlen(pzClass)+1;
  lenS3    = lstrlen(pzCaption)+1;

  AktSize = StatSize+lenS1+lenS2+lenS3;

  hMem = GlobalAlloc(GMEM_MOVEABLE, (DWORD) AktSize);
  if(hMem)
  {
     pMem = GlobalLock(hMem);
     pDlg = (DialogHeader_t *) pMem;

     pDlg->lStyle      = lStyle;
     pDlg->nItemNumber = 0;
     pDlg->X           = X;
     pDlg->Y           = Y;
     pDlg->Cx          = Cx;
     pDlg->Cy          = Cy;

     lstrcpy(pMem+StatSize,pzMenuName);
     lstrcpy(pMem+StatSize+lenS1,pzClass);
     lstrcpy(pMem+StatSize+lenS1+lenS2,pzCaption);

     GlobalUnlock(hMem);
     Offset = AktSize;
     return TRUE;
  }
  return FALSE;
}
```

The CreateDlgHeader function stores a dialog header structure in memory and initializes it with the values that were passed to it. The function then returns a handle to this memory location, which serves as the template for creating a dialog box.

4.16.3 Additional control elements

We have implemented a second function to insert control elements in the dialog box. This function is called CreateDlgItem and has the following parameters:

- A handle to the memory location where the DLGTEMPLATE structure is stored.
- The ID number for the newly created control.
- The class of the new control.
- The location of the control in the dialog box. The coordinates of the upper left corner must be given along with the height and width.
- Title text for the control.
- Number of extra bytes to reserve.

The CreateDlgItem function uses the handle passed to it to reallocate a memory region that is large enough to store the description of the new control element and the existing DLGTEMPLATE structure. In addition, the field that stores the number of controls in the dialog box is updated. After the function is successfully completed, a handle to the new dialog box template is returned.

CreateDlgItem can be used to add new control elements to dynamic dialog boxes at will. The new elements will be appended to the existing template. The figure below illustrates how this works.

After using CreateDlgHeader and CreateDlgItem to create and store the dialog box template in memory, the dialog box itself can be created.

As we already mentioned, the dialog box creation functions differ in the second parameter. If we want to create a modal dialog box, we call the DialogBoxIndirect function and pass the handle to the DLGTEMPLATE structure to it. We have already discussed the other parameters as they are used when creating static dialog boxes:

- Handle for the current application instance.
- Handle for the parent window.
- Long pointer to the callback function of the dialog box (remember that dialog box functions must be defined as EXPORT in the module definition file *.DEF!).

```
/*********************************************************************
 C r e a t e D l g I t e m ()
 ============================
 This function fills in the dialog item structure and allocates the global
 memory range from which the new size is taken, If the <nCtrlClass>
 parameter is passed a NULL, <lStyle> is assigned a predefined control
 element in numeric form, assigning class and style descriptions
 to the structure.

Parameters:
            CtrlId          Control element identifier
            lStyle          Style of new control element
            nCtrlClass      Class of new control element
            X,Y             Upper left corner coordinates
            Cx,Cy           Element height and width
            pzText          Text of the control element
            nExtraBytes     Number of extra bytes

 Return values:
            HANDLE   Returns handle to the global memory range. This range
                     must be locked before access. Handle is NULL if not
                     enough memory can be allocated.
*********************************************************************/

BOOL FAR PASCAL CreateDlgItem(int CtrlId, LONG lStyle, BYTE nCtrlClass,
                     int X, int Y, int Cx, int Cy,
                     LPSTR pzText, BYTE nExtraBytes)
{
  LPSTR            pMem;
  DialogItem_t     *pDlg;
  DialogHeader_t   *pDlgHeader;
  int              StatSize, lenS, AktSize;
```

```
BYTE           *pByte;
HANDLE         hNewMem;

StatSize = sizeof(DialogItem_t);
lenS     = lstrlen(pzText)+1;
AktSize  = StatSize + lenS + nExtraBytes+1;
hNewMem  = GlobalReAlloc(hMem, (DWORD) Offset+AktSize, GMEM_MOVEABLE);
if(hNewMem)
{
   hMem = hNewMem;
   pMem = GlobalLock(hMem);
   pDlg = (DialogItem_t *)(pMem+Offset);
   pDlg->CtrlId = CtrlId;
   if(nCtrlClass == NULL)
   {
      SetDlgItemStyle((int) lStyle, &(pDlg->lStyle), &(pDlg->nCtrlClass));
   }
   else
   {
      pDlg->lStyle      = lStyle;
      pDlg->nCtrlClass = nCtrlClass;
   }
   pDlg->X          = X;
   pDlg->Y          = Y;
   pDlg->Cx         = Cx;
   pDlg->Cy         = Cy;
   lstrcpy(pMem+Offset+StatSize, pzText);
   pByte = (BYTE *) (pMem+Offset+StatSize+lenS);
   *pByte = nExtraBytes;
   pDlgHeader = (DialogHeader_t *) pMem;
   (pDlgHeader->nItemNumber)++;
   Offset += AktSize;
   GlobalUnlock(hMem);
   return TRUE;
 }
 return FALSE;
}
```

To create a modeless dialog box, the GlobalLock function locks the memory block where the DLGTEMPLATE structure is stored. You must also pass a long pointer, to this memory location, to the CreateDialogIndirect function.

As you practice creating dialog boxes in this way, you will see how powerful it is. You'll be able to create applications that allow the user to create and change dialog box templates according to their own wishes. You can also create dialog boxes with custom menu bars.

4.17 Source Code: DYN_DEMO.EXE

DYNDLG.H include file

```
/*****************************************************************************
 D Y N D L G . H
 ===============
 This header file contains all Defines, data structures and function proto-
 types needed to create modal and modeless dialog boxes.
 *****************************************************************************/


/*------------------------< Function prototyping >----------------------*/

BOOL FAR PASCAL CreateDlgHeader(
                LONG  lStyle,         // Dialog box style
                int   X,              // X-position of upper left corner
                int   Y,              // Y-position of upper left corner
                int   Cx,             // Dialog box width
                int   Cy,             // Dialog box height
                LPSTR pzResource,     // Dialog box resource name
                LPSTR pzClass,        // Dialog box class
                LPSTR pzCaption);     // Dialog box caption

BOOL FAR PASCAL CreateDlgItem(
                int   CtrlId,         // Control element identifier
                LONG  lStyle,         // Control element style
                BYTE  nCtrlClass,     // Control element class
                int   X,              // X-position
                int   Y,              // Y-position
                int   Cx,             // Width
                int   Cy,             // Height
                LPSTR pzText,         // Control text
                BYTE  nExtraBytes);   // Number of extra bytes

void SetDlgItemStyle(int Id, LONG FAR *lStyle, BYTE FAR *nCtrlClass);

HANDLE FinishDlgHeader(void);

/*--------------------< Undocumented WINDOWS functions >-----------------*/

LPSTR FAR PASCAL lstrcpy(LPSTR,LPSTR);

int FAR PASCAL  lstrlen(LPSTR);
```

```
/*------------------------< Default dialog box class >---------------------*/
#define DEFAULTDLGCLASS  "#32770"

#define BUTTONCLASS      0x80
#define EDITCLASS        0x81
#define STATICCLASS      0x82
#define LISTBOXCLASS     0x83
#define SCROLLBARCLASS   0x84


/*-------------------< Predefined control style classes >------------------*/

#define ICON                1
#define RECTANGLE           2
#define VERTSCROLLBAR       3
#define HORZSCROLLBAR       4
#define BLACKBOX            5
#define LEFTTEXT            6
#define CENTERTEXT          7
#define RIGHTTEXT           8
#define GROUPBOX            9
#define CHECKBOX            10
#define LEFTCHECKBOX        11
#define PUSHBUTTON          12
#define DEFPUSHBUTTON       13
#define RADIOBUTTON         14
#define TRISTATEBUTTON      15
#define RIGHTEDIT           16
#define LEFTEDIT            17
#define CENTEREDIT          18
#define MULTIPLEEDIT        19
#define SORTLISTBOX         20
#define NOSORTLISTBOX       21
#define AUTOCHECKBOX        22


/*---------------------------< DialogHeader >--------------------------*/

typedef struct
{
   long lStyle;            // Dialog box style
   BYTE nItemNumber;       // Number of controls in the dialog box
   int  X;                 // X-coordinate of upper left corner of box
   int  Y;                 // Y-coordinate of upper left corner of box
   int  Cx;                // Box width
   int  Cy;                // Box height

   /*-------------------------------------------------------------
```

```
      Variable portion of DialogHeader structure

      char pzMenuName[]      Resource identifier of menu bar
      char pzClass[]         Class name
      char pzCaption[]       Caption

   ------------------------------------------------------------*/
} DialogHeader_t;


/*-----------------------------< DialogItem >---------------------------*/

typedef struct
{
   int  X;                  // Control element X-coordinate
   int  Y;                  // Control element Y-coordinate
   int  Cx;                 // Control element width
   int  Cy;                 // Control element height
   int  CtrlId;             // Control identifier
   long lStyle;             // Control element style
   BYTE nCtrlClass;         // Control element class

   /*------------------------------------------------------------

      Variable portion of DialogItem structure

      char pzText[]        Control text
      BYTE nExtraBytes[]   ExtraBytes for additional information

   ------------------------------------------------------------*/
} DialogItem_t;
```

DYN_DEMO.H include file

```
#define  MI_QUIT     100
#define  MI_MODAL    101
#define  MI_MODELESS 102
#define  MI_SELECT   103
```

DYN_DEMO.RC resource file

```
#include <windows.h>
#include "dyn_demo.h"

Menu   MENU
```

```
        Begin
           MENUITEM "E&xit",               MI_QUIT
            POPUP "&Dialog Box"
            Begin
              MENUITEM "Modal...",         MI_MODAL
              MENUITEM "Modeless...",      MI_MODELESS
            End
        End

DlgMenu MENU
        Begin
         MENUITEM "&Close",   MI_QUIT
            POPUP "C&heck Box"
            Begin
              MENUITEM "Toggle Select",  MI_SELECT
            End
        End
```

DYN_DEMO.DEF module definition file

```
NAME            DYN_DEMO
DESCRIPTION     'Demonstrates dynamic dialog box generation'
STUB            'winstub.exe'
EXETYPE         WINDOWS

CODE            PRELOAD MOVEABLE
DATA            PRELOAD MOVEABLE MULTIPLE

HEAPSIZE        0x4000
STACKSIZE       0x4000

EXPORTS         DialogboxFkt
                WindowProc
```

DYN_DEMO.MAK MAKE file

```
Mod  = S
Warn = 3

.c.obj:
   cl -W$(Warn) -c -Gsw -Os -Zp -A$(Mod) $*.c

.rc.res:
   rc -r $*.rc

ALL: dyn_demo.exe
```

```
dyn_demo.obj:  dyn_demo.c

dyndlg.obj:    dyndlg.c dyndlg.h

dyn_demo.res:  dyn_demo.rc

dyn_demo.exe:  dyn_demo.obj dyndlg.obj dyn_demo.res dyn_demo.def
               link dyn_demo+dyndlg,,,LIBW+$(Mod)LIBCEW/NOD,dyn_demo.def
               rc dyn_demo.res
```

DYNDLG.C source code

```
/************************************************************************
 D Y N D L G . C
 ===============
 This file contains all the functions needed to create dynamic modal and
 modeless dialog boxes.
************************************************************************/

#include <windows.h>
#include "dyndlg.h"

static int Offset;

extern HANDLE hMem;

/***********************************************************************
 C h a r s 2 P i x e l
 =====================

 This function computes character-defined dimensions of a dialog box
 (column/line position of the upper left corner, width/height in pixels).

 Parameters:
           X,Y     Column and row of upper left corner
           Cx,Cy   Dialog box width and height based on num of characters

 Return values:
           None
***********************************************************************/
void Chars2Pixel(int *x, int *y, int *cx, int *cy)
{
   *cx = *cx * 4 + 10; // Width same size as in DIALOG.EXE
   *cy = *cy * 8 + 10; // Height same size as in DIALOG.EXE
   *x  = *x  * 4;
   *y  = *y  * 8;
```

```
}


/***********************************************************************
 C r e a t e D l g H e a d e r
 =============================

 This function allocates a range in global memory and inserts the dialog
 header structure.

 Parameters:
            lStyle          Style of new dialog box
            X,Y             Upper left corner coordinates of box
            Cx,Cy           Height and width of dialog box
            pzMenuName      Name of menu resources in application's .RC file
            pzClass         Class name of dialog box
            pzCaption       Caption of dialog box

 Return values:
            HANDLE   Returns handle to the global memory range. This range
                     must be locked before access. Handle is NULL if not
                     enough memory can be allocated.
***********************************************************************/
BOOL FAR PASCAL CreateDlgHeader(LONG lStyle,
                       int X, int Y, int Cx, int Cy,
                       LPSTR pzMenuName,
                       LPSTR pzClass,
                       LPSTR pzCaption)
{
  LPSTR                 lpMem;
  DialogHeader_t FAR *  lpDlg;
  int                   StatSize,
                        AktSize, lenS1, lenS2, lenS3;

  StatSize = sizeof(DialogHeader_t);   // Size of static portion
  lenS1    = lstrlen(pzMenuName)+1;
  lenS2    = lstrlen(pzClass)+1;
  lenS3    = lstrlen(pzCaption)+1;

  AktSize = StatSize+lenS1+lenS2+lenS3;

  hMem = GlobalAlloc(GMEM_MOVEABLE, (DWORD) AktSize);
  if(hMem)
  {
     lpMem = GlobalLock(hMem);
     lpDlg = (DialogHeader_t FAR *) lpMem;

     lpDlg->lStyle      = lStyle;
```

```
    lpDlg->nItemNumber = 0;
    lpDlg->X           = X;
    lpDlg->Y           = Y;
    lpDlg->Cx          = Cx;
    lpDlg->Cy          = Cy;

    lstrcpy(lpMem+StatSize,pzMenuName);
    lstrcpy(lpMem+StatSize+lenS1,pzClass);
    lstrcpy(lpMem+StatSize+lenS1+lenS2,pzCaption);

    GlobalUnlock(hMem);
    Offset = AktSize;
    return TRUE;
  }
  return FALSE;
}

/**************************************************************************
 C r e a t e D l g I t e m
 =========================

 This function fills in the dialog item structure and allocates the global
 memory range from which the new size is taken. If the <nCtrlClass>
 parameter is passed a NULL, <lStyle> is assigned a predefined control
 element in numeric form, assigning class and style descriptions
 to the structure.

 Parameters:
             CtrlId          Control element identifier
             lStyle          Style of new control element
             nCtrlClass      Class of new control element
             X,Y             Upper left corner coordinates
             Cx,Cy           Element height and width
             pzText          Text of the control element
             nExtraBytes     Number of extra bytes

 Return values:
             HANDLE   Returns handle to the global memory range. This range
                      must be locked before access. Handle is NULL if not
                      enough memory can be allocated.
**************************************************************************/
BOOL FAR PASCAL CreateDlgItem(int CtrlId, LONG lStyle, BYTE nCtrlClass,
                      int X, int Y, int Cx, int Cy,
                      LPSTR pzText, BYTE nExtraBytes)
{
  LPSTR                  lpMem;
  DialogItem_t   FAR *   lpDlg;
  DialogHeader_t FAR *   lpDlgHeader;
```

```
  int                     StatSize, lenS, AktSize;
  BYTE            FAR*    lpByte;
  HANDLE                  hNewMem;

  StatSize = sizeof(DialogItem_t);
  lenS     = lstrlen(pzText)+1;

  AktSize  = StatSize + lenS + nExtraBytes+1;

  hNewMem = GlobalReAlloc(hMem, (DWORD) Offset+AktSize, GMEM_MOVEABLE);
  if(hNewMem)
  {
     hMem = hNewMem;
     lpMem = GlobalLock(hMem);
     lpDlg = (DialogItem_t FAR *)(lpMem+Offset);

     lpDlg->CtrlId = CtrlId;

     if(nCtrlClass == NULL)
     {
        SetDlgItemStyle((int) lStyle, (LONG FAR *) &(lpDlg->lStyle),
                                      (BYTE FAR *) &(lpDlg->nCtrlClass));
     }
     else
     {
        lpDlg->lStyle     = lStyle;
        lpDlg->nCtrlClass = nCtrlClass;
     }
     lpDlg->X           = X;
     lpDlg->Y           = Y;
     lpDlg->Cx          = Cx;
     lpDlg->Cy          = Cy;

     lstrcpy(lpMem+Offset+StatSize, pzText);

     lpByte = (BYTE FAR *) (lpMem+Offset+StatSize+lenS);
     *lpByte = nExtraBytes;

     lpDlgHeader = (DialogHeader_t FAR *) lpMem;
     (lpDlgHeader->nItemNumber)++;

     Offset += AktSize;

     GlobalUnlock(hMem);
     return TRUE;
  }
  return FALSE;
}
```

```
/**************************************************************************
 S e t D l g I t e m S t y l e
 =============================

 This function eases user access to control elements, by filling
 standard elements with identifying number <Id>, as well as the
 structure fields <lStyle> and <CtrlClass>.

 Parameters:
           Id:         Defined control element ID numbers for
                       Listbox, Editbox, Buttons, etc.
           CtrlClass:  Filled by the function
           lStyle:     Filled by the function

 Return values: None
**************************************************************************/
void SetDlgItemStyle(int Id, LONG FAR * lStyle, BYTE FAR * CtrlClass)
{
   switch(Id)
   {
      case ICON:                      // Icon
         *CtrlClass = STATICCLASS;
         *lStyle    = SS_ICON | WS_BORDER | WS_CHILD | WS_VISIBLE;
      break;

      case RECTANGLE:                 // Rectangle
         *CtrlClass = STATICCLASS;
         *lStyle    = SS_BLACKFRAME | WS_CHILD | WS_VISIBLE;
      break;

      case VERTSCROLLBAR:             // Vertical scroll bars
         *CtrlClass = SCROLLBARCLASS;
         *lStyle    = SBS_VERT | WS_CHILD | WS_VISIBLE;
      break;

      case HORZSCROLLBAR:             // Horizontal scroll bar
         *CtrlClass = SCROLLBARCLASS;
         *lStyle    = SBS_HORZ | WS_CHILD | WS_VISIBLE;
      break;

      case BLACKBOX:                  // Black box
         *CtrlClass = STATICCLASS;
         *lStyle    = SS_BLACKRECT | WS_CHILD | WS_VISIBLE;
      break;

      case LEFTTEXT:                  // Left-justified text
         *CtrlClass = STATICCLASS;
```

```
   *lStyle     = SS_LEFT | WS_BORDER | WS_CHILD | WS_VISIBLE;
break;

case CENTERTEXT:                 // Centered text
   *CtrlClass = STATICCLASS;
   *lStyle     = SS_CENTER | WS_BORDER | WS_CHILD | WS_VISIBLE;
break;

case RIGHTTEXT:                  // Right-justified text
   *CtrlClass = STATICCLASS;
   *lStyle     = SS_RIGHT | WS_BORDER | WS_CHILD | WS_VISIBLE;
break;

case GROUPBOX:                   // Group box
   *CtrlClass = BUTTONCLASS;
   *lStyle     = BS_GROUPBOX | WS_CHILD | WS_VISIBLE;
break;

case CHECKBOX:                   // Check box
   *CtrlClass = BUTTONCLASS;
   *lStyle     = BS_AUTOCHECKBOX | WS_TABSTOP | WS_CHILD | WS_VISIBLE;
break;

case LEFTCHECKBOX:               // Check box with left-justified text
   *CtrlClass = BUTTONCLASS;
   *lStyle     = BS_LEFTTEXT | BS_AUTOCHECKBOX | WS_TABSTOP | WS_CHILD
                              | WS_VISIBLE;
break;

case AUTOCHECKBOX:               // Automatic check box
   *CtrlClass = BUTTONCLASS;
   *lStyle     = BS_AUTOCHECKBOX | WS_TABSTOP | WS_CHILD | WS_VISIBLE;
break;

case PUSHBUTTON:                 // Push button
   *CtrlClass = BUTTONCLASS;
   *lStyle     = BS_PUSHBUTTON | WS_TABSTOP | WS_CHILD | WS_VISIBLE;
break;

case DEFPUSHBUTTON:              // Default push button
   *CtrlClass = BUTTONCLASS;
   *lStyle     = BS_DEFPUSHBUTTON | WS_TABSTOP | WS_CHILD | WS_VISIBLE;
break;

case RADIOBUTTON:                // Radio button
   *CtrlClass = BUTTONCLASS;
   *lStyle     = BS_RADIOBUTTON | WS_TABSTOP | WS_CHILD | WS_VISIBLE;
break;
```

```
        case TRISTATEBUTTON:            // 3 state button (auto)
           *CtrlClass = BUTTONCLASS;
           *lStyle    = BS_AUTO3STATE | WS_TABSTOP | WS_CHILD | WS_VISIBLE;
        break;

        case LEFTEDIT:                  // Edit box with left-justified text
           *CtrlClass = EDITCLASS;
           *lStyle    = ES_LEFT | WS_BORDER | WS_TABSTOP | WS_CHILD | WS_VISIBLE;
        break;

        case CENTEREDIT:                // Edit box with centered text
           *CtrlClass = EDITCLASS;
           *lStyle    = ES_CENTER | WS_BORDER | WS_TABSTOP | WS_CHILD | WS_VISIBLE;
        break;

        case RIGHTEDIT:                 // Edit box with right-justified text
           *CtrlClass = EDITCLASS;
           *lStyle    = ES_RIGHT | WS_BORDER | WS_TABSTOP | WS_CHILD | WS_VISIBLE;
        break;

        case MULTIPLEEDIT:              // Multiple-line edit box
           *CtrlClass = EDITCLASS;
           *lStyle    = ES_LEFT | ES_MULTILINE | ES_NOHIDESEL | ES_AUTOVSCROLL
                        | ES_AUTOHSCROLL | WS_VSCROLL | WS_HSCROLL
                        | WS_BORDER | WS_TABSTOP | WS_CHILD | WS_VISIBLE;
        break;

        case SORTLISTBOX:               // List box with sorted entries
           *CtrlClass = LISTBOXCLASS;
           *lStyle    = LBS_STANDARD | WS_BORDER | WS_TABSTOP | WS_CHILD
                        | WS_VISIBLE;
        break;

        case NOSORTLISTBOX:             // List box with unsorted entries
           *CtrlClass = LISTBOXCLASS;
           *lStyle    = LBS_NOTIFY | WS_BORDER | WS_TABSTOP | WS_CHILD
                        | WS_VISIBLE;
        break;
    }
}
```

DYN_DEMO.C source code

```
/***************************************************************************

 D Y N _ D E M O . C    Main module for sample application which creates
                        dynamic (during runtime) DIALOG BOXES

***************************************************************************/
#include        <windows.h>
#include        <string.h>
#include        "dyndlg.H"
#include        "dyn_demo.h"


HANDLE        hInstance;
HWND          hwMain;
HFONT         hFont;
HDC           hDC;
char          zAppName[] = "Demo: Dynamic Dialog Boxes";


BYTE          *pzAppTitle;
BYTE          *pzNoMemory;
HWND          hShowWnd;
HANDLE        hMem;           // Handle to Dialog box structure


BOOL BuildDialog(HWND hWnd)
{

  CreateDlgHeader( WS_BORDER  | WS_CAPTION | WS_DLGFRAME | WS_VSCROLL |
                   WS_HSCROLL | WS_SYSMENU | WS_GROUP    | WS_TABSTOP |
                   WS_SIZEBOX | WS_VISIBLE | WS_POPUP,
                   24, 20, 160, 120,
                   "DlgMenu",
                   "",
                   "Dialogbox");

  if(!hMem)
  {
     MessageBox(GetFocus(), "Not enough memory", "Dialog Header",
                MB_OK);
     return FALSE;
  }
          //    Id    lStyle    Class        X    Y   CX   CY  Text Bytes
  CreateDlgItem(1000,(int) DEFPUSHBUTTON, 0, 65, 90, 35, 12, "OK",    0x00);
  CreateDlgItem(3002,(int) LEFTCHECKBOX,  0, 10, 45, 35, 12, "Left", 0x00);
```

```
  CreateDlgItem(3003,(int) CHECKBOX,        0, 115,45, 35, 12, "Right",0x00);

  if(!hMem)
  {
     MessageBox(GetFocus(), "Not enough memory", "Dialog Item",
                MB_OK);
     return FALSE;
  }
  return TRUE;
}


/***************************************************************************

 Dialogbox function for controlling the dynamic box

 ### Callback Function ###
***************************************************************************/

BOOL FAR PASCAL DialogboxFkt(HWND hDlg, unsigned msg, WORD wP, LONG lP)
{
  switch (msg)
  {
      case WM_INITDIALOG:
         return TRUE;

      case WM_COMMAND:
         switch(wP)
         {
             case MI_QUIT:                  // End menu item
             case 1000:                     // OK button
                EndDialog(hDlg,TRUE);
                break;

             case MI_SELECT:
                CheckDlgButton(hDlg,3002,
                               IsDlgButtonChecked(hDlg,3002) ? 0 : 1);
                CheckDlgButton(hDlg,3003,
                               IsDlgButtonChecked(hDlg,3003) ? 0 : 1);
                break;

             default: return FALSE;
         }
         break;
      default: return FALSE;
   }
   return FALSE;
}
```

```
/**************************************************************************

 W i n d o w P r o c
 ===================

 ### Window function of Mainwindow ###

**************************************************************************/

long FAR PASCAL WindowProc(HWND hWnd, unsigned msg, WORD wP, LONG lP)
{
   FARPROC     lpDlg;
   LPSTR       lpDynDlg;

   switch (msg)
   {
      case WM_COMMAND:
         switch(wP)
         {
             case MI_MODELESS:
                if (BuildDialog(hWnd))
                {
                  lpDlg = MakeProcInstance(DialogboxFkt, hInstance);
                  if(lpDlg)
                  {
                    lpDynDlg = GlobalLock(hMem);
                    CreateDialogIndirect(hInstance, lpDynDlg, hWnd, lpDlg);
                  }
                }
                break;

             case MI_MODAL:
                if (BuildDialog(hWnd))
                {
                  lpDlg = MakeProcInstance(DialogboxFkt, hInstance);
                  if(lpDlg)
                     DialogBoxIndirect(hInstance, hMem, hWnd, lpDlg);
                  FreeProcInstance(lpDlg);
                }
                break;


             case MI_QUIT:        // Exit ...
                if(MessageBox(hWnd, (LPSTR)"Exit program - are you sure?",
                              (LPSTR)"Exit Program",
                     MB_ICONQUESTION | MB_YESNO | MB_DEFBUTTON1 |
                     MB_APPLMODAL) == IDYES)
```

```
                DestroyWindow(hWnd);
            break;
         }
         break;

      case WM_DESTROY:               /* End application */
         FreeProcInstance((FARPROC) lpDlg);
         PostQuitMessage(NULL);
         break;

      default:
         return(DefWindowProc(hWnd, msg, wP, lP));
   }
   return (NULL);
}


/********************************************* Main function of application */
int PASCAL WinMain (HANDLE hInst, HANDLE hPrevInstance, LPSTR lpszCmdLine,
                    int nCmdShow)
{
  MSG          msg ;
  WNDCLASS     wndclass ;

  if (!hPrevInstance)
  {
     wndclass.style          = CS_VREDRAW | CS_HREDRAW;
     wndclass.lpfnWndProc    = WindowProc ;
     wndclass.cbClsExtra     = 0 ;
     wndclass.cbWndExtra     = 0 ;
     wndclass.hInstance      = hInst;
     wndclass.hIcon          = NULL;
     wndclass.hCursor        = LoadCursor (NULL, IDC_ARROW);
     wndclass.hbrBackground = GetStockObject (WHITE_BRUSH) ;
     wndclass.lpszMenuName  = NULL ;
     wndclass.lpszClassName = zAppName ;

     if (!RegisterClass (&wndclass))
         return FALSE;

     hInstance = hInst ;

     hwMain = CreateWindow (zAppName, zAppName, WS_OVERLAPPEDWINDOW,
                            CW_USEDEFAULT, 0, CW_USEDEFAULT, 0, NULL,
                            LoadMenu(hInstance,(LPSTR) "Menu"),
                            hInstance, NULL) ;

     ShowWindow(hwMain, SW_SHOWNORMAL);
```

```
    UpdateWindow (hwMain);
  }

  if(hPrevInstance)
    return FALSE;

  while(GetMessage (&msg, NULL, 0, 0))
  {
    TranslateMessage (&msg) ;
    DispatchMessage (&msg) ;
  }
  return msg.wParam;
}
```

5 Displaying Graphics

In this chapter we'll discuss a topic that is very important for the user and often causes many problems for programmers—graphics. Graphics play a tremendous role in all Windows applications, and many SDK functions are part of the previously mentioned Windows GDI (Graphics Device Interface).

5.1 Coordinate Systems

It is very difficult to show all of the various parts of the GDI in one section or in one single demo program. Therefore, we will concentrate on a few basic aspects. These will include the coordinate systems and mapping modes used by the GDI.

Logical and physical screens

The major problem of an all-purpose graphics interface is how to reconcile the concepts of the logical graphics screen and the physical graphics screen. A universal graphics program that would run in as many graphics environments as possible would most likely use a logical coordinate system. Since screens display in two dimensions, width and height, a two-dimensional coordinate system is required.

Many of you may remember Cartesian coordinate system from school math. Cartesian coordinates consist of two theoretically endless axes perpendicular to one another. The point at which they cross is known as the origin. The axes are usually named x and y, where the x axis is horizontal and the y axis is vertical. The two axes divide the plane in which they are located into four regions known as quadrants.

Normally the upper right quadrant is labeled as quadrant 1. The other quadrants are numbered in counterclockwise order. The values used in each quadrant differ by sign. For example, the x and y values in quadrant 1 are positive, while the x and y values in quadrant 3 are negative. The programmer must describe the points, lines and objects of a picture within a coordinate system. Then the picture can be displayed on the screen using the capabilities of the Windows GDI.

GDI coordinates

The GDI works with an internal coordinate system similar to the one previously described. This logical coordinate system has x and y axes perpendicular to one another. The coordinates on the x axis extend from -32768 on the left side of the origin to +32767 on the right. The y coordinates extend from -32768 above the origin to +32767 below the origin. Unlike the Cartesian coordinate system, this coordinate system places its negative y values above the x axis.

The 32K limits to the x and y coordinates result from the way the GDI represents coordinates as integers. The GDI logical coordinate system must then be translated to the physical limits of the screen as defined by the graphics card the computer is using. To accomplish this, the GDI has two mapping modes. The term mapping refers to relating the logical GDI coordinate system to the so-called viewport.

Viewport

The viewport is the rectangular screen region that will contain the portion of the logical coordinate system to be displayed within a given window. This part of the logical coordinate system is known as a logical window. The mapping modes affect the way the logical window is displayed on the screen in the viewport. The mapping factor determines how many logical units make up a pixel on the screen. The mapping factor is also responsible for setting the window origin for each window and for aligning the two window axes so that the picture can be displayed on the screen. The logical window describes the picture in logical coordinates, whereas the viewport window uses viewport coordinates (also known as device coordinates).

The current measurements of the viewport in a certain window can always be obtained with the GetClientRect function:

```
void GetClientRect (HWND hWnd, LPRECT lpRect);
```

hWnd is the window handle. lpRect is a long pointer to a rectangular structure. lpRect stores the four coordinates that define the viewport measurements (lpRect->left, lpRect->top, lpRect->right, lpRect->bottom).

Client area coordinates always relate to the upper left corner of a window. This corner (the viewport origin) is always given the coordinates (0,0). Therefore, lpRect->right defines the width and lpRect->bottom defines the height of the viewport in pixels.

5.2 GDI Mapping Modes

Most character functions of the GDI expect logical coordinates as parameters, but there are some that use device coordinates. The GDI has functions for converting coordinates from one system to the other (DPtoLP, LPtoDP). Windows takes the mapping mode into consideration during the conversion. The following section contains descriptions of all eight mapping modes used by Windows.

MM_TEXT

This mapping mode is turned on by default in the GDI. In MM_TEXT mode, one logical unit corresponds to one pixel on the screen. Positive logical x coordinates are counted to the right of the viewport origin and positive y coordinates are counted below the viewport origin. The name MM_TEXT reflects the way text is normally output - from left to right continuing downward. The effects of GDI functions on the mapping measurements or the orientation of the axes are ignored in MM_TEXT mode.

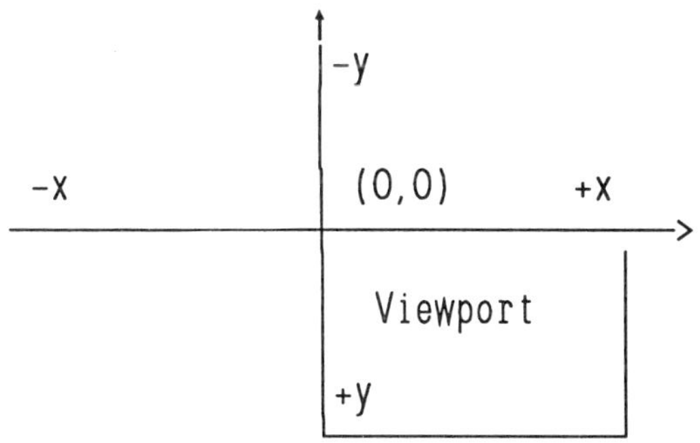

You can set the MM_TEXT mapping mode with the SetMapMode function, which is also used to set all other mapping modes:

```
int SetMapMode (HDC hDC, int nMapMode)
```

hDC is the handle to a display context to which the mapping mode relates. nMapMode is a value defined in the include file WINDOWS.H. The constant value MM_TEXT is entered here for the MM_TEXT mapping mode. The value returned by the function corresponds to the previous mapping mode of the display context.

MM_ANISOTROPIC

In this mode, you can use GDI functions to influence the mapping scale and the orientation of the y axis. The relationship between the dimensions of the logical window and the viewport is set with the SetWindowExt and SetViewportExt functions, which set the x and y extents.

```
DWORD SetWindowExt (HDC hDC, int xWinExtent, int yWinExtent);
DWORD SetViewportExt (HDC hDC, int xViewExtent, int yViewExtent);
```

These functions set the dimensions and orientation of the x and y sides of the logical window and the viewport. The values themselves aren't significant; they have to be considered relative to one another. hDC is the handle to a display context. xWinExtent is a positive or negative integer value that determines the width of the logical window. yWinExtent gives the corresponding window height. xViewExtent is the width of the viewport and yViewExtent is its height. The GDI evaluates the ratios.

```
xWinExtent      yWinExtent         xViewExtent     yViewExtent
----------- and -----------    or  ----------- and -----------
xViewExtent     yViewExtent        xWinExtent      yWinExtent
```

These ratios are used as scaling factors. Depending on whether the scaling factor gives a positive or negative value, the corresponding window axis and viewport axis will point in the same direction or the opposite direction. Here is an example: If xWinExtent is 10 and xViewExtent is 100, then one logical unit in the x axis will equal 10 pixels on screen, and 10 logical units will equal 100 pixels, etc. If an application uses the Cartesian coordinate system for the logical coordinates and uses positive y coordinates for drawing a picture (quadrants 1 and 2), then the picture will not be visible on the screen if a positive y scaling factor and a viewport origin in the upper left corner is used. This is because positive y values are located below the x axis in the viewport. To fix this situation, you can either multiply the scaling factor by -1 or use negative logical y coordinates.

The MM_ANISOTROPIC mode will not always maintain shapes because of the independent x and y scaling factors. This means that a circle in the logical window will be displayed as an ellipse in the viewport, and a square will be displayed as a rectangle. This mapping mode is best suited for evenly filling the client area of a window with a picture. The logical units are converted into pixels for use on the x and y axes of the viewport by the GDI.

MM_ISOTROPIC

This mode is used when you want to maintain the shape of a picture. Windows accomplishes this by using one scaling factor throughout the mapping operation. The other scaling factor is changed by the GDI depending on the aspect ratio of the graphics card being used. This will correct the viewport extents and display the picture correctly regardless of the graphics card. The most common graphics cards have pixels that are taller than they are wide. The GDI uses the aspect ratio to scale the x and y axes in order to correct the hardware-dependent pixel size. Remember that since the mapping of the MM_ISOTROPIC mode is dependent upon the aspect ratio, it is somewhat limited in this sense.

The logical window and viewport extents can only be changed in the MM_ISOTROPIC and MM_ANISOTROPIC modes. The other mapping modes can change the origin of the logical window and the viewport by using the SetWindowOrg and SetViewportOrg GDI functions.

```
DWORD SetWindowOrg (HDC hDC, int xWindowOrg, yWindowOrg);
```

hDC is the handle for the display context to which the function pertains. xWindowOrg and yWindowOrg represent the new coordinates of the window origin in logical units. The low word of the function result contains the previous x coordinate, and the high word contains the previous y coordinate of the window origin.

You can visualize the way this function works by mapping the point (xWinOrg, yWinOrg) in the logical coordinate system to the point (0, 0) in the viewport coordinate system. All other points in the logical coordinate system are mapped in the same way. For example, a circle around the logical origin would appear as a circle around the viewport origin. The following sequence sets the window origin so that the center point of the logical coordinate system maps to the client area center in window hWind:

```
HWND hWnd
RECT rClientRect;
     ...
GetClientRect(hWnd, (LPRECT) &rClientRect);
SetWindowOrg(GetDC(hWnd), -rClientRect.right/2, -rClientRect.bottom/2);
     ...
```

After setting the window and viewport extents, the following function draws a filled circle with its center point in the center of the client area, with a radius of ten logical units:

```
Ellipse(hDC, -10, -10, 10, 10);
```

As the name suggests, the SetViewportOrg function sets the origin of the viewport:

```
DWORD SetViewportOrg (HDC hDC, int xViewportOrg, int yViewportOrg);
```

hDC is the display context. xViewportOrg and yViewportOrg are the new coordinates of the viewport origin in device coordinates. The function result contains the previous x coordinate in the low word and the previous y coordinate in the high word.

How do we visualize the effect of this function? As opposed to the SetWindowOrg function, SetViewportOrg maps the logical point (0, 0) to the viewport point (xViewportOrg, yViewportOrg). If we want to use SetViewportOrg in the same way as the example above, the function call would look like this:

```
HWND hWnd
RECT rClientRect;
     ...
GetClientRect(hWnd, (LPRECT) &rClientRect);
SetViewportOrg(GetDC(hWnd), rClientRect.right/2, rClientRect.bottom/2);
     ...
```

After using the SetWindowOrg, SetViewportOrg, SetWindowExtent and SetViewportExtent functions for a given display context, Windows takes over the work of mapping and scaling automatically for every logical point. So the programmer only has to worry about the logical picture.

Metric mapping modes

Before we proceed, let's discuss the other five mapping modes:

MM_HIENGLISH;
MM_HIMETRIC
MM_LOENGLISH
MM_LOMETRIC
MM_TWIPS

These mapping modes allow you to scale pictures with physical units of measure. For example, in the MM_HIENGLISH mapping mode, 1000 logical units equal one inch. The MM_LOENGLISH mode sets 100 logical units equal to one inch. In the MM_HIMETRIC mode, 100 logical units equal one millimeter. There are 10 logical units per millimeter in MM_LOMETRIC mode. The MM_TWIPS mode sets one logical unit equal to 1/1440 inch. This corresponds to one point, the unit of measure used with type sizes and fonts. This mode is most useful when working with fonts and text output. All five of these mapping modes have positive y values above the x axis as with the Cartesian coordinate system. This is different from the MM_TEXT mode, which maps positive y values below the x axis. Because these modes use physical units of measure, it's not possible to scale the window and viewport origins.

5.3 Application: GDIDEMO.EXE

Now that you have some background information on mapping modes and GDI programming, let's use a practical example to apply what we've learned. Our demo program is called GDIDEMO.EXE. It displays graphics to the client area of the main window using all eight mapping modes. The program also allows you to set the foreground and background colors and demonstrates how the GDI uses graphics resources such as pens and brushes. Other aspects of the program include evaluating mouse events within a window function and using cascading menus and submenus.

Basic structure

Let's start by describing the basic structure of the GDIDEMO.EXE program. The InitFirstInstance function registers the window class of the main window for the first instance, which is similar to the other demo programs we have seen. In this case, we do not allow further instances of the program to be started. If this function call is successful, we initiate the creation of some graphics resources. The resources most frequently used by the GDI include brushes and pens. The GDI uses brushes to fill in the background or other regions in the client area. Pens are used to draw lines and other figures. Most GDI functions automatically use the brush and pen currently selected in the display context. A display context can contain only one brush and one pen at any time.

5.3.1 Brushes and colors

The GDI has several functions for creating brushes. In this program, we will use CreateSolidBrush. This function creates a colored brush with no pattern:

```
HBRUSH CreateSolidBrush (COLORREF rgbColor);
```

The function result is a handle to the brush resource that is created. The dwColor parameter is of type COLORREF, which is used in many GDI functions that require the specification of colors. A COLORREF value is type DWORD (unsigned long). This is indicated in the WINDOWS.H include file. Only the three lowest words are required for coding the color. The highest (fourth) byte indicates how to interpret the COLORREF value.

If the fourth byte contains a zero, the COLORREF value represents an explicit RGB value. Every screen color can be expressed as a mixture of red, green and blue - the primary colors of light. Each individual color component can have a value from 0 to 255. The lowest intensity of the color is 0 and the highest is 255. A color consisting of R=0, G=0 and B=0 will result in the deepest black, whereas R=255, G=255 and B=255 will produce a bright, pure white. This is the same way colors are displayed on your color TV. Each point on the screen is a mixture of red, green and blue light generated by the picture tube. The order in which the color components are given in a COLORREF value are red in the first (lowest) byte, green in the second byte and blue in the third byte.

You don't have to work with bits and bytes in order to read or write a COLORREF value. Instead, you can simply use the RGB macro:

```
COLORREF RGB (BYTE nRed, BYTE nGreen, BYTE nBlue);
```

This macro accepts the three color components as parameters and returns a value of type COLORREF. If the fourth byte of the COLORREF value contains 1, then the COLORREF value is an index in a logical color palette. If the fourth byte contains 2, then the COLORREF value is a palette-relative RGB value. These different COLORREF types only matter when you are using a logical color palette. We will discuss this in more detail when we cover the Windows color palette manager.

We will use the array ahBrushes ("a" stands for array) in the GDIDEMO.EXE program to create red, green, blue, white and black brushes. For example, the following creates a red brush:

```
ahBrushes[0] = CreateSolidBrush(RGB(255, 0, 0);
```

Another way to create brushes is with the CreateHatchBrush function:

```
HBRUSH CreateHatchBrush (int nStyle, COLORREF dwColor);
```

dwColor is a color value of type COLORREF. This represents the color that will be used for the lines in the pattern. nStyle gives the style, or pattern of the brush. The following style values can be used:

HS_BDIAGONAL	45 degree diagonal pattern (from top left to right bottom)
HS_CROSS	cross hatching (90 degree angle)
HS_DIAGCROSS	diagonal cross hatching (45 degree angle)
HS_FDIAGONAL	45 degree diagonal (from bottom left to top right)
HS_HORIZONTAL	horizontal hatching
HS_VERTICAL	vertical hatching

5.3.2 Pens

Now let's look at pens. The CreatePen function creates a pen:

```
HPEN CreatePen (int nStyle, int nWidth, COLORREF dwColor);
```

The function result HPEN is a handle to the newly created pen. NULL is returned if the pen could not be created. nStyle is the pen style. The following values can be used ("value" represents the define value from the WINDOWS.H include file):

Style	Value	Description
PS_SOLID	0	solid line
PS_DASH	1	dashed line
PS_DOT	2	dotted line
PS_DASHDOT	3	dash-dot pattern
PS_DASHDOTDOT	4	dash-dot-dot pattern
PS_NULL	5	not visible
PS_INSIDEFRAME	6	fills a graphics figure

nWidth is the width of the pen in logical units.

In our program, we will use the variable ahPens to create five pens with the same colors mentioned above.

5.3.3 Initializing a menu

Next, the main window is displayed on the screen and the program enters the message loop. So we'll continue our discussion of the program in the window function of the main window - MainWinProc. The WM_CREATE message, which is sent to the main window before it is displayed on the screen, triggers some initialization work. We retrieve a handle to the main window menu and store it in the variable hMainMenu. Next, we get a handle to the "Colors" submenu of the main menu. This is done with the help of the GetSubMenu function:

```
// Get handle from color submenu
hColorMenu = GetSubMenu(hMainMenu, 2);
```

The GetSubMenu function expects two parameters: The handle for the main menu and an integer value that represents the position of the submenu within the main menu. The first submenu is 0. The function result is the handle to the specified submenu. We have declared hMainMenu and the hColorMenu variables as static within the MainWinProc function. Otherwise these variables would lose their values after a message was processed. Here is a tip that can save you a lot of time debugging: You should check all variables within a window function or any other callback function to determine whether they should be initialized each time the function is run or if they should retain their values. If a variable is to retain its value, it must be declared as either global or static within the callback function.

Menu item check

The next step in the GDIDEMO.EXE program is to check some menu items. The MM_TEXT mapping mode is used by default. Black background and white foreground are used for the cascading **Foreground** and **Background** menus. At the same time you check the menu items, you must also initialize the nCurMapMode, nCurFgColor and nCurBgColor variables with the corresponding values. The height (nCurWindowYExtent) and width (nCurWindowXExtent) extents of the logical window are set to 1000 units each.

Now let's see how each menu item that could appear in the wP parameter of the WM_COMMAND message is handled. The MI_QUIT and MI_ABOUT items are used to exit the program and display an about box. These items do not require any further explanation here, since they were completely described in the previous demo program. One of the MI_MM_... menu items is sent to the MainWndProc function when the user selects a mapping mode from the Mapping Mode menu. The value MI_MM_TEXT+1 is subtracted from the ID of the corresponding menu item and the result is stored in the variable nCurMapMode:

```
// Convert to a define-value from WINDOWS.H
nCurMapMode = wP-MI_MM_TEXT+1;
```

The variable nCurMapMode will now contain a value that matches that of the corresponding mapping mode from the WINDOWS.H include file. The MM_TEXT mapping mode has the value 1 and MM_ANISOTROPIC has the value 8. Next, a FOR loop is processed for each menu item to determine whether or not it should be checked:

```
for (i=MI_MM_TEXT; i<=MI_MM_ANISOTROPIC; i++)
{
  if (i == wP)          // Check selected entry
    CheckMenuItem(hMainMenu, i, MF_CHECKED);
  else                  // Do not check other entries
    CheckMenuItem(hMainMenu, i, MF_UNCHECKED);
}
```

The next step is to use the InvalidateRect function to create a WM_PAINT message for the main window. This enables the paint function PaintGrafik to make the client area of the main window correspond to the selected mapping mode. We will look at the PaintGrafik function in more detail later.

The MI_FG_... menu items are processed in the WM_COMMAND message when a foreground color is selected. A FOR loop is used again to check the corresponding menu item. The MI_BG_... menu items, which indicate the selection of a background color, are processed in the same way. After each of these message types, a WM_PAINT message is sent by the InvalidateRect function to update the client area.

5.3.4 Displaying the picture

Now we'll look at the WM_PAINT message in detail. As mentioned above, this message calls the PaintGrafik function, which is responsible for updating the client area of the main window. As usual, we start by getting a display context handle with the BeginPaint function. Next, we use the GetClientRect function to get the current dimensions, in device coordinates, of the main window client area. The values returned are stored in the rClientRect rectangle structure.

Then we set the mapping mode for the display context according to the contents of the nCurMapMode variable:

```
// Set current mapping mode
SetMapMode (hDC, nCurMapMode);
```

The current mapping mode is also displayed in the title bar of the main window by using the SetWindowText function:

```
// Display mapping mode in main window title bar
wsprintf(szTitleBar, "%s - %s Mapping Mode",
                    (LPSTR)szApplName, (LPSTR)aszMapModes[nCurMapMode-1]);
SetWindowText(hWnd, (LPSTR)szTitleBar);
```

```
void SetWindowText (HWND hWnd, LPSTR lpszText);
```

hWnd is a window or control handle. If it is a control, the text is displayed inside the control itself rather than in the title line. lpsz is a long pointer to a character string ending in "\0".

Next, the logical window and the viewport origins are set. We will assume that the viewport origin will be in the center of the client area so that we can use a four quadrant coordinate system. The logical window origin is defined at coordinates (0, 0).

```
nCurViewXExtent    = rClientRect.right;     // Viewport dimensions
nCurViewYExtent    = rClientRect.bottom;
ptCurViewOrg.x     = nCurViewXExtent/2;     // Set viewport origin
ptCurViewOrg.y     = nCurViewYExtent/2;
ptCurWindowOrg.x   = 0;                     // Set window origin
ptCurWindowOrg.y   = 0;

// Determine viewport origin
```

```
SetViewportOrg(hDC, ptCurViewOrg.x, ptCurViewOrg.y);

// Determine window origin
SetWindowOrg(hDC,

ptCurWindowOrg.x, ptCurWindowOrg.y);
```

We must determine the mapping mode in order to proceed with the next step, since the GDI takes the viewport and window extents into consideration only in the MM_ISOTROPIC and MM_ANISOPTROPIC modes. The values returned by the GetClientRect function are used to set the dimensions of the viewport so that they exactly match the height and width of the client area. The y value is then multiplied by the variable nCurYDirection. This value of this variable is toggled between 1 and -1 by pressing the right mouse button. The negative value will display the picture normally on the screen and the positive value will display the picture upside down. Toggling the display in this fashion will only work in the MM_ISOTROPIC and MM_ANISOTROPIC mapping modes. The window extents are set to nCurWindowXExtent and nCurWindowYExtent (1000 logical units each).

```
if ((nCurMapMode == MM_ISOTROPIC) || (nCurMapMode == MM_ANISOTROPIC))
{
  // Determine window dimensions
  SetWindowExt(hDC, nCurWindowXExtent, nCurWindowYExtent);
  SetViewportExt(hDC, nCurViewXExtent, nCurYDirection*nCurViewYExtent);
  // Determine Viewport dimensions
  SetViewportExt(hDC, nCurViewXExtent, nCurYDirection*nCurViewYExtent);
}
```

Next, we set the foreground (pen) and background (brush) colors:

```
// Set background color
SelectObject(hDC, ahBrushes[nCurBgColor]);

// Set foreground color
SelectObject(hDC, ahPens[nCurFgColor]);
```

The SelectObject function selects the current brush and pen from the display context. The GDI uses these resources to paint the client area.

Mapping mode

Before we actually use the GDI functions to display our picture, we must determine if the MM_TEXT mapping mode has been selected, since this will affect whether our y coordinates must be positive or negative. For example, the statement to draw a rectangle in the first quadrant using a mapping mode other than MM_TEXT is:

```
Rectangle(hDC, 30, 130, 130, 30);
```

The same statement for the MM_TEXT mapping mode would be:

```
Rectangle(hDC, 30, -130, 130, -30);
```

Except for the orientation of the y axis, the GDI functions can be used identically regardless of the mapping mode.

```
// Draw coordinate cross and graphic elements
if (nCurMapMode != MM_TEXT)
{
  Ellipse(hDC, -200, 200, 200, -200);         // Circle
  MoveTo(hDC, -200, 0);
  LineTo(hDC, 200, 0);                        // X-axis
  MoveTo(hDC, 0, 200);
  LineTo(hDC, 0, -200);                       // Y-axis

  // Square in first quadrant
  Rectangle(hDC, 30, 130, 130, 30);
  // Circle in second quadrant
  Arc(hDC, -130, 130, -30, 30, -30, 30, -30, 30);
  // Square with rounded corners in third quadrant
  RoundRect(hDC, -130, -30, -30, -130, 20, 20);
  // Triangle in fourth quadrant
  Polyline(hDC, (LPPOINT)aptTriangle, 4);

  Polygon(hDC, (LPPOINT)aptVertTriangle, 3);  // Arrow at end of Y-axis
  Polygon(hDC, (LPPOINT)aptHorzTriangle, 3);  // Arrow at end of X-axis
}
else // Use Y-value multiplied by -1 in MM_TEXT mode
{
  Ellipse(hDC, -200, -200, 200, 200);
  MoveTo(hDC, -200, 0);
  LineTo(hDC, 200, 0);
  MoveTo(hDC, 0, -200);
  LineTo(hDC, 0, 200);
  Rectangle(hDC, 30, -130, 130, -30);
  Arc(hDC, -130, -130, -30, -30, -30, -30, -30, -30);
  RoundRect(hDC, -130, 30, -30, 130, 20, 20);
```

```
    Polyline(hDC, (LPPOINT)aptTmTriangle, 4);
    Polygon(hDC, (LPPOINT)aptVertTmTriangle, 3);
    Polygon(hDC, (LPPOINT)aptHorzTmTriangle, 3);
  }
```

Ellipse

Our first GDI function is Ellipse, which we'll use to draw a circle, with a diameter of 200 logical units, around the origin of the coordinate plane:

```
Ellipse(hDC, -200, 200, 200, -200);
BOOL Ellipse (HDC hDC, int xUpperLeft, int yUpperLeft, int xLowerRight, int
yLowerRight);
```

hDC is the display context handle. The four parameters that follow hDC are the coordinates of the rectangle that defines the boundaries of the ellipse. (xUpperLeft, yUpperLeft) represents the upper left corner and (xLowerRight, yLowerRight) represents the lower right corner. The height or width of this rectangle may not exceed 32767 logical units. This limit also applies to many other GDI functions. The result of this function indicates whether or not the ellipse was successfully drawn (TRUE or FALSE). After the ellipse (or circle if the height and width of the defining rectangle are the same) is drawn with the selected pen, the figure is filled in with the selected brush. This is also why we draw the coordinate axes after the circle. Otherwise, the axes would be colored over by the brush of the Ellipse function.

MoveTo and LineTo

The MoveTo and LineTo GDI functions are used to draw the axes of the coordinate plane. In the example below, we are assuming a mapping mode other than MM_TEXT is being used:

```
MoveTo(hDC, -200, 0);
LineTo(hDC, 200, 0);                          // X-axis
MoveTo(hDC, 0, 200);
LineTo(hDC, 0, -200);                         // Y-axis
```

The MoveTo function allows us to establish the current position of the GDI. The current position is used by many GDI functions (such as LineTo) as the starting point for graphics output. You can also think of this as the location of the graphics cursor.

We use the MoveTo function to set the current position to the point (200, 0), which is located 200 logical units below the origin on the x axis. From here, the LineTo function will use the current pen to draw a line to the logical point (200, 0), which is located on the positive segment of the x axis. Since the LineTo function always relates to the current position, it only needs to receive the endpoint of the line that you want to draw. The y axis of the coordinate plane is then drawn in the same way.

Now let's look at the other figures we can draw with GDI functions:

```
// Square in first quadrant
Rectangle(hDC, 30, 130, 130, 30);
// Circle in second quadrant
Arc(hDC, -130, 130, -30, 30, -30, 30, -30, 30);
// Square with rounded corners in third quadrant
RoundRect(hDC, -130, -30, -30, -130, 20, 20);
// Triangle in fourth quadrant
Polyline(hDC, (LPPOINT)aptTriangle, 4);

Polygon(hDC, (LPPOINT)aptVertTriangle, 3);    // Arrow at end of X-axis
Polygon(hDC, (LPPOINT)aptHorzTriangle, 3);    // Arrow at end of Y-axis
```

Rectangle

The Rectangle function draws rectangular figures:

```
BOOL Rectangle (HDC hDC, int xUpperLeft, int yUpperLeft, int xLowerRight, int
yLowerRight);
```

The parameters are the same as those used in the Ellipse function, except that the rectangle defined by the coordinates is actually drawn instead of just defining the boundaries of an ellipse. The rectangle is then filled in with the current brush.

RoundRect

The RoundRect function draws a rectangle with rounded corners:

```
BOOL RoundRect (HDC hDC, int xUpperLeft, int yUpperLeft, int xLowerRight, int
yLowerRight, int nEllipseWidth, int nEllipseHeight);
```

The first five parameters correspond to those of the rectangle function. nEllipseWidth and nEllipseHeight define the width and height of the ellipse used to draw the rounded corners of the figure. The figure is again filled in with the current brush.

Arc

The Arc function draws elliptical curves:

```
BOOL Arc (HDC hDC, int xUpperLeft, int yUpperLeft, int xLowerRight, int
yLowerRight, int xArcStart, int yArcStart, int xArcEnd, int yArcEnd);
```

The coordinates (xUpperLeft, yUpperLeft) and (xLowerRight, yLowerRight) define the center of the arc and the rectangle that defines its boundaries. The arc begins at coordinates (xArcStart, yArcStart) and proceeds counterclockwise to (xArcEnd, yArcEnd). Since an arc does not define an enclosed region, there is nothing to fill in with the brush. The function result is TRUE if the arc is successfully drawn; otherwise it is FALSE.

Our program uses the Arc function to draw a circle (a special kind of elliptical arc):

```
Arc(hDC, -130, 130, -30, 30, -30, 30, -30, 30);
```

PolyLine

Next is the PolyLine function:

```
BOOL PolyLine (HDC hDC, LPPOINT lpPoints, int nPoints);
```

This function connects several points with a line. lpPoints is a long pointer to an array that contains nPoints elements of type POINT. The GDI connects all the given points in order, starting with the first element of the array. We use the PolyLine function to draw a triangle in our program:

```
Polyline(hDC, (LPPOINT)aptTriangle, 4);
```

Even though a triangle consists of only three sides, we must give the PolyLine function four points. This ensures that the PolyLine function will draw a closed figure.

Polygon

The Polygon function works differently:

```
BOOL Polygon (HDC hDC, LPPOINT lpPoints, int nPoints);
```

Although the parameters correspond to those of the PolyLine function, the two functions use them differently. The Polygon function is able to connect open line segments and form a polygon.

We use this function in our program in order to draw arrows at the upper end of the x axis and the right end of the y axis:

```
Polygon(hDC, (LPPOINT)aptVertTriangle, 3);    // Arrow at end of X-axis
Polygon(hDC, (LPPOINT)aptHorzTriangle, 3);    // Arrow at end of Y-axis
```

This time we only need three points to define the triangles we want to draw. The three points are defined in the aptVertTriangle and aptHorzTriangle arrays. The polygons are filled in according to the selected polygon fill mode.

After these two triangles are drawn at the ends of the x and y axes, the BeginPaint function is called to free the display context and the paint function's work is completed.

5.3.5 Reading mouse messages

Now let's see how the window function MainWinProc handles other messages. The WM_RBUTTONDOWN message is sent to indicate a mouse event:

```
case WM_RBUTTONDOWN:          // Right mouse button pressed
  // Return Y-axis orientation
  nCurYDirection = -nCurYDirection;
```

When the mouse event occurs Windows sends all mouse messages to the window function of the window, in which the mouse cursor is located. Or the SetCapture function can be used to capture all mouse events even if the mouse cursor is located in another window.

The WM_RBUTTONDOWN message is sent to a window when the user presses the right mouse button. In our program, this event changes the sign of the variable nYCurDirection, which will switch the orientation of the y axis in mapping modes MM_ANISOTROPIC and MM_ISOTROPIC. This turns the displayed picture upside down in the client area.

Here is a summary of the most frequently used mouse messages:

WM_LBUTTONDOWN
: Left mouse button pressed.

WM_LBUTTONUP
: Left mouse button released.

WM_LBUTTONDBLCLK
: Double-click on left mouse button; this message will only be sent to windows defined with the CS_DBLCLKS style.

WM_RBUTTONDOWN
: Right mouse button pressed.

WM_RBUTTONUP
: Right mouse button released.

WM_RBUTTONDBLCLK
: Double-click on right mouse button; this message will only be sent to windows defined with the CS_DBLCLKS style.

WM_MBUTTONDOWN
: Middle mouse button pressed.

WM_MBUTTONUP
: Middle mouse button released.

WM_MBUTTONDBLCLK
: Double-click on middle mouse button; this message will only be sent to windows defined with the CS_DBLCLKS style.

WM_MOUSEMOVE
: Indicate a mouse movement; the current mouse cursor position is given by the lParam parameter.

The current mouse cursor position, in the client area, is always indicated by the value of the lParam parameter in a mouse message. The x coordinate is given by the low word and the y coordinate by the high word. These coordinates are given relative to the upper left corner of the window that receives the message. The MAKEPOINT macro provides an easy way to convert the lParam value to a POINT data structure:

```
POINT MAKEPOINT (DWORD dwMousePos);
```

The wParam parameter also plays a part in mouse messages. This parameter indicates whether the user was holding the <Shift> or <Ctrl> key while the mouse button was pressed. wParam can be a combination of the following values:

MK_SHIFT	<Shift> pressed
MK_CONTROL	<Control> pressed
MK_LBUTTON	Left mouse button pressed
MK_MBUTTON	Middle mouse button pressed
MK_RBUTTON	Right mouse button pressed

Let's discuss some of the special features of mouse messages in more detail. A double-click on a window will only send a WM_xBUTTONDBLCLK message to a window if its window class was registered with the CS_DBLCLKS window style (x stands for L, M or R). If this is the case, the sequence of events following a double-click is as follows: Windows sends a WM_xBUTTONDOWN message followed by a WM_xBUTTONUP message. This combination represents a single click of the mouse button. At this time, the application cannot tell whether the user intends to double-click the mouse button or to stop with a single click. The WM_xBUTTONDBLCLK and WM_xBUTTONUP messages are sent after the second click, and the application will then know that a double-click was intended.

What happens when the user moves the mouse quickly across the screen? Does this mean that the application's message loop will be overwhelmed with WM_MOUSEMOVE messages? Actually, Windows doesn't simply add all new WM_MOUSEMOVE messages to the end of the message queue as it does with other message types. Instead, Windows checks to see if there is already a WM_MOUSEMOVE message in the queue. If there is, Windows simply changes the wParam and lParam parameters of the existing message.

Let's return to the SetCapture function for a moment. This function is used when you want to know about all mouse events, including those that occur within other windows. The SetCapture function call looks like this:

```
HWND SetCapture (HWND hWnd);
```

hWnd is the window that is to receive all mouse messages after the function call. The function result indicates which window was previously receiving mouse messages (this will be NULL if no window was receiving messages).

It is important to release the SetCapture function as soon as possible after the desired messages have been captured so that other windows or applications can process mouse messages as needed. The ReleaseCapture function handles this:

```
void ReleaseCapture (void);
```

After calling this function, mouse messages will again be sent to the window containing the mouse cursor, at the time the mouse event occurs.

5.3.6 Releasing resources

Now we can discuss how the WM_DESTROY message is handled in the GDIDEMO.EXE program. In this program we have created several GDI resources which occupy valuable memory in the Windows system. When a user exits the application, we can use the WM_DESTROY message as our cue to do some clean up work. This includes destroying all GDI resources and freeing the memory that was allocated to them:

```
case WM_DESTROY:
  // Release allocated GDI resources
  for (i=0; i<MAXBRUSHES; i++)
    DeleteObject(ahBrushes[i]);
  for (i=0; i<MAXPENS; i++)
    DeleteObject(ahPens[i]);

  // Send WM_QUIT if window is destroyed
  PostQuitMessage(0);
  break;
```

The DeleteObject function frees objects such as brushes, pens, bitmaps, fonts, regions and palettes (we will talk more about regions and palettes later):

```
BOOL DeleteObject (HANDLE hObject);
```

hObjcct is a handle for one of the objects named above. Remember that none of the standard objects used by Windows may be destroyed in this way. Also, you cannot delete any objects that are currently selected in a display context. The result of this function indicates whether the resources were freed (TRUE) or not (FALSE).

This concludes our introduction of graphics output with the GDIDEMO.EXE program. You should now be familiar with the workings of the GDI. We will build on this knowledge and do some additional GDI programming in the next chapter with the "eyes" application.

5.4 Source Code: GDIDEMO.EXE

GDIDEMO.H include file

```
/* Stringtable Defines */

#define IDS_APPLNAME            1

/* Application icon */

#define IDDIALOGICON          50

/* File menu */

#define MI_QUIT              100
#define MI_ABOUT             101

/* Mapping menu */

#define MI_MM_TEXT           200
#define MI_MM_LOMETRIC       201
#define MI_MM_HIMETRIC       202
#define MI_MM_LOENGLISH      203
#define MI_MM_HIENGLISH      204
#define MI_MM_TWIPS          205
#define MI_MM_ISOTROPIC      206
#define MI_MM_ANISOTROPIC 207

/* Color menu */

#define MI_FG_RED            300
#define MI_FG_GREEN          301
#define MI_FG_BLUE           302
#define MI_FG_WHITE          303
#define MI_FG_BLACK          304
#define MI_BG_RED            305
#define MI_BG_GREEN          306
#define MI_BG_BLUE           307
#define MI_BG_WHITE          308
#define MI_BG_BLACK          309

/* Dialog box control IDs */

/* Other defines */
```

GDIDEMO.RC resource file

```
#include <windows.h>

#include "gdidemo.h"

IDDIALOGICON ICON gdidemo.ico    ; Icon

rcinclude gdidemo.dlg            ; Contains dialog box definitions

STRINGTABLE
BEGIN
  IDS_APPLNAME,       "GDIDemo"  ; Application name
END

MainMenu MENU
BEGIN
  POPUP "&File"
  BEGIN
    MENUITEM "E&xit",    MI_QUIT
    MENUITEM SEPARATOR
    MENUITEM "A&bout GDIDemo...",  MI_ABOUT
  END
  POPUP "&Mapping"
  BEGIN
    MENUITEM "&Text Mode",          MI_MM_TEXT
    MENUITEM SEPARATOR
    MENUITEM "&Anisotropic",       MI_MM_ANISOTROPIC
    MENUITEM "&Isotropic",         MI_MM_ISOTROPIC
    MENUITEM SEPARATOR
    MENUITEM "&LOMETRIC",            MI_MM_LOMETRIC
    MENUITEM "&HIMETRIC",            MI_MM_HIMETRIC
    MENUITEM "L&OENGLISH",           MI_MM_LOENGLISH
    MENUITEM "HI&ENGLISH",           MI_MM_HIENGLISH
    MENUITEM "T&WIPS",               MI_MM_TWIPS
  END
  POPUP "&Color"
  BEGIN
    POPUP "&Foreground"
    BEGIN
      MENUITEM "&Red",             MI_FG_RED
      MENUITEM "&Green",            MI_FG_GREEN
      MENUITEM "&Blue",            MI_FG_BLUE
      MENUITEM "&White",            MI_FG_WHITE
      MENUITEM "B&lack",         MI_FG_BLACK
    END
    POPUP "&Background"
```

```
    BEGIN
      MENUITEM "&Red",                MI_BG_RED
      MENUITEM "&Green",               MI_BG_GREEN
      MENUITEM "&Blue",               MI_BG_BLUE
      MENUITEM "&White",               MI_BG_WHITE
      MENUITEM "B&lack",            MI_BG_BLACK
    END
  END
END ; MainMenu
```

GDIDEMO.DLG dialog box file

```
ABOUTDLG DIALOG LOADONCALL MOVEABLE DISCARDABLE 72, 15, 157, 104
CAPTION "About GDIDemo"
STYLE WS_BORDER | WS_CAPTION | WS_DLGFRAME | WS_SYSMENU | DS_MODALFRAME |
WS_POPUP
BEGIN
    CONTROL "GDIDemo", -1, "static", SS_CENTER | WS_CHILD, 58, 5, 37, 10
    CONTROL "Version 1.00", -1, "static", SS_CENTER | WS_CHILD, 46, 20, 62, 10
    CONTROL "Copyright  1990", -1, "static", SS_CENTER | WS_CHILD, 36, 35, 86, 11
    CONTROL "Abacus", -1, "static", SS_CENTER | WS_CHILD, 40, 51, 79, 11
    CONTROL "OK", IDOK, "button", BS_DEFPUSHBUTTON | WS_TABSTOP | WS_CHILD, 66,
86, 24, 12
    CONTROL IDDIALOGICON, -1, "static", SS_ICON | WS_CHILD, 13, 25, 16, 27
    CONTROL "by D.Honekamp && P. Wilken", 106, "static", SS_CENTER | WS_CHILD,
30, 66, 102, 11
END
```

GDIDEMO.DEF module definition file

```
NAME           GDIDEMO

DESCRIPTION  'GDI Demo Program'

EXETYPE      WINDOWS

CODE           PRELOAD MOVEABLE DISCARDABLE
DATA           PRELOAD MOVEABLE MULTIPLE

HEAPSIZE     8000
STACKSIZE    8000

EXPORTS
             MainWndProc   @1
             MdfAboutProc  @2
```

GDIDEMO.MAK MAKE file

```
Model = S
Warn   = 3
Linker = link

all: gdidemo.exe

gdidemo.res: gdidemo.h gdidemo.rc gdidemo.dlg
  rc -r gdidemo.rc

gdidemo.obj: gdidemo.h gdidemo.c
  cl -c -A$(Model) -W$(Warn) -Gsw -Zpe -Os gdidemo.c

gdidemo.exe: gdidemo.obj gdidemo.def gdidemo.res
  $(Linker) /NOD /al:16 gdidemo,gdidemo.exe,,libw+$(Model)libcew,gdidemo.def
  rc gdidemo.res
```

GDIDEMO.C source code

```
/****************************************************************************
 GDIDEMO.C
 =========

 This program demonstrates the basics of graphics applications using the
 GDI (Graphics Device Interface) SDK functions of Windows.

 Specifics:     GDI coordinate system
                Mapping modes
                Brushes and pens
                Color specification
 ***************************************************************************/

/* -------------------------< Include files >--------------------------- */

#include <windows.h>
#include <stdio.h>
#include <string.h>
#include <stdlib.h>
#include <io.h>

#include "gdidemo.h"

/* -----------------------------< Defines >------------------------------ */

#define MAXNAMELENGTH 30                      // Max. length of application names
```

```
#define MAXBRUSHES     5                       // Number of brushes used
#define MAXPENS        5                       // Number of pens used

/* -------------------------< Global variables >-------------------------- */

HANDLE          hInst;                         // Instance of application
HWND            hwMain;                        // Main window
char            szApplName[MAXNAMELENGTH];     // Application name
FARPROC         lpfnModal,                     // For modal dialog boxes
                lpfnModeless;                  // For modeless dialog boxes
int             nCurMapMode,                   // Current mapping mode
                nCurWindowXExtent,             // Current window width
                nCurWindowYExtent,             // Current window height
                nCurViewXExtent,               // Current viewport width
                nCurViewYExtent,               // Current viewport height
                nCurFgColor,                   // Current foreground color
                nCurBgColor,                   // Current background color
                nCurYDirection = -1;           // Current Y-axis direction
POINT           ptCurWindowOrg,                // Current window origin
                ptCurViewOrg;                  // Current viewport origin
HBRUSH          ahBrushes[MAXBRUSHES];         // Array for brushes used
HPEN            ahPens[MAXPENS];               // Array for pens used
POINT           aptVertTriangle[3] =           // Arrow along Y-axis
                     { { -15, 180 },
                       {   0, 200 },
                       {  15, 180 } },
                aptHorzTriangle[3] =           // Arrow along X-axis
                     { { 180,  15 },
                       { 200,   0 },
                       { 180, -15 } },
                aptVertTmTriangle[3] =         // Arrow along Y-axis (MM_TEXT)
                     { { -15, -180 },
                       {   0, -200 },
                       {  15, -180 } },
                aptHorzTmTriangle[3] =         // Arrow along X-axis (MM_TEXT)
                     { { 180,  -15 },
                       { 200,   0  },
                       { 180,   15 } },
                aptTriangle[4] =
                     { {  80, -30  },
                       {  130,-130 },
                       {  30, -130 },
                       {  80, -30  } },
                aptTmTriangle[4] =
                     { {  80,  30  },
                       {  130, 130 },
                       {  30,  130 },
                       {  80,  30  } };
```

```
// Text for window menu bar
char * aszMapModes[8] = { "MM_TEXT",      "MM_LOMETRIC",  "MM_HIMETRIC",
                          "MM_LOENGLISH", "MM_HIENGLISH", "MM_TWIPS",
                          "MM_ISOTROPIC", "MM_ANISOTROPIC" };

/* ----------------------< Function prototypes >------------------------ */

int  InitFirstInstance (HANDLE, HANDLE, int);
LONG FAR PASCAL MainWndProc (HWND, unsigned, WORD, LONG);
BOOL FAR PASCAL MdfAboutProc (HWND, unsigned, WORD, LONG);
void PaintGraphic (HWND);

/***************************************************************************
 W i n M a i n ()
 ================

 The WinMain function is the main function for every Windows program. WinMain
 is the equivalent of the main() function found in standard C programs, and
 represents the "point or entry" for program execution.

 Parameters:

   HANDLE hInstance:     Current instance handle of the application.
   HANDLE hPrevInstance: Previous instance handle of the application. NULL
                         if the current instance is the first instance.
   LPSTR  lpszCmdLine:   Long pointer to the string placed after the program
                         name during program execution.
   int    nCmdShow:      Parameter which specifies the application window's
                         appearance when the program starts.

 Return values:

   int:                  The wParam parameter for the last message received.
 ***************************************************************************/

int PASCAL WinMain (HANDLE hInstance,  HANDLE hPrevInstance,
                    LPSTR lpszCmdLine, int nCmdShow)
{
  MSG   msg;                        // Message variable

  if (!hPrevInstance)               // Initialization of first instance
  {
    if (!InitFirstInstance(hInstance, hPrevInstance, nCmdShow))
      return NULL;

    // Create brushes
    ahBrushes[0] = CreateSolidBrush(RGB(255, 0, 0));          // Red
    ahBrushes[1] = CreateSolidBrush(RGB(0, 255, 0));          // Green
```

```
    ahBrushes[2] = CreateSolidBrush(RGB(0, 0, 255));          // Blue
    ahBrushes[3] = CreateSolidBrush(RGB(255, 255, 255));      // White
    ahBrushes[4] = CreateSolidBrush(RGB(0, 0, 0));            // Black

    // Create pens
    ahPens[0]    = CreatePen(PS_SOLID, 1, RGB(255, 0, 0));     // Red
    ahPens[1]    = CreatePen(PS_SOLID, 1, RGB(0, 255, 0));     // Green
    ahPens[2]    = CreatePen(PS_SOLID, 1, RGB(0, 0, 255));     // Blue
    ahPens[3]    = CreatePen(PS_SOLID, 1, RGB(255, 255, 255)); // White
    ahPens[4]    = CreatePen(PS_SOLID, 1, RGB(0, 0, 0));       // Black
  }
  else                              // No other instances allowed
  {
    return NULL;
  }

  hInst  = hInstance;                              // Declaration of global
                                                   // instance variable

  hwMain = CreateWindow(szApplName,                // Window class name
                        szApplName,                // Window title
                        WS_OVERLAPPEDWINDOW |      // Overlapped window with
                        WS_VSCROLL,                // scroll bars
                        CW_USEDEFAULT,             // X-position (default)
                        CW_USEDEFAULT,             // Y-position (default)
                        CW_USEDEFAULT,             // Window width (default)
                        CW_USEDEFAULT,             // Window height (default)
                        NULL,                      // No parent window
                        LoadMenu(hInstance, "MainMenu"),
                        hInstance,                 // Instance of application
                        NULL);                     // No extra parameters

   if (!hwMain)
     return NULL;

  /* ---------------------< Display main window >----------------------- */

   ShowWindow(hwMain, nCmdShow);                   // Make window visible
   UpdateWindow(hwMain);                           // Update window

  /* ----------------------< Message  loop >---------------------------- */

  while (GetMessage(&msg, NULL, 0, 0))             // Message reading
  {
      TranslateMessage(&msg);                      // Message translation
      DispatchMessage(&msg);                       // Message -> windows
  }
  return (msg.wParam);                             // End application
```

```
} // WinMain

/****************************************************************************
 I n i t F i r s t I n s t a n c e ()
 ====================================

 This function initializes the first instance of the "GDIDemo" application.

 Parameters:

   HANDLE hInstance:     Current instance handle of the application.
   HANDLE hPrevInstance: Previous instance handle of the application. NULL
                         if the current instance is the first instance.
   int    nCmdShow:      Parameter which specifies the application window's
                         appearance when the program starts.

 Return values;

   int                   Null if the "GDIDemo" window class registers.
                         Otherwise, a value other than NULL.
 ****************************************************************************/

int InitFirstInstance (HANDLE hInstance, HANDLE hPrevInstance, int nCmdShow)
{
  WNDCLASS MainWndClass;                    // Main window class

  // Load application name from resource file
  LoadString(hInstance, IDS_APPLNAME, (LPSTR)szApplName, MAXNAMELENGTH-1);

  // Specify window class information
  MainWndClass.lpszClassName = szApplName;                // Window class
  MainWndClass.hInstance     = hInstance;                 // Instance
  MainWndClass.lpfnWndProc   = MainWndProc;               // Window function
  MainWndClass.style         = CS_HREDRAW | CS_VREDRAW;
  MainWndClass.lpszMenuName  = (LPSTR) NULL;              // No menu
  MainWndClass.hCursor       = LoadCursor(NULL, IDC_ARROW); // Mouse cursor
  MainWndClass.hIcon         = LoadIcon(hInstance,
MAKEINTRESOURCE(IDDIALOGICON));
  MainWndClass.hbrBackground = GetStockObject(WHITE_BRUSH); // White background
  MainWndClass.cbClsExtra    = 0;                         // No extra bytes
  MainWndClass.cbWndExtra    = 0;                         // No extra bytes

  // Registering "GDIDemo" window class
  return (RegisterClass(&MainWndClass));
} // InitFirstInstance

/****************************************************************************
 M a i n W n d P r o c ()
```

```
========================

This function acts as the main window function. All messages are sent to
this window.

Parameters:

  HWND     hWnd:     Window handle.
  unsigned msg:      Message type.
  WORD     wP:       Message-dependent 16 bit value
  LONG     lP:       Message-dependent 32 bit value

Return values:

  LONG               0L if the window function has sent the message.
                     Otherwise, the return value from the DefWindowProc
                     default window function.
***************************************************************************/

LONG FAR PASCAL MainWndProc (HWND hWnd, unsigned msg, WORD wP, LONG lP)
{
   static  HMENU hMainMenu;        // Main menu handle variable
   static  HMENU hColorMenu;       // Color menu handle variable
   int     nResult;                // Return value from DialogBox function
   WORD    i;

   switch (msg)
   {
     case WM_CREATE:               // For creating window
       // Get handle from main menu
       hMainMenu = GetMenu(hWnd);

       // Get handle from color submenu
       hColorMenu = GetSubMenu(hMainMenu, 2);

       // Initialize menu items
       CheckMenuItem(hMainMenu, MI_MM_TEXT, MF_CHECKED);

       // Initialize foreground color (black) and background color (white)
       CheckMenuItem(GetSubMenu(hColorMenu, 0), MI_FG_BLACK, MF_CHECKED);
       CheckMenuItem(GetSubMenu(hColorMenu, 1), MI_BG_WHITE, MF_CHECKED);

       // Initialize important GDI parameters
       nCurMapMode        = MM_TEXT;            // Mapping mode
       nCurWindowXExtent = 1000;                // Window dimensions
       nCurWindowYExtent = 1000;
       nCurFgColor        = MI_FG_BLACK;        // Foreground color
       nCurBgColor        = MI_BG_WHITE;        // Background color
```

```
    break;

  case WM_DESTROY:
    // Release allocated GDI resources
    for (i=0; i<MAXBRUSHES; i++)
      DeleteObject(ahBrushes[i]);
    for (i=0; i<MAXPENS; i++)
      DeleteObject(ahPens[i]);

    // Send WM_QUIT if window is destroyed
    PostQuitMessage(0);
    break;

  case WM_RBUTTONDOWN:          // Right mouse button pressed
    // Return Y-axis orientation
    nCurYDirection = -nCurYDirection;

    // Create WM_PAINT message
    InvalidateRect(hWnd, NULL, TRUE);
    break;

  case WM_COMMAND:              // Messages from menu bar
    switch (wP)
    {
      case MI_QUIT:             // End program
        PostMessage(hwMain, WM_SYSCOMMAND, SC_CLOSE, 0L);
        break;

      case MI_ABOUT:            // Call "About GDIDemo" dialog box
        lpfnModal = MakeProcInstance(MdfAboutProc, hInst);
        nResult = DialogBox(hInst, "ABOUTDLG", hwMain, lpfnModal);
        FreeProcInstance(lpfnModal);
        break;

      case MI_MM_TEXT:          // Change mapping mode
      case MI_MM_ANISOTROPIC:
      case MI_MM_ISOTROPIC:
      case MI_MM_LOMETRIC:
      case MI_MM_HIMETRIC:
      case MI_MM_LOENGLISH:
      case MI_MM_HIENGLISH:
      case MI_MM_TWIPS:
        // Convert to a define-value from WINDOWS.H
        nCurMapMode = wP-MI_MM_TEXT+1;

        for (i=MI_MM_TEXT; i<=MI_MM_ANISOTROPIC; i++)
        {
          if (i == wP)          // Check selected entry
```

```
          CheckMenuItem(hMainMenu, i, MF_CHECKED);
        else                // Do not check other entries
          CheckMenuItem(hMainMenu, i, MF_UNCHECKED);
      }
      // Create WM_PAINT message
      InvalidateRect(hWnd, NULL, TRUE);
      break;

    case MI_FG_RED:         // Change foreground color
    case MI_FG_GREEN:
    case MI_FG_BLUE:
    case MI_FG_WHITE:
    case MI_FG_BLACK:
      nCurFgColor = wP-MI_FG_RED;

      for (i=MI_FG_RED; i<=MI_FG_BLACK; i++)
      {
        if (i == wP)        // Check selected entry
          CheckMenuItem(GetSubMenu(hColorMenu, 0), i, MF_CHECKED);
        else                // Do not check other entries
          CheckMenuItem(GetSubMenu(hColorMenu, 0), i, MF_UNCHECKED);
      }
      // Create WM_PAINT message
      InvalidateRect(hWnd, NULL, TRUE);
      break;

    case MI_BG_RED:         // Change background color
    case MI_BG_GREEN:
    case MI_BG_BLUE:
    case MI_BG_WHITE:
    case MI_BG_BLACK:
      nCurBgColor = wP-MI_BG_RED;

      for (i=MI_BG_RED; i<=MI_BG_BLACK; i++)
      {
        if (i == wP)        // Check selected entry
          CheckMenuItem(GetSubMenu(hColorMenu, 1), i, MF_CHECKED);
        else                // Do not check other entries
          CheckMenuItem(GetSubMenu(hColorMenu, 1), i, MF_UNCHECKED);
      }
      // Create WM_PAINT message
      InvalidateRect(hWnd, NULL, TRUE);
      break;

     default:
       break;
  }
  break;
```

```
    case WM_PAINT:                // Client area update needed
      PaintGraphic(hWnd);
      break;

    default: // Pass other messages to default window function
      return (DefWindowProc(hWnd, msg, wP, lP));
      break;
  }
  return 0L;
} // MainWndProc

/*****************************************************************************
 M d f A b o u t P r o c ()
 ==========================

 This function processes messages for the "About GDIDemo" dialog box.

 Parameters:

   HWND     hDlg:     Dialog box handle.
   unsigned msg:      Message type.
   WORD     wP:       Message-dependent 16 bit value.
   LONG     lP:       Message-dependent 32 bit value.

 Return values:

   BOOL               TRUE if the dialog function contains the given message.
                      Otherwise, FALSE.
 *****************************************************************************/

BOOL FAR PASCAL MdfAboutProc (HWND hDlg, unsigned msg, WORD wP, LONG lP)
{
  switch (msg)
  {
    case WM_INITDIALOG:           // Dialog box display message
      return TRUE;                // Do not execute initialization
      break;

    case WM_COMMAND:              // Dialog box control message
      switch (wP)
      {
        case IDOK:                // Click on OK button
          EndDialog(hDlg, TRUE);
          return TRUE;
          break;

        default:                  // Other messages
```

```
          return FALSE;
          break;
      }
      break;

    case WM_SYSCOMMAND:         // Message from dialog box system menu
      switch (wP)
      {
        // ALT+F4, double-click system menu or select "Close" from system
        // menu

        case SC_CLOSE:
          EndDialog(hDlg, TRUE);
          return TRUE;
          break;

        default:                // Other system menu messages
          return FALSE;
          break;
      }
      break;

    default:                    // Other messages
        return FALSE;
        break;
  }
} // MdfAboutProc

/*****************************************************************************
 P a i n t G r a p h i c ()
 ========================

 This function is needed for redrawing the client area of the main window.

 Parameters:

   HWND    hWnd:    Window handle.

 Return values:    None.
 *****************************************************************************/

 void PaintGraphic (HWND hWnd)
 {
   PAINTSTRUCT ps;                    // Client are information
   HDC                 hDC;           // Display context handle
   RECT         rClientRect;          // Client area rectangle
   char         szTitleBar[80];       // Main window title bar text
```

```
hDC = BeginPaint(hWnd, &ps);      // Get main window display context

// Determine client area dimensions
GetClientRect(hWnd, &rClientRect);

// Set current mapping mode
SetMapMode (hDC, nCurMapMode);

// Display mapping mode in main window title bar
wsprintf(szTitleBar, "%s - %s Mapping Mode",
                     (LPSTR)szApplName, (LPSTR)aszMapModes[nCurMapMode-1]);
SetWindowText(hWnd, (LPSTR)szTitleBar);

nCurViewXExtent   = rClientRect.right;     // Viewport dimensions
nCurViewYExtent   = rClientRect.bottom;
ptCurViewOrg.x    = nCurViewXExtent/2;     // Set viewport origin
ptCurViewOrg.y    = nCurViewYExtent/2;
ptCurWindowOrg.x  = 0;                     // Set window origin
ptCurWindowOrg.y  = 0;

// Determine viewport origin
SetViewportOrg(hDC, ptCurViewOrg.x, ptCurViewOrg.y);

// Determine window origin
SetWindowOrg(hDC, ptCurWindowOrg.x, ptCurWindowOrg.y);

if ((nCurMapMode == MM_ISOTROPIC) || (nCurMapMode == MM_ANISOTROPIC))
{
  // Determine window dimensions
  SetWindowExt(hDC, nCurWindowXExtent, nCurWindowYExtent);

  // Determine Viewport dimensions
  SetViewportExt(hDC, nCurViewXExtent, nCurYDirection*nCurViewYExtent);
}

// Set background color
SelectObject(hDC, ahBrushes[nCurBgColor]);

// Set foreground color
SelectObject(hDC, ahPens[nCurFgColor]);

// Draw coordinate cross and graphic elements
if (nCurMapMode != MM_TEXT)
{
  Ellipse(hDC, -200, 200, 200, -200);          // Circle
  MoveTo(hDC, -200, 0);
  LineTo(hDC, 200, 0);                         // X-axis
  MoveTo(hDC, 0, 200);
```

```
    LineTo(hDC, 0, -200);                           // Y-axis

    // Square in first quadrant
    Rectangle(hDC, 30, 130, 130, 30);
    // Circle in second quadrant
    Arc(hDC, -130, 130, -30, 30, -30, 30, -30, 30);
    // Square with rounded corners in third quadrant
    RoundRect(hDC, -130, -30, -30, -130, 20, 20);
    // Triangle in fourth quadrant
    Polyline(hDC, (LPPOINT)aptTriangle, 4);

    Polygon(hDC, (LPPOINT)aptVertTriangle, 3);    // Arrow at end of X-axis
    Polygon(hDC, (LPPOINT)aptHorzTriangle, 3);    // Arrow at end of Y-axis
  }
  else // Use Y-value multiplied by -1 in MM_TEXT mode
  {
    Ellipse(hDC, -200, -200, 200, 200);
    MoveTo(hDC, -200, 0);
    LineTo(hDC, 200, 0);
    MoveTo(hDC, 0, -200);
    LineTo(hDC, 0, 200);
    Rectangle(hDC, 30, -130, 130, -30);
    Arc(hDC, -130, -130, -30, -30, -30, -30, -30, -30);
    RoundRect(hDC, -130, 30, -30, 130, 20, 20);
    Polyline(hDC, (LPPOINT)aptTmTriangle, 4);
    Polygon(hDC, (LPPOINT)aptVertTmTriangle, 3);
    Polygon(hDC, (LPPOINT)aptHorzTmTriangle, 3);
  }

  EndPaint(hWnd, &ps);          // Release display context
} // PaintGraphic
```

6 Color and Bitmaps

Chapter 5 provided a general introduction to GDI. In this chapter we will cover some additional aspects of GDI programming, such as:

1) The Windows color palette manager

2) Regions

3) Bitmaps and bitmap animation

We will also look at the following subjects:

1) The Windows timer

2) Dynamically changing menus

The demo application we'll discuss in this chapter is called EYES.EXE. The program draws two stylized eyes on the screen. The pupils of these eyes follow the movements of the mouse cursor around the screen. EYES.EXE will run in multiple instances. A dialog box allows the user to change the colors of the background, the eyes and the pupils. This is done by using the Windows 3 color palette manager.

The description of this program may sound familiar to you. There is a shareware program called EyeCon, which performs the same task. Also, a similar program called XEYES is provided with some versions of X-Window (a graphical interface for UNIX) as an entertainment program. Even though the workings of this program may seem simple on the surface, the implementation of these functions under Windows requires some real programming finesse.

6.1 The Windows Color Palette Manager

As we mentioned above, the EYES.EXE application uses the Windows color palette manager. This utility was included as a feature of the SDK starting with Windows Version 3.0. It acts as an interface between the colors an application wishes to use and the actual color capabilities of the hardware available on the PC running the application (CGA, Hercules, EGA, VGA, TIGA, etc.).

Even the most complex graphics card can only display a set number of colors on the screen at any given time. The number of colors and the colors themselves depend on the graphics mode selected. The hardware palette is the color set that the graphics card makes available to an application program. The colors that Windows can make available to the application is called the system palette.

The Windows palette manager works basically like this: An application should be able to work with a desired logical color palette, regardless of what other applications may be running at the time. As long as the color needs of the various applications do not conflict, the palette manager can supply the required colors directly from the system palette.

As soon as the applications need to display more colors on the screen than are available through the system palette, the palette manager implements a color mapping algorithm. When the algorithm is applied, the palette manager tries to select colors, from the system palette, that are closest to the application's desired colors. This minimizes the loss of color on the screen.

The window that has the input priority also has the highest priority for accessing colors from the system palette. The palette manager assures that the color needs of this window are satisfied first by the system palette. If all available colors in the system palette are used, then the mapping process takes over and uses the colors that come closest to the desired colors. The palette manager will also attempt to provide the desired colors to the other windows that do not have the input focus, but at a lower priority.

The way the palette manager works is similar to the Windows font manager. Both try to fulfill the requirements of applications.

However, the application cannot be sure that its wishes will be met exactly. This is because Windows is a multitasking system. So a single application cannot have exclusive access to all operating system resources.

With proper planning, you can easily overcome this limitation and program your applications to fully utilize the way the font and palette managers work.

Now let's discuss the practical aspects of working with the Windows palette manager. In order to use the palette manager, an application must create a logical color palette Under Windows. A logical color palette is simply viewed as another GDI resource.

To see how this works, let's study the source code of the EYES.EXE application. After the usual preparations, such as registering the window class of the main program for the first instance of the application, the InitPalette function is called. This function allocates a logical color palette with three entries used for the background of the "Eyes" window, the eye color and the pupil color:

```
    // Allocate memory on the local heap for a logical
....// palette with MAXCOLORS entries
    pLogPal = (NPLOGPALETTE) LocalAlloc(LMEM_FIXED,
                                        (sizeof(LOGPALETTE) +
                                        (sizeof(PALETTEENTRY)*MAXCOLORS)));
```

The LocalAlloc function dynamically allocates memory, on the local heap, for the three colors. Normally, the LocalAlloc function returns a handle used with a LocalLock function call to return a pointer to the memory region. But in this case, we passed LMEM_FIXED as a parameter value. So the allocated memory region is fixed and the handle that is returned by LocalAlloc can be used directly as a near pointer (16 bit). There is more information on this procedure in the chapter on Windows memory management.

We then cast the returned pointer to type NPLOGPALETTE and store it in the variable pLogPal. NPLOGPALETTE is a near pointer to a LOGPALETTE structure. This structure describes a logical color palette and is defined in WINDOWS.H as follows:

```
/* Logical Palette */
typedef struct tagLOGPALETTE {
```

```
    WORD          palVersion;
    WORD          palNumEntries;
    PALETTEENTRY          palPalEntry[1];
} LOGPALETTE;
```

palVersion is the current Windows version of the palette structure. The 0x300 palNumEntries indicates how many entries of type PALETTEENTRY are in the palPalEntry array. This explains the memory allocations above: We need enough space for a structure of type LOGPALETTE and for MAXCOLORS palette entries of type PALETTEENTRY.

The following step initializes the LOGPALETTE structure:

```
    pLogPal->palVersion     = 0x300;      // Version number
    pLogPal->palNumEntries  = MAXCOLORS;  // Number of entries
```

Next comes the initialization of all palette entries. The PALETTEENTRY data structure is defined in WINDOWS.H as follows:

```
typedef struct tagPALETTEENTRY
{
  BYTE peRed;     // red component
  BYTE peGreen;   // green component
  BYTE peBlue;    // blue component
  BYTE peFlags;   // palette entry mode
} PALETTEENTRY;
```

The palette entry mode peFlags tells the palette manager how to handle the entry. One of the following values can be used:

PC_EXPLICIT — The low word of the entry represents a direct index to the hardware palette of the output device.

PC_NOCOLLAPSE — The palette manager should attempt to store a color value (defined by peRed, peGreen and peRed) in an unused entry in the system palette so that it will also be available for other applications. If there are no free entries in the table, the requested color will be created over an existing system palette entry.

PC_RESERVED — The palette manager should not attempt to make the requested color available to other applications when color mapping.

The peRed, peGreen and peBlue fields of the PALETTEENTRY structure define a color value the same way the RGB macro does. The three primary colors red, green and blue are mixed in various proportions by assigning a value from 0 to 255 for each color component.

We will select PC_NOCOLLAPSE as the entry mode:

```
// Initialization of palette entries
for (i=0; i<MAXCOLORS; i++)
{
  pLogPal->palPalEntry[i].peFlags = PC_NOCOLLAPSE;      // entry mode
}
```

After this, the individual color fields are initialized. The EYES.EXE application has its own initialization file: EYES.INI. If this file is available in the Windows directory, it is accessed and the initialization information is read. This works in much the same way as the WIN.INI file. Our EYES.INI file looks like this:

```
[eyes]
background.red=255
background.green=0
background.blue=0
eyes.red=0
eyes.green=255
eyes.blue=0
pupils.red=0
pupils.green=0
pupils.blue=255
```

The [eyes] segment contains keywords for the red, green and blue components of the background color, the eyes and the pupils. The initialization value is separated from the keyword by an equal sign in each case. Although this segment could also be stored in the WIN.INI file, Microsoft recommends creating private initialization files for other applications. This allows Windows to read the WIN.INI file quickly when you start the system.

How do we access this initialization file? The SDK functions GetProfileString and GetProfileInt access WIN.INI, and

GetPrivateProfileString and GetPrivateProfileInt access private initialization files (in Windows 3.0 and higher). The ...ProfileString functions are used specifically for accessing character strings, and the ...ProfileInt functions are used to access integer values.

For example, here is how the GetPrivateProfileInt function is used in the EYES.EXE program:

```
WORD GetPrivateProfileInt (LPSTR lpszApplication, LPSTR lpszKey, int
nDefaultValue, LPSTR lpszInitFile);
```

lpszApplication is a long pointer to the application name, which is stored in square brackets in the initialization file (for example "[eyes]"). lpszKey is a long pointer to the keyword that is linked to the initialization value with an equal sign (for example "background.red" in the line 'background.red=255'). nDefaultValue is an integer value set by the programmer that the function will use if the keyword indicated by lpszKey cannot be found. lpszInitFile is a long pointer to the pathname where the private initialization file can be found.

If a relative pathname is given (for example "eyes.ini"), then Windows will only look in the Windows directory. This is where the WIN.INI file is located. The current directory will not be searched. If the keyword was found, the function will return the positive integer value that follows the keyword, or it will return zero if no value or a negative value was found. If the keyword was not found, the function returns the value nDefaultValue.

In our program, the GetPrivateProfileInt function assigns RGB values to the entries in the allocated logical palette:

```
// Background (default color: white)
pLogPal->palPalEntry[BACKGROUND].peRed   =
  (BYTE) GetPrivateProfileInt("eyes", "background.red", 255, "EYES.INI");
pLogPal->palPalEntry[BACKGROUND].peGreen =
  (BYTE) GetPrivateProfileInt("eyes", "background.green", 255, "EYES.INI");
pLogPal->palPalEntry[BACKGROUND].peBlue  =
  (BYTE) GetPrivateProfileInt("eyes", "background.blue", 255, "EYES.INI");
                 ...
```

After initializing the palette entries, we must instruct Windows to use these settings to create the palette that will be used in the rest of the program. We also have to get a handle for the palette. The CreatePalette functions handle this for us:

```
// create logical color palette set color values
hCurPal = CreatePalette((LPLOGPALETTE)pLogPal);
```

HPALETTE is specified as follows:

```
HPALETTE CreatePalette (LPLOGPALETTE lpLogPal);
```

lpLogPal is a long pointer to a LOGPALETTE data structure. The function result is of type HPALETTE (handle to a logical palette) or NULL if the color palette could not be created. The handle to the palette is hCurPal, which can be used in the rest of the program just like any other GDI resource handle. For example, the handle can be used to select this palette in a display context and then free it with DeleteObject after it has been used.

6.2 The Windows Timer

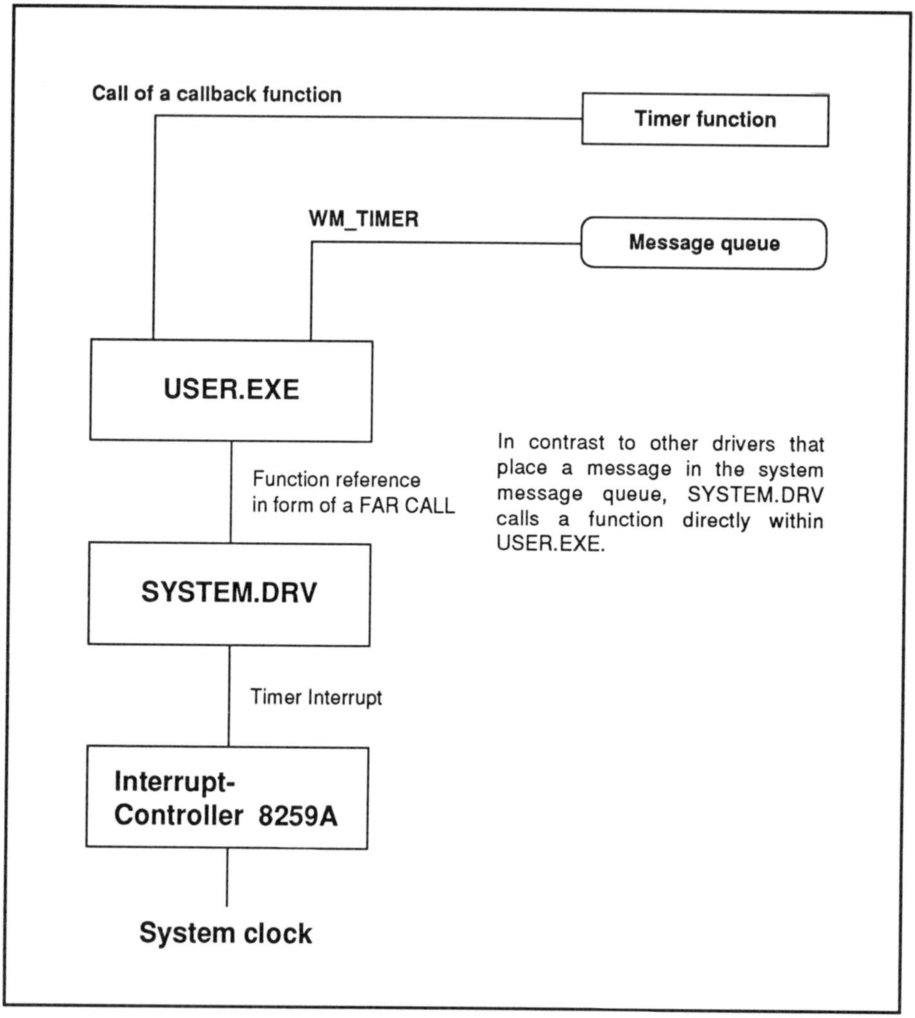

Handling the timer under Windows

Let's stop for a moment to consider the logical flow of the program. After the color palette is created and the main window is displayed on screen, the Windows timer is started:

```
if (!SetTimer(hwMain, 1, TIMERINTERVAL, NULL)) // Set timer
{
  LoadString(hInst, IDS_NOMORETIMERS, (LPSTR)szMBString,
                    sizeof(szMBString)-1);
  MessageBox(hwMain, szMBString, szApplName, MB_OK | MB_ICONEXCLAMATION);
  return FALSE;
}
```

As the name indicates, the SetTimer function sets the timer, which controls the periodic movement of the pupils. Right now we'll discuss the SetTimer function only briefly. The next chapter will present more information about this function.

```
WORD SetTimer (HWND hWnd, int nEventID, WORD wInterval, FARPROC lpfnTimerFunc);
```

hWnd is the handle for the window that will be sent a WM_TIMER message every wInterval milliseconds. nEventID is a timerID, which uniquely identifies the timer and must be greater than zero (similar to the child ID used to identify a child window with the CreateWindow function). lpfnTimerFunc is either NULL if the hWnd parameter is used, or it is the procedure instance address of a callback function that Windows will call every wInterval milliseconds (the accuracy of the time interval depends on the resolution of your system clock). If the result returned by the SetTimer function is zero, then the time could not be started. Under Windows, the timer can be running up to 16 separate instances at any given time.

We use the SetTimer function to send a WM_TIMER message to the MainWndProc function every TIMERINTERVAL milliseconds. If the timer cannot be loaded again, then we load a message string for the MessageBox function from the string table of the resource file so that an appropriate error message will be displayed. Otherwise, the program enters the message loop as usual.

6.3 Accelerators

We need to take a closer look at the message loop for this application. The EYES.EXE program presents the first use of the accelerator in this book. The accelerator defines certain key combinations that allow you to select certain menu items quickly:

```
while (GetMessage((LPMSG)&msg, NULL, 0, 0))    // Message reading
{
  if (!TranslateAccelerator(hwMain, hAccelTable, (LPMSG)&msg))
  {
    TranslateMessage((LPMSG)&msg);              // Message translation
    DispatchMessage((LPMSG)&msg);               // Message -> Windows
  }
}
```

The **About Eyes...** and **Palette...** items can be selected directly with the key combinations <Ctrl>+<A> and <Ctrl>+<P>. To define these hotkeys, we must add the accelerator table to the resource file EYES.RC:

```
Eyes ACCELERATORS
BEGIN
  "^A", MI_ABOUT
  "^P", MI_PALETTE
END
```

An accelerator table begins with the name of the table followed by the keyword ACCELERATORS. The familiar BEGIN...END section is next. Accelerator hotkey combinations are defined within this section. Each combination must be associated with a menu item. The format of each entry is:

```
"Accelerator combination", menu_ID [,TYPES]
```

The accelerator combination can be a simple ASCII character in double quotes or it can be a virtual key (a function key such as <F1>). If the caret symbol (^) precedes the character, the <Ctrl> key must be pressed along with the character key to select the associated menu item. If you want to define a simple ASCII character as an accelerator key, you must enter the value "ASCII" in the type field. Otherwise the character will only activate the menu item if it is pressed while the <Shift> key is held. If the accelerator key is a function key, you must enter "VIRTKEY" in the type field. "ALT" in the type field means that the <Alt> key must be pressed with the character key, and "SHIFT" means that you must press the <Shift> key along with the character key.

After defining the accelerator table in the resource file, you must also use the LoadAccelerators function in the first instance of the program in order to load the accelerator table from the resource file and to get a handle for the loaded table:

```
// Load accelerator table
hAccelTable = LoadAccelerators(hInstance, szApplName);
```

Finally, as we saw above, you must expand the message loop with the TranslateAccelerator function. This function must be called before the TranslateMessage and DispatchMessage functions. It recognizes WM_KEYUP and WM_KEYDOWN messages and checks these against the defined accelerator hot key combinations. When an accelerator combination is encountered, the window that contains the menu item for the accelerator combination is sent a WM_COMMAND or a WM_SYSCOMMAND (for system menus) message. The corresponding window function processes this message and returns to the TranslateAccelerator function. This procedure is similar to that used with SendMessage.

If the TranslateAccelerator function returns a value of 0, then an accelerator combination was not processed. This means the message will be processed "normally" by TranslateMessage and DispatchMessage. Otherwise, these functions can no longer be called with the processed message.

6.4 Dynamic Menu Changes

Next we'll examine handling messages in the window function MainWndProc; We'll concentrate on the WM_CREATE message, which performs initialization work. This time we have not specified any explicit menu resources in the "eyes.rc" resource file. Instead, we will dynamically expand the system menu for this application by two menu items. We use the GetSystemMenu function to retrieve a handle to a copy of the system menu:

```
// Get handle to copy of system menu
hSystemMenu = GetSystemMenu(hWnd, FALSE);
```

The first parameter of the GetSystemMenu function is a handle to the window that will contain the system menu. The second parameter is given as either TRUE or FALSE. If it is FALSE, the function returns a handle to a copy of the system menu. The application can change this copy as desired. If this parameter is TRUE, then the copy of the system menu is destroyed and a handle to the original system menu is returned.

The next step involves expanding the system menu with a new entry. To visually separate the new entry, first we'll add a vertical line to the end of the menu:

```
// Add separation line to end of menu
AppendMenu(hSystemMenu, MF_SEPARATOR, 0, (LPSTR)NULL);
```

The AppendMenu function does this. This is one of many functions that can be used to dynamically change menus at run time. Windows 2.x had the ChangeMenu function, which handled all changes, such as inserting, appending, changing, removing or deleting menu entries. This function will still run under Windows 3.0 in order to maintain upward compatibility, but you should always use the 3.0 menu functions for new applications. Under Windows 3.0, the features of the ChangeMenu function have been split among several individual functions. The following are the most important (the names are self-explanatory):

AppendMenu

DeleteMenu

InsertMenu

ModifyMenu

RemoveMenu

As an example, let's take a closer look at the AppendMenu function:

```
BOOL AppendMenu (HMENU hMenu, WORD wItemMode, WORD wItemID, LPSTR lpItem);
```

hMenu is a handle to the menu involved. wItemMode indicates whether the new menu item should also be displayed after it has been appended. This parameter can contain a combination of the values MF_BITMAP (the menu item is displayed as a bitmap), MF_CHECKED (the item is checked), MF_DISABLED (the item cannot be selected), MF_ENABLED (the item is free to be selected), MF_GRAYED (the item is displayed in gray), MF_MENUBREAK (the item is placed in a new line or column), MF_MENUBARBREAK (the item is separated from others with a vertical line), MF_OWNERDRAW (application is responsible for drawing menu items), MF_POPUP (wItemID contains the ID of a pull-down menu), MF_SEPARATOR (displays a horizontal separation line), MF_STRING (lpItem is a long pointer to a character string that will be used as the menu item) or MF_UNCHECKED (the item is not checked). wItemId contains either the ID of the new menu entry or the ID of a pull-down menu, depending on the value of wItemMode parameter. The meaning of lpItem depends on the wItemMode parameter. For example, MF_BITMAP would mean the menu entry is a bitmap. The bitmap handle will then be found in LOWORD(lpItem). MF_STRING would indicate that the menu item is a character string. In this case, lpItem is a long pointer to a character string ending in '\0'. For MF_OWNERDRAW, lpItem is a value that can be used by the application to associate its own data with the menu item. This value can be queried by processing WM_DRAWITEM and WM_MEASUREITEM system messages. The result of the AppendMenu function is TRUE if it is successfully executed; otherwise it is FALSE.

Let's take a closer look at MF_OWNERDRAW menu items. The application itself is responsible for drawing this type of menu item. Windows sends the application two special messages to help take care of this. The WM_MEASUREITEM message is sent before an MF_OWNERDRAW menu item or an OWNERDRAW control is displayed. In this message, the lParam parameter points to a MEASUREITEMSTRUCT data structure, which contains field for the type, the control ID (for a control) or the menu ID (for a menu entry), the width and height of the object, and an additional parameter DWORD which is reserved for private data. The application is responsible for filling out this structure with the desired values. Windows sends a WM_DRAWITEM message when the appearance of an OWNERDRAW menu item or control has changed and must be partially or completely redrawn. In this message, lParam is a long pointer to a DRAWITEMSTRUCT data structure. Like MEASUREITEMSTRUCT, this structure contains information on the object type (menu item or control), the object ID and additional fields. From these, the application can determine whether the object needs to be completely or only partially redrawn. It will know where the input focus is and whether or not the object is selected. One very important field passes a handle to the display context of the object. The application can then use this for drawing. This data structure also contains a rectangle that defines the limits of the object and a DWORD field for passing private data.

After adding our separation line, the AppendMenu function is called again to append the "Palette...\tCTRL+P" menu item. The ID for this item is MI_PALETTE and its accelerator combination is "CTRL+P". The "\t" stands for the tab character. This means that the accelerator combination for the menu item will be displayed on the right side of the menu. Selecting this menu item will open a color palette selection dialog box with three scroll bars:

```
// Append Palette... menu item
AppendMenu(hSystemMenu, MF_STRING, MI_PALETTE, (LPSTR)"Palette...\tSTRG+P");
```

The same mechanism appends the "About Eyes...\tCTRL+A" menu item. This item will open the about box with the accelerator combination "CTRL+A":

```
// Append About Eyes... menu item
AppendMenu(hSystemMenu, MF_STRING, MI_ABOUT, (LPSTR)"Info .ber Eyes...\tSTRG+A");
```

Finally, we will demonstrate how to add menu items using the InsertMenu function. We will use this function to insert a separation line between the "**Palette...**" and "**About Eyes...**" menu items:

```
// Add separation line between MI_PALETTE and MI_ABOUT
InsertMenu(hSystemMenu, MI_ABOUT, MF_SEPARATOR | MF_BYCOMMAND, 0, (LPSTR)NULL);
```

The syntax of the InsertMenu function is similar to that of the AppendMenu function:

```
BOOL InsertMenu (HMENU hMenu, WORD wPos, WORD wItemMode, WORD wItemID, LPSTR
lpItem);
```

hMenu, wItemID and lpItem have the same meanings as with the AppendMenu function. wItemMode can also have the values MF_BYCOMMAND or MF_BYPOSITION. MF_BYCOMMAND means that wPos contains the ID of the menu item before which the new menu item will be inserted. MF_BYPOSITION means that wPos contains the position of the menu item before which the new item will be inserted. Menu positions are integer values, where 0 indicates the first menu item. A value of -1 means that the new entry will be inserted as the last entry in the menu (which really seems to make the AppendMenu function unnecessary...).

6.5 Bitmaps

Let's leave the subject of dynamic menus for now and look at how some parameters, that are important for the rest of the program, are calculated. First, we need the size of the client area for an application window that has been expanded to its maximum size. These values are needed to calculate the dimensions of the bitmap that stores the background of the pupils, which is used later during the animation. This is accomplished with the GetSystemMetrics function. This function is useful for retrieving various screen parameters:

```
// Calculate maximum bitmap size
SetRect(&rMaxRect, 0, 0, GetSystemMetrics(SM_CXFULLSCREEN),
        GetSystemMetrics(SM_CYFULLSCREEN));
```

The GetSystemMetrics function has the following syntax:

```
int GetSystemMetrics (int nIndex);
```

nIndex indicates which screen parameter the function should return. Some of the most important values for nIndex are:

SM_CXSCREEN	Screen width in pixels
SM_CYSCREEN	Screen height in pixels
SM_CXFULLSCREEN	Width of client area in full-size window
SM_CYFULLSCREEN	Height of client area in full-size window
SM_CXMIN	Minimum window height
SM_CXMAX	Maximum window height
SM_CYCAPTION	Height of window title bar
SM_CYMENU	Height of single-line menu bar

We will use the indices SM_CXFULLSCREEN and SM_CYFULLSCREEN to calculate the dimensions of the client area for a full-size window. These values will then be assigned to the variable rMaxRect.

We should note here that the entire EYES.EXE program uses only the standard MM_TEXT mapping mode. Therefore, there is an equivalence between the client area coordinates and the logical coordinates that simplifies programming functions that use client area coordinates as parameters or that return them as results.

In the next step, we will calculate some parameters that will be used to logically divide the client area of the main window for displaying the eyes and the pupils:

```
nBorderLeft      = nBorderRight  = rMaxRect.right / 16;
nBorderTop       = nBorderBottom = rMaxRect.bottom / 8;
nEllipseWidth    = rMaxRect.right/2-nBorderRight-nBorderLeft;
nEllipseHeight   = rMaxRect.bottom-nBorderBottom-nBorderTop;
nMaxEyeWidth     = (nEllipseWidth+nEllipseHeight)/6;
```

The figure "Client Area Parameters" shows these values. nMaxEyeWidth is the diameter of a pupil when the client area of the window is expanded to full size. This value is required for some of the bitmap functions.

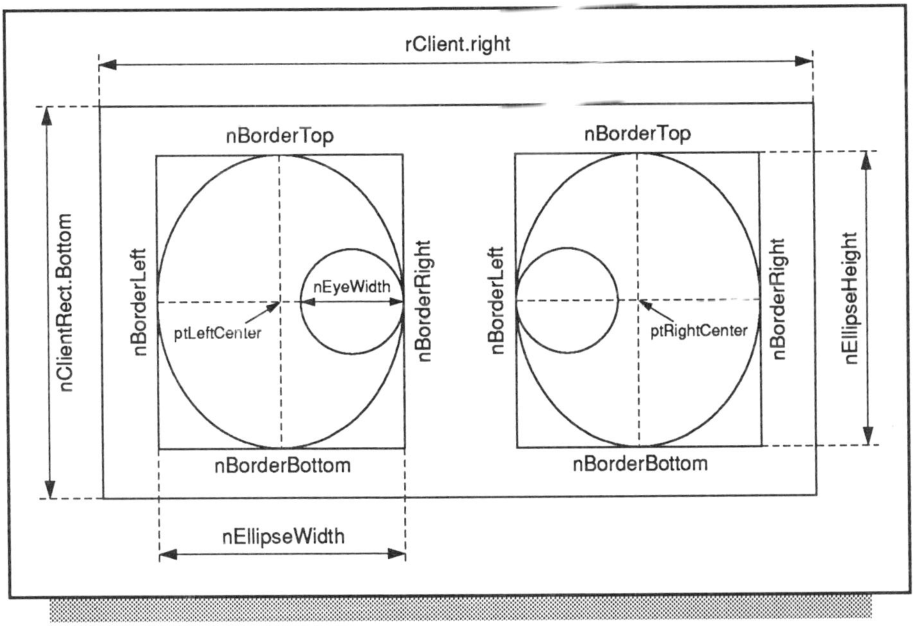

Client area parameters

Before using bitmaps, a compatible display context must be set up:

```
hDC = GetDC(hWnd);

// Create compatible display context
hBkGrDC = CreateCompatibleDC(hDC);
```

Think of a compatible display context as a memory block that represents part of the physical output area. It is associated with an output device (such as the screen). It is necessary to route all output through a single function that is aware of the special features of the graphics hardware. For example, if bitmaps were created for a color screen but they must be displayed on a monochrome monitor, they must be converted. On a color screen, one pixel is represented by four bits (pixel on/off plus the information on each color component). However, on a monochrome screen only one bit is required to display a pixel (pixel on/off). The term "bit plane" is also used to describe the number of bits required to display a pixel. The CreateCompatibleDC function creates a compatible display context:

```
HDC CreateCompatibleDC (HDC hDC);
```

hDC is the handle to a "normal" display context that is assigned to a certain output device. hDC can also be NULL, in which case a compatible display context for the entire screen will be created. This function returns a handle to the compatible display context. In all cases, the output device identified by the hDC parameter must be able to manipulate bitmaps.

The GetDeviceCaps function retrieves information about the hardware capabilities of a given output device. This ability to work with bitmaps can be queried with the value RC_BITBLT (which represents Raster Capability: Bit Block Transfer) in the second parameter:

```
if (GetDeviceCaps(hDC, RC_BITBLT))
{
  // Device can be assigned a compatible display context
}
else
{
  // Device cannot be assigned a compatible display context
}
```

After creating a compatible display context, we must create compatible bitmaps before we can perform any bitmap operations:

```
// Create compatible bitmaps
hBkGrLeftBitmap  = CreateCompatibleBitmap(hDC, nMaxEyeWidth, nMaxEyeWidth);
hBkGrRightBitmap = CreateCompatibleBitmap(hDC, nMaxEyeWidth, nMaxEyeWidth);
```

```
ReleaseDC(hWnd, hDC);
break;
```

The CreateCompatibleBitmap function receives the display context of an output device as the first parameter. The second and third parameters are the width and height of the bitmap to be created. These dimensions are given in bits. If the function is successful, it returns a handle of type HBITMAP. If the bitmap could not be created, the function returns NULL. A bitmap created in this way is compatible with the output device given by hDC. This means that it uses the same number of bit planes to describe a pixel. A bitmap created with CreateCompatibleBitmap can be selected within a compatible display context. This is usually required for operations that involve moving bitmaps.

After a compatible display context for the background of the left and right pupils has been created and the display context for the main window is freed, the WM_CREATE message has completed its work.

6.6 Regions

The WM_SIZE message is handled in the MainWndProc function. A WM_SIZE message is always sent to a window when its size changes. Windows passes the new status of the window in the wParam parameter (SIZEFULLSCREEN: maximum size, SIZEICONIC: reduced to an icon, SIZENORMAL: neither maximum size nor reduced to an icon). lParam gives the new width (LOWORD) and height (HIWORD) of the window. This message creates the regions that we will use later for determining the position of the pupils:

```
case WM_SIZE: // Window size change
     GetDimensions(hWnd);
     hLeftOuterRgn = CreateEllipticRgn(nBorderLeft, nBorderTop,
                              (rRect.right/2)-nBorderRight,
                              rRect.bottom-nBorderBottom);
     hLeftInnerRgn = CreateEllipticRgn(nBorderLeft+nEyeWidth,
                                 nBorderTop+nEyeWidth,
                                 (rRect.right/2)-nBorderRight-nEyeWidth,
                                 rRect.bottom-nBorderBottom-nEyeWidth);
          ...
```

Before we create regions, the GetDimensions function is called to calculate some of the important client area parameters.

The left and right borders are set to 1/16 of the width of the client area while the top and bottom borders are set to 1/8 of the height of the client area:

```
GetClientRect(hWnd, (LPRECT) &rRect);

// Setting the borders
nBorderLeft     = nBorderRight  = rRect.right / 16;
nBorderTop      = nBorderBottom = rRect.bottom / 8;
```

Next, the center points of the left and right eyes are calculated:

```
// Center point of left eye
ptLeftCenter.x  = rRect.right/4;
ptLeftCenter.y  = rRect.bottom/2;

// Center point of right eye
ptRightCenter.x = 3*rRect.right/4;
ptRightCenter.y = rRect.bottom/2;
```

Finally, the height and width of the eye ellipses are calculated along with the diameter of the pupils:

```
// Eye dimensions
nEllipseWidth    = rRect.right/2-nBorderRight-nBorderLeft;
nEllipseHeight   = rRect.bottom-nBorderBottom-nBorderTop;

// Pupil diameters
   nEyeWidth        = (nEllipseWidth+nEllipseHeight)/6;
} // GetDimensions
```

Now that we have adjusted these values to fit the current size of the client area, we can get back to creating our regions. A region is an area within a window that the GDI can manipulate as a graphic object. Regions are GDI resources. Just like other GDI resources, they can be created with the help of certain functions and then freed again with the DeleteObject function. The GDI recognizes different shapes of regions: rectangles, rectangles with rounded corners, ellipses and polygons. There are several operations that can be performed on regions. For example, you can combine two regions into one (CombineRegion) or compare two regions (EqualRegion), fill in a region with a brush (FillRegion), frame a region (FrameRegion) or invert its contents (InvertRegion). An entire region can be moved with the OffsetRegion function.

In the EYES.EXE program, we will only be interested in elliptical regions. The CreateEllipticRgn function creates such a region:

```
HRGN CreateEllipticRgn (int xUpperLeft, int xUpperLeft, int xLowerRight, int
yLowerRight);
```

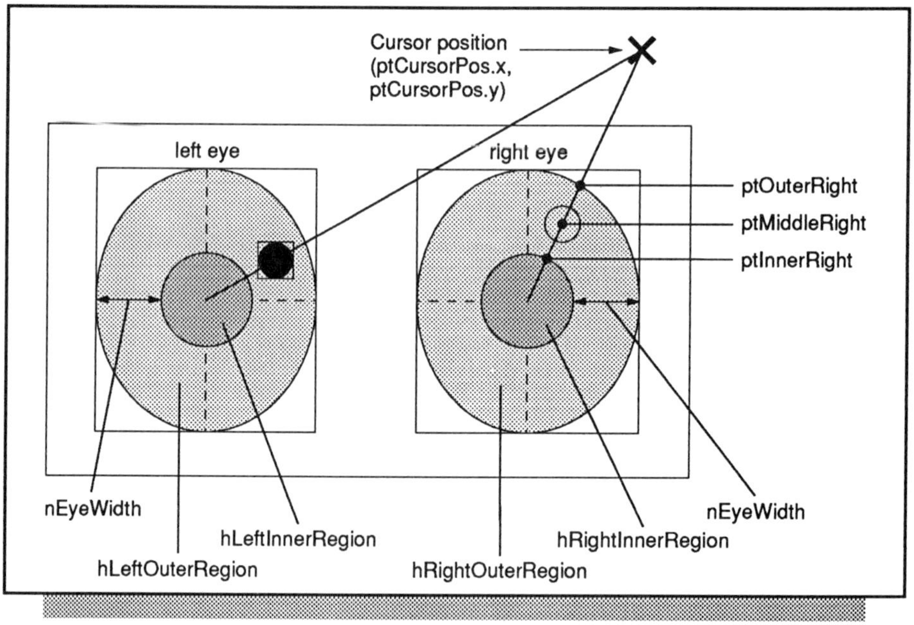

Ellptical regions

The four parameters of this function represent the coordinates, of the four corners of the rectangle, that defines the ellipse. These are device coordinates, such as those used with the GetClientRect function. If we were using a mapping mode other than MM_TEXT, these coordinates would have to be converted, perhaps with the DPtoLP function. The function result is of type HRGN. This is a handle to the newly created region. The result is NULL if the region could not be created. The meanings of the four regions hLeftInnerRegion, hLeftOuterRegion, hRightInnerRegion and hRightOuterRegion are explained in the figure "Elliptical Regions".

6.7 Screen Output

Now we will discuss the WM_PAINT message. This message triggers a call to the paint function PaintEyes. This is the function that paints the eyes in the client area of the main window. First the display context must be prepared with the BeginPaint function. After this, the logical color palette we created with the InitPalette function will be used. This palette is selected within the display context of the main window.

```
// Select color palette in display context
SelectPalette(hDC, hCurPal, FALSE);
```

The SelectObject function is not used to select a palette in a display context. (This function was already described for selecting bitmaps, brushes, fonts, pens and regions.) Instead, we use the SelectPalette function:

```
HPALETTE SelectPalette (HDC hDC, HPALETTE hPal, BOOL bBackgroundMode);
```

hDC is the handle to the display context in which the palette associated with the handle hPal will be selected. bBackgroundMode gives the background mode of the palette. If this parameter is FALSE, then the palette becomes a foreground palette if the window indicated by hDC has the input focus. If this parameter is TRUE, then the palette is always a background palette. Remember that the palette manager gives the foreground palette higher priority than the background palette when selecting colors from the system palette.

As with the SelectObject function, the value returned by this function is a handle to the palette that was previously selected in the display context (NULL if an error occurs).

Selecting the hCurPal palette in the display context of the main window is an important step, but we still need the RealizePalette function before we can actually use the palette.

Calling this function handles the process of mapping the colors of the display context to the system palette colors:

```
// Realize color palette
RealizePalette(hDC);
```

After calling GetDimensions to update the eye parameters, we use the CreateSolidBrush function to create a brush that we will use to clear the background of the window:

```
hEraseBrush = CreateSolidBrush(PALETTEINDEX(BACKGROUND));
```

This time no explicit RGB colors are used. Instead, we use palette index values. You may remember that a COLORREF value can be an RGB value (RGB macro), a palette index value (PALETTEINDEX macro) or a palette-relative RGB value (PALETTERGB macro).

A palette index value uses the number of the color entry to select a color from a logical palette. In the Eyes program we have defined the colors as follows: BACKGROUND (0), EYES (1) and PUPILS (2). This means that the background will use the first color entry from the palette indicated by hCurPal, the eyes will use the second and the pupils the third.

If we use the PALETTERGB macro, then we must specify the three color component values as with the RGB macro. The palette manager would then respond by giving us the three colors from the system palette that come close to matching these.

After we have created the background brush, we use it with the FillRect function to fill in the client area. The brush is then deleted again:

```
FillRect(hDC, &rRect, hEraseBrush); // Clear background
DeleteObject(hEraseBrush);
```

Next, we must display the eyes:

```
// Select eye brush in display context
hEyeBrush = CreateSolidBrush(PALETTEINDEX(EYES));
hSaveBrush = SelectObject(hDC, hEyeBrush);

// Draw left eye
Ellipse(hDC, nBorderLeft, nBorderTop,
           (rRect.right/2)-nBorderRight, rRect.bottom-nBorderBottom);

// Draw right eye
Ellipse(hDC, (rRect.right/2)+nBorderLeft, nBorderTop,
           rRect.right-nBorderRight, rRect.bottom-nBorderBottom);
```

```
DeleteObject(SelectObject(hDC, hSaveBrush));
```

Now comes the good part - calculating the pupil position based on the current mouse cursor position and moving the pupils as the mouse cursor moves.

Let's go through this procedure one step at a time. First, we call the SetPositions function. This function is responsible for calculating the pupil position. The first thing it does is query the current location of the mouse cursor:

```
// Determine current cursor position in screen coordinates
GetCursorPos((LPPOINT)&ptCursorPos);
ScreenToClient(hWnd, (LPPOINT)&ptCursorPos);
```

Regardless of the mapping mode, the GetCursorPos function returns the position of the cursor in screen coordinates relative to the upper left corner of the screen. Since we would rather use client area coordinates for our subsequent operations, we will use the ScreenToClient function to make this conversion. This function takes the POINT data structure, indicated by the long pointer in the second parameter, and converts the screen coordinates here into client area coordinates of the hWnd window. The ClientToScreen function can be used for conversions in the other direction (client area coordinates -> screen coordinates).

After this preparation, we need the LineDDA function. This function can only be used in connection with a callback function:

```
lpfnProc = MakeProcInstance(LineFunc, hInst);

bInnerPtDone = FALSE;
bOuterPtDone = FALSE;
LineDDA(ptLeftCenter.x, ptLeftCenter.y, ptCursorPos.x, ptCursorPos.y, lpfnProc,
(LPSTR)"left");

     ...
FreeProcInstance(lpfnProc);
```

The LineDDA function has the following syntax:

```
void LineDDA (int xStart, int yStart, int xEnd, int yEnd, FARPROC lpCallbackFct,
LPSTR lpData);
```

This function starts at point (xStart, yStart) and processes each point in order up to the endpoint (xEnd, yEnd). The endpoint itself is not processed. For each point on the line, LineDDA calls the function that is linked to the procedure instance address lpCallbackFct with a MakeProcInstance call. The coordinates of the point are passed along with the lpData parameter, which the application can use to store additional data.

In our program, we use the LineFunc function as the callback function. This is declared as a callback function as follows (and exported in the module definition file "eyes.def"):

```
void FAR PASCAL LineFunc (short X, short Y, LPSTR lpData);
```

The LineFunc function first checks to see whether the lpData parameter contains the string "left" (left eye) or "right" (right eye):

```
if (lstrcmp(lpData, (LPSTR)"left") == 0) // Left eye
{
  ...
}
else                                     // Right eye
{
  ...
}
```

Let's look at the first part of this section of code. Starting with the center point of the left eye (ptLeftCenter.x, ptLeftCenter.y), the function sequentially runs through all points until it reaches the current cursor location (ptCursorPos.x, ptCursorPos.y). For each point, the function checks to see if the variable bInnerPtDone has been set (this variable is initialized to FALSE) to determine if the point is outside of the region defined by hLeftInnerRegion:

```
if (!bInnerPtDone && !PtInRegion(hLeftInnerRegion, X, Y))
{
...
```

When the first point that lies outside of hLeftInnerRegion is found, the ptInnerLeft variable is set to this value and bInnerPtDone is set to TRUE:

```
ptInnerLeft.x = X;
ptInnerLeft.y = Y;
bInnerPtDone = TRUE;
```

The next task is to find the first point on the line, from the center of the eye to the cursor location, that lies outside of the hLeftOuterRgn region:

```
if (!bOuterPtDone && !PtInRegion(hLeftOuterRgn, X, Y))
{
  ptOuterLeft.x = X;
  ptOuterLeft.y = Y;
  bOuterPtDone = TRUE;
}
```

The corresponding calculations are made for the right eye. After the LineDDA function (with the help of the LineFunc callback function) has determined the points ptInnerLeft and ptOuterLeft for the left eye and ptInnerRight and ptOuterRight for the right eye, they are passed to the SetPosition function.

Now we need to determine which quadrant (as seen from the center point of the eye) contains these points:

```
// First quadrant (upper right)
if ((ptCursorPos.x > ptLeftCenter.x) && (ptCursorPos.y < ptLeftCenter.y))
   {
     ptMiddleLeft.x = (ptOuterLeft.x-ptInnerLeft.x)/2+ptInnerLeft.x;
     ptMiddleLeft.y = ptInnerLeft.y-(ptInnerLeft.y-ptOuterLeft.y)/2;
   }

// Second quadrant (upper left)
if ((ptCursorPos.x < ptLeftCenter.x) && (ptCursorPos.y < ptLeftCenter.y))
{
  ptMiddleLeft.x = ptInnerLeft.x-(ptInnerLeft.x-ptOuterLeft.x)/2;
  ptMiddleLeft.y = ptInnerLeft.y-(ptInnerLeft.y-ptOuterLeft.y)/2;
}
   ...
```

ptMiddleLeft is the point that represents the center point of the left pupil. It is calculated as half the distance between the x and y coordinates of ptInnerLeft and ptOuterLeft. This means that it is the mid-point of the line connecting these two points. ptMiddleRight is calculated in the same way.

Now that we have the center points of the pupils, we can use SetPosition to calculate the rectangles rLeftEye and rRightEye, which define the pupils:

```
SetRect(&rLeftEye, ptMiddleLeft.x-(nEyeWidth/2), ptMiddleLeft.y-(nEyeWidth/2),
        ptMiddleLeft.x+(nEyeWidth/2), ptMiddleLeft.y+(nEyeWidth/2));

...

SetRect(&rRightEye, ptMiddleRight.x-(nEyeWidth/2), ptMiddleRight.y-(nEyeWidth/2),
        ptMiddleRight.x+(nEyeWidth/2), ptMiddleRight.y+(nEyeWidth/2));
```

This completes the actual calculation of the coordinates. The next steps in the PaintEyes function are as follows:

1) Store the pupil backgrounds in their new locations

2) Draw the pupils at these locations

The bitmaps hBkGrLeftBitmap and hBkGrRightBitmap have been previously prepared for storing the backgrounds by using the SaveBackgrounds function:

```
SelectObject(hBkGrDC, hBkGrLeftBitmap);
// Save background of left pupil as bitmap
BitBlt(hBkGrDC, 0, 0, nEyeWidth, nEyeWidth,
                hDC, rLeftEye.left, rLeftEye.top, SRCCOPY);

SelectObject(hBkGrDC, hBkGrRightBitmap);
// Save background of right pupil as bitmap
BitBlt(hBkGrDC, 0, 0, nEyeWidth, nEyeWidth,
                hDC, rRightEye.left, rRightEye.top, SRCCOPY);
```

First, the bitmaps are selected within the compatible display context hBkGrDC with the SelectObject function. Then the BitBlt function copies the pupils from the display context of the main window to the compatible display context. This function is designed for moving bitmaps:

```
BOOL BitBlt (HDC hToDC, int xUpperLeftTo, int yUpperLeftTo,
             int nWidth, int nHeight,
             HDC hFromDC, int xUpperLeftFrom, int yUpperLeftFrom,
             DWORD dwROP);
```

As you can see, the BitBlt function expects many parameters. hToDC is the handle to the display context to which the bitmap is to be copied. hFromDC is the display context that originally contains the bitmap. The point (xUpperLeftFrom, yUpperLeftFrom) represents the upper left corner of the bitmap in hFromDC. (xUpperLeftTo, yUpperLeftTo) is the destination point within the hToDC display context. The size of the bitmap in the source and destination display context must be equal (width: nWidth logical units, height: nHeight logical units). When the function is successfully executed, it returns a value of TRUE. Otherwise, FALSE is returned.

The dwROP parameter deserves special attention. This parameter represents a raster operation code parameter (ROP), which defines the relationship between the bits of the source and the destination bitmaps and the brush (Pattern) of the destination bitmap. The ROP used for bitmap operations is a composite of three values and is therefore referred to as a tertiary ROP. Theoretically, there are 256 possible combinations for a tertiary ROP (2 to the 8th power). In practice, you will not need nearly as many values. There is a total of 15 ROP values defined in the WINDOWS.H include file. Some examples of the more common values are:

SRCCOPY	copy the source bitmap directly without alterations
MERGECOPY	join the bits of the source and destination bitmaps with an AND operator
SRCPAINT	join the bits of the source and destination bitmaps with an OR operator
SRCINVERT	join the bits of the source and destination bitmaps with an XOR (exclusive OR) operator
DSTINVERT	the destination bitmap is inverted
PATCOPY	the destination bitmap gets a copy of the brush pattern
PATINVERT	the bits of the destination bitmap are joined to the brush pattern with an XOR operator
BLACKNESS	all pixels of the destination bitmap are set to black
WHITENESS	all pixels of the destination bitmap are set to white

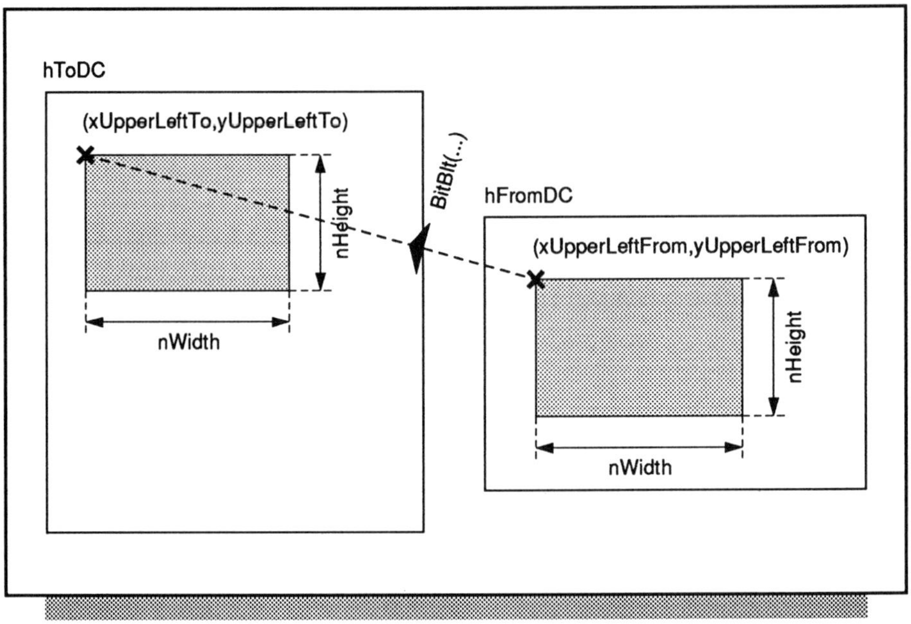

BitBlt parameters

BitBlt is not the only function that can be used for moving or combining bitmaps. We should also mention the PatBlt and StretchBlt functions. StretchBlt is used for enlarging or shrinking a bitmap while moving it. You can also use this function to invert a bitmap by using opposite signs on nFromWidth and nToWidth and/or nFromHeight and nToHeight. These parameters represent, in logical units, the width and height of the source bitmap (nFromWidth, nFromHeight) and the width and height of the destination bitmap (nToWidth, nToHeight):

```
BOOL StretchBlt (HDC hToDC, int xUpperLeftTo, int yUpperLeftTo,
                 int nToWidth, int nToHeight,
                 HDC hFromDC, int xUpperLeftFrom, int yUpperLeftFrom,
                 int nFromWidth, int nFromHeight,
                 DWORD dwROP);
```

Obviously when you shrink a bitmap, you will lose some of the information located in the source bitmap. With the SetStretchBltMode you can vary the algorithm Windows uses to move bits during the shrinking process:

```
int SetStretchBltMode (HDC hDC, int nMode);
```

hDC is a display context handle. nMode can take one of the following values: BLACKONWHITE (black pixels are given higher priority than white), WHITEONBLACK (white pixels are given higher priority) or COLORONCOLOR (no priority to white or black pixels). This function returns the value of the previous mode.

The PatBlt function is not used for moving bitmaps. Instead, it fills a rectangular region of a display context with a certain pattern. The pattern depends on the brush currently selected in the display context and on the raster operations code.

```
BOOL PatBlt (HDC hDC, int xToUpperLeft, yToUpperLeft, int nWidth, int nHeight,
DWORD dwROP);
```

xTo and yTo define the upper left corner of the rectangle nWidth logical units wide and nHeight logical units high within the display context indicated by hDC. Only the following five values are needed for the raster operations code: DSTINVERT, PATCOPY, PATINVERT, BLACKNESS and WHITENESS.

Now let's look at item 2 in the PaintEyes function. This is where the pupils are actually drawn. The PaintPupils function is used:

```
void PaintPupils (HDC hDC)
{
  // Select color palette in display context
  SelectPalette(hDC, hCurPal, FALSE);
  // Realize color palette
  RealizePalette(hDC);
  hPupilBrush = CreateSolidBrush(PALETTEINDEX(PUPILS)); // Pupil brush
  hSaveBrush = SelectObject(hDC, hPupilBrush);
  Ellipse(hDC, rLeftEye.left, rLeftEye.top, rLeftEye.right, rLeftEye.bottom);
  Ellipse(hDC, rRightEye.left, rRightEye.top, rRightEye.right, rRightEye.bottom);
  DeleteObject(SelectObject(hDC, hSaveBrush));
} // PaintPupils
```

After selecting the palette hCurPal in the display context and executing it, the function creates the pupils brush. The PUPILS values serve as index values in the logical palette. The pupils themselves are then drawn with two calls to the Ellipse function.

The work of the PaintEyes function is completed by calling the EndPaint function. Now let's take a look at the WM_TIMER message.

As previously mentioned, this message is sent to the window function of the main window every TIMERINTERVAL milliseconds. When this message is received, the position of the pupils must be set to the current position of the mouse cursor. How do we do this?

The easiest way is to call the InvalidateRect function to invalidate the client area of the main window and force the PaintEyes function to be called. However, this method has a distinct disadvantage: the constant re-painting of the client area causes the screen to flicker. Obviously this will quickly annoy the user. To avoid this, we can add this commonly used animation technique to the PaintEyes function:

1) Retrieve the previously stored pupil bitmap background

2) Calculate the new pupil position

3) Save the new pupil bitmap background

4) Draw the pupil in the new position

The actual code sequence used in the WM_TIMER message looks like this:

```
case WM_TIMER:      // Message from the timer
  {
    if (!bLocked) // Blocked by a dialog box?
    {
      // Check for cursor position change
      GetCursorPos((LPPOINT)&ptNewCursorPos);
      ScreenToClient(hWnd, (LPPOINT)&ptNewCursorPos);

     if ((ptNewCursorPos.x != ptCursorPos.x) ||
        (ptNewCursorPos.y != ptCursorPos.y))
     {
       hDC = GetDC(hWnd);
       GetBackgrounds(hDC);      // Retrieve old pupil backgrounds
       SetPositions(hWnd);       // Calculate new pupil positions
       SaveBackgrounds(hDC);     // Save new pupil backgrounds
       PaintPupils(hDC);         // Redraw pupils
       ReleaseDC(hWnd, hDC);
     }
    }
  }
break;
```

First, we check if the bLocked variable is TRUE. When the About... and Palette dialog boxes are called, this variable is set to TRUE in order to prevent movement of the pupils while these dialog boxes are open. When bLocked is FALSE, then the program checks to make sure the mouse has moved. If it hasn't, then the pupils don't have to move. If the mouse cursor position has changed, GetDC retrieves the display context. Then GetBackgrounds is called to copy the saved pupil backgrounds back to the client area:

```
SelectObject(hBkGrDC, hBkGrLeftBitmap);
// Copy old background back to left pupil
BitBlt(hDC, rLeftEye.left, rLeftEye.top, nEyeWidth, nEyeWidth,
       hBkGrDC, 0, 0, SRCCOPY);

SelectObject(hBkGrDC, hBkGrRightBitmap);
// Copy old background back to right pupil
BitBlt(hDC, rRightEye.left, rRightEye.top, nEyeWidth, nEyeWidth,
       hBkGrDC, 0, 0, SRCCOPY);
```

The GetBackgrounds function is similar to SaveBackgrounds, only the source and destination display contexts are reversed. After the old background is restored, SetPositions calculates the new pupil positions. After this, the PaintPupils function is called to draw the pupils on screen. The display context is freed, which completes the procedure for moving the pupils.

6.8 Palettes in Practice

Let's now take a look at what happens within the modal "Color Palette" dialog box. The dialog function MdfPaletteProc is associated with this dialog box. The control elements within it are three vertical scroll bars used to set the red, green and blue color values (IDs: SB_RED, SB_GREEN and SB_BLUE). Under the scroll bar for each color is a static control that displays a number value from 0 to 255 as set by the scroll bar (IDs: SS_RVALUE, SS_GVALUE and SS_BVALUE). On the right side of the dialog box is a group box containing three radio buttons used to determine whether the color being set is to be used for the background, the eyes or the pupils (IDs: RB_BACKGROUND, RB_EYES and RB_PUPILS). In the lower right corner of the dialog box is the "Color" group box, which contains a control of type SS_RIGHT | WS_CHILD. This control displays the color created by the red, green and blue components set with the scroll bars. In addition, the "Color Palette" dialog box also contains the obligatory OK button for leaving the dialog box.

Initialization

The WM_INITDIALOG message is processed in the MdfPaletteProc function, triggering some initialization work. The handle for the SS_COLOR rectangle is stored in the variable hColorRect. The variable nRBIndex stores the currently selected color index. This variable is initialized to 0. After this, the window handles for the three scroll bar controls are stored in the aScrollbars array. The SetScrollRange sets the scroll range to 0 - 255 for each scroll bar.

After the initialization, the scroll bars must be set to the values that create the currently selected color. In order to do this, the color palette must be accessed with the GetPaletteEntries function:

```
    GetPaletteEntries(hCurPal, nRBIndex, 1, &PaletteEntry);
```

```
WORD GetPaletteEntries (HPALETTE hPal, WORD wFirst, WORD wCount, LPPALETTENTRY
lpPalEntries);
```

The GetPaletteEntries function retrieves wCount colors starting with the index value wFirst, from the logical palette indicated by hPal. These entries are made available to the application by storing them in the PALETTENTRY data structure, indicated by the long pointer lpPalEntries. The value returned by the function is the number of entries copied from the palette.

When accessing the hCurPal palette, we are interested in only one color entry at a time. This entry is stored in the PaletteEntry variable. The fields of this variable are required when calling the SetScrollbars function. This function receives, as parameters, a handle to the dialog box and the three color component values:

```
SetScrollbars(hDlg,
              (int) PaletteEntry.peRed,   // red component
              (int) PaletteEntry.peGreen, // green component
              (int) PaletteEntry.peBlue); // blue component
```

****

For each color component, the SetScrollbars function sets the indicator within the scroll bar to the position defined by SetScrollPos and then enters the associated value in the static control found beneath the scroll bar (SS_RVALUE, SSGVALUE or SS_BVALUE):

```
void SetScrollbars (HWND hDlg, int RValue, int GValue, int BValue)
{
  SetScrollPos(GetDlgItem(hDlg, SB_RED), SB_CTL, RValue, TRUE);
  SetDlgItemInt(hDlg, SS_RVALUE, RValue, FALSE);
  SetScrollPos(GetDlgItem(hDlg, SB_GREEN), SB_CTL, GValue, TRUE);
  SetDlgItemInt(hDlg, SS_GVALUE, GValue, FALSE);
  SetScrollPos(GetDlgItem(hDlg, SB_BLUE), SB_CTL, BValue, TRUE);
  SetDlgItemInt(hDlg, SS_BVALUE, BValue, FALSE);
} // SetScrollbars
```

Next, the background radio button is turned on and the current color in the SS_COLOR rectangle is displayed:

```
CheckRadioButton(hDlg, RB_BACKGROUND, RB_PUPILS, RB_BACKGROUND);
// Display new color in SS_COLOR rectangle
SetDlgItemText(hDlg, SS_COLOR, "");
```

This routine displays the SS_COLOR rectangle's current color in a rather roundabout way. The SetDlgItemText function would normally be called to display text in a control. But since we use empty quotes "" as a parameter, no text is given to display. Windows interprets this by assuming that the character display region of the control needs to be updated and the necessary messages are sent. In particular, a WM_CTLCOLOR message must be sent before a control can be updated or re-painted. This gives an application a chance to set the color that will be used for the background or foreground of the text message.

Controls

You should remember the following when handling the WM_CTLCOLOR message: Windows uses the wParam parameter of this message to store a handle for the display context of the control that is affected. The lParam parameter contains two values: LOWORD(lParam) contains a handle to the control itself and HIWORD(lParam) contains a value that indicates the type of control. The following values are possible:

CTLCOLOR_BTN	Button control
CTLCOLOR_DLG	Dialog box control
CTLCOLOR_EDIT	Edit box control
CTLCOLOR_LISTBOX	List box control
CTLCOLOR_MSGBOX	Message box control
CTLCOLOR_SCROLLBAR	Scroll bar control
CTLCOLOR_STATIC	Static control

The low word of the lP parameter is compared to the handle for the hColorRect control. If the values are not the same, the function returns a result of FALSE. This indicates that this particular message is dealing with a different control, which we are not interested in:

```
case WM_CTLCOLOR:                    // Before control display
  if (LOWORD(lP) == hColorRect)      // from color rectangle?
  {
     // process message
            ...
  }
  else
    return FALSE;
```

If the message does involve the SS_COLOR rectangle, we select the hCurPal palette in the display context for this control. The palette is also realized with RealizePalette. Then we create a brush using the color containing the palette index number indicated by nRBIndex:

```
SelectPalette((HDC)wP, hCurPal, FALSE);
RealizePalette((HDC)wP);
hBrush = CreateSolidBrush(PALETTEINDEX(nRBIndex));
```

Now comes the tricky part of processing a WM_CTLCOLOR message. If a non-standard brush has been selected or if the SetBkColor function has been used, Windows will expect that the origin of the brush being used has been reconciled with the origin of the display context. In addition, a handle to the brush must be returned as the function result:

```
ptPoint.x = ptPoint.y = 0;
ClientToScreen(hDlg, &ptPoint);
SetBrushOrg((HDC)wP, ptPoint.x, ptPoint.y);
UnrealizeObject(hBrush);
SetBkColor((HDC)wP, PALETTEINDEX(nRBIndex));
return (hBrush);              // Return handle to brush
```

What do we mean by reconciling the origin of a brush? Internally, the GDI associates a rectangular bit pattern with a brush. The same pattern is repeated until the region is filled. As long as the region being filled doesn't move, there are no problems. But if part of the fill region is moved and Windows wants to update a different part of the fill region with the same bit pattern, it's possible that the bit pattern no longer fits properly in the two different parts of the fill region (think of the problems involved with matching patterns while hanging wall paper). Windows provides the SetBrushOrg and UnrealizeObject functions to help deal with these problems:

```
DWORD SetBrushOrg (HDC hDC, int xNewOrigin, int yNewOrigin);
```

SetBrushOrg sets the origin of the brush, selected in the display context indicated by hDC, to the point (xNewOrigin, yNewOrigin). xNewOrigin and yNewOrigin are given in screen coordinates and can have values from 0 to 7. The previous brush origin is returned as the result.

In the program, the ClientToScreen function converts the point variable ptPoint, with logical coordinates (0,0), to screen coordinates. These screen coordinates are then passed to the SetBrushOrg function.

```
BOOL UnrealizeObject (HANDLE hBrushOrPalette);
```

hBrushOrPalette can be a handle to a brush or a palette. In the case of a brush, the function will initialize the origin of the brush and use this value the next time the brush is selected. The brush may not be selected in a display context at the time the function is called. In the case of a palette, the function will ensure that the palette is completely regenerated from the system palette the next time the RealizePalette function is called.

After calling the UnrealizeObject function, the brush origins have been properly reconciled and SetBkColor can be used to set the background color of the SS_COLOR control. After the handle of the brush that was used is returned, we are finished processing the WM_CTLCOLOR message.

The next step is handling the WM_VSCROLL message. This message is sent to MdfPaletteProc when one of the vertical scroll bars is clicked by the user:

```
case WM_VSCROLL:                    // Scroll bar message
  // Set scroll position
  nScrollPos = GetScrollPos(HIWORD(lP), SB_CTL);
  switch (wP)
  {
    case SB_LINEUP:
      nScrollValue = -1;
      break;
    case SB_LINEDOWN:
      nScrollValue = 1;
      break;
      ...
```

First the current scroll position must be determined. We call the GetScrollPos function by passing the scroll bar handle in HIWORD(lP) and the value SB_CTL (before we would have used SB_HORZ or SB_VERT) as the scroll bar type. The result is stored in nScrollPos. Then, depending on whether the user clicked an arrow or the indicator, the nScrollValue variable will contain a value that indicates how far the scroll bar should be moved (negative values: move up, positive values: move down). This value must be between 0 and 255:

```
// Calculate scroll value
nScrollValue = max(-nScrollPos, min(nScrollValue, 255-nScrollPos));
```

The nScrollPos variable is then changed as determined by nScrollValue and the scroll thumb is moved:

```
if (nScrollValue)
{
  nScrollPos += nScrollValue;
  // Set new scroll position
  SetScrollPos(HIWORD(lP), SB_CTL, nScrollPos, TRUE);
```

The ID of the scroll bar control is needed to determine the ID of the accompanying SS_?VALUE static control. The GetWindowWord function is used:

```
wControlId = GetWindowWord(HIWORD(lP), GWW_ID);
```

The GetWindowWord function returns certain information about a window depending on the value of the second parameter. The first parameter must be the window handle. The second parameter is an index value that indicates a location in an area where Windows has stored information about that particular window. The following values can be used:

GWW_ID — The function returns the ID of a control.

GWW_HINSTANCE — The function returns the instance handle with which the window is associated.

GWW_HWNDPARENT — The function returns a handle to the parent window.

The static control ID value obtained with this function allows us to display the selected color value as a decimal number under the corresponding scroll bar:

```
// Display new color value
SetDlgItemInt(hDlg, SS_RVALUE+wControlId-SB_RED, nScrollPos, FALSE);
```

Now we can split the current color into its red, green and blue components by querying the scroll positions:

```
// Determine color component values
RValue = GetScrollPos(aScrollbars[0], SB_CTL);
GValue = GetScrollPos(aScrollbars[1], SB_CTL);
BValue = GetScrollPos(aScrollbars[2], SB_CTL);
```

These values are needed to fill the PaletteEntry variable:

```
PaletteEntry.peRed   = (BYTE)RValue;
PaletteEntry.peGreen = (BYTE)GValue;
PaletteEntry.peBlue  = (BYTE)BValue;
PaletteEntry.peFlags = PC_NOCOLLAPSE;
```

Setting color entries

Now we must call the SetPaletteEntries function to store the new color entry in the hCurPal palette:

```
// Set palette entry
SetPaletteEntries(hCurPal, nRBIndex, 1, &PaletteEntry);
```

The last action involved in processing a WM_VSCROLL message is updating the SS_COLOR rectangle to show the new color to the user:

```
// Display new color in SS_COLOR rectangle
SetDlgItemText(hDlg, SS_COLOR, "");
```

The last message we'll discuss here affects the radio buttons:

```
case RB_BACKGROUND:         // Message from radio buttons
case RB_EYES:
case RB_PUPILS:
  nRBIndex = wP-RB_BACKGROUND;
  GetPaletteEntries(hCurPal, nRBIndex, 1, &PaletteEntry);
  // Set scroll positions
  SetScrollbars(hDlg,
               (int) PaletteEntry.peRed,    // Red component
               (int) PaletteEntry.peGreen,  // Green component
               (int) PaletteEntry.peBlue);  // Blue component
// Display color in SS_COLOR rectangle
SetDlgItemText(hDlg, SS_COLOR, "");
return FALSE;
break;
```

The nRBIndex variable is set to correspond to the active radio button. The entry responsible for the desired color is retrieved from the color palette, the scroll positions change accordingly and the SS_COLOR rectangle is updated.

The WM_DESTROY message frees allocated GDI resources. Bitmaps, regions and the color palette are deleted by the DeleteObject function. The compatible display context hBkGrDC must be deleted with the DeleteDC function. The KillTimer function stops the timer so that it can be used by other applications. This function expects a window handle and the timer ID as parameters.

You may want to add improvements to this application, such as adding a second timer so the eyes will "blink", or displaying the pupils in 3D.

6.9 Source Code: EYES.EXE

EYES.H include file

```
#define IDS_APPLNAME        1
#define IDS_NOMORETIMERS 2

/* IDs for additional entries in system menu */
#define MI_ABOUT          10
#define MI_PALETTE        11

/* IDs for PALETTEBOX dialog box */
#define SS_RED            100
#define SS_GREEN          101
#define SS_BLUE           102
#define SS_RVALUE         105
#define SS_GVALUE         106
#define SS_BVALUE         107
#define SS_COLOR          108
#define SB_RED            110
#define SB_GREEN          111
#define SB_BLUE           112
#define RB_BACKGROUND     115
#define RB_EYES           116
#define RB_PUPILS         117

/* General Defines */
#define TIMERINTERVAL     800
#define MAXCOLORS         3
#define MAXLENGTH         20

/* Color palette indices for background, eyeballs and pupils */
#define BACKGROUND        0
#define EYES              BACKGROUND+1
#define PUPILS            BACKGROUND+2
```

EYES.RC resource file

```
#include <windows.h>
#include "eyes.h"

rcinclude eyes.dlg

STRINGTABLE
BEGIN
```

```
  IDS_APPLNAME,      "Eyes" ; Application name
  IDS_NOMORETIMERS, "No more timers available"
END

Eyes ACCELERATORS
BEGIN
  "^A", MI_ABOUT
  "^P", MI_PALETTE
END
```

EYES.DLG dialog box file

```
ABOUTDLG DIALOG LOADONCALL MOVEABLE DISCARDABLE 72, 15, 157, 104
CAPTION "About Eyes"
STYLE WS_BORDER | WS_CAPTION | WS_DLGFRAME | WS_SYSMENU | DS_MODALFRAME |
WS_POPUP
BEGIN
    CONTROL "Eyes", -1, "static", SS_CENTER | WS_CHILD, 58, 5, 37, 10
    CONTROL "Version 1.00", -1, "static", SS_CENTER | WS_CHILD, 46, 20, 62, 10
    CONTROL "Copyright  1990", -1, "static", SS_CENTER | WS_CHILD, 36, 35, 86, 11
    CONTROL "Abacus", -1, "static", SS_CENTER | WS_CHILD, 40, 51, 79, 11
    CONTROL "OK", 1, "button", BS_DEFPUSHBUTTON | WS_TABSTOP | WS_CHILD, 66, 86,
24, 12
    CONTROL "by D.Honekamp && P. Wilken", 106, "static", SS_CENTER | WS_CHILD,
30, 66, 102, 11
END

PALETTEDLG DIALOG LOADONCALL MOVEABLE DISCARDABLE 37, 22, 161, 110
CAPTION "Palette"
STYLE WS_BORDER | WS_CAPTION | WS_DLGFRAME | WS_SYSMENU | WS_POPUP
BEGIN
    CONTROL "Red", 100, "static", SS_LEFT | WS_CHILD, 6, 8, 17, 10
    CONTROL "Green", 101, "static", SS_LEFT | WS_CHILD, 35, 8, 22, 8
    CONTROL "Blue", 102, "static", SS_LEFT | WS_CHILD, 67, 8, 16, 8
    CONTROL "Text", 110, "scrollbar", SBS_VERT | WS_CHILD, 8, 21, 9, 46
    CONTROL "Text", 111, "scrollbar", SBS_VERT | WS_CHILD, 39, 21, 9, 46
    CONTROL "Text", 112, "scrollbar", SBS_VERT | WS_CHILD, 71, 21, 8, 46
    CONTROL "###", 105, "static", SS_LEFT | WS_CHILD, 6, 72, 16, 8
    CONTROL "###", 106, "static", SS_LEFT | WS_CHILD, 37, 72, 16, 8
    CONTROL "###", 107, "static", SS_LEFT | WS_CHILD, 69, 72, 16, 9
    CONTROL "Background", 115, "button", BS_AUTORADIOBUTTON | WS_TABSTOP |
WS_CHILD, 101, 22, 53, 12
    CONTROL "Eyes", 116, "button", BS_AUTORADIOBUTTON | WS_TABSTOP | WS_CHILD,
101, 40, 35, 12
    CONTROL "Pupils", 117, "button", BS_AUTORADIOBUTTON | WS_TABSTOP | WS_CHILD,
101, 57, 40, 12
```

```
    CONTROL "Object", -1, "button", BS_GROUPBOX | WS_TABSTOP | WS_CHILD, 96, 7,
59, 65
    CONTROL "OK", 1, "button", BS_DEFPUSHBUTTON | WS_TABSTOP | WS_CHILD, 22, 88,
43, 14
    CONTROL "Color", -1, "button", BS_GROUPBOX | WS_TABSTOP | WS_CHILD, 96, 74,
59, 26
    CONTROL "", 108, "static", SS_RIGHT | WS_CHILD, 102, 88, 48, 11
END
```

EYES.DEF module definition file

```
NAME         EYES

DESCRIPTION  'Eyes Program'

EXETYPE      WINDOWS

CODE         PRELOAD MOVEABLE DISCARDABLE
DATA         PRELOAD MOVEABLE MULTIPLE

HEAPSIZE     6000
STACKSIZE    6000

EXPORTS
             MainWndProc    @1
             MdfAboutProc   @2
             MdfPaletteProc @3
             LineFunc       @4
```

EYES.MAK MAKE file

```
Model = S
Warn   = 3
Linker = link

all: eyes.exe

eyes.res: eyes.h eyes.rc eyes.dlg
  rc -r eyes.rc

eyes.obj: eyes.h eyes.c
  cl -c -A$(Model) -W$(Warn) -Gsw -Zpe -Os eyes.c

eyes.exe: eyes.obj eyes.def eyes.res eyes.def
  $(Linker) /NOD /al:16 eyes,eyes.exe,,libw+$(Model)libcew,eyes.def
  rc eyes.res
```

EYES.C source code

```
/*************************************************************************
 EYES.C
 ======

 This program addresses the following problems that occur in GDI programming:

 Color palettes
 Regions
 Bitmaps
 Timer-controlled execution
 Dynamic menu changes
 ************************************************************************/

/* -------------------------< Include files >---------------------------- */
#include <windows.h>
#include <stdio.h>
#include <string.h>
#include <stdlib.h>

#include "eyes.h"

/* ------------------------< Global variables >------------------------- */

HANDLE        hInst,                  // Instance of application
              hAccelTable;            // Handle for accelerator table
HWND          hwMain;                 // Main window
char          szApplName[20],         // Application name
              szMBString[255];        // Message box info
HRGN          hLeftOuterRgn,          // LineDDA regions
              hRightOuterRgn,
              hLeftInnerRgn,
              hRightInnerRgn;
POINT         ptInnerLeft,            // LineDDA points
              ptInnerRight,
              ptOuterLeft,
              ptOuterRight,
              ptMiddleRight,          // Center point of right pupil
              ptMiddleLeft,           // Center point of left pupil
              ptCursorPos,            // Mouse cursor position
              ptLeftCenter,           // Center point of left eye
              ptRightCenter,          // Center point of right eye
              ptNewCursorPos;         // New cursor position
BOOL          bInnerPtDone,           // LineDDA marker
              bOuterPtDone,
              bLocked = FALSE;        // TRUE when dialog box is called
```

```
short         nBorderLeft,          // Left border
              nBorderTop,           // Top border
              nBorderRight,         // Right border
              nBorderBottom,        // Bottom border
              nEllipseWidth,        // Eye width
              nEllipseHeight,       // Eye height
              nEyeWidth,            // Current pupil size
              nMaxEyeWidth;         // Maximum pupil size
RECT          rRect,                // Generic rectangle
              rLeftEye,             // Rectangle for left pupil
              rRightEye;            // Rectangle for right pupil
HDC           hBkGrDC;              // Handle to compatible display context
HBRUSH        hEraseBrush,          // Erase brush
              hEyeBrush,            // Eye brush
              hPupilBrush,          // Pupil brush
              hSaveBrush;           // Save brush
HBITMAP       hBkGrLeftBitmap,      // Bitmap handle for left pupil
              hBkGrRightBitmap;     // Bitmap handle for right pupil
NPLOGPALETTE  pLogPal;              // Pointer to logical color palette
HPALETTE      hCurPal;              // Handle to current color palette
HMENU         hSystemMenu;          // System menu handle
FARPROC       lpfnModal,            // Used by modal dialog boxes
              lpfnProc;             // Generally used for Callback functions

/* ----------------------< Function prototypes >----------------------- */

int  InitFirstInstance (HANDLE ,HANDLE, int);
LONG FAR PASCAL MainWndProc  (HWND, unsigned, WORD, LONG);
void FAR PASCAL LineFunc (short, short, LPSTR);
BOOL FAR PASCAL MdfAboutProc (HWND, unsigned, WORD, LONG);
BOOL FAR PASCAL MdfPaletteProc (HWND, unsigned, WORD, LONG);
BOOL InitPalette (void);
void GetDimensions (HWND);
void SetPositions (HWND);
void SaveBackgrounds (HDC);
void GetBackgrounds (HDC);
void PaintPupils (HDC);
void PaintEyes (HWND);
void SetScrollbars (HWND, int, int, int);

/*****************************************************************************
 W i n M a i n ()
 ================

 The WinMain function is the main function for every Windows program. WinMain
 is the equivalent of the main() function found in standard C programs, and
 represents the "point of entry" for program execution.
```

```
 Parameters:

   HANDLE hInstance:     Current instance handle of the application.
   HANDLE hPrevInstance: Previous instance handle of the application. NULL
                         if the current instance is the first instance.
   LPSTR  lpszCmdLine:   Long pointer to the string placed after the program
                         name during program execution.
   int    nCmdShow:      Parameter which specifies the application window's
                         appearance when the program starts.

 Return values:

   int:                  The wParam parameter for the last message received.
 ***************************************************************************/

int PASCAL WinMain (HANDLE hInstance,  HANDLE hPrevInstance,
                    LPSTR lpszCmdLine, int nCmdShow)
{
  MSG        msg;                   // Message variable

  if (!hPrevInstance)               // Initialization of first instance
  {
    if (!InitFirstInstance(hInstance, hPrevInstance, nCmdShow))
      return NULL;
    // Load accelerator table
    hAccelTable = LoadAccelerators(hInstance, szApplName);
  }
  else                               // Initialization of multiple instances
  {
    GetInstanceData(hPrevInstance, szApplName, 20);
  }

  /* ----------------< Initialization of all instances >---------------- */
  hInst   = hInstance;                              // Global instance variable

  // Create logical color palette
  InitPalette();

  hwMain = CreateWindow(szApplName,                 // Window class name
                        szApplName,                 // Window caption
                        WS_OVERLAPPEDWINDOW,        // Overlapped window
                        CW_USEDEFAULT,              // X-position (default)
                        CW_USEDEFAULT,              // Y-position (default)
                        CW_USEDEFAULT,              // Initial X-size (default)
                        CW_USEDEFAULT,              // Initial Y-size (default)
                        NULL,                       // No parent window
                        NULL,                       // Use class menu
                        hInstance,                  // Instance of application
```

```
                        NULL);                  // No creation parameters

  if (!hwMain)
    return NULL;

  ShowWindow(hwMain, nCmdShow);                 // Make window visible
  UpdateWindow(hwMain);                         // Update window

  if (!SetTimer(hwMain, 1, TIMERINTERVAL, NULL)) // Set timer
  {
    LoadString(hInst, IDS_NOMORETIMERS, (LPSTR)szMBString,
                      sizeof(szMBString)-1);
    MessageBox(hwMain, szMBString, szApplName, MB_OK | MB_ICONEXCLAMATION);
    return FALSE;
  }

 /* -------------------------< Message  loop >-------------------------- */
 while (GetMessage((LPMSG)&msg, NULL, 0, 0))   // Message reading
 {
   if (!TranslateAccelerator(hwMain, hAccelTable, (LPMSG)&msg))
   {
     TranslateMessage((LPMSG)&msg);             // Message translation
     DispatchMessage((LPMSG)&msg);              // Message -> Windows
   }
 }
 /* -------------------- < End of application > ---------------------- */
 return (msg.wParam);
} // WinMain

/***************************************************************************
 I n i t F i r s t I n s t a n c e ()
 ====================================

 This function initializes the first instance of the "Eyes" application.

 Parameters:

   HANDLE hInstance:     Current instance handle of the application.
   HANDLE hPrevInstance: Previous instance handle of the application. NULL
                         if the current instance is the first instance.
   int    nCmdShow:      Parameter which specifies the application window's
                         appearance when the program starts.

 Return values:

   int                   NULL if the "Eyes" window class registers.
                         Otherwise, a value other than NULL.
***************************************************************************/
```

```
int InitFirstInstance (HANDLE hInstance, HANDLE hPrevInstance, int nCmdShow)
{
  WNDCLASS MainWndClass;                         // Main window class

  /* -----------< Load application name from resource file >-------------- */

  LoadString(hInstance, IDS_APPLNAME, (LPSTR)szApplName, 20);

  /* ---------------< Specify window class information >------------------ */

  MainWndClass.lpszClassName = szApplName;               // Window class
  MainWndClass.hInstance     = hInstance;                // Instance
  MainWndClass.lpfnWndProc   = MainWndProc;              // Window function
  MainWndClass.style         = CS_HREDRAW | CS_VREDRAW;
  MainWndClass.lpszMenuName  = (LPSTR) NULL;             // No menu
  MainWndClass.hCursor       = LoadCursor(NULL, IDC_ARROW); // Mouse cursor
  MainWndClass.hIcon         = NULL;       // Use client area as icon
  MainWndClass.hbrBackground = GetStockObject(WHITE_BRUSH);
  MainWndClass.cbClsExtra    = 0;                        // No extra bytes
  MainWndClass.cbWndExtra    = 0;                        // No extra bytes

  /* ----------------< Registering "Eyes" window class >------------------ */

  return (RegisterClass(&MainWndClass));
} // InitFirstInstance

/************************************************************************
 I n i t P a l e t t e ()
 ========================

 This function creates a logical color palette.

 Parameters:                    None

 Return values:

   BOOL              TRUE if the color palette can be generated.
                     Otherwise, FALSE.
 ************************************************************************/

BOOL InitPalette (void)
{
  int i;

    // Allocate memory on the local heap for a logical
    // palette with MAXCOLORS entries
    pLogPal = (NPLOGPALETTE) LocalAlloc(LMEM_FIXED,
```

```
                                    (sizeof(LOGPALETTE) +
                                    (sizeof(PALETTEENTRY)*MAXCOLORS)));

pLogPal->palVersion     = 0x300;      // Version number
pLogPal->palNumEntries  = MAXCOLORS;  // Number of entries

// Initialization of palette entries
for (i=0; i<MAXCOLORS; i++)
{
  pLogPal->palPalEntry[i].peFlags = PC_NOCOLLAPSE;     // Entry mode
}

/*********************************************************************
 The EYES.INI initialization contains the color values for pupils, eyes
 and background. These values are accepted if EYES.INI is found in the
 WINDOWS directory. Otherwise, default values are used.
 *********************************************************************/

// Background (default color: white)
pLogPal->palPalEntry[BACKGROUND].peRed   =
  (BYTE) GetPrivateProfileInt("eyes", "background.red", 255, "EYES.INI");
pLogPal->palPalEntry[BACKGROUND].peGreen =
  (BYTE) GetPrivateProfileInt("eyes", "background.green", 255, "EYES.INI");
pLogPal->palPalEntry[BACKGROUND].peBlue  =
  (BYTE) GetPrivateProfileInt("eyes", "background.blue", 255, "EYES.INI");

// Eyeball ellipses (default color: white)
pLogPal->palPalEntry[EYES].peRed   =
  (BYTE) GetPrivateProfileInt("eyes", "eyes.red", 255, "EYES.INI");
pLogPal->palPalEntry[EYES].peGreen =
  (BYTE) GetPrivateProfileInt("eyes", "eyes.green", 255, "EYES.INI");
pLogPal->palPalEntry[EYES].peBlue  =
  (BYTE) GetPrivateProfileInt("eyes", "eyes.blue", 255, "EYES.INI");

// Pupils (default color: black)
pLogPal->palPalEntry[PUPILS].peRed   =
  (BYTE) GetPrivateProfileInt("eyes", "pupils.red", 0, "EYES.INI");
pLogPal->palPalEntry[PUPILS].peGreen =
  (BYTE) GetPrivateProfileInt("eyes", "pupils.green", 0, "EYES.INI");
pLogPal->palPalEntry[PUPILS].peBlue  =
  (BYTE) GetPrivateProfileInt("eyes", "pupils.blue", 0, "EYES.INI");

// Create logical color palette set color values
hCurPal = CreatePalette((LPLOGPALETTE)pLogPal);

if (hCurPal)
  return TRUE;
else
```

```
    return FALSE;
} // InitPalette

/****************************************************************************
 M a i n W n d P r o c ()
 =======================

 This function acts as the main window function. All messages are sent to
 this window.

 Parameters:

   HWND     hWnd:     Window handle.
   unsigned msg:      Message type.
   WORD     wP:       Message-dependent 16 bit value
   LONG     lP:       Message-dependent 32 bit value

 Return values:

   LONG               0L if the window function has sent the message.
                      Otherwise, the return value from the DefWindowProc
                      default window function.

 ***************************************************************************/

LONG FAR PASCAL MainWndProc (HWND hWnd, unsigned msg, WORD wP, LONG lP)
{
  HDC      hDC;
  RECT     rMaxRect;
  int           nResult;        // Return value for DialogBox function

   switch (msg)
   {
     case WM_CREATE:
       // Get handle to copy of system menu
       hSystemMenu = GetSystemMenu(hWnd, FALSE);

       // Add separation line to end of menu
       AppendMenu(hSystemMenu, MF_SEPARATOR, 0, (LPSTR)NULL);

       // Append Palette menu item
       AppendMenu(hSystemMenu, MF_STRING, MI_PALETTE,
                               (LPSTR)"Palette...\tCtrl+P");

       // Append About Eyes... menu item
       AppendMenu(hSystemMenu, MF_STRING, MI_ABOUT,
                               (LPSTR)"About Eyes...\tCtrl+A");
```

```
        // Add separation line between MI_PALETTE and MI_ABOUT
        InsertMenu(hSystemMenu, MI_ABOUT, MF_SEPARATOR | MF_BYCOMMAND,
                                0, (LPSTR)NULL);

        // Calculate maximum bitmap size
        SetRect(&rMaxRect, 0, 0, GetSystemMetrics(SM_CXFULLSCREEN),
                GetSystemMetrics(SM_CYFULLSCREEN));

        nBorderLeft     = nBorderRight  = rMaxRect.right / 16;
        nBorderTop      = nBorderBottom = rMaxRect.bottom / 8;
        nEllipseWidth   = rMaxRect.right/2-nBorderRight-nBorderLeft;
        nEllipseHeight  = rMaxRect.bottom-nBorderBottom-nBorderTop;
        nMaxEyeWidth    = (nEllipseWidth+nEllipseHeight)/6;

        hDC = GetDC(hWnd);

        // Create compatible display context
        hBkGrDC = CreateCompatibleDC(hDC);
        // Create compatible bitmaps
        hBkGrLeftBitmap  = CreateCompatibleBitmap(hDC, nMaxEyeWidth,
nMaxEyeWidth);
        hBkGrRightBitmap = CreateCompatibleBitmap(hDC, nMaxEyeWidth,
nMaxEyeWidth);
        ReleaseDC(hWnd, hDC);
        break;

      case WM_DESTROY:
        KillTimer(hWnd, 1);                 // Kill timer
        DeleteObject(hCurPal);              // Release color palette
        DeleteDC(hBkGrDC);                  // Release compatible DC
        DeleteObject(hBkGrLeftBitmap);      // Release bitmaps
        DeleteObject(hBkGrRightBitmap);
        DeleteObject(hLeftOuterRgn);        // Release regions
        DeleteObject(hLeftInnerRgn);
        DeleteObject(hRightOuterRgn);
        DeleteObject(hRightInnerRgn);
        PostQuitMessage(0);                 // Send WM_QUIT message
        break;

      case WM_SYSCOMMAND:                   // Message from system menu
        switch (wP)
        {
          case MI_ABOUT:                    // "About Eyes..."
            bLocked = TRUE;
            lpfnModal = MakeProcInstance(MdfAboutProc, hInst);
            nResult = DialogBox(hInst, "ABOUTDLG", hwMain, lpfnModal);
            FreeProcInstance(lpfnModal);
            bLocked = FALSE;
```

```
        InvalidateRect(hWnd, NULL, TRUE);
        UpdateWindow(hWnd);
        break;

      case MI_PALETTE:                  // Color configuration dialog box
        bLocked = TRUE;
        lpfnModal = MakeProcInstance(MdfPaletteProc, hInst);
        nResult = DialogBox(hInst, "PALETTEDLG", hwMain, lpfnModal);
        FreeProcInstance(lpfnModal);
        bLocked = FALSE;
        InvalidateRect(hWnd, NULL, TRUE);
        UpdateWindow(hWnd);
        break;

      default:
        return (DefWindowProc(hWnd, msg, wP, lP));
        break;
    }
    break;

  case WM_PAINT:     // Client area redraw needed
    PaintEyes(hWnd);
    break;

  case WM_NCPAINT:   // Client area redraw NOT needed
    InvalidateRect(hWnd, NULL, TRUE);
    return (DefWindowProc(hWnd, msg, wP, lP));
    break;

  case WM_TIMER:     // Message from the timer
    {
      if (!bLocked) // Blocked by a dialog box?
      {
        // Check for cursor position change
        GetCursorPos((LPPOINT)&ptNewCursorPos);
        ScreenToClient(hWnd, (LPPOINT)&ptNewCursorPos);

        if ((ptNewCursorPos.x != ptCursorPos.x) ||
          (ptNewCursorPos.y != ptCursorPos.y))
        {
          hDC = GetDC(hWnd);
          GetBackgrounds(hDC);     // Retrieve old pupil backgrounds
          SetPositions(hWnd);      // Calculate new pupil positions
          SaveBackgrounds(hDC);    // Save new pupil backgrounds
          PaintPupils(hDC);        // Redraw pupils
          ReleaseDC(hWnd, hDC);
        }
      }
```

```
      }
      break;

    case WM_SIZE: // Window size change
        GetDimensions(hWnd);
        hLeftOuterRgn = CreateEllipticRgn(nBorderLeft, nBorderTop,
                            (rRect.right/2)-nBorderRight,
                            rRect.bottom-nBorderBottom);
        hLeftInnerRgn = CreateEllipticRgn(nBorderLeft+nEyeWidth,
                              nBorderTop+nEyeWidth,
                              (rRect.right/2)-nBorderRight-nEyeWidth,
                              rRect.bottom-nBorderBottom-nEyeWidth);
        hRightOuterRgn = CreateEllipticRgn((rRect.right/2)+nBorderLeft,
                            nBorderTop,
                            rRect.right-nBorderRight,
                            rRect.bottom-nBorderBottom);
        hRightInnerRgn = CreateEllipticRgn(rRect.right/2+nBorderLeft+nEyeWidth,
                              nBorderTop+nEyeWidth,
                              rRect.right-nBorderRight-nEyeWidth,
                              rRect.bottom-nBorderBottom-nEyeWidth);
        break;

    default:
      return (DefWindowProc(hWnd, msg, wP, lP));
      break;
  }
  return 0L;
} // MainWndProc

/***************************************************************************
 M d f A b o u t P r o c ()
 ==========================

 This function processes messages for the "About Eyes..." dialog box.

 Parameters:

   HWND     hDlg:      Dialog box handle.
   unsigned msg:       Message type.
   WORD     wP:        Message-dependent 16 bit value
   LONG     lP.        Message-dependent 32 bit value

 Return values:

   BOOL                TRUE if the dialog function contains the given message.
                       Otherwise, FALSE.
 ***************************************************************************/
```

```
BOOL FAR PASCAL MdfAboutProc (HWND hDlg, unsigned msg, WORD wP, LONG lP)
{
  switch (msg)
  {
    case WM_INITDIALOG:         // Dialog box display message
      return TRUE;              // Do not execute initialization
      break;

    case WM_COMMAND:            // Dialog box control message
      switch (wP)
      {
        case IDOK:              // Click on OK button
          EndDialog(hDlg, TRUE);
          return TRUE;
          break;

        default:                // Other messages
          return FALSE;
          break;
      }
      break;

    case WM_SYSCOMMAND:         // Menu from dialog box system menu
      switch (wP)
      {
        // ALT+F4, double-click system menu or select "Close" from system
        // menu to select

        case SC_CLOSE:
          EndDialog(hDlg, TRUE);
          return TRUE;
          break;

        default:                // Other system menu messages
          return FALSE;
          break;
      }
      break;

    default:                    // Other messages
        return FALSE;
        break;
  }
} // MdfAboutProc

/*********************************************************************
  S e t S c r o l l b a r s ()
  ============================
```

```
  This function sets the color scroll bar thumbs in positions
  corresponding to their respective color components.
************************************************************************/

void SetScrollbars (HWND hDlg, int RValue, int GValue, int BValue)
{
  SetScrollPos(GetDlgItem(hDlg, SB_RED), SB_CTL, RValue, TRUE);
  SetDlgItemInt(hDlg, SS_RVALUE, RValue, FALSE);
  SetScrollPos(GetDlgItem(hDlg, SB_GREEN), SB_CTL, GValue, TRUE);
  SetDlgItemInt(hDlg, SS_GVALUE, GValue, FALSE);
  SetScrollPos(GetDlgItem(hDlg, SB_BLUE), SB_CTL, BValue, TRUE);
  SetDlgItemInt(hDlg, SS_BVALUE, BValue, FALSE);
} // SetScrollbars

/***********************************************************************
 M d f P a l e t t e P r o c ()
 ==============================

 This function processes messages for the "Palette..." dialog box.

 Parameters:

   HWND     hDlg:     Dialog box handle.
   unsigned msg:      Message type.
   WORD     wP:       Message-dependent 16 bit value
   LONG     lP:       Message-dependent 32 bit value

 Return values:

   BOOL               TRUE if the dialog function contains the given message.
                      Otherwise, FALSE.
 ************************************************************************/

BOOL FAR PASCAL MdfPaletteProc (HWND hDlg, unsigned msg, WORD wP, LONG lP)
{
  int             i,
                  nScrollPos,          // scroll bar thumb position
                  nScrollValue,        // Scroll value
                  RValue,              // Red component
                  GValue,              // Green component
                  BValue;              // Blue component
  WORD            wControlId;          // Control ID
  PALETTEENTRY    PaletteEntry;        // Color palette entry
  static int      nRBIndex;            // Radio button index
  static POINT    ptPoint;             // Point
  static HWND     hColorRect;          // SS_COLOR rectangle's control handle
  static HBRUSH   hBrush;              // Brush handle for SS_COLOR rectangle
```

```
static HWND          aScrollbars[3]; // Scroll bar handle field

switch (msg)
{
  case WM_INITDIALOG:        // Dialog box display message
    hColorRect = GetDlgItem(hDlg, SS_COLOR);
    nRBIndex = 0;
    for (i=0; i<3; i++)
    {
      // Set scroll bar thumbs
      aScrollbars[i] = GetDlgItem(hDlg, SB_RED+i);
      // Set scroll area
      SetScrollRange(aScrollbars[i], SB_CTL, 0, 255, FALSE);
    }
    GetPaletteEntries(hCurPal, nRBIndex, 1, &PaletteEntry);
    // Set thumb positions
    SetScrollbars(hDlg,
                  (int) PaletteEntry.peRed,    // Red component
                  (int) PaletteEntry.peGreen, // Green component
                  (int) PaletteEntry.peBlue); // Blue component
    CheckRadioButton(hDlg, RB_BACKGROUND, RB_PUPILS, RB_BACKGROUND);
    // Display new color in SS_COLOR rectangle
    SetDlgItemText(hDlg, SS_COLOR, "");
    SetFocus(GetDlgItem(hDlg, IDOK));
              hBrush = 0;      // Still no brush created

    return FALSE;
    break;

  case WM_CTLCOLOR:                  // Before control display
    if (LOWORD(lP) == hColorRect)    // From color rectangle?
    {
      SelectPalette((HDC)wP, hCurPal, FALSE);
      RealizePalette((HDC)wP);
               if (hBrush)           // Remove access to old brush
                   DeleteObject(hBrush);
      hBrush = CreateSolidBrush(PALETTEINDEX(nRBIndex));
      ptPoint.x = ptPoint.y = 0;
      ClientToScreen(hDlg, &ptPoint);
      SetBrushOrg((HDC)wP, ptPoint.x, ptPoint.y);
      UnrealizeObject(hBrush);
      SetBkColor((HDC)wP, PALETTEINDEX(nRBIndex));
      return (hBrush);               // Return handle to brush
    }
    else
      return FALSE;

    case WM_VSCROLL:                 // Scroll bar message
```

```
// Set scroll position
nScrollPos = GetScrollPos(HIWORD(lP), SB_CTL);
switch (wP)
{
  case SB_LINEUP:
    nScrollValue = -1;
    break;
  case SB_LINEDOWN:
    nScrollValue = 1;
    break;
  case SB_PAGEUP:
    nScrollValue = -8;
    break;
  case SB_PAGEDOWN:
    nScrollValue = 8;
    break;
  case SB_THUMBPOSITION:
    nScrollValue = LOWORD(lP)-nScrollPos;
    break;
  default:
    nScrollValue = 0;
    break;
}
// Calculate scroll value
nScrollValue = max(-nScrollPos, min(nScrollValue, 255-nScrollPos));
if (nScrollValue)
{
  nScrollPos += nScrollValue;
  // Set new scroll position
  SetScrollPos(HIWORD(lP), SB_CTL, nScrollPos, TRUE);
  wControlId = GetWindowWord(HIWORD(lP), GWW_ID);
  // Display new color value
  SetDlgItemInt(hDlg, SS_RVALUE+wControlId-SB_RED, nScrollPos, FALSE);

  // Determine color component values
  RValue = GetScrollPos(aScrollbars[0], SB_CTL);
  GValue = GetScrollPos(aScrollbars[1], SB_CTL);
  BValue = GetScrollPos(aScrollbars[2], SB_CTL);

  PaletteEntry.peRed   = (BYTE)RValue;
  PaletteEntry.peGreen = (BYTE)GValue;
  PaletteEntry.peBlue  = (BYTE)BValue;
  PaletteEntry.peFlags = PC_NOCOLLAPSE;

  // Set palette entry
  SetPaletteEntries(hCurPal, nRBIndex, 1, &PaletteEntry);
  // Display colors in SS_COLOR rectangle
  SetDlgItemText(hDlg, SS_COLOR, "");
```

```
      }
      break;

    case WM_COMMAND:              // Dialog box control message
      switch (wP)
      {
        case IDOK:                // Click on OK button
                      if (hBrush)            // Remove brush access
                          DeleteObject(hBrush);
          EndDialog(hDlg, TRUE); // Close dialog box
          return TRUE;
          break;

        case RB_BACKGROUND:       // Message from radio buttons
        case RB_EYES:
        case RB_PUPILS:
          nRBIndex = wP-RB_BACKGROUND;
          GetPaletteEntries(hCurPal, nRBIndex, 1, &PaletteEntry);
          // Set scroll positions
          SetScrollbars(hDlg,
                      (int) PaletteEntry.peRed,   // Red component
                      (int) PaletteEntry.peGreen, // Green component
                      (int) PaletteEntry.peBlue); // Blue component
          // Display color in SS_COLOR rectangle
          SetDlgItemText(hDlg, SS_COLOR, "");
          return FALSE;
          break;

        default:
          return FALSE;
          break;
      }
      break;

    case WM_SYSCOMMAND:          // Message from dialog box system menu
      switch (wP)
      {
        // ALT+F4, double-click system menu or select "Close" from system
        // menu to select

        case SC_CLOSE:
                      PostMessage(hDlg, WM_COMMAND, IDOK, 0L);
          return TRUE;
          break;

        default:                // Other system menu messages
          return FALSE;
          break;
```

```
      }
      break;

    default:                      // Other messages
        return FALSE;
        break;
  }
} // MdfPaletteProc

/***************************************************************************
 L i n e F u n c ()
 ==================

 Callback function of the LineDDA function.

 Parameters:

   short  X       X-coordinate of currently processed points
   short  Y       Y-coordinate of currently processed points
   LPSTR  lpData  Long pointer to data received from application

  Return values:   None.
 ***************************************************************************/

void FAR PASCAL LineFunc (short X, short Y, LPSTR lpData)
{
  if (lstrcmp(lpData, (LPSTR)"left") == 0) // Left eye
  {
    if (!bInnerPtDone && !PtInRegion(hLeftInnerRgn, X, Y))
    {
      ptInnerLeft.x = X;
      ptInnerLeft.y = Y;
      bInnerPtDone = TRUE;
    }
    if (!bOuterPtDone && !PtInRegion(hLeftOuterRgn, X, Y))
    {
      ptOuterLeft.x = X;
      ptOuterLeft.y = Y;
      bOuterPtDone = TRUE;
    }
    return;
  }
  else                                     // Right eye
  {
    if (!bInnerPtDone && !PtInRegion(hRightInnerRgn, X, Y))
    {
      ptInnerRight.x = X;
      ptInnerRight.y = Y;
```

```
        bInnerPtDone = TRUE;
      }
      if (!bOuterPtDone && !PtInRegion(hRightOuterRgn, X, Y))
      {
        ptOuterRight.x = X;
        ptOuterRight.y = Y;
        bOuterPtDone = TRUE;
      }
      return;
    }
} // LineFunc

/*****************************************************************************
 G e t D i m e n s i o n s ()
 ============================

 This function calculates important parameters.

 Parameters:

   HWND  hWnd   Window handle

 Return values:  None.
 *****************************************************************************/

void GetDimensions (HWND hWnd)
{
   GetClientRect(hWnd, (LPRECT) &rRect);

   // Setting the borders
   nBorderLeft      = nBorderRight  = rRect.right / 16;
   nBorderTop       = nBorderBottom = rRect.bottom / 8;

   // Center point of left eye
   ptLeftCenter.x   = rRect.right/4;
   ptLeftCenter.y   = rRect.bottom/2;

   // Center point of right eye
   ptRightCenter.x = 3*rRect.right/4;
   ptRightCenter.y = rRect.bottom/2;

   // Eye dimensions
   nEllipseWidth    = rRect.right/2-nBorderRight-nBorderLeft;
   nEllipseHeight   = rRect.bottom-nBorderBottom-nBorderTop;

   // Pupil diameters
   nEyeWidth        = (nEllipseWidth+nEllipseHeight)/6;
} // GetDimensions
```

```
/***************************************************************************
 S e t P o s i t i o n s ()
 ==========================

 This function computes positions of the pupils.

 Parameters:
   HWND  hWnd        Window handle

 Return values:  None.
 ***************************************************************************/

void SetPositions (HWND hWnd)
{
   // Determine current cursor position in screen coordinates
   GetCursorPos((LPPOINT)&ptCursorPos);
   ScreenToClient(hWnd, (LPPOINT)&ptCursorPos);

   lpfnProc = MakeProcInstance(LineFunc, hInst);

   bInnerPtDone = FALSE;
   bOuterPtDone = FALSE;
   LineDDA(ptLeftCenter.x, ptLeftCenter.y, ptCursorPos.x, ptCursorPos.y,
           lpfnProc, (LPSTR)"left");

   // First quadrant (upper right)
   if ((ptCursorPos.x > ptLeftCenter.x) && (ptCursorPos.y < ptLeftCenter.y))
   {
     ptMiddleLeft.x = (ptOuterLeft.x-ptInnerLeft.x)/2+ptInnerLeft.x;
     ptMiddleLeft.y = ptInnerLeft.y-(ptInnerLeft.y-ptOuterLeft.y)/2;
   }

   // Second quadrant (upper left)
   if ((ptCursorPos.x < ptLeftCenter.x) && (ptCursorPos.y < ptLeftCenter.y))
   {
     ptMiddleLeft.x = ptInnerLeft.x-(ptInnerLeft.x-ptOuterLeft.x)/2;
     ptMiddleLeft.y = ptInnerLeft.y-(ptInnerLeft.y-ptOuterLeft.y)/2;
   }

   // Third quadrant (lower left)
   if ((ptCursorPos.x < ptLeftCenter.x) && (ptCursorPos.y > ptLeftCenter.y))
   {
     ptMiddleLeft.x = ptInnerLeft.x-(ptInnerLeft.x-ptOuterLeft.x)/2;
     ptMiddleLeft.y = (ptOuterLeft.y-ptInnerLeft.y)/2+ptInnerLeft.y;
   }

   // Fourth quadrant (lower right)
```

```
  if ((ptCursorPos.x > ptLeftCenter.x) && (ptCursorPos.y > ptLeftCenter.y))
  {
    ptMiddleLeft.x = (ptOuterLeft.x-ptInnerLeft.x)/2+ptInnerLeft.x;
    ptMiddleLeft.y = (ptOuterLeft.y-ptInnerLeft.y)/2+ptInnerLeft.y;
  }

  SetRect(&rLeftEye, ptMiddleLeft.x-(nEyeWidth/2), ptMiddleLeft.y-(nEyeWidth/2),
          ptMiddleLeft.x+(nEyeWidth/2), ptMiddleLeft.y+(nEyeWidth/2));

  bInnerPtDone = bOuterPtDone = FALSE;
  LineDDA(ptRightCenter.x, ptRightCenter.y, ptCursorPos.x, ptCursorPos.y,
          lpfnProc, (LPSTR)"right");

  // First quadrant (upper right)
  if ((ptCursorPos.x > ptRightCenter.x) && (ptCursorPos.y < ptRightCenter.y))
  {
    ptMiddleRight.x = (ptOuterRight.x-ptInnerRight.x)/2+ptInnerRight.x;
    ptMiddleRight.y = ptInnerRight.y-(ptInnerRight.y-ptOuterRight.y)/2;
  }

  // Second quadrant (upper left)
  if ((ptCursorPos.x < ptRightCenter.x) && (ptCursorPos.y < ptRightCenter.y))
  {
    ptMiddleRight.x = ptInnerRight.x-(ptInnerRight.x-ptOuterRight.x)/2;
    ptMiddleRight.y = ptInnerRight.y-(ptInnerRight.y-ptOuterRight.y)/2;
  }

  // Third quadrant (lower left)
  if ((ptCursorPos.x < ptRightCenter.x) && (ptCursorPos.y > ptRightCenter.y))
  {
    ptMiddleRight.x = ptInnerRight.x-(ptInnerRight.x-ptOuterRight.x)/2;
    ptMiddleRight.y = (ptOuterRight.y-ptInnerRight.y)/2+ptInnerRight.y;
  }

  // Fourth quadrant (lower right)
  if ((ptCursorPos.x > ptRightCenter.x) && (ptCursorPos.y > ptRightCenter.y))
  {
    ptMiddleRight.x = (ptOuterRight.x-ptInnerRight.x)/2+ptInnerRight.x;
    ptMiddleRight.y = (ptOuterRight.y-ptInnerRight.y)/2+ptInnerRight.y;
  }

  SetRect(&rRightEye, ptMiddleRight.x-(nEyeWidth/2), ptMiddleRight.y-
(nEyeWidth/2),
          ptMiddleRight.x+(nEyeWidth/2), ptMiddleRight.y+(nEyeWidth/2));

  FreeProcInstance(lpfnProc);
} // SetPositions
```

```
/****************************************************************************
 S a v e B a c k g r o u n d s ()
 ================================

 This function saves the client area background before redrawing the pupils.

 Parameters:

   HDC          hDC         Window display context

 Return values:   None.
 ****************************************************************************/

void SaveBackgrounds (HDC hDC)
{
   SelectObject(hBkGrDC, hBkGrLeftBitmap);
   // Save background of left pupil as bitmap
   BitBlt(hBkGrDC, 0, 0, nEyeWidth, nEyeWidth,
          hDC, rLeftEye.left, rLeftEye.top, SRCCOPY);

   SelectObject(hBkGrDC, hBkGrRightBitmap);
   // Save background of right pupil as bitmap
   BitBlt(hBkGrDC, 0, 0, nEyeWidth, nEyeWidth,
          hDC, rRightEye.left, rRightEye.top, SRCCOPY);
} // SaveBackgrounds

/****************************************************************************
 G e t B a c k g r o u n d s ()
 ==============================

 This function restores the pupil backgrounds stored by SaveBackgrounds.

 Parameters:

   HDC    hDC    Window display context

 Return values:   None.
 ****************************************************************************/

void GetBackgrounds (HDC hDC)
{
  SelectObject(hBkGrDC, hBkGrLeftBitmap);
  // Copy old background back to left pupil
  BitBlt(hDC, rLeftEye.left, rLeftEye.top, nEyeWidth, nEyeWidth,
         hBkGrDC, 0, 0, SRCCOPY);

  SelectObject(hBkGrDC, hBkGrRightBitmap);
  // Copy old background back to right pupil
```

```
  BitBlt(hDC, rRightEye.left, rRightEye.top, nEyeWidth, nEyeWidth,
         hBkGrDC, 0, 0, SRCCOPY);
} // GetBackgrounds

/*****************************************************************************
 P a i n t P u p i l s ()
 ========================

 This function redraws the pupils.

 Parameters:

   HDC    hDC:    Window display context.

 Return values:    None.
 *****************************************************************************/

void PaintPupils (HDC hDC)
{
  // Select color palette in display context
  SelectPalette(hDC, hCurPal, FALSE);
  // Realize color palette
  RealizePalette(hDC);
  hPupilBrush = CreateSolidBrush(PALETTEINDEX(PUPILS)); // Pupil brush
  hSaveBrush = SelectObject(hDC, hPupilBrush);
  Ellipse(hDC, rLeftEye.left, rLeftEye.top, rLeftEye.right, rLeftEye.bottom);
  Ellipse(hDC, rRightEye.left, rRightEye.top, rRightEye.right, rRightEye.bottom);
  DeleteObject(SelectObject(hDC, hSaveBrush));
} // PaintPupils

/*****************************************************************************
 P a i n t E y e s ()
 ====================

 This function is needed for redrawing the client area of the main window.

 Parameters:

   HWND   hWnd:     Window handle.

 Return values:     None.
 *****************************************************************************/

 void PaintEyes (HWND hWnd)
 {
   PAINTSTRUCT ps;
   HDC         hDC;
```

```
  hDC = BeginPaint(hWnd, &ps);    // Get main window display context

  // Select color palette in display context
  SelectPalette(hDC, hCurPal, FALSE);
  // Realize color palette
  RealizePalette(hDC);

  GetDimensions(hWnd);                     // Determine eye dimensions

  hEraseBrush = CreateSolidBrush(PALETTEINDEX(BACKGROUND));
  FillRect(hDC, &rRect, hEraseBrush);  // Clear background
  DeleteObject(hEraseBrush);

  // Select eye brush in display context
  hEyeBrush   = CreateSolidBrush(PALETTEINDEX(EYES));
  hSaveBrush  = SelectObject(hDC, hEyeBrush);

  // Draw left eye
  Ellipse(hDC,    nBorderLeft, nBorderTop,
                  (rRect.right/2)-nBorderRight, rRect.bottom-nBorderBottom);
  // Draw right eye
  Ellipse(hDC,    (rRect.right/2)+nBorderLeft, nBorderTop,
                  rRect.right-nBorderRight, rRect.bottom-nBorderBottom);

  DeleteObject(SelectObject(hDC, hSaveBrush));

  SetPositions(hWnd);               // Calculate new pupil position
  SaveBackgrounds(hDC);             // Save new pupil backgrounds
  PaintPupils(hDC);                 // Redraw pupils

  EndPaint(hWnd, &ps);
} // PaintEyes
```

7 The Address Book Application

Windows' predefined window classes offer nearly unlimited potential for most applications. But occasionally, you may need a special control or a window that looks a certain way.

Windows would not be the powerful programming environment that it is if it did not enable you to create custom features. Among other things, you can:

1) define and register a new control

2) use subclassing to change the way the window functions of standard controls (list boxes, edit boxes etc.) work

In this chapter, we'll present an application that demonstrates how to combine standard controls, custom controls, controls that have been altered by subclassing, dialog boxes and GDI graphic elements to create new effects.

When using control elements, remember that Microsoft has certain standards for how they must behave. The user of any Windows application should be able to expect that a control will work the same from all programs. So, make changes to these standards very carefully.

7.1 Overview

The demo program we will create in this chapter is called ADDRBOOK.EXE. From the outside, this appears to be a compact application. The main window has two menus listed in the main window bar: **File** and **Dialog Boxes**. The familiar **Exit** and **About Address Book...** items are found under the first menu.

The **Dialog Boxes** menu contains only one item: **Address Book**. When this item is selected, a dialog box that looks like an open address book with three entry fields on each page and index letters in the margins of the pages will appear on the screen.

The three graphic "binder rings" give this dialog box the appearance of a looseleaf address book. Also, the upper part of each page is separated from the three entry boxes (which are actually edit boxes) by a horizontal line. This dividing line contains an index letter which is displayed in a larger font size than the system font.

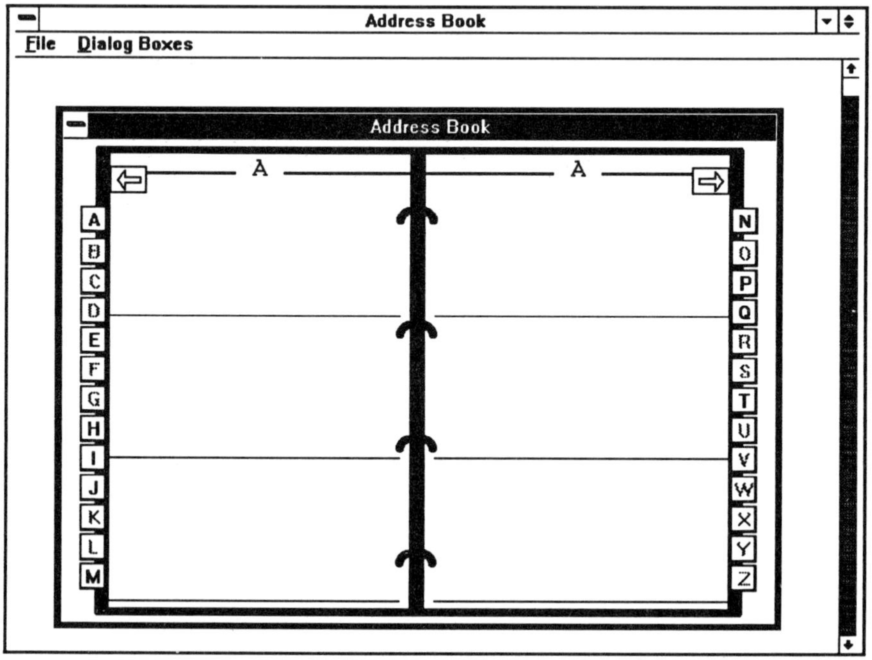

The ADDRBOOK.EXE application

The upper portions of the left and right pages of the address book dialog box contain controls that are displayed as arrows. The arrow on the left page points left, and the one on the right page points right. These arrows allow the user to page forward and backward through the address book.

We compromised on several points in order to keep this application from getting too large. First, we could have made the dialog box look even more like a "real" address book, but this would have complicated things without providing any new functionality for us to study. Second, you can enter data in the dialog box, but you cannot save it. A truly useful address book application would be able to further process the entries made in the dialog box.

We invite you to let your creativity run wild in expanding the address book application. In this chapter, we will concentrate on presenting the new points about Windows programming that we want to demonstrate.

When you reach the end of this chapter, you'll notice that the source code is split between two files: ADDRBOOK.C and ADDRUTIL.C. If you work with large Windows programs, eventually you'll have to learn how to break an application up into several smaller source code files. Splitting an application into logical modules makes good sense, and it eases the Windows memory manager's tasks of handling the program and selecting the most appropriate memory model.

Memory models

A separate .C file is converted to an .OBJ module by the compiler. If the SMALL memory model is used, all object modules are linked in a single code segment. In memory models that require more than one code segment (MEDIUM and LARGE), each module compiled from the C source code is assigned to a separate data segment. This allows you to specify a different memory management option (MOVEABLE, DISCARDABLE, etc), in the module definition file, for the application. This means that the Windows memory manager can manage the application more flexibly and with less memory. If you define all code segments as MOVABLE and DISCARDABLE, then all you need to run the application is enough memory to handle the largest code segment.

You must be very careful, however, when you split an application into several modules. In the worst case, the memory manager will always be busy swapping code segments if you call functions that are stored in different modules. The general guideline is that a compiled module should not be larger than about 5K. In Protected Mode, the segment size of 4K is perfect for this. The MMU of the 80386 uses a 4K page size.

The ADDRBOOK.C and ADDRUTIL.C modules are split in such a way that ADDRBOOK.C contains the basic Windows functionality and ADDRUTIL.C contains the functions used to manage the address book dialog box. Let's begin with the Windows functions found in the ADDRBOOK.C module.

7.2 Defining Custom Controls

Most of the following has already been discussed. One special item is the way window class is registered in the InitFirstInstance function:

```
// Registering the "Address book" window class
RegisterClass(&MainWndClass);

// Registering a custom window class
return(RegisterBookCtrl(hInstance));
```

After we register the window class of the main window, we call the RegisterBookCtrl function. This function is found in the ADDRUTIL.C module. It is used to register window classes for custom controls. The first step is to define the fields of the type WNDCLASS window class variable wc for a control with the class name "LEXBUTTON":

```
WNDCLASS wc;

wc.lpszClassName   = "LEXBUTTON";
wc.style           = CS_HREDRAW | CS_VREDRAW | CS_DBLCLKS;
wc.hInstance       = hInst;
wc.lpfnWndProc     = fwLexButton;
wc.hCursor         = LoadCursor(NULL, IDC_ARROW);
wc.hIcon           = NULL;
wc.lpszMenuName    = NULL;
wc.hbrBackground   = (HBRUSH) GetStockObject(WHITE_BRUSH);
wc.cbClsExtra      = 0;
wc.cbWndExtra      = sizeof(BOOL); // Saves enabled/disabled status

if(!RegisterClass(&wc))
   return FALSE;
```

Controls of window class "LEXBUTTON" are used to represent the index tabs on the address book. These controls are simple rectangles that can contain text. Similar to any normal pushbutton control, they can be clicked, disabled and enabled. The window function fwLexButton is responsible for the LEXBUTTON control. We will examine this function in detail later. Note that this time we will use the cbWndExtra field, which is reserved for special purposes. We use this field for a type BOOL variable that indicates whether a window of the LEXBUTTON window class is enabled or disabled.

Next, we define and register a window class called "L_ARROW":

```
wc.lpszClassName   = "L_ARROW";
wc.style           = CS_HREDRAW | CS_VREDRAW | CS_DBLCLKS;
wc.hInstance       = hInst;
wc.lpfnWndProc     = fwLeftArrow;
wc.hCursor         = LoadCursor(NULL, IDC_ARROW);
wc.hIcon           = NULL;
wc.lpszMenuName    = NULL;
wc.hbrBackground   = (HBRUSH) GetStockObject(WHITE_BRUSH);
wc.cbClsExtra      = 0;
wc.cbWndExtra      = sizeof(BOOL); // Saves enabled/disabled status

if(!RegisterClass(&wc))
   return FALSE;
```

This is the same procedure used to define and register the LEXBUTTON window class. fwLeftArrow is the window function for the L ARROW window class. Our program will only use one control of type L_ARROW. This is the left arrow that appears on the left page of the address book and is used to page back through the address book. When it is clicked, a message box also opens to indicate that you are paging backwards.

Window class R_ARROW is very similar to L_ARROW. The R_ARROW window class is used to display the right arrow control, which pages forward through the address book when clicked.

```
wc.lpszClassName   = "R_ARROW";
wc.style           = CS_HREDRAW | CS_VREDRAW | CS_DBLCLKS;
wc.hInstance       = hInst;
wc.lpfnWndProc     = fwRightArrow;
wc.hCursor         = LoadCursor(NULL, IDC_ARROW);
wc.hIcon           = NULL;
wc.lpszMenuName    = NULL;
wc.hbrBackground   = (HBRUSH) GetStockObject(WHITE_BRUSH);
wc.cbClsExtra      = 0;
wc.cbWndExtra      = sizeof(BOOL); // Saves enabled/disabled status

if(!RegisterClass(&wc))
   return FALSE;
return TRUE;
```

The InitFirstInstance function returns after successfully registering all window classes. In the WinMain function, the CreateWindow function is called to create the main window. Then a handle to the main menu is retrieved and the "Address Book" and "Dialog Boxes" menu items are initialized:

```
/* ----------------------< Initialization tasks >---------------------- */

// Get handle to main menu
hMainMenu = GetMenu(hwMain);
CheckMenuItem(hMainMenu, MI_ADDRBOOK, MF_UNCHECKED);
```

After this, the main window is displayed and the program moves into the message loop. The window function of the main window MainWndProc does not have much to do in this application. The most interesting message is under the "Address Book" menu item, which displays the address book dialog box when clicked:

```
case MI_ADDRBOOK:           // Call the "Address Book" dialog box
  if (!bDlgModeless)        // Dialog box must be displayed
  {
    lpfnModeless = MakeProcInstance(NdfAddressBookProc, hInst);
    hDlgModeless = CreateDialog(hInst, "ADDRESSBOOK", hwMain, lpfnModeless);
    if (hDlgModeless)
    {
      ShowWindow(hDlgModeless, SW_SHOWNORMAL);
      bDlgModeless = TRUE;
      // Check menu entry
      CheckMenuItem(hMainMenu, MI_ADDRBOOK, MF_CHECKED);
    }
    else
      MessageBox(GetFocus(), "Address dialog box could not be opened",
                 szApplName, MB_OK | MB_ICONEXCLAMATION);
  }
  else                      // Dialog box must be destroyed
  {
    DestroyWindow(hDlgModeless);
    FreeProcInstance(lpfnModeless);
    bDlgModeless = FALSE;
    hDlgModeless = NULL;
    // Remove checkmark
    CheckMenuItem(hMainMenu, MI_ADDRBOOK, MF_UNCHECKED);
  }
  break;
```

The address book dialog box is modeless, as we can see from the use of the CreateDialog function. We use the same method for handling this dialog box that we saw in the "DBOXDEMO" application. The boolean variable bDlgModeless, the window handle hDlgModeless and the procedure instance variable lpfnModeless are used to create and delete this dialog box.

Now let's discuss the functions of the ADDRUTIL.C module. The focal point of this module is the dialog function NdfAddressBookProc. This is the dialog function for the address book window. Since this function has no menu of its own, most of the messages it processed originate from the controls of the address book dialog box. The controls represent child windows of the address book dialog box.

Notice that the CreateWindow function is not used anywhere in the ADDRUTIL.C module to create windows of class LEXBUTTON, L_ARROW or R_ARROW. Instead, Windows (or more precisely, the resource compiler rc.exe) is informed of the position, width and height of the controls using the DIALOG command of the address book dialog box within the ADDRBOOK.DLG file:

```
ADDRESSBOOK DIALOG LOADONCALL MOVEABLE DISCARDABLE 20, 30, 270, 180
CAPTION "Address Book"
STYLE WS_BORDER | WS_CAPTION | WS_DLGFRAME | WS_SYSMENU | WS_VISIBLE |
DS_LOCALEDIT | DS_MODALFRAME | WS_POPUP
BEGIN
   CONTROL "",  3000, "l_arrow", 0 | WS_CHILD, 18, 10, 14, 10
   CONTROL "",  3001, "r_arrow", 0 | WS_CHILD, 238, 10, 14, 10
   CONTROL "A", 2000, "lexbutton", 0 | WS_CHILD, 7, 25, 10, 10
   CONTROL "B", 2001, "lexbutton", 0 | WS_CHILD, 7, 37, 10, 10
   CONTROL "C", 2002, "lexbutton", 0 | WS_CHILD, 7, 48, 10, 10
   CONTROL "D", 2003, "lexbutton", 0 | WS_CHILD, 7, 59, 10, 10
   CONTROL "E", 2004, "lexbutton", 0 | WS_CHILD, 7, 70, 10, 10
   CONTROL "F", 2005, "lexbutton", 0 | WS_CHILD, 7, 81, 10, 10
   CONTROL "G", 2006, "lexbutton", 0 | WS_CHILD, 7, 92, 10, 10
   CONTROL "H", 2007, "lexbutton", 0 | WS_CHILD, 7, 103, 10, 10
   CONTROL "I", 2008, "lexbutton", 0 | WS_CHILD, 7, 114, 10, 10
   CONTROL "J", 2009, "lexbutton", 0 | WS_CHILD, 7, 125, 10, 10
   CONTROL "K", 2010, "lexbutton", 0 | WS_CHILD, 7, 136, 10, 10
   CONTROL "L", 2011, "lexbutton", 0 | WS_CHILD, 7, 147, 10, 10
   CONTROL "M", 2012, "lexbutton", 0 | WS_CHILD, 7, 158, 10, 10
   CONTROL "N", 2013, "lexbutton", 0 | WS_CHILD, 253, 25, 10, 10
   CONTROL "O", 2014, "lexbutton", 0 | WS_CHILD, 253, 37, 10, 10
   CONTROL "P", 2015, "lexbutton", 0 | WS_CHILD, 253, 48, 10, 10
   CONTROL "Q", 2016, "lexbutton", 0 | WS_CHILD, 253, 59, 10, 10
   CONTROL "R", 2017, "lexbutton", 0 | WS_CHILD, 253, 70, 10, 10
   CONTROL "S", 2018, "lexbutton", 0 | WS_CHILD, 253, 81, 10, 10
```

```
    CONTROL "T", 2019, "lexbutton", 0 | WS_CHILD, 253, 92, 10, 10
    CONTROL "U", 2020, "lexbutton", 0 | WS_CHILD, 253, 103, 10, 10
    CONTROL "V", 2021, "lexbutton", 0 | WS_CHILD, 253, 114, 10, 10
    CONTROL "W", 2022, "lexbutton", 0 | WS_CHILD, 253, 125, 10, 10
    CONTROL "X", 2023, "lexbutton", 0 | WS_CHILD, 253, 136, 10, 10
    CONTROL "Y", 2024, "lexbutton", 0 | WS_CHILD, 253, 147, 10, 10
    CONTROL "Z", 2025, "lexbutton", 0 | WS_CHILD, 253, 158, 10, 10
    CONTROL "", 4000, "edit", ES_LEFT | ES_MULTILINE | WS_TABSTOP | WS_CHILD, 19,
28, 108, 36
    CONTROL "", 4001, "edit", ES_LEFT | ES_MULTILINE | WS_TABSTOP | WS_CHILD, 19,
75, 108, 36
    CONTROL "", 4002, "edit", ES_LEFT | ES_MULTILINE | WS_TABSTOP | WS_CHILD, 19,
120, 108, 36
    CONTROL "", 4003, "edit", ES_LEFT | ES_MULTILINE | WS_TABSTOP | WS_CHILD, 144,
28, 108, 36
    CONTROL "", 4004, "edit", ES_LEFT | ES_MULTILINE | WS_TABSTOP | WS_CHILD, 144,
75, 108, 36
    CONTROL "", 4005, "edit", ES_LEFT | ES_MULTILINE | WS_TABSTOP | WS_CHILD, 144,
120, 108, 36
END
```

Our discussion of the rest of this application will begin with the WM_INITDIALOG message. This message is sent to the dialog box before it is displayed. If we had real address data in our address book we should initialize the index tabs on the address book in such a way that the user would automatically know which pages contain address entries.

We do this simply by enabling the LEXBUTTON controls for the pages that have entries and disabling those for the pages that don't have entries. A disabled LEXBUTTON control is displayed in gray, just like any other disabled pushbutton control. This means that the control cannot be activated.

Since we are not going to load any real data in our application, we will use the random number generator to initialize the index letters in our address book:

```
case WM_INITDIALOG:
   // Initialize random number generator
   srand((unsigned)time(NULL));

   // Enable or disable all indices except "A"
   for (i=1; i<26; i++)
   {
```

```
  if (rand() % 2)
    EnableWindow(GetDlgItem(hDlg,ID_LEX+i), FALSE);
  else
    EnableWindow(GetDlgItem(hDlg,ID_LEX+i), TRUE);
}
// Make "A" the current index letter
AktReg = ID_LEX;
EnableWindow(GetDlgItem(hDlg,ID_LEX), TRUE);
```

The C run time function srand is used to initialize the random number generator with the number of seconds that have elapsed since 1/1/1970. Then the EnableWindow function initializes the LEXBUTTON controls from "B" to "Z" to enabled or disabled depending on whether the random number returned by the rand function is odd or even.

The letter "A" isn't included in this process. It is always initialized to enabled. Its ID value ID_LEX is assigned to the variable AktReg, which makes it the current index letter.

7.3 LEXBUTTON Window Functions

Let's take a closer look at how the fwLexButton window function processes messages sent to a LEXBUTTON control. The WM_ENABLE message is sent to a window when it is enabled (in which case wP != 0) or disabled (wP == 0). When a window function receives this message, it calls the SetWindowWord function in order to set the extra bytes that were reserved for status information on the window. This value will be TRUE for a disabled LEXBUTTON and FALSE for an enabled LEXBUTTON. Later, this status will be used by the DrawLexButton function when the LEXBUTTON is actually drawn:

```
case WM_ENABLE:          // wP == NULL disable button, otherwise enable
  SetWindowWord(hWnd, 0, wP==NULL ? TRUE : FALSE);  // Save status
  InvalidateRect(hWnd, NULL, FALSE);
break;
```

The bSelected variable is initialized to FALSE when a WM_CREATE message is processed. If the mouse cursor is in a LEXBUTTON control and the left mouse button is pressed, the resulting WM_LBUTTONDOWN message will set the value of bSelected to TRUE. The LEXBUTTON then calls the SetCapture function to handle all subsequent mouse messages. The InvalidateRect function is called to invalidate the entire client area of the LEXBUTTON, which leads to the generation of a WM_PAINT message:

```
case WM_LBUTTONDOWN:      // Left mouse button pressed
  bSelected = TRUE;
  SetCapture(hWnd);
  GetClientRect(hWnd, &rect);
  InvalidateRect(hWnd, NULL, FALSE);
  break;
```

When the WM_PAINT message is received, the window function calls the BeginPaint function to get a display context. Then the text stored in the .DLG file is read into the LEXBUTTON control:

```
/*-- < Read the text defined as control in DLG file >---*/
iTxtLen = GetWindowTextLength(hWnd);
hWinTxt = LocalAlloc(LMEM_MOVEABLE, iTxtLen+1);
pWinTxt= LocalLock(hWinTxt);
GetWindowText(hWnd, pWinTxt,iTxtLen+1);
```

We do not use a fixed buffer to store the text of the control. Instead, we use the LocalAlloc function to dynamically allocate memory on the local heap. The number of bytes we need to allocate is determined by calling the GetWindowTextLength function. One additional byte is required for the "\0" that appears at the end of the text string.

As soon as pWinTxt points to the text string to be displayed within the control, we can use the DrawLexButton function to draw it. Then the reserved hWinTxt handle and allocated memory are freed:

```
/*----------------< Draw the control >--------------------*/
DrawLexButton(hWnd, hDC, GetWindowWord(hWnd, 0), bSelected, pWinTxt);
LocalUnlock(hWinTxt);
LocalFree(hWinTxt);
```

The DrawLexButton paint function creates a pen resource, selects it in the display context of the control, then draws a rectangle around the entire client area:

```
// Create pen
hPen = CreatePen(PS_SOLID, 2, RGB(0, 0, 0));
hOldPen = SelectObject(hDC,hPen);
// Set dimensions
GetClientRect(hWnd, &rcClient);
Rectangle(hDC, rcClient.left, rcClient.top,
               rcClient.right, rcClient.bottom);
```

The size of the text string is calculated with the help of the GetTextExtent function. Depending on whether the LEXBUTTON in question is selected (bSelected == TRUE) or not (bSelected == FALSE), a black or white background brush is selected in the display context and the text color is set to white, or some other color, with the help of the GetSysColor function:

```
lTextExt = GetTextExtent(hDC, szText, strlen(szText));
if(bSelected)     // The control has been selected
{
   hOldBrush = SelectObject(hDC, GetStockObject(BLACK_BRUSH));
   SetTextColor(hDC, RGB(255,255,255));
   SetBkColor(hDC, RGB(0,0,0));
}
else
{
   hOldBrush = SelectObject(hDC, GetStockObject(WHITE_BRUSH));
   SetTextColor(hDC, GetSysColor(COLOR_WINDOWTEXT));
```

```
}
```

The GetSysColor function expects an integer value as a parameter. This value can be used to get the color of the text or one of the other important system colors, for example:

COLOR_BACKGROUND	background color of the desktop window
COLOR_WINDOW	background color of windows
COLOR_WINDOWFRAME	color of window frames
COLOR_CAPTIONTEXT	color of window caption text
COLOR_GRAYTEXT	color of the text used for disabled controls

The result of the GetSysColor function is a DWORD RGB color value. The SetSysColor function is then used to set this color. SetSysColor has the following syntax:

```
void SetSysColors (int nCount, LPINT lpWhichColors, DWORD FAR * lpNewColors);
```

nCount tells how many colors are to be changed by the function. lpWhichColors is a long pointer to an array of COLOR_... system color values containing nCount entries. lpNewColors points to a corresponding array with nCount new RGB color values that are to replace the current system colors in the lpWhichColors array.

This sets the background and foreground colors. Now, if the control is enabled, the DrawLexButton function will draw a new rectangle around the client area and fill it with the selected background brush, to display the reverse video effect when you click a LEXBUTTON:

```
// Draw rectangle for control
Rectangle(hDC, rcClient.left, rcClient.top,
            rcClient.right, rcClient.bottom);
```

The bGrayed parameter gives the current enabled/disabled status of the LEXBUTTON as obtained with the GetWindowWord(hWnd, 0) function. If this value is TRUE, the GrayString function is called in order to display the control as grayed. Otherwise, the TextOut function is used:

```
if(bGrayed)
{
// Display text in gray
GrayString(hDC, GetStockObject(BLACK_BRUSH), NULL,
                (DWORD) (LPSTR) szText, strlen(szText),
```

```
                (rcClient.right / 2) - (LOWORD(lTextExt) / 2),
                (rcClient.bottom / 2) - (HIWORD(lTextExt) / 2),
                0,0);
}
else
{
 // Display text normally
 TextOut(hDC, (rcClient.right / 2) - (LOWORD(lTextExt) / 2),
           (rcClient.bottom / 2) - (HIWORD(lTextExt) / 2),
           szText, strlen(szText));
}
```

The GrayString function is actually rather complex:

```
BOOL GrayString (HDC hDC, HBRUSH hBrush, FARPROC lpDrawString, DWORD dwData, int
nLength, int xPos, int yPos, int nWidth, int nHeight);
```

hBrush is the handle for the brush used for the gray value. If lpDrawString is NULL, then the GrayString function uses the TextOut function to output the text. In this case, dwData must be a long pointer to the output text. Otherwise, lpDrawString indicates the procedure instance address of a custom callback function for text output. dwData contains all data that must be given to this output function. nLength is the length of the output text string. If this parameter is 0, then dwData must point to a string ending in "\0" and the length is automatically determined. xPos and yPos determine the position where text output will begin. nWidth and nHeight are the width and height of the rectangle within which the text will be drawn. If this parameter is 0, then the GrayText function calculates a suitable rectangle based on the TEXTMETRICS values of the font currently selected in the display context and the length of the output string.

Instead of the GrayString function, we could have used the SetTextColor function with a GetSysColor(COLOR_GRAYTEXT) color value. The difference is that for some output devices the function result of the GetSysColor(COLOR_GRAYTEXT) can be 0, which is black, because the device cannot directly display gray scales. The GrayString function works on this type of output device as well by internally copying the gray text to a monochrome bitmap, either with TextOut or with the custom callback text output function.

Windows then executes a PatBlt function call on this bitmap using a gray pattern brush. This operation reduces the black pixels in the bitmap by about half. Then the BitBlt function is called with a certain raster operations code in order to copy the bitmap to the hDC display context of the GrayString function. The selected raster operations code takes the black pixels, in the bitmap, that arc not part of the text and changes their color to that assigned to the hBrush brush. A black brush is used here in order to obtain a true gray tone. After the text is output to the control, the original brush and pen are selected in the display context and the resources are deleted:

```
  // Release resources
  SelectObject(hDC, hOldPen);
  DeleteObject(hPen);
  SelectObject(hDC, hOldBrush);
  SetTextColor(hDC, GetSysColor(COLOR_WINDOWTEXT));
} // DrawLexButton
```

We will now see how the WM_MOUSEMOVE message is handled within the fwLexButton window function. WM_MOUSEMOVE messages are only of interest when the LEXBUTTON is selected:

```
case WM_MOUSEMOVE:        // Mouse movement
  if(!bSelected) break;
```

If the mouse movement takes place within the client area of the control, no status change is necessary:

```
  if(PtInRect(&rect, MAKEPOINT(lP)))
    break;
```

The PtInRect function returns a value of TRUE if the mouse cursor is within the defined rectangle; otherwise it returns FALSE. The MAKEPOINT macro converts the lP parameter of the message into a POINT data structure. If the mouse cursor is outside the client area of the LEXBUTTON, then the status must be changed from "selected" to "not selected". The InvalidateRect function then redraws the control:

```
bSelected = FALSE;
InvalidateRect(hWnd, &rect, FALSE);
break;
```

The LEXBUTTON status should also change when the user releases the left mouse button. The capture of all mouse messages should then be stopped with the ReleaseCapture function. After the control is redrawn, the PostMessage function sends a WM_COMMAND message, containing the ID of the clicked LEXBUTTON, to the address book dialog box:

```
case WM_LBUTTONUP:          // Left mouse button released
  bSelected = FALSE;
  ReleaseCapture();
  InvalidateRect(hWnd, NULL, FALSE);
  UpdateWindow(hWnd);
  PostMessage(GetParent(hWnd), WM_COMMAND,
              GetWindowWord(hWnd, GWW_ID), 0L);
  break;
```

When a message is received from a LEXBUTTON, the dialog function NdfAddressBookProc saves the ID of the control in the AktReg variable. After this, the DrawBook function is called, with the value TRUE, in the bCaptionOnly parameter so that only the caption of the dialog box is redrawn to show the new index letter:

```
case WM_COMMAND:
  switch (wP)
  {
    // LEXBUTTON message
    case ID_LEX:    // From A ...
    case ID_LEX+1:  case ID_LEX+2:  case ID_LEX+3:
    case ID_LEX+4:  case ID_LEX+5:  case ID_LEX+6:
    case ID_LEX+7:  case ID_LEX+8:  case ID_LEX+9:
    case ID_LEX+10: case ID_LEX+11: case ID_LEX+12:
    case ID_LEX+13: case ID_LEX+14: case ID_LEX+15:
    case ID_LEX+16: case ID_LEX+17: case ID_LEX+18:
    case ID_LEX+19: case ID_LEX+20: case ID_LEX+21:
    case ID_LEX+22: case ID_LEX+23: case ID_LEX+24:
    case ID_LEX+25: // ... to Z

      AktReg = wP;
      {
        HDC hDC;

        hDC = GetDC(hDlg);
        // Redraw caption
        DrawBook(hDlg, hDC, AktReg, TRUE);
        ReleaseDC(hDlg, hDC);
        CurIndex = Alphabet[AktReg-ID_LEX];
      }
      return TRUE;
      break;
```

7.4 Subclassing

We will look at the DrawBook function in greater detail later. For now, let's return to the WM_INITDIALOG message of the NdfAddressBookProc function. After the LEXBUTTONs are enabled or disabled according to the random number generator, the program moves on to the six edit boxes, within the dialog box, that make up the subclass. Each edit box allows the user to enter address information in notebook form, like the following:

```
Last Name, First Name
Street Address
City, State and Zip
Area Code/Phone Number
```

The edit boxes of the subclass should be related in such a way that pressing the <Enter> key does not end the processing of an edit box. Instead, the cursor will jump to the next edit box in the series. Subclassing works for these edit boxes in the following way:

We need a way to get around the window function for edit boxes of this window class. Messages sent to the edit boxes must first be processed by a special window function. This function will then decide whether the message can simply be routed to the "real" window function or if some sort of special handling is required for this message:

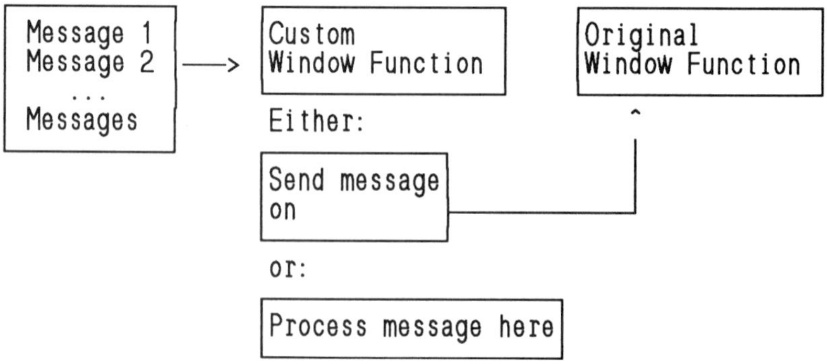

Subclassing principle

The first step in realizing this procedure in your code is to set up a procedure instance address for the new window function:

```
lpprocNewEditProc = MakeProcInstance((FARPROC) fwEditPreProcess,
                                     hInst);
if (lpprocNewEditProc == NULL)
  return FALSE;
```

Our special window function is called fwEditPreProcess. Like all window functions, it is declared as LONG FAR PASCAL and exported to the module definition file of the application. Next, we get the window handle of the first edit box. This is needed by the SetWindowLong function to save the procedure instance address of the original edit box window function and to record the new window function for the window class:

```
hEditCtl = GetDlgItem(hDlg, ID_EDADDR);
lpprocOldEditProc = (FARPROC) SetWindowLong(hEditCtl, GWL_WNDPROC,
                                   (LONG) lpprocNewEditProc);
```

The SetWindowLong function has the following syntax:

```
LONG SetWindowLong (HWND hWnd, int nOffset, DWORD dwNewValue);
```

This function replaces the value of nOffset, in the window class structure of the hWnd window, with the value of the dwNewValue parameter. There are several possible values for nOffset. GWL_EXSTYLE changes the expanded style and GWL_STYLE changes the normal style of the window. The GWL_WNDPROC value is used for subclassing. In our case, dwNewValue contains the procedure instance address of the new window function. The function result is the address of the previous window function.

After saving the original window function in the lprocOldEditProc variable, the fwEditPreProcess function is set as the window function for the remaining edit boxes:

```
for (i=1; i<6; i++)
{
 hEditCtl = GetDlgItem(hDlg, ID_EDADDR+i);
 SetWindowLong(hEditCtl, GWL_WNDPROC,
              (LONG) lpprocNewEditProc);
}
return TRUE;
```

The changes made by the subclassing procedure are cancelled if the window function receives a WM_DESTROY message:

```
case WM_DESTROY:
   /*----------------< Cancel subclassing >-------------*/

   for (i=0; i<6; i++)
   {
      SetWindowLong(GetDlgItem(hDlg, ID_EDADDR+i), GWL_WNDPROC,
                    (LONG) lpprocOldEditProc);
   }
   FreeProcInstance(lpprocNewEditProc);
   return TRUE;
   break;
```

Now we'll take a closer look at the fwEditPreProcess function. Window functions for controls don't automatically receive all types of Windows messages that concern them. For example, pressing the tab key or the cursor keys will not generate a message since these keys have special meanings within controls. Windows provides the WM_GETDLGCODE message, which enables the window functions for controls to overcome this limitation.

The wParam and lParam parameters are not used with the WM_GETDLGCODE message. Windows only cares about the value that is returned by the window function and passed to the message. Some interesting function results are:

DLGC_WANTMESSAGE	Report all keyboard input. The window function then becomes responsible for sending information on to the control
DLGC_WANTCHARS	Report WM_CHAR messages
DLGC_WANTARROWS	Report pressing of cursor keys
DLGC_WANTTAB	Report pressing the tab key

We will use the DLGC_WANTMESSAGE result to query the keyboard input:

```
switch (msg)
{
  case WM_GETDLGCODE:
    return DLGC_WANTMESSAGE; // Report every keyboard input (also CR)
```

Within the fwEditPreProcess function, we are especially interested in WM_CHAR messages:

```
case WM_CHAR:
  switch (wP)
  {
    case 0x0D: // Convert CR -> CR/LF
      SendCharToEdit(lpprocOldEditProc, hWnd, '\r', 0L);
      SendCharToEdit(lpprocOldEditProc, hWnd, '\n', 0L);
      break;
```

When a message of this type is returned, the wP parameter is examined to determine whether the <Enter> key was pressed. If it was, the SendCharToEdit function is used to send a carriage return/linefeed to the original edit box function. This sequence of events causes the cursor to move to the next line, within the edit box that has the input focus, so that the user can continue to enter data.

The SendCharToEdit function simulates the three messages that are normally created by Windows when a key is pressed:

```
CallWindowProc(lpEdit, hWnd, WM_KEYDOWN, c,lP);
CallWindowProc(lpEdit, hWnd, WM_CHAR, c,lP);
CallWindowProc(lpEdit, hWnd, WM_KEYUP, c,lP);
```

If the key pressed was not a carriage return, then the fwEditPreProcess function calls the original edit box window function using the parameters it received:

```
// All other characters routed to original window function
default:
  return(CallWindowProc(lpprocOldEditProc, hWnd, msg, wP, lP));
```

7.5 Drawing the Book

After subclassing, we come to the DrawBook function. This function is responsible for how the address book dialog box looks. DrawBook is called when the NdfAddressBookProc dialog function receives a WM_PAINT message:

```
case WM_PAINT:   // Redraw part of dialog box
  hDC = BeginPaint(hDlg, &ps);
  DrawBook(hDlg, hDC, AktReg, FALSE);
  EndPaint(hDlg, &ps);
  return TRUE;
  break;
```

The four parameters of the DrawBook function are the dialog box window handle hWnd, the accompanying display context hDC, the current index letter AktReg and the boolean variable bCaptionOnly, which indicates whether the entire address book (bCaptionOnly == FALSE) or only the caption with the index letter (bCaptionOnly == TRUE) should be repainted.

This function's first job is to calculate all important dimensions of the dialog box. The variables used for the address book can be taken from the following figure:

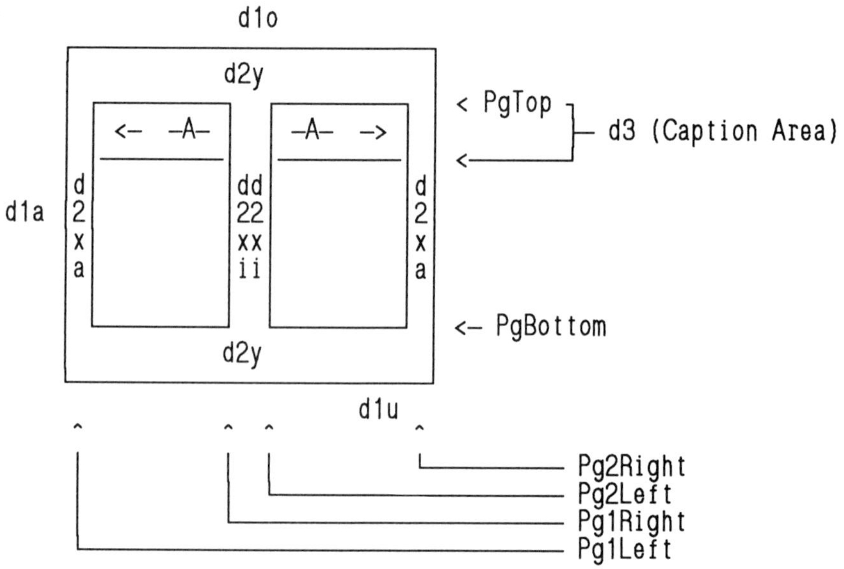

After these values are determined, the GetTextMetrics and GetClientRect functions are used to retrieve the current font parameters and the dimensions of the client area:

```
/*------------------< Dialog box dimensions >-------------------*/

GetTextMetrics(hDC, &tm);
GetClientRect(hWnd, &rcClient);
```

After this, the GetDialogBaseUnits function is called to set the dialog box base units:

```
// Get current dialog box base units
lBaseUnits = GetDialogBaseUnits();
```

The GetDialogBaseUnits function returns a LONG value. The low value is the current dialog box width unit. This is equal to 1/4 of the current width, in pixels, of one character displayed in the dialog box. Windows uses the system font as the basis for this calculation. The high part of the result is the current dialog box height unit. This is 1/8 the height of the current height, in pixels, of a letter displayed in the dialog box.

We use the base units obtained in this way to calculate the width and height, in pixels, of the address book dialog box:

```
// Calculate dialog box dimensions
BoxHeight = HIWORD(lBaseUnits/8) * CYADDRDLG;
BoxWidth  = LOWORD(lBaseUnits/4) * CXADDRDLG;
```

CYADDRDLG and CXADDRDLG are the values for the height and width of the dialog box as defined in the resource file ADDRBOOK.DLG and in the include file ADDRBOOK.H.

In the next step we set the mapping mode to MM_ANISOTROPIC. Also, the window and viewpoint origins and extensions for the display context are set:

```
/*----------------------< Set mapping mode >-----------------------*/

SetMapMode(hDC, MM_ANISOTROPIC);
SetWindowOrg(hDC, 0, 0);
SetWindowExt(hDC, BoxWidth, BoxHeight);
SetViewportOrg(hDC,0,0);
```

```
SetViewportExt(hDC,rcClient.right,rcClient.bottom);
```

And we also have to set up the paint resources:

```
/*-------------------< Create paint resources >-------------------*/

hB6Pen    = CreatePen(0,6, RGB(0, 0, 0));
hB2Pen    = CreatePen(0,2, RGB(0, 0, 0));
hB1Pen    = CreatePen(0,1, RGB(0, 0, 0));
hOldPen   = SelectObject(hDC, hB1Pen);
hOldBrush = SelectObject(hDC, GetStockObject(BLACK_BRUSH));
```

After the important address book dimensions are calculated, we jump to the CAPTION label with a goto statement if the bCaptionOnly parameter indicates that only the caption of the window should be repainted:

```
/*------------------< Calculate page dimensions >---------------------*/

mp        = BoxWidth / 2;
Pg1Left   = d1a + d2xa;
PgTop     = d1o + d2y;
Pg1Right  = mp  - d2xi;
PgBottom  = BoxHeight-d1u-d2y;
Pg2Left   = mp  + d2xi;
Pg2Right  = BoxWidth-d1a-d2xa;

if(bCaptionOnly)              // Only the captions are redrawn
   goto CAPTION;              // Uh-oh, a goto...
```

If the entire address book is to be repainted, the function begins by drawing the "binding" with the RoundRect function:

```
/*---------------------< Draw the "binding" >------------------*/

RoundRect(hDC, d1a, d1o,
               BoxWidth-d1a,BoxHeight-d1u,
               d1o,d1o);
```

Next comes the left page:

```
/*----------------------< Draw the left page >-------------------*/

SelectObject(hDC, GetStockObject(WHITE_BRUSH));
RoundRect(hDC, Pg1Left, PgTop, Pg1Right, PgBottom, d2y, d2y);
```

```
SelectObject(hDC,hB2Pen);
```

The line that separates the caption is drawn as follows:

```
/*----------------------< Dividing line for caption >----------------------*/

MoveTo(hDC, Pg1Left,  PgTop + d3);
LineTo(hDC, Pg1Right, PgTop + d3);

SelectObject(hDC, hB1Pen);
d4 = (PgBottom-PgTop-d3-d1u) / 3;
```

Next comes the lines that divide the individual edit boxes on the left page:

```
/*--------------------< Line between edit boxes 1 and 2 >-------------------*/

MoveTo(hDC, Pg1Left,     PgTop+d3+d4);
LineTo(hDC, Pg1Right-ar, PgTop+d3+d4);

/*--------------------< Line between edit boxes 2 and 3 >-------------------*/

MoveTo(hDC, Pg1Left,     PgTop+d3+2*d4);
LineTo(hDC, Pg1Right-ar, PgTop+d3+2*d4);

/*------------------< Line below the third edit box >-----------------------*/

MoveTo(hDC, Pg1Left,     PgTop+d3+3*d4);
LineTo(hDC, Pg1Right-ar, PgTop+d3+3*d4);
```

The same procedure is repeated for the right page. When both pages are drawn, the "binding rings" between the two pages can be added. This is done with four calls to the Arc GDI function:

```
/*--------------------< Draw "binder rings" >-----------------------*/

SelectObject(hDC, hB6Pen);

d5 = (PgBottom-PgTop)/4;
for(i=0;i<=3;i++)
{
   int y;

   y=PgTop+d5/2+i*d5;
   Arc(hDC, mp-d2y-ar, y,
            mp+d2y+ar, y+2*ar,
```

```
            mp+d2y+ar, y+ar,
            mp-d2y-ar, y+ar);
}
```

This completes the graphic work required to draw the address book. The paint resources can now be deleted:

```
/*--------------------< Delete paint resources >------------------*/

SelectObject(hDC, hOldBrush);
SelectObject(hDC, hOldPen);
DeleteObject(hB6Pen);
DeleteObject(hB2Pen);
DeleteObject(hB1Pen);
```

We are still missing the display of the current index letter in the caption area of both pages. We have used the goto statement to jump to the CAPTION label again. The program jumps to this label whenever the caption area has to be drawn.

```
/*---------------------------< Draw caption >--------------------------*/

CAPTION:
{
  char buf[80];
  LONG lTextLength;
  HFONT hOldFont;
```

We want to use a special font to display the index letter. The height of the letters in this font should be greater than the height of the current font tm.tmheight but less than 1.5 times this value. The variables iFontHeight and iMaxFontHeight are loaded with these values:

```
// Lower limit of caption font height is the normal font height
iFontHeight = tm.tmHeight;
// Upper limit of caption font height = 1.5 times the normal font height
iMaxFontHeight = tm.tmHeight+(tm.tmHeight/2);
```

Next, the EnumFonts function is called. This function uses a callback function to display a list of possible fonts:

```
// List fonts
lpFontProc = MakeProcInstance(CalcFont, hInst);
EnumFonts(hDC, "Courier", lpFontProc, NULL);
FreeProcInstance(lpFontProc);
```

The EnumFonts function has the following syntax:

```
int EnumFonts (HDC hDC, LPSTR lpszFontName, FARPROC lpCallback, LPSTR lpData);
```

The EnumFonts function calls the callback function, indicated by the lpCallback procedure instance address, for all fonts, with the names indicated by lpszFontName, that are available to the display context hDC. If lpszFontName is NULL, then all fonts available to the display context are listed. The lpData parameter is used to pass any other required data to the callback function.

We have used "Courier" as our font name and CalcFont as the callback function. A callback function for EnumFonts expects four parameters:

```
int FAR PASCAL CalcFont (LPLOGFONT lpLogFont, LPTEXTMETRIC lpTextMetric,
                         short nType, LPSTR lpData)
```

lpLogFont is a long pointer to a LOGFONT data structure. This structure contains 14 fields that define important characteristics of the font. Here are some of the most important fields:

short lfHeight	Average character height in logical units.
short lfWidth	Average character width in logical units.
short lfEscapement	Direction in which the character is drawn in relation to a 360 degree coordinate system. This value refers to the x axis of the first quadrant and proceeds in 1/10 degree increments in a counterclockwise direction. A value of 900 would indicate a character drawn straight up and down. It only makes sense to use this field with vector fonts, since these can be flexibly scaled and rotated.
short lfOrientation	Gives the orientation of the character relative to the x axis of a coordinate system as with lfEscapement. A value of 450 would mean that the character would be displayed at a 45 degree angle. This field is also only meaningful with vector fonts.

short lfWeight	Gives the point density, or weight, of a character. The possible values range from 0 (invisible) to 1000, but only a limited number of values have any practical use. 400 represents normal weight and 700 is "bold" text. There are additional FW_ values in increments of 100 defined in WINDOWS.H, such as FW_THIN (100), FW_MEDIUM (500) or FW_BLACK (900).
BYTE lfCharSet	Gives the character set type. Possible values are:
ANSI_CHARSET	ANSI character set
OEM_CHARSET	OEM character set
SYMBOL_CHARSET	Character set containing special symbols. The Japanese versions of Windows also have the SHIFTJIS_CHARSET Japanese character set.
BYTE lfFaceName[LF_FACESIZE]	Gives the font name. If this field is NULL, Windows takes the default font name.

lpTextMetric is a long pointer to a TEXTMETRIC data structure. We are already familiar with this structure from an earlier program. nType is a short integer value that gives more precise information on the font type. The following predefined constants can be combined:

```
nType & RASTER_FONTTYPE     TRUE  -> raster font
                            FALSE -> vector font
nType & DEVICE_FONTTYPE     TRUE  -> device font
                            FALSE -> GDI font
```

Although raster fonts can only be used in certain sizes with certain output devices, vector fonts can be scaled as desired. Device fonts are associated with a certain output device (for example, the character set available to a printer). They are not available to the GDI as .FON files. GDI fonts are character sets defined in .FON files. The GDI can use them to create output for just about any device that can be controlled at the pixel level.

lpData is a long pointer to any data that the application may have available to pass to the callback function.

Windows will call the callback function until no more fonts are available to be listed or until the function returns a value of 0.

The CalcFont function returns a value of 1 as soon as a device-dependent font is encountered:

```
if (nType & DEVICE_FONTTYPE)
  return 1;
```

Otherwise, we get a handle to the display context of the main window. Then we use the CreateFontIndirect function to convert the passed LOGFONT data structure into a logical font. A handle for this font is then stored in hNewFont:

```
else
{
  hDC     = GetDC(hwMain);
  // Create new font...
  hNewFont = CreateFontIndirect(lpLogFont);
```

We must use the Windows font mapper if we want to select this logical font in a display context. The font mapper is similar to the palette manager. It attempts to fulfill all requests as closely as possible by using the available system resources. However, it's possible that the selected font does not entirely meet your requirements. We select the font in the display context of the main window:

```
// ...and select font in display context
hOldFont = SelectObject(hDC, hNewFont);
```

The height of the font is then checked to ensure that it's the proper size. If it is, then we are satisfied with this font and we store its handle in the hCaptionFont variable and free the display context. The function will now return a value of 0 so that Windows will not list any additional fonts. If the height of the font was found to be inappropriate, then the old font is selected back in the display context. The display context is freed and the function returns a value of 1 so that other available fonts will continue to be listed:

```
// Check font size
```

```
if ((lpLogFont->lfHeight >  iFontHeight) &&
     (lpLogFont->lfHeight <= iMaxFontHeight))
{ // Yes -> assign font handle hCaptionFont
  hCaptionFont = SelectObject(hDC, hOldFont);
  ReleaseDC(hwMain, hDC);
  return 0; // Result 0 -> no more fonts
}
else         // No -> re-select old font
{
  DeleteObject(SelectObject(hDC, hOldFont));
  ReleaseDC(hwMain, hDC);
  return 1; // List additional fonts
}
```

Within the DrawBook function, the font indicated by the handle stored in hCaptionFont is selected in the display context of the address book dialog box. Then the current index letter is displayed in the center of the caption area on both pages of the address book (hopefully with an acceptable font):

```
  // Select font in display context
  hOldFont = SelectObject(hDC, hCaptionFont);

  // Display current index character in caption area
  wsprintf(buf," %c ", Alphabet[AktReg-ID_LEX]);
  lTextLength = GetTextExtent(hDC, buf, strlen(buf));

  // First page
  TextOut(hDC, Pg1Left+(Pg1Right-Pg1Left)/2-
               (LOWORD(lTextLength)/2), PgTop+1,
               buf, strlen(buf));

  // Second page
  TextOut(hDC, Pg2Left+(Pg2Right-Pg2Left)/2-
               (LOWORD(lTextLength/2)), PgTop+1,
               buf, strlen(buf));
  DeleteObject(SelectObject(hDC, hOldFont));
}
```

This completes the work of the DrawBook function. There are four functions left to discuss in the ADDRUTIL.C module: The window functions fwLeftArrow and fwRightArrow and the accompanying paint functions DrawLeftArrow and DrawRightArrow. These functions handle the arrow controls used to page through the address book.

We won't discuss the window functions in detail here because they work the same way as the fwLexButton function. Instead, we will discuss the DrawLeftArrow function. This function is responsible for painting the L_ARROW control. The function DrawRightArrow works analogously.

As with other outputs in the address book application, the arrow controls also use the MM_ANISOTROPIC mapping mode. The logical coordinate system represents the entire client area with dimensions of 120 x 80:

```
GetClientRect(hWnd,&rClientRect);
SetMapMode(hDC, MM_ANISOTROPIC);
SetWindowOrg(hDC, 0, 0);
SetWindowExt(hDC, 120, 80);
SetViewportOrg(hDC,0,0);
SetViewportExt(hDC,rClientRect.right,rClientRect.bottom);
```

We will use the Polygon function to display the arrows themselves. The required points are stored in the POINT array ArrowPt. The arrow is surrounded by an imaginary rectangle that defines its boundaries:

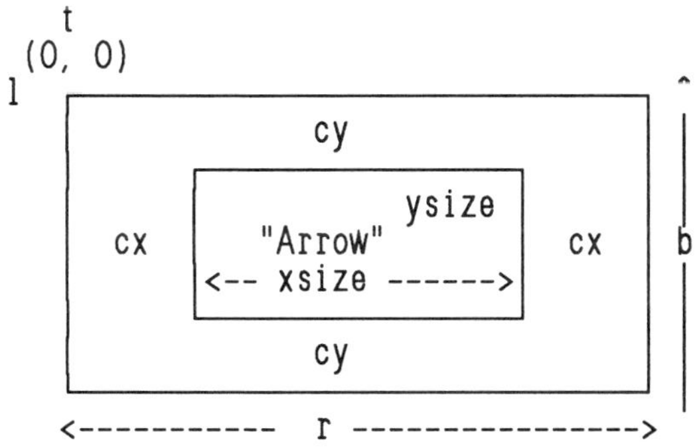


```
ArrowPt[0].x = cx+xsize;            // Left arrow
ArrowPt[0].y = cy+ysize/3*2;
ArrowPt[1].x = cx+xsize/3;
ArrowPt[1].y = cy+ysize/3*2;
ArrowPt[2].x = cx+xsize/3;
ArrowPt[2].y = cy+ysize;
ArrowPt[3].x = cx;
ArrowPt[3].y = cy+ysize/2;
ArrowPt[4].x = cx+xsize/3;
ArrowPt[4].y = cy;
```

```
ArrowPt[5].x = cx+xsize/3;
ArrowPt[5].y = cy+ysize/3;
ArrowPt[6].x = cx+xsize;
ArrowPt[6].y = cy+ysize/3;
```

The mechanism for enabling and disabling the control works the same as with the LEXBUTTON control.

One final word on the address book application. We have seen that Windows allows you to use custom controls and subclassing of window functions in a practically unlimited fashion to create different kinds of applications. As a Windows developer, however, you must remember that users of Windows applications have come to expect things to look and behave a certain way. Carefully consider any diversions from the way "normal" Windows applications behave. This is important so that you can maintain the standard "look and feel" of Windows applications that currently exists in software from many different manufacturers.

Here is a good rule of thumb: You have done a good job in maintaining the Windows standard if a user familiar with other Windows software can use your application once and feel comfortable with how the interface looks and works.

7.6 Source Code: ADDRBOOK.EXE

ADDRBOOK.H include file

```
/* Stringtable defines */

#define IDS_APPLNAME        1

/* Application icon */

#define IDDIALOGICON    50

/* File menu */

#define MI_QUIT         100
#define MI_ABOUT        101

/* Dialog Boxes menu */

#define MI_ADDRBOOK     110

/* Dialog box control IDs */

#define ID_LEX       2000   /* First LEXBUTTON "A" */
#define ID_LEFT      3000   /* Left arrow          */
#define ID_RIGHT     3001   /* Right arrow         */
#define ID_EDADDR    4000   /* First Edit box      */

/*-----------------------< General  defines >--------------------------*/

#define MAXCHARS         255    /* Number of characters                */
#define MAXADDREDIT      6      /* Number of edit fields in address book */
#define MAXADDREDLENGTH 26      /* Max. num. of characters per Edit line */
#define MAXADDREDLINES   4      /* Max. num. of lines per Edit box       */
#define MAXFIELDLENGTH  30      /* Field length */

/*------------< DEFINES for the Address Book dialog box >--------------*/

#define XADDRDLG  20            /* X-position Address dialog box        */
#define YADDRDLG  30            /* Y-position Address dialog box        */
#define CXADDRDLG 270           /* X-extension Address dialog box       */
#define CYADDRDLG 180           /* Y-extension Address dialog box       */
#define XLLEXADDR 7             /* X-position of left Lexbuttons        */
#define XRLEXADDR 253           /* X-position of right Lexbuttons       */
#define CXLEXADDR 10            /* X-extensions of Lexbuttons           */
#define CYLEXADDR 10            /* Y-extensions of Lexbuttons           */
```

```
#define XLEFTARROW 18          /* X-position of left arrow              */
#define XRIGHTARROW 238        /* X-position of right arrow             */
#define YLRARROW  6            /* Y-positions of left & right arrows    */
#define CXLRARROW 14           /* X-extension of arrows                 */
#define CYLRARROW 10           /* Y-extension of arrows                 */
#define XLNEWLEX 127           /* X-position of left x-Lexbuttons       */
#define XRNEWLEX 138           /* X-position of right x-Lexbuttons      */
#define CXNEWLEX 6             /* X-extension of x-Lexbuttons           */
#define CYNEWLEX 10            /* Y-extension of x-Lexbuttons           */
#define XLEDITADDR 19          /* X-position of left Edit boxes         */
#define XREDITADDR 144         /* X-position of right Edit boxes        */
#define CXEDITADDR 108         /* X-extensions of Edit boxes            */
#define CYEDITADDR 36          /* Y-extensions of Edit boxes            */

/*--------------------< Functions  in addrutil.c >----------------------*/

LONG FAR PASCAL fwLexButton (HWND, WORD, WORD, LONG);
LONG FAR PASCAL fwLeftArrow (HWND, WORD, WORD, LONG);
LONG FAR PASCAL fwRightArrow (HWND, WORD, WORD, LONG);
LONG FAR PASCAL fwEditPreProcess(HWND, WORD, WORD, LONG);
BOOL FAR PASCAL fdAdressBook (HWND, WORD, WORD, LONG);
BOOL RegisterBookCtrl (HANDLE);
```

ADDRBOOK.RC resource file

```
#include <windows.h>
#include "addrbook.h"

IDDIALOGICON ICON addrbook.ico   ; Application icon

rcinclude addrbook.dlg           ; Contains dialog box definitions

STRINGTABLE
BEGIN
  IDS_APPLNAME,       "Address Book"  ; Name of application
END

MainMenu MENU
BEGIN
  POPUP "&File"
  BEGIN
    MENUITEM "E&xit",        MI_QUIT
    MENUITEM SEPARATOR
    MENUITEM "A&bout Address Book...", MI_ABOUT
  END
  POPUP "&Dialog Boxes"
  BEGIN
```

```
    MENUITEM "&Address Book...",          MI_ADDRBOOK
  END
END ; MainMenu
```

ADDRBOOK.DLG dialog box file

```
ADDRESSBOOK DIALOG LOADONCALL MOVEABLE DISCARDABLE 20, 30, 270, 180
CAPTION "Address Book"
STYLE WS_BORDER | WS_CAPTION | WS_DLGFRAME | WS_SYSMENU | WS_VISIBLE |
DS_LOCALEDIT | DS_MODALFRAME | WS_POPUP
BEGIN
    CONTROL "", 3000, "l_arrow", 0 | WS_CHILD, 18, 10, 14, 10
    CONTROL "", 3001, "r_arrow", 0 | WS_CHILD, 238, 10, 14, 10
    CONTROL "A", 2000, "lexbutton", 0 | WS_CHILD, 7, 25, 10, 10
    CONTROL "B", 2001, "lexbutton", 0 | WS_CHILD, 7, 37, 10, 10
    CONTROL "C", 2002, "lexbutton", 0 | WS_CHILD, 7, 48, 10, 10
    CONTROL "D", 2003, "lexbutton", 0 | WS_CHILD, 7, 59, 10, 10
    CONTROL "E", 2004, "lexbutton", 0 | WS_CHILD, 7, 70, 10, 10
    CONTROL "F", 2005, "lexbutton", 0 | WS_CHILD, 7, 81, 10, 10
    CONTROL "G", 2006, "lexbutton", 0 | WS_CHILD, 7, 92, 10, 10
    CONTROL "H", 2007, "lexbutton", 0 | WS_CHILD, 7, 103, 10, 10
    CONTROL "I", 2008, "lexbutton", 0 | WS_CHILD, 7, 114, 10, 10
    CONTROL "J", 2009, "lexbutton", 0 | WS_CHILD, 7, 125, 10, 10
    CONTROL "K", 2010, "lexbutton", 0 | WS_CHILD, 7, 136, 10, 10
    CONTROL "L", 2011, "lexbutton", 0 | WS_CHILD, 7, 147, 10, 10
    CONTROL "M", 2012, "lexbutton", 0 | WS_CHILD, 7, 158, 10, 10
    CONTROL "N", 2013, "lexbutton", 0 | WS_CHILD, 253, 25, 10, 10
    CONTROL "O", 2014, "lexbutton", 0 | WS_CHILD, 253, 37, 10, 10
    CONTROL "P", 2015, "lexbutton", 0 | WS_CHILD, 253, 48, 10, 10
    CONTROL "Q", 2016, "lexbutton", 0 | WS_CHILD, 253, 59, 10, 10
    CONTROL "R", 2017, "lexbutton", 0 | WS_CHILD, 253, 70, 10, 10
    CONTROL "S", 2018, "lexbutton", 0 | WS_CHILD, 253, 81, 10, 10
    CONTROL "T", 2019, "lexbutton", 0 | WS_CHILD, 253, 92, 10, 10
    CONTROL "U", 2020, "lexbutton", 0 | WS_CHILD, 253, 103, 10, 10
    CONTROL "V", 2021, "lexbutton", 0 | WS_CHILD, 253, 114, 10, 10
    CONTROL "W", 2022, "lexbutton", 0 | WS_CHILD, 253, 125, 10, 10
    CONTROL "X", 2023, "lexbutton", 0 | WS_CHILD, 253, 136, 10, 10
    CONTROL "Y", 2024, "lexbutton", 0 | WS_CHILD, 253, 147, 10, 10
    CONTROL "Z", 2025, "lexbutton", 0 | WS_CHILD, 253, 158, 10, 10
    CONTROL "", 4000, "edit", ES_LEFT | ES_MULTILINE | WS_TABSTOP | WS_CHILD, 19,
 28, 108, 36
    CONTROL "", 4001, "edit", ES_LEFT | ES_MULTILINE | WS_TABSTOP | WS_CHILD, 19,
 75, 108, 36
    CONTROL "", 4002, "edit", ES_LEFT | ES_MULTILINE | WS_TABSTOP | WS_CHILD, 19,
 120, 108, 36
    CONTROL "", 4003, "edit", ES_LEFT | ES_MULTILINE | WS_TABSTOP | WS_CHILD,
 144, 28, 108, 36
```

```
    CONTROL "", 4004, "edit", ES_LEFT | ES_MULTILINE | WS_TABSTOP | WS_CHILD,
144, 75, 108, 36
    CONTROL "", 4005, "edit", ES_LEFT | ES_MULTILINE | WS_TABSTOP | WS_CHILD,
144, 120, 108, 36
END

ABOUTDLG DIALOG LOADONCALL MOVEABLE DISCARDABLE 72, 15, 157, 104
CAPTION "About AddrBook"
STYLE WS_BORDER | WS_CAPTION | WS_DLGFRAME | WS_SYSMENU | DS_MODALFRAME |
WS_POPUP
BEGIN
    CONTROL "AddrBook", -1, "static", SS_CENTER | WS_CHILD, 56, 5, 41, 10
    CONTROL "Version 1.00", -1, "static", SS_CENTER | WS_CHILD, 46, 20, 62, 10
    CONTROL "Copyright  1990", -1, "static", SS_CENTER | WS_CHILD, 36, 35, 86, 11
    CONTROL "Abacus", -1, "static", SS_CENTER | WS_CHILD, 40, 50, 79, 11
    CONTROL "OK", 1, "button", BS_DEFPUSHBUTTON | WS_TABSTOP | WS_CHILD, 67, 86,
24, 12
    CONTROL "", -1, "static", SS_ICON | WS_CHILD, 13, 25, 16, 27
    CONTROL "by D.Honekamp && P. Wilken", 106, "static", SS_CENTER | WS_CHILD,
30, 66, 102, 11
END
```

ADDRBOOK.DEF module definition file

```
NAME          ADDRBOOK

DESCRIPTION   'Address Book Application'

EXETYPE       WINDOWS

CODE           PRELOAD MOVEABLE DISCARDABLE
DATA           PRELOAD MOVEABLE MULTIPLE

HEAPSIZE      8000
STACKSIZE     8000

EXPORTS
              MainWndProc
              MdfAboutProc
              NdfAddressBookProc
              fwLexButton
              fwEditPreProcess
              fwRightArrow
              fwLeftArrow
              CalcFont
```

ADDRBOOK.MAK MAKE file

```
Model  = S
Warn   = 3
Linker = link

all: addrbook.exe

addrbook.res: addrbook.h addrbook.rc addrbook.dlg
  rc -r addrbook.rc

addrbook.obj: addrbook.h addrbook.c
  cl -c -A$(Model) -W$(Warn) -Gsw -Zpe -Os addrbook.c

addrutil.obj: addrbook.h addrutil.c
  cl -c -A$(Model) -W$(Warn) -Gsw -Zpe -Os addrutil.c

addrbook.exe: addrbook.obj addrutil.obj addrbook.def addrbook.res
  $(Linker) /NOD /al:16
addrbook+addrutil,addrbook.exe,,libw+$(Model)libcew,addrbook.def
  rc addrbook.res
```

ADDRBOOK.C source code

```
/***************************************************************************
 ADDRBOOK.C
 ==========

 This program generates a user-defined dialog box. This box features many
 custom controls as well as edit boxes. The dialog box appears as a
 three-ring binder, with index characters running along the left and right
 margins of the address book. This effect was created by instructing the
 application to draw the dialog box and control it using unused areas of
 memory.
 The six edit boxes in this application are not Windows standard: They are
 generated using subclassing. Pressing <Enter> moves the cursor to the next
 line of text.
 ***************************************************************************/

/* -------------------------< Include files >--------------------------- */

#include <windows.h>
#include <stdio.h>
#include <string.h>
#include <stdlib.h>
#include <io.h>
```

```
#include "addrbook.h"

/* -----------------------< Global variables >--------------------------- */

HANDLE        hInst;                        // Instance of application
HWND          hwMain,                       // Main window
              hDlgModeless = NULL,          // Modeless dialog box handle
              hDlgModal = NULL;             // Modal dialog box handle
HMENU         hMainMenu;                    // Main menu handle
char          szApplName[MAXFIELDLENGTH];   // Application name
BOOL          bDlgModeless = FALSE;         // Marker for modeless
                                            // dialog box
FARPROC       lpfnModal,                    // Used by modal dialog boxes
              lpfnModeless;                 // Used by modeless dialog boxes

/* ----------------------< Function prototypes >------------------------- */

extern BOOL FAR PASCAL NdfAddressBookProc (HWND, unsigned, WORD, LONG);
extern BOOL RegisterBookCtrl (HANDLE);

LONG FAR PASCAL MainWndProc   (HWND, unsigned, WORD, LONG);
BOOL FAR PASCAL MdfAboutProc  (HWND, unsigned, WORD, LONG);
int  InitFirstInstance (HANDLE ,HANDLE, int);
void PaintAddressBook (HWND);

/************************************************************************
 W i n M a i n ()
 ================

 The WinMain function is the main function for every Windows program. WinMain
 is the equivalent of the main() function found in standard C programs, and
 represents the "point of entry" for program execution.

 Parameters:

   HANDLE hInstance:     Current instance handle of the application.
   HANDLE hPrevInstance: Previous instance handle of the application. NULL
                         if the current instance is the first instance.
   LPSTR  lpszCmdLine:   Long pointer to the string placed after the program
                         name during program execution.
   int    nCmdShow:      Parameter which specifies the application window's
                         appearance when the program starts.

 Return values:

   int:                  The wParam parameter for the last message received.
 ***********************************************************************/
```

```
int PASCAL WinMain (HANDLE hInstance,  HANDLE hPrevInstance,
                    LPSTR lpszCmdLine, int nCmdShow)
{
  MSG   msg;                        // Message variable

  if (!hPrevInstance)               // Initialization of first instance
  {
    if (!InitFirstInstance(hInstance, hPrevInstance, nCmdShow))
      return NULL;

  }
  else                              // No additional instances allowed
  {
    return NULL;
  }

  hInst  = hInstance;               // Declaration of global
                                    // instance variable

  hwMain = CreateWindow(szApplName,              // Window class name
                        szApplName,              // Window caption
                        WS_OVERLAPPEDWINDOW |    // Overlapped window
                        WS_VSCROLL,              // with scroll bars
                        CW_USEDEFAULT,           // X-position (default)
                        CW_USEDEFAULT,           // Y-position (default)
                        CW_USEDEFAULT,           // Initial X-size (default)
                        CW_USEDEFAULT,           // Initial Y-size (default)
                        NULL,                    // No parent window
                        LoadMenu(hInstance, "MainMenu"),
                        hInstance,               // Instance of application
                        NULL);                   // No creation parameters

   if (!hwMain)
     return NULL;

  /* ----------------------< Initialization tasks >---------------------- */

  // Get handle to main menu
  hMainMenu = GetMenu(hwMain);
  CheckMenuItem(hMainMenu, MI_ADDRBOOK, MF_UNCHECKED);

  /* ---------------------< Display  main  window >---------------------- */

   ShowWindow(hwMain, nCmdShow);                 // Make window visible
   UpdateWindow(hwMain);                         // Update window

  /* ------------------------< Message  loop >-------------------------- */
```

```
  while (GetMessage(&msg, NULL, 0, 0))          // Message reading
  {
    if (!(hDlgModeless != NULL &&               // Dialog box active?
         IsDialogMessage(hDlgModeless, &msg)))  // Dialog box message?
    {
      TranslateMessage(&msg);                   // Message translation
      DispatchMessage(&msg);                    // Message -> Windows
    }
  }
  return (msg.wParam);                          // End application
} // WinMain

/*************************************************************************
 I n i t F i r s t I n s t a n c e ()
 ====================================

 This function initializes the first instance of "Address Book" application.

 Parameters:

   HANDLE hInstance:     Current instance handle of the application.
   HANDLE hPrevInstance: Previous instance handle of the application. NULL
                         if the current instance is the first instance.
   int    nCmdShow:      Parameter which specifies the application window's
                         appearance when the program starts.

 Return values:

   int                   NULL if the window classes register.
                         Otherwise, a value other than NULL.
 *************************************************************************/

int InitFirstInstance (HANDLE hInstance, HANDLE hPrevInstance, int nCmdShow)
{
  WNDCLASS MainWndClass;                        // Main window class

  // Load application name from the resource file
  LoadString(hInstance, IDS_APPLNAME, (LPSTR)szApplName, 20);

  // Specify window class information
  MainWndClass.lpszClassName = szApplName;                   // Window class
  MainWndClass.hInstance     = hInstance;                    // Instance
  MainWndClass.lpfnWndProc   = MainWndProc;                  // Window function
  MainWndClass.style         = CS_HREDRAW | CS_VREDRAW;
  MainWndClass.lpszMenuName  = (LPSTR) NULL;                 // No menu
  MainWndClass.hCursor       = LoadCursor(NULL, IDC_ARROW);  // Mouse cursor
```

```
  MainWndClass.hIcon          = LoadIcon(hInstance,
MAKEINTRESOURCE(IDDIALOGICON));
  MainWndClass.hbrBackground = GetStockObject(WHITE_BRUSH); // White background
  MainWndClass.cbClsExtra    = 0;                           // No extra bytes
  MainWndClass.cbWndExtra    = 0;                           // No extra bytes

  // Registering the "Address Book" window class
  RegisterClass(&MainWndClass);

  // Registering a custom window class
  return(RegisterBookCtrl(hInstance));
} // InitFirstInstance

/****************************************************************************
 M a i n W n d P r o c ()
 =======================

 This function acts as the main window function. All messages are sent to
 this window.

 Parameters:

   HWND     hWnd:     Window handle.
   unsigned msg:      Message type.
   WORD     wP:       Message-dependent 16 bit value
   LONG     lP:       Message-dependent 32 bit value

 Return values:

   LONG               0L if the window function has sent the message.
                      Otherwise, the return value from the DefWindowProc
                      default window function.
 ****************************************************************************/

LONG FAR PASCAL MainWndProc (HWND hWnd, unsigned msg, WORD wP, LONG lP)
{
   int       nResult;            // Return value for DialogBox function

   switch (msg)
   {
     case WM_DESTROY:
       PostQuitMessage(0);       // Send WM_QUIT if window is destroyed
       break;

     case WM_COMMAND:            // Messages from menu bar
       switch (wP)
       {
         case MI_QUIT:           // End program
```

```
          PostMessage(hwMain, WM_SYSCOMMAND, SC_CLOSE, 0L);
          break;

        case MI_ABOUT:            // Call "About Address Book" dialog box
          lpfnModal = MakeProcInstance(MdfAboutProc, hInst);
          nResult = DialogBox(hInst, "ABOUTDLG", hwMain, lpfnModal);
          FreeProcInstance(lpfnModal);
          break;

        case MI_ADDRBOOK:         // Call the "Address Book" dialog box
          if (!bDlgModeless)      // Dialog box must be displayed
      {
          lpfnModeless = MakeProcInstance(NdfAddressBookProc, hInst);
          hDlgModeless = CreateDialog(hInst, "ADDRESSBOOK", hwMain,
lpfnModeless);
          if (hDlgModeless)
          {
            ShowWindow(hDlgModeless, SW_SHOWNORMAL);
            bDlgModeless = TRUE;
            // Check menu entry
            CheckMenuItem(hMainMenu, MI_ADDRBOOK, MF_CHECKED);
          }
          else
           MessageBox(GetFocus(), "Address Book dialog box could not be opened",
                      szApplName, MB_OK | MB_ICONEXCLAMATION);
        }
        else                    // Dialog box must be destroyed
        {
          DestroyWindow(hDlgModeless);
          FreeProcInstance(lpfnModeless);
          bDlgModeless = FALSE;
          hDlgModeless = NULL;
          // Remove checkmark
          CheckMenuItem(hMainMenu, MI_ADDRBOOK, MF_UNCHECKED);
        }
        break;

       default:
         break;
      }
      break;

    case WM_PAINT:              // Client area update needed
      PaintAddressBook(hWnd);
      break;

    default: // Pass other messages to default window function
      return (DefWindowProc(hWnd, msg, wP, lP));
```

```
      break;
  }
  return 0L;
} // MainWndProc

/*************************************************************************
 M d f A b o u t P r o c ()
 ==========================

 This function processes messages for the "About Address Book" dialog box.

 Parameters:

   HWND      hDlg:     Dialog box handle.
   unsigned msg:       Message type.
   WORD      wP:       Message-dependent 16 bit value
   LONG      lP:       Message-dependent 32 bit value

 Return values:

   BOOL                TRUE if the dialog function contains the given message.
                       Otherwise, FALSE.
 *************************************************************************/

BOOL FAR PASCAL MdfAboutProc (HWND hDlg, unsigned msg, WORD wP, LONG lP)
{
  switch (msg)
  {
    case WM_INITDIALOG:         // Dialog box display message
      return TRUE;              // Do not execute initialization
      break;

    case WM_COMMAND:            // Dialog box control message
      switch (wP)
      {
      case IDOK:                // Click on OK button
        EndDialog(hDlg, TRUE);
        return TRUE;
        break;

      default:                  // Other messages
        return FALSE;
        break;
      }
      break;

    case WM_SYSCOMMAND:         // Message from dialog box system menu
      switch (wP)
```

```
      {
      // ALT+F4, double-click system menu or select "Close" from system
      // menu to select

      case SC_CLOSE:
        EndDialog(hDlg, TRUE);
        return TRUE;
        break;

      default:                    // Other system menu messages
        return FALSE;
        break;
      }
      break;

    default:                      // Other messages
      return FALSE;
      break;
  }
} // MdfAboutProc

/****************************************************************************
 P a i n t A d d r e s s B o o k ()
 ==================================

 This function is needed to repaint the main window client area.

 Parameters:

   HWND    hWnd:    Window handle.

 Return values:     None.
 ****************************************************************************/

void PaintAddressBook (HWND hWnd)
{
  PAINTSTRUCT ps;                // Client area information
  HDC         hDC;               // Display context handle

  hDC = BeginPaint(hWnd, &ps); // Get main window display context

  // Client area output eventually appears in main window from here

  EndPaint(hWnd, &ps);           // Release display context
} // PaintAddressBook
```

ADDRUTIL.C source code

```
/************************************************************************

 A D D R U T I L . C
 ===================

 This source contains all the functions needed by the "Address Book"
 dialog box. It creates custom controls and adds graphic elements to the
 dialog box.
************************************************************************/

/*-----------------------------< Includes>----------------------------------*/

#include <windows.h>
#include <stdlib.h>
#include <string.h>
#include <time.h>
#include "addrbook.h"

/*---------------------------< External variables >-----------------------*/

extern HWND       hwMain;              // Main window handle
extern HANDLE     hInst;               // Instance handle
extern char       szApplName[];        // Program name

/*-------------------------< Global variables >---------------------------*/

char    Alphabet[] = "ABCDEFGHIJKLMNOPQRSTUVWXYZ";
char    CurIndex;                      // Current starting character
int     iFontHeight,                   // Font size for index characters
        iMaxFontHeight;                // Maximum font size
HFONT   hCaptionFont,                  // Index character fonts
        hOldFont;
FARPROC lpprocNewEditProc,             // For edit box subclassing
        lpprocOldEditProc;
HANDLE  hEditCtl;                      // Edit box handle
BOOL    bNewPage = FALSE;              // Data record for new page

/*-------------------------< Function prototypes >------------------------*/

void DrawLexButton (HWND, HDC, BOOL, BOOL, PSTR);
void DrawBook (HWND, HDC, int, BOOL);
void SendCharToEdit (FARPROC, HWND, char, LONG);
void DrawLeftArrow (HWND, HDC, BOOL);
void DrawRightArrow (HWND, HDC, BOOL);
LONG FAR PASCAL fwLexButton(HWND, WORD, WORD, LONG);
```

```
LONG FAR PASCAL fwEditPreProcess(HWND, WORD, WORD, LONG);
LONG FAR PASCAL fwRightArrow (HWND, WORD, WORD, LONG);
LONG FAR PASCAL fwLeftArrow (HWND, WORD, WORD, LONG);
BOOL FAR PASCAL MdfNewIndex(HWND, WORD, WORD, LONG);
BOOL FAR PASCAL NdfAddressBookProc (HWND, WORD, WORD, LONG);
int  FAR PASCAL CalcFont (LPLOGFONT, LPTEXTMETRIC, short, LPSTR);
BOOL RegisterBookCtrl (HANDLE);

/*****************************************************************************
 C a l c F o n t ()
 ==================

 This function acts as the callback function for the EnumFonts function. It
 checks available fonts until it finds a font of the proper height (global
 variables iFontHeight and iMaxFontHeight provide upper and lower limits).

 Parameters:

   LPLOGFONT      lpLogFont      Long pointer to a LOGFONT data structure
   LPTEXTMETRICS  lpTextMetrics  Long pointer to a TEXTMETRIC data structure
   short          nType          Gives type of font for search
   LPSTR          lpData         Long pointer to data eventually passed by
                                 the EnumFonts function

 Return values:

   int            0 if the desired font is found. Otherwise, 1.
 *****************************************************************************/

int FAR PASCAL CalcFont (LPLOGFONT lpLogFont, LPTEXTMETRIC lpTextMetric,
                         short nType, LPSTR lpData)
{
   HFONT  hNewFont;
   HDC    hDC;

   if (nType & DEVICE_FONTTYPE)
     return 1;
   else
   {
     hDC    = GetDC(hwMain);
     // Create new font...
     hNewFont = CreateFontIndirect(lpLogFont);

     // ... and select font in display context
     hOldFont = SelectObject(hDC, hNewFont);

     // Check font size
     if ((lpLogFont->lfHeight >  iFontHeight) &&
```

```
      (lpLogFont->lfHeight <= iMaxFontHeight))
    { // Yes -> assign font handle hCaptionFont
      hCaptionFont = SelectObject(hDC, hOldFont);
      ReleaseDC(hwMain, hDC);
      return 0; // Result 0 -> no more fonts
    }
    else        // No -> re-select old font
    {
      DeleteObject(SelectObject(hDC, hOldFont));
      ReleaseDC(hwMain, hDC);
      return 1; // List additional fonts
    }
  }
} // CalcFont

/**************************************************************************
 D r a w L e x B u t t o n ()
 ============================

 This function processes the WM_PAINT message for the custom control
 "LEXBUTTON".
                                      -----
                                      | A |
                                      -----
 Parameters:
  HWND       hWnd       Window handle
  HDC        hDC        Display context handle
  BOOL       bGrayed    TRUE when grayed
  BOOL       bSelected  TRUE when selectable by mouse - can appear inverse
  PSTR       szText     Text that should be placed in box

 Return values:         None.
**************************************************************************/

void DrawLexButton(HWND hWnd, HDC hDC, BOOL bGrayed, BOOL bSelected, PSTR szText)
{
  RECT    rcClient;          // Client area rectangle
  HBRUSH  hOldBrush;         // Brush handle
  HPEN    hOldPen,           // Pen handles
          hPen;
  LONG    lTextExt;          // For GetTextExtent function

  // Create pen
  hPen = CreatePen(PS_SOLID, 2, RGB(0, 0, 0));
  hOldPen = SelectObject(hDC,hPen);

  // Set dimensions
  GetClientRect(hWnd, &rcClient);
```

```
  // Draw rectangle for control
  Rectangle(hDC, rcClient.left, rcClient.top,
            rcClient.right, rcClient.bottom);

  // Center text in control
  lTextExt = GetTextExtent(hDC, szText, strlen(szText));
  if(bSelected)     // The control has been selected
  {
    hOldBrush = SelectObject(hDC, GetStockObject(BLACK_BRUSH));
    SetTextColor(hDC, RGB(255,255,255));
    SetBkColor(hDC, RGB(0,0,0));
  }
  else
  {
    hOldBrush = SelectObject(hDC, GetStockObject(WHITE_BRUSH));
    SetTextColor(hDC, GetSysColor(COLOR_WINDOWTEXT));
  }
  // Draw rectangle as control
  Rectangle(hDC, rcClient.left, rcClient.top,
            rcClient.right, rcClient.bottom);
  if(bGrayed)
  {
    // Display text in gray
    GrayString(hDC, GetStockObject(BLACK_BRUSH), NULL,
                    (DWORD) (LPSTR) szText, strlen(szText),
                    (rcClient.right / 2) - (LOWORD(lTextExt) / 2),
                    (rcClient.bottom / 2) - (HIWORD(lTextExt) / 2),
                    0,0);
  }
  else
  {
   // Display text normally
   TextOut(hDC, (rcClient.right / 2) - (LOWORD(lTextExt) / 2),
                (rcClient.bottom / 2) - (HIWORD(lTextExt) / 2),
                szText, strlen(szText));
  }

  // Release resources
  SelectObject(hDC, hOldPen);
  DeleteObject(hPen);
  SelectObject(hDC, hOldBrush);
  SetTextColor(hDC, GetSysColor(COLOR_WINDOWTEXT));
} // DrawLexButton

/************************************************************************
 f w L e x B u t t o n ()
 ========================
```

```
This function represents the window function for user-defined "LEXBUTTON"
control elements. This type of control generates a rectangle similar to a
check box, which contains a centered character. This character appears as
either grayed or selectable, depending on its status. If it is selectable,
the user can click on it as he or she would click on a push button.

Parameters:

 Standard message structure

Return values:

  LONG          0L if the window function has processed the message.
                Otherwise, the return value from the DefWindowProc
                default window function.
***************************************************************************/

LONG FAR PASCAL fwLexButton(HWND hWnd, WORD msg, WORD wP, LONG lP)
{
   static RECT rect;
   static BOOL bSelected;

   switch(msg)
   {
     case WM_CREATE:
      bSelected = FALSE;
     break;

     case WM_ENABLE:         // wP == NULL? disable button, otherwise enable
       SetWindowWord(hWnd, 0, wP==NULL ? TRUE : FALSE);  // Save status
       InvalidateRect(hWnd, NULL, FALSE);
     break;

     case WM_MOUSEMOVE:      // Mouse movement
       if(!bSelected) break;
       if (PtInRect(&rect, MAKEPOINT(lP)))
       break;
       bSelected = FALSE;
       InvalidateRect(hWnd, &rect, FALSE);
       break;

     case WM_LBUTTONDOWN:    // Left mouse button pressed
       bSelected = TRUE;
       SetCapture(hWnd);
       GetClientRect(hWnd, &rect);
       InvalidateRect(hWnd, NULL, FALSE);
       break;
```

```
      case WM_LBUTTONUP:      // Left mouse button released
        bSelected = FALSE;
        ReleaseCapture();
        InvalidateRect(hWnd, NULL, FALSE);
        UpdateWindow(hWnd);
        PostMessage(GetParent(hWnd), WM_COMMAND,
                    GetWindowWord(hWnd, GWW_ID), 0L);
        break;

      case WM_PAINT:            // Repaint needed
        {
        HDC          hDC;
        PAINTSTRUCT  ps;
        int          iTxtLen;
        HANDLE       hWinTxt;
        PSTR         pWinTxt;

        hDC = BeginPaint(hWnd, &ps);

        /*-- < Read the text defined as control in DLG file >---*/
        iTxtLen = GetWindowTextLength(hWnd);
        hWinTxt = LocalAlloc(LMEM_MOVEABLE, iTxtLen+1);
        pWinTxt= LocalLock(hWinTxt);
        GetWindowText(hWnd, pWinTxt,iTxtLen+1);

        /*----------------< Draw the control >--------------------*/
        DrawLexButton(hWnd, hDC, GetWindowWord(hWnd, 0), bSelected, pWinTxt);
        LocalUnlock(hWinTxt);
        LocalFree(hWinTxt);
        EndPaint(hWnd, &ps);
        }
        break;

      default: // More trouble with the default function...
       return DefWindowProc(hWnd, msg, wP, lP);
      break;
    }
    return 0L;
} // fwLexButton

/***************************************************************************
 D r a w B o o k ()
 ==================

 This function processes the WM_PAINT message for the "Address Book" dialog
 box. It draws the necessary graphic elements in the box's client area.

                       dlo
```

```
     +---------------------------------+
     |              d2y                |
     |   +----------+  +----------+    |    <-- PgTop -+
     |   | <-   -A- |  | -A-   -> |    |               |-- d3 (Caption Area)
     |   |----------|  |----------|    |    -----------+
     | d |          |dd|          | d  |
d1a  | 2 |          |22|          | 2  |
     | x |          |xx|          | x  |
     | a |          |ii|          | a  |
     |   |          |  |          |    |
     |   |          |  |          |    |
     |   +----------+  +----------+    |    <-- PgBottom
     |              d2y                |
     +---------------------------------+
                   d1u
       ^          ^  ^          ^
       |          |  |          |__________ Pg2Right
       |          |  |______________________ Pg2Left
       |          |_________________________ Pg1Right
       |____________________________________ Pg1Left

 Parameters:

  HWND  hWnd          Window handle
  HDC   hDC           Display context handle
  int   AktReg        ID of the last LexButton clicked
  BOOL  bCaptionOnly  TRUE if only the caption should be redrawn.
                      FALSE if the entire box should be redrawn.

 Return values:       None.
*************************************************************************/

void DrawBook(HWND hWnd, HDC hDC, int AktReg, BOOL bCaptionOnly)
{
  TEXTMETRIC tm;
  RECT    rcClient;
  HBRUSH  hOldBrush;
  HPEN    hOldPen, hB1Pen, hB2Pen, hB6Pen;
  LONG    lBaseUnits;
  FARPROC lpFontProc;

  int     BoxHeight,  // Window height
          BoxWidth,   // Window width
          ar =   8,   // Radius for arc

       /*----< Spacing between window border and "binder cover" >---- */

       d1o =  5,    // Top
```

```
      d1a =  25,  // Horizontal
      d1u =  5,   // Bottom

      /*-----< Spacing between "binder cover" and page margin >------- */

      d2y  =  5,  // Vertical
      d2xi =  5,  // Horizontal (inner)
      d2xa = 10,  // Horizontal (outer)
      d3  =  15,  // Spacing between top of page and separator
      mp,         // Center of window
      d4,         // Spacing between edit box separation lines
      d5,i,       // Spacing between rings
      d7 = 6,
      PgTop,   PgBottom,    // Page top and page bottom
      Pg1Left, Pg1Right,    // Left and right margins (left page)
      Pg2Left, Pg2Right;    // Left and right margins (right page)

/*--------------------< Dialog box dimensions >----------------------*/

GetTextMetrics(hDC, &tm);
GetClientRect(hWnd, &rcClient);

// Get current dialog box base units
lBaseUnits = GetDialogBaseUnits();

// Calculate dialog box dimensions
BoxHeight  = HIWORD(lBaseUnits/8) * CYADDRDLG;
BoxWidth   = LOWORD(lBaseUnits/4) * CXADDRDLG;

/*-----------------------< Set mapping mode >---------------------------*/

SetMapMode(hDC, MM_ANISOTROPIC);
SetWindowOrg(hDC, 0, 0);
SetWindowExt(hDC, BoxWidth, BoxHeight);
SetViewportOrg(hDC,0,0);
SetViewportExt(hDC,rcClient.right,rcClient.bottom);

/*--------------------< Create paint resources >----------------------*/

hB6Pen     = CreatePen(0,6, RGB(0, 0, 0));
hB2Pen     = CreatePen(0,2, RGB(0, 0, 0));
hB1Pen     = CreatePen(0,1, RGB(0, 0, 0));
hOldPen    = SelectObject(hDC, hB1Pen);
hOldBrush  = SelectObject(hDC, GetStockObject(BLACK_BRUSH));

/*-----------------< Calculate page dimensions >----------------------*/

mp       = BoxWidth / 2;
```

```
PglLeft   = dla + d2xa;
PgTop     = dlo + d2y;
PglRight = mp   - d2xi;
PgBottom = BoxHeight-dlu-d2y;
Pg2Left  = mp   + d2xi;
Pg2Right = BoxWidth-dla-d2xa;

if(bCaptionOnly)              // Only the captions are redrawn
   goto CAPTION;              // Uh-oh, a goto...

/*-------------------------< Draw the "binding" >-----------------------*/

RoundRect(hDC, dla, dlo,
          BoxWidth-dla,BoxHeight-dlu,
          dlo,dlo);

/*-------------------------< Draw the left page >-----------------------*/

SelectObject(hDC, GetStockObject(WHITE_BRUSH));
RoundRect(hDC, PglLeft, PgTop, PglRight, PgBottom, d2y, d2y);

SelectObject(hDC,hB2Pen);

/*----------------------< Dividing line for caption >--------------------*/

MoveTo(hDC, PglLeft,  PgTop + d3);
LineTo(hDC, PglRight, PgTop + d3);

SelectObject(hDC, hB1Pen);
d4 = (PgBottom-PgTop-d3-dlu) / 3;

/*-----------------< Line between edit boxes 1 and 2 >------------------*/

MoveTo(hDC, PglLeft,     PgTop+d3+d4);
LineTo(hDC, PglRight-ar, PgTop+d3+d4);

/*-----------------< Line between edit boxes 2 and 3 >------------------*/

MoveTo(hDC, PglLeft,     PgTop+d3+2*d4);
LineTo(hDC, PglRight-ar, PgTop+d3+2*d4);

/*-----------------< Line below the third edit box >--------------------*/

MoveTo(hDC, PglLeft,     PgTop+d3+3*d4);
LineTo(hDC, PglRight-ar, PgTop+d3+3*d4);

/*---------------------< Draw the right page >-------------------------*/
```

```
RoundRect(hDC, Pg2Left, PgTop, Pg2Right, PgBottom, d2y, d2y);

SelectObject(hDC, hB2Pen);
MoveTo(hDC, Pg2Left,
PgTop + d3);
LineTo(hDC, Pg2Right,PgTop + d3);

SelectObject(hDC, hB1Pen);

/*-----------------< Line between edit boxes 1 and 2 >-------------------*/

MoveTo(hDC, Pg2Left+ar, PgTop+d3+d4);
LineTo(hDC, Pg2Right,   PgTop+d3+d4);

/*-----------------< Line between edit boxes 2 and 3 >-------------------*/

MoveTo(hDC, Pg2Left+ar, PgTop+d3+2*d4);
LineTo(hDC, Pg2Right,   PgTop+d3+2*d4);

/*-----------------< Line below the third edit box >---------------------*/

MoveTo(hDC, Pg2Left+ar, PgTop+d3+3*d4);
LineTo(hDC, Pg2Right,   PgTop+d3+3*d4);

/*----------------------< Draw "binder rings" >-------------------------*/

SelectObject(hDC, hB6Pen);

d5 = (PgBottom-PgTop)/4;
for(i=0;i<=3;i++)
{
   int y;

   y=PgTop+d5/2+i*d5;
   Arc(hDC, mp-d2y-ar, y,
          mp+d2y+ar, y+2*ar,
          mp+d2y+ar, y+ar,
          mp-d2y-ar, y+ar);
}

/*-----------------------< Delete paint resources >---------------------*/

SelectObject(hDC, hOldBrush);
SelectObject(hDC, hOldPen);
DeleteObject(hB6Pen);
DeleteObject(hB2Pen);
DeleteObject(hB1Pen);
```

```
  /*---------------------------< Draw caption >---------------------------*/

  CAPTION:
  {
    char buf[80];
    LONG lTextLength;
    HFONT hOldFont;

    // Lower limit of caption font height is the normal font height
    iFontHeight = tm.tmHeight;
    // Upper limit of caption font height = 1.5 times the normal font height
    iMaxFontHeight = tm.tmHeight+(tm.tmHeight/2);

    // List fonts
    lpFontProc = MakeProcInstance(CalcFont, hInst);
    EnumFonts(hDC, "Courier", lpFontProc, NULL);
    FreeProcInstance(lpFontProc);

    // Select font in display context
    hOldFont = SelectObject(hDC, hCaptionFont);

    // Display current index character in caption area
    wsprintf(buf," %c ", Alphabet[AktReg-ID_LEX]);
    lTextLength = GetTextExtent(hDC, buf, strlen(buf));

    // First page
    TextOut(hDC, Pg1Left+(Pg1Right-Pg1Left)/2-
                 (LOWORD(lTextLength)/2), PgTop+1,
                 buf, strlen(buf));

    // Second page
    TextOut(hDC, Pg2Left+(Pg2Right-Pg2Left)/2-
                 (LOWORD(lTextLength/2)), PgTop+1,
                 buf, strlen(buf));
    DeleteObject(SelectObject(hDC, hOldFont));
  }
} // DrawBook

/**************************************************************************
 N d f A d d r e s s B o o k P r o c ()
 ======================================

 This function processes messages for the "Address Book" dialog box.

 Parameters:

  Standard message structure
```

```
 Return values:

  BOOL      TRUE if the message is sent. Otherwise, FALSE.
*************************************************************************/

BOOL FAR PASCAL NdfAddressBookProc (HWND hDlg, WORD msg, WORD wP, LONG lP)
{
   HDC              hDC;            // Display context handle
   PAINTSTRUCT      ps;             // Paint information
   static int       AktReg;         // Current starting character index
   int              i;

   switch(msg)
   {
     case WM_INITDIALOG:
      // Initialize random number generator
      srand((unsigned)time(NULL));

      // Enable or disable all indices except "A"
      for (i=1; i<26; i++)
      {
        if (rand() % 2)
          EnableWindow(GetDlgItem(hDlg,ID_LEX+i), FALSE);
        else
          EnableWindow(GetDlgItem(hDlg,ID_LEX+i), TRUE);
      }
      // Make "A" the current index letter
      AktReg = ID_LEX;
      EnableWindow(GetDlgItem(hDlg,ID_LEX), TRUE);

      /* ---------- <Implement subclassing for edit boxes > ------------ */

      lpprocNewEditProc = MakeProcInstance((FARPROC) fwEditPreProcess,
                                           hInst);
      if (lpprocNewEditProc == NULL)
        return FALSE;
      hEditCtl = GetDlgItem(hDlg, ID_EDADDR);
      lpprocOldEditProc = (FARPROC) SetWindowLong(hEditCtl, GWL_WNDPROC,
                                                  (LONG) lpprocNewEditProc);
      for (i=1; i<6; i++)
      {
       hEditCtl = GetDlgItem(hDlg, ID_EDADDR+i);
       SetWindowLong(hEditCtl, GWL_WNDPROC,
                     (LONG) lpprocNewEditProc);
      }
      return TRUE;

     case WM_DESTROY:
```

```
/*---------------------< Cancel subclassing >------------------*/

for (i=0; i<6; i++)
{
   SetWindowLong(GetDlgItem(hDlg, ID_EDADDR+i), GWL_WNDPROC,
                 (LONG) lpprocOldEditProc);
}
FreeProcInstance(lpprocNewEditProc);
return TRUE;
break;

case WM_COMMAND:
  switch (wP)
  {
  // LEXBUTTON message
  case ID_LEX:     // From A ...
  case ID_LEX+1:  case ID_LEX+2:  case ID_LEX+3:
  case ID_LEX+4:  case ID_LEX+5:  case ID_LEX+6:
  case ID_LEX+7:  case ID_LEX+8:  case ID_LEX+9:
  case ID_LEX+10: case ID_LEX+11: case ID_LEX+12:
  case ID_LEX+13: case ID_LEX+14: case ID_LEX+15:
  case ID_LEX+16: case ID_LEX+17: case ID_LEX+18:
  case ID_LEX+19: case ID_LEX+20: case ID_LEX+21:
  case ID_LEX+22: case ID_LEX+23: case ID_LEX+24:
  case ID_LEX+25: // ... to Z

    AktReg = wP;
    {
      HDC hDC;

      hDC = GetDC(hDlg);
      // Redraw caption
      DrawBook(hDlg, hDC, AktReg, TRUE);
      ReleaseDC(hDlg, hDC);

      CurIndex = Alphabet[AktReg-ID_LEX];
    }
    return TRUE;
    break;

  case ID_LEFT:    // Left arrow
    MessageBox(GetFocus(), "Page back", szApplName,
               MB_OK | MB_ICONASTERISK);
    return TRUE;
    break;

  case ID_RIGHT:  // Right arrow
    MessageBox(GetFocus(), "Page forward", szApplName,
```

```
                     MB_OK | MB_ICONASTERISK);
          return TRUE;
          break;

        default:
          return FALSE;
          break;
        }
        break;

      case WM_PAINT:  // Redraw part of dialog box
        hDC = BeginPaint(hDlg, &ps);
        DrawBook(hDlg, hDC, AktReg, FALSE);
        EndPaint(hDlg, &ps);
        return TRUE;
        break;

    case WM_SYSCOMMAND:          // Message from dialog box system menu
      switch (wP)
      {
      // ALT+F4, double-click system menu or select "Close" from system
      // menu

      case SC_CLOSE:             // Close address book
        PostMessage(hwMain, WM_COMMAND, MI_ADDRBOOK, 0L);
        return TRUE;
        break;

      default:                   // Other system menu messages
        return FALSE;
        break;
      }
      break;

     default:
       return FALSE;
       break;
   }
} // NdfAddressBookProc

/***************************************************************************
 D r a w L e f t A r r o w ()
 ============================

 This function draws the user-defined control element 'L_ARROW'.

     +-------+
     |  <==  |
```

```
    +-------+

 Parameters:

  HWND  hWnd       Window handle
  HDC   hDC        Display context handle
  BOOL  bSelected  TRUE if arrow is clicked using the left mouse button.
                   Arrow then appears in inverse video.

 Return values:    None
***************************************************************************/

void DrawLeftArrow(HWND hWnd, HDC hDC, BOOL bSelected)
{
  RECT    rClientRect;
  HBRUSH  hOldBrush = NULL;
  HPEN    hOldPen = NULL;
  POINT   ArrowPt[7];
  int     xsize, ysize,
        l,t,r,b,
        cx,cy;

  GetClientRect(hWnd,&rClientRect);
  SetMapMode(hDC, MM_ANISOTROPIC);
  SetWindowOrg(hDC, 0, 0);
  SetWindowExt(hDC, 120, 80);
  SetViewportOrg(hDC,0,0);
  SetViewportExt(hDC,rClientRect.right,rClientRect.bottom);

  t= 0;  l= 0;  r=120;  b=80;  cx=r/6;  cy=b/6;

  xsize=r-l-2*cx;
  ysize=b-t-2*cy;

  ArrowPt[0].x = cx+xsize;              // Left arrow
  ArrowPt[0].y = cy+ysize/3*2;
  ArrowPt[1].x = cx+xsize/3;
  ArrowPt[1].y = cy+ysize/3*2;
  ArrowPt[2].x = cx+xsize/3;
  ArrowPt[2].y = cy+ysize;
  ArrowPt[3].x = cx;
  ArrowPt[3].y = cy+ysize/2;
  ArrowPt[4].x = cx+xsize/3;
  ArrowPt[4].y = cy;
  ArrowPt[5].x = cx+xsize/3;
  ArrowPt[5].y = cy+ysize/3;
  ArrowPt[6].x = cx+xsize;
  ArrowPt[6].y = cy+ysize/3;
```

```
  if(GetWindowWord(hWnd, 0))            // Control grayed
     hOldBrush = SelectObject(hDC, GetStockObject(GRAY_BRUSH));
  else
  {
     if(bSelected)
     {
      hOldBrush = SelectObject(hDC, GetStockObject(BLACK_BRUSH));
      hOldPen   = SelectObject(hDC, GetStockObject(WHITE_PEN));
     }
     else
      hOldBrush = SelectObject(hDC, GetStockObject(WHITE_BRUSH));
  }
  Rectangle(hDC, l,t,r,b);
  Polygon(hDC, ArrowPt,7);
  SelectObject(hDC, hOldBrush);
  if (hOldPen)
    SelectObject(hDC, hOldPen);
} // DrawLeftArrow

/***************************************************************************
 D r a w R i g h t A r r o w ()
 ==============================

 This function draws the user-defined control element 'R_ARROW'.

     +-------+
     |  ==>  |
     +-------+

 Parameters:

  HWND  hWnd       Window handle
  HDC   hDC        Display context handle
  BOOL  bSelected  TRUE if arrow is clicked using the left mouse button.
                   Arrow then appears in inverse video.

 Return values:    None
***************************************************************************/

void DrawRightArrow (HWND hWnd, HDC hDC, BOOL bSelected)
{
  RECT    rClientRect;
  HBRUSH  hOldBrush = NULL;
  HPEN    hOldPen = NULL;
  POINT   ArrowPt[7];
  int     xsize, ysize, l,t,r,b,cx,cy;
```

```
  GetClientRect(hWnd,&rClientRect);
  SetMapMode(hDC, MM_ANISOTROPIC);
  SetWindowOrg(hDC, 0, 0);
  SetWindowExt(hDC, rClientRect.right,rClientRect.bottom);
  SetWindowExt(hDC, 120, 80);
  SetViewportOrg(hDC,0,0);
  SetViewportExt(hDC,rClientRect.right,rClientRect.bottom);

  t= 0;  l= 0;  r=120;  b=80;  cx=r/6;  cy=b/6;
  xsize=r-l-2*cx;
  ysize=b-t-2*cy;

  ArrowPt[0].x = cx;                   // Right arrow
  ArrowPt[0].y = cy+ysize/3*2;
  ArrowPt[1].x = cx+xsize/3*2;
  ArrowPt[1].y = cy+ysize/3*2;
  ArrowPt[2].x = cx+xsize/3*2;
  ArrowPt[2].y = cy+ysize;
  ArrowPt[3].x = cx+xsize;
  ArrowPt[3].y = cy+ysize/2;
  ArrowPt[4].x = cx+xsize/3*2;
  ArrowPt[4].y = cy;
  ArrowPt[5].x = cx+xsize/3*2;
  ArrowPt[5].y = cy+ysize/3;
  ArrowPt[6].x = cx;
  ArrowPt[6].y = cy+ysize/3;

  if(GetWindowWord(hWnd, 0))           // Control grayed
     hOldBrush = SelectObject(hDC, GetStockObject(GRAY_BRUSH));
  else
  {
     if(bSelected)
     {
      hOldBrush = SelectObject(hDC, GetStockObject(BLACK_BRUSH));
      hOldPen   = SelectObject(hDC, GetStockObject(WHITE_PEN));
     }
     else
      hOldBrush = SelectObject(hDC, GetStockObject(WHITE_BRUSH));
  }
  Rectangle(hDC, l,t,r,b);
  Polygon(hDC, ArrowPt,7);
  SelectObject(hDC, hOldBrush);
  if (hOldPen)
    SelectObject(hDC, hOldPen);
} // DrawRightArrow

/***************************************************************************
 f w L e f t A r r o w ()
```

```
 ========================

 This function makes a new control element available. It generates a
 rectangle containing an arrow pointing to the left.

 Parameters:

  Standard message structure

 Return values:

  BOOL      TRUE if button is pressed. Otherwise, FALSE.
***************************************************************************/

LONG FAR PASCAL fwLeftArrow (HWND hWnd, WORD msg, WORD wP, LONG lP)
{
   static BOOL bSelected;          // Selection marker
   static RECT rClientRect;        // Client area rectangle

   switch(msg)
   {
     case WM_CREATE:               // For displaying control
      bSelected = FALSE;
     break;

     case WM_ENABLE:               // wP == NULL disable button, otherwise enable
      SetWindowWord(hWnd, 0, wP==NULL ? TRUE : FALSE);  // Save status
      InvalidateRect(hWnd, NULL, FALSE);
     break;

     case WM_MOUSEMOVE:            // Mouse movement
     {
      if(!bSelected) break;
      if (PtInRect(&rClientRect, MAKEPOINT(lP)))
        break;
      bSelected = FALSE;
      InvalidateRect(hWnd, &rClientRect, FALSE);
      break;
     }

     case WM_LBUTTONDOWN:  // Left mouse button pressed
      bSelected = TRUE;
      SetCapture(hWnd);
      GetClientRect(hWnd, &rClientRect);
      InvalidateRect(hWnd, NULL, FALSE);
      break;

     case WM_LBUTTONUP:    // Left mouse button released
```

```
      bSelected = FALSE;
      ReleaseCapture();
      InvalidateRect(hWnd, NULL, FALSE);
      UpdateWindow(hWnd);
      // Inform window
      PostMessage(GetParent(hWnd), WM_COMMAND, ID_LEFT, 0L);
      break;

      case WM_PAINT:      // Control repaint needed
       {
        HDC hDC;
        PAINTSTRUCT ps;

        hDC = BeginPaint(hWnd, &ps);

        DrawLeftArrow(hWnd, hDC, bSelected);

        EndPaint(hWnd, &ps);
       }
     break;

     default:             // Pass other information
      return DefWindowProc(hWnd, msg, wP, lP);
     break;
   }
   return FALSE;
} // fwLeftArrow

/***************************************************************************
 f w R i g h t A r r o w ()
 ==========================

 This function makes a new control element available. It generates a
 rectangle containing an arrow pointing to the right.

 Parameters:

  Standard message structure

 Return values:

  BOOL      TRUE if button is pressed. Otherwise, FALSE.
***************************************************************************/

LONG FAR PASCAL fwRightArrow (HWND hWnd, WORD msg, WORD wP, LONG lP)
{
   static BOOL bSelected;  // Selection marker
   static RECT rClientRect;       // Client area rectangle
```

```
switch(msg)
{
  case WM_CREATE:      // For displaying control
   bSelected = FALSE;
  break;

  case WM_ENABLE:      // wP == NULL disable button, otherwise enable
                          // Save status
   SetWindowWord(hWnd, 0, wP==NULL ? TRUE : FALSE);
   InvalidateRect(hWnd, NULL, FALSE);
  break;

  case WM_MOUSEMOVE:     // Mouse movement
  {
   if(!bSelected) break;
   if (PtInRect(&rClientRect, MAKEPOINT(lP)))
     break;
   bSelected = FALSE;
   InvalidateRect(hWnd, &rClientRect, FALSE);
   break;
  }

  case WM_LBUTTONDOWN:  // Left mouse button pressed
   bSelected = TRUE;
   SetCapture(hWnd);
   GetClientRect(hWnd, &rClientRect);
   InvalidateRect(hWnd, NULL, FALSE);
   break;

  case WM_LBUTTONUP:     // Left mouse button released
   bSelected = FALSE;
   ReleaseCapture();
   InvalidateRect(hWnd, NULL, FALSE);
   UpdateWindow(hWnd);
   // Inform window
   PostMessage(GetParent(hWnd), WM_COMMAND, ID_RIGHT, 0L);
   break;

  case WM_PAINT:         // Control repaint needed
   {
     HDC         hDC;
     PAINTSTRUCT ps;

     hDC = BeginPaint(hWnd, &ps);

     DrawRightArrow(hWnd, hDC, bSelected);

     EndPaint(hWnd, &ps);
```

```
      }
     break;

     default:            // Pass other information
      return DefWindowProc(hWnd, msg, wP, lP);
     break;
   }
   return FALSE;
} // fwRightArrow

/**********************************************************************
 R e g i s t e r B o o k C t r l ()
 ==================================

 This function registers all custom control elements needed by the
 address book. These are:

    LEXBUTTON     Rectangular button containing a centered character
    L_ARROW       Left arrow
    R_ARROW       Right arrow

 Parameters:

  HANDLE  hInst   Current instance handle of application

 Return values:

  BOOL            TRUE if the class can be registered, otherwise FALSE
**********************************************************************/

BOOL RegisterBookCtrl (HANDLE hInst)
{
   WNDCLASS wc;

   wc.lpszClassName  = "LEXBUTTON";
   wc.style          = CS_HREDRAW | CS_VREDRAW | CS_DBLCLKS;
   wc.hInstance      = hInst;
   wc.lpfnWndProc    = fwLexButton;
   wc.hCursor        = LoadCursor(NULL, IDC_ARROW );
   wc.hIcon          = NULL;
   wc.lpszMenuName   = NULL;
   wc.hbrBackground  = (HBRUSH) GetStockObject( WHITE_BRUSH );
   wc.cbClsExtra     = 0;
   wc.cbWndExtra     = sizeof(BOOL); // Saves enabled/disabled status

   if(!RegisterClass(&wc))
      return FALSE;
```

```
   wc.lpszClassName  = "L_ARROW";
   wc.style          = CS_HREDRAW | CS_VREDRAW | CS_DBLCLKS;
   wc.hInstance      = hInst;
   wc.lpfnWndProc    = fwLeftArrow;
   wc.hCursor        = LoadCursor(NULL, IDC_ARROW );
   wc.hIcon          = NULL;
   wc.lpszMenuName   = NULL;
   wc.hbrBackground  = (HBRUSH) GetStockObject( WHITE_BRUSH );
   wc.cbClsExtra     = 0;
   wc.cbWndExtra     = sizeof(BOOL); // Saves enabled/disabled status

   if(!RegisterClass(&wc))
      return FALSE;

   wc.lpszClassName  = "R_ARROW";
   wc.style          = CS_HREDRAW | CS_VREDRAW | CS_DBLCLKS;
   wc.hInstance      = hInst;
   wc.lpfnWndProc    = fwRightArrow;
   wc.hCursor        = LoadCursor(NULL, IDC_ARROW );
   wc.hIcon          = NULL;
   wc.lpszMenuName   = NULL;
   wc.hbrBackground  = (HBRUSH) GetStockObject( WHITE_BRUSH );
   wc.cbClsExtra     = 0;
   wc.cbWndExtra     = sizeof(BOOL); // Saves enabled/disabled status

   if(!RegisterClass(&wc))
      return FALSE;
   return TRUE;
} // RegisterBookCtrl

/*************************************************************************
 S e n d C h a r T o E d i t ()
 ==============================

 This function simulates character input in the edit box designated hEdit.
 This is achieved by sending the WM_KEYDOWN, WM_CHAR and WM_KEYUP messages.

 Parameters:

   FARPROC   lpEdit    Pointer to the original edit box window function
   HWND      hWnd      Edit box window handle
   char      c         Character to be inserted

 Return values:        None
 *************************************************************************/

void SendCharToEdit (FARPROC lpEdit, HWND hWnd, char c, LONG lP)
{
```

```
   CallWindowProc(lpEdit, hWnd, WM_KEYDOWN, c,lP);
   CallWindowProc(lpEdit, hWnd, WM_CHAR, c,lP);
   CallWindowProc(lpEdit, hWnd, WM_KEYUP, c,lP);
} // SendCharToEdit

/*************************************************************************
 f w E d i t P r e P r o c e s s ()
 ==================================

 This function prepares the system for subclassing the edit boxes in the
 address book application.

 Parameter:

  Standard message structure

 Return values:

  Original edit box window function's return value, or WM_GETDLGCODE value
*************************************************************************/

LONG FAR PASCAL fwEditPreProcess (HWND hWnd, WORD msg, WORD wP, LONG lP)
{
  switch (msg)
  {
    case WM_GETDLGCODE:
      return DLGC_WANTMESSAGE; // Report every keyboard input (also CR)

    case WM_CHAR:
      switch (wP)
      {
      case 0x0D: // Convert CR -> CR/LF
        SendCharToEdit(lpprocOldEditProc, hWnd, '\r', 0L);
        SendCharToEdit(lpprocOldEditProc, hWnd, '\n', 0L);
        break;

      // All other characters routed to original window function
      default:
        return(CallWindowProc(lpprocOldEditProc, hWnd, msg, wP, lP));
        break;
      }
      break;

    default: // Call original function
      return(CallWindowProc(lpprocOldEditProc, hWnd, msg, wP, lP));
      break;
  }
} // fwEditPreProcess
```

8 The Multiple Document Interface

The multiple document interface allows the user to work with many objects of different types or the same object in different formats using several child windows.

The first application to take advantage of this possibility was Microsoft's spreadsheet program Excel as implemented under Windows 2.xx. The MDI was thoroughly described in the documentation for the Windows 2.xx SDK, but Excel was the only program to take advantage of it for a long time. One reason for this is that using the MDI requires some real programming acrobatics and thorough, detailed knowledge of Windows. One problem that is encountered when implementing the MDI is displaying more than one active window. Normally, Windows will display all windows as grayed except the one that currently has the input focus.

As with many other features of Windows, the MDI was updated with many improvements when Windows 3 was released. After Microsoft equipped the OS/2 file manager with MDI, it included this capability with the Windows File Manager and Program Manager.

The developers also made improvements to the SDK to provide the Windows programmer with tools that would make it easier to create new applications, which could take advantage of the MDI without extraordinary programming efforts.

Windows 3 is a successful environment for MS-DOS machines. The MDI is now also part of more and more standard applications employed by all Windows users. Consequently, in the future it will become even more important for developers of new Windows applications to use this interface. In the following sections we will explain the basic workings of an MDI application. The practical capabilities of the demo program listed in this chapter will be kept intentionally simple so that we can focus on the MDI implementation.

8.1 Anatomy of an MDI Application

An MDI application consists of three basic components:

1) Frame window

2) Client window

3) Child window

Each of these is explained below.

MDI frame window

The frame window is similar to the main window of a standard Windows application. It has a title bar, a system menu and icons for changing the window size. But the similarities end here. Although the frame window also has a menu bar, it is different from that of a "normal" application.

As we will see, a major feature of the MDI is its object-oriented concept. In this case, the objects can be items, such as documents, tables or graphics, that are displayed in MDI child windows (also called document windows in the following discussion).

The items in the frame window menu enable or disable the various objects available to the system. The frame window uses a context sensitive menu bar, which means that the items listed will always pertain to the currently active document window (of which there can be only one at any given time). The title bars of both the frame window and the active document window are lit to indicate this. The context sensitive frame window menu will enable or disable different items, or even change completely in order to correspond to the objects available in the currently active document window.

MDI client window

The entire client area of the frame window forms another window called the client window. The standard color for this window is pale yellow. It is an important part of every MDI application.

The client window area defines the space in which the document windows can move. Neither the child windows nor their icons can be displayed outside the client window area, but both can be moved anywhere within it. The "full size" display of any of the child windows is also limited by the size of the client window.

As far as the programmer is concerned, the client window is comparable to a control element. The window function for the MDI found in the Application Programmer Interface (API) has taken over much of the work that formerly had to be coded by hand. An example of this is the way in which we manage document windows.

This is a good time to introduce another MDI component: the **Window** popup menu. The popup menu is part of every MDI menu. Among other things, it contains three items used for managing document windows. This menu also contains a list of all open documents and their ID numbers and names. When you select an item from this list, a mark will appear to indicate which document is selected. The corresponding document will be moved to the foreground and given the input focus. The client window maintains this list by adding new documents that are opened and removing documents as they are closed.

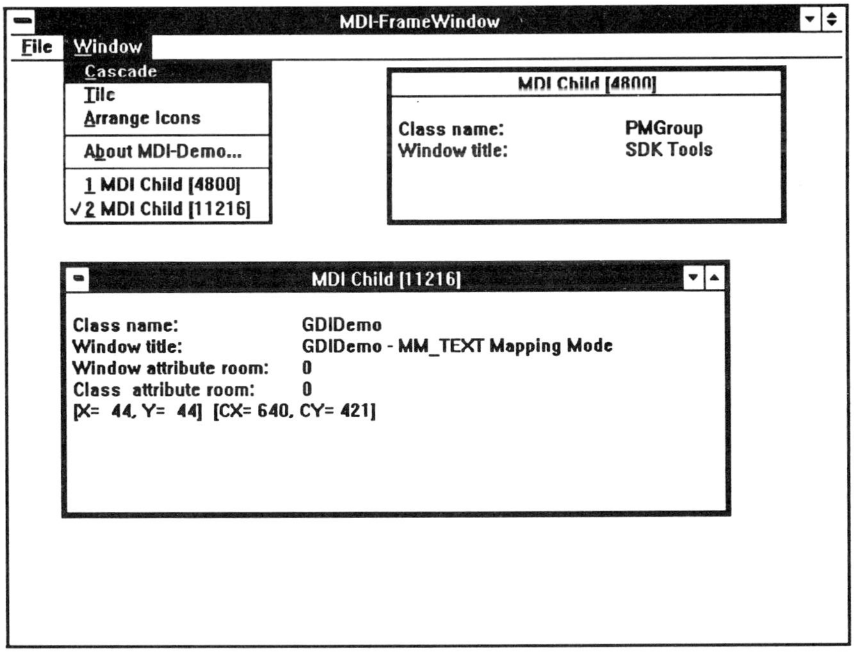

The open MDI ***Window*** *menu*

Now back to arranging windows. We will distinguish between overlapping (CASCADE) or adjacent (TILE, because they are arranged like tiles in a floor) windows. Cascading windows overlap in such a way that only the title bar of each window can be seen except for the current window, which is entirely visible.

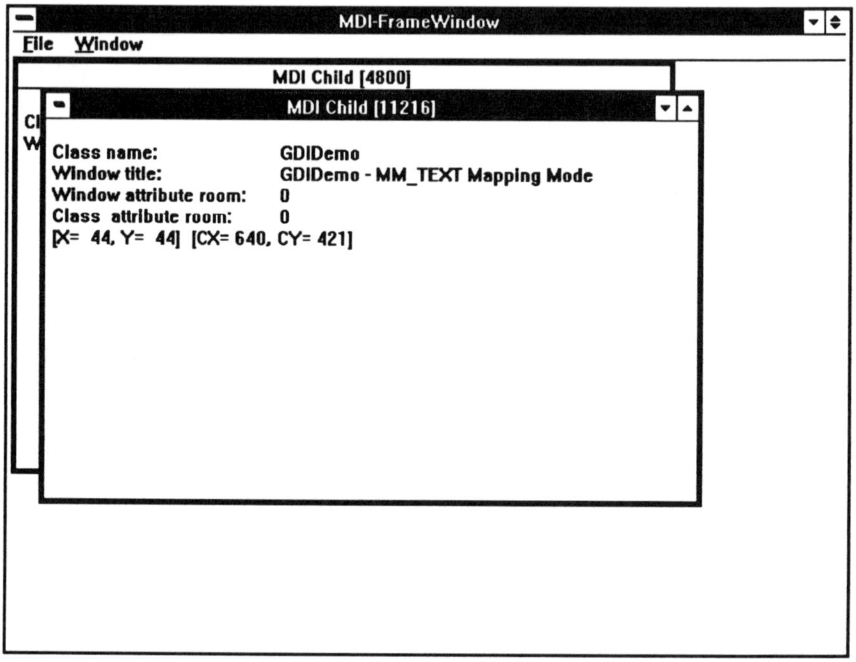

MDI windows arranged with CASCADE

Windows arranged with TILE do not overlap.

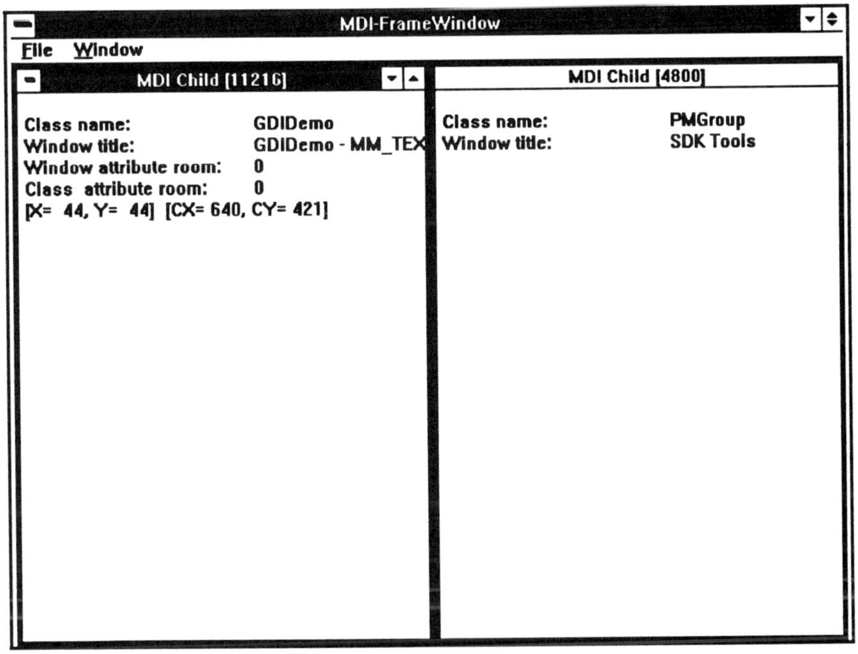

MDI windows arranged with TILE

The user selects the desired window arrangement from the popup menu. The SDK under Windows 2.xx required the programmer to set up the arrangement of the document windows. Now the proper message needs to be sent to the client window (WM_MDICASCADE or WM_MDITILE).

We have seen that it is now much easier to arrange the child windows of MDI applications. We should also note that it is the responsibility of the client window to manage the document windows. We will discuss this in more detail later when we cover default window functions.

Child windows

MDI child windows also look like "normal" main windows. They have a system menu and icons for changing the size of the window. As we already mentioned, however, the size and mobility of child windows are limited by the client window. A child window cannot be moved outside the client window, nor can its maximized (full size) display exceed the borders of the client window. When you display a child window at full size, the document window's title bar is replaced and the title of the child window is displayed in the title bar of the frame window. The icon for the child window's system menu is moved to the start of the menu bar and the icon for sizing the window is moved to the far right.

As opposed to main windows, document windows have an additional menu bar that corresponds to the menu bar of the frame window.

A document window distinguishes itself from other document windows by its icon. The window can be reduced to an icon and moved anywhere within the client window.

The window class of the document window has a special meaning when creating an MDI application. When you are working with several different object types, you should specify a different window class for each one. The advantages of this will become clear as we discuss object-related data handling.

The modified message loop

Our list of special MDI components is completed with the message loop. As opposed to a "normal" message loop, the MDI message loop is modified to include the TranslateMDISysAccel function. This function acts as a filter to trap all MDI "hotkeys" entered from the keyboard. You can then check to see if the application has attached a meaning to the particular hotkey being processed. If it hasn't, then the TranslateMessage and DispatchMessage functions are called.

```
while(GetMessage(&msg,0,0,0))
{
   if(!TranslateMDISysAccel(hwClient),&msg) &&
      !TranslateAccelerator(hwFrame, hAccelTable, &msg))
   {
      TranslateMessage(&msg);
      DispatchMessage(&msg);
   }
}
```

8.1.1 Object-related data handling

Now that you are familiar with the important components of an MDI application, we can discuss object-related data handling. The MDI concept supports object-oriented programming to an even greater extent than Windows by itself. Since the same window function is used to process data objects of the same type, we must find a mechanism for managing object-related information. The window title in a spreadsheet program, or perhaps the name of a word processing document are examples of object-related information.

Normally, each object is displayed in its own window. This means that we can use the separate windows to manage the data associated with each object. Windows has two different ways we can do this. One is to use the window structure of the document window to store a number of extra bytes that contain the object-related data. A second way is to define properties. Under Windows, properties are data structures that can be associated with a given window. They are managed in a property list.

Expanding the window structure

The WNDCLASS data structure allows you to reserve room for private window-related data when the window class is registered. The cbWndExtra field in the WNDCLASS data structure gives the size of the private data block in bytes. When the window class is registered, Windows adds a block of this size to the end of the window structure.

The data in this private block is addressed using an index. Depending on the access function used, this index is either a 2 byte (WORD) or 4 byte (LONG) offset. An index value of zero would therefore address the first two (with WORD) or four (with LONG) bytes.

```
cbWndExtra - 8;
Room for up
to eight bytes
of private data
```

Byte offset	Index by... LONG	WORD
0-1	0	0
2-3	0	1
4-5	1	2
6-7	1	3

Extra bytes appended to the window structure

The access function pairs used to address the private data are Set/GetWindowWord and Set/GetWindowLong. The names of the functions indicate the type of offset addressing used (WORD or LONG).

```
/*---< Store data in extra bytes >---*/

nOldValue = SetWindowWord(hWnd, nIndex, wValue); // as WORD

lOldValue = SetWindowLong(hWnd, nIndex, lValue); // as LONG

/*---< Read data from extra bytes >---*/

nValue = GetWindowWord(hWnd, nIndex);         // as WORD

lValue = GetWindowLong(hWnd, lIndex);         // as LONG
```

The property list

A property is any data structure that can be associated with a window. The application stores these data structures in a memory block. The SetProp function uses the handle to such an object together with a unique ID (in the form of an ANSI character string) to enter the object in the corresponding window's property list. A property list is set up on the USER heap by the Windows USER.EXE module when a window is created. The property list for a window starts out empty.

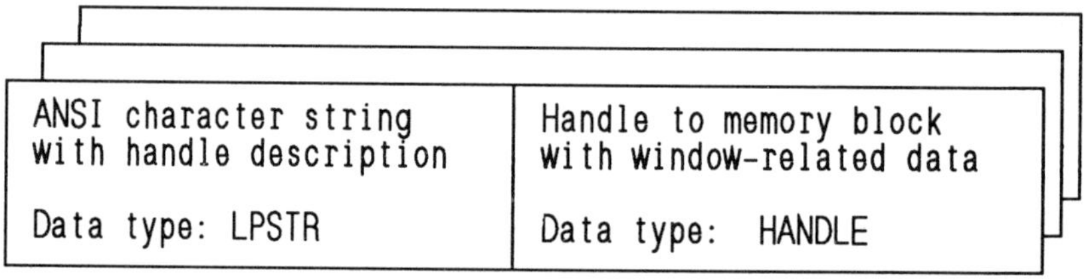

Elements of a property list

```
/* Types and variable declarations */

typedef struct tagDemoStruct;
{
   /*
      from the user-defined data structure
      containing window-related information
   */
} DemoStruct;
```

```
HANDLE hMem;              // handle to memory block
PSTR   pMem;              // NEAR pointer to the memory block
DemoStruct * pDemo;       // pointer to the DemoStruct structure

char   szEntry[] = "DEMOENTRY"

/*---< Enter elements in the property list >--- */
hMem = LocalAlloc(LHND, sizeof(DemoStruct)); // allocate
pMem = LocalLock(hMem);                      // lock
pMem = (PSTR) pDemo;                         // initialize
LocalFree(hMem);                             // free
SetProp(hWnd,(LPSTR) szEntry, hMem);         // enter in the list
```

You can now access a data object according to its unique ID. This is passed together with the window handle to the GetProp function. When this function encounters an entry with this ID in the property list, it returns the corresponding memory handle. After locking this handle and "casting", you can access this data structure like any other C structure. This eliminates the need to address individual data with offset indices as we learned to do before with the ExtraBytes of the window class structure. Unfortunately we pay for this advantage with speed, since direct access to the ExtraBytes with an offset is usually faster.

Another important point is that other applications can access the property list of a window and, therefore, its data objects. All that is required is a valid handle for the window. As a general rule, however, properties should only be used by the application that created them, excepting global objects like GDI paint resources.

```
/*---< Accessing an element in the property list >--- */
hMem  = GetProp(hWnd, (LPSTR) szEntry); // get handle
pMem  = LocalLock(hMem);                // ...lock...
pDemo = (DemoStruct *) pMem;            // and cast for the rest of the
                                        // processing
```

The EnumProps function can show us the entries in the property list. This function gets passed a handle, to the window whose property list you want to see, and a pointer to a callback function. As long as the process is not aborted by returning a NULL, all list entries are then passed to this callback function.

The callback function uses the PASCAL function call sequence. There are two groups of parameters, depending on the segment attributes of the data segment. For applications and DLLs with FIXED data segments, the following parameters are used:

```
int FAR PASCAL CallBackFunc(HWND hWnd, LPSTR lpEntry, HANDLE hMem)
```

For applications and DLLs with MOVEABLE data segments, there are two differences in the parameters. A dummy parameter is added, and a PSTR is used instead of an LPSTR to store the ANSI string:

```
int FAR PASCAL CallBackFunc(HWND hWnd, WORD wDummy, PSTR  pEntry, HANDLE hMem)
```

Like all other callback functions, this one must also be listed under EXPORTS in the module definition file.

```
/*---< Displaying the elements of a property list >---*/
FARPROC  lpCallBackFunc;       // procedure instance address of callback function
lpCallBackFunc = MakeProcInstance((FARPORC) CallBackFunc, hInst);
EnumProps(hWnd, lpCallBackFunc); // display of elements
FreeProcInstance(lpCallBackFunc);
```

It is the application's responsibility to remove all entries it has made to the list and free the allocated memory before the application is ended (with the receipt of a WM_DESTROY message). Since Windows itself uses the property list to store information that is needed internally, the application must be careful to delete only those elements which it entered itself.

If an application does not clean up after itself in the property list, then the entries it made will remain in the list until the end of the Windows session. Since space is at a premium on the USER heap, this can lead to a heap overrun. So you shouldn't use the property list to store large amounts of data for longer times. A better way to store larger quantities of data is to allocate a memory block on the global heap and then use SetWindowWord to store a handle to this block in the window structure, or SetProp to store the handle in the property list.

```
/*---< Delete entries from the property list >---*/
if(hMem = RemoveProp(hWnd, (LPSTR) szEntry))
{
   // element deleted from list
   LocalFree(hMem);                 // free memory block
}
else // element not found in list ...
```

8.2 Implementing an MDI Application

Now that we understand the important components of an MDI application and know a little about the mechanism for handling object-related data, we can examine the basic steps involved in actually creating an MDI application.

Register window classes

Let's begin by registering the window class of the MDI frame window. This class isn't different than any other main window. Registering the frame window class:

```
WndClass.style         = CS_VREDRAW | CS_HREDRAW ;
WndClass.lpfnWndProc   = FrameWndProc ;
WndClass.cbClsExtra    = 0 ;
WndClass.cbWndExtra    = 0 ;
WndClass.hInstance     = hInst ;
WndClass.hIcon         = LoadIcon (hInst, (LPSTR) "FrameIcon") ;
WndClass.hCursor       = LoadCursor (NULL, IDC_ARROW);
WndClass.hbrBackground = COLOR_APPWORKSPACE + 1;
WndClass.lpszMenuName  = (LPSTR) "Menu";
WndClass.lpszClassName = (LPSTR) "MDIFRAME" ;
```

Next, we will register the window class used for document windows. If all child windows are intended to display the same object type, then you only have to register one window class. If you want to display different types of objects in various child windows, then you should register a different window class for each object type.

As we already mentioned, you must decide whether or not you want to reserve extra room for additional data in the window structure at the time the window class is registered. In our MDI example, we will reserve WNDEXTRABYTES in the window structure. Later, we will store a handle here for the window to which the document window will pass information. Registering the document window class:

```
WndClass.style         = 0 ;
WndClass.lpfnWndProc   = ChildWndProc ;
WndClass.cbWndExtra    = CBWNDDATA;      // Room for
                                         // window-specific data
WndClass.hIcon         = LoadIcon (hInst, (LPSTR) "ChildIcon") ;
WndClass.hCursor       = NULL;
WndClass.lpszMenuName  = NULL;           // MDI child window has
                                         // no menu
WndClass.lpszClassName = (LPSTR) "MDICHILD" ;
```

We do not have to register a window class for the client window. This uses the MDICLIENT window class, which is already defined in the API.

Modify the message loop

After all required window classes are registered, we have to modify the message loop as described above.

Create the frame window and client window

Now we are getting to the heart of an MDI application. The first thing we will do is use the CreateWindow function to create the MDI frame window. The parameters we will pass to the function are the same as those for creating a "normal" main window. The use of the CreateWindow function implies calling the window function of the frame window with a WM_CREATE message. The frame window function will then use this message to create the client window.

To do this we must first initialize a data structure of type CLIENTCREATESTRUCT. This structure contains two fields. The first, hWindowMenu, receives a handle to the popup menu window. The following code statement shows how we obtain this handle:

```
ClientCreate.hWindowMenu =  GetSubMenu(hwMenu, MI_WINDOW);
```

The second field is called idFirstChild. It should be filled with the ID of the first document window. This ID is later sent to the frame window as the wParam parameter of a WM_COMMAND message when the corresponding document window is selected from the list in the popup menu. Additional child windows are numbered in sequence starting from idFirstChild. When a document window is closed, the child window IDs are renumbered so that there are no gaps.

After the CREATECLIENTSTRUCT data structure is initialized, we can use CreateWindow to create the client window. Note that the WS_CLIPCHILDREN bit is set in the style specification for the window. The following code creates the client window:

```
/************************************************************************
 C r e a t e M d i C l i e n t W i n d o w
 ========================================

 This function creates the MDI Clientwindow.

 Parameters:
 HWND          MDI window handle
```

```
 Return values:
 BOOL          TRUE if the client window could be created. Otherwise, FALSE
************************************************************************/
BOOL CreateMdiClientWindow(HWND hWnd)
{
   CLIENTCREATESTRUCT  ClientCreate;      // MDI ClientWindow data structure
                                          // through which window creation is
                                          // accessed
   ClientCreate.hWindowMenu =  GetSubMenu(hwMenu, MI_WINDOW);
   ClientCreate.idFirstChild = FIRSTCHILDID;

   hwClient = CreateWindow ("MDICLIENT",    // Predefined window class
                            NULL,
                            CLIENTWINDOWSTYLE,
                            0, 0, 0, 0,
                            hWnd,
                            1,
                            hInst,
                            (LPSTR) &ClientCreate) ;
   if(!hwClient)
       return FALSE;

   ShowWindow(hwClient, SW_SHOW);
   return TRUE;
}
```

Before discussing the document windows in more detail, we must make a few more comments about the window function of the frame window. As we already know, there are some significant differences between MDI and standard applications.

One of these differences is that some of the messages that aren't processed by the frame window are not automatically sent to DefWndProc as usual. Instead, some messages get routed to the DefFrameProc, which is specially written for the MDI. The messages we are especially interested in are WM_SIZE and WM_COMMAND. Re-routing certain WM_COMMAND messages to the window function that controls the child windows is what allows the child windows to be activated using the popup menu.

Creating a document window

As with the client window, we will also use a special data structure, called the MDICREATESTRUCT structure, to create a document window. Document windows are not created with CreateWindow. Instcad, the MDICREATESTRUCT is properly initialized and then a WM_MDICREATE message is sent to the client window to trigger the creation of a document window. The lParam parameter of the MDICREATE message contains a LONG pointer to the MDICREATESTRUCT.

The following initializes the MDICREATESTRUCT data structure by sending the WM_MDICREATE message to the client window:

```
/*************************************************************************
 C r e a t e M d i C h i l d W i n d o w
 =======================================

 This function creates a new MDI child window.

 Parameters:
 long        LOWORD of this parameter contains the handle to the
             selected window.
*************************************************************************/
void CreateMdiChildWindow(long lP)
{
   MDICREATESTRUCT    MdiCreate;      // Data structure for creating an
                                      // MDI child window

   wsprintf(szBuffer,"MDI Child [%d]",LOWORD(lP));    // Title bar
   MdiCreate.szClass = (LPSTR) "MDICHILD";
   MdiCreate.szTitle = (LPSTR) szBuffer;
   MdiCreate.style   = WS_CHILD;
   MdiCreate.hOwner  = hInst;          // Instance handle for application
                                       // being created

   MdiCreate.x       = CW_USEDEFAULT; // X-position of MDI child window
   MdiCreate.y       = CW_USEDEFAULT; // Y-position "   "    "     "
   MdiCreate.cx      = CW_USEDEFAULT; // Width      "   "    "     "
   MdiCreate.cy      = CW_USEDEFAULT; // Height     "   "    "     "
   MdiCreate.lParam  = lP;
   SendMessage(hwClient, WM_MDICREATE, 0,
                             (LONG) (LPMDICREATESTRUCT) &MdiCreate);
}
```

Messages that aren't processed by the window function of the document window are sent to the special MDI function DefMDIChildProc instead of DefWndProc.

We have already discussed object-related data as it pertains to document windows. Now we will take a look at how you can pass this special information to a document window when it is created.

The key is the lParam parameter of the MDICREATESTRUCT data structure. This is a 32 bit pointer to the memory block that contains the special data to be passed to the child window. The client window receives this data along with the MDICREATE message and wraps the MDICREATESTRUCT structure, indicated by the lParam parameter, into a CREATESTRUCT structure. It then passes the entire thing to the document window in the form of a WM_CREATE message. This mechanism is illustrated in the following figure:

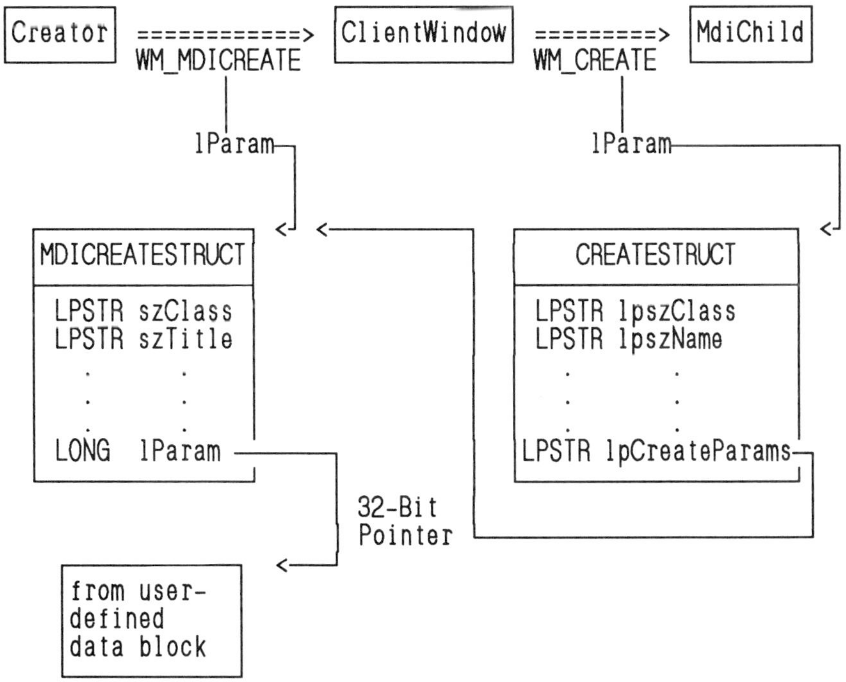

Passing data to create a document window

The following code segment shows what the child window must do in order to access this special data when processing the WM_CREATE message.

In our MDI demo application, we have used this mechanism to pass a window handle to the document window. The child window then keeps this handle in the ExtraBytes of the window structure.

The following code accesses data, during the creation of a document window, using the long parameter lP:

```
case WM_CREATE:
{
   LPCREATESTRUCT    lpCreate;
   LPMDICREATESTRUCT lpMdiCreate;

   /*----------< Data in extra bytes of window class >----------*/

   lpCreate    = (LPCREATESTRUCT)    lP;
   lpMdiCreate = (LPMDICREATESTRUCT) lpCreate->lpCreateParams;
   SetWindowWord(hWnd, GWW_HWINFO, LOWORD(lpMdiCreate->lParam));
```

The process described above for creating a document window is a good example of how child windows are controlled within MDI applications.

The client window is responsible for managing things. In addition to the messages which we've already seen, that are used to arrange document windows, the client window also processes messages for creating and terminating windows. It takes messages, such as WM_MDICREATE or WM_MDIDESTROY, from the application and sends them on as WM_CREATE or WM_DESTROY messages to the appropriate child window.

Although this usually pertains to the currently active child window, other events (such as ending the application) can lead to messages being sent to all document windows.

To send messages to all document windows, the corresponding handles must be available. It is comforting to know that Windows internally maintains a list of these. This list can be accessed with the EnumWindows function.

This function will pass all window handles, belonging to the application, one after the other to a callback function. This procedure continues until the value zero is returned to interrupt it.

The following code calls the Enum function:

```
lpEnumFunc = MakeProcInstance((FARPROC) FillWindowList, hInst);
EnumWindows(lpEnumFunc, 0L);
FreeProcInstance(lpEnumFunc);
```

The following code is an example of a callback function:

```
/************************************************************************
 F i l l W i n d o w L i s t                    ### Callback function ###
 ===========================

 This function executes a callback from the EnumWindows function.
 FillWindowList enters the titles of all parent and child windows in the
 combo box found in the SELECTWINDOW dialog box.

 Parameters:
 HWND          Handles to respective parent windows
 LONG          LOWORD == 0: Parent window listing
               LOWORD == 1: Child window listing

 Return values:
 BOOL FAR PASCAL    Listing stops if NULL is returned.
************************************************************************/
BOOL FAR PASCAL FillWindowList(HWND hWnd, LONG lParam)
{
    char szText[MAXLEN];
    int  mode;

    mode = LOWORD(lParam);
    if(GetClassName(hWnd, (LPSTR) szText, MAXLEN) == 0)
       lstrcpy((LPSTR) szText, (LPSTR) "<undefined>");
    wsprintf((LPSTR) szBuffer,"%5d %s",hWnd, (LPSTR) szText);
    SendMessage(GetDlgItem(hwSelBox, LB_PARENTS+mode), LB_ADDSTRING, 0,
                (LONG) (LPSTR) szBuffer);
    return TRUE;
}
```

Unfortunately, the handles returned in this way are not just those belonging to document windows. This process also returns handles to the titles of child windows that are displayed as icons. Since these cannot be handled as document windows, they must be filtered out. This can be done with the GetWindow function. This function is passed the handle in question along with the value "GW_OWNER". A result of zero indicates a document window while a value greater than zero indicates an icon title.

We will complete our discussion of the basic structure of MDI applications with an overview of the parent/child relationship using the program manager as an example:

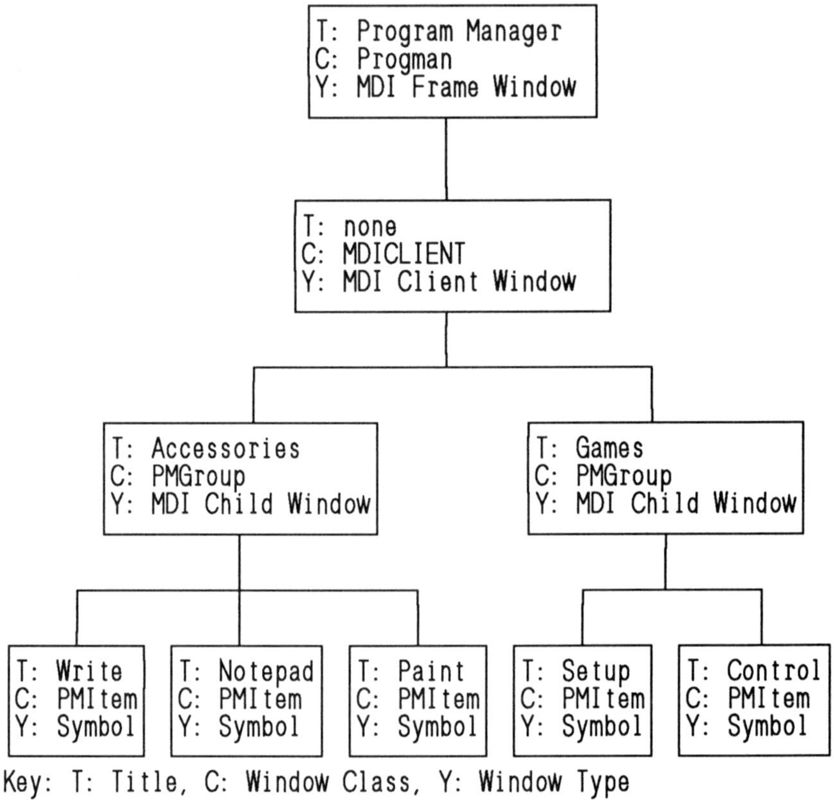

Program manager (presented as parent/child relationship)

8.3 Source Code: MDI_DEMO.EXE

MDI_DEMO.H include file

```
/***************************************************************************
 MDI_DEMO.H    Header file for MDI_Demo application
***************************************************************************/


/***************************************************************************
 Defines one of many MDI child windows with corresponding user-defined
 data structure. The handle to this data structure is entered in the
 existing Property list. This entry is identified as "PROBDEMOENTRY".
***************************************************************************/
typedef struct tagPropertyStruct
{
  int   xSize,        // Current client area width
        ySize,        // Current client area height
        nMaxLines,    // Current number of possible output lines
        nLine,        // Current output line
        nCharHeight,  // Character height
        nCharWidth;   // Character width
} PropertyStruct;

#define MAXLEN        80
#define CBWNDDATA      2            // Room for window structure data
#define GWW_HWINFO     0            // First WORD index to extra bytes in
                                    // the window structure

#define MI_ABOUT     100
#define MI_QUIT      101
#define MI_CREATE    102
#define MI_SELECT    103

#define MI_CASCADE   110
#define MI_TILE      112
#define MI_ARRANGE   113
#define MI_CLOSEALL  114

#define LB_PARENTS   120
#define LB_CHILDS    121

#define FIRSTCHILDID 1000
#define MI_WINDOW    1              // Position of Window popup menu
#define CLIENTWINDOWSTYLE    WS_CHILD|WS_CLIPCHILDREN|WS_VSCROLL|WS_HSCROLL
```

MDI_RC.H include file

```
/*************************************************************************
 MDI_DEMO.H    Header file for MDI_Demo application
*************************************************************************/


/*************************************************************************
 Defines one of many MDI child windows with corresponding user-defined
 data structure. The handle to this data structure is entered in the
 existing Property list. This entry is identified as "PROBDEMOENTRY".
*************************************************************************/
typedef struct tagPropertyStruct
{
  int   xSize,        // Current client area width
        ySize,        // Current client area height
        nMaxLines,    // Current number of possible output lines
        nLine,        // Current output line
        nCharHeight,  // Character height
        nCharWidth;   // Character width
} PropertyStruct;

#define MAXLEN       80
#define CBWNDDATA    20            // Room for window structure data
#define GWW_HWINFO    0            // First WORD index to extra bytes in
                                   // the window structure
#define MI_WINDOW     1            // Position of Window popup menu

#define MI_ABOUT    100
#define MI_QUIT     101
#define MI_CREATE   102
#define MI_SELECT   103

#define MI_CASCADE  110
#define MI_TILE     112
#define MI_ARRANGE  113
#define MI_CLOSEALL 114

#define EB_TITLE    120
#define ST_HWND     121

#define FIRSTCHILDID 1000
```

MDI_DEMO.RC resource file

```
#include <windows.h>
#include "mdi_demo.h"
rcinclude mdi_demo.dlg

FrameIcon   ICON    MDIFRAME.ICO
ChildIcon   ICON    MDICHILD.ICO
DialogIcon ICON     MDI_DEMO.ICO

Menu  MENU
   Begin
       POPUP "&File"
       Begin
         MENUITEM "&Select Window",                   MI_SELECT
         MENUITEM SEPARATOR
         MENUITEM "&Close All MDI Windows",           MI_CLOSEALL
         MENUITEM SEPARATOR
         MENUITEM "E&xit...",                         MI_QUIT
       End

       POPUP "&Window"
       Begin
         MENUITEM "&Cascade",                         MI_CASCADE
         MENUITEM "&Tile",                            MI_TILE
         MENUITEM "&Arrange Icons",                   MI_ARRANGE
         MENUITEM SEPARATOR
         MENUITEM "A&bout MDI-Demo...",               MI_ABOUT
       End
   End
```

MDI_DEMO.DLG dialog box file

```
ABOUTBOX DIALOG LOADONCALL MOVEABLE DISCARDABLE 57, 25, 200, 121
STYLE WS_DLGFRAME | WS_POPUP
BEGIN
    CONTROL "M D I _ D e m o", 101, "static", SS_CENTER | WS_CHILD, 5, 17, 187,
12
    CONTROL "Copyright  1991", 103, "static", SS_CENTER | WS_CHILD, 0, 58, 189,
10
    CONTROL "Abacus", 104, "static", SS_CENTER | WS_CHILD, 0, 68, 189, 11
    CONTROL "Authors: D.Honekamp && P.Wilken", 106, "static", SS_CENTER |
WS_CHILD, 0, 86, 188, 11
    CONTROL "OK", 1, "button", BS_DEFPUSHBUTTON | WS_CHILD, 75, 104, 44, 12
END
```

```
SELECTWINDOW DIALOG LOADONCALL MOVEABLE DISCARDABLE 41, 19, 228, 136
CAPTION "Window Selection"
STYLE WS_BORDER | WS_CAPTION | WS_DLGFRAME | WS_POPUP
BEGIN
    CONTROL "Parent Window:", 102, "static", SS_LEFT | WS_CHILD, 12, 14, 48, 8
    CONTROL "Child Window", 104, "static", SS_LEFT | WS_CHILD, 137, 14, 43, 9
    CONTROL "OK", 1, "button", BS_DEFPUSHBUTTON | WS_TABSTOP | WS_CHILD, 12, 118,
48, 11
    CONTROL "Cancel", 2, "button", BS_PUSHBUTTON | WS_TABSTOP | WS_CHILD, 172,
118, 48, 11
    CONTROL "", 120, "listbox", LBS_NOTIFY | LBS_SORT | LBS_STANDARD | WS_BORDER
| WS_VSCROLL | WS_CHILD, 11, 25, 120, 81
    CONTROL "", 121, "listbox", LBS_NOTIFY | LBS_SORT | LBS_STANDARD | WS_BORDER
| WS_VSCROLL | WS_CHILD, 138, 25, 82, 81
END
```

MDI_DEMO.DEF module definition file

```
NAME            Mdi_Demo
DESCRIPTION     'Sample MDI application'
EXETYPE         WINDOWS
STUB            'winstub.exe'

CODE            PRELOAD MOVEABLE

DATA            PRELOAD MOVEABLE MULTIPLE

HEAPSIZE        0x2000
STACKSIZE       0x2000

EXPORTS         FrameWndProc
                ChildWndProc
                MdfAboutBox
                MdfSelectWindow
                ScanPropList
                FillWindowList
```

MDI_DEMO.MAK MAKE file

```
Mod  = S
Warn = 3

.c.obj:
   cl -W$(Warn) -c -Fc -Os -Zpe -Gw -A$(Mod) $*.c

.rc.res:
```

```
   rc -r $*.rc

ALL: mdi_demo.exe

mdi_demo.obj: mdi_demo.c    mdi_demo.def   mdi_demo.h

mdi_prop.obj: mdi_prop.c    mdi_demo.h

mdi_info.obj: mdi_info.c    mdi_demo.h

mdi_demo.res: mdi_demo.rc   mdi_demo.dlg

mdi_demo.exe: mdi_demo.obj mdi_prop.obj mdi_info.obj mdi_demo.res mdi_demo.def
              link
mdi_demo+mdi_prop+mdi_info,,,LIBW+$(Mod)LIBCEW/NOE/NOD,mdi_demo.def;
              rc mdi_demo.res
```

MDI_DEMO.C source code

```
/**************************************************************************

 M D I _ D E M O . C    Main module for MDI_Demo application

**************************************************************************/

#include        <windows.h>
#include        "Mdi_DEMO.H"

HANDLE      hInst;                      // Handle for application instance
HANDLE      hAccelTable;                // Accelerator table handle

HMENU       hwMenu;                     // Main menu handle
HWND        hwFrame;                    // MDI border window handle
HWND        hwClient;                   // MDI client window handle
HWND        hwNdf;                      // Modeless dialog box handle

FARPROC     lpTmpProc,
            lpSelectProc;               // Pointer to modeless dialog box
                                        // function for window selection
int         nChildNr    = 0,
            aktion;

char        szAppName[]    = "MDI-FrameWindow",
            szPropEntry [] = "PROPDEMOENTRY",
            szBuffer[MAXLEN+1];

/*** Function prototypes ***/
```

```
BOOL FAR PASCAL MdfAboutBox(     HWND hDlg, unsigned msg, WORD wP, LONG lP);
LONG FAR PASCAL ChildWndProc(    HWND hWnd, unsigned msg, WORD wP, LONG lP);
LONG FAR PASCAL FrameWndProc(    HWND hWnd, unsigned msg, WORD wP, LONG lP);
BOOL CreateMdiClientWindow(HWND hWnd);
void CreateMdiChildWindow(long lP);
void DestroyMdiChildren(void);
int PASCAL WinMain (HANDLE hInstance, HANDLE hPrevInstance,
                    LPSTR lpszCmdLine, int nCmdShow);

/*** Function prototypes from MDI_PROP.C module ***/
int FAR PASCAL ScanPropList(HWND hWnd, WORD wDummy, PSTR pString,
                                                        HANDLE hData);
BOOL AddPropEntry(HWND hWnd, LPCREATESTRUCT lpCreate);

/*** Function prototypes from MDI_INFO.C module ***/
void Writeln(HWND hWnd, LPSTR lpText);
void DisplayClassInfo(HWND hWnd);
BOOL FAR PASCAL MdfSelectWindow(HWND hDlg, unsigned msg, WORD wP, LONG lP);

/***********************************************************************
 M d f A b o u t B o x                        ### Dialog box function ###
 =====================

 This function processes the "About" dialog box
***********************************************************************/
BOOL FAR PASCAL MdfAboutBox(HWND hDlg, unsigned msg, WORD wP, LONG lP)
{
   switch(msg)
   {
      case WM_COMMAND:
         switch(wP)
         {
            case IDOK:
               EndDialog(hDlg,TRUE);
               return TRUE;
            default:
               return FALSE;
         }
      default:
         return FALSE;
   }
}

/************************************************************************
 C h i l d W n d P r o c                         ### Callback function ###
 =======================

 M D I - C h i l d W i n d o w   F u n c t i o n
```

```
*************************************************************************/
LONG FAR PASCAL ChildWndProc(HWND hWnd, unsigned msg, WORD wP, LONG lP)
{
   HDC                 hDC;
   HANDLE              hMem;           // Property object handle
   PSTR                pMem;           // Pointer to object memory range
   PAINTSTRUCT         Ps;
   PropertyStruct *    pPropStruct;    // Pointer to property data structure

   switch (msg)
   {
      case WM_CREATE:
      {
         LPCREATESTRUCT     lpCreate;
         LPMDICREATESTRUCT lpMdiCreate;

         /*----------< Data in extra bytes of window class >----------*/
         /*
            This example assigns the  handle of the previously  selected
            window to the extra bytes of the window class structure. The
            necessary space appears at edge of window class registration.
            IP parameters can then be accessed from this handle.

            lP --> CREATESTRUCT
                    .lpCreateParams --> MDICREATESTRUCT
                                          .lParam   our handle in LOWORD
         */

         lpCreate    = (LPCREATESTRUCT)    lP;
         lpMdiCreate = (LPMDICREATESTRUCT) lpCreate->lpCreateParams;
         SetWindowWord(hWnd, GWW_HWINFO, LOWORD(lpMdiCreate->lParam));

         /*----------------< Data in property list >-----------------*/
         /*
            Every MDI child window needs a data structure which contains
            important information in 'writeln'. The handle to this data
            structure is passed to this window's property list
         */
         return AddPropEntry(hWnd, lpCreate);
      }  // WM_CREATE
      break;

      case WM_SIZE:
         if(hMem = GetProp(hWnd, (LPSTR) szPropEntry))
         {
            if(pMem = LocalLock(hMem))
            {
               pPropStruct = (PropertyStruct *) pMem;
```

```
                pPropStruct->ySize   = HIWORD(lP);
                LocalUnlock(hMem);
            }
        }
        return DefMDIChildProc(hWnd, WM_SIZE, wP, lP);
    break;

    case WM_MDIACTIVATE:
        /*
            The wP parameter informs the current window whether it is
            active (=TRUE) or inactive (=FALSE). The IP parameter
            contains handles to two MDI child windows.
            LOWORD(lP)    Handle to the child window to be activated
            HIWORD(lP)    Handle to the child window to be deactivated
        */
        if(wP)  // Window is active...
            InvalidateRect(hWnd, NULL, TRUE);
        return DefMDIChildProc(hWnd, WM_MDIACTIVATE, wP, lP);
    break;

    case WM_PAINT:
        hDC = BeginPaint(hWnd, (LPPAINTSTRUCT) &Ps);
        DisplayClassInfo(hWnd);
        EndPaint(hWnd, (LPPAINTSTRUCT) &Ps);
    break;

    case WM_DESTROY:
    {
        static FARPROC lpScanPropList;
        lpScanPropList = MakeProcInstance(ScanPropList, hInst);
        EnumProps(hWnd, lpScanPropList);
        FreeProcInstance(lpScanPropList);
        return DefMDIChildProc(hWnd, WM_DESTROY, wP, lP);
    }
    break;

    default:
      /*
        Attention: Unlike standard window functions, all unprocessed
        messages  are  passed  to  MDI  child  windows  using  the
        "DefMDIChildProc" function, rather than  to  parent  windows
        using the "DefWindProc" function.
      */
      return DefMDIChildProc(hWnd, msg, wP, lP);
   break;
  }
}
```

```
/**********************************************************************
 C r e a t e M d i C l i e n t W i n d o w
 ==========================================

 This function creates the MDI Clientwindow.

 Parameters:
 HWND         MDI window handle

 Return values:
 BOOL         TRUE if the client window could be created. Otherwise, FALSE
**********************************************************************/
BOOL CreateMdiClientWindow(HWND hWnd)
{
   CLIENTCREATESTRUCT  ClientCreate;      // MDI ClientWindow data structure
                                          // through which window creation is
                                          // accessed
   /*
      Get handle to "Window" popup menu from the MDI-FrameWindow menu bar.
      This menu automatically adds the title of MDI child windows to
      MDI window functions when open, and removes the title when closed.
   */
   ClientCreate.hWindowMenu =  GetSubMenu(hwMenu, MI_WINDOW);

   /*
      Default to a number for the first MDI child window. This number is
      sent to the FrameWindow by a WM_COMMAND message, when the MDI child
      window is selected from entries in the "Window" popup menu.
   */
   ClientCreate.idFirstChild = FIRSTCHILDID;

   hwClient = CreateWindow ("MDICLIENT",    // Predefined window class
                           NULL,
                           CLIENTWINDOWSTYLE,
                           0, 0, 0, 0,
                           hWnd,
                           1,
                           hInst,
                           (LPSTR) &ClientCreate) ;
   if(!hwClient)
      return FALSE;

   ShowWindow(hwClient, SW_SHOW);
   return TRUE;
}


/**********************************************************************
```

```
 C r e a t e M d i C h i l d W i n d o w
 =======================================

 This function creates a new MDI child window.

 Parameters:
 long         LOWORD of this parameter contains the handle to the
              selected window.
***************************************************************************/
void CreateMdiChildWindow(long lP)
{
   MDICREATESTRUCT    MdiCreate;     // Data structure for creating an
                                     // MDI child window

   wsprintf(szBuffer,"MDI Child [%d]",LOWORD(lP));    // Title bar
   MdiCreate.szClass = (LPSTR) "MDICHILD";
   MdiCreate.szTitle = (LPSTR) szBuffer;
   MdiCreate.style   = WS_CHILD;
   MdiCreate.hOwner  = hInst;          // Instance handle for application
                                       // being created

   MdiCreate.x       = CW_USEDEFAULT; // X-position of MDI child window
   MdiCreate.y       = CW_USEDEFAULT; // Y-position "    "    "     "
   MdiCreate.cx      = CW_USEDEFAULT; // Width      "    "    "     "
   MdiCreate.cy      = CW_USEDEFAULT; // Height     "    "    "     "

   /*
       The lParam parameter can be used as a LONG pointer to
       user-defined data.

       In this example, LOWORD contains the IP parameter for the handle
       to the window selected by double-clicking. This handle is passed
       on the MDI child function, and is stored in the extra bytes of
       the window structure by processing the WM_CREATE message.
   */
   MdiCreate.lParam  = lP;

   /*
     Attention: Unless we state otherwise, the CreateWindow function
     should not be used to create an MDI child window. Furthermore,
     This involves filling a variable of type MDICREATESTRUCT, and
     sending a LONG pointer to the client window in the form of a
     WM_MDICREATE message.
   */
   SendMessage(hwClient, WM_MDICREATE, 0,
                                 (LONG) (LPMDICREATESTRUCT) &MdiCreate);
}
```

```
/*************************************************************************
 D e s t r o y M d i C h i l d r e n
 ===================================

 This function destroys all MDI child windows.
*************************************************************************/
void DestroyMdiChildren(void)
{
   HWND hwChild;

   ShowWindow(hwClient, SW_HIDE);     // Client window hidden to avoid
                                      // unnecessary repainting

   while(hwChild = GetWindow(hwClient, GW_CHILD))
   {
      /*
         The list of Window manager-handled child windows searches for
         MDI child windows, and these are destroyed by the
         WM_MDIDESTROY message
      */

      while(hwChild && GetWindow(hwChild,GW_OWNER))
      {
            /*
               The previous window handle is a handle to the subtitle window
               if an icon, rather than an MDI window. Since this window
               shouldn't be handled like an MDI window, it is passed on...
            */
            hwChild = GetWindow(hwChild,GW_HWNDNEXT);
      }

      if(hwChild)
      {
           /*
              If the handle indicates an MDI child window, a
              WM_MDIDESTROY message is sent to the client window...
           */
           SendMessage(hwClient, WM_MDIDESTROY, hwChild, 0L);
      }
      else break;
   }
   ShowWindow(hwClient, SW_NORMAL);  // Make client window visible
}

/*************************************************************************
 F r a m e W n d P r o c                          ### Callback function ###
 =======================
```

```
 M D I - F r a m e W i n d o w   F u n c t i o n
************************************************************************/
LONG FAR PASCAL FrameWndProc(HWND hWnd, unsigned msg, WORD wP, LONG lP)
{
   switch (msg)
   {
      case WM_CREATE:
         return CreateMdiClientWindow(hWnd);    // Create client window...
         break;

      case WM_DESTROY:                          // End application
         DestroyMdiChildren();
         PostQuitMessage(NULL);
         break;

      case WM_COMMAND:
         switch (wP)
         {
             case MI_QUIT:                      // End program...
                if(MessageBox(hWnd, (LPSTR)"Do you really want to exit?",
                            (LPSTR)"Exit Program",
                    MB_ICONQUESTION | MB_YESNO | MB_DEFBUTTON1 |
                    MB_APPLMODAL) == IDYES)
                DestroyWindow(hWnd);
             break;

             case MI_ABOUT:                     // About box
                lpTmpProc = MakeProcInstance((FARPROC)MdfAboutBox, hInst);
                aktion = DialogBox(hInst, "ABOUTBOX", hWnd, lpTmpProc);
                FreeProcInstance(lpTmpProc);
             break;

             case MI_SELECT:               // Window selection dialog box
                lpSelectProc = MakeProcInstance((FARPROC) MdfSelectWindow,
                                                 hInst);
                hwNdf = DialogBox(hInst, (LPSTR)"SELECTWINDOW",
                                                 hwFrame, lpSelectProc);
                FreeProcInstance(lpSelectProc);
             break;

             case MI_CLOSEALL:        // Close all MDI windows
                DestroyMdiChildren();
             break;

             /*-----< Menu commands for MDI window arrangement >------*/
             case MI_CASCADE:         // Cascade MDI child windows
                SendMessage(hwClient, WM_MDICASCADE, 0, 0L);
             break;
```

```
            case MI_TILE:            // Tile MDI child windows
               SendMessage(hwClient, WM_MDITILE, 0, 0L);
            break;

            case MI_ARRANGE:         // Arrange MDI icons
               SendMessage(hwClient, WM_MDIICONARRANGE, 0, 0L);
            break;

            default:
               return DefFrameProc(hWnd, hwClient, WM_COMMAND, wP, lP);
            break;
         }// switch wP

      default:
         /*
           Attention: Unlike standard window functions, all unprocessed
           messages from an MDI FrameWindow function are sent to the
           "DefFrameProc" function rather than the "DefWindowProc"
           function.
         */
         return DefFrameProc(hWnd, hwClient, msg, wP, lP);
      break;
   }
   return (NULL);
}

/*************************************************************************
 Initialize an MDI application
*************************************************************************/
int PASCAL WinMain (HANDLE hInstance, HANDLE hPrevInstance,
                    LPSTR lpszCmdLine, int nCmdShow)
{
  MSG          msg ;
  WNDCLASS     WndClass;

  hInst  = hInstance;      // Save current instance

  /*---------< Register MDIFrame window class >-------*/
  if (!hPrevInstance)
  {
     WndClass.style          = CS_VREDRAW | CS_HREDRAW ;
     WndClass.lpfnWndProc    = FrameWndProc ;
     WndClass.cbClsExtra     = 0 ;
     WndClass.cbWndExtra     = 0 ;
     WndClass.hInstance      = hInst ;
     WndClass.hIcon          = LoadIcon (hInst, (LPSTR) "FrameIcon") ;
     WndClass.hCursor        = LoadCursor (NULL, IDC_ARROW);
```

```
    WndClass.hbrBackground = COLOR_APPWORKSPACE + 1;
    WndClass.lpszMenuName  = (LPSTR) "Menu";
    WndClass.lpszClassName = (LPSTR) "MDIFRAME" ;

    if (!RegisterClass (&WndClass))
        return FALSE;

    /*--------< Register MDIChild window class >------*/
    WndClass.style          = 0 ;
    WndClass.lpfnWndProc    = ChildWndProc ;
    WndClass.cbWndExtra     = CBWNDDATA;      // Room for
                                              // window-specific data
    WndClass.hIcon          = LoadIcon (hInst, (LPSTR) "ChildIcon") ;
    WndClass.hCursor        = NULL;
    WndClass.lpszMenuName   = NULL;           // MDI child window has
                                              // no menu
    WndClass.lpszClassName = (LPSTR) "MDICHILD" ;

    if (!RegisterClass (&WndClass))
        return FALSE;
}

/*---------------------< Create MDI frame window >-------------------*/
hwMenu  = LoadMenu(hInst, (LPSTR) "Menu");
hwFrame = CreateWindow ((LPSTR) "MDIFRAME", (LPSTR) szAppName,
                        WS_OVERLAPPEDWINDOW | WS_CLIPCHILDREN,
                        0, 0, CW_USEDEFAULT, CW_USEDEFAULT,
                        NULL,
                        hwMenu,
                        hInst, NULL) ;

if(!hwFrame)
    return FALSE;

ShowWindow(hwFrame, SW_SHOW);
UpdateWindow(hwFrame);

/*---------------< Direct modified message loop >-------------*/

while(GetMessage (&msg, NULL, 0, 0))
{
    if( /*--- Passing MDI (keyboard) input codes to the
              appropriate MDI window                    ---*/
       !TranslateMDISysAccel(hwClient, &msg)
       && !TranslateAccelerator(hwFrame, hAccelTable, &msg))
    {
       /*--- "normal" message processing ---*/
       TranslateMessage (&msg) ;
```

```
        DispatchMessage (&msg) ;
      }
  }
  return msg.wParam;
} // WinMain
```

MDI_INFO.C source code

```
/************************************************************************
 MDI_INFO    This module contains all functions for window selection
             and structure data display.
************************************************************************/
#include <Windows.h>
#include <stdio.h>
#include "MDI_DEMO.H"

/*** External variables ***/
extern char   szPropEntry[];
extern HANDLE hInst;

/*** Local variables ***/
HWND   hwSelBox;
char   szBuffer[MAXLEN+1];
int    nTabs[1];

/*** Function prototypes ***/
void CreateMdiChildWindow(long lP);
void Writeln(HWND hWnd, LPSTR lpText, BOOL bClrScrn);
void DisplayClassInfo(HWND hWnd);
BOOL FAR PASCAL FillParentList(HWND hWnd, LONG lParam);
BOOL FAR PASCAL MdfSelectWindow(HWND hDlg, unsigned msg, WORD wP, LONG lP);

/************************************************************************
 F i l l W i n d o w L i s t                  ### Callback function ###
 ===========================

 This function executes a callback from the EnumWindows function.
 FillWindowList enters the titles of all parent and child windows in the
 combo box found in the SELECTWINDOW dialog box.

 Parameters:
 HWND          Handles to respective parent windows
 LONG          LOWORD == 0: Parent window listing
               LOWORD == 1: Child window listing

 Return values:
 BOOL FAR PASCAL    Listing stops if NULL is returned.
```

```
***************************************************************************/
BOOL FAR PASCAL FillWindowList(HWND hWnd, LONG lParam)
{
    char szText[MAXLEN];
    int  mode;

    mode = LOWORD(lParam);
    if(GetClassName(hWnd, (LPSTR) szText, MAXLEN) == 0)
       lstrcpy((LPSTR) szText, (LPSTR) "<undefined>");
    wsprintf((LPSTR) szBuffer,"%5d %s",hWnd, (LPSTR) szText);
    SendMessage(GetDlgItem(hwSelBox, LB_PARENTS+mode), LB_ADDSTRING, 0,
                (LONG) (LPSTR) szBuffer);
    return TRUE;
}

/**************************************************************************
 M d f S e l e c t W i n d o w         ### modal dialog box function ###
 ==============================

 This is the window function for processing the window selection mask
*************************************************************************/
BOOL FAR PASCAL MdfSelectWindow(HWND hDlg, unsigned msg, WORD wP, LONG lP)
{
   static HWND hwCurListBox;
   HWND        hwSelected;
   FARPROC     lpEnumFunc;

   switch(msg)
   {
      case WM_INITDIALOG:
         hwSelBox = hDlg;
         SendMessage(GetDlgItem(hDlg,LB_PARENTS), LB_RESETCONTENT, 0, 0L);
         SendMessage(GetDlgItem(hDlg,LB_CHILDS), LB_RESETCONTENT, 0, 0L);
         lpEnumFunc = MakeProcInstance((FARPROC) FillWindowList, hInst);
         EnumWindows(lpEnumFunc, 0L);
         FreeProcInstance(lpEnumFunc);
         EnableWindow(GetDlgItem(hDlg, IDOK), FALSE);
      break;

      case WM_COMMAND:
         switch(wP)
         {
            case IDCANCEL:
               EndDialog(hDlg,FALSE);
               return TRUE;
            break;

            case IDOK:
```

```
            SendMessage(hwCurListBox, LB_GETTEXT,
                        (WORD) SendMessage(hwCurListBox, LB_GETCURSEL, 0, 0L),
                        (LONG) (LPSTR) szBuffer);
              sscanf(szBuffer,"%5d",&hwSelected);
            if(hwSelected)
            {
                CreateMdiChildWindow(MAKELONG(hwSelected, 0));
                EndDialog(hDlg, TRUE);
             }
            return TRUE;
          break;

          case LB_PARENTS:
            if(HIWORD(lP) == LBN_DBLCLK)
            {
              hwCurListBox = LOWORD(lP);
              SendMessage(hwCurListBox, LB_GETTEXT,
                          (WORD) SendMessage(hwCurListBox, LB_GETCURSEL,
0,0L),
                          (LONG) (LPSTR) szBuffer),
              sscanf(szBuffer,"%5d",&hwSelected);
              if(hwSelected)
              {
                EnableWindow(GetDlgItem(hDlg, IDOK), TRUE);
                SendMessage(GetDlgItem(hDlg,LB_CHILDS),
                        LB_RESETCONTENT, 0, 0L);
                lpEnumFunc = MakeProcInstance((FARPROC) FillWindowList,
                                                               hInst);
                EnumChildWindows(hwSelected,lpEnumFunc, MAKELONG(1,0));
                FreeProcInstance(lpEnumFunc);
              }
            }
          break;

          case LB_CHILDS:
            hwCurListBox = GetDlgItem(hDlg, wP);
            if(HIWORD(lP) == LBN_DBLCLK)
              SendMessage(hDlg, WM_COMMAND, IDOK, 0L);
          break;
        }
      break;

      default:
        return FALSE;
    }
}

/***************************************************************************
```

```
 D i s p l a y C l a s s I n f o
 ================================

 This function interprets the window class structure of the hWnd-specified
 window. The information contained therein is displayed through the
 hWnd-specified MDI child window.

 Parameters:
 HWND       hWnd   Handle to current MDI child window
***************************************************************************/
void DisplayClassInfo(HWND hWnd)
{
   HANDLE    hInstance;          // Handle to application instance, created
                                 // by window classes
   WNDCLASS WndClass;            // Window class
   HWND     hwInfo;              // Handle to window containing the desired
                                 // information
   RECT     Rect;

   char     szTemp[MAXLEN+1],
            szClass[MAXLEN+1];

   /*
     Handle to information, from which the extra bytes of the MDI window
     structure are unpacked
   */
   hwInfo = (HWND) GetWindowWord(hWnd, GWW_HWINFO);

   /* Get name of window class */
   if(!GetClassName(hwInfo, (LPSTR) szClass, MAXLEN))
      return ;
   wsprintf((LPSTR) szBuffer,"Class name:\t%s",(LPSTR) szClass);
   Writeln(hWnd, (LPSTR) szBuffer, TRUE);

   /* Get window title, if available */
   if(!GetWindowText(hwInfo, (LPSTR) szTemp, MAXLEN))
      lstrcpy((LPSTR) szTemp,(LPSTR) "<Untitled>");
   wsprintf((LPSTR) szBuffer,"Window title:\t%s", (LPSTR) szTemp);
   Writeln(hWnd, (LPSTR) szBuffer, FALSE);

   /* Unpack instance handle */
   hInstance = GetWindowWord(hwInfo, GWW_HINSTANCE);

   /* Get window class structure */
   GetClassInfo(hInstance, (LPSTR) szClass, (LPWNDCLASS) &WndClass);
   wsprintf((LPSTR) szBuffer,"Window attribute room:\t%-4d",
                                                   WndClass.cbWndExtra);
   if((szClass[0] != '#') && !GetParent(hwInfo))
```

```
    {
       Writeln(hWnd, (LPSTR) szBuffer, FALSE);
       wsprintf((LPSTR) szBuffer,"Class  attribute room:\t%-4d",
                                                 WndClass.cbClsExtra);
       Writeln(hWnd, (LPSTR) szBuffer, FALSE);

       GetWindowRect(hwInfo, (LPRECT) &Rect);
       wsprintf((LPSTR) szBuffer,"[X=%4d, Y=%4d]  [CX=%4d, CY=%4d]", Rect.left,
                                       Rect.top, Rect.right, Rect.bottom);
       Writeln(hWnd, (LPSTR) szBuffer, FALSE);
    }
}

/***************************************************************************
 W r i t e l n
 =============
 This function displays its given string in the next free line of the
 client area. If the output reaches the last possible output line, the
 output moves up by one line. The new last line overwrites the old contents
 of the last line.

 Parameters:
 HWND         Output window handle
 LPSTR        String to be displayed
 BOOL         Indicates whether client area should be cleared
***************************************************************************/
void Writeln(HWND hWnd, LPSTR lpText, BOOL bClrScrn)
{
   HDC              hDC;
   HANDLE           hMem;
   PSTR             pMem;
   RECT             Rect;
   PropertyStruct * pPropStruct;

   if(hMem = GetProp(hWnd, (LPSTR) szPropEntry))
   {
      if(pMem = LocalLock(hMem))
      {
         pPropStruct = (PropertyStruct *) pMem;
         nTabs[0]    = 25 * pPropStruct->nCharWidth;
         hDC  = GetDC(hWnd);
         if(bClrScrn)
         {
            GetClientRect(hWnd, (LPRECT) &Rect);
            FillRect(hDC, (LPRECT) &Rect, GetStockObject(WHITE_BRUSH));
            pPropStruct->nLine = 0;
         }
```

```
        if(pPropStruct->nLine++ >=   // Current line > max. number of lines
                  pPropStruct->ySize / pPropStruct->nCharHeight - 1)
           pPropStruct->nLine = 0;
        /*------------------< Delete line contents >---------------*/
        Rect.left   = 0;
        Rect.top    = pPropStruct->nLine * pPropStruct->nCharHeight;
        Rect.bottom = Rect.top + pPropStruct->nCharHeight;
        Rect.right  = pPropStruct->xSize;
        FillRect(hDC, (LPRECT) &Rect, GetStockObject(WHITE_BRUSH));
        /*-------------------< Display new line >----------------*/
        TabbedTextOut(hDC, 5, Rect.top, lpText, lstrlen(lpText), 1,
                     (LPINT) nTabs, 5);
        ReleaseDC(hWnd, hDC);
        LocalUnlock(hMem);
     }
  }
}
```

MDI_PROP.C source code

```
#include <windows.h>
#include "mdi_demo.h"

/*** External variables ***/
extern HANDLE hInst;
extern HWND   hwFrame, hwClient;
extern char   szPropEntry[];

/*** Function prototyping ***/
int FAR PASCAL ScanPropList(HWND hWnd, WORD wDummy, PSTR pString,
                                                  HANDLE hData);
BOOL AddPropEntry(HWND hWnd, LPCREATESTRUCT lpCreate);

/***********************************************************************
 S c a n P r o p L i s t                        ### Callback function ###
 =======================

 This function lists all available entries in the property list, and
 removes any specified by the application. This callback function is only
 suitable for applications with MOVEABLE data segments.

 Parameters
 HWND
 WORD         Dummy parameter
 PSTR         Specifies identifier of the current list entry
 HANDLE       Handle to current data object
**********************************************************************/
```

```
int FAR PASCAL ScanPropList(HWND hWnd, WORD wDummy, PSTR pString,
                                                   HANDLE hData)
{
   if(lstrcmp((LPSTR) pString, (LPSTR) szPropEntry) == NULL)
   {
      // Entry found...
      LocalFree(hData);                      // Free data object
      RemoveProp(hWnd, (LPSTR) pString);    // Remove entry from list
      return NULL;                           // Cancel list search
   }
}


/**************************************************************************
 A d d P r o p E n t r y
 =======================

 This function inserts an entry in the property list for every MDI child
 window. The identifier for this entry is placed in szPropEntry.

 Parameters:
 HWND         Handle to current MDI child window
 LPCREATE     Pointer to the Create structure, which is passed to the
              MDI child window functions by a WM_CREATE message, in the
              form of an lP parameter.

 Return values:
 BOOL         TRUE if the function was needed. Otherwise, FALSE.
**************************************************************************/
BOOL AddPropEntry(HWND hWnd, LPCREATESTRUCT lpCreate)
{
   HDC                hDC;
   HANDLE             hMem;
   PSTR               pMem;
   TEXTMETRIC         TxtMetric;
   PropertyStruct *   pPropStruct;

   if(hMem = LocalAlloc(LHND, sizeof(PropertyStruct)))
   {
      if(pMem = LocalLock(hMem))
      {
         pPropStruct = (PropertyStruct *) pMem;
         pPropStruct->ySize = lpCreate->cy;
         pPropStruct->xSize = lpCreate->cx;
         pPropStruct->nLine = 0;
         hDC = GetDC(hWnd);
         GetTextMetrics(hDC, (LPTEXTMETRIC) &TxtMetric);
         pPropStruct->nCharWidth  = TxtMetric.tmAveCharWidth;
```

```
            pPropStruct->nCharHeight = TxtMetric.tmHeight +
TxtMetric.tmExternalLeading;
            ReleaseDC(hWnd,hDC);
            LocalUnlock(hMem);
            return SetProp(hWnd,(LPSTR) szPropEntry, hMem);
        }
    }
}
```

9 The Clipboard

This chapter discusses one of the most widely used features of Microsoft Windows—the clipboard.

9.1 How the Clipboard Works

The clipboard is a system-wide resource for sharing data with other applications. If you have ever worked with a Windows word processing program such as Windows Write or Word for Windows, then you are probably familiar with the procedure for moving blocks of text. You mark the desired block and select the **Cut** menu item from the **Edit** menu. The marked block of text then disappears from the screen. Next, you move the cursor to the place where you would like to insert the block of text and select the **Paste** item from the **Edit** menu. The same procedure can move a text block to a different instance of the same application, or a completely different application.

If you have ever wondered how this works, the answer is the clipboard. The clipboard temporarily stores the block of text between the **Cut** and **Paste** menu items. Actually, the data is not stored itself. Instead, the object handle (a handle to the global memory element that stores the data) is placed in the clipboard. The EDIT window class defined in the Windows API also uses the clipboard to store text blocks that it is moving or copying. In general, the clipboard is a useful tool for temporarily storing data while moving or copying it between applications.

Note: The Windows 3 clipboard can move data between MS-DOS programs such as Multiplan and Word. In addition, you can also move data between MS-DOS programs and Windows programs. The only limitation is that the data must be in text format.

Data exchange between Windows applications is not limited to ASCII text, as we can see from looking at the WINDOWS.H file. The constants for various other data formats are defined here. The prefix 'CF_' stands for clipboard format. Here is a list of the clipboard data formats that are predefined in WINDOWS.H:

0x001 CF_TEXT — This is the standard Windows text format. It uses the ANSI character set. Each line ends with CR/LF (carriage return and line feed). The end of text is indicated by a NULL symbol ('\0').

0x002 CF_BITMAP — Bitmap format. The accompanying object handle is a bitmap handle (HBITMAP).

0x003 CF_METAFILEPICT
Metafile format. The data is stored in a format defined by the METAFILEPICT data structure.

0x004 CF_SYLK — Microsoft Symbolic Link Format.

0x005 CF_DIF — Data Interchange Format from Software Arts.

0x006 CF_TIFF — Tag Image File Format.

0x007 CF_OEMTEXT
Text in ASCII format, often used by non-Windows applications. Each line ends with CR/LF, and the text ends with NULL ('\0').

0x008 CF_DIB — The data is stored in a format defined by the BITMAPINFO data structure.

0x009 CF_PALETTE
Color palette format.

In addition to these standard formats, there are other constants defined that allow data objects with custom attributes or formatting (such as bold or underline) to be stored in the clipboard.

Custom clipboard formats

A custom data format pertains to a data object that has been assigned some application-specific attributes. This includes text blocks created by word processing applications. This type of data object is identified as CF_OWNERDISPLAY.

0x080 CF_OWNERDISPLAY
When an application stores a data object with this format in the clipboard, it indicates that it is able to display the data again using the format

(including special attributes) of the new client area (i.e., where the contents will be "pasted"). We will discuss this subject in more detail later.

Another type of custom data object includes data with a standard format, such as bitmap, but protected from general access. These format types are indicated by CF_DSPBITMAP, CF_DSPTEXT or CF_DSPMETAPICTFILE. They are handled just like their namesakes CF_TEXT, CF_BITMAP or CF_METAFILEPICT. The special types are used when you want to share data using the clipboard, but you do not want the data to be generally available.

An example of this would be bitmap transfer between two instances of the same application. A bitmap with format CF_DSPBITMAP is stored in the clipboard by one instance. The second instance then accesses the data by specifying the format CF_DSPBITMAP. If, in the meantime, some other application tries to access the clipboard contents with CF_BITMAP, access will be denied.

0x081 CF_DSPTEXT
Private text

0x082 CF_DSPBITMAP
Private bitmap

0x083 CF_DSPMETAFILEPICT
Private metafile picture

The third type of private data object is an unspecified format used strictly within an application. There is no general specification for such an object. There is a group of constants reserved for this data, ranging from CF_PRIVATEFIRST to CF_PRIVATELAST.

0x200 CF_PRIVATEFIRST
First private format ID

0x2FF CF_PRIVATELAST
Last private format ID

Data objects of other formats are freed by the clipboard. Data objects with IDs between 0x200 and 0x2FF (private formats) must be freed by the application using GlobalFree().

9.2 Registering Clipboard Formats

In addition to the predefined clipboard formats listed above, it is also possible for you to register other data formats. This is done by calling:

```
wNewFormatId = RegisterClipboardFormat((LPSTR)"New_Format");
```

0xC000 - 0xFFFF	The ID number returned by the RegisterClipboardFormat function will be between 0xC000 and 0xFFFF.

After registering the new format, it will be valid system-wide. It can then be used in the same ways as the predefined formats. If you store data in the clipboard using this format, then the format ID will also be found in the list of available formats when you call:

```
wNextFormat = EnumClipboardFormats(wFormat);
```

The format name can be accessed by any clipboard user with:

```
nLength = GetClipboardFormatName(wNewFormatId, lpFormatName,
                                 nMaxLength);
```

If the RegisterClipboardFormat function is used by several applications (or application instances) then Windows will make sure that all applications get the same ID number for the format. This format ID will remain valid for the entire Windows session.

9.3 Working with the Clipboard

The Windows API provides the programmer with several functions for working with the clipboard. But since the clipboard is a system-wide resource that can be accessed by only one application at a time, there are several points you should remember.

9.3.1 Opening the clipboard

There are two basic operations when working with the clipboard: Reading an object from the clipboard or storing an object in the clipboard. You can either pass something to the clipboard or get something from it. The second operation requires that an object is already stored there.

For either operation, an application must first open the clipboard. This is done with the function:

```
hClpBrd = OpenClipboard(hWnd);
```

This function returns a handle to the clipboard as long as it has not been opened by another application. In this case, the function result would be NULL.

Note: At this point, we must remind you that Windows applications are running in a multitasking environment based on the message-polling principle. As a result, an application will retain CPU until it frees it itself by calling the proper function. These functions include GetMessage, PeekMessage, SendMessage and MessageBox. When these functions are called by an application, the functions will jump to the Windows kernel, which then assigns the freed CPU to other applications. When an application opens the clipboard, this type of function call should not be permitted. This prevents some other application, which would then get the freed CPU, from attempting to use OpenClipboard() to access the clipboard. Windows manages these extra attempts to open the clipboard by returning NULL instead of a clipboard handle.

9.3.2 Copying data to the clipboard

Once opened, we can think about storing a data object in the clipboard. We will describe the basic procedure here. Later, we will show you how to optimize this procedure when an application has to support many different data objects or particularly large data objects. But we will begin by storing a data object in ANSI format.

Before we begin, we must remove any old contents from the clipboard with the EmptyClipboard() function. Next, each data format gets its own global memory block and the object is copied there. The corresponding object handles are then passed to the clipboard using the SetClipboardData function. The final step is to close the clipboard again so that other applications can access it. The complete code sequence for storing an object in the clipboard looks like the following:

```
char      szAnsiText[] = "This is the ANSI text" ;

HWND      hWnd;              // Application's window handle
HANDLE    hAnsiText;         // Handle for global memory block
                             // for storing CF_TEXT data

LPSTR     lpGmemAnsi;        // Pointer to the global memory block


/*---------------< Store data in clipboard >-----------*/

if(OpenClipboard(hWnd))
{
   // Empty clipboard
   EmptyClipboard();
   // Allocate global memory blocks
   hAnsiText = GlobalAlloc(GHND, sizeof(szAnsiText));
   // Lock memory blocks and copy data
   lpGmemAnsi = GlobalLock(hAnsiText);
   lstrcpy(lpGmemAnsi, (LPSTR) szAnsiText);
   // Unlock memory blocks
   GlobalUnlock(hAnsiText);
   // Store data in clipboard
   SetClipboardData(CF_TEXT, hAnsiText);
   // Close clipboard
   CloseClipboard();
}
```

When an application calls the SetClipboardData function, it gives up ownership of the clipboard. From this time on, the object handle that was passed to SetClipboardData as a parameter should no longer be used to access the data.

If the data must be accessed for some reason, you should either store a private copy somewhere else or use the handle, returned by SetClipboardData, for read access to the clipboard. In most cases, the data indicated by the object handle will remain the same after it has been stored in the clipboard. However, it is possible that the data could be moved during the SetClipboardData function call and the memory block indicated by the object handle could be freed.

So the result of the SetClipboardData function should always be used as the new handle for the data.

Another restriction to the application is that it isn't allowed to free the global memory block that it allocated for the data object. Since this task is taken over by the clipboard, you must not lock any memory blocks unnecessarily. All memory blocks must be unlocked by the time the clipboard is closed again.

Data objects that were passed to the clipboard by means of private ID numbers (constants between 0x200 CF_PRIVATEFIRST and 0x2FF CF_PRIVATELAST) are an exception. The application is responsible for freeing the memory blocks used for these types of data objects.

Summary

1) Open clipboard
2) Delete old contents of clipboard
3) Allocate and lock global memory block
4) Place data object in clipboard
5) Free memory block
6) Store information
    6.1) Pass format ID and object handle
    6.2) Store the object handle returned (when applicable)
7) Close clipboard

9.3.3 Retrieving data from the clipboard

Any application in possession of a valid clipboard handle can access the contents of the clipboard. There are various ways to do this.

One way is to query the formats that are stored in the clipboard. This is done with the following statements:

```
wFormat = 0;              // Initialization
while (wFormat = EnumClipboardFormats(wFormat))
{
   /*
     Format processing ...
   */
};
```

Depending on the value of wFormat, the EnumClipboardFormats function will return the format IDs from the format list starting with the next number. wFormat must always be a value that is contained in the list. If you want to begin at the start of the format list, then wFormat must be 0. When the end of the list is reached, EnumClipboardFormats will return a value of 0.

After listing the available formats, it is up to the application to determine what format will be used to get the data object.

Another way of accessing the data in the clipboard can be used when the application is interested in only one specific data format. You can use:

```
bFormatFound = IsClipboardFormatAvailable(CF_...);
```

to determine whether anything of the desired format is stored in the clipboard.

In Version 3, you can also check the contents of the clipboard using a custom priority list. In this list, the format IDs of interest to the application are stored in an integer array in order of priority. A WORD FAR * pointer to this array and the number of entries are passed to the GetPriorityClipboardFormat function.

```
int PrioList[] = { CF_TEXT, CF_OEMTEXT, CF_BITMAP };
wFormat = GetPriorityClipboardFormat((WORD FAR *) PrioList, 3);
```

The result of this function specifies the highest priority data format, found in the clipboard, that corresponds to one from the priority list. 0 indicates that the clipboard is empty, and -1 means that none of the data formats given in the priority list were found in the clipboard.

To access the desired data object, we must call the GetClipboardData function. The ID number of the desired data format is passed, as a parameter, to it. The function then returns a handle to the global memory block that contains the data.

Remember that this handle will only be valid between the time you call the GetClipboardData() function and the CloseClipboard() function. So we recommend copying the data to a private memory block for further use. Locking the data object for a long time is also not advisable.

Complete the access to the clipboard data by calling CloseClipboard(). This function closes the clipboard and makes it possible for other applications to access it again. The entire code sequence will look like the following:

```
HWND      hWnd;            // Application's window handle
int       nFormatId;       // Clipboard format ID
                           // e.g.  CF_TEXT, CF_BITMAP, etc ...

HANDLE    hClpbdData,      // Handle for global memory block
                           // of the data object
          hPrivatData;     // Handle for private memory block

LPSTR     lpClpbdData,     // Pointer to global data
          lpPrivateData;   // Pointer to private copy

/*----------------< Reading data from the clipboard >-----------*/

if(OpenClipboard(hWnd))
{
   // The clipboard was successfully opened
   if(IsClipboardFormatAvailable(nFormatId))
   {
      // Clipboard contains data of the desired format
      hClpData = GetClipboardData(nFormatId);
      // Allocate private memory block
      hPrivateData = GlobalAlloc(GHND, GlobalSize(hClpData);
      // Lock memory blocks and copy clipboard data
      lpPrivateData= GlobalLock(hPrivateData);
```

```
        lpClpData     = GlobalLock(hClpData);
        lstrcpy(lpPrivateData,lpClpData); // For CF_TEXT/CF_OEMTEXT
        // Unlock memory blocks
        GlobalUnlock(hClpbdData);
        GlobalUnlock(hPrivateData);
    }
    CloseClipboard();
}
```

When the copy of the data object is no longer needed, this memory block is freed with:

```
GlobalFree(hPrivateData);
```

The object handle returned by GetClipboardData cannot be freed by the application because it belongs to the clipboard.

Summary

1) Open clipboard
2) Check to see if it contains data in the desired format
3) Get handle to this data object
4) Copy data object to private memory block
5) Close clipboard

9.4 The Clipboard Viewer Chain

When an application opens the clipboard, it becomes a clipboard viewer until the time it closes the clipboard. If an application wants to remain informed of the clipboard contents after it has closed it, then the application can enter itself in the clipboard viewer chain. This is done by calling the function:

```
hNextViewer = SetClipboardViewer(hNewViewer);
```

This function makes this application the first in the viewer chain by storing the application handle in hFirstViewer. The previous first application's handle is stored in hNextViewer, the second viewer is stored in the chain. If there was no other viewer in the chain, hNextViewer will be NULL. It is advisable to store this handle in a static variable.

You must do a couple of things in order to use the viewer chain properly. Windows itself only stores the handle to the first member of the chain. So the whole chain will only work if each member routes the messages it receives on to the next member. The window handle for the next application is given to a new application when it is entered in the chain.

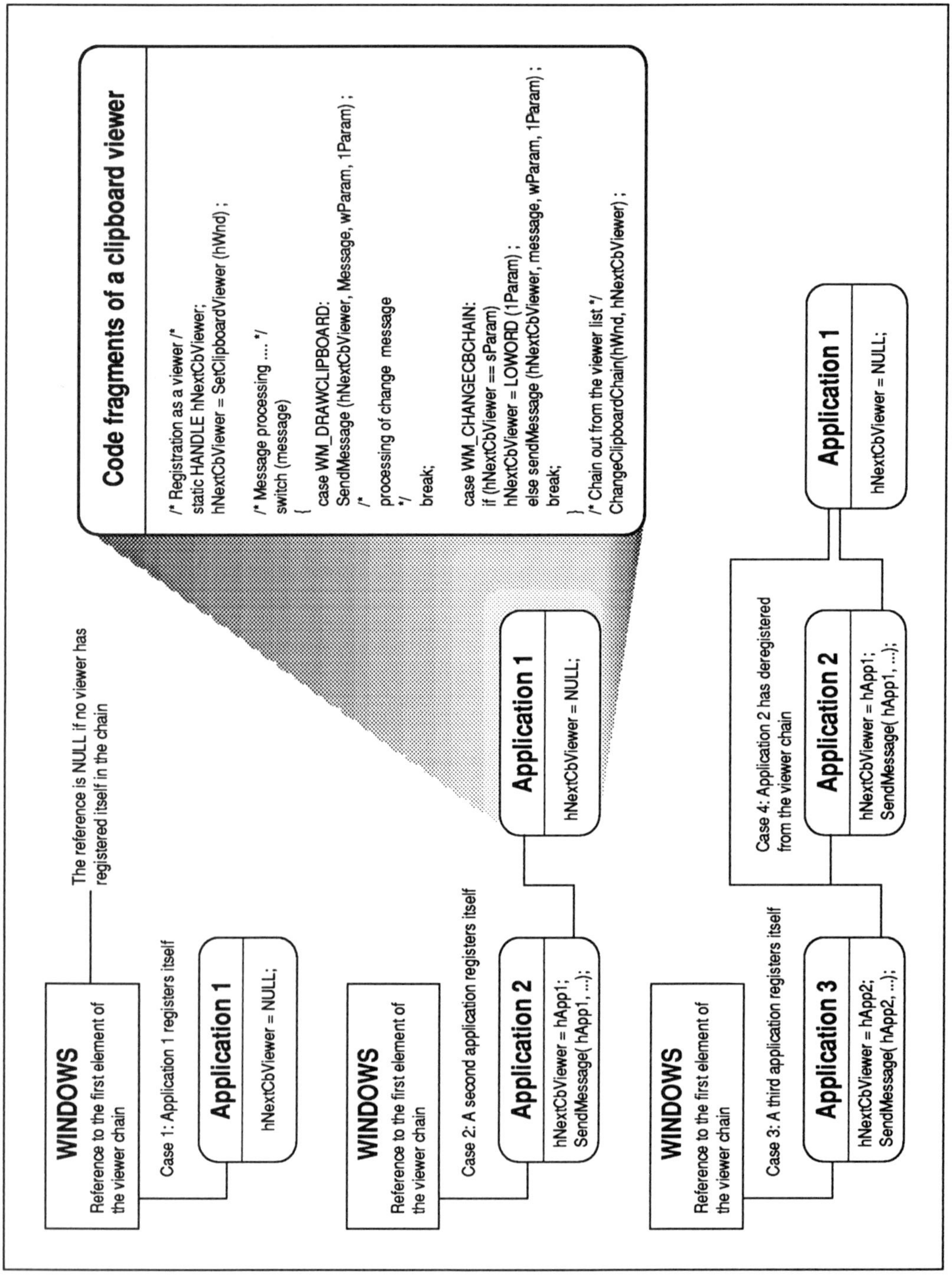

Structure of the clipboard viewer chain

When an application is entered in the viewer chain, Windows will keep it informed of the contents of the clipboard as well as the contents of the viewer chain. Two messages are used for this.

WM_DRAWCLIPBOARD
Changes in the clipboard contents

Windows uses this message to inform the first application in the chain about any changes in the clipboard contents. The first viewer then routes this message on to the next application in the chain with:

```
SendMessage(hNextViewer, message, wParam, lParam);
```

This application will then forward the message to the next, and so forth. If an application fails to send the message on, then the viewer chain is broken.

WM_CHANGECBCHAIN
Remove from chain

An application can remove itself from the clipboard viewer chain by calling ChangeClipboardChain. Required parameters are the handles to the application's own window and to the next application.

```
ChangeClipboardChain(hOwnWnd, hNextViewer);
```

This function call causes Windows to send a WM_CHANGECBCHAIN message to the first application in the clipboard viewer chain. The wParam parameter of this message contains a handle to the window that wants to remove itself from the chain. The window that wants to leave the chain stores the handle, to the application that follows it in the chain, in the low word of the lParam parameter (LOWORD(lParam)).

Every member of the chain will check the wParam parameter and compare the value with the handle of the window that follows it. If the comparison is successful, the next window wants to leave the chain. This means that the handle stored in LOWORD(lParam) will become the next window in the chain and its handle is stored in static memory. All subsequent WM_DRAWCLIPBOARD messages are sent to the new window. If the comparison is unsuccessful, the message is simply sent to the next window in the viewer chain.

9.5 Multiple Data Formats

We have already seen what is needed to store a data object in the clipboard. As long as a data object is in only one format, and as long as it does not require large amounts of storage space, the procedure described earlier in this chapter is suitable. But if you need to store multiple formats, such as a block consisting of ASCII text, ANSI text and a bitmap, Windows has another procedure for saving data. Instead of storing the object in global memory in all formats supported by the owner, the owner tells the clipboard directly which data formats needed to support the object. This is done by calling the SetClipboardData function using NULL handles instead of object handles. A function call for ASCII text would look like the following:

```
SetClipboardData(CF_TEXT, NULL);
```

After the required formats have been entered, CloseClipboard() is called. Now when a viewer asks for a special data object, from the clipboard, by calling GetClipboardData(), this function will find the NULL handle instead of the object handle. This tells the GetClipboardData function to use SendMessage to send a WM_RENDERFORMAT message to the owner. This tells the clipboard owner to store the data in global memory using the data format specified by the wParam parameter, and to return the corresponding object handle to GetClipboardData. This function then passes the handle on to the viewer. This entire procedure is transparent to the viewer, as if the clipboard had simply returned the object handle as is done with "normal" clipboard data retrieval.

Another message that the clipboard owner has to process is WM_RENDERALLFORMATS. Unlike WM_RENDERFORMAT, this message instructs the owner to return object handles for all formats requested by the clipboard. WM_RENDERALLFORMATS is sent to the owner just before the application ends. This message gives the clipboard owner a chance to store data in global memory and pass the corresponding object handles to the clipboard. The clipboard contents remain valid while the application is running. Whether an application will react to a WM_RENDERALLFORMATS message in this way or whether it will ignore it depends on the formats of data objects. If these formats are meaningless to other applications after the clipboard owner application has ended, then no reaction is needed.

9.6 Data Displayed by the Owner

The format ID CF_OWNERDISPLAY refers to data objects that the viewer cannot access directly. A viewer can, however, ask the owner to display the object in the viewer's client area.

Let's clarify this with an example. We have marked a text block in Word for Windows and copied it to the clipboard. When another application opens the clipboard, it will find (among others) the formats CF_TEXT, CF_OEMTEXT and CF_OWNERDISPLAY. If this application requests the data in CF_TEXT or CF_OEMTEXT format, it will receive a handle, to the data, from the clipboard. The application can then copy the text block to a private memory block and process it as desired. The data object will free all format codes, such as bold or underline.

The other application can also use the CF_OWNERDISPLAY format to display the data exactly as it was displayed in Word for Windows. But in this case the application does not receive a handle to the data object. So it cannot store a copy of the data in its own buffer.

But before the text block can be cleanly displayed in the viewer's client area, there are a couple of things both the viewer and the owner should do.

First, let's look at the responsibilities of the owner.

The owner indicates that it can display private data objects in the viewer's client area by sending the CF_OWNERDISPLAY format ID to the clipboard. This is done by calling the function:

```
SetClipboardData(CF_OWNERDISPLAY, NULL);
```

without passing a valid object handle.

From then on, the owner must be prepared to react to the following messages:

WM_SIZECLIPBOARD
: The clipboard viewer uses this message to inform the owner that it has changed its window size. The new dimensions are stored in a RECT

data structure in global memory, and the handle for this structure is stored in the LOWORD of the lParam parameter. The wParam parameter identifies the clipboard viewer.

WM_PAINTCLIPBOARD
: The clipboard viewer uses this message to inform the owner that the viewer client area must be redrawn. A PAINTSTRUCT data structure is stored in global memory, and the handle to it is stored in the LOWORD of lParam. The wParam parameter identifies the clipboard viewer here as well.

By comparing the RECT data, from the last WM_SIZECLIPBOARD message, with the data in rcPaint (part of the PAINTSTRUCT structure), the owner can decide whether the entire client area or just part of it must be redrawn.

If the owner receives a WM_SIZECLIPBOARD message with a RECT structure that indicates an empty rectangle (0,0,0,0), the viewer application has been reduced to an icon or ended.

WM_VSCROLLCLIPBOARD
WM_HSCROLLCLIPBOARD
: These messages tell the owner that it must update the client area.

Now we will take a look at how these messages are generated by the viewer.

In order to display the data object, the viewer sends two successive messages:

1) First, the viewer sends a WM_SIZECLIPBOARD message. The RECT structure indicates the current dimensions of the client area. These are obtained with GetClientRect.

2) Next, the viewer clears its client area by declaring it invalid with InvalidateRect. This triggers a WM_PAINT message. The viewer processes this message and retrieves the current

PAINTSTRUCT structure with BeginPaint. This is then sent to the owner in the form of a WM_PAINTCLIPBOARD message.

The owner will then respond by displaying the clipboard contents in the viewer's client area. From this point on, the viewer must capture certain messages in order to be able to route them to the owner.

The details of this procedure are given in the following code excerpt.

```
case WM_VSCROLL:
   if(bPrivateFormatSelected)
      SendMessage(hClpOwner, WM_VSCROLLCLIPBOARD, hWnd,
                  MAKELONG(wP,LOWORD(lP)));
break;

case WM_HSCROLL:
   if(bPrivateFormatSelected)
      SendMessage(hClpOwner, WM_HSCROLLCLIPBOARD, hWnd,
                  MAKELONG(wP,LOWORD(lP)));
break;

case WM_SIZE:
   if(bPrivateFormatSelected)
      ServePrivateFormat(hWnd,1,lP);  // ==> WM_SIZECLIPBOARD
break;

case WM_PAINT:
   BeginPaint(...);
   if(bPrivateFormatSelected)
      ServePrivateFormat(hWnd,2,0L); // ==> WM_PAINTCLIPBOARD
   EndPaint(...);
```

Comments: The bPrivateFormatSelected flag indicates that the application has selected the CF_OWNERDISPLAY format. The custom function ServePrivateFormat is responsible for correctly storing the RECT or PAINTSTRUCT data structure in a global memory block and for passing it on to the owner as a WM_SIZECLIPBOARD or WM_PAINTCLIPBOARD message.

9.7 *.CLP Files

Now that we have seen how different applications can exchange data using the clipboard, let's take a look at how we can take the clipboard contents and store it in a file.

Starting in Version 3, a specific protocol stores data objects, from the clipboard, in a file. The structure used consists of three parts: A header, the format descriptor and the actual data. If the data object uses more than one format, then the different data format descriptors follow the header. The corresponding data comes last (see the figures listed in the next section).

The clipboard file structure (*.CLP)

File Header

Offset	Description	Type	Comments:
0- 1	CLP_ID	WORD	File type ID: 0xC350
2- 3	wFormatCount	WORD	Number of formats found in file

First Format Descriptor Block (length = 89 bytes)

Offset	Description	Type	Comments:
4- 5	wFormatId	WORD	ID of first format
6- 9	lDataLength	LONG	Length of format data in bytes
10-13	lDataOffset	LONG	Position of first byte in file relative to start of file
14-92	szPrivateName	s[79]	If this is a private data format, name is entered here

Second Format Descriptor Block (length=89 bytes)

Offset	Description	Type	Comments:
4- 5	wFormatId	WORD	ID of first format
6- 9	lDataLength	LONG	Length of format data in bytes
10-13	lDataOffset	LONG	Position of first byte in file relative to start of file
14-92	szPrivateName	s[79]	If this is a private data format, name is entered here

.
.
.

nth Format Descriptor Block

n*89 + 4 to n*89 + 4+l	Data block in format 1 l = Length of data block in bytes

n*89+4+l+1	Data block in format 2

.
.
.

	Data block in format n

Clipboard file structure (.CLP)*

You'll find more information and the listings for a demo application in Chapter 14 of this book.

10 The Timer

The timer is one of the most important components - not only for Windows, but for PCs in general. The timer, or more precisely the timer chip (Intel 8259), plays a role in all different kinds of processing, such as RAM refresh cycles and the system clock. Every 54.95 ms, or 18.2 times per second, the timer chip sends a signal to the interrupt controller via IRQ0. From there, the CPU is informed in the usual way (see the section on serial ports). The CPU is then responsible for calling the interrupt processing routines.

A device driver realizes this procedure in Windows. It is called SYSTEM.DRV, and it replaces the standard MS-DOS timer interrupt function in the interrupt vector table when Windows is started.

However, we must remember that a PC running under Windows is still a fully functional MS-DOS machine. So one of SYSTEM.DRV's tasks is to route the clock impulses directly to the original MS-DOS interrupt function. Only after this has happened can SYSTEM.DRV begin its real work.

Windows also installs special device drivers for processing keyboard and serial port interrupts (KEYBOARD.DRV and COMM.DRV). When an interrupt of the proper type is received, these drivers send a corresponding message to the USER.EXE module. In so doing, the message is routed to the appropriate system message loop.

SYSTEM.DRV differs from these device drivers in this point. Instead of sending a message, it branches directly to a FAR CALL in the USER.EXE module and executes a function there.

Before we describe actual timer events, let's take a moment to look at the timer itself. The timer is handled as a resource under Windows. Like display contexts or the clipboard, the timer is also a limited resource. There is a total of 16 timers available system-wide. An application activates the timer by calling the SetTimer function. There are two types of timers you can select. With one type of timer, a message is sent to the message loop of an application. With the other type, USER.EXE calls the function for processing the timer event directly.

10.1 Timer Activation: Window Method

Here are the parameters used to activate a timer with the SetTimer function when sending WM_TIMER messages to a particular window:

HWND parameter
Handle for the window receiving the WM_TIMER message.

int parameter
ID number assigned by the application to the activated timer. This ID number is to be saved for accessing the timer later.

WORD parameter
The time period to wait before triggering the WM_TIMER message. The time is given in milliseconds. Valid values are from 55 ms to 65535 ms. The minimum of 55 ms is a limitation of the timer chip itself, since it sends out a timer impulse every 54.95 ms. This is the smallest unit of time, and all time values are internally converted to integer multiples of this value.

FARPROC parameter
In this case, we set this parameter to NULL. We will take a closer look at how it works when we demonstrate the second method for activating the timer.

Multiple timers
Because there is a limited number of timers available system-wide, we must evaluate the result of the SetTimer function. If this result is not zero, then there was another timer available to be activated. If the result is zero, then all timers are currently being used. The complete SetTimer function call looks like this:

```
if(!SetTimer(hWnd, 1, 2000, NULL))
{
   /*
     No timers available now ...
     Try again later
   */
}
else
/*
   Timer was successfully activated
*/
```

After activating the timer, Windows sends WM_TIMER messages, in the specified interval, to the application identified by the window handle. The messages are placed in the application's message loop as usual.

10.2 Timer Activation: Callback Method

Windows also provides another way of activating the timer. Instead of sending a message, you can call the timer event function directly. To do this, we must use parameter 4 to pass the procedure instance address of the function that will process the timer events.

Since this function is called directly by Windows, its parameters are pre-defined.

```
/*----------- Definition of the callback function -------------*/

WORD FAR PASCAL TimerEventFunction(HWND hWnd, WORD Msg,
                                   int TimerId, DWORD dwTime)
{
   /*
     this function is called by Windows directly
     when the timer is activated
   */
}
```

The required procedure instance address of the TimerEventFunction is obtained as usual with the MakeProcInstance function. Since it is a callback function, TimerEventFunction must also be exported in the DEF file.

```
/*------------------ Required variables -------------------*/

FARPROC    lpTimerEventFunction;       // --> EXPORT
                                       //     in *.DEF-File
HANDLE     hInst;                      // application
                                       // instance address


/*---------Set procedure instance address ------------*/

lpTimerEventFunction = MakeProcInstance(TimerEventFunction,
                                        hInst);
```

After the procedure instance address is set, the timer can be activated. When the timer is running, USER.EXE calls TimerEventFunction directly.

```
/*------------------ Activate timer --------------------*/

if(!SetTimer(hWnd, 1, 2000, lpTimerEventFunction))
{
   /*
     no timer currently available
     try again later
   */
}
else
/*
   timer was successfully activated
*/
```

Comments: With the timer activations we have seen so far, the timer ID is set by the application. However, there may be cases when the application doesn't want to bother with assigning and managing this ID. In these instances, Windows can give the timer a unique ID itself. This is done by setting parameters 1 and 2, in the SetTimer function call, to zero when activating the timer. When the timer is successfully activated, the function will return the timer ID.

```
if(TimerId = SetTimer(NULL, 0, 2000, lpTimerEventFunction))
{
   /*
     no timers available now...
     try again later
   */
}
else
/*
   timer was successfully activated
*/
```

Now that we know how to activate the timer, we should also learn how to deactivate it. The KillTimer function is called with the corresponding window handle and timer ID as parameters:

```
if(KillTimer(hWnd, TimerId))
{
  /*
    timer was successfully deactivated
  */
}
else
{
```

```
  /*
    no timer with the specified ID was found
  */
}
```

Now let's return to the point where we leave the USER.EXE module after SYSTEM.DRV has used a FAL CALL to execute a function there. This function's job is to decrement, by 1, each timer counter activated by the application each time it is called. When the timer was activated, the timer counter was initialized to the next highest integer value resulting from the quotient of the delay time and the interval of the timer interrupt.

Let's clarify this with an example. Assume a timer is activated as follows:

```
SetTimer(hWnd, 1, 2000, NULL);
```

This means that a timer interrupt will be sent every 54.95 ms. So the next highest integer value resulting from the delay time divided by the interrupt interval is:

```
2000 ms / 54.95 ms = 36.
```

Therefore, the actual delay time will be 36 * 54.95 ms = 1978.2 ms. The timer counter was initialized with the value 36 in this case.

If a timer runs out, which means the timer counter reaches the value zero, then the timer event function is called or a WM_TIMER message is sent, depending on how the timer was activated.

Since the WM_TIMER message does not interrupt the current processing of the CPU, you cannot be assured that the delay time you set will always be kept. If another application ties up the CPU for a while, the signal will be delayed. So it's possible that the timer interval will go by several times before the application that receives the message can access the CPU and react to the message.

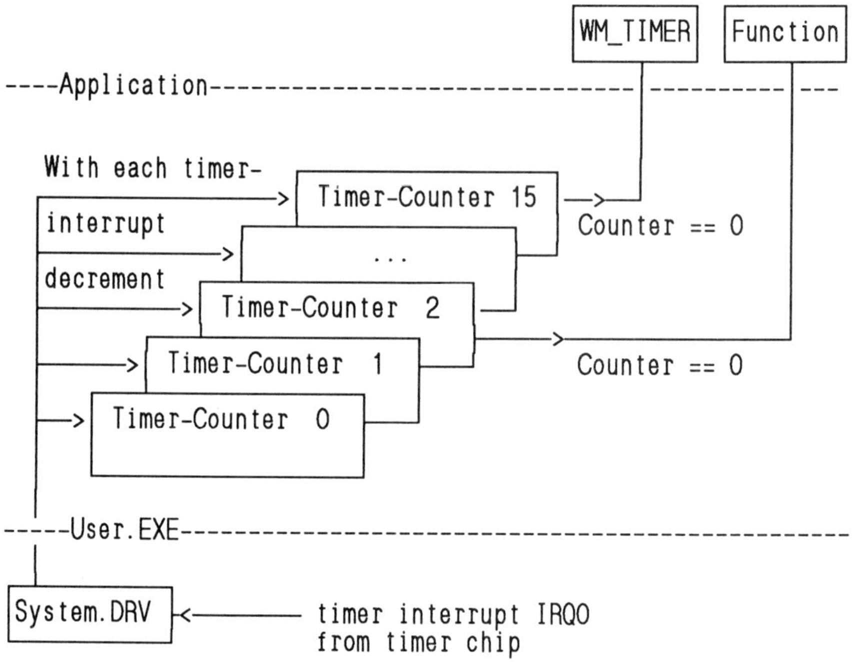

Processing the timer interrupt

However, Windows will prevent the application from having to process several waiting WM_TIMER messages in such a case. These messages are held back so that the application only processes the last one to be received.

Example

Let's assume application A activates a timer that sends a message to the application every 500 ms. This will happen as intended if the application receives some CPU time in intervals less than 500 ms. But if application B is running a calculation that takes 1.8 seconds, for example, then application A will not get any CPU access during this time, even though its timer counter will have elapsed three times. So USER.EXE was not able to enter these three events in the application's message loop. Instead, they are collected in a WM_TIMER message, which is sent to application A when the CPU is available again.

10.3 Description of a Timer Program

Chapter 14 contains an application named CLPDEMO.EXE, which demonstrates the information we have presented about working with timers. Each time the application is started, the About box containing the copyright is displayed before the main window appears.

This is donc by calling:

```
SendMessage(hWnd, WM_COMMAND, MI_ABOUT, NULL);
```

while processing the WM_CREATE message. The message is sent to the window to simulate selecting the menu item that produces the About box.

At the time of initialization, the About box function activates a timer with a delay of several milliseconds.

When the WM_TIMER message is received, four bitmaps are created and the About box is closed again.

Another use for the timer is in controlling the ports. You can use the timer here to periodically check the receiving buffer for any characters that may have been sent. This example shows how a function can be called directly as a result of the timer running out.

10.4 Timer Functions

```
WORD SetTimer(HWND hWnd, int nEventId, WORD wDelay, FARPROC lpTimerFunction)
```

Activating a timer

```
BOOL KillTimer(HWND hWnd, int nEventId)
```

Deactivating a timer

Message produced: WM_TIMER (0x0113)

The timer ID is stored in the wParam parameter. If a timer function was assigned to the timer when it was activated, then the lParam parameter will contain a pointer to this function. In this case, the function is called by Windows directly, and no WM_TIMER message is sent to the application's message loop.

More details on this subject are presented with the listing in Chapter 14.

11 Dynamic Data Exchange (DDE)

Under Windows, Dynamic Data Exchange (DDE) is a complex and very powerful mechanism that allows different applications to communicate directly with one another. DDE's capabilities far surpass simple data transfer, which can be performed with the clipboard.

DDE protocol

DDE uses a standard protocol for all Windows applications, which allows software from different developers to communicate. DDE may also present the foundation for a new type of program. Up until now, several developers have attempted to combine applications such as word processing, spreadsheet and database management into a single super package. Unfortunately these integrated packages always had to make certain compromises.

With DDE, it's possible to combine the capabilities of specialized programs into an integrated environment. For example, combining the packages Word for Windows, Superbase 4 and Excel under DDE would make the best of each program available, resulting in a very powerful working environment.

11.1 Atoms

Let's define some of the components of the DDE protocol. An *atom* is a unique ID number for a character string. The string itself is located in a table (an array), and the atom is the index for the string in this array. Each character string is unique and appears only once. The technical literature refers to this type of structure as a *hash table.*

Windows has two types of atom tables—private and global. Even though the first type is not particularly relevant to DDE, we will describe it briefly anyway.

Private atoms

Any application can create a private atom table on the local heap using the InitAtomTable function. Access to this table is limited to the application that created it. As a parameter, this function receives the size of the table (number of columns). This must be a whole number.

```
/*--- Allocating a private atom table on the local heap ---*/
BOOL InitAtomTable(nTableEntries)
```

The AddAtom function then enters character strings in the table. The parameter for this function is a pointer to the character string being added. The atom that identifies the string, in the table, is returned when the function is successfully completed.

```
/*---- Storing a string in a private atom table ----*/
nAtom = AddAtom((LPSTR) "I am a character string");
```

If you call the AddAtom function more than once with the same character string, it will return the same atom. Multiple calls to the function increments the reference counter kept for each table entry. The AddAtom function is case sensitive.

There are two different ways to access a character string stored in the atom table. The GetAtomName function copies the string, indicated by the atom in the first parameter, to the buffer variable indicated with the second parameter. The total number of characters to be copied is limited by the third parameter.

```
/*--- Read string from a private atom table ---*/
nCopied = GetAtomName(nAtom, lpPuffer, nMaxChars);
```

The function result indicates how many characters were actually copied. If the result is zero, the atom was invalid.

The other way to access the atom table is with the GetAtomHandle function, which returns a handle to the specified character string.

```
/*--- Get handle to an atom table string ---*/
hMem = GetAtomHandle(nAtom);
```

The function result is a handle for the local heap, which can be interpreted with the LocalLock function. If the function result is zero, then the atom was invalid.

The next function used in dealing with atoms is DeleteAtom. This function receives, as a parameter, the atom that you wish to delete. If this atom is found in the table, the DeleteAtom function decrements its reference counter. Only when the reference counter reaches zero is the character string actually removed from the table.

```
/*--- Delete a string from a private atom table ---*/
while(DeleteAtom(nAtom));
```

To ensure that the string is indeed deleted from the table, the while loop calls the DeleteAtom function until the reference counter equals zero. If you know the character string that you want to access but you do not know its atom, the FindAtom function can help. This function receives a pointer to the character string as a parameter and returns the corresponding atom as long as the string was found in the table.

```
/*--- Finding an atom by its character string ---*/
nAtom = FindAtom(lpString);
```

Global atoms

The global atom table is very important to the DDE. There is only one global atom table for the entire system, and it can be accessed by all applications. Since each string is identified by exactly one atom, any application can use the proper atom to access a given string. This relates to DDE because atoms can be included in DDE messages (usually in the high or low word of lParam) in order to move character strings between applications. The DDE protocol specifies which partner in the communication must then delete the atom.

Let's look at the functions used to manipulate the global atom table. As you can see from the following list, almost all private atom functions have global equivalents. The function names are the same, with "Global" prefixes added:

```
nAtom   = GlobalAddAtom(lpString);
nCopied = GlobalGetAtomName(nAtom, lpString, nMaxChars);
nAtom   = GlobalDeleteAtom(nAtom);
nAtom   = GlobalFindAtom(lpString);
```

These functions all work the same way as their private atom table counterparts. The InitAtom function has no global counterpart, because the size of the global atom table is set at 37 columns. However, this does not limit the global atom table to 37 entries. The range of valid global atom handles extends from 0xC000 to 0xFFF, for a maximum of 16384 atoms.

11.2 Exchanging Global Data Objects

Global atoms represent one way that data (in the form of character strings) can be transferred from one application to another.

Shared memory

Another medium for data exchange is shared memory. As the name suggests, this refers to a memory region that can be accessed by several programs simultaneously. This region can be used in such a way that data stored there by one application can be read by another application.

Unlike other operating systems, such as UNIX, the Windows memory manager does not directly support this kind of shared memory region. This means that an application isn't allowed to work with the global handles of other applications. For example, you cannot access another application's handles by calling GlobalLock, nor can you use global handles in your own messages between applications in order to exchange data.

At this point, you may recall some of your own experiences where you were able to successfully use these methods. It is true that they will work for systems without EMS memory. But Microsoft cautions that, in order to maintain compatibility with EMS systems and future Windows versions, DDE is the only mechanism for exchanging global handles between applications.

In order to use DDE for data exchange, global handles must be stored on the global heap in a certain way. This is the responsibility of the sender. The size of the object being sent and the GMEM_MOVEABLE and GMEM_DDE_SHARE flags are passed to the GlobalAlloc function, which allocates an appropriate memory block. The memory block is locked upon receipt of a valid handle, and the data is copied.

Before the data can then be sent to the receiver, it must be freed. DDE messages are usually sent with the PostMessage function. The only exception is WM_DDE_INITIATE and its answering message WM_DDE_ACK. These are sent with the SendMessage function.

```
/* Allocating memory for a DDE data object */

if(hData = GlobalAlloc(GMEM_DDE_SHARE | GMEM_MOVEABLE,
                       sizeof( ... )))
{
   if(lpData = GlobalLock(hData))       // Lock memory block
   {
       lstrcpy(lpData, ...);            // Copy data
       GlobalUnlock(hData);             // Free block
       PostMessage(...);                // Send data
   }
   else // Error message GlobalLock
}
else  // Error message GlobalAlloc
```

After the object has been sent and processed by the receiver, we have to address whether the server or the client is responsible for "cleaning up," or deleting the object. Unfortunately, there is no simple answer to this question. Basically, the party that receives a negative ACKnowledge must check to see if it pertains to a message that contains a data object. If it does, then the corresponding object must be deleted. Also, a server must delete data objects presented to it by a WM_DDE_POKE message.

A client that receives an object by a WM_DDE_DATA message decides whether or not to delete the object based on the fRelease flag within the DDEDATA structure. If the fRelease flag was set by the server, then the data object must be deleted. The client is relieved of this duty if it answers the data message with a negative ACKnowledge.

11.3 The DDE Protocol

Before applications can exchange data, they must establish a connection. The structure of this connection is described in three hierarchical steps in the DDE protocol.

11.3.1 The structure of a DDE session

Initialization

A DDE session is initiated with a WM_DDE INITIATE message. However, some preparations must be made before such a message can be sent.

The WM_DDE_INITIATE message allows the receiving application to generally specify what applications it will communicate with and what topics will be the subject.

The topic and the name of the application are specified by storage in global atoms. If no limitations are to be set, then both of these atoms will contain zero. If the communication is intended for any application, then the low word of lParam is set to NULL. The same is true for the topic, if any topic can be used.

```
aTopic   = GlobalAddAtom(lpTopic);
aAppName = GlobalAddAtom(lpAppName);
```

The simplest thing to do is to send the message, as a broadcast message, to all applications currently running. This is done by entering -1 in place of the window handle that would normally identify the receiver to the SendMessage function.

```
/* Broadcast message to all applications ... */
SendMessage(-1, WM_DDE_INITIATE, hClient,
            MAKELONG(aAppName, aTopic));
```

When an application capable of participating in a DDE session receives a WM_DDE_INITIATE message, it checks the application name and the topic to see if it is being addressed. If it is, it responds with a positive acknowledge message. The SendMessage function is used to send this WM_DDE_ACK message back to the client. You should note that this is the only case in which the DDE protocol allows a WM_DDE_ACK message to be sent with SendMessage. Normally, the PostMessage function must be used.

If the client receives a positive acknowledgement to its WM_DDI_INITIATE query, then it saves the window handle of its communication partner. This handle was received in the wParam parameter of the WM_DDE_ACK message. The client then uses this handle to forward all subsequent messages directly to the server.

11.3.2 Types of data exchange

With these first steps, we have identified two applications that are able to communicate with one another on a certain topic. Now let's get more specific and determine exact contents of the communication.

First, the client must specify what type of communications channel, or link, will be established between the server and client. There are four types:

One-time data exchange using DDE

With a one-time data exchange, the client can send the server an unrequested data object with a WM_DDE_POKE message. Or the client can query the server with a WM_DDE_REQUEST message to determine what data object it wants.

```
/* Send unrequested data object to server ... */

PostMessage(hServer, WM_DDE_POKE, hClient,
            MAKELONG(hData, aItem);

/* Data object requested by server ... */

PostMessage(hServer, WM_DDE_REQUEST, hClient,
            MAKELONG(h
```

Setting up links

A link is a special connection to the server. The server uses the link to send a WM_DDE_DATA message to the client to indicate that the value of a specific data object has changed. This type of message must be sent by the server each time the value of a data object changes. The server can be released from this obligation only if the client sends a WM_DDE_UNADVISE message.

The WM_DDE_ADVISE message is used for setting up a link. The low word of the lParam parameter contains a handle to a

DDEADVISE data structure, and the high word contains the atom used to access the description of the data object in question.

The DDEADVISE data structure contains several flags that determine how data will flow through the link.

We have already seen that the server sends a WM_DDE_DATA message to the client when the value of a data object changes. If the fAckReg flag in the DDEADVISE structure is set, then the server must wait for a response from the client before sending another message. This procedure prevents the client from being overwhelmed with change messages from the server.

The fDeferUpd flag also prevents the client from being swamped by changing data objects. The status of this flag (TRUE or FALSE) determines whether a hot or warm link will be set up:

Hot link

With a hot link, the server sends the client a handle to the data object along with the message that indicates the change in the data object. This handle is stored in the low word of the lParam parameter in the WM_DDE_DATA message.

```
// CLIENT: setting up a hot link ...

lpOptions->cfFormat = CF_TEXT;  // Desired data format
lpOptions->fAckReg  = TRUE;     // Flow control on
lpOptions->fDeferUpd= FALSE;    // Deliver data object immediately
PostMessage(hServer, WM_DDE_ADVISE, hClient,
          MAKELONG(hOptions, aItem));

// SERVER: sending a change message ...

DDEDATA FAR * lpData;           // Pointer to DDEDATA structure

/*
   DDEDATA - create proper structure ...

   The actual data object is appended to the header of the
   DDEDATA structure starting at word 3
*/

lpData->fRequested = FALSE;      // No answer to REQUEST
lpData->fAckReq    = TRUE;       // Client must respond with ACK
lpData->fRelease   = TRUE;       // Client must delete data object
```

```
/* Update message with hot link */
PostMessage(hClient, WM_DDE_DATA, hServer,
            MAKELONG(hData, aItem));        // With data handle
```

Warm link

Like a hot link, a warm link provides a connection for the server to inform the client of a change in the data object with a WM_DDE_DATA. However, with a warm link the WM_DDE_DATA message will not contain a handle to the data object. It is up to the client to say whether or not it is interested in the current value of the data object. If so, the client uses a WM_DDE_REQUEST message to explicitly request this from the server. The server then responds with a WM_DDE_DATA message with the fRequested flag of the DDEDATA structure set to TRUE. This indicates that the new WM_DDE_DATA message is in response to a request from the client. This new message will then contain a handle to the data object in the low word of lParam and a handle to the DDEDATA structure in the high word of lParam.

```
// CLIENT: setting up a warm link ...

lpOptions->cfFormat = CF_TEXT;      // Desired data format
lpOptions->fAckReg  = TRUE;         // Flow control on
lpOptions->fDeferUpd= TRUE;         // Data object requested separately
PostMessage(hServer, WM_DDE_ADVISE, hClient,
            MAKELONG(hOptions, aItem));

/* Update message with warm link */
PostMessage(hClient, WM_DDE_DATA, hServer,
           MAKELONG(0, aItem));             // Without data handle
```

Closing a link

When the client is no longer interested in a data object, it can tell the server to stop sending the change messages, which effectively results in closing the link.

```
/* Closing a link ... */

PostMessage(hServer, WM_DDE_UNADVISE, hClient,
            MAKELONG(0, aItem));
```

If more than one link was opened by the client, they can all be closed with a single message by setting the aItem atom to zero.

```
/* Closing all links ... */

PostMessage(hServer, WM_DDE_UNADVISE, hClient,
            MAKELONG(0, 0));
```

Remote command execution

WM_DDE_EXECUTE is a special DDE message type that allows the client to send commands for execution by the server. Our DDE demo program, which creates a DDE connection to the Windows Program Manager, contains a good example of this. An important requirement for this type of link is that the server has some sort of macro language available that the client can use to send instructions to the server.

11.3.3 Terminating a DDE session

A DDE session can be terminated by the client or the server at any time. So both applications must be prepared to receive and process a WM_DDE_TERMINATE message. The application that wants to end the sessions sends the message to its communication partner.

```
/* Terminate a DDE session ... */

PokeMessage(hDdePartner, WM_DDE_TERMINATE, hWnd, 0L);
```

When an application receives a WM_DDE_TERMINATE message, it must respond with a WM_DDE_TERMINATE message. Other responses, especially negative or wait acknowledge messages, are not allowed.

It is the responsibility of any application taking part in a DDE session to properly terminate this session before the application itself ends.

11.4 Application: DDE_EXE.EXE

As a demo program, we have selected a program that communicates with the Windows memory manager using DDE. The Program Manager has a DDE interface, which allows other Windows applications to request the following actions:

Create new program groups

The following command instructs the Program Manager to create a new program group called "GroupName" with the path name "Path":

```
CreateGroup(GroupName, Path)
```

If a program group with this name already exists, then the Program Manager will activate the corresponding window.

Delete a program group

The following command instructs the Program Manager to delete the program group indicated by "GroupName":

```
DeleteGroup(GroupName)
```

Show the contents of a program group

The following command displays the window indicated by "GroupName" in the specified Format (maximized, minimized or normal):

```
ShowGroup(GroupName,Format)
```

Add new programs to a group

The following command allows an application to add a new program to a program group created with CreateGroup:

```
AddItem(ProgramName,Description,
        IconPath, IconIndex,
        xPos, yPos)
```

"ProgramName" must be given, but all other parameters are optional.

You can also specify the path and any parameters for the program start, just as if you were working with the Program Manager directly. The "Description" parameter represents the text that will be displayed underneath the program icon in the group window. "IconPath" is the path for the icon. If this is a DOS application, you can use the "IconIndex" parameter to specify which of the five internal Program Manager icons will be used to represent the application. The "xPos" and "yPos" parameters determine where the icon will be displayed in the group window. If these parameters are not specified, the Program Manager will position the icon in the next free space.

After the Program Manager's DDE interface has been set up, the program is fairly self-explanatory. Once a link has been established to the Program Manager, it will function as a server. The demo program will then send various WM_DDE_EXECUTE messages to initiate some of the actions described above.

11.5 DDE Message Tables

This section contains tables that list DDE messages according to use.

The column DDE Message contains a brief description of the message. The prefix WM_DDE must precede the message in order for it to be a valid DDE message. This column also indicates the direction of the message. "C ==> S" indicates a message from client to server and "S ==> C" indicates server to client. And finally, this column indicates whether the message is sent with SendMessage or PostMessage.

The second column, labeled "Description", briefly explains the purpose of the message.

The third and fourth columns indicate what information is contained in the high and/or low words of the lParam parameter. The associated data structure is also indicated where applicable.

Starting a DDE session			
DDE Message	Description	LO(lParam)	HI(lParam)
INITIATE C <=> S SendMessage	Request to establish a communication link	aApplication	aTopic
ACK C <=> S SendMessage	Acknowledges receipt of messages such as: WM_DDE_INITIATE ---> WM_DDE_EXECUTE ---> Others ... --->	 aApplication wStatus wStatus Structure DDEACK Fields: fAck, fBusy, bAppReturn-Code	 aTopic hCommand aItem
TERMINATE C <=> S Postmessage	End a link session established with INITIATE	reserved	reserved

Permanent Data Exchange (continuous update)
a) Hot Link (fDeferUpd == 0) includes data
b) Warm Link (fDeferUpd == 1) data must be requested

DDE Message	Description	LO(lParam)	HI(lParam)
ADVISE C ==> S PostMessage	Client requests the server to send a message whenever the specified data object changes. If the fDeferUpd flag is not set, then the object indicated by aItem is passed along with the message. If the flag is set, data must be requested separately with a REQUEST query to the server.	hOptions Structure: DDEADVISE< Fields: fAckReq fDeferUpd	aItem
DATA S ==> C PostMessage	The server informs the client that the object indicated by aItem has changed.	hData Structure: DDEDATA< Fields: fAckReq fRelease fRequested cfFormat Data starts with third word	aItem
REQUEST C ==> S PostMessage	Asks the server to send the object indicated by aItem	cfFormat	aItem
UNADVISE C ==> S PostMessage	Ends the request for permanent updates to changes in the value of the object indicated by aItem	reserved	aItem

Transferring unrequested data objects to the server			
DDE Message	Description	LO(lParam)	HI(lParam)
POKE C ==> S PostMessage	The client uses this message to send unrequested data to the server	hData → Structure: DDEPOKE Fields fRelease cfFormat	aItem

Remote control of a server application			
DDE Message	Description	LO(lParam)	HI(lParam)
EXECUTE C ==> S PostMessage	The client uses this message to send a command sequence to the server	reserved	hCommand

11.6 Source Code: DDE_EXE.EXE

DDE_.H include file

```
/*******************************
 DDE_EXE.H
 *******************************/


#define MI_ABOUT           100
#define MI_DDEINIT         101
#define MI_DDETERM         102
#define MI_QUIT            103

#define MI_CREATEGROUP     110
#define MI_SHOWGROUP       111
#define MI_DELETEGROUP     112
#define MI_ADDITEM         113


#define EB_NAME            120
#define EB_CMD             121
#define EB_PATH            122
#define EB_GROUP           123
#define EB_ICON            124
#define EB_HORZ            125
#define EB_VERT            126
#define CB_ICON            129
#define RB_RESTORE         130
#define RB_MIN             131
#define RB_MAX             132
#define RB_CURRENT         133
#define CB_ACTIVATE        139
#define CB_SAVE            140
```

DDE_EXE.RC resource file

```
#include <windows.h>
#include "dde_exe.h"

rcinclude DDE_EXE.dlg

AppIcon  ICON  DDE_EXE.ICO

Menu  MENU
```

```
    Begin
        MENUITEM "¬",                         MI_ABOUT

        POPUP "&File"
        Begin
          MENUITEM "&Create DDE Link",    MI_DDEINIT
          MENUITEM "&Remove DDE Link",     MI_DDETERM        GRAYED
          MENUITEM SEPARATOR
          MENUITEM "E&xit Program...",  MI_QUIT
        End

        POPUP "&Edit"
        Begin
          MENUITEM "&Create Group",        MI_CREATEGROUP    GRAYED
          MENUITEM "&Show Group",       MI_SHOWGROUP      GRAYED
          MENUITEM "&Delete Group",        MI_DELETEGROUP    GRAYED
          MENUITEM SEPARATOR
          MENUITEM "Add &Program",    MI_ADDITEM        GRAYED
        End
    End
```

DDE.DLG dialog box file

```
NEWPROG DIALOG LOADONCALL MOVEABLE DISCARDABLE 86, 26, 148, 89
CAPTION "New Program"
STYLE WS_BORDER | WS_CAPTION | WS_DLGFRAME | WS_POPUP
BEGIN
    CONTROL "Description:", 100, "static", SS_LEFT | WS_CHILD, 7, 30, 46, 8
    CONTROL "Command Line:", 101, "static", SS_LEFT | WS_CHILD, 7, 52, 45, 8
    CONTROL "", 102, "edit", ES_LEFT | WS_BORDER | WS_TABSTOP | WS_CHILD, 60, 28,
79, 12
    CONTROL "", 103, "edit", ES_LEFT | WS_BORDER | WS_TABSTOP | WS_CHILD, 60, 49,
79, 12
    CONTROL "OK", 104, "button", BS_DEFPUSHBUTTON | WS_TABSTOP | WS_CHILD, 7, 73,
45, 12
    CONTROL "Cancel", 105, "button", BS_PUSHBUTTON | WS_TABSTOP | WS_CHILD, 92,
73, 45, 12
    CONTROL "Group Name:", 106, "static", SS_LEFT | WS_CHILD, 7, 10, 50, 8
    CONTROL "", 107, "edit", ES_LEFT | WS_BORDER | WS_TABSTOP | WS_CHILD, 60, 9,
79, 12
END

NEWGROUP DIALOG LOADONCALL MOVEABLE DISCARDABLE 87, 34, 145, 76
CAPTION "Add Program Group"
STYLE WS_BORDER | WS_CAPTION | WS_DLGFRAME | WS_POPUP
BEGIN
    CONTROL "Description:", 100, "static", SS_LEFT | WS_CHILD, 8, 17, 47, 8
```

```
    CONTROL "Path:", 101, "static", SS_LEFT | WS_CHILD, 7, 39, 36, 8
    CONTROL "", 102, "edit", ES_LEFT | WS_BORDER | WS_TABSTOP | WS_CHILD, 60, 15,
79, 12
    CONTROL "", 103, "edit", ES_LEFT | WS_BORDER | WS_TABSTOP | WS_CHILD, 60, 36,
79, 12
    CONTROL "OK", 104, "button", BS_DEFPUSHBUTTON | WS_TABSTOP | WS_CHILD, 7, 60,
45, 12
    CONTROL "Cancel", 105, "button", BS_PUSHBUTTON | WS_TABSTOP | WS_CHILD, 94,
60, 45, 12
END

DELGROUP DIALOG LOADONCALL MOVEABLE DISCARDABLE 87, 34, 145, 62
CAPTION "Delete Program Group"
STYLE WS_BORDER | WS_CAPTION | WS_DLGFRAME | WS_POPUP
BEGIN
    CONTROL "Description:", 100, "static", SS_LEFT | WS_CHILD, 7, 17, 47, 8
    CONTROL "", 102, "edit", ES_LEFT | WS_BORDER | WS_TABSTOP | WS_CHILD, 60, 16,
79, 12
    CONTROL "OK", 104, "button", BS_DEFPUSHBUTTON | WS_TABSTOP | WS_CHILD, 8, 46,
45, 12
    CONTROL "Cancel", 105, "button", BS_PUSHBUTTON | WS_TABSTOP | WS_CHILD, 94,
46, 45, 12
END

SHOWGROUP DIALOG LOADONCALL MOVEABLE DISCARDABLE 87, 34, 145, 96
CAPTION "Display Program Group"
STYLE WS_BORDER | WS_CAPTION | WS_DLGFRAME | WS_POPUP
BEGIN
    CONTROL "Description:", 100, "static", SS_LEFT | WS_CHILD, 7, 17, 47, 8
    CONTROL "", 102, "edit", ES_LEFT | WS_BORDER | WS_TABSTOP | WS_CHILD, 60, 16,
79, 12
    CONTROL "OK", 104, "button", BS_DEFPUSHBUTTON | WS_TABSTOP | WS_CHILD, 8, 79,
45, 12
    CONTROL "Cancel", 105, "button", BS_PUSHBUTTON | WS_TABSTOP | WS_CHILD, 91,
78, 45, 12
    CONTROL "Icon", 106, "button", BS_GROUPBOX | WS_TABSTOP | WS_CHILD, 8, 33,
131, 40
    CONTROL "Maximize", 107, "button", BS_RADIOBUTTON | WS_TABSTOP | WS_CHILD,
13, 58, 41, 12
    CONTROL "Minimize", 108, "button", BS_RADIOBUTTON | WS_TABSTOP | WS_CHILD,
85, 59, 39, 12
    CONTROL "Normal Format", 109, "button", BS_RADIOBUTTON | WS_TABSTOP |
WS_CHILD, 13, 44, 70, 12
END
```

DDE_EXE.DLG dialog box file

```
CREATEGROUP DIALOG LOADONCALL MOVEABLE DISCARDABLE 87, 34, 145, 76
CAPTION "Add Program Group"
STYLE WS_BORDER | WS_CAPTION | WS_DLGFRAME | WS_POPUP
BEGIN
    CONTROL "Description:", -1, "static", SS_LEFT | WS_CHILD, 8, 17, 47, 8
    CONTROL "Path:", -1, "static", SS_LEFT | WS_CHILD, 7, 39, 36, 8
    CONTROL "", 120, "edit", ES_LEFT | WS_BORDER | WS_TABSTOP | WS_CHILD, 60, 15,
79, 12
    CONTROL "", 122, "edit", ES_LEFT | WS_BORDER | WS_TABSTOP | WS_CHILD, 60, 36,
79, 12
    CONTROL "OK", 1, "button", BS_DEFPUSHBUTTON | WS_TABSTOP | WS_CHILD, 7, 60,
45, 12
    CONTROL "Cancel", 2, "button", BS_PUSHBUTTON | WS_TABSTOP | WS_CHILD, 94, 60,
45, 12
END

DELETEGROUP DIALOG LOADONCALL MOVEABLE DISCARDABLE 87, 34, 145, 62
CAPTION "Delete Program Group"
STYLE WS_BORDER | WS_CAPTION | WS_DLGFRAME | WS_POPUP
BEGIN
    CONTROL "Description:", -1, "static", SS_LEFT | WS_CHILD, 7, 17, 47, 8
    CONTROL "", 120, "edit", ES_LEFT | WS_BORDER | WS_TABSTOP | WS_CHILD, 60, 16,
79, 12
    CONTROL "OK", 1, "button", BS_DEFPUSHBUTTON | WS_TABSTOP | WS_CHILD, 8, 46,
45, 12
    CONTROL "Cancel", 2, "button", BS_PUSHBUTTON | WS_TABSTOP | WS_CHILD, 94, 46,
45, 12
END

SHOWGROUP DIALOG LOADONCALL MOVEABLE DISCARDABLE 86, 24, 145, 123
CAPTION "Show Program Group"
STYLE WS_BORDER | WS_CAPTION | WS_DLGFRAME | WS_POPUP
BEGIN
    CONTROL "Description:", -1, "static", SS_LEFT | WS_CHILD, 7, 17, 47, 8
    CONTROL "", 120, "edit", ES_LEFT | WS_BORDER | WS_TABSTOP | WS_CHILD, 60, 16,
79, 12
    CONTROL "Icon", -1, "button", BS_GROUPBOX | WS_TABSTOP | WS_CHILD, 8, 33,
131, 63
    CONTROL "Current Size", 133, "button", BS_AUTORADIOBUTTON | WS_TABSTOP |
WS_CHILD, 14, 57, 58, 12
    CONTROL "Maximize", 132, "button", BS_AUTORADIOBUTTON | WS_TABSTOP |
WS_CHILD, 14, 69, 41, 12
    CONTROL "Minimize", 131, "button", BS_AUTORADIOBUTTON | WS_TABSTOP |
WS_CHILD, 14, 82, 39, 12
```

```
    CONTROL "Default Size", 130, "button", BS_AUTORADIOBUTTON | WS_TABSTOP |
WS_CHILD, 14, 44, 59, 12
    CONTROL "Activate Group", 139, "button", BS_AUTOCHECKBOX | WS_TABSTOP |
WS_CHILD, 68, 82, 70, 12
    CONTROL "OK", 1, "button", BS_DEFPUSHBUTTON | WS_TABSTOP | WS_CHILD, 9, 106,
45, 12
    CONTROL "Cancel", 2, "button", BS_PUSHBUTTON | WS_TABSTOP | WS_CHILD, 91,
105, 45, 12
END

ADDITEM DIALOG LOADONCALL MOVEABLE DISCARDABLE 28, 17, 266, 118
CAPTION "Add Program"
STYLE WS_BORDER | WS_CAPTION | WS_DLGFRAME | WS_POPUP
BEGIN
    CONTROL "Description:", -1, "static", SS_LEFT | WS_CHILD, 16, 20, 46, 8
    CONTROL "Command Line:", -1, "static", SS_LEFT | WS_CHILD, 15, 45, 38, 8
    CONTROL "", 120, "edit", ES_LEFT | WS_BORDER | WS_TABSTOP | WS_CHILD, 65, 17,
79, 12
    CONTROL "", 121, "edit", ES_LEFT | WS_BORDER | WS_TABSTOP | WS_CHILD, 65, 44,
79, 12
    CONTROL "OK", 1, "button", BS_DEFPUSHBUTTON | WS_TABSTOP | WS_CHILD, 14, 103,
45, 12
    CONTROL "Cancel", 2, "button", BS_PUSHBUTTON | WS_TABSTOP | WS_CHILD, 211,
102, 45, 12
    CONTROL "Icon", 111, "button", BS_GROUPBOX | WS_TABSTOP | WS_CHILD, 154, 9,
104, 87
    CONTROL "Name of Icon File:", -1, "static", SS_LEFT | WS_CHILD, 159, 65, 70,
8
    CONTROL "", 124, "edit", ES_LEFT | WS_BORDER | WS_TABSTOP | WS_CHILD, 160,
77, 89, 12
    CONTROL "Icon Index (for ProgMan Files)", 114, "static", SS_LEFT | WS_CHILD,
158, 23, 98, 8
    CONTROL "", 129, "combobox", CBS_DROPDOWNLIST | WS_VSCROLL | WS_CHILD, 159,
35, 95, 86
    CONTROL "Position", -1, "button", BS_GROUPBOX | WS_TABSTOP | WS_CHILD, 12,
64, 132, 32
    CONTROL "Horizontal:", -1, "static", SS_LEFT | WS_CHILD, 19, 81, 37, 8
    CONTROL "Vertical:", -1, "static", SS_LEFT | WS_CHILD, 88, 82, 28, 8
    CONTROL "", 125, "edit", ES_LEFT | WS_BORDER | WS_TABSTOP | WS_CHILD, 59, 79,
22, 12
    CONTROL "", 126, "edit", ES_LEFT | WS_BORDER | WS_TABSTOP | WS_CHILD, 118,
80, 22, 12
END

ABOUTBOX DIALOG LOADONCALL MOVEABLE DISCARDABLE 58, 24, 193, 97
STYLE WS_DLGFRAME | WS_POPUP
BEGIN
    CONTROL "Remote Control", 101, "static", SS_CENTER | WS_CHILD, 1, 7, 187, 12
```

```
    CONTROL "Copyright  1990", 103, "static", SS_CENTER | WS_CHILD, 0, 38, 189,
10
    CONTROL "Abacus", 104, "static", SS_CENTER | WS_CHILD, 0, 47, 189, 11
    CONTROL "Authors: D.Honekamp && P.Wilken", 106, "static", SS_CENTER |
WS_CHILD, 0, 66, 188, 11
    CONTROL "OK", 1, "button", BS_DEFPUSHBUTTON | WS_TABSTOP | WS_CHILD, 75, 81,
41, 12
    CONTROL "Remote Program Manager Control using DDE EXECUTE Instructions", 105,
"static", SS_CENTER | WS_CHILD, 0, 18, 193, 18
END
```

DDE_EXE.DEF module definition file

```
NAME            DDE_EXE
DESCRIPTION     'Sample program - Dynamic Data Exchange under Windows'
EXETYPE         WINDOWS
STUB            'winstub.exe'

CODE            PRELOAD MOVEABLE

DATA            PRELOAD MOVEABLE MULTIPLE

HEAPSIZE        0x2000
STACKSIZE       0x3000

EXPORTS         WndProc
                MdfAboutBox
                MdfCreateGroup
                MdfDeleteGroup
                MdfShowGroup
                MdfAddItem
```

DDE_EXE.MAK MAKE file

```
Mod  = S
Warn = 3

.c.obj:
   cl -W$(Warn) -c -Os -Zpe -Gw -A$(Mod) $*.c

.rc.res:
   rc -r $*.rc

all: dde_exe.exe

dde_exe.obj:   dde_exe.c
```

```
dde_dlg.obj:   dde_dlg.c

dde_dde.obj:   dde_dde.c

dde_exe.res:   dde_exe.rc   dde_exe.dlg

dde_exe.exe:   dde_exe.obj  dde_dlg.obj  dde_dde.obj dde_exe.res dde_exe.def
              link
dde_exe+dde_dlg+dde_dde,,,LIBW+$(Mod)LIBCEW/NOE/NOD,dde_exe.def;
              rc dde_exe.res
```

DDE_EXE.C source code

```
/**************************************************************************

 D D E _ E X E . C      Main module of DDE sample application

**************************************************************************/

#include        <windows.h>
#include        <dde.h>
#include        <string.h>
#include        <stdio.h>
#include        "dde_exe.h"

/*-----------------------< Global variables >-------------------------*/
FARPROC      lpTmpProc;
HANDLE       hInst;
HMENU        hwMenu;              // Handle for main menu
HWND         hProgMan = 0;        // Handle for Program Manager
HWND         hClient;             // Handle for main window
char         szAppName[] = "Remote Control";
extern int   nMode;

/*---------------------------< Prototyping >--------------------------*/
void DdeExecute(HWND hServer, LPSTR lpCmd);
BOOL DdeInitiate(void);
BOOL DdeTerminate(void);
void ProcessDdeAck(HANDLE, LONG);
long FAR PASCAL MdfCreateGroup(HWND hDlg, unsigned msg, WORD wP, LONG lP);
long FAR PASCAL MdfDeleteGroup(HWND hDlg, unsigned msg, WORD wP, LONG lP);
long FAR PASCAL MdfShowGroup(HWND hDlg, unsigned msg, WORD wP, LONG lP);
long FAR PASCAL MdfAddItem(HWND hDlg, unsigned msg, WORD wP, LONG lP);
long FAR PASCAL MdfAboutBox(HWND hDlg, unsigned msg, WORD wP, LONG lP);

/**************************************************************************
```

```
 E n a b l e D d e M e n u I t e m s
 ===================================

 Depending on the bFlag parameter status, this grays or enables menu items
 dealing with DDE data.
*************************************************************************/
void EnableDdeMenuItems(BOOL bFlag)
{
   EnableMenuItem(hwMenu, MI_DDEINIT,     bFlag==TRUE ? MF_GRAYED:MF_ENABLED);
   EnableMenuItem(hwMenu, MI_DDETERM,     bFlag==TRUE ? MF_ENABLED:MF_GRAYED);
   EnableMenuItem(hwMenu, MI_CREATEGROUP,bFlag==TRUE ? MF_ENABLED:MF_GRAYED);
   EnableMenuItem(hwMenu, MI_SHOWGROUP,   bFlag==TRUE ? MF_ENABLED:MF_GRAYED);
   EnableMenuItem(hwMenu, MI_DELETEGROUP,bFlag==TRUE ? MF_ENABLED:MF_GRAYED);
   EnableMenuItem(hwMenu, MI_ADDITEM,     bFlag==TRUE ? MF_ENABLED:MF_GRAYED);
   EnableMenuItem(hwMenu, MI_QUIT,        bFlag==TRUE ? MF_GRAYED:MF_ENABLED);
}

/************************************************************************
 W n d P r o c                ### Callback function ###
 =============

 M a i n W i n d o w     F u n c t i o n
*************************************************************************/
long FAR PASCAL WndProc(HWND hWnd, unsigned msg, WORD wP, LONG lP)
{
   int         aktion;

   switch (msg)
   {
      case WM_DESTROY:                /* End application */
         PostQuitMessage(NULL);
      break;

      /****************************** Process DDE messages ***/
      case WM_DDE_ACK:
         ProcessDdeAck((HWND) wP,lP);
      break;

      case WM_DDE_TERMINATE:
         if(wP == hProgMan)           // Message from the Program Manager?
         {                            // Yes: Then process it
            hProgMan = 0;             // No more active DDE links
            PostMessage(wP, WM_DDE_TERMINATE, hClient, 0L);
            EnableDdeMenuItems(FALSE);
         }
      break;

      /*
```

```
   All other DDE messages are relevant to an EXECUTE communication.

*/

case WM_COMMAND:
{
  switch (wP)
  {
     case MI_QUIT:       // End program...
        if(MessageBox(hWnd, (LPSTR)"Do you really want to exit?",
                   (LPSTR)"Exit Program",
             MB_ICONQUESTION | MB_YESNO | MB_DEFBUTTON1 |
             MB_APPLMODAL) == IDYES)
        DestroyWindow(hWnd);
     break;

     case MI_ABOUT:
        lpTmpProc = MakeProcInstance((FARPROC)MdfAboutBox, hInst);
        aktion = DialogBox(hInst, "ABOUTBOX", hWnd, lpTmpProc);
        FreeProcInstance(lpTmpProc);
     break;

     case MI_DDEINIT:
        EnableDdeMenuItems(TRUE);
        DdeInitiate();
     break;

     case MI_DDETERM:
        EnableDdeMenuItems(FALSE);
        DdeTerminate();
     break;

   case MI_CREATEGROUP:              // Create new program group
        lpTmpProc = MakeProcInstance((FARPROC)MdfCreateGroup, hInst);
        aktion = DialogBox(hInst, "CREATEGROUP", hWnd, lpTmpProc);
        FreeProcInstance(lpTmpProc);
        break;

   case MI_SHOWGROUP:                // Show program group
        lpTmpProc = MakeProcInstance((FARPROC)MdfShowGroup, hInst);
        aktion = DialogBox(hInst, "SHOWGROUP", hWnd, lpTmpProc);
        FreeProcInstance(lpTmpProc);
        break;

   case MI_DELETEGROUP:              // Delete program group
        lpTmpProc = MakeProcInstance((FARPROC)MdfDeleteGroup, hInst);
        aktion = DialogBox(hInst, "DELETEGROUP", hWnd, lpTmpProc);
        FreeProcInstance(lpTmpProc);
```

```
            break;

        case MI_ADDITEM:                // Add item to program group
            lpTmpProc = MakeProcInstance((FARPROC)MdfAddItem, hInst);
            aktion = DialogBox(hInst, "ADDITEM", hWnd, lpTmpProc);
            FreeProcInstance(lpTmpProc);
            break;

            default: break;
        }// switch wP
      }// case WM_COMMAND
      default:
          return(DefWindowProc(hWnd, msg, wP, lP));
   }
   return (NULL);
}

/**************************************************************************
 W i n M a i n
 =============

 Main function of Windows application
**************************************************************************/
int PASCAL WinMain (HANDLE hInstance, HANDLE hPrevInstance, LPSTR lpszCmdLine,
                    int nCmdShow)
{
  MSG          msg ;
  WNDCLASS     wndclass ;

  if (!hPrevInstance)
  {
     wndclass.style          = CS_VREDRAW | CS_HREDRAW ;
     wndclass.lpfnWndProc    = WndProc ;
     wndclass.cbClsExtra     = 0 ;
     wndclass.cbWndExtra     = 0 ;
     wndclass.hInstance      = hInstance ;
     wndclass.hIcon          = LoadIcon (hInstance,(LPSTR) "AppIcon") ;
     wndclass.hCursor        = LoadCursor (NULL, IDC_ARROW);
     wndclass.hbrBackground = GetStockObject (WHITE_BRUSH) ;
     wndclass.lpszMenuName  = NULL;
     wndclass.lpszClassName = szAppName ;

     if (!RegisterClass (&wndclass))
         return FALSE;

     hInst = hInstance;
     hwMenu = LoadMenu(hInst, "Menu");
     hClient = CreateWindow (szAppName, szAppName,
```

```
                            WS_OVERLAPPEDWINDOW | WS_CLIPSIBLINGS,
                            320, 270, 300, 200, NULL,
                            hwMenu,
                            hInstance, NULL) ;

      ShowWindow(hClient, SW_SHOWNORMAL);
      UpdateWindow (hClient);
   }

   if(hPrevInstance)
      return FALSE;

   /*-------------< Message loop >----------*/

   while(GetMessage (&msg, NULL, 0, 0))
   {
      TranslateMessage (&msg) ;
      DispatchMessage (&msg) ;
   }
   return msg.wParam;
}
```

DDE_DDE.C source code

```
/*************************************************************************
 D D E _ D D E . C     This module contains all DDE functions needed
                       by the DDE EXECUTE processes
*************************************************************************/

#include <windows.h>
#include <dde.h>

#define  fACK   0x8000

/*--------------------------< Global variables >-----------------------*/
extern HWND  hClient;
extern HWND  hProgMan;

char   szBuffer[80];

int    nMode = 0;    /*
                      Current DDE link status:

                      0: No DDE link to Program Manager active
                      1: Wait to quit a WM_DDE_INITIATE message
                      2: ACK contained in INIT
                      3: Wait to quit a WM_DDE_EXECUTE message
```

```
                     4: ACK contained in EXECUTE
                     5: Self-terminate DDE link, wait for WM_DDE_TERMINATE
                        response from the server
                   */

/*------------------------------< Prototyping >------------------------*/
void DdeExecute(LPSTR lpCmd);
BOOL DdeInitiate(void);
BOOL DdeTerminate(void);
void ProcessDdeAck(HWND, LONG);

/***********************************************************************
 M e m E r r o r B o x
 =====================
 This function generates a message box that advises the user that not
 enough memory is available for the operation.
***********************************************************************/
void MemErrorBox(void)
{
   MessageBox(GetFocus(),
      (LPSTR) "Not enough memory \navailable for DDE shared memory",
      (LPSTR) "Memory Error",
      MB_SYSTEMMODAL |  MB_OK | MB_ICONSTOP);
}

/***********************************************************************
 D d e T e r m i n a t e
 =======================

 This function ends a previously set DDE link with the Program Manager.

 Global variables
 hProgMan          Handle for Program Manager
 hClient           Handle for an application
 nMode             Status variable
***********************************************************************/
BOOL DdeTerminate(void)
{
   return PostMessage(hProgMan, WM_DDE_TERMINATE, hClient, 0L);
}

/***********************************************************************
 D d e I n i t i a t e
 =====================

 This function sets a DDE link to the Program Manager. After the link, it
 is possible to communicate with the Program Manager using commands in the
 form of WM_DDE_EXECUTE messages. The Program Manager reports the results
```

```
 of execution in the form of positive or negative WM_DDE_ACK messages.

 To create the DDE link with the Program Manager and the Clients, the
 application and topic names must be placed in the WM_DDE_INITIATE
 telegram "PROGMAN".

 Global variables
 hClient             Handle for client application
 nMode               Status variable
*********************************************************************/
BOOL DdeInitiate(void)
{
   ATOM   aApp, aTopic;

   aApp   = GlobalAddAtom((LPSTR) "PROGMAN");
   aTopic = GlobalAddAtom((LPSTR) "PROGMAN");

   SendMessage(-1, WM_DDE_INITIATE, hClient, MAKELONG(aApp, aTopic));
   GlobalDeleteAtom(aApp);
   GlobalDeleteAtom(aTopic);
   return TRUE;
}

/*********************************************************************
 D d e E x e c u t e
 ===================

 This function sends a previously server-specific EXECUTE command, which
 lpCmd specifies, to the hServer identified DDE server application.

 Global variables
 hClient             Handle for client application
 hProgMan            Handle for Program Manager
 nMode               Status variable

 Parameters
 LPSTR  lpCmd        Specifies command string
*********************************************************************/
void DdeExecute(LPSTR lpCmd)
{
   HANDLE hMem;
   LPSTR  lpMem;

   hMem = GlobalAlloc(GMEM_DDESHARE, lstrlen(lpCmd)+1);
   if(hMem)
   {
      lpMem = GlobalLock(hMem);      // Reserve shared memory
      lstrcpy(lpMem, lpCmd);         // Copy data
```

```
      GlobalUnlock(hMem);               // Release shared memory
      if(!PostMessage(hProgMan,         // Send message to server
                WM_DDE_EXECUTE, hClient, MAKELONG(0, hMem)))
      {
         GlobalFree(hMem);              // Error during message passing
      }
   }
   else
   {
      MemErrorBox();                    // Not enough memory
   }
}

/**************************************************************************
 P r o c e s s D d e A c k
 =========================
 This function processes all WM_DDE_ACK messages received. The global
 status variable <nMode> states the status of ACK.

 Global variables
 int        nMode

 Parameters
 HWND       hSender     Handle for sender of ACK message. This handle is
                        placed in the wParam Parameter of the
                        WM_DDE_ACK message.
 LONG       lP          lParam Parameter of WM_DDE_ACK message. The
                        interpretation depends on nMode
**************************************************************************/
void ProcessDdeAck(HWND hSender, LONG lP)
{
   ATOM     aApp;
   ATOM     aTopic;
   HANDLE   hMem;
   WORD     wStatus;
   char     szServerName[21];

   if(!hProgMan)
   {
      // Initialization phase ...
      aApp   = LOWORD(lP);
      aTopic = HIWORD(lP);
      GlobalGetAtomName(aApp, (LPSTR) szServerName, 20);
      if(lstrcmp((LPSTR) szServerName, (LPSTR) "PROGMAN") == 0)
      {
          // Answer comes from Program Manager
          MessageBox(hClient,
             (LPSTR) "DDE link to\nProgram Manager set",
```

```
                (LPSTR) "DDE Status",
                MB_OK | MB_APPLMODAL);
            hProgMan = hSender;
        }
        GlobalDeleteAtom(aApp);
        GlobalDeleteAtom(aTopic);
    }
    else
    {
        // Quit a WM_DDE_EXECUTE message
        hMem     = HIWORD(lP);              // Handle for data object
        wStatus  = LOWORD(lP);

        if(wStatus & fACK)
        {                                   // Positive ACKnowledge
            MessageBox(hClient,
                (LPSTR) "DDE access executed correctly!",
                (LPSTR) "DDE Status",
                MB_APPLMODAL | MB_ICONEXCLAMATION | MB_OK);
        }
        else
        {                                   // Negative ACKnowledge
            MessageBox(hClient,
                (LPSTR) "DDE access could not be\nexecuted correctly!",
                (LPSTR) "DDE Status",
                MB_APPLMODAL | MB_ICONEXCLAMATION | MB_OK);
        }
        GlobalFree(hMem);                   // Free shared memory
    }
}
```

DDE_DLG.C source code

```
/************************************************************************

 D D E _ D L G . C      This module contains all dialog box functions

************************************************************************/

#include <windows.h>
#include <dde.h>
#include "dde_exe.h"

/*---------------------------< Prototyping >---------------------------*/
void DdeExecute(LPSTR lpCmd);
BOOL DdeInitiate(void);
BOOL DdeTerminate(void);
```

```
void ProcessDdeAck(HWND, LONG);
BOOL FAR PASCAL MdfCreateGroup(HWND hDlg, unsigned msg, WORD wP, LONG lP);
BOOL FAR PASCAL MdfDeleteGroup(HWND hDlg, unsigned msg, WORD wP, LONG lP);
BOOL FAR PASCAL MdfShowGroup(HWND hDlg, unsigned msg, WORD wP, LONG lP);
BOOL FAR PASCAL MdfAddItem(HWND hDlg, unsigned msg, WORD wP, LONG lP);
BOOL FAR PASCAL MdfAboutBox(HWND hDlg, unsigned msg, WORD wP, LONG lP);

/*---------------------------< Local variables >-----------------------*/
static int    nShowCommand;      // Current display type for group
static char   szDdeCmd[256];     // Command buffer for Program Manager
              szGrpName[30],
              szGrpPath[63],
              szPrgName[30],
              szCommand[80],
              szIconPath[63];

char* szaIcons[10]  = {  "MDI LOGO",             // Names for Program
                         "DOS Fullscreen",       // Manager-integral
                         "DOS TextWindow",       // icons
                         "Spreadsheet",
                         "Windows Application",
                         "Telephone Logo",
                         "Empty Window",
                         "Document Window",
                         "Window Logo",
                         "MDI Logo" };
int nMaxLength = 79;

/*********************************************************************
 M d f A b o u t B o x                       ### Dialog box function ###
 =====================

 This is the window function for processing the About box
*********************************************************************/
BOOL FAR PASCAL MdfAboutBox(HWND hDlg, unsigned msg, WORD wP, LONG lP)
{
   switch(msg)
   {
      case WM_COMMAND:
         switch(wP)
         {
            case IDOK:
               EndDialog(hDlg,TRUE);
               return TRUE;
            default:
               return FALSE;
         }
      default:
```

```
            return FALSE;
      }
}

/*********************************************************************
 M d f C r e a t e G r o u p                    ### Dialog box function ###
 ===========================

 This is the window function for processing the CREATEGROUP dialog box.
 Its task is to prompt the user for all necessary group parameters.
 *********************************************************************/
BOOL FAR PASCAL MdfCreateGroup(HWND hDlg, unsigned msg, WORD wP, LONG lP)
{
   switch(msg)
   {
      case WM_INITDIALOG:
         SetDlgItemText(hDlg, EB_NAME, (LPSTR) szGrpName);
         SetDlgItemText(hDlg, EB_PATH, (LPSTR) szGrpPath);
      break;

      case WM_COMMAND:
         switch(wP)
         {
            case IDOK:
               GetDlgItemText(hDlg, EB_NAME, (LPSTR) szGrpName, nMaxLength);
               GetDlgItemText(hDlg, EB_PATH, (LPSTR) szGrpPath, nMaxLength);
               wsprintf((LPSTR) szDdeCmd,(LPSTR)"[CreateGroup(%s,%s)]",
                        (LPSTR) szGrpName, (LPSTR) szGrpPath);
               DdeExecute((LPSTR) szDdeCmd); // Command to Program Manager
               /*
                  Continue without a break...
               */
            case IDCANCEL:
               EndDialog(hDlg,TRUE);
               return wP==IDOK ? TRUE : FALSE;
            break;

            default:
               return FALSE;
         }
      default:
         return FALSE;
   }
}

/*********************************************************************
 M d f D e l e t e G r o u p                    ### Dialog box function ###
 ===========================
```

```
 This is the window function for processing the DELETEGROUP dialog box.
 It prompts for the names of program groups the user wants deleted, then
 sends an appropriate telegram to the Program Manager
************************************************************************/
BOOL FAR PASCAL MdfDeleteGroup(HWND hDlg, unsigned msg, WORD wP, LONG lP)
{
   switch(msg)
   {
      case WM_INITDIALOG:
         SetDlgItemText(hDlg, EB_NAME, NULL);
      break;

      case WM_COMMAND:
         switch(wP)
         {
            case IDOK:
               GetDlgItemText(hDlg, EB_NAME, (LPSTR) szGrpName, nMaxLength);
               wsprintf((LPSTR) szDdeCmd, (LPSTR)"[DeleteGroup(%s)]",
                        (LPSTR) szGrpName);
               DdeExecute((LPSTR) szDdeCmd); // Command to Program Manager
               /*
                  Continue without a break ...
               */
            case IDCANCEL:
               EndDialog(hDlg,TRUE);
               return wP==IDOK ? TRUE : FALSE;
            break;

            default:
               return FALSE;
         }
      default:
         return FALSE;
   }
}

/************************************************************************
 M d f S h o w G r o u p                      ### Dialog box function ###
 =======================

 This is the window function for processing the SHOWGROUP dialog box.
 It prompts for the names of program groups the user wants shown as icons
 and sends an appropriate telegram to the Program Manager
************************************************************************/
BOOL FAR PASCAL MdfShowGroup(HWND hDlg, unsigned msg, WORD wP, LONG lP)
{
  BOOL        bActive = FALSE;
```

```
int         nShowType;

 switch(msg)
 {
    case WM_INITDIALOG:
       SetDlgItemText(hDlg, EB_NAME, (LPSTR) szGrpName);
       CheckRadioButton(hDlg, RB_RESTORE, RB_CURRENT,
                        nShowCommand + RB_RESTORE);
       CheckDlgButton(hDlg, CB_ACTIVATE, bActive);
    break;

    case WM_COMMAND:
       switch(wP)
       {
          case RB_RESTORE:
          case RB_MIN:
          case RB_MAX:
          case RB_CURRENT:
             nShowCommand = wP-RB_RESTORE;
          break;


          case IDOK:
             bActive=IsDlgButtonChecked(hDlg, CB_ACTIVATE);
             switch(nShowCommand)
             {
                case 0:    // Normal screen
                   nShowType = (bActive==TRUE) ? 1 : 4;
                break;

                case 1:    // Icon
                   nShowType = (bActive==TRUE) ? 2 : 7;
                break;

                case 2:    // Maximized
                   nShowType = 3;
                break;

                case 3:    // Current size
                   nShowType = (bActive==TRUE) ? 5 : 8;
                break;
             }
             GetDlgItemText(hDlg, EB_NAME, (LPSTR) szGrpName, nMaxLength);
             wsprintf((LPSTR) szDdeCmd,(LPSTR)"[ShowGroup(%s,%d)]",
                      (LPSTR) szGrpName, nShowType);

             DdeExecute((LPSTR) szDdeCmd); // Command to Program Manager
             /*
```

```
                Continue without a break ...
              */
            case IDCANCEL:
              EndDialog(hDlg,TRUE);
              return wP==IDOK ? TRUE : FALSE;
            break;
          }
      default:
        return FALSE;
  }
}

/***********************************************************************
 M d f A d d I t e m                          ### Dialog box function ###
 ===================

***********************************************************************/
BOOL FAR PASCAL MdfAddItem(HWND hDlg, unsigned msg, WORD wP, LONG lP)
{
  static int  i, nIconIndex, nYpos, nXpos;
  static HWND hComboBox;
  BOOL        bTranslated;

   switch(msg)
   {
      case WM_INITDIALOG:
         SetDlgItemText(hDlg, EB_NAME, NULL);
         SetDlgItemText(hDlg, EB_CMD , NULL);
         SetDlgItemText(hDlg, EB_ICON, (LPSTR) "PROGMAN");
         SetDlgItemInt(hDlg,  EB_HORZ, 0, FALSE);
         SetDlgItemInt(hDlg,  EB_VERT, 0, FALSE);
         hComboBox = GetDlgItem(hDlg, CB_ICON);
         for(i=0;i<=9;i++)
         {
            SendMessage(hComboBox, CB_ADDSTRING, 0,
                        (LONG) (LPSTR) szaIcons[i]);
         }
         SendMessage(hComboBox, CB_SELECTSTRING, -1, (LONG) (LPSTR) "DOS");
      break;

      case WM_COMMAND:
         switch(wP)
         {
            case IDOK:
               GetDlgItemText(hDlg, EB_NAME, (LPSTR) szPrgName, 29);
               GetDlgItemText(hDlg, EB_CMD,  (LPSTR) szCommand, 79);
               GetDlgItemText(hDlg, EB_ICON, (LPSTR) szIconPath,62);
               nYpos = GetDlgItemInt(hDlg, EB_HORZ, &bTranslated, FALSE);
```

```
            nXpos = GetDlgItemInt(hDlg, EB_VERT, &bTranslated, FALSE);
            nIconIndex = (int)SendMessage(hComboBox, CB_GETCURSEL, 0, 0L);
            wsprintf((LPSTR) szDdeCmd,
                     (LPSTR) "[AddItem(%s,%s,%s,%d,%d,%d)]",
                     (LPSTR) szCommand,
                     (LPSTR) szPrgName,
                     (LPSTR) szIconPath,
                     nIconIndex, nXpos, nYpos);
            DdeExecute((LPSTR) szDdeCmd); // Command to Program Manager
            /*
               Continue without a break ...
            */
         case IDCANCEL:
            EndDialog(hDlg,TRUE);
            return wP==IDOK ? TRUE : FALSE;
         break;

         default:
            return FALSE;
      }
   default:
      return FALSE;
   }
}
```

12 Filter Functions (Hooks)

If you have spent much time working with Windows or with the Windows Software Development Kit (SDK), then you may already be familiar with two very helpful tools. The first, SPY.EXE, is often very useful for debugging applications. The second, the Recorder, allows you to record a sequence of events and then play back this sequence. This can be very useful for such things as creating a demo that executes automatically.

Hooks

This chapter will be devoted to studying these and similar programs. The key to this type of help program lies in the use of hook functions. These consist of various filters that can be placed between Windows and applications.

The hook intercepts all messages and passes them through a filter function before sending them on to the receiving application for processing. The phrase "all messages" actually depends on the filter type used, as we will see in our discussion of each filter type.

Most filter types operate system-wide, meaning they filter all messages that appear on the system. So these filters must always be available to Windows. To guarantee that these functions will always be available, they are implemented as DLL (dynamic library link) functions (see Chapter 15 for more information on DLLs). This is done by declaring the code segment for the function as FIXED in the module definition file.

The only exception to this rule is WH_MSGFILTER. This filter is limited to the application that created it and it can only operate within this application.

Note:

Since filters represent a bottleneck in the system processing, they should only be used when you are trying to trap errors or debug an application during development or troubleshooting. There may also be some special applications that effectively utilize filters in their normal operations.

As a general rule, you should not leave filters installed any longer than is absolutely necessary.

A filter function is simply a callback function. Its parameters are as follows:

```
FAR PASCAL FilterFunction(int nCode, WORD wParam, DWORD lParam)
```

The result is either nothing (void) or an integer value. Be careful when you are using the various filter functions. The syntax is always the same, but the parameters used are specific to the filter type.

As with any other callback function, filter functions must be declared under EXPORTS in the module definition file (*.DEF) of the DLL or the application.

12.1 Filter Types

Now let's take a look at each of the filter types, and what they do.

12.1.1 WH_CALLWNDPROC

SendMessage filter

If you install this filter, all messages sent with the SendMessage function will first be captured by the filter function. The filter function can then be used to change the message in any way, which is normally not recommended and must be done carefully.

After leaving the filter function, the (modified) message will be directed on to the window that was intended to receive it. Filter functions must exist as part of a library.

With this type of filter, the actual message information is stored in a special data structure not predefined in WINDOWS.H. We will call this structure CWPMSG (CallWndProcMeSsaGe) and define it as follows:

```
typedef struct tagCWPMSG
{
   WORD  hlParam, // Hi word of the lParam
                     of the actual message
         llParam, // Lo word of the lParam
                     of the actual message
         wParam,  // wParam parameter of the message
         wMsg,    // Message type
         hWnd;    // Window handle for receiving window
} CWPMSG;
```

The lParam parameter of the filter function is a FAR pointer to this type of data structure. To access the components of this structure, we use a local FAR pointer of type CWPMSG and cast lParam.

```
CWPMSG FAR * lpCwpMsg;               // Private pointer

...

lpCwpMsg = (CWPMSG FAR *) lParam;    // Cast lParam parameter

...
```

```
lpCwpMsg->...                        // access fields in structure
```

The filter function doesn't return a result. It is of type VOID FAR PASCAL.

12.1.2 WH_GETMESSAGE

GetMessage filter

This filter is activated each time an application calls the GetMessage function. Just as with the SendMessage filter, this filter can capture messages and analyze and/or change them. After leaving the filter function, the (modified) message from the GetMessage function is given back to the application.

In this case, the hooked message is stored in the normal MSG structure, which is defined in WINDOWS.H. The lParam parameter of the filter function references this data structure with a FAR pointer. Access to the individual fields of the structure is accomplished using private FAR pointers of type MSG.

```
MSG FAR * lpMsg;                // Private pointer to MSG structure

...

lpMsg = (MSG FAR *) lParam;     // Cast lParam of filter function

...

lpMsg->...                      // Access fields of data structure
```

This filter function does not return a result because it is type VOID FAR PASCAL.

12.1.3 WH_KEYBOARD

Filter all keyboard input

This filter is activated by the GetMessage or PeekMessage functions and the filter function is called whenever a WM_KEYUP or WM_KEYDOWN message is encountered. This filter can therefore be used to check all keyboard input.

You can extract exact information on the keyboard event that triggered the filter by evaluating the 32 bit lParam parameter of the filter function. This parameter contains the following information:

Bit	Meaning
0 - 15	Key strike counter (LOWORD(lParam))
16 - 23	Scan code for the key pressed
24	Flag for extended key
25 - 26	not used
27 - 28	01: if <Alt> key was pressed 00: if <Alt> key was not pressed
30	Key status prior to sending of message: 1: Key was down 0: Key was up
31	Continuing status of the key: 1: Key was released 0: Key was held down

Key information obtained with the WH_KEYBOARD filter

With this filter type, it is possible to start an application with a hot key. This means that a certain key combination (such as <Shift>+<F1>), which is defined by you, will start application XYZ.

The result of this filter function tells Windows whether to process the message further (result == 0) or throw it away (result ==1). This filter function returns values of type int FAR PASCAL.

12.1.4 WH_MSGFILTER

Application-specific filter

This filter allows you to check all messages sent in conjunction with dialog boxes, message boxes or menus before they are sent on to the message loop of the application. The filter works only on one specific application, and it must be installed by this application itself.

Since this filter function is limited to a single application, it can also be implemented as part of an application. This means that it does not have to be set up in a DLL like the other filter functions.

12.1.5 WH_SYSMSGFILTER

System-wide filter

This filter is activated by the same messages as the WM_MSGFILTER, but its effect is system-wide. This means that the applicable messages from all applications running will pass through the filter.

12.1.6 WH_JOURNALRECORD

Recording message sequences

This pair of filters allows you to record a sequence of messages and then play it back at a later time. The Windows tool RECORDER.EXE is a good example of what can be accomplished with these two filter types.

When events are recorded, the WH_JOURNALRECORD filter is installed. It copies all messages received and stores them in a file before sending them on to be processed by the application.

At a later time, you can then replay this sequence of events with the help of the WH_JOURNALPLAYBACK filter. This filter is called by Windows when an application requests a certain event. The filter function will then play back the stored message to Windows one by one. Windows controls the playback with the nCode parameter. Each time Windows calls the filter function with nCode == HC_SKIP, the next message in the sequence is delivered.

Delay

Along with the message, the filter function gives Windows a time delay value that tells Windows how long to wait before processing the message. If this value is zero, then Windows processes the message immediately. This allows you to control the execution of programs with exact time intervals, which is very helpful for running tests or presenting demos.

One final note: Windows will ignore all mouse and keyboard input as long as the playback filter is installed. This filter function pair must also be stored in a library.

12.2 Installation and Removal

Now that we have learned about all of the filter types, we can discuss how to actually install a filter.

As a demo program, we will implement an application that filters out all DDE (Dynamic Data Exchange between Windows applications) messages and displays text descriptions of them in the client area of the main window. This will be very useful for closely monitoring communications between applications when we take a closer look at DDE later.

Capturing DDE messages

We already know that DDE messages are sent either with SendMessage or PostMessage. So we must install a filter type that will capture these messages. For SendMessage messages, we know that we can use the WH_CALLWNDPROC filter, which is activated when SendMessage is called.

Now we have to find a filter that will capture PostMessage messages. Since there is no special PostMessage filter, we will use the WH_GETMESSAGE filter, which is activated when the "posted" message is read from the application's message loop with a GetMessage call.

We also have to implement two filter functions to accompany these filters. You can study the source code to CPHOOK.C to see how this is done. At the moment, we are more interested in the procedure for installing filters.

First, we must obtain the procedure instance addresses of the two DLL filter functions. This is done by calling GetProcAddress. The parameters for this function are the DLL handle and a pointer to the name of the filter function.

```
lpfFilterFunction = GetProcAddress(hDll,lpFunctionName);
```

You can get the DLL handle after it has been loaded in the application that is using it. This happens with the following command:

```
hDll = LoadLibrary((LPSTR)"HOOK.DLL");
```

You will need to supply the filename of the DLL.

For cases where the filter function is implemented as part of the application (see WM_MSGFILTER), you can obtain the procedure instance address in the usual way with the MakeProcInstance function.

```
FARPROC lpFilterFunction;          // Procedure instance address
HANDLE  hInst;                     // Application instance

lpFilterFunction = MakeProcInstance(FilterFunction, hInst);
```

Once we have the procedures instance addresses, we can activate the filters. The SetWindowsHook function is used for this. The parameters required by this function are the ID number of the filter type and the instance address of the filter function. Here is the relevant excerpt from the HOOK.DLL source code:

```
/*-----------------------< Activate filter >------------------*/
 lpfWhCallWndProc    = GetProcAddress(hLib, (LPSTR) "WhCallWndProc");
 lpfPrevCallWndProc = SetWindowsHook(WH_CALLWNDPROC, lpfWhCallWndProc);

 if(lpfWhCallWndProc)
 {
    lpfWhGetMessage   = GetProcAddress(hLib, (LPSTR) "WhGetMessage");
    lpfPrevGetMessage= SetWindowsHook(WH_GETMESSAGE, lpfWhGetMessage);

    if(lpfWhGetMessage)
    {
       hDbgWnd = hWnd;
       return TRUE;    // Both windows properly activated
    }
 }
```

We mentioned that filters represent bottlenecks to system processing, and your application's performance will suffer while filters are installed. Except for certain specialized applications, the use of filters should therefore be reserved for debugging and error trapping during development. You should not leave a filter installed any longer than is absolutely necessary.

Here is the procedure for removing a filter:

```
/*---------------------< De-activate filter >------------------*/
        UnhookWindowsHook(WH_GETMESSAGE,  lpfWhGetMessage);
        UnhookWindowsHook(WH_CALLWNDPROC, lpfWhCallWndProc);
```

If an application has installed a filter and fails to deactivate it before the application itself is terminated, a system crash may occur.

This concludes our discussion of Windows filter types. You will be able to better understand the practical use of filters by studying the demo program. Here's a summary of all the filter types:

Filter Name	Define	Type	Description
WH_CALLWNDPROC lParam: CWPMSG FAR*	4	DLL	Window function filter Captures all messages sent with SendMessage
WH_GETMESSAGE lParam: MSG FAR *	3	DLL	Message filter becomes active each time GetMessage is called
WH_KEYBOARD lParam: 32-Bit status information	2	DLL	Koyboard filter becomes active when an application calls GetMessage or PeekMessage and there is a WM_KEYUP or WM_KEYDOWN message to be processed
WH_MSGFILTER lParam: MSG FAR *	-1	APP or DLL	Message filter limited to all dialog box, messagebox or menu messages for a particular application
WH_SYSMSGFILTER lParam: MSG FAR *	6	DLL	System-wide message filter for all dialog box, message box or menu messages
WH_JOURNALRECORD lParam: MSG FAR *	0	DLL	Records sequence of events Windows calls this function whenever an event exists in the event queue
WH_JOURNALPLAYBACK lParam: MSG FAR *	1	DLL	Windows calls this function when requested for an event The filter's job then sends the next event message
WH_CBT WH_WINDOWMGR	5 7		Unspecified filter types

Notes: DLL:Filter function implemented in DLL
APP:Filter function implemented within application

12.3 Summary of Hook Functions

```
FARPROC SetWindowsHook(int nFilterTyp, FARPROC lpfFilter)
```

This function installs a filter of type nFilter. The lpfFilter parameter gives the procedure instance address of the filter function to be installed. The result of the SetWindowsHook function is the procedure instance address of a previously installed filter (if available). This value is stored in static memory and a pointer to this memory location is passed to the DefHookProc function in the fourth parameter.

```
DWORD DefHookProc(int nCode, WORD wParam, DWORD lParam,
                  FARPROC FAR * lplpfNextFilter)
```

This function is called by a filter function when Windows passes a negative nCode parameter. The filter function will call DefHookProc without any further processing of the message.

The DefHookProc function calls the next filter function in the chain of installed filter functions.

The function result is dependent upon the nCode parameter.

```
BOOL UnhookWindowsHook(int nFilterTyp, FARPROC lpfFilter)
```

This function removes the filter function indicated by the lpfFilter parameter. The filter function must have been installed with SetWindowsHook.

A function result other than zero indicates that the filter function was successfully removed from the system.

```
BOOL CallMsgFilter(lpMsg, nCode)
```

This function can be used to pass a filter-specific code (nCode) and the message, indicated by lpMsg from an MSG data structure, to the current filter function.

The function result indicates whether the message was processed (TRUE) or not (FALSE).

12.4 Source Code: CPHOOK.EXE

CPHOOKRC.H include file

```
/**********************************************************************
 CpHookRc.H            Resource definition file for Hook Demo
**********************************************************************/

/*------------------------------< Defines >--------------------------------*/
#define MI_ABOUT    200
#define MI_QUIT     201
#define MI_INSTALL  202
#define MI_REMOVE   203
```

CPHOOK.RC resource file

```
#include <windows.h>
#include "cphookrc.h"
rcinclude cphook.dlg
AppIcon  ICON    CPHOOK.ICO

Menu  MENU
   Begin
       MENUITEM "",                        MI_ABOUT

       POPUP "&File"
       Begin
       MENUITEM "&Install Filter"         MI_INSTALL
       MENUITEM "&Remove Filter",         MI_REMOVE GRAYED
       MENUITEM SEPARATOR
       MENUITEM "E&xit...",               MI_QUIT
       End
END
```

CPHOOK.DLG

```
ABOUTBOX DIALOG LOADONCALL MOVEABLE DISCARDABLE 58, 24, 193, 97
STYLE WS_DLGFRAME | WS_POPUP
BEGIN
    CONTROL "Captain Hook", 101, "static", SS_CENTER | WS_CHILD, 1, 6, 187, 12
    CONTROL "Copyright  1990", 103, "static", SS_CENTER | WS_CHILD, 0, 38, 189,
10
    CONTROL "Abacus", 104, "static", SS_CENTER | WS_CHILD, 75, 47, 37, 11
```

```
    CONTROL "Authors: D.Honekamp && P.Wilken", 106, "static", SS_CENTER |
WS_CHILD, 0, 66, 188, 11
    CONTROL "OK", 1, "button", BS_DEFPUSHBUTTON | WS_TABSTOP | WS_CHILD, 75, 81,
41, 12
    CONTROL "DDE Message Filter", 105, "static", SS_CENTER | WS_CHILD, 19, 22,
157, 8
END
```

CPHOOK.DEF module definition file

```
NAME            CpHook
DESCRIPTION 'Demo Application of message filters (hooks)'
EXETYPE         WINDOWS
STUB            'winstub.exe'

CODE            PRELOAD MOVEABLE

DATA            PRELOAD MOVEABLE MULTIPLE

HEAPSIZE        0x2000
STACKSIZE       0x2000

EXPORTS         WndProc
                MdfAboutBox
```

CPHOOK.MAK MAKE file

```
Mod  = S
Warn = 3

.c.obj:
   cl -W$(Warn) -c -Od -Zpei -Gw -A$(Mod) $*.c

.rc.res:
   rc -r $*.rc

ALL: cphook.exe


cphook.obj:    cphook.c

cphook.res:    cphook.rc   cphook.dlg

cphook.exe:    cphook.obj  cphook.res cphook.def
               link /CO cphook,,,LIBW+$(Mod)LIBCEW+HOOK.LIB/NOE/NOD,cphook.def;
               rc cphook.res
```

CPHOOK.C source code

```
/*************************************************************************

 C P H O O K . C       Main module for CAPTAIN HOOK, application
                       demonstrating Windows hooks

*************************************************************************/

#include        <windows.h>
#include        <string.h>
#include        <stdio.h>
#include        <dde.h>
#include        "CpHookRc.H"

/*---------------------------< Prototyping >----------------------------*/
BOOL FAR PASCAL MdfAboutBox(HWND hDlg, unsigned msg, WORD wP, LONG lP);
BOOL FAR PASCAL InstallDdeFilter(HANDLE hLib, HWND hWnd, BOOL bInstall);
long FAR PASCAL WndProc(HWND hWnd, unsigned msg, WORD wP, LONG lP);
int PASCAL WinMain (HANDLE hInstance, HANDLE hPrevInstance, LPSTR lpszCmdLine,
                    int nCmdShow);

/*------------------------< Global variables >--------------------------*/
HANDLE       hInst,               // Handle for Application instance
             hLib;                // Handle for HOOK.DLL
HMENU        hwMenu;              // Handle for main menu
HWND         hwMain;              // Handle for main window
char         szAppName[] = "Captain Hook";
BOOL         bHooksActive = FALSE;

/************************************************************************
 M d f A b o u t B o x                       ### Dialog box function ###
 =====================

 This is the window function for processing the About box
************************************************************************/
BOOL FAR PASCAL MdfAboutBox(HWND hDlg, unsigned msg, WORD wP, LONG lP)
{
   switch(msg)
   {
      case WM_COMMAND:
         switch(wP)
         {
            case IDOK:
               EndDialog(hDlg,TRUE);
               return TRUE;
            default:
```

```
                return FALSE;
            }
        default:
            return FALSE;
    }
}

/*************************************************************************
 W n d P r o c                               ### Callback function ###
 =============

 M a i n W i n d o w   F u n c t i o n
*************************************************************************/
long FAR PASCAL WndProc(HWND hWnd, unsigned msg, WORD wP, LONG lP)
{
   int          aktion;
   FARPROC      lpTmpProc;

   switch (msg)
   {
      case WM_DESTROY:                   /* End application */
         if(bHooksActive)
            InstallDdeFilter(hLib, hWnd, FALSE);
         PostQuitMessage(NULL);
      break;

      case WM_COMMAND:
      {
        switch (wP)
        {
           case MI_QUIT:            // End program ...
              if(MessageBox(hWnd, (LPSTR)"Do you really want to exit?",
                         (LPSTR)"Exit Program",
                  MB_ICONQUESTION | MB_YESNO | MB_DEFBUTTON1 |
                  MB_APPLMODAL) == IDYES)
              DestroyWindow(hWnd);
           break;

           case MI_ABOUT:
              lpTmpProc = MakeProcInstance((FARPROC)MdfAboutBox, hInst);
              aktion = DialogBox(hInst, "ABOUTBOX", hWnd, lpTmpProc);
              FreeProcInstance(lpTmpProc);
           break;

           case MI_INSTALL:     // Installing WH_CALLWNDPROC filters
              if(InstallDdeFilter(hLib, hWnd, TRUE))
              {
                 EnableMenuItem(hwMenu, MI_REMOVE,  MF_ENABLED);
```

```
                EnableMenuItem(hwMenu, MI_INSTALL, MF_GRAYED);
                EnableMenuItem(hwMenu, MI_QUIT,    MF_GRAYED);
                bHooksActive = TRUE;
             }
             else
                MessageBox(hWnd,
                   (LPSTR)"Filter function could\nnot be installed",
                   (LPSTR)"Hook Error",
                   MB_ICONEXCLAMATION | MB_OK | MB_DEFBUTTON1);
          break;

          case MI_REMOVE:     // Removing WH_CALLWNDPROC filters
             if(InstallDdeFilter(hLib, hWnd, FALSE))
             {
                EnableMenuItem(hwMenu, MI_REMOVE,  MF_GRAYED);
                EnableMenuItem(hwMenu, MI_INSTALL, MF_ENABLED);
                EnableMenuItem(hwMenu, MI_QUIT,    MF_ENABLED);
                bHooksActive = FALSE;
             ]
          break;
       }// switch wP

     }// case WM_COMMAND
     default:
         return(DefWindowProc(hWnd, msg, wP, lP));
  }
  return (NULL);
}

/**************************************************************************
 W i n M a i n
 =============

 Main function of Windows application
**************************************************************************/
int PASCAL WinMain (HANDLE hInstance, HANDLE hPrevInstance, LPSTR lpszCmdLine,
                    int nCmdShow)
{
  MSG         msg ;
  WNDCLASS    wndclass ;

  if (!hPrevInstance)
  {
     wndclass.style          = CS_VREDRAW | CS_HREDRAW ;
     wndclass.lpfnWndProc    = WndProc ;
     wndclass.cbClsExtra     = 0 ;
     wndclass.cbWndExtra     = 0 ;
     wndclass.hInstance      = hInstance ;
```

```
    wndclass.hIcon          = LoadIcon (hInstance,(LPSTR) "AppIcon") ;
    wndclass.hCursor        = LoadCursor (NULL, IDC_ARROW);
    wndclass.hbrBackground = GetStockObject (WHITE_BRUSH) ;
    wndclass.lpszMenuName  = NULL;
    wndclass.lpszClassName = szAppName ;

    if (!RegisterClass (&wndclass))
        return FALSE;

    hInst = hInstance;
    hwMenu = LoadMenu(hInst, "Menu");
    hwMain = CreateWindow (szAppName, szAppName, WS_OVERLAPPEDWINDOW,
                        20, 0, 600, 200, NULL,
                        hwMenu,
                        hInstance, NULL) ;

    ShowWindow(hwMain, SW_SHOWNORMAL);
    UpdateWindow (hwMain);
  }
  if(hPrevInstance)
    return FALSE;

  hLib   = LoadLibrary((LPSTR) "HOOK.DLL");
  if(hLib == NULL)
  {
    MessageBox(hwMain, (LPSTR)"HOOK.DLL not found",
                       (LPSTR)"Hook Error",
                       MB_ICONEXCLAMATION | MB_OK | MB_DEFBUTTON1);

    return FALSE;
  }

  /*-------------< Message loop >----------*/

  while(GetMessage (&msg, NULL, 0, 0))
  {
    TranslateMessage (&msg) ;
    DispatchMessage (&msg) ;
  }
  return msg.wParam;
}
```

12.5 Source Code: HOOK.DLL

HOOK.DEF module definition file

```
LIBRARY hook

DESCRIPTION 'DLL with WH_SYSMSGFILTER filter function'

EXETYPE WINDOWS

CODE PRELOAD FIXED
DATA PRELOAD SINGLE

HEAPSIZE       0

EXPORTS
   WhCallWndProc      @1
   WhGetMessage       @2
   InstallDdeFilter   @3
   WEP                @4 RESIDENTNAME
```

HOOK.MAK MAKE file

```
Mod  = S
Warn = 3

.rc.res:
        rc -r $*.rc

all: hook.dll

hook.obj:    hook.c
  cl -c -A$(Mod)w -W$(Warn) -Gsw -Zpe -Os $*.c

hook.dll: hook.c hook.obj hook.def
  link /NOD /al:16 hook, hook.dll,, $(Mod)dllcew libw, hook.def
  implib hook.lib hook.def
  rc hook.dll
  copy hook.dll ..
  copy hook.lib ..
```

HOOK.C source code

```
/**************************************************************************
```

```
 H O O K . C          Main module of HOOK.DLL, a dynamic link library
                      (DLL) with hook filter functions.

***************************************************************************/

#include        <windows.h>
#include        <string.h>
#include        <dde.h>

#define   fACK       0x8000
#define   fWARM      0x4000
#define   fACKREQ    0x8000
#define   fRELEASE   0x2000
#define   fREQUEST   0x1000

/*----------------------------< Prototyping >----------------------------*/
void  FAR PASCAL WhCallWndProc(int nCode, WORD wP, DWORD lP);
void  FAR PASCAL WhGetMessage(int nCode, WORD wP, DWORD lP);
BOOL  FAR PASCAL InstallDdeFilter(HANDLE hLib, HWND hWnd, BOOL bInstall);
VOID  FAR PASCAL WEP(int nParam);

/*-----------------------< Data type  definition >-----------------------*/
typedef struct tagCWPMSG
{                  // Data structure returns messages
   WORD  hlParam, // HIGHWORD(lParam) of lParam parameter for message
         llParam, // LOWWORD(lParam) of lParam parameter for message
         wParam,  // wParam parameter for message
         wMsg,    // Message type
         hWnd;    // Window handle specified for message
} CWPMSG;

/*------------------------< Global  variables >-------------------------*/

static FARPROC   lpfWhCallWndProc,    // Instance address of filter function
                 lpfWhGetMessage,
                 lpfPrevCallWndProc,  // Address of PrevCall function
                 lpfPrevGetMessage;

static int    nLine = 0;              // Current output line
static HWND   hDbgWnd;

char          szTxt[256];

char* szaDdeMsg[11] = { "INITIATE",
                        "TERMINATE",
                        "WARM_LINK",
                        "HOT_LINK",
```

```
                          "REQUEST",
                          "SER_DATA",
                          "CLT_POKE",
                          "POS_ACK",
                          "NEG_ACK",
                          "EXECUTE",
                          "LINK_TERM" } ;

/*************************************************************************
 W r i t e l n
 =============

 This function displays the passed string in the next available line of
 the client area. If the function reaches the last line of the client
 area, the text is placed in the last line, overwriting the old line.

 Parameters:
 HWND        Output window handle
 LPSTR       Passed string
*************************************************************************/
void Writeln(HWND hWnd, LPSTR lpText)
{
   HDC          hDC;
   RECT         Rect;
   TEXTMETRIC   TxtMetric;
   int          nCharHeight,    // Character height
                nCharWidth;     // Character width

   hDC = GetDC(hWnd);
   GetTextMetrics(hDC, (LPTEXTMETRIC) &TxtMetric);
   nCharWidth  = TxtMetric.tmAveCharWidth;
   nCharHeight = TxtMetric.tmHeight + TxtMetric.tmExternalLeading;

   GetClientRect(hWnd, (LPRECT) &Rect);

   if(nLine++ >= Rect.bottom/nCharHeight - 1)
      nLine = 0;

   /*--------------------< Clear old line contents >------------------*/
   Rect.top    = nLine * nCharHeight;
   Rect.bottom = Rect.top + nCharHeight;
   FillRect(hDC, (LPRECT) &Rect, GetStockObject(WHITE_BRUSH));

   /*----------------------< Display  text >-------------------------*/
   TextOut(hDC, 5, Rect.top, lpText, lstrlen(lpText));

   /*--------------------< Delete next line >------------------------*/
   Rect.top    = (nLine+1) * nCharHeight;
```

```
   Rect.bottom = Rect.top + nCharHeight;
   FillRect(hDC, (LPRECT) &Rect, GetStockObject(WHITE_BRUSH));
   ReleaseDC(hWnd, hDC);
}

/**************************************************************************
 W h C a l l W n d P r o c                        ### Callback function ###
 =========================

 This function is the filter function of type WH_CALLWNDPROC. It waits
 for messages sent using SendMessage.

 The following messages are used by DDE protocol:

 WM_DDE_INITIATE and the response WM_DDE_ACK.
**************************************************************************/
void FAR PASCAL WhCallWndProc(int nCode, WORD wP, DWORD lP)
{
  CWPMSG FAR *pWndMsg;        // Pointer to a message data structure to be
                              // used with the WH_CALLWNDPROC filter only.
                              // Other filters use the standard
                              // MSG data structure.
  char        szApp[31],
              szTopic[31];
  int         nMsg;

  if(nCode < 0)
  {
     // Pass message without further processing...
     DefHookProc(nCode, wP, lP, (FARPROC FAR *) &lpfPrevCallWndProc);
  }
  else
  {
    /*
       Get access to the user-defined CWPMSG data structure, which contains
       information about the message-controlled filters
    */

    pWndMsg = (CWPMSG FAR *) lP; // NOTE: lP is a FAR pointer

    switch(pWndMsg->wMsg)
    {
       case WM_DDE_INITIATE:       // Create DDE link
         GlobalGetAtomName(pWndMsg->hlParam, (LPSTR) szTopic, 30);
         GlobalGetAtomName(pWndMsg->llParam, (LPSTR) szApp,  30);
         wsprintf((LPSTR) szTxt, (LPSTR)"%4x ==> %4x  %s  A=%s  T=%s",
                  pWndMsg->wParam,
                  pWndMsg->hWnd,
```

```
                (LPSTR) szaDdeMsg[0],
                (LPSTR) szApp,
                (LPSTR) szTopic);
        Writeln(hDbgWnd, (LPSTR) szTxt);
      break;

      case WM_DDE_ACK:                       // Exit message
        nMsg = (pWndMsg->llParam & fACK) ? 7 : 8; // Positive : Negative ACK
        GlobalGetAtomName(pWndMsg->hlParam, (LPSTR) szTopic, 30);
        GlobalGetAtomName(pWndMsg->llParam, (LPSTR) szApp,  30);
        wsprintf((LPSTR) szTxt, (LPSTR)"%4x ==> %4x  %s  A=%s  T=%s",
                pWndMsg->wParam,
                pWndMsg->hWnd,
                (LPSTR) szaDdeMsg[nMsg],
                (LPSTR) szApp,
                (LPSTR) szTopic);
        Writeln(hDbgWnd, (LPSTR) szTxt);
      break;
    }
  }
}

/***********************************************************************
 W h G e t M e s s a g e
 =======================

 This filter function filters complete messages, read from the applications
 by the GetMessage function call.

 The DDE protocol handle can filter all functions when sent by PostMessage.
 ***********************************************************************/
void FAR PASCAL WhGetMessage(int nCode, WORD wP, DWORD lP)
{
  MSG FAR *pMsg;
  char           szItem[61];
  int            nMsg;          // Index: Message type
  WORD           llParam,       // Least significant word of lParam
                 hlParam;       // Most significant word of lParam
  LPSTR          lpCommand;

  if(nCode < 0)
  {
    // Pass message without processing...
    DefHookProc(nCode, wP, lP, (FARPROC FAR *) &lpfPrevGetMessage);
  }
  else
  {
    /*
```

```
      Get access to MSG data structure, which contains information about
      the message-controlled filters
   */

   pMsg = (MSG FAR *) lP; // NOTE: lP is a FAR pointer to the MSG structure

   hlParam = HIWORD(pMsg->lParam);
   llParam = LOWORD(pMsg->lParam);

   switch(pMsg->message)
   {
      case WM_DDE_TERMINATE:        // Terminate DDE link
        wsprintf((LPSTR) szTxt, (LPSTR)"%4x ==> %4x  %s",
                 pMsg->wParam,
                 pMsg->hwnd,
                 (LPSTR) szaDdeMsg[1]);
        Writeln(hDbgWnd, (LPSTR) szTxt);
      break;

      case WM_DDE_ADVISE:           // Direct permanent link to server
        GlobalGetAtomName(hlParam, (LPSTR) szItem, 30);
        nMsg = (llParam & fWARM) ? 2 : 3;  // WARM : HOT Link
        wsprintf((LPSTR) szTxt, (LPSTR)"%4x ==> %4x  %s  [%s]",
                 pMsg->wParam,
                 pMsg->hwnd,
                 (LPSTR) szaDdeMsg[nMsg],
                 (LPSTR) szItem);
        Writeln(hDbgWnd, (LPSTR) szTxt);
      break;

      case WM_DDE_UNADVISE:         // Remove permanent link
        GlobalGetAtomName(hlParam, (LPSTR) szItem, 30);
        wsprintf((LPSTR) szTxt, (LPSTR)"%4x ==> %4x  %s  [%s]",
                 pMsg->wParam,
                 pMsg->hwnd,
                 (LPSTR) szaDdeMsg[10],
                 (LPSTR) szItem);
        Writeln(hDbgWnd, (LPSTR) szTxt);
      break;

      case WM_DDE_DATA:             // Update message from server
        GlobalGetAtomName(hlParam, (LPSTR) szItem, 30);
        wsprintf((LPSTR) szTxt, (LPSTR)"%4x ==> %4x  %s  [%s]",
                 pMsg->wParam,
                 pMsg->hwnd,
                 (LPSTR) szaDdeMsg[5],
                 (LPSTR) szItem);
        Writeln(hDbgWnd, (LPSTR) szTxt);
```

```
      break;

      case WM_DDE_POKE:            // Un-requested data sent to client
        GlobalGetAtomName(hlParam, (LPSTR) szItem, 30);
        wsprintf((LPSTR) szTxt, (LPSTR)"%4x ==> %4x  %s  [%s]",
                 pMsg->wParam,
                 pMsg->hwnd,
                 (LPSTR) szaDdeMsg[6],
                 (LPSTR) szItem);
        Writeln(hDbgWnd, (LPSTR) szTxt);
      break;


      case WM_DDE_EXECUTE:         // Remote command execution
         lpCommand = GlobalLock(hlParam);
         wsprintf((LPSTR) szTxt, (LPSTR)"%4x ==> %4x  %s  %-75s",
                  pMsg->wParam,
                  pMsg->hwnd,
                  (LPSTR) szaDdeMsg[9],
                  lpCommand);
         GlobalUnlock(hlParam);
         Writeln(hDbgWnd, (LPSTR) szTxt);
      break;

      case WM_DDE_REQUEST:
         GlobalGetAtomName(hlParam, (LPSTR) szItem, 30);
         wsprintf((LPSTR) szTxt, (LPSTR)"%4x==>%4x  %s  [%s]",
                 pMsg->wParam,
                 pMsg->hwnd,
                 (LPSTR) szaDdeMsg[5],
                 (LPSTR) szItem);
         Writeln(hDbgWnd, (LPSTR) szTxt);
      break;

      case WM_DDE_ACK:                           // Exit message
         nMsg = (llParam & fACK) ? 7 : 8;        // Positive : Negative ACK
         GlobalGetAtomName(hlParam, (LPSTR) szItem, 30);
         wsprintf((LPSTR) szTxt, (LPSTR)"%4x ==> %4x  %s  I=%s",
                 pMsg->wParam,
                 pMsg->hwnd,
                 (LPSTR) szaDdeMsg[nMsg],
                 (LPSTR) szItem);
         Writeln(hDbgWnd, (LPSTR) szTxt);
      break;
    }
  }
}
```

```
/***************************************************************************
 I n s t a l l D d e F i l t e r
 ===============================

 This function calls filters of type WH_CALLWNDPROC and WH_GETMESSAGE,
 depending on whether the <bInstll> flag is installed or not.
 InstallDdeFilter requires the window handle of the function called. This
 uses the Writeln() function to write the filtered messages to the client
 area of the application. The handle to the DLL is also passed. This
 handle contains the application called by LoadLibrary("HOOK.DLL").
***************************************************************************/
BOOL FAR PASCAL InstallDdeFilter(HANDLE hLib, HWND hWnd, BOOL bInstall)
{
   if(bInstall)
   {
     /*-----------------------< Activate filter >------------------*/
      lpfWhCallWndProc    = GetProcAddress(hLib, (LPSTR) "WhCallWndProc");
      lpfPrevCallWndProc = SetWindowsHook(WH_CALLWNDPROC, lpfWhCallWndProc);

      if(lpfWhCallWndProc)
      {
         lpfWhGetMessage  = GetProcAddress(hLib, (LPSTR) "WhGetMessage");
         lpfPrevGetMessage= SetWindowsHook(WH_GETMESSAGE, lpfWhGetMessage);

         if(lpfWhGetMessage)
         {
            hDbgWnd = hWnd;
            return TRUE;
         }
      }
   }
   else
   {
      /*----------------------< De-activate filter >------------------*/
      if(lpfWhGetMessage)
      {
         UnhookWindowsHook(WH_GETMESSAGE,  lpfWhGetMessage);
         UnhookWindowsHook(WH_CALLWNDPROC, lpfWhCallWndProc);
         hDbgWnd = NULL;
         return TRUE;
      }
   }
   return FALSE;
}

/*****************************************************************************
 W E P ()
 ========
```

```
 This is the DLL shutdown function. It requires no parameters.
 *************************************************************************/

VOID FAR PASCAL WEP (int bSystemExit)
{
  if (bSystemExit)
  {
    // System shutdown
  }
  else
  {
    // DLL use counter = NULL
  }
} // WEP
```

13 Printing

This chapter discusses printers, how MS-DOS controls printed output and how Windows controls printed output.

13.1 Printing under DOS

Do you remember the first time you were faced with the problem of putting the output of your program on paper? You were probably overjoyed to discover that printer output under MS-DOS was no problem at all. The operating system allows you to address the printer as a file. In C dialects for MS-DOS there is usually a corresponding stream, named stdprn, that is already predefined. So you don't even have to open the pseudo file that represents the printer. This equivalence between file and output device enabled your program to use the same functions to write to the screen, a file or to the printer.

Unfortunately, it's only that easy if you confine yourself to printing pure text. As soon as you want to harness the capabilities of your printer for text formatting and font design, or output graphics and special characters, you find yourself struggling with the printer's designers. Many dot-matrix printers obey commands in accordance with the Epson ESC/P standard, but no two printers will react to the same control sequence in the same way. Take the following printer command:

```
ESC 'A' 1
```

This command gives you a line spacing of 1/72 inch on 9 pin printers, and a line spacing of 1/60 inch on 24 pin printers. In general: The more elaborate and polished the printout, the more you notice the differences, big and small, between various printers. Meanwhile, this has resulted in current word processing and graphic software supplied with dozens, or even hundreds, of printer drivers.

13.2 Printing under Windows

Under Windows, programmers are just as protected from printer-specific qualities as they are from details of the video adapter connected to the computer. Printing requires a certain amount of preparation in your program, but the actual text and graphic output functions work, regardless of whether you send output to the screen, a file or the printer. However, as we will see later, the developers at Microsoft didn't achieve absolute transparency either. The GDI (Graphics Device Interface), which provides all of the functions for text and graphic output, provides this (far-reaching) device independence. The GDI accesses hardware through device drivers, rather than performing direct hardware access.

13.2.1 Device independence through GDI

You always start GDI access by getting a handle to a device context. As a rule, GetDC() or BeginPaint() accesses the device context assigned to the window where your output will appear. Windows are automatically equipped with a device context when they are created; so you don't need to worry about generating device contexts for windows yourself. On the other hand, if you want to access the printer, you must create an appropriate device context first by using the CreateDC() function.

The device context is a precise description of the assigned device driver's current status. It contains information about colors, character modes, graphic objects such as brushes, pens or fonts, etc. The device context represents a connection between an application, the GDI and the device driver.

When the GDI is instructed to perform a graphic function, it reads the device driver to ensure that the operation may be performed independently. The driver answers 'yes' if a supported device with the necessary function exists (e.g., video adapters with graphic capabilities), or if the operation must be emulated. Otherwise, the GDI must divide the character operation into smaller tasks executable by the driver. For instance, ellipses are usually created by drawing short lines, or by placing individual pixels. This concept allows different devices, such as screens, printers or plotters, to be used for output.

13.2.2 The printer is not a screen

Unfortunately, this means that a Windows application must be concerned about the specific characteristics of the output device it is using. In some cases it is only possible to approximate the emulation of a feature, and the results may not be what you expected. For example, the GDI can simulate colors by grading (mixing) colors. However, high contrast colors don't necessarily result in high contrast patterns. The situation becomes worse when you print because patterns print differently than they look on the screen due to the higher resolution of the printer. Besides, this technique only works on color surfaces. The GDI resorts to the most similar available color in the output device when printing lines or text. With most printers, this simply means a choice between black and white.

There are other aspects that make it necessary for you to consider the output device in your program. For instance, under Windows it's even possible to hook up a printer that is not capable of printing graphics. Even though GetDeviceCaps() is rarely used to check graphics capabilities for the screen, in most cases you can't avoid calling this function to check your printer. We'll discuss this in more detail later. Also, when you work with printers or plotters there are error sources that you don't have with the screen. The printer might be offline (disconnected) or out of paper. Memory shortages or lack of space on the hard drive can also create printing problems.

Another thing to consider: There are no windows on the paper. When several applications access the screen simultaneously, they never intrude because each program can only write to its own window. GDI limits the output to the screen area allocated to the program. However, you can't overlap printer output from several different programs this way. On the contrary, you have to divide the printer output into separate documents or print tasks. Also, you can't create a new page of your document by simply overwriting the previous page as you do on the screen. Instead, you have to use form-feeding. Windows provides one new function to implement this additionally required program logic: Escape().

13.2.3 Escape(): Printer access

The Escape() function is the interface between your program and the printer. While the GDI graphic functions perform the actual printer output (what you see in black and white afterwards), Escape() governs the administrative aspect. This function tells the printer the beginning and end of a document, so you can separate the individual print tasks.

Different variants allow access to specific characteristics of each device, such as paper feed selection on a multiple sheet feeder. Finally, you can use this function to ask for information about the printer directly from the driver. For example, you could determine the paper size or the orientation of the paper (portrait or landscape).

13.2.4 Summary of the printing process

GDIs, printer drivers and the Print Manager, which you usually activate in the WIN.INI file, must work together in a rather complicated way in order for the output of your program to appear on the printer. Here's what this process looks like:

1) You determine the current printer from the WIN.INI file.

2) You use this information to create a device context for the printer. GDI loads and initializes the printer driver (a DLL) if this hasn't already been done.

3) The Escape() subfunction STARTDOC starts a new print task. The GDI passes this call directly to the printer driver. The printer driver performs all of the necessary initialization and informs the GDI when it is finished. The GDI then tries to load the Print Manager, unless it has been deactivated in the WIN.INI file.

4) You output the first page of your document by calling the appropriate GDI functions. The GDI places these function references in a temporary metafile either in the TEMP directory or in the root directory of drive C:.

5) When the first page of your document is finished, use the Escape() subfunction, NEWFRAME, to request a form-feed.

6) Now the GDI begins sending your output to the printer driver. The driver translates the function references from the metafile into instructions that the printer can understand (i.e., a series of control sequences and data or a Postscript text). The GDI places the output of the printer driver in the printer file.

7) The Print Manager then sends this printer file to the printer, deleting it afterwards. The GDI deletes the metafile.

8) After outputting the last page of your document, you conclude the print task with the Escape() subfunction, ENDDOC.

Much of this process runs transparently. As far as your program is concerned, the printing process finishes as soon as the GDI has created the temporary files. During the actual printing, your program continues running, as usual.

Some variations are possible. You could deactivate the Print Manager by making the appropriate entry in the WIN.INI file (spooler=no in the [windows] section). It makes sense to do this if you already have another spooler installed, such as a hardware solution.

One spooler is generally faster than two spoolers. In such a case, the GDI sends the output of the printer driver directly to the printer. No printer file is created.

During the entire printer output, however, Windows is "frozen" (i.e., the printing process runs exclusively in the foreground), which makes it impossible to swap tasks. You can solve this problem with an abort function, which we will explain in more detail later. Instead of aborting the printing process, this function enables multitasking in Windows again.

You can also influence the production of metafiles. When the graphic function references are being translated to a printer file, it can result in large amounts of data. Depending on the printer resolution, it can result in more than a megabyte.

For this reason, the GDI doesn't transfer all of the function references to the printer driver at once, but instead divides a page into several sections, called bands. For each of these bands, the metafile is sent to the driver, whereby clipping is set to the appropriate section of the page.

If the printer doesn't need banding, the metafiles stop being created and the GDI references go directly to the driver. A Windows program can also take banding into its own hands. As we will see, this is a practical technique for printing bitmaps.

You must put bitmaps in both the metafile and the printer file. That takes time and under the right circumstances, could exceed the capacity of the TEMP directory if the directory is installed on a virtual directory. If your program takes over the banding, it creates a separate, small metafile for each band. We will explain the necessary program logic in a later chapter.

13.3 The Minimum Solution

WINPRINT (Version 1) is a first approach to redirecting the output of a Windows application to the printer. Although the solution works, it has a number of disadvantages that we will discuss later. What is presented here is the minimum effort required for printing. The project consists of the following files:

- WINPRINT.C contains those parts of the program that have nothing to do with printer output: Logging on the window class, creating windows, the message loops as well as the window function of the application window. The menu contains the pop up menu called **Program**, which contains the items **Print** (start a sample printout), **Exit** and **About WINPRINT...**.

- DOPRINT.C contains the functions for printing. We will discuss this file in detail.

- WINPRINT.RC is the resource file. It defines the menu and the **About WINPRINT...** dialog box, and imports the application icon.

- WINPRINT.H contains some global definitions, such as the application names, etc.

- RESOURCE.H contains the definitions necessary for the resource file.

- WINPRINT.DEF is the module definition file for the linker.

- WINPRINT.ICO is cut from a Desktop bitmap of the Windows system and doesn't serve any particular purpose.

- MAKEFILE helps connect everything into a whole. You can run either MAKE from the Microsoft C 5.1 package or the newer NMAKE of the C 6.0 compiler.

When you choose **Print** in the **Program** menu, it calls the DoPrint() function in the DOPRINT module. This is where the preparations for printing begin.

What you need

Each output from the GDI requires a handle to a device context. So the first thing you do is create such a device context for the printer:

```
hDC = CreateDC(lpszDriverName, lpszDeviceName,     lpszOutputPort, lpInitData);
```

The fourth argument, lpInitData, is usually set to NULL. This instructs the printer to accept the settings that the user made in the system control. You have to discover the other arguments from the WIN.INI file first. In the [windows] section there is a line called "device= ... ", which contains the names of the current printer, its driver and the port to which the printer is connected:

```
[windows]  .  .    [diverse entries]  .device=Epson 24-pin,EPSON24,LPT1:
```

This line specifies the default printer, as the user might select a printer from the control panel in Windows. The function GetPrinterDC() reads this description from the WIN.INI file and divides it into the three required strings. You use strtok() from the standard library of the C compiler to divide the string into three "tokens". Remember that the first entry, the device name, can have spaces, which is why only the comma is specified as a separator here. All of the other entries can be separated by commas and/or spaces. Of course, the function also has to take into consideration that there is no printer set as the standard printer or that the entry could be incorrect. In such a case, it returns the invalid handle, NULL.

After calling GetPrinterDC(), the printer driver is loaded and the device context is installed. DoPrint() now announces a new print task using the escape() function. Here's what the syntax looks like:

```
int Escape( HDC    hPrnDC,     /* Handle of the printer DC    */
            int    nEscape     /* Subfunction              */
            int    nCount,     /* Number of bytes in InData    */
            LPSTR lpInData,    /* Pointer to input data */
            LPSTR lpOutData    /* Pointer to output data */         );
```

nEscape stands for the desired subfunction. WINDOWS.H defines symbolic constants for all of the available escape functions. There are several dozen of them, but not every driver supports all of them. Escape() returns 0 if you call it with a subfunction number that the driver does not support. A negative value is returned for all other errors. However, you can also determine in advance whether an escape subfunction is available:

```
int nEscape;
int nResult;
nEscape = ENABLEDUPLEX;
nResult = Escape(hDC, QUERYESCSUPPORT, sizeof(int), (LPSTR)&nEscape, NULL);
```

You use these lines to check whether the current printer is able to print on both sides of a piece of paper. Remember that you cannot directly transfer the function number that you would like to check, since Escape() always expects a pointer to the input data. The data (structures) to which lpInData and lpOutData are pointing depend on the subfunction. The SDK Reference Manual gives a list of all the printer escapes. In our program it's not necessary to ask such a question, since the program only calls subfunctions that are mandatory for each driver.

The subfunction STARTDOC announces a print task. lpInData points to a character string up to 31 characters long (plus null bytes) that contains the name of the document. Later, the document can be identified by this name in the display of the Print Manager. The name of the program should also be included here. That's all the preparation you need. PrintPage() outputs a sample page consisting of both text and graphics. This function is a beautiful example of device independence under Windows, because it doesn't matter to Windows whether hDC belongs to the device context of a printer, plotter or the screen. Just for fun, you can expand the window function MainWndProc() in WINPRINT.C by inserting the following case instructions in the "switch (wMsg)" block:

```
case WM_PAINT :
   {
      PAINTSTRUCT ps;
      HDC         hDC;
      RECT        rc;
      hDC = BeginPaint(hWnd, &ps);
      GetClientRect(hWnd, &rc);
      PrintPage(hDC, rc.right, rc.bottom);
      EndPaint(hWnd, &ps);
   }
   break;
case WM_SIZE :
   InvalidateRect(hWnd, NULL, TRUE);
   break;
```

The response to WM_SIZE makes the entire window surface invalid and results in a message, from WM_PAINT, that redraws the entire window surface. This is necessary because PrintPage() makes the size of the drawing dependent on the size of the entire character surface, which in this case is the size of the window interior.

After it returns from PrintPage(), the output for your program is closed. You still have to inform the Print Manager of this. The escape function, NEWFRAME, concludes the current page. As a result, the GDI references to translation are passed to the printer driver. Since there aren't any more pages, the subfunction ENDDOC also ends the document. NEWFRAME and ENDDOC don't need any more parameters. Remember to call ENDDOC only when there haven't been any errors. In case of an error the GDI concludes the print task.

The usual clean-up work comes at the end. All you have to do is use the DeleteDC() function to remove the device context of the printer again.

Shortcomings

Mindlessly calling WINPRINT won't hurt your system. If you expanded MainWndProc(), you will discover that the printout matches the summary in the WinPrint window. So where's the problem? The big disadvantage of this program is its "stinginess". While it is printing, the rest of the system is frozen. So none of the other programs get any computer time, and you can't switch to a different task. This is especially annoying if you started a longer printout. It's even worse if the Print Manager in the WIN.INI file is switched off. Bottom Line: You'll have to take an extended break from your work on the computer because you can't abort the printing process either.

13.3.1 Source code: WINPRINT (Version 1)

RESOURCE.H include file

```
/****************************************************************************/
/*** RESOURCE.H                                                          ***/
/***                                                                     ***/
/*** Resource IDs                                                        ***/
/***                                                                     ***/
/*** (c) 1991 by Abacus                                                  ***/
/*** Author: H. Huptasch                                                 ***/
/****************************************************************************/


#define ID_ABOUT     100
#define ID_QUIT      101
#define ID_WORK      102
```

WINPRINT.H include file

```
/****************************************************************************/
/*** WINPRINT.H                                                          ***/
/***                                                                     ***/
/*** Global definitions and declarations                                 ***/
/***                                                                     ***/
/*** (c) 1991 by Abacus                                                  ***/
/*** Author: H. Huptasch                                                 ***/
/****************************************************************************/

#define CLASS_NAME   "WinPrintClass"
#define APPL_NAME    "WinPrint"
#define MENU_NAME    "WinPrintMenu"
#define ICON_NAME    "WinPrintIcon"
#define ABOUTBOX     "AboutBox"

/* Instance handle of application                                           */

extern HANDLE hInst;

/* Printed output function prototypes                                       */

BOOL DoPrint(HWND);
void PrintPage(HDC, int, int);
```

WINPRINT.RC resource file

```
/*************************************************************************/
/*** WINPRINT.RC                                                      ***/
/***                                                                  ***/
/*** (c) 1991 by Abacus                                               ***/
/*** Author: H. Huptasch                                              ***/
/*************************************************************************/

#include <windows.h>
#include "resource.h"

WinPrintIcon ICON winprint.ico

WinPrintMenu MENU
BEGIN
   POPUP "&Program"
   BEGIN
      MENUITEM "&Print",         ID_WORK
      MENUITEM "E&xit",           ID_QUIT
      MENUITEM SEPARATOR
      MENUITEM "A&bout WINPRINT...", ID_ABOUT
   END
END

AboutBox DIALOG LOADONCALL MOVEABLE DISCARDABLE 10, 9, 144, 78
STYLE WS_DLGFRAME | WS_POPUP
BEGIN
   ICON           "WinPrintIcon",            -1,     8,  8,  16, 21,  SS_ICON
   CTEXT          "WinPrint",                -1,    24,  4, 120,  8
   CTEXT          " 1991 Abacus",           -1,    24, 14, 120,  8
   CTEXT          "Author: Heiko Huptasch",  -1,    24, 22, 120,  8
   CTEXT          "Version 1.0",             -1,    24, 36, 120,  8
   DEFPUSHBUTTON  "OK",                      IDOK, 58, 56,  52, 14,  WS_GROUP
END
```

WINPRINT.DEF module definition file

```
NAME         WINPRINT
EXETYPE      WINDOWS
DESCRIPTION 'WINPRINT - A Windows application by Abacus (c) 1991'

STUB         'WINSTUB.EXE'

CODE         MOVEABLE DISCARDABLE
DATA         PRELOAD MOVEABLE MULTIPLE
```

```
HEAPSIZE    1024
STACKSIZE   4096

SEGMENTS
   _TEXT    PRELOAD
   WINPRINT PRELOAD
   DOPRINT  LOADONCALL

EXPORTS
   MainWndProc
   AboutProc
```

MAKEFILE

```
# Creation of WINPRINT.EXE
#
# MAKEFILE for Microsoft's MAKE or NMAKE
#
# (c) 1991 by Abacus
# Author: H. Huptasch


# Object file list

OBJECTS  =  winprint.obj doprint.obj


# Define compiler and necessary switches

CC       =  cl
CFLAGS   =  -AM -Osw -Gsw -Zpe -W3 -NT$* -DLINT_ARGS -D_WINDOWS

.c.obj:
   $(CC) -c $(CFLAGS) $*.c


#Flexible lists

MAKE_ALL:      winprint.exe

winprint.res:  winprint.rc winprint.ico resource.h
   rc -r winprint.rc

winprint.obj:  winprint.c  winprint.h  resource.h

doprint.obj:   doprint.c   winprint.h
```

```
winprint.exe:  $(OBJECTS)  winprint.res winprint.def
   link /NOD/NOE/A:16 $(OBJECTS), , nul, libw mlibcew, winprint
   rc winprint.res
```

DOPRINT.C source code

```
/****************************************************************************/
/*** DOPRINT.C                                                           ***/
/***                                                                     ***/
/*** Printer output module for WINPRINT.                                 ***/
/*** The method presented here is a minimal solution. It works, but is   ***/
/*** not the standard for proper Windows programming.                    ***/
/***                                                                     ***/
/*** (c) 1991 by Abacus                                                  ***/
/*** Author: H. Huptasch                                                 ***/
/****************************************************************************/

#include <windows.h>
#include <string.h>

#include "winprint.h"

/****************************************************************************/
/*** Prototypes                                                          ***/
/****************************************************************************/

static HDC      GetPrinterDC(void);

/****************************************************************************/
/*** DoPrint                                                             ***/
/***                                                                     ***/
/*** Minimal interaction with the printer driver                         ***/
/****************************************************************************/

BOOL DoPrint(HWND hWnd)
{
   static char szMessage[] = "MiniPrint - Demo Printout";
   HDC         hPrnDC;
   int         nEscError;
   int         xPage, yPage;

   /* Create device context for the printer                                */

   if ((hPrnDC = GetPrinterDC()) == NULL)
      return (FALSE);
   /* Send maximum printable height and width in pixels                    */
```

```
   xPage   = GetDeviceCaps(hPrnDC, HORZRES);
   yPage   = GetDeviceCaps(hPrnDC, VERTRES);

   /* Display printing in progress                                        */

   nEscError = Escape(hPrnDC, STARTDOC, sizeof(szMessage)-1, szMessage, NULL);
   if (nEscError > 0)
   {
      PrintPage(hPrnDC, xPage, yPage);

      /* Page break, display printing in progress if all is going well.    */

      nEscError = Escape(hPrnDC, NEWFRAME, 0, NULL, NULL);

      if (nEscError > 0)
         Escape(hPrnDC, ENDDOC, 0, NULL, NULL);
   }

   DeleteDC(hPrnDC);

   return (nEscError > 0);
}

/**************************************************************************/
/*** GetPrinterDC                                                      ***/
/***                                                                   ***/
/*** Creates device context for default printer as stated in WIN.INI.  ***/
/**************************************************************************/

static HDC GetPrinterDC(void)
{
   char  szDevice[64];
   char *pDevice, *pDriver, *pOutput;

   GetProfileString("windows", "device", "", szDevice, 64);

   if ( (pDevice = strtok(szDevice, ",")) &&
        (pDriver = strtok(NULL,     ", ")) &&
        (pOutput = strtok(NULL,     ", ")) )
      return (CreateDC(pDriver, pDevice, pOutput, NULL));
   else
      return (NULL);
}

/**************************************************************************/
/*** PrintPage                                                         ***/
/***                                                                   ***/
/*** Prepares a demo page.                                             ***/
```

```
/*** This function acts independently of the output device. It can        ***/
/*** work just as well for the screen as for the printer.                 ***/
/***************************************************************************/

void PrintPage(HDC hDC, int xPage, int yPage)
{
   char  szText[] = "Hello, Printer!";
   int   xPrint;
   int   yPrint;
   DWORD dwExtent;
   POINT Extent;

   /* Place margins around printable area                                  */
   xPrint = (xPage * 8) / 10;
   yPrint = (yPage * 8) / 10;

   /* Store device context                                                 */
   SaveDC(hDC);

   /* MM_ISOTROPIC mapping mode eases creation of circles and squares.     */
   /* Otherwise, you would have to convey many parameters to the device.   */

   SetMapMode(hDC, MM_ISOTROPIC);
   SetWindowExt(hDC, 1000, 1000);
   SetViewportExt(hDC, xPrint, -yPrint);
   SetViewportOrg(hDC, xPage / 2, yPage / 2);

   Rectangle(hDC, -500, 500, 500, -500);

   Ellipse(hDC, -480,  480, -240,  240);
   Ellipse(hDC,  240,  480,  480,  240);
   Ellipse(hDC, -480, -240, -240, -480);
   Ellipse(hDC,  240, -240,  480, -480);

   MoveTo(hDC,    0,  450);
   LineTo(hDC, -360, -210);
   LineTo(hDC,  360, -210);
   LineTo(hDC,    0,  450);

   dwExtent = GetTextExtent(hDC, szText, sizeof(szText) - 1);
   Extent = MAKEPOINT(dwExtent);
   TextOut(hDC, -Extent.x / 2, Extent.y / 2, szText, sizeof(szText) - 1);

   /* Restore original device context status                               */

   RestoreDC(hDC, -1);
}
```

WINPRINT.C source code

```
/***************************************************************************/
/*** WINPRINT.C                                                         ***/
/***                                                                    ***/
/*** Framework program for printer output.                              ***/
/*** Contains initialization, main loop and application window functions.***/
/***                                                                    ***/
/*** (c) 1991 by Abacus                                                 ***/
/*** Author: H. Huptasch                                                ***/
/***************************************************************************/

#include <windows.h>
#include <string.h>

#include "winprint.h"
#include "resource.h"

/***************************************************************************/
/*** Global variables                                                   ***/
/***************************************************************************/

/* To avoid changing an application handle, it is best to declare the    */
/* handle as a global variable.                                          */

HANDLE hInst;

/***************************************************************************/
/*** Prototypes                                                         ***/
/***************************************************************************/


int  PASCAL       WinMain(HANDLE, HANDLE, LPSTR, int);

/* Local functions for this module                                       */

static BOOL       InitClass(HANDLE);
static void       CallAbout(HWND);

/* Callback functions; must be exported to .DEF file as well             */

LONG FAR PASCAL   MainWndProc(HWND, WORD, WORD, DWORD);
BOOL FAR PASCAL   AboutProc(HWND, WORD, WORD, DWORD);

/***************************************************************************/
/*** WinMain                                                            ***/
/***************************************************************************/
```

```
int PASCAL WinMain(HANDLE hNewInst, HANDLE hPrevInst,
                   LPSTR lpCmdLine, int nCmdShow)
{
   HWND hWnd;
   MSG  msg;


   if (!hPrevInst)
      if (!InitClass(hNewInst))
         return (NULL);

   hInst = hNewInst;

   hWnd  = CreateWindow( CLASS_NAME,
                         APPL_NAME,
                         WS_OVERLAPPEDWINDOW,         /* window style      */
                         CW_USEDEFAULT,               /* x position        */
                         CW_USEDEFAULT,               /* y position        */
                         CW_USEDEFAULT,               /* width             */
                         CW_USEDEFAULT,               /* height            */
                         NULL,                        /* parent handle     */
                         NULL,                        /* menu or child ID  */
                         hNewInst,                    /* instance          */
                         NULL );                      /* additional info   */

   if (!hWnd)
      return (NULL);

   ShowWindow(hWnd, nCmdShow);
   UpdateWindow(hWnd);

   while (GetMessage(&msg, NULL, NULL, NULL))
   {
      TranslateMessage(&msg);
      DispatchMessage(&msg);
   }

   return (msg.wParam);
}

/*************************************************************************/
/*** InitClass:                                                        ***/
/*************************************************************************/

static BOOL InitClass(HANDLE hInstance)
{
   HANDLE    hMemory;
```

```
   PWNDCLASS pWndClass;
   BOOL      bSuccess;

   if ((hMemory = LocalAlloc(LPTR, sizeof(WNDCLASS))) != NULL)
   {
      pWndClass = (PWNDCLASS)LocalLock(hMemory);

      pWndClass->style         = NULL;
      pWndClass->lpfnWndProc   = MainWndProc;
      pWndClass->hInstance     = hInstance;
      pWndClass->hIcon         = LoadIcon(hInstance, ICON_NAME);
      pWndClass->hCursor       = LoadCursor(NULL, IDC_ARROW);
      pWndClass->hbrBackground = COLOR_WINDOW + 1;
      pWndClass->lpszMenuName  = MENU_NAME;
      pWndClass->lpszClassName = CLASS_NAME;

      bSuccess = RegisterClass(pWndClass);

      LocalUnlock(hMemory);
      LocalFree(hMemory);
   }
   else
      bSuccess = FALSE;

   return (bSuccess);
}

/**************************************************************************/
/*** MainWndProc                                                       ***/
/**************************************************************************/

LONG FAR PASCAL MainWndProc(HWND hWnd, WORD wMsg, WORD wParam, DWORD lParam)
{
   BOOL  bCallDefProc;

   bCallDefProc = FALSE;

   switch (wMsg)
   {
      case WM_CREATE :
         break;

      case WM_COMMAND :
         switch (wParam)
         {
            case ID_ABOUT :
               CallAbout(hWnd);
               break;
```

```
            case ID_QUIT :
               PostMessage(hWnd, WM_CLOSE, 0, 0L);
               break;

            case ID_WORK :
               DoPrint(hWnd);
               break;

            default:
               bCallDefProc = TRUE;
         }
         break;


      /*** Activate the following case instructions if you want output   ***/
      /*** to appear on the screen as well.                               ***/

      /* The drawing size varies with the window size; the program redraws */
      /* the graphic each time the window size changes.                    */

      /*
      case WM_PAINT :
         {
            PAINTSTRUCT ps;
            HDC         hDC;
            RECT        rc;

            hDC = BeginPaint(hWnd, &ps);
            GetClientRect(hWnd, &rc);
            PrintPage(hDC, rc.right, rc.bottom, 1);
            EndPaint(hWnd, &ps);
         }
         break;

      case WM_SIZE :
         InvalidateRect(hWnd, NULL, TRUE);
         break;
      */

      case WM_DESTROY :
         PostQuitMessage(0);
         break;

      default :
         bCallDefProc = TRUE;
   }
```

```
   return (bCallDefProc ? DefWindowProc(hWnd, wMsg, wParam, lParam) : NULL);
}

/*****************************************************************************/
/*** CallAbout                                                            ***/
/*****************************************************************************/

static void CallAbout(HWND hWnd)
{
   FARPROC lpProcAbout;

   lpProcAbout = MakeProcInstance(AboutProc, hInst);
   DialogBox(hInst, ABOUTBOX, hWnd, lpProcAbout);
   FreeProcInstance(lpProcAbout);
}

/*****************************************************************************/
/*** AboutBox                                                             ***/
/*****************************************************************************/

BOOL FAR PASCAL AboutProc(HWND hDlg, WORD wMsg, WORD wParam, DWORD lParam)
{
   switch (wMsg)
   {
      case WM_INITDIALOG :
         return (TRUE);

      case WM_COMMAND :
         if (wParam == IDOK)
         {
            EndDialog(hDlg, NULL);
            return (TRUE);
         }
         break;
   }

   return (FALSE);
}
```

13.4 Message Loops and Printers

WINPRINT1 is in desperate need of revision. A more "partnerlike" relationship with system resources (here: CPU time) and an opportunity for the user to abort a lengthy process, such as printing, are indispensable improvements to a Windows program. We'll make those improvements in the next version, WINPRINT (Version 2), which is listed later in this chapter.

Multitasking in Windows is "non-preemptive". The system itself cannot interrupt a task that is running. Instead, the system must wait until the task voluntarily returns control. In Windows the preferred method for doing this is to call GetMessage(), PeekMessage() or WaitMessage(). Fortunately, the programmers of Microsoft protected us from having to insert calls of PeekMessage() in every function for printer output. They provided a central mechanism for this: the abort function. The GDI accesses this callback function cyclically when processing the escape function called NEWFRAME (i.e., while it transfers the temporary metafile that it created from your GDI calls to the printer driver). The format of this function is precisely defined:

```
BOOL FAR PASCAL AbortProc(HDC hDC, int nCode);
```

Since you are calling the abort function from Windows, it has to be defined as FAR PASCAL. It also has to be listed in the definition file under EXPORTS. In the program, you use the escape function, SETABORTPROC, to tell Windows the address of the abort function:

```
FARPROC fnAbortProc;fnAbortProc = MakeProcInstance(AbortProc, hInstance);
Escape(hPrnDC, SETABORTPROC, 0, (LPSTR)fnAbortProc, NULL);
```

You have to call before opening the document with STARTDOC. As with all callback functions, you cannot directly specify the address of the function. Instead, you use the pointer that returns MakeProcInstance(). This is important so that the function can access the right data segment when it is called from Windows. Here's an example of an abort function:

```
BOOL FAR PASCAL AbortProc(HDC hDC, int nCode)
{
   MSG msg;
```

```
    while (PeekMessage(&msg, NULL, 0, 0, PM_REMOVE))
    {
        TranslateMessage(&msg);
        DispatchMessage(&msg);
    }
    return (TRUE);
}
```

That was a genuine message loop. As long as there are messages for the program pending, PeekMessage() removes them from the waiting queue (therefore PM_REMOVE) and distributes them to the window of the application. As soon as all of the messages have been processed, the function returns to the GDI. Before it does so, however, PeekMessage() gives the system an opportunity to transfer the control to another program. Already, with this simple form of the abort function, the system blockade is lifted during printing.

You're probably wondering how the function got its name. Consider the function header. When you call AbortProc(), the GDI passes the argument "nCode" among other things. This is an error message: 0, if there is no error, or SP_OUTOFDISK if the GDI no longer finds enough room for its temporary files. This can happen from time to time, because the printer driver has to create a temporary file too, the printer file.

Memory problems

The hard drive can run out of memory with extensive documents or if there are multiple print tasks in the Print Manager's queue. What happens after an SP_OUTOFDISK error depends on the return value of the abort function. If the function returns FALSE, it aborts the print task. The temporary files are deleted, and Escape-NEWFRAME returns with the error code, SP_APPABORT. However, if the function returns TRUE, the printing process is not aborted. This is the usual procedure. Since the system now has an opportunity to change tasks, it also gives the Print Manager a chance to output the current printer file from its waiting queue. That frees memory space on the hard drive. So the return value TRUE signals that your program is ready to wait until there is enough room available to continue printing.

13.5 Status Display and Abort Options

By re-establishing multitasking you've already done as much as you can to make a neatly programmed Windows application out of WINPRINT. While the program is printing, it is not using the system exclusively. So the user can change to another application if he/she wants. More importantly, the Print Manager can work while the printer driver is still busy creating the printer file. However, there is still one problem facing the user if he/she mistakenly triggered a lengthy printout.

Aborting

The Print Manager offers the only option for aborting. The print task, however, doesn't appear there until the first time NEWFRAME is called, which is after the first page is completed. It could take some time for the first page to be completed, especially if the page contains bitmaps, which results in large amounts of data in the metafile. Of course, it's also possible that the Print Manager might not even be activated. WINPRINT needs its own device that lets the user abort. You use a modeless dialog box.

The more common modal dialog boxes suspend a program until the user edits and quits with either [OK] or [Abort] (you can still change to a different application, though). The Windows dialog manager assumes control of the dialog box in collaboration with the window function of the box. The function DialogBox() doesn't return until the dialog is finished, and the main program can continue running.

Modeless dialog boxes are more like regular windows. You use an analog call—CreateDialog()—to create them, and they get their messages from the waiting queue of the application, through its message loop. This furnishes the application with messages and allows it to continue unrestricted. You can create a modeless dialog box rather quickly:

```
FARPROC fnDlgProc;
HWND    hPrnDlg;
fnDlgProc = MakeProcInstance(PrintDlgBox, hInstance);
hPrnDlg   = CreateDlg(hInstance, "PrintDlgBox", hWnd, fnDlgProc);
```

Once again: MakeProcInstance() determines the address of the window function and you have to export PrintDlgBox() in the DEF file. If you furnish the dialog box in the resource file with the WS_VISIBLE flag, it appears on the screen right after you call CreateDlg(). Otherwise you have to use ShowWindow() first to make it visible.

The dialog box can also do this itself in response to the WM_INITDIALOG message. The actual task of PrintDlgBox() is simple. The box waits until the user presses a cancel button. It then leaves a message for the main program and quits. The message loop in the abort function still has to be modified so that this all works.

Although PeekMessage() also has to take the messages for the modeless dialog box from the applications waiting queue, you cannot use DispatchMessage() to pass them to the dialog box. If you did call DispatchMessage(), you would bypass the dialog manager, which saves you a lot of work in managing the dialogs (e.g., the dialog manager switches from one control element to another by pressing the <Tab> key).

The function IsDialogMessage() determines whether a message is intended for the modeless dialog box and, if necessary, processes the message with the help of the dialog manager. Of course, the notice, from the dialog box, indicating that the user has aborted the printing process also must be considered. It's also easy to put that in the abort function, which then finally lives up to its name. Here's what the function would look like:

```
BOOL FAR PASCAL AbortProc(HDC hDC, int nCode)
{
   MSG msg;
   while (!bUserAbort && PeekMessage(&msg, NULL, 0, 0, PM_REMOVE))
   {
      if (!hPrnDlg || !IsDialogMessage(hPrnDlg, &msg))
      {
         TranslateMessage(&msg);
         DispatchMessage(&msg);
      }
   }
   return (!bUserAbort);
}
```

As you can see, you can only call IsDialogMessage() if the modeless dialog box exists. The easiest way to achieve this is by making the handle of the box global, and immediately setting it to zero when the box closes. IsDialogMessage() returns FALSE if the message was not intended for the dialog box so that TranslateMessage() and DispatchMessage() can process it. Basically, it's a question of the same procedure that you use in WinMain() when you put a modeless dialog box somewhere in your program.

Nothing about this box is specific to the printing process. The abort function is complete. You not only leave the message loop when PeekMessage() can no longer find any messages in the waiting queue, but also when PrintDlgBox() sets the global variable bUserAbort to TRUE. In this case, AbortProc() returns the value FALSE, causing the GDI to cancel the print task and allow Escape NEWFRAME, with the error code SP_APPABORT, to return.

13.6 Error Handling and Printing

WINPRINT (Version 1) uses a very simple response to errors. DoPrint() quits and returns to MainWndProc() if it receives a value of FALSE. In MainWndProc(), the value is finally discarded. This is not as bad as it might seem because the GDI or the Print Manager already informs the user of many errors. However, since this isn't always the case, a program should also contain a few lines about error handling. The GDI knows two ways to inform you about errors. One way is the second argument, nCode, when you call the abort function. Here, the value SP_OUTOFDISK signals that there isn't enough memory on the hard drive. The other way is the return value of Escape(). The function Escape() always returns a positive value in cases of success, and returns a NULL when you call it with an unsupported subfunction number. Negative values mean that a printing error has occurred. The following error codes are defined in WINDOWS.H:

SP_ERROR	General error
SP_APPABORT	Cancelled from program
SP_OUTOFDISK	Out of disk space
SP_OUTOFMEMORY	Out of memory space
SP_USERABORT	Cancelled from Print Manager

More about errors

SP_APPABORT appears when the abort function cancels the print task. SP_OUTOFMEMORY can occur when the metafile is being translated to a printer file so the escape function NEWFRAME precedes SP_OUTOFMEMORY (this also applies to SP_OUTOFDISK when an abort function has not been announced). SP_USERABORT comes from the Print Manager when the user deletes a print task there, and SP_ERROR simply indicates an error. Each of these error codes has a flag named SP_NOTREPORTED. When this flag is deleted, the GDI has already informed the user of the error; otherwise you can do this now. SP_NOTREPORTED has the value 0x4000, so its error codes are always negative.

13.7 Expanding WINPRINT

If you install all of the changes, which we've discussed so far, to WINPRINT (Version 1), you get a program that looks like WINPRINT (Version 2). The project is made up of the same files as WINPRINT (Version 1), with some changes:

- WINPRINT.C contains the program sections that don't have anything to do with printer output, so WINPRINT.C remains unchanged.
- DOPRINT.C contains the functions for printing. This file is subject to the most changes.
- WINPRINT.RC is the resource file. It also includes the definition of the modeless dialog box, PrintDlgBox.
- WINPRINT.H contains the function prototypes. That's why this file is also affected by a small change to PrintPage().
- RESOURCE.H remains unchanged in spite of the new dialog box, since the new dialog box only uses IDs predefined in WINDOWS.H.
- WINPRINT.DEF is expanded in the EXPORT section by the abort function and the dialog box window function.
- WINPRINT.ICO remains unchanged.
- MAKEFILE remains unchanged.

If you take a look at DOPRINT.C, you will be able to easily identify the solutions discussed in the previous sections.

How the program works

The DoPrint() function starts as usual by creating a device context for the printer and then determining the dimensions of the printed surface. After that, it creates the dialog box for aborting the process and the GDI is made aware of the abort function. Remember that EnableWindow() calls the application window. It is absolutely necessary. By implementing the abort function, the main window is provided with messages even during the printing process.

This enables the user to use the menu to start printer output again, even while output is running, to delete the data to be printed from the program or even quit the whole program. Of course, you could take the appropriate precautions for such cases, but since WINPRINT (Version 2) does not, the main window of the application is deactivated until the document is passed entirely to the GDI.

Aborting the program

We have already discussed the abort function in an earlier section. The dialog box window function is also rather simple. Since you can place the dialog box anywhere on the screen, it's a good idea to enter the name of the program, to which it belongs, in the title bar of the dialog box. You can do this directly in the resource file, or as a response to WM_INITDIALOG by using the SetWindowText() function. You can also use SetWindowText() to append notices to the names about different instances of the program. Also, this is where you deactivate the **Close** item in the system menu. You should have this dialog box as long as the program prints. The only other message to which PrintDlgProc() has to respond is WM_COMMAND, which is triggered by the only button in the box, the cancel button. That's why you don't have to examine the parameter, wParam. The abort is noted in the global variable, bUserAbort, then the main window is activated again and the dialog box is deleted. You should follow this sequence so Windows doesn't activate another program after removing the dialog box, which would cause your program to disappear in the background. It's also important to set hDlgPrint to zero. The abort function requires this information so that it doesn't continue dispatching messages to IsDialogMessage().

The control system for printout in DoPrint() is no different than the procedure in WINPRINT (Version 1). However, for purposes of demonstration, it was expanded by a loop for outputting several pages. In essence, however, it is the same. Use STARTDOC to announce the document. NEWFRAME causes a formfeed at the end of each page. ENDDOC displays the end of the document, except if an error occurs, when the GDI aborts the document. Keep in mind that PrintPage() now - also for demonstration purposes - expects a page number as an additional argument. You also have to make this change in WINPRINT.H. And if you want to have the output appear in the window as a response to a WM_PAINT message in MainWndProc(), then you still have to adapt the call of PrintPage() in WINPRINT.C. The necessary changes for outputting on the screen are mentioned in the description of WINPRINT (Version 1).

The end of the printing process

After the printing process is over, you have to put things back in order. If the user cancelled the printing procedure using the dialog box, then the box has already removed itself. (In this case, it's not necessary to allocate SP_APPABORT to nEscError—its only purpose is to choose an appropriate error text in GetErrorText().) In all other cases, DoPrint() has to end the dialog box. The sequence of EnableWindow() and DestroyWindow() is also significant here. After that, call FreeProcInstance() for both the abort function and the window function and use DeleteDC() to remove the device context.

The last section of DoPrint() runs if an error has occurred. The only time a message outputs is when the bit SP_NOTREPORTED displays that this has not yet happened. GetErrorText(), which is a simple function for outputting a message, uses a table to translate the error number into a string. WINPRINT (Version 2) doesn't do anything if the GDI has already reported the error. Other programs might require more steps here. The only reason you set the SP_NOTREPORTED bits in the else branch is to assign one of the error codes defined in WINDOWS.H to the nEscError variable (the error numbers are always defined by a set bit).

WINPRINT (Version 2) implements a control system of the printing process that is easy to use in serious applications. Due to the extensive separation of management and execution of printer output, it is easy to integrate the DoPrint() function into your own programs. As a rule, this requires inserting your own functions in the appropriate control structure at the end of DoPrint(). The functions described here are suitable for a great majority of the cases where you have to print the data of your programs. However, there are still other advanced techniques that we will discuss in the remaining sections of this chapter.

13.7.1 Source code: WINPRINT (Version 2)

RESOURCE.H include file

```
/****************************************************************************/
/*** RESOURCE.H                                                          ***/
/***                                                                     ***/
/*** Resource IDs                                                        ***/
/***                                                                     ***/
/*** (c) 1991 by Abacus                                                  ***/
/*** Author: H. Huptasch                                                 ***/
/****************************************************************************/


#define ID_ABOUT     100
#define ID_QUIT      101
#define ID_WORK      102
```

WINPRINT.H include file

```
/****************************************************************************/
/*** WINPRINT.H                                                          ***/
/***                                                                     ***/
/*** Global definitions and declarations                                 ***/
/***                                                                     ***/
/*** (c) 1991 by Abacus                                                  ***/
/*** Author: H. Huptasch                                                 ***/
/****************************************************************************/

#define CLASS_NAME   "WinPrintClass"
#define APPL_NAME    "WinPrint"
#define MENU_NAME    "WinPrintMenu"
#define ICON_NAME    "WinPrintIcon"
#define ABOUTBOX     "AboutBox"

/* Instance handle of application                                        */

extern HANDLE hInst;

/* Printed output function prototypes                                    */

BOOL DoPrint(HWND);
void PrintPage(HDC, int, int, int);
```

WINPRINT.RC resource file

```
/*************************************************************************/
/*** WINPRINT.RC                                                      ***/
/***                                                                  ***/
/*** (c) 1991 by Abacus                                               ***/
/*** Author: H. Huptasch                                               ***/
/*************************************************************************/

#include <windows.h>
#include "resource.h"

WinPrintIcon ICON winprint.ico

WinPrintMenu MENU
BEGIN
   POPUP "&Program"
   BEGIN
      MENUITEM "&Print",          ID_WORK
      MENUITEM "E&xit",            ID_QUIT
      MENUITEM SEPARATOR
      MENUITEM "A&bout WINPRINT...", ID_ABOUT
   END
END

AboutBox DIALOG LOADONCALL MOVEABLE DISCARDABLE 10, 9, 144, 78
STYLE WS_DLGFRAME | WS_POPUP
BEGIN
   ICON           "WinPrintIcon",              -1,    8,  8,  16, 21,  SS_ICON
   CTEXT          "WinPrint",                  -1,   24,  4, 120,  8
   CTEXT          " 1991 Abacus",              -1,   24, 14, 120,  8
   CTEXT          "Author: Heiko Huptasch",    -1,   24, 22, 120,  8
   CTEXT          "Version 1.0",               -1,   24, 36, 120,  8
   DEFPUSHBUTTON  "OK",                        IDOK, 58, 56,  52, 14,  WS_GROUP
END

PrintDlgBox DIALOG LOADONCALL MOVEABLE DISCARDABLE 40, 40, 120, 40
STYLE WS_POPUP | WS_CAPTION | WS_SYSMENU | WS_VISIBLE
BEGIN
   CTEXT          "Printing in progress",  -1,        4, 6, 120, 12
   DEFPUSHBUTTON  "Cancel",                IDCANCEL, 44, 22, 32, 14, WS_GROUP
END
```

WINPRINT.DEF module definition file

```
NAME          WINPRINT
```

```
EXETYPE     WINDOWS
DESCRIPTION 'WINPRINT - A Windows application by ABACUS (c) 1991'

STUB        'WINSTUB.EXE'

CODE        MOVEABLE DISCARDABLE
DATA        PRELOAD MOVEABLE MULTIPLE

HEAPSIZE    1024
STACKSIZE   4096

SEGMENTS
   _TEXT    PRELOAD
   WINPRINT PRELOAD
   DOPRINT  LOADONCALL

EXPORTS
   MainWndProc
   AboutProc
   AbortProc
   PrintDlgProc
```

MAKEFILE

```
# Creation of WINPRINT.EXE
#
# MAKEFILE for Microsoft's MAKE or NMAKE
#
# (c) 1991 by Abacus
# Author: H. Huptasch


# Object file list

OBJECTS  =  winprint.obj doprint.obj


# Define compiler and necessary switches

CC       =  cl
CFLAGS   =  -AM -Osw -Gsw -Zpe -W3 -NT$* -DLINT_ARGS -D_WINDOWS

.c.obj:
   $(CC) -c $(CFLAGS) $*.c


#Flexible lists
```

```
MAKE_ALL:       winprint.exe

winprint.res:   winprint.rc winprint.ico resource.h
   rc -r winprint.rc

winprint.obj:   winprint.c  winprint.h  resource.h

doprint.obj:    doprint.c   winprint.h

winprint.exe:   $(OBJECTS)  winprint.res winprint.def
   link /NOD/NOE/A:16 $(OBJECTS), , nul, libw mlibcew, winprint
   rc winprint.res
```

DOPRINT.C source code

```
/*************************************************************************/
/*** DOPRINT.C                                                        ***/
/***                                                                  ***/
/*** Printer output module for WINPRINT.                              ***/
/*** The DoPrint() function sends output to single-page or           ***/
/*** multiple-page documents.                                         ***/
/***                                                                  ***/
/*** (c) 1991 by Abacus                                               ***/
/*** Author: H. Huptasch                                              ***/
/*************************************************************************/

#include <windows.h>
#include <string.h>

#include "winprint.h"

/*************************************************************************/
/*** Global variables module                                          ***/
/*************************************************************************/

static BOOL bUserAbort;
static HWND hDlgPrint;

/*************************************************************************/
/*** Prototypes                                                       ***/
/*************************************************************************/

static HDC      GetPrinterDC(void);
static LPSTR    GetErrorText(int);

/* Callback functions; must also be exported to .DEF file           */
```

```
BOOL FAR PASCAL PrintDlgProc(HWND, WORD, WORD, DWORD);
BOOL FAR PASCAL AbortProc(HDC, int);

/*************************************************************************/
/*** PrintDlgProc                                                      ***/
/***                                                                   ***/
/*** Modeless dialog box window function, through which the user can  ***/
/*** cancel the printing process.                                      ***/
/*************************************************************************/

BOOL FAR PASCAL PrintDlgProc(HWND hDlg, WORD wMsg, WORD wParam, DWORD lParam)
{
   switch (wMsg)
   {
      case WM_INITDIALOG:
         SetWindowText(hDlg, APPL_NAME);
         EnableMenuItem(GetSystemMenu(hDlg, FALSE), SC_CLOSE, MF_GRAYED);
         break;

      case WM_COMMAND:
         bUserAbort = TRUE;
         EnableWindow(GetParent(hDlg), TRUE);
         DestroyWindow(hDlg);
         hDlgPrint = 0;
         break;

      default:
         return (FALSE);
   }

   return (TRUE);
}

/*************************************************************************/
/*** AbortProc                                                         ***/
/***                                                                   ***/
/*** Print Manager callback functions.                                 ***/
/*** It's possible to abort printing, but not necessary.               ***/
/*************************************************************************/

BOOL FAR PASCAL AbortProc(HDC hPrnDC, int nCode)
{
   MSG msg;

   while (!bUserAbort && PeekMessage(&msg, NULL, 0, 0, PM_REMOVE))
   {
      if (!hDlgPrint || !IsDialogMessage(hDlgPrint, &msg))
```

```
        {
           TranslateMessage(&msg);
           DispatchMessage(&msg);
        }
    }

    return (!bUserAbort);

    /* Or abort because of error:

    return (!(bUserAbort || nCode == SP_OUTOFDISK));
    */
}

/****************************************************************************/
/*** DoPrint                                                              ***/
/***                                                                      ***/
/*** Interaction with the printer driver                                  ***/
/****************************************************************************/

#define N_PAGES    2  /* Number of pages to be printed.                      */

BOOL DoPrint(HWND hWnd)
{
   static char szMessage[] = "WinPrint - Demo Printout";
   HDC          hPrnDC;
   FARPROC      fpAbortProc;
   FARPROC      fpDlgPrint;
   int          nEscError;
   int          xPage, yPage;

   /* Create device context for the printer                                 */

   if ((hPrnDC = GetPrinterDC()) == NULL)
      return (FALSE);

   /* Send maximum printable height and width in pixels                     */

   xPage  = GetDeviceCaps(hPrnDC, HORZRES);
   yPage  = GetDeviceCaps(hPrnDC, VERTRES);

   /* Install dialog box and Abort function
*/

   EnableWindow(hWnd, FALSE);

   bUserAbort  = FALSE;
```

```
    fpDlgPrint   = MakeProcInstance(PrintDlgProc, hInst);
    hDlgPrint    = CreateDialog(hInst, "PrintDlgBox", hWnd, fpDlgPrint);

    fpAbortProc = MakeProcInstance(AbortProc, hInst);
    Escape(hPrnDC, SETABORTPROC, 0, (LPSTR)fpAbortProc, NULL);

    /* Display printing in progress
*/

    nEscError = Escape(hPrnDC, STARTDOC, sizeof(szMessage)-1, szMessage, NULL);
    if (nEscError > 0)
    {
       int i;

       i = 1;

       while (i <= N_PAGES && (nEscError > 0))
       {
          PrintPage(hPrnDC, xPage, yPage, i++);
          nEscError = Escape(hPrnDC, NEWFRAME, 0, NULL, NULL);
       }

       if (nEscError > 0)
          Escape(hPrnDC, ENDDOC, 0, NULL, NULL);
    }

    if (!bUserAbort)
    {
       /* Dialog box must be removed if this occurs                        */

       EnableWindow(hWnd, TRUE);
       DestroyWindow(hDlgPrint);
    }
    else if (nEscError > 0)
       nEscError = SP_APPABORT;    /* For GetErrorText()                   */

    FreeProcInstance(fpDlgPrint);
    FreeProcInstance(fpAbortProc);
    DeleteDC(hPrnDC);

    if (nEscError <= 0)
    {
       if (nEscError & SP_NOTREPORTED)
       {
          char szMsg[80];

          wsprintf(szMsg, "Printer Error: %0.60s!", GetErrorText(nEscError));
          MessageBox(hWnd, szMsg, APPL_NAME, MB_OK | MB_ICONEXCLAMATION);
```

```
      }
      else
      {
         nEscError |= SP_NOTREPORTED;

         /* The error was displayed, but other dimensions may be needed.    */
      }
   }

   return ((nEscError > 0) || bUserAbort);
}

/***************************************************************************/
/*** GetPrinterDC                                                       ***/
/***                                                                    ***/
/*** Creates a default printer device context, as stated in WIN.INI.    ***/
/***************************************************************************/

static HDC GetPrinterDC(void)
{
   char  szDevice[64];
   char *pDevice, *pDriver, *pOutput;

   GetProfileString("windows", "device", "", szDevice, 64);

   if ( (pDevice = strtok(szDevice, ",")) &&
        (pDriver = strtok(NULL,     ", ")) &&
        (pOutput = strtok(NULL,     ", ")) )
      return (CreateDC(pDriver, pDevice, pOutput, NULL));
   else
      return (NULL);
}

/***************************************************************************/
/*** PrintPage                                                          ***/
/***                                                                    ***/
/*** Prepares a demo page.                                              ***/
/*** This function acts independently of the output device. It can     ***/
/*** work just as well for the screen.                                  ***/
/***************************************************************************/

void PrintPage(HDC hDC, int xPage, int yPage, int nPage)
{
   char  szText[32];
   int   xPrint;
   int   yPrint;
   DWORD dwExtent;
   POINT Extent;
```

```
   /* Place margins around printable area                                    */

   xPrint = (xPage * 8) / 10;
   yPrint = (yPage * 8) / 10;

   /* Store device context                                                   */

   SaveDC(hDC);

   /* MM_ISOTROPIC mapping mode eases creation of circles and squares.       */
   /* Otherwise, you would have to convey many parameters to the device.     */

   SetMapMode(hDC, MM_ISOTROPIC);
   SetWindowExt(hDC, 1000, 1000);
   SetViewportExt(hDC, xPrint, -yPrint);
   SetViewportOrg(hDC, xPage / 2, yPage / 2);

   Rectangle(hDC, -500, 500, 500, -500);

   Ellipse(hDC, -480,  480, -240,  240);
   Ellipse(hDC,  240,  480,  480,  240);
   Ellipse(hDC, -480, -240, -240, -480);
   Ellipse(hDC,  240, -240,  480, -480);

   MoveTo(hDC,    0,  450);
   LineTo(hDC, -360, -210);
   LineTo(hDC,  360, -210);
   LineTo(hDC,    0,  450);

   wsprintf(szText, "Page %d", nPage);
   dwExtent = GetTextExtent(hDC, szText, lstrlen(szText));
   Extent = MAKEPOINT(dwExtent);
   TextOut(hDC, -Extent.x / 2, Extent.y / 2, szText, lstrlen(szText));

   /* Restores original device context status
*/

   RestoreDC(hDC, -1);
}

/***************************************************************************/
/*** GetErrorText                                                        ***/
/***                                                                     ***/
/*** Translates Print Manager error codes into error messages.           ***/
/***************************************************************************/

LPSTR GetErrorText(int nErrorCode)
{
```

```
    static char *szErrText[] =
    {
        "General error",
        "Aborted by user",
        "Aborted by SPOOLER",
        "TMP directory is full",
        "Not enough memory"
    };

    return (szErrText[~nErrorCode]);
}
```

WINPRINT.C source code

```
/***************************************************************************/
/*** WINPRINT.C                                                         ***/
/***                                                                    ***/
/*** Framework program for printer output.                              ***/
/*** Contains initialization, main loop and application window functions.***/
/***                                                                    ***/
/*** (c) 1991 by Abacus                                                 ***/
/*** Author: H. Huptasch                                                ***/
/***************************************************************************/

#include <windows.h>
#include <string.h>

#include "winprint.h"
#include "resource.h"

/***************************************************************************/
/*** Global variables                                                   ***/
/***************************************************************************/

/* To avoid changing an application handle, it is best to declare the     */
/* handle as a global variable.                                           */

HANDLE hInst;

/***************************************************************************/
/*** Prototypes                                                         ***/
/***************************************************************************/


int  PASCAL       WinMain(HANDLE, HANDLE, LPSTR, int);

/* Local functions for this module                                        */
```

```
static BOOL       InitClass(HANDLE);
static void       CallAbout(HWND);

/* Callback functions; must be exported to .DEF file as well              */

LONG FAR PASCAL   MainWndProc(HWND, WORD, WORD, DWORD);
BOOL FAR PASCAL   AboutProc(HWND, WORD, WORD, DWORD);

/*************************************************************************/
/*** WinMain                                                           ***/
/*************************************************************************/

int PASCAL WinMain(HANDLE hNewInst, HANDLE hPrevInst,
                   LPSTR lpCmdLine, int nCmdShow)
{
   HWND hWnd;
   MSG  msg;


   if (!hPrevInst)
      if (!InitClass(hNewInst))
         return (NULL);

   hInst = hNewInst;

   hWnd  = CreateWindow( CLASS_NAME,
                         APPL_NAME,
                         WS_OVERLAPPEDWINDOW,          /* window style      */
                         CW_USEDEFAULT,                /* x position        */
                         CW_USEDEFAULT,                /* y position        */
                         CW_USEDEFAULT,                /* width             */
                         CW_USEDEFAULT,                /* height            */
                         NULL,                         /* parent handle     */
                         NULL,                         /* menu or child ID  */
                         hNewInst,                     /* instance          */
                         NULL );                       /* additional info   */

   if (!hWnd)
      return (NULL);

   ShowWindow(hWnd, nCmdShow);
   UpdateWindow(hWnd);

   while (GetMessage(&msg, NULL, NULL, NULL))
   {
      TranslateMessage(&msg);
      DispatchMessage(&msg);
   }
```

```
   return (msg.wParam);
}

/**************************************************************************/
/*** InitClass:                                                       ***/
/**************************************************************************/

static BOOL InitClass(HANDLE hInstance)
{
   HANDLE    hMemory;
   PWNDCLASS pWndClass;
   BOOL      bSuccess;

   if ((hMemory = LocalAlloc(LPTR, sizeof(WNDCLASS))) != NULL)
   {
      pWndClass = (PWNDCLASS)LocalLock(hMemory);

      pWndClass->style         = NULL;
      pWndClass->lpfnWndProc   = MainWndProc;
      pWndClass->hInstance     = hInstance;
      pWndClass->hIcon         = LoadIcon(hInstance, ICON_NAME);
      pWndClass->hCursor       = LoadCursor(NULL, IDC_ARROW);
      pWndClass->hbrBackground = COLOR_WINDOW + 1;
      pWndClass->lpszMenuName  = MENU_NAME;
      pWndClass->lpszClassName = CLASS_NAME;

      bSuccess = RegisterClass(pWndClass);

      LocalUnlock(hMemory);
      LocalFree(hMemory);
   }
   else
      bSuccess = FALSE;

   return (bSuccess);
}

/**************************************************************************/
/*** MainWndProc                                                      ***/
/**************************************************************************/

LONG FAR PASCAL MainWndProc(HWND hWnd, WORD wMsg, WORD wParam, DWORD lParam)
{
   BOOL  bCallDefProc;

   bCallDefProc = FALSE;

   switch (wMsg)
```

```
{
   case WM_CREATE :
      break;

   case WM_COMMAND :
      switch (wParam)
      {
         case ID_ABOUT :
            CallAbout(hWnd);
            break;

         case ID_QUIT :
            PostMessage(hWnd, WM_CLOSE, 0, 0L);
            break;

         case ID_WORK :
            DoPrint(hWnd);
            break;

         default:
            bCallDefProc = TRUE;
      }
      break;


   /*** Activate the following case instructions if you want output   ***/
   /*** to appear on the screen as well.                                ***/

   /* The drawing size varies with the window size; the program redraws */
   /* the graphic each time the window size changes.                     */

   /*
   case WM_PAINT :
      {
         PAINTSTRUCT ps;
         HDC         hDC;
         RECT        rc;

         hDC = BeginPaint(hWnd, &ps);
         GetClientRect(hWnd, &rc);
         PrintPage(hDC, rc.right, rc.bottom, 1);
         EndPaint(hWnd, &ps);
      }
      break;

   case WM_SIZE :
      InvalidateRect(hWnd, NULL, TRUE);
      break;
```

```
      */

      case WM_DESTROY :
         PostQuitMessage(0);
         break;

      default :
         bCallDefProc = TRUE;
   }

   return (bCallDefProc ? DefWindowProc(hWnd, wMsg, wParam, lParam) : NULL);
}

/*************************************************************************/
/*** CallAbout                                                         ***/
/*************************************************************************/

static void CallAbout(HWND hWnd)
{
   FARPROC lpProcAbout;

   lpProcAbout = MakeProcInstance(AboutProc, hInst);
   DialogBox(hInst, ABOUTBOX, hWnd, lpProcAbout);
   FreeProcInstance(lpProcAbout);
}

/*************************************************************************/
/*** AboutBox                                                          ***/
/*************************************************************************/

BOOL FAR PASCAL AboutProc(HWND hDlg, WORD wMsg, WORD wParam, DWORD lParam)
{
   switch (wMsg)
   {
      case WM_INITDIALOG :
         return (TRUE);

      case WM_COMMAND :
         if (wParam == IDOK)
         {
            EndDialog(hDlg, NULL);
            return (TRUE);
         }
         break;
   }

   return (FALSE);
}
```

13.8 Banding

One nice feature of WINPRINT (Version 1) or WINPRINT (Version 2) is the device independence of the output. PrintPage() can output its drawing on the screen or the printer. In the second case, the GDI creates a metafile, for each page, that can be sent to the printer driver several times. The repetition isn't significant here. Since the metafile that PrintPage() creates is two dozen bytes in size, it is not anything to worry about. It's a little different for pages of complex structure.

Metafiles and memory

A drawing from a CAD program, which is intended for a large format plotter, can be composed of several thousand objects, and would then result in a metafile of the same size. Above all, however, outputting bitmaps increases the size of the metafile drastically. The main memory requirements also increase with larger graphics, and can interfere with the total performance of the Windows system, especially when more than one application is active at the same time. There is a solution for such cases: Divide the page into small sections that can be output one after the other, so that you only have to store the description of the current section in the buffer. This technique is called banding.

You use the Escape() function to implement banding. The subfunction NEXTBAND successively gives you the coordinates of the current section in a RECT structure. As soon as you get back an empty rectangle, you know that the page has been completely output. NEXTBAND doesn't just inform you of the coordinates of each band, but also about the clipping. You can output the complete drawing after each call of this escape subfunction. In the metafile you would only reach the area of the current band.

For WINPRINT (Version 2) that means that you could achieve banding simply by calling PrintPage() once for each NEXTBAND pass. In practice, however, you use the clipping information that the NEXTBAND call makes available to draw only the objects that are either partially or fully in the current band. This can mean a considerable savings in time when you output complex graphics. Unfortunately, the collaboration between the main memory and the disk memory also has the disadvantage of decreased device independence. Not all drivers support this technique. You have to ask in advance whether the subfunction NEXTBAND is available and take the appropriate measures depending on the answer.

Adding banding to WINPRINT

The application WINPRINT (Version 3) contains the necessary logic for using banding. It consists of the same files as WINPRINT (Version 2). The essential changes affect the PrintPage() function in the module DOPRINT.C, whose prototype you also have to adapt in WINPRINT.H. For reasons of efficiency, the banding is executed here. In DoPrint() you have to adapt the call of PrintPage(), and you have to consider that when you use banding, you cannot close the page with NEWFRAME. (This would create a second formfeed, since NEXTBAND has already executed this function after the last band was output.) This simplifies the output loop in DoPrint() to the following form:

```
nEscError = Escape(hPrnDC, STARTDOC, sizeof(szMessage)-1, szMessage, NULL);
if (nEscError > 0)
{
   int i;

   i = 1;

   while (i <= N_PAGES && (nEscError > 0))
      nEscError = PrintPage(hPrnDC, xPage, yPage, i++);

   if (nEscError > 0)
      Escape(hPrnDC, ENDDOC, 0, NULL, NULL);
}
```

There is more to say about PrintPage(). Above all, however: The function creates the same output as in previous versions of the program. Banding, and the additional measures for improving runtime behavior, are like hunting for sparrows using cannons. In real applications you have to determine whether the techniques are of any practical use through experiments.

PrintPage() begins with similar steps. The current status of the device context is saved in order to set up a new coordinate system that prevents circles from being made into ellipses. After that, the process is different. Since the display of the page now takes place in a loop that could run for a long time (around 40 times with an NEC 24-pin printer and standard typing paper), it makes sense to perform constant calculations first. Here, this refers to determining the descriptive rectangle for text output. Before entering the output loop, you still have to check whether the device you are addressing even supports banding:

```
int nNextband = NEXTBAND;
if (Escape(hDC, QUERYESCSUPPORT, sizeof(int), (LPSTR)&nNextband, NULL))
   /* Banding is supported */
```

Note the necessary detour using the variable nNextband. If banding is not supported (e.g., for output on the screen that you can activate in WINPRINT.C), PrintPage() will simulate it. The RECT structure, which otherwise would have initialized with the coordinates of the first band, is filled with the values of the entire print surface, making it a "band" that includes the entire working area. nNextband is still set to null so that we will be able to distinguish genuine banding from simulated banding later. nEscError also has to be positive, in order for the loop to run through once. Banding is usually supported for output to a printer, and the coordinates of the first section are located in rcBand.

The following loop will run until rcBand contains an empty rectangle (use IsRectEmpty() to determine this) or until an error pops up. The device context has to be reinitialized in each cycle of the loop. That seems surprising at first, but is understandable if you think of the processes in the background. Each time you call NEXTBAND it transfers the previous metafile (if there is one) to the printer driver and creates a new metafile for the current band.

However, all of the information about earlier GDI calls are lost, including information about the calls that change the device context. If you forget this circumstance, you may have serious trouble. In our case, for example, it would mean that the coordinates used in the GDI calls do not match the set system. If you got any output at all, it would only be distorted and incomplete. You also have to reselect all required character objects (pens, brushes etc.) each time in the device context.

Next is the consideration of the clipping information, mentioned at the beginning, in order to draw only the objects that come into play for the current band. Here you have to consider that NEXTBAND places device specific coordinates in rcBand. If you don't work in mapping mode, you have to convert these coordinates to your logical coordinate system first. That's what DPtoLP() is used for. LPtoDP()

helps the transformation in the opposite direction. Now you can draw all the objects that are cutting the present band. Unfortunately you can't call on the Windows function, IntersectRect(), for a decision because it cannot manage the reverse direction of the vertical axis (in PrintPage() the y axis runs from bottom to top instead of top to bottom). Because of this, there is a separate function for this purpose, called RcIntersect(), which is better adapted to the requirements of PrintPage() in your call.

Banding and abort function

Something strange happens at the end of the loop. After determining the coordinates of the next band, it calls the abort function. This happens because the GDI no longer performs this task when you take banding into your own hands. That's why fpAbortProc was defined globally, instead of locally, in DoPrint(). The variable is actually a FARPROC variable and is only changed to a pointer to the abort function in order to suppress a warning from the compiler. This type definition is located at the beginning of the DOPRINT.C file.

If you need several GDI calls in order to output a band, then you should designate several calls of the abort function in the loop. This guarantees that the dialog box will respond to user input without too much delay because the dialog box only gets messages when the abort function is executed. This measure is only required for genuine banding, but it wouldn't hurt otherwise, either. During simulated banding, PrintPage() does exactly what NEXTBAND would do if the page were completely output: It triggers a formfeed and returns an empty rectangle to rcBand.

Incidentally, there's a very good reason why the return value of the Escape() call NEWFRAME is not examined more closely here. Video drivers are one of the drivers that NEXTBAND does not support. The NEWFRAME function doesn't offer them either. Just to be on the safe side, you would have to use QUERYESCSUPPORT to determine whether NEWFRAME is available. Whether Escape() ignores functions that are not supported is up to the programmer's taste and skill.

That's how PrintPage() uses banding. In this example, you could retain device independence at the expense of readability. However, occasionally it might be more practical to write separate functions for outputting to different devices. This is especially true if you use escape subfunctions that cannot be used with every device driver.

13.8.1 Source code: WINPRINT (Version 3)

RESOURCE.H include file

```
/******************************************************************************/
/*** RESOURCE.H                                                             ***/
/***                                                                        ***/
/*** Resource IDs                                                           ***/
/***                                                                        ***/
/*** (c) 1991 by Abacus                                                     ***/
/*** Author: H. Huptasch                                                    ***/
/******************************************************************************/


#define ID_ABOUT     100
#define ID_QUIT      101
#define ID_WORK      102
```

WINPRINT.H include file

```
/******************************************************************************/
/*** WINPRINT.H                                                             ***/
/***                                                                        ***/
/*** Global definition and declarations                                     ***/
/***                                                                        ***/
/*** (c) 1991 by Abacus                                                     ***/
/*** Author: H. Huptasch                                                    ***/
/******************************************************************************/

#define CLASS_NAME   "WinPrintClass"
#define APPL_NAME    "WinPrint"
#define MENU_NAME    "WinPrintMenu"
#define ICON_NAME    "WinPrintIcon"
#define ABOUTBOX     "AboutBox"

/* Instance handle of application                                           */

extern HANDLE hInst;

/* Printed output function prototypes                                       */

BOOL DoPrint(HWND);
int  PrintPage(HDC, int, int, int);
```

WINPRINT.RC resource file

```
/****************************************************************************/
/*** WINPRINT.RC                                                          ***/
/***                                                                      ***/
/*** (c) 1991 by Abacus                                                   ***/
/*** Author: H. Huptasch                                                  ***/
/****************************************************************************/

#include <windows.h>
#include "resource.h"

WinPrintIcon ICON winprint.ico

WinPrintMenu MENU
BEGIN
   POPUP "&Program"
   BEGIN
      MENUITEM "&Print",        ID_WORK
      MENUITEM "E&xit",          ID_QUIT
      MENUITEM SEPARATOR
      MENUITEM "A&bout WINPRINT...", ID_ABOUT
   END
END

AboutBox DIALOG LOADONCALL MOVEABLE DISCARDABLE 10, 9, 144, 78
STYLE WS_DLGFRAME | WS_POPUP
BEGIN
   ICON           "WinPrintIcon",             -1,    8,  8,  16, 21,  SS_ICON
   CTEXT          "WinPrint",                 -1,   24,  4, 120,  8
   CTEXT          " 1991 Abacus",             -1,   24, 14, 120,  8
   CTEXT          "Author: Heiko Huptasch",   -1,   24, 22, 120,  8
   CTEXT          "Version 1.0",              -1,   24, 36, 120,  8
   DEFPUSHBUTTON  "OK",                       IDOK, 58, 56,  52, 14,  WS_GROUP
END

PrintDlgBox DIALOG LOADONCALL MOVEABLE DISCARDABLE 40, 40, 120, 40
STYLE WS_POPUP | WS_CAPTION | WS_SYSMENU | WS_VISIBLE
BEGIN
   CTEXT          "Printing in progress",    -1,    4, 6, 120, 12
   DEFPUSHBUTTON  "Cancel",                 IDCANCEL, 44, 22, 32, 14, WS_GROUP
END
```

WINPRINT.DEF module definition file

```
NAME        WINPRINT
EXETYPE     WINDOWS
DESCRIPTION 'WINPRINT - A Windows application by Abacus (c) 1991'

STUB        'WINSTUB.EXE'

CODE        MOVEABLE DISCARDABLE
DATA        PRELOAD MOVEABLE MULTIPLE

HEAPSIZE    1024
STACKSIZE   4096

SEGMENTS
   _TEXT    PRELOAD
   WINPRINT PRELOAD
   DOPRINT  LOADONCALL

EXPORTS
   MainWndProc
   AboutProc
   AbortProc
   PrintDlgProc
```

MAKEFILE

```
# Creation of WINPRINT.EXE
#
# MAKEFILE for Microsoft's MAKE or NMAKE
#
# (c) 1991 by Abacus
# Author: H. Huptasch


# Object file list

OBJECTS  =  winprint.obj doprint.obj


# Define compiler and necessary switches

CC       =  cl
CFLAGS   =  -AM -Osw -Gsw -Zpe -W3 -NT$* -DLINT_ARGS -D_WINDOWS

.c.obj:
```

```
   $(CC) -c $(CFLAGS) $*.c


#Flexible lists

MAKE_ALL:      winprint.exe

winprint.res:  winprint.rc winprint.ico resource.h
   rc -r winprint.rc

winprint.obj:  winprint.c  winprint.h  resource.h

doprint.obj:   doprint.c   winprint.h

winprint.exe:  $(OBJECTS)  winprint.res winprint.def
   link /NOD/NOE/A:16 $(OBJECTS), , nul, libw mlibcew, winprint
   rc winprint.res
```

DOPRINT.C source code

```
/******************************************************************************/
/*** DOPRINT.C                                                              ***/
/***                                                                        ***/
/*** Printer output module for WINPRINT.                                    ***/
/*** The DoPrint() function sends output to single-page or                  ***/
/*** multiple-page documents.                                               ***/
/***                                                                        ***/
/*** (c) 1991 by Abacus                                                     ***/
/*** Author: H. Huptasch                                                    ***/
/******************************************************************************/

#include <windows.h>
#include <string.h>

#include "winprint.h"

/******************************************************************************/
/*** Global variables module                                                ***/
/******************************************************************************/

static BOOL    bUserAbort;
static HWND    hDlgPrint;
static FARPROC fpAbortProc;

/******************************************************************************/
/*** Prototypes                                                             ***/
/******************************************************************************/
```

```
static HDC      GetPrinterDC(void);
static LPSTR    GetErrorText(int);
static BOOL     RcIntersect(RECT *, int, int, int, int);

/* Callback functions; must also be exported to .DEF file                 */

BOOL FAR PASCAL PrintDlgProc(HWND, WORD, WORD, DWORD);
BOOL FAR PASCAL AbortProc(HDC, int);

/* Type of a pointer to the Abort function                                */

typedef BOOL FAR PASCAL ABORTPROC(HDC, int);
typedef ABORTPROC FAR *FPABORTPROC;

/***********************************************************************/
/*** PrintDlgProc                                                    ***/
/***                                                                 ***/
/*** Modeless dialog box window function, through which the user can ***/
/*** cancel the printing process.                                    ***/
/***********************************************************************/

BOOL FAR PASCAL PrintDlgProc(HWND hDlg, WORD wMsg, WORD wParam, DWORD lParam)
{
   switch (wMsg)
   {
      case WM_INITDIALOG:
         SetWindowText(hDlg, APPL_NAME);
         EnableMenuItem(GetSystemMenu(hDlg, FALSE), SC_CLOSE, MF_GRAYED);
         break;

      case WM_COMMAND:
         bUserAbort = TRUE;
         EnableWindow(GetParent(hDlg), TRUE);
         DestroyWindow(hDlg);
         hDlgPrint = 0;
         break;

      default:
         return (FALSE);
   }

   return (TRUE);
}

/***********************************************************************/
/*** AbortProc                                                       ***/
/***                                                                 ***/
/*** Print Manager callback functions.                               ***/
```

```
/*** It's possible to abort printing, but not necessary.                ***/
/**************************************************************************/

BOOL FAR PASCAL AbortProc(HDC hPrnDC, int nCode)
{
   MSG msg;

   while (!bUserAbort && PeekMessage(&msg, NULL, 0, 0, PM_REMOVE))
   {
      if (!hDlgPrint || !IsDialogMessage(hDlgPrint, &msg))
      {
         TranslateMessage(&msg);
         DispatchMessage(&msg);
      }
   }

   return (!bUserAbort);

   /* Or abort because of error:

   return (!(bUserAbort || nCode == SP_OUTOFDISK));
   */
}

/**************************************************************************/
/*** DoPrint                                                            ***/
/***                                                                    ***/
/*** Interaction with the printer driver                                ***/
/**************************************************************************/

#define N_PAGES   1  /* Number of pages to be printed.                     */

BOOL DoPrint(HWND hWnd)
{
   static char szMessage[] = "WinPrint - Demo Printout";
   HDC          hPrnDC;
   FARPROC      fpDlgPrint;
   int          nEscError;
   int          xPage, yPage;

   /* Create device context for the printer                               */

   if ((hPrnDC = GetPrinterDC()) == NULL)
      return (FALSE);

   /* Send maximum printable height and width in pixels                    */

   xPage  = GetDeviceCaps(hPrnDC, HORZRES);
```

```
yPage   = GetDeviceCaps(hPrnDC, VERTRES);

/* Install dialog box and Abort function                              */

EnableWindow(hWnd, FALSE);

bUserAbort   = FALSE;

fpDlgPrint   = MakeProcInstance(PrintDlgProc, hInst);
hDlgPrint    = CreateDialog(hInst, "PrintDlgBox", hWnd, fpDlgPrint);

fpAbortProc = MakeProcInstance(AbortProc, hInst);
Escape(hPrnDC, SETABORTPROC, 0, (LPSTR)fpAbortProc, NULL);

/* Display printing in progress                                       */

nEscError = Escape(hPrnDC, STARTDOC, sizeof(szMessage)-1, szMessage, NULL);
if (nEscError > 0)
{
   int i;

   i = 1;

   while (i <= N_PAGES && (nEscError > 0))
      nEscError = PrintPage(hPrnDC, xPage, yPage, i++);

   if (nEscError > 0)
      Escape(hPrnDC, ENDDOC, 0, NULL, NULL);
}

if (!bUserAbort)
{
   /* Dialog box must be removed if this occurs                       */

   EnableWindow(hWnd, TRUE);
   DestroyWindow(hDlgPrint);
}
else if (nEscError > 0)
   nEscError = SP_APPABORT;    /* For GetErrorText()                  */

FreeProcInstance(fpDlgPrint);
FreeProcInstance(fpAbortProc);
DeleteDC(hPrnDC);

if (nEscError <= 0)
{
   if (nEscError & SP_NOTREPORTED)
   {
```

```
         char szMsg[80];

         wsprintf(szMsg, "Printer Error: %0.60s!", GetErrorText(nEscError));
         MessageBox(hWnd, szMsg, APPL_NAME, MB_OK | MB_ICONEXCLAMATION);
      }
      else
      {
         nEscError |= SP_NOTREPORTED;

         /* The error was displayed, but other dimensions may be needed.   */
      }
   }

   return ((nEscError > 0) || bUserAbort);
}

/****************************************************************************/
/*** GetPrinterDC                                                        ***/
/***                                                                     ***/
/*** Creates a default printer device context, as stated in WIN.INI.     ***/
/****************************************************************************/

static HDC GetPrinterDC(void)
{
   char  szDevice[64];
   char *pDevice, *pDriver, *pOutput;

   GetProfileString("windows", "device", "", szDevice, 64);

   if ( (pDevice = strtok(szDevice, ",")) &&
        (pDriver = strtok(NULL,     ", ")) &&
        (pOutput = strtok(NULL,     ", ")) )
      return (CreateDC(pDriver, pDevice, pOutput, NULL));
   else
      return (NULL);
}

/****************************************************************************/
/*** PrintPage                                                           ***/
/***                                                                     ***/
/*** Prepares a demo page.                                               ***/
/*** This function acts independently of the output device. It can       ***/
/*** work just as well for the screen.                                   ***/
/*** The introduction to banding is not self-explanatory: The solution   ***/
/*** is not very elegant.                                                ***/
/****************************************************************************/

int PrintPage(HDC hDC, int xPage, int yPage, int nPage)
```

```
{
   char  szText[32];
   int   xPrint;
   int   yPrint;
   DWORD dwExtent;
   RECT  rcTxt;
   int   nTxtLen;
   RECT  rcBand;
   int   nNextband;
   int   nEscError;

   /* Place margins around printable area                                    */

   xPrint = (xPage * 8) / 10;
   yPrint = (yPage * 8) / 10;

   /* Store device context                                                   */

   SaveDC(hDC);

   /* MM_ISOTROPIC mapping mode eases creation of circles and squares.       */
   /* Otherwise, you would have to convey many parameters to the device.     */

   SetMapMode(hDC, MM_ISOTROPIC);
   SetWindowExt(hDC, 1000, 1000);
   SetViewportExt(hDC, xPrint, -yPrint);
   SetViewportOrg(hDC, xPage / 2, yPage / 2);

   /* Unchangeable code section from the loop                                */

   nTxtLen       = wsprintf(szText, "Page %d", nPage);
   dwExtent      = GetTextExtent(hDC, szText, lstrlen(szText));
   rcTxt.left    = -(int)LOWORD(dwExtent) / 2;
   rcTxt.top     = HIWORD(dwExtent) / 2;
   rcTxt.right   = rcTxt.left + LOWORD(dwExtent);
   rcTxt.bottom = rcTxt.top - (int)HIWORD(dwExtent);

   /* Determines whether device supports banding                             */

   nNextband = NEXTBAND;
   if (!Escape(hDC, QUERYESCSUPPORT, sizeof(int), (LPSTR)&nNextband, NULL))
   {
      /* To use the same coding for banding, a band is drawn along the      */
      /* perimeter of the printable area.                                    */

      nEscError     = 1;
      rcBand.left   = 0;
      rcBand.top    = 0;
```

```
      rcBand.right  = xPage;
      rcBand.bottom = yPage;
      nNextband     = 0;      /* Indicator for "No banding!"              */
   }
   else
      nEscError = Escape(hDC, NEXTBAND, 0, NULL, (LPSTR)&rcBand);

   while (nEscError > 0 && !IsRectEmpty(&rcBand))
   {
      /* Device context must be re-initialized for every band!           */

      SetMapMode(hDC, MM_ISOTROPIC);
      SetWindowExt(hDC, 1000, 1000);
      SetViewportExt(hDC, xPrint, -yPrint);
      SetViewportOrg(hDC, xPage / 2, yPage / 2);

      /* Convert device coordinates into logical coordinates             */

      DPtoLP(hDC, (LPPOINT)&rcBand, 2);

      /* "Complex" graphic operations should only be executed when you   */
      /* want to change the current band.                                */

      if (RcIntersect(&rcBand, -500, 500, 500, -500))
         Rectangle(hDC, -500, 500, 500, -500);

      if (RcIntersect(&rcBand, -480, 480, -240, 240))
         Ellipse(hDC, -480,  480, -240,  240);
      if (RcIntersect(&rcBand, 240, 480, 480, 240))
         Ellipse(hDC,  240,  480,  480,  240);
      if (RcIntersect(&rcBand, -480, -240, -240, -480))
         Ellipse(hDC, -480, -240, -240, -480);
      if (RcIntersect(&rcBand, 240, -240, 480, -480))
         Ellipse(hDC,  240, -240,  480, -480);

      if (RcIntersect(&rcBand, -360, 450, 360, -210))
      {
         MoveTo(hDC,    0,  450);
         LineTo(hDC, -360, -210);
         LineTo(hDC,  360, -210);
         LineTo(hDC,    0,  450);
      }

      if (RcIntersect(&rcBand, rcTxt.left, rcTxt.top, rcTxt.right, rcTxt.bottom))
         TextOut(hDC, rcTxt.left, rcTxt.top, szText, nTxtLen);

      /* If banding is supported, you can abort to draw the next band.   */
      /* Otherwise, the output will be ready.                            */
```

```
      if (nNextband)
      {
         nEscError = Escape(hDC, NEXTBAND, 0, NULL, (LPSTR)&rcBand);
         (*(FPABORTPROC)fpAbortProc)(hDC, 0);
      }
      else
      {
         Escape(hDC, NEWFRAME, 0, NULL, NULL);
         SetRectEmpty(&rcBand);
      }
   }

   /* Restores original device context status                          */

   RestoreDC(hDC, -1);

   return (nEscError);
}

/***********************************************************************/
/*** RcIntersect                                                     ***/
/***                                                                 ***/
/*** Determines whether a rectangle is described by single coordinates ***/
/*** overlapping a RECT structure. The extract is not returned.      ***/
/*** IntersectRect() cannot be used because PrintPage() exchanges the ***/
/*** vertical coordinate axes.                                       ***/
/***********************************************************************/

static BOOL RcIntersect(RECT *pRect, int left, int top, int right, int bottom)
{
   BOOL bHorz, bVert;

   bHorz = (left > pRect->left ? left   < pRect->right : right > pRect->left);
   bVert = (top  > pRect->top  ? bottom < pRect->top   : top   > pRect->bottom);

   return (bHorz && bVert);
}

/***********************************************************************/
/*** GetErrorText                                                    ***/
/***                                                                 ***/
/*** Translates Print Manager error codes into error messages.       ***/
/***********************************************************************/

LPSTR GetErrorText(int nErrorCode)
{
   static char *szErrText[] =
   {
```

```
        "General error",
        "Aborted by user",
        "Aborted by SPOOLER",
        "TMP directory is full",
        "Not enough memory"
    };

    return (szErrText[~nErrorCode]);
}
```

WINPRINT.C source code

```
/*****************************************************************************/
/*** WINPRINT.C                                                            ***/
/***                                                                       ***/
/*** Framework program for printer output.                                 ***/
/*** Contains initialization, main loop and application window functions.***/
/***                                                                       ***/
/*** (c) 1991 by Abacus                                                    ***/
/*** Author: H. Huptasch                                                   ***/
/*****************************************************************************/

#include <windows.h>
#include <string.h>

#include "winprint.h"
#include "resource.h"

/*****************************************************************************/
/*** Global variables                                                      ***/
/*****************************************************************************/

/* To avoid changing an application handle, it is best to declare the      */
/* handle as a global variable.                                            */

HANDLE hInst;

/*****************************************************************************/
/*** Prototypes                                                            ***/
/*****************************************************************************/


int  PASCAL       WinMain(HANDLE, HANDLE, LPSTR, int);

/* Local functions for this module                                         */

static BOOL       InitClass(HANDLE);
```

```
static void       CallAbout(HWND);

/* Callback functions; must be exported to .DEF file as well              */

LONG FAR PASCAL   MainWndProc(HWND, WORD, WORD, DWORD);
BOOL FAR PASCAL   AboutProc(HWND, WORD, WORD, DWORD);

/**************************************************************************/
/*** WinMain                                                           ***/
/**************************************************************************/

int PASCAL WinMain(HANDLE hNewInst, HANDLE hPrevInst,
                   LPSTR lpCmdLine, int nCmdShow)
{
   HWND hWnd;
   MSG  msg;


   if (!hPrevInst)
      if (!InitClass(hNewInst))
         return (NULL);

   hInst = hNewInst;

   hWnd  = CreateWindow( CLASS_NAME,
                         APPL_NAME,
                         WS_OVERLAPPEDWINDOW,           /* window style      */
                         CW_USEDEFAULT,                 /* x position        */
                         CW_USEDEFAULT,                 /* y position        */
                         CW_USEDEFAULT,                 /* width             */
                         CW_USEDEFAULT,                 /* height            */
                         NULL,                          /* parent handle     */
                         NULL,                          /* menu or child ID  */
                         hNewInst,                      /* instance          */
                         NULL );                        /* additional info   */

   if (!hWnd)
      return (NULL);

   ShowWindow(hWnd, nCmdShow);
   UpdateWindow(hWnd);

   while (GetMessage(&msg, NULL, NULL, NULL))
   {
      TranslateMessage(&msg);
      DispatchMessage(&msg);
   }
```

```
   return (msg.wParam);
}

/*************************************************************************/
/*** InitClass:                                                        ***/
/*************************************************************************/

static BOOL InitClass(HANDLE hInstance)
{
   HANDLE    hMemory;
   PWNDCLASS pWndClass;
   BOOL      bSuccess;

   if ((hMemory = LocalAlloc(LPTR, sizeof(WNDCLASS))) != NULL)
   {
      pWndClass = (PWNDCLASS)LocalLock(hMemory);

      pWndClass->style         = NULL;
      pWndClass->lpfnWndProc   = MainWndProc;
      pWndClass->hInstance     = hInstance;
      pWndClass->hIcon         = LoadIcon(hInstance, ICON_NAME);
      pWndClass->hCursor       = LoadCursor(NULL, IDC_ARROW);
      pWndClass->hbrBackground = COLOR_WINDOW + 1;
      pWndClass->lpszMenuName  = MENU_NAME;
      pWndClass->lpszClassName = CLASS_NAME;

      bSuccess = RegisterClass(pWndClass);

      LocalUnlock(hMemory);
      LocalFree(hMemory);
   }
   else
      bSuccess = FALSE;

   return (bSuccess);
}

/*************************************************************************/
/*** MainWndProc                                                       ***/
/*************************************************************************/

LONG FAR PASCAL MainWndProc(HWND hWnd, WORD wMsg, WORD wParam, DWORD lParam)
{
   BOOL  bCallDefProc;

   bCallDefProc = FALSE;

   switch (wMsg)
```

```
{
   case WM_CREATE :
      break;

   case WM_COMMAND :
      switch (wParam)
      {
         case ID_ABOUT :
            CallAbout(hWnd);
            break;

         case ID_QUIT :
            PostMessage(hWnd, WM_CLOSE, 0, 0L);
            break;

         case ID_WORK :
            DoPrint(hWnd);
            break;

         default:
            bCallDefProc = TRUE;
      }
      break;


   /*** Activate the following case instructions if you want output   ***/
   /*** to appear on the screen as well.                                ***/

   /* The drawing size varies with the window size; the program redraws */
   /* the graphic each time the window size changes.                    */

   /*
   case WM_PAINT :
      {
         PAINTSTRUCT ps;
         HDC         hDC;
         RECT        rc;

         hDC = BeginPaint(hWnd, &ps);
         GetClientRect(hWnd, &rc);
         PrintPage(hDC, rc.right, rc.bottom, 1);
         EndPaint(hWnd, &ps);
      }
      break;

   case WM_SIZE :
      InvalidateRect(hWnd, NULL, TRUE);
      break;
```

```
      */

      case WM_DESTROY :
         PostQuitMessage(0);
         break;

      default :
         bCallDefProc = TRUE;
   }

   return (bCallDefProc ? DefWindowProc(hWnd, wMsg, wParam, lParam) : NULL);
}

/************************************************************************/
/*** CallAbout                                                        ***/
/************************************************************************/

static void CallAbout(HWND hWnd)
{
   FARPROC lpProcAbout;

   lpProcAbout = MakeProcInstance(AboutProc, hInst);
   DialogBox(hInst, ABOUTBOX, hWnd, lpProcAbout);
   FreeProcInstance(lpProcAbout);
}

/************************************************************************/
/*** AboutBox                                                         ***/
/************************************************************************/

BOOL FAR PASCAL AboutProc(HWND hDlg, WORD wMsg, WORD wParam, DWORD lParam)
{
   switch (wMsg)
   {
      case WM_INITDIALOG :
         return (TRUE);

      case WM_COMMAND :
         if (wParam == IDOK)
         {
            EndDialog(hDlg, NULL);
            return (TRUE);
         }
         break;
   }

   return (FALSE);
}
```

13.9 Printer Driver Control

Deep in the insides of the system control/printer there is a dialog box that lets you make different basic settings for the printer. For example, you can choose a setting for the kind of paper format used, choose between portrait or landscape and also select any extra character sets. The system control doesn't create this dialog box. The box belongs to the printer driver. Depending on the driver you set, the dialog box places different settings at your disposal. The selection of the paper format is the most popular setting because almost all printers allow more than one format. Other options are rarely used, such as choosing between color or monochrome print or choosing among one of several sheet feeds. Since the settings the user makes here are kept in the WIN.INI file, they are system wide and permanent for most drivers. These settings communicate the exact configuration of the printer to the system.

For some applications, however, it would be extremely practical if you could adapt these settings according to your own requirements. A spread sheet might need to print paper in landscape format, while an office application might need to control the different sheet feeds in order to automatically print envelopes, letterheads and forms. Windows offers two methods of making settings for the printer.

13.9.1 You don't have to do it all yourself...

You're already familiar with the easy solution provided by the standard applications that come with each Windows package. Windows Write and Windows Paintbrush let you call the dialog box of the printer driver using the **Printer Setup...** item in the **File** menu. Making a setting here is the same as making it in the system control. The settings are system wide, which means that they apply to all applications equally and are saved in the WIN.INI file. So they are kept until the next change.

The global character of these settings doesn't mean that calling **Printer Setup...** would change the parameters of a program that is in the process of printing. Instead of being updated continuously, the printer parameters are set once when a device context is created. You have to call the dialog box of the driver before your program, CreateDC(), is executed.

The procedure is quite simple. You find the [device=] entry of the WIN.INI file and use something like strtok() to divide it into its three components. By doing that, you have also laid the groundwork for calling CreateDC() later. Now you have to load the device driver. Windows does not create the dialog box for printer installation. Furthermore, each device makes a function, that controls the dialog with the user, available. This function is called DeviceMode().

Windows device drivers are dynamic link libraries (DLLs) that you load by entering LoadLibrary(). You already determined the driver name from WIN.INI, but you have to add the .DRV extension for LoadLibrary(), so the function can find the library. The return value of LoadLibrary() is a handle for the driver if it is greater than or equal to 32. Smaller values are error codes.

After loading the device driver, all you need is the address of the DeviceMode() function in the driver, which you get from GetProcAddress(). The first argument is the handle of the DLL; the second argument is the name of the function. Incidentally, it doesn't matter whether you write in uppercase or lowercase, all input is converted to uppercase letters. As an alternative you could also select the function using the PROC_OLDDEVICEMODE constant, which is defined in DRIVINIT.H. After returning from DeviceMode(), remember to call FreeLibrary().

Calling FreeLibrary() decrements the reference count of the DLL so that the library can be removed from the memory if it is no longer needed. In this way you can expand OldDevmode() so that you create a device context, with the data in pDriver, pDevice and pOutput, whose handle the function should then return. Here's the listing for ODEVMODE.C as it appears on the companion diskette.

```
void OldDevmode(HWND hWnd)
{   char        szDevice[64];
   char        szDriver[14];
   char       *pDevice, *pDriver, *pOutput;
   HANDLE      hDriver;
   FARPROC     fpDevmode;
   GetProfileString("windows", "device", "", szDevice, 64);
   if ( !(pDevice = strtok(szDevice, ",")) ||
        !(pDriver = strtok(NULL,     ", ")) ||
        !(pOutput = strtok(NULL,     ", ")) )
      return;
```

```
/* No valid default printer entered                    */
 lstrcpy(szDriver, pDriver);
 lstrcat(szDriver, ".DRV");
 if ((hDriver = LoadLibrary(szDriver)) < 32)
    return;  /* Driver could not be loaded?!                    */
 if ((fpDevmode = GetProcAddress(hDriver, "DeviceMode")) == NULL)
 {
    FreeLibrary(hDriver);
    return;
/* This function should always be available!     */
 }
 (*fpDevmode)(hWnd, hDriver, (LPSTR)pDevice, (LPSTR)pOutput);
 FreeLibrary(hDriver);}
```

As easy as this solution is, it does have two disadvantages. We already mentioned one of them, which is that all of the settings made here permanently influence the entire system. The other disadvantage is that you have to show the user a big dialog box of the printer driver just to have the user choose, for example, between landscape and portrait.

13.9.2 ...But you can

A number of printer settings are accessible using subfunctions of Escape() so that you don't have to go to the dialog box of the printer driver to change them. The most important of these subfunctions are:

GETSETPAPERORIENT
: Can switch between landscape and portrait as well as determine the current setting.

ENUMPAPERMETRICS
: Supplies a list of all the paper formats supported by the printer driver.

GETSETPAPERMETRICS
: Sets a new paper format and gives back the previous format.

SETCOPYCOUNT
: Determines how many copies of each page are to be printed. This refers to copies created by the hardware. For example, laser printers

usually have an option for printing multiple copies of a page.

DRAFTMODE	Selects the quality of the print. Pin printers can usually switch between draft mode and LQ (letter quality) mode, while laser printers often only let you change the resolution for graphics.
ENABLEDUPLEX	Switches on Duplex printing, if the printer supports it.

Using these escape functions is somewhat complex, since there is no common convention for calling them. Also, you have to use QUERYESCSUPPORT beforehand to check their availability, since not all drivers support these options. The following code sequence sets the printer to landscape format (e.g., to output a wide table), and then resets the previous orientation:

```
nEscape = GETSETPRINTORIENT;
if (Escape(hDC, QUERYESCSUPPORT, sizeof(int), (LPSTR)&nEscape, NULL))
{
   nOrient = Escape(hDC, GETSETPRINTORIENT, 0, NULL, NULL);
   sOrient.dwOrient = 2;
   Escape(hDC, GETSETPRINTORIENT, sizeof(ORIENT), (LPSTR)&sOrient, NULL);
   /* ... */
   sOrient.dwOrient = nOrient;
   Escape(hDC, GETSETPRINTORIENT, sizeof(ORIENT), (LPSTR)&sOrient, NULL);
}
```

Under Windows 2.xx this was the only way to change the basic settings of a printer that was program controlled. It was always possible that the active printer would not be able to understand the Escapes. That's why, under Windows 3, they expanded the specification for device drivers. Drivers for Version 3 have two new functions that make changing printer settings a lot more flexible: DeviceCapabilities() and ExtDeviceMode(). As with DeviceMode(), these are functions that are in the driver DLL, not Windows functions. That's why they are only available if the driver has been completely updated to Version 3. Unfortunately, this is not the case for all of the drivers that are supplied with Windows 3. However, this should improve in time.

A data structure called DEVMODE plays an important part in using ExtDeviceMode(). It is defined in DRIVINIT.H in the following way:

```
typedef struct
{
   /* DEVMODE-Header */
   char  dmDeviceName[32];
   WORD  dmSpecVersion;
   WORD  dmDriverVersion;
   WORD  dmSize;
   WORD  dmDriverExtra;
   DWORD dmFields;
   /* Public settings */
   short dmOrientation;
   short dmPaperSize;
   short dmPaperLength;
   short dmPaperWidth;
   short dmScale;
   short dmCopies;
   short dmDefaultSource;
   short dmPrintQuality;
   short dmColor;
   short dmDuplex;
   /* Private Data */
   BYTE  dmDriverData[];
}
 DEVMODE;
```

The values that the individual fields of the structure can include are defined, in DRIVINIT.H, as symbolic constants (actually, DRIVINIT.H is made up almost exclusively of these #defines). As you can see, DEVMODE is subdivided into three parts. The header must always be filled if you want to use this structure as input for ExtDeviceMode(), but the function can take over this work for you using a special call. The following fields include the values of the settings that you want to change.

You don't have to fill all of the fields. In dmFields, bitflags record which fields contain valid values. Of course, you must consider whether the printer even offers the desired settings. You don't need to worry about the third part of the structure, dmDriverData. It contains driver oriented data that usually are undocumented. The area size depends on the driver. Use ExtDeviceMode() or DeviceCapabilities() to determine the size. We'll explain how to use these functions with an example. NewDevmode() shows the basic procedure.

After reading the information on the current printer from WIN.INI, use LoadLibrary() to load the printer driver and use GetProcAddress() to determine the addresses of both functions, if they are available. As we already mentioned, genuine Windows 3 drivers are still the exception. If you do have an appropriate driver loaded, you can call xtDeviceMode() for the first time. The syntax is:

```
int ExtDeviceMode( HWND      hWnd,
                   HANDLE    hDriver,
                   LPDEVMODE lpDevModeOut,
                   LPSTR     lpDevice,
                   LPSTR     lpOutput,
                   LPDEVMODE lpDevModeIn,
                   LPSTR     lpProfile,
                   WORD      wMode
                 );
```

hWnd is a window handle that is used to display the dialog box of the driver. This window activates at the end of the dialog box. hDriver is the handle of the device driver, which is supplied by LoadLibrary(). lpDevice and lpOutput stand for the device and the output port. Up to now we have used strtok() from the WIN.INI file to extract this information. lpDevModeOut points to a DEVMODE structure where the function can enter the current settings if DM_COPY is specified as the mode. lpDevModeIn points to a structure that contains input data for the function if DM_MODIFY is selected as the mode. Specify the mode in wMode. The following values are possible:

DM_COPY	Writes the current settings of the driver to lpDevModeOut.
DM_MODIFY	Changes the current settings in accordance with the information in lpDevModeIn. This change is local, so it won't influence any other running programs. It's not kept in the WIN.INI file either.
DM_UPDATE	Writes changed settings from lpDevModeIn to the WIN.INI file. In other words, you can use it to make global, permanent changes.
DM_PROMPT	Prompts the driver to show its installation box.

You can also combine these values. For example, DM_PROMPT | DM_COPY shows the dialog box of the driver and writes the settings of the user to lpDevModeOut. DM_MODIFY | DM_PROMPT | DM_COPY would initialize the dialog box first with the information from lpDevModeIn. DM_PROMPT | DM_UPDATE is like calling the old function, DeviceMode(). It displays the dialog box and places the new settings in the WIN.INI file, but the program doesn't find out about the settings. Access to WIN.INI is the standard behavior when lpProfile is set equal to NULL. As an alternative, you could also specify the name of another file (e.g., to realize settings that are both application oriented and permanent).

In the example, the first call of ExtDeviceMode() is for determining the size of the DEVMODE structure. Remember that at the end of this structure is a data field whose size depends on its driver. Then you set wMode equal to null and call the function. This information is used to place DEVMODE on the heap. In the following example, the output of the printer is supposed to be set to draft quality. The simplest way to do this is to first initialize DEVMODE with the current settings of the driver. The header of the structure is also correctly set, which is important for being able to use it as input for ExtDeviceMode(). The driver oriented data are also entered in dmDriverData. Before you start changing entries in the DEVMODE structure, you should be sure that the printer supports the capacity in question. DoDevmode() calls the DeviceCapabilities() function to do this. Here is the syntax:

```
DWORD DeviceCapabilities( LPSTR     lpDevice,
                          LPSTR     lpOutput,
                          WORD      nIndex,
                          LPSTR     lpDataOut,
                          LPDEVMODE lpDevMode
                        );
```

lpDevice and lpOutput represent the output device and the port to which it is connected. You use nIndex to tell the function which information you want. DRIVINIT.H defines a number of symbolic constants for this purpose. Some subfunctions produce several return values. These data are copied to the buffer, to which lpDataOut is pointing. You can determine the required size by calling the function with lpDataOut equals NULL. If lpDevMode is equal to NULL, the function takes all data from the current settings of the printer driver.

As an alternative you can also specify the address of a DEVMODE structure. DeviceCapabilities() then evaluates the address.

NewDevmode() only wants to know whether the selected printer is capable of setting the output quality. The function number for this is DC_FIELDS; lpDataOut and lpDevMode are both set to NULL. The return value is a long word that matches the dmFields entry in DEVMODE. A bit called DM_PRINTQUALITY indicates that the print quality of this device can vary. There is an easier way to obtain this information. The previous call of ExtDeviceMode(), with the mode DM_COPY, has already written the current setting to lpDM. Because of that, the flags of all the valid fields in the structure are now available using lpDM->dmFields. DeviceCapabilities() can also get you information that cannot be easily read out of DEVMODE.

If you were successful, NewDevmode() can now set the printer to draft quality. To do this, enter the value DMRES_DRAFT in lpDM->dmPrintQuality and set lpDM->dmFields to DM_PRINTQUALITY. You could also omit the last step, since in this case the other fields of the structure also contain valid (and desirable) values. However, you should always mark the components that actually should be changed. ExtDeviceMode() then conducts the new DEVMODE structure to the printer driver.

It's advantageous to specify DM_MODIFY|DM_COPY as the mode and use lpDM for both the input and output data. For example, if the printer doesn't have draft quality, the original setting is entered back in lpDM and you still have a valid value in this structure. This could be the case with a laser printer that has different graphic resolutions (DMRES_LOW = 75 dpi, DMRES_MEDIUM = 150 dpi and DMRES_HIGH = 300 dpi), but doesn't provide draft quality for text output. So lpDM points to a valid DEVMODE structure that can be passed as a fourth argument to CreateDC().

The rest of the printer output runs as usual. When your output is finished, remember to use FreeLibrary() to free the printer driver. NewDevmode() also has to deallocate the memory for the DEVMODE structure. If you study the listing for this example, you will discover that things aren't quite as complicated as they first seem. On the other hand, DeviceCapabilities() and ExtDeviceMode() make up several different functions, which makes the operation complex. One reason they didn't provide several smaller functions for the various tasks is that each of these functions would require a separate entry point in the DLL. Then you would have to use GetProcAddress() to assign a separate pointer to each function. Although the example doesn't show all of the aspects of these functions, it does show you enough so that you can manage by using the SDK manuals.

Here's the listing for NDEVMODE.C, as it appears on your companion diskette for this book.

```
void NewDevmode(HWND hWnd)
{
   char          szDevice[64];
   char          szDriver[14];
   char         *pDevice, *pDriver, *pOutput;
   HANDLE        hDriver;
   HANDLE        hDM;
   LPDEVMODE     lpDM;
   LPFNDEVMODE   fpExtDM;
   LPFNDEVCAPS   fpDevCap;
   int           nDM;
   DWORD         dwFields;
   HDC           hDC;
   GetProfileString("windows", "device", "", szDevice, 64);
   if ( !(pDevice = strtok(szDevice, ","))  ||
        !(pDriver = strtok(NULL,     ", ")) ||
        !(pOutput = strtok(NULL,     ", ")) )
      return;
  /* No valid default printer entered                 */
   lstrcpy(szDriver, pDriver);
   lstrcat(szDriver, ".DRV");
   if ((hDriver = LoadLibrary(szDriver)) < 32)
      return;
  /* Driver could not be loaded?!                         */
   fpExtDM  = GetProcAddress(hDriver, "ExtDeviceMode");
   fpDevCap = GetProcAddress(hDriver, "DeviceCapabilities");
   if (!(fpExtDM && fpDevCap))  {      FreeLibrary(hDriver);
      return;  /* No real Windows 3 driver                         */
   }
   /* Determine size of DEVMODE                                     */
   nDM = (*fpExtDM)(hWnd, hDriver, NULL, pDevice, pOutput, NULL, NULL, 0);
   if (!(hDM = GlobalAlloc(GMEM_MOVEABLE | GMEM_ZEROINIT, (long)nDM)))
   {
      FreeLibrary(hDriver);
      return;
  /* It won't run without enough memory                          */
   }
```

```
lpDM = (LPDEVMODE)GlobalLock(hDM);
/* User can now work with ExtDeviceMode()                              */
/* Read current parameters                                           */
(*fpExtDM)(hWnd, hDriver, lpDM, pDevice, pOutput, NULL, NULL, DM_COPY);
/* Set printer to draft mode if possible                         */
dwFields = (*fpDevCap)(pDevice, pOutput, DC_FIELDS, NULL, NULL);
if (dwFields & DM_PRINTQUALITY)
{
   lpDM->dmPrintQuality = DMRES_DRAFT;
   lpDM->dmFields       = DM_PRINTQUALITY;
   (*fpExtDM)(hWnd, hDriver, lpDM, pDevice, pOutput, lpDM, NULL,
              DM_MODIFY | DM_COPY);
}
/* lpDM contains DEVMODE for CreateDC()                                */
hDC = CreateDC(pDriver, pDevice, pOutput, (LPSTR)lpDM);
GlobalUnlock(hDM);
/* ... */
DeleteDC(hDC);
GlobalFree(hDM);
FreeLibrary(hDriver);}
```

13.10 Multiple Printers

The GetPrinterDC() function from the previous sample programs creates one device context for the default printer entered under "device=" in the [windows] section of the WIN.INI file. However, with some programs, the user must set the proper printer before printing. For example, if a CAD program is being used, a plotter should be used instead of a daisy wheel printer. Although you could use a simple prompt, which asks the user to select the appropriate output device by using the system control, there is a better solution. Fortunately, it's possible to integrate such a selection to an application.

Printer selection

You will need two things for this: a list of available output devices and information on the device, driver name and the assigned output port for the device you select. You can get both pieces of information by using the same function:

```
char szDevices[2048];
GetProfileString("devices", NULL, "", szDevices, sizeof(szDevices));
```

The first argument of GetProfileString() represents the section of the WIN.INI file to which the entry you are searching for belongs. The second argument is the name of the entry itself (the item to the left of the equal sign). If the second argument is equal to NULL, then you called the enumerating (listing) form of GetProfileString(). The function enters the names (not the values), of all available entries of this section, in the target buffer szDevices. Each entry is separated by a zero byte. You recognize the last entry by the zero byte that follows.

```
char *pDevices;
HWND  hListBox;
   [Create listbox and fill szDevices with values]pDevice = szDevices;
while (*pDevice)
{
   SendMessage(hListBox, LB_ADDSTRING, 0, pDevice);
   pDevice += lstrlen(pDevice) + 1;
}
```

These lines include all the entries of the [devices] section in a list box. The program uses this list box to determine the user's choice. The problem with the enumerating form of GetProfileString() is that you don't know beforehand how many entries there are and how much space is taken up by their names. You must ensure that the buffer is big enough. The return value of GetProfileString() is the number of characters actually sent to the buffer—the last zero byte is not counted. If the buffer is too small, the function returns the maximum length that you specified in the fifth argument (in the example: sizeof(szDevices)). In the enumerating form, you would get the maximum length minus two as the return value in this case.

As we mentioned, szDevices now contains the names of all the entries in the [devices] section, but not the device description to the right of the equal sign. To get to the device description, you must call GetProfileString() again, specifying a pointer to the name of the desired device as your second argument.

```
char szDevice[64];char szPrinter[64];nIndex = (int)SendMessage(hListBox,
LB_GETCURSEL, 0, 0));SendMessage(hListBox, LB_GETTEXT, nIndex,
szDevice);GetProfileString("devices", szDevice, "", szPrinter,
sizeof(szPrinter));
```

This is the continuation of the example above. The selected entry is read out of the listbox and passed on to GetProfileString(). szPrinter now contains the information necessary for creating a device context through CreateDC(). You can use strtok() to separate the information, as shown in the GetPrinterDC() function from WINPRINT (Version 1) or WINPRINT (Version 2).

This selection of an alternative output device is local (i.e., other applications are not affected by it). If you wanted to set the standard printer for the entire system, you would have to enter the definition in szPrinter, along with WriteProfileString(), under the keyword "device=" in the [windows] section of the WIN.INI file:

```
WriteProfileString("windows", "device", szPrinter);
```

However, usually you shouldn't do this unless your program is explicitly designed for such purposes.

13.11 Using Fonts

You may have gotten the impression that printer output and screen output are so different from one another that the expression "device independence" no longer seems appropriate. Actually, it requires some work in your program to utilize all the options of the printer. However, not every program requires you to use all the measures introduced here. Often it's sufficient to send the output to the standard printer, just as many programs can get along without adapting to the basic settings of the printer.

If you want to use certain properties, which aren't available in every printer, it is often possible (and wise) to check the options when you start the program. For instance, you can only choose between landscape and portrait mode if the connected printer can actually execute the switch. The required settings are made before printing when you create the device context. The output itself can often be independent of the target device; the same GDI functions are called. One group of these functions is very important to printing in Windows. We are talking about working with fonts, or character sets, which we'll discuss in detail.

Under MS-DOS, different font attributes can be used to improve the appearance of your printouts. Underlining, bold or italic fonts are examples of this (reasonably priced printers that offer a selection of different fonts have only recently been available). You set these text attributes by sending printer oriented control characters to the device. Under Windows, you won't find functions, such as SetTextBold() or UnderlineText(), for switching attributes.

Under Windows, you have to create a separate font for each of these text displays. From a typographical standpoint this makes sense, since, for instance, an italic font is really different from a regular font that is only slanted. For you the programmer, this means you will have to change the way you think. Fortunately, you will be able to use the same procedure to create both the "fake" italic font of a screen or pin printer and the "real" italic font of a (PostScript) laser printer.

13.11.1 Font selection

If you have already experimented with fonts for screen output, then you are familiar with the basic procedure. As a GDI function, it makes no difference to CreateFont() whether you create a character set for the screen or for some other device. The function doesn't even know which device the font is intended for. You don't determine this until you use SelectObject() to load it into a device context. The GDI then tries to select the font that most closely matches the arguments specified by CreateFont() based on all of the fonts available for this device.

If you want to do a lot with text displays, such as underlining, it's much better to create the font using CreateFontIndirect(). To do this, first fill out a LOGFONT structure, whose components match the arguments for CreateFont(), and then pass the structure on to CreateFontIndirect(). To activate the italic font, all you have to do is set the appropriate flag in LOGFONT and call CreateFontIndirect() again with this changed structure.

To let the user choose among several fonts, your program must create a list of available fonts. You can install the names of the character sets in a menu. However, since you can install many fonts in a system, it's better to fill a list box or combo box with this information.

Here's the listing of ENUMFONT.C as it appears on the companion diskette for this book:

```
extern HANDLE hInst;

int FAR PASCAL FontFunc(LPLOGFONT, LPTEXTMETRIC, int, LPSTR);

void GetFonts(HDC hDC, HWND hListBox)
{
   FARPROC fpFonts;

   fpFonts = MakeProcInstance(FontFunc, hInst);
   SendMessage(hListBox, WM_REDRAW, FALSE, 0L);
   EnumFonts(hDC, NULL, fpFonts, (LPSTR)(DWORD)hListBox);
   SendMessage(hListBox, WM_REDRAW, TRUE, 0L);
   InvalidateRect(hListBox, NULL, TRUE);
   FreeProcInstance(fpFonts);
}
```

```
int FAR PASCAL FontFunc(LPLOGFONT lpLF, LPTEXTMETRIC lpTM, int nType, LPSTR
lpData)
{
   HWND hListBox;
   char szName[LF_FACESIZE + 2];
   int  nIndex;

   hListBox = (HANDLE)LOWORD(lpData);

   szName[0] = (nType & DEVICE_FONTTYPE ? '*' : ' ');
   szName[1] = ' ';
   lstrcpy(szName + 2, lpLF->lfFaceName);
   nIndex   = (int)SendMessage(hListBox, LB_ADDSTRING, 0, (long)(lpLF-
>lfFaceName);
   SendMessage(hListBox, LB_SETITEMDATA, nIndex, (long)nType);

   return (TRUE);
}
```

FontFunc() is a callback function that the GDI calls once for each character set that it finds. That's why you have to export this function to the .DEF file of your program. Also, you have to call MakeProcInstance() in order to get a pointer to the function. EnumFonts() lets you pass any parameter to the callback function. Here, it's a handle to the list box that is supposed to accept the font names. Both messages sent to the list box are for suppressing the screen glint that would result if the list box were updated for each new entry. InvalidateRect() does not redraw the entire list box until the action is finished.

FontNames() utilizes the information passed to it in the argument, nType. If the bit RASTER_FONTTYPE is set in it, then the font is a raster font; otherwise it is a vector font. The bit DEVICE_FONT designates a character set installed in the printer; otherwise the font is supplied by the GDI. This value is first linked to the corresponding font name in the list box, so that it will also be available later. Then the printer-specific fonts in the list box are marked with an asterisk in front of them. Although you seldom see anything like this, it is interesting information for the user. Above all, it makes a considerable difference in the printing speed of dot matrix printers, whether you use a resident font of the printer or whether a GDI font in the form of a graphic is output. Since EnumFonts() was called without specifying a character set name (the second parameter is equal to NULL), the GDI calls the callback function only once for each font. To obtain a list of the different sizes each font is available in, you must call EnumFonts() again and specify the font name. You can use the LB_GETTEXT message to read the name from the list box. In our case, remember that the first two characters are not part of the font name.

13.11.2 Problems

We have already hinted that when you use CreateFont() or CreateFontIndirect() to create a font, you can specify exactly what the character set you want to use will look like. Among these specifications are the size and information about whether the font is proportional or if all of the characters in the font have the same width. You can also define attributes, such as underlining or slanting, or specify a font name that instructs the system to use a certain character set. Since there are so many possible combinations of these specifications, not all of these describable fonts are available in one system.

SelectObject() loads the font that comes closest to your description in the device context. This decision depends on the device. Suppose that you define a 15 point character set. It's possible that a 14 point font is selected in the device context of the screen, while, in the device context of the printer, a 16 point font is selected. That's the end of "WYSIWYG" (What You See Is What You Get). When you format text in this font for screen output, a page will be able to hold a lot more information than the printer will be able to print. Word wrapping and page breaks won't match at all. There's nothing you can do to remedy this problem. Even if the screen and the printer have the same fonts (e.g., output with GDI vector fonts), there will still be visible inaccuracies due to the different resolutions of both devices. However, there are two techniques that help ease this problem.

13.11.3 Logical Twips mapping mode

If you want your program to display, as accurately as possible, what the printout will look like, the first thing you should do is set up a common coordinate system for the screen and the printer. Then you can skip the constant conversions from screen coordinates to printer coordinates, or the conversion takes place in the GDI. There are several mapping modes that set the logical coordinate system on the basis of physical size. For MM_LOMETRIC and MM_HIMETRIC a unit is 0.1 or 0.01 millimeters while for MM_LOENGLISH and MM_HIENGLISH a unit is 0.01 or 0.001 inches.

For fonts, the most widespread unit of measure is the point, which is approximately 1/72 inch. The GDI also provides a mapping mode for this. MM_TWIPS creates logical coordinates that are 1/1440 inches large or one twentieth of a point, which is what Twip stands for. This would be a practical solution except that an inch is bigger to the screen than to the rest of the world. In Windows this phenomenon is called the "logical inch". You can use the GetDeviceCaps() function to determine the dimensions of your screen in inches and in pixels and calculate the resolution from the two. For a VGA card in standard mode, the following horizontal resolution results:

```
HORZRES / (HORZSIZE / 25.4) = LOGPIXELSX  640   / (  208    / 25.4) = 78.15 dpi
```

If you ask GetDeviceCaps() for the resolution, you get LOGPIXELSX=96 dpi. Now, if you calculate back the screen size, you get:

```
(HORZRES / LOGPIXELSX) * 25.4 = HORZSIZE(  640   /     96    ) * 25.4 = 169 mm
```

The screen shows an enlarged section of the document. The reason for this artificial increase in the resolution is the display of the fonts. While an 8 point font would be easy to read on paper, on the screen the same font would result in a character size of about six times five pixels. On most monitors, this is too small to work with. So you cannot use MM_TWIPS as a mapping mode. But it's not too difficult to create your own mode that takes the logical coordinates of the screen into consideration.

```
/***************************************************************************/
/*** MMLogicalTwips                                                     ***/
/***                                                                    ***/
/*** Installs a coordinate system in the device context, using the      ***/
/*** twip (1 twip= 1/1440") as the unit of measurement.                 ***/
/***************************************************************************/

static void MMLogicalTwips(HDC hDC)
{
   int xLogpixels;
   int yLogpixels;
```

```
    xLogpixels = GetDeviceCaps(hDC, LOGPIXELSX);
    yLogpixels = GetDeviceCaps(hDC, LOGPIXELSY);
    SetMapMode(hDC, MM_ANISOTROPIC);
    SetWindowExt(hDC, 1440, 1440);
    SetViewportExt(hDC, xLogpixels, yLogpixels);
}
```

Our choice of MM_ANISOTROPIC takes into consideration the fact that the logical resolution of many video cards is different horizontally and vertically (e.g., 96 to 72 dpi on an EGA card). It is the only mapping mode that allows different scaling for both coordinate axles. At the beginning of your work session, call this function both for the device context of the screen as well as the printer. Since you are now working in the same coordinate system in both devices, you can also use the same LOGFONT structure to create a character set for the screen and the printer; you specify the font size in the components in logical units as with all coordinate specifications. You can create a ten point font in both cases by using logfont.lfHeight=200 (10 * 20).

13.11.4 Double formatting

As you already know, this does not mean that you get the same physical character set each time you load this (logical) font in the printer or screen device context. Use GetTextMetrics() to determine how close the font, selected by GDI, matches your description. This function fills the TEXTMETRIC structure with specifications that you can compare with the corresponding values in the LOGFONT structure. While differences in appearance pose only an optical problem, you have to provide special measures if the selected font of the screen is a different size than the font of the printer.

Although you won't be able to have perfect WYSIWYG under these conditions, the word wrapping and page break in both displays will match. You can achieve this by using the printer font for the wrap/break. Only after the text is set on individual lines can you format it with the screen font. You also use this font for output. This procedure is demonstrated in the JUSTIFY program listed at the end of this chapter.

The file organization of the project is exactly the same as in previous examples. The PrintPage() function in the DOPRINT.C module contains everything that relates to this subject. It displays a short text in justified format. The output appears on the screen and, if requested, on the printer. The second argument, hOutDC, determines which device context the output are directed to. The first argument, hPrnDC must always be the handle to the device context of the printer. The dimensions of its character set form the foundation of formatting. Use wFontSize to specify the desired font size in points.

Coordinate setup

You set up the common coordinate system for both devices right at the beginning. You are already familiar with the function that you use for this, MMLogicalTwips(). After that you generate the font. The specifications are kept rather vague; memset() sets all of the entries to null, the default values of the GDI. The only thing you define is the font size and that it is a proportional character set. You call GetTextMetrics() afterwards to determine the necessary amount for the line feed. As you can see, the font of the printer is also used for this. The formatting itself is relatively easy. The text will run through, word by word, until its width is greater than the set line width. The space is assumed as the word limit.

It's important to delete the transfer counter of the GDI by using SetTextJustification(hPrnDC, 0, 0) before calling GetTextExtent(). The GDI notes any truncation errors, that might occur, in this counter in order to consider them if called a second time. This is very useful when a line of text is made up of several partial lines (especially if different fonts are used in these partial lines). In our case, though, there can't be any carryover. As soon as the line becomes too wide, or you reach the end of the text, the loop stops.

The position of the word wrapping is marked by pEnd. It is the last space found in the line. This position tells you how much text the printer can display in the line. Now you have to format the line again for the output device. This time, though, you use hOutDC. You also use SetTextJustification() to justify the text. This function removes the spaces between the end of the text line and the right margin. SetTextJustification() then re-distributes these spaces equally within the line, padding the spaces between words.

This technique is easy to use. Except for using the printer and screen DC at the same time, it's no different than simple output on the screen. How well the screen display matches the printout depends on how similar the character sets are that the GDI selected for both devices. If the screen font is too small in proportion to the printer font, there will be greater distances between the words than in the printout. However, this isn't a major problem.

It's worse if the screen font is more than just slightly too large. Then the text won't even fit in the space provided for it. Instead of justified text, you get a ragged right margin, and/or the lines run into each other. If you are using a VGA card in standard resolution and a printer driver for a 24 pin printer, you can observe this effect when you select 8 points in the **Font Size** menu of the JUSTIFY program.

```
/**********************************************************************/
/*** PrintPage                                                      ***/
/***                                                                ***/
/*** Prints the sample text in justified format. Line breaks on the ***/
/*** screen correspond to those on the printer (WYSIWYG).           ***/
/**********************************************************************/

static char szText[] =
   "The PrintLines() function shows an example of text formatted so that "
   "line breaks are ignored and spaces are inserted to justify the text in "
   "screen and printed output. The trick to this lies in formatting the "
   "output before it reaches either output device.";

void PrintPage(HDC hPrnDC, HDC hOutDC, WORD wFontSize)
{
   int      nOutDC;
   int      nPrnDC;
   LOGFONT lf;
   HFONT    hFont;
   TEXTMETRIC tm;
   DWORD    dwExtent;
   char    *pText, *pStart, *pEnd;
   int      nSpace;
   int      x, y;
   WORD     wLineWidth;

   /* Store current device context                                      */


   nOutDC = SaveDC(hOutDC);
   nPrnDC = SaveDC(hPrnDC);

   /* Set coordinate system                                             */

   MMLogicalTwips(hOutDC);
```

```
MMLogicalTwips(hPrnDC);

/* Create proportional font - size is of particular interest.          */

memset(&lf, 0, sizeof(LOGFONT));
lf.lfHeight          = wFontSize * 20;
lf.lfPitchAndFamily = VARIABLE_PITCH;
hFont                = CreateFontIndirect(&lf);
SelectObject(hOutDC, hFont);
SelectObject(hPrnDC, hFont);
GetTextMetrics(hPrnDC, &tm);

x = y = 1440 / 2;        /* Insert 1/2" (720 twips) left and top margins */
wLineWidth = 5 * 1440;   /* Specify 5" (7200 twips) line width           */

/* Divide text into lines; breaks are removed and replaced with spaces */
/* if the text width is less than the specified line width.            */
/* This formatting is based on printer fonts.                          */

pText = szText;

while (*pText)
{
   while (*pText && *pText == ' ')
      ++pText;

   pStart = pText;
   nSpace = 0;

   do
   {
      if (!*(pEnd = pText))
         break;                   /* End of text                          */

      while (*pText && *pText++ != ' ')
         ;

      ++nSpace;

      SetTextJustification(hPrnDC, 0, 0);
      dwExtent = GetTextExtent(hPrnDC, pStart, pText - pStart - 1);
   } while (LOWORD(dwExtent) < wLineWidth);

   /* The way this loop is designed, the counter slightly overshoots    */
   /* the goal.                                                         */

   if (*pText)
      --nSpace;
```

```
        if (*pEnd)
            --pEnd;
        else
            nSpace = 0;     /* Last line not justified                          */

        /* Formatting executes in the output device's context.                */

        SetTextJustification(hOutDC, 0, 0);
        dwExtent = GetTextExtent(hOutDC, pStart, pEnd - pStart);
        if (nSpace > 1)
            SetTextJustification(hOutDC, wLineWidth - LOWORD(dwExtent), nSpace - 1);
        TextOut(hOutDC, x, y, pStart, pEnd - pStart);

        y += tm.tmHeight + tm.tmExternalLeading;
        pText = pEnd;
    }

    RestoreDC(hPrnDC, nPrnDC);
    RestoreDC(hOutDC, nOutDC);
    DeleteObject(hFont);
}
```

Aside from the PrintPage() function, JUSTIFY is barely different than WINPRINT (Version 2). (It's not worth using banding, as you did in WINPRINT (Version 3).) Windows always manages the printing process according to the same system, which is realized in DoPrint() and its auxiliary function in the DOPRINT.C model. The necessary adjustments concern the user interface (the printer dialog box and error handling), as well as the interface for the data output function, PrintPage(). This is where problems can start, when you are creating output data (whether graphics or text) and you want to have different devices display your data as identically as possible. Using JUSTIFY is one technique for displaying text and graphics on more than one device. Other problems, such as reproducing colors on a monochrome printer, are still waiting for your solution.

13.11.5 Source code: JUSTIFY

RESOURCE.H include file

```
/**************************************************************************/
/*** RESOURCE.H                                                        ***/
/***                                                                   ***/
/*** Resource IDs                                                      ***/
/***                                                                   ***/
/*** (c) 1991 Abacus                                                   ***/
/*** Author: H. Huptasch                                               ***/
/**************************************************************************/


#define ID_ABOUT      100
#define ID_QUIT       101
#define ID_WORK       102

#define ID_FONT08     8
#define ID_FONT10     10
#define ID_FONT12     12
#define ID_FONT14     14
#define ID_FONT16     16
```

JUSTIFY.H include file

```
/**************************************************************************/
/*** JUSTIFY.H                                                         ***/
/***                                                                   ***/
/*** Global definitions and declarations                               ***/
/***                                                                   ***/
/*** (c) 1991 by Abacus                                                ***/
/*** Author: H. Huptasch                                               ***/
/**************************************************************************/

#define CLASS_NAME    "JustifyClass"
#define APPL_NAME     "Justify"
#define MENU_NAME     "JustifyMenu"
#define ICON_NAME     "JustifyIcon"
#define ABOUTBOX      "AboutBox"

/* Instance handle of application                                        */

extern HANDLE hInst;
```

```
/* Function prototypes for printed output                              */

HDC  GetPrinterDC(void);
BOOL DoPrint(HWND, WORD);
void PrintPage(HDC, HDC, WORD);
```

JUSTIFY.RC resource file

```
/*************************************************************************/
/*** JUSTIFY.RC                                                        ***/
/***                                                                   ***/
/*** (c) 1991 by Abacus                                                ***/
/*** Author: H. Huptasch                                               ***/
/*************************************************************************/

#include <windows.h>
#include "resource.h"

JustifyIcon ICON justify.ico

JustifyMenu MENU
BEGIN
   POPUP "&Program"
   BEGIN
      MENUITEM "&Print",        ID_WORK
      MENUITEM "E&xit",          ID_QUIT
      MENUITEM SEPARATOR
      MENUITEM "A&bout JUSTIFY...",  ID_ABOUT
   END
   POPUP "&Font Size"
   BEGIN
      MENUITEM " &8 Points",         ID_FONT08
      MENUITEM "1&0 Points",         ID_FONT10
      MENUITEM "1&2 Points",         ID_FONT12
      MENUITEM "1&4 Points",         ID_FONT14, CHECKED
      MENUITEM "1&6 Points",         ID_FONT16
   END
END

AboutBox DIALOG LOADONCALL MOVEABLE DISCARDABLE 10, 9, 144, 78
STYLE WS_DLGFRAME | WS_POPUP
BEGIN
   ICON          "JustifyIcon",              -1,    8,  8,  16, 21,  SS_ICON
   CTEXT         "Justify",                  -1,   24,  4, 120,  8
   CTEXT         " 1991 Abacus",            -1,   24, 14, 120,  8
   CTEXT         "Author: Heiko Huptasch",   -1,   24, 22, 120,  8
   CTEXT         "Version 1.0",              -1,   24, 36, 120,  8
```

```
   DEFPUSHBUTTON  "OK",                     IDOK, 58, 56,  52, 14,  WS_GROUP
END

PrintDlgBox DIALOG LOADONCALL MOVEABLE DISCARDABLE 40, 40, 120, 40
STYLE WS_POPUP | WS_CAPTION | WS_SYSMENU | WS_VISIBLE
BEGIN
   CTEXT          "Printing in progress",  -1,        4, 6, 120, 12
   DEFPUSHBUTTON  "Cancel",                IDCANCEL, 44, 22, 32, 14, WS_GROUP
END
```

JUSTIFY.DEF module definition file

```
NAME        JUSTIFY
EXETYPE     WINDOWS
DESCRIPTION 'JUSTIFY - A Windows application by Abacus (c) 1991'

STUB        'WINSTUB.EXE'

CODE        MOVEABLE DISCARDABLE
DATA        PRELOAD MOVEABLE MULTIPLE

HEAPSIZE    1024
STACKSIZE   4096

SEGMENTS
   _TEXT    PRELOAD
   JUSTIFY  PRELOAD
   DOPRINT  LOADONCALL

EXPORTS
   MainWndProc
   AboutProc
   AbortProc
   PrintDlgProc
```

MAKEFILE

```
# Create JUSTIFY.EXE
#
# MAKEFILE for Microsoft's MAKE or NMAKE
#
# (c) 1991 by Abacus
# Author: H. Huptasch


# Object file list
```

```
OBJECTS  = justify.obj doprint.obj


# Define compiler and necessary switches

CC       = cl
CFLAGS   = -AM -Osw -Gsw -Zpe -W3 -NT$* -DLINT_ARGS -D_WINDOWS

.c.obj:
   $(CC) -c $(CFLAGS) $*.c


#Flexible lists

MAKE_ALL:    justify.exe

justify.res: justify.rc justify.ico resource.h
   rc -r justify.rc

justify.obj: justify.c  justify.h   resource.h

doprint.obj: doprint.c  justify.h

justify.exe: $(OBJECTS) justify.res justify.def
   link /NOD/NOE/A:16 $(OBJECTS), , nul, libw mlibcew, justify
   rc justify.res
```

DOPRINT.C source code

```
/****************************************************************************/
/*** DOPRINT.C                                                           ***/
/***                                                                     ***/
/*** Printer output module for JUSTIFY.                                  ***/
/*** The PrintPage() function shows how to format text, ignoring line    ***/
/*** breaks, both on screen and printer.                                 ***/
/***                                                                     ***/
/*** (c) 1991 by Abacus                                                  ***/
/*** Author: H. Huptasch                                                 ***/
/****************************************************************************/

#include <windows.h>
#include <string.h>

#include "justify.h"
```

```
/*************************************************************************/
/*** Global variable module                                            ***/
/*************************************************************************/

static BOOL bUserAbort;
static HWND hDlgPrint;

/*************************************************************************/
/*** Prototypes                                                        ***/
/*************************************************************************/

static void     MMLogicalTwips(HDC);
static LPSTR    GetErrorText(int);

/* Callback functions must also be exported in .DEF file!              */

BOOL FAR PASCAL PrintDlgProc(HWND, WORD, WORD, DWORD);
BOOL FAR PASCAL AbortProc(HDC, int);

/*************************************************************************/
/*** PrintDlgProc                                                      ***/
/***                                                                   ***/
/*** Window function for modeless dialog box, allowing the user to     ***/
/*** cancel the printing procedure.                                    ***/
/*************************************************************************/

BOOL FAR PASCAL PrintDlgProc(HWND hDlg, WORD wMsg, WORD wParam, DWORD lParam)
{
   switch (wMsg)
   {
      case WM_INITDIALOG:
         SetWindowText(hDlg, APPL_NAME);
         EnableMenuItem(GetSystemMenu(hDlg, FALSE), SC_CLOSE, MF_GRAYED);
         break;

      case WM_COMMAND:
         bUserAbort = TRUE;
         EnableWindow(GetParent(hDlg), TRUE);
         DestroyWindow(hDlg);
         hDlgPrint = 0;
         break;

      default:
         return (FALSE);
   }

   return (TRUE);
}
```

```
/**************************************************************************/
/*** AbortProc                                                          ***/
/***                                                                    ***/
/*** Callback function for the Print Manager.                          ***/
/*** Printing can be cancelled if an error occurs (optional).          ***/
/**************************************************************************/

BOOL FAR PASCAL AbortProc(HDC hPrnDC, int nCode)
{
   MSG msg;

   while (!bUserAbort && PeekMessage(&msg, NULL, 0, 0, PM_REMOVE))
   {
      if (!hDlgPrint || !IsDialogMessage(hDlgPrint, &msg))
      {
         TranslateMessage(&msg);
         DispatchMessage(&msg);
      }
   }

   return (!bUserAbort);

   /* Or cancel due to error:
   return (!(bUserAbort || nCode == SP_OUTOFDISK));
   */
}

/**************************************************************************/
/*** DoPrint                                                            ***/
/***                                                                    ***/
/*** Interaction with printer driver                                    ***/
/**************************************************************************/

BOOL DoPrint(HWND hWnd, WORD wFontSize)
{
   static char szMessage[] = "Justify - Demo Printout";
   HDC         hPrnDC;
   FARPROC     fpAbortProc;
   FARPROC     fpDlgPrint;
   int         nEscError;

   /* Add a device context for the printer first                         */

      if ((hPrnDC = GetPrinterDC()) == NULL)
      return (FALSE);

   /* Install dialog box and abort function                              */
```

```
EnableWindow(hWnd, FALSE);

bUserAbort   = FALSE;

fpDlgPrint   = MakeProcInstance(PrintDlgProc, hInst);
hDlgPrint    = CreateDialog(hInst, "PrintDlgBox", hWnd, fpDlgPrint);

fpAbortProc = MakeProcInstance(AbortProc, hInst);
Escape(hPrnDC, SETABORTPROC, 0, (LPSTR)fpAbortProc, NULL);

/* Display print process                                              */

nEscError = Escape(hPrnDC, STARTDOC, sizeof(szMessage)-1, szMessage, NULL);
if (nEscError > 0)
{
   PrintPage(hPrnDC, hPrnDC, wFontSize);
   nEscError = Escape(hPrnDC, NEWFRAME, 0, NULL, NULL);

   if (nEscError > 0)
      Escape(hPrnDC, ENDDOC, 0, NULL, NULL);
}

if (!bUserAbort)
{
   /* In this case, dialog box must still be removed                  */

   EnableWindow(hWnd, TRUE);
   DestroyWindow(hDlgPrint);
}
else if (nEscError > 0)
   nEscError = SP_APPABORT;    /* For GetErrorText()                  */

FreeProcInstance(fpDlgPrint);
FreeProcInstance(fpAbortProc);
DeleteDC(hPrnDC);

if (nEscError <= 0)
{
   if (nEscError & SP_NOTREPORTED)
   {
      char szMsg[80];

      wsprintf(szMsg, "Printer Error %0.60s", GetErrorText(nEscError));
      MessageBox(hWnd, szMsg, APPL_NAME, MB_OK | MB_ICONEXCLAMATION);
   }
}

return ((nEscError > 0) || bUserAbort);
```

```
}

/***********************************************************************/
/*** GetPrinterDC                                                    ***/
/***                                                                 ***/
/*** Creates a default printer device context as stated in WIN.INI.  ***/
/***********************************************************************/

HDC GetPrinterDC(void)
{
   char  szDevice[64];
   char *pDevice, *pDriver, *pOutput;

   GetProfileString("windows", "device", "", szDevice, 64);

   if ( (pDevice = strtok(szDevice, ",")) &&
        (pDriver = strtok(NULL,     ", ")) &&
        (pOutput = strtok(NULL,     ", ")) )
      return (CreateDC(pDriver, pDevice, pOutput, NULL));
   else
      return (NULL);
}

/***********************************************************************/
/*** MMLogicalTwips                                                  ***/
/***                                                                 ***/
/*** Installs a coordinate system in the device context, using the   ***/
/*** twip (1 twip= 1/1440") as the unit of measurement.              ***/
/***********************************************************************/

static void MMLogicalTwips(HDC hDC)
{
   int xLogpixels;
   int yLogpixels;

   xLogpixels = GetDeviceCaps(hDC, LOGPIXELSX);
   yLogpixels = GetDeviceCaps(hDC, LOGPIXELSY);
   SetMapMode(hDC, MM_ANISOTROPIC);
   SetWindowExt(hDC, 1440, 1440);
   SetViewportExt(hDC, xLogpixels, yLogpixels);
}

/***********************************************************************/
/*** PrintPage                                                       ***/
/***                                                                 ***/
/*** Prints the sample text in justified format. Line breaks on the  ***/
/*** screen correspond to those on the printer (WYSIWYG).            ***/
/***********************************************************************/
```

```
static char szText[] =
   "The PrintLines() function shows an example of text formatted so that "
   "line breaks are ignored and spaces are inserted to justify the text in "
   "screen and printed output. The trick to this lies in formatting the "
   "output before it reaches either output device.";

void PrintPage(HDC hPrnDC, HDC hOutDC, WORD wFontSize)
{
   int        nOutDC;
   int        nPrnDC;
   LOGFONT lf;
   HFONT    hFont;
   TEXTMETRIC tm;
   DWORD    dwExtent;
   char    *pText, *pStart, *pEnd;
   int        nSpace;
   int        x, y;
   WORD     wLineWidth;

   /* Store current device context                                         */


   nOutDC = SaveDC(hOutDC);
   nPrnDC = SaveDC(hPrnDC);

   /* Set coordinate system                                                */

   MMLogicalTwips(hOutDC);
   MMLogicalTwips(hPrnDC);

   /* Create proportional font - size is of particular interest.          */

   memset(&lf, 0, sizeof(LOGFONT));
   lf.lfHeight           = wFontSize * 20;
   lf.lfPitchAndFamily = VARIABLE_PITCH;
   hFont                 = CreateFontIndirect(&lf);
   SelectObject(hOutDC, hFont);
   SelectObject(hPrnDC, hFont);
   GetTextMetrics(hPrnDC, &tm);

   x = y = 1440 / 2;        /* Insert 1/2" (720 twips) left and top margins */
   wLineWidth = 5 * 1440;   /* Specify 5" (7200 twips) line width           */

   /* Divide text into lines; breaks are removed and replaced with spaces */
   /* if the text width is less than the specified line width.            */
   /* This formatting is based on printer fonts.                          */

   pText = szText;
```

```
    while (*pText)
    {
       while (*pText && *pText == ' ')
          ++pText;

       pStart = pText;
       nSpace = 0;

       do
       {
          if (!*(pEnd = pText))
             break;              /* End of text                              */

          while (*pText && *pText++ != ' ')
             ;

          ++nSpace;

          SetTextJustification(hPrnDC, 0, 0);
          dwExtent = GetTextExtent(hPrnDC, pStart, pText - pStart - 1);
       } while (LOWORD(dwExtent) < wLineWidth);

       /* The way this loop is designed, the counter slightly overshoots    */
       /* the goal.                                                          */

       if (*pText)
          --nSpace;
       if (*pEnd)
          --pEnd;
       else
          nSpace = 0;     /* Last line not justified                        */

       /* Formatting executes in the output device's context.               */

       SetTextJustification(hOutDC, 0, 0);
       dwExtent = GetTextExtent(hOutDC, pStart, pEnd - pStart);
       if (nSpace > 1)
          SetTextJustification(hOutDC, wLineWidth - LOWORD(dwExtent), nSpace - 1);
       TextOut(hOutDC, x, y, pStart, pEnd - pStart);

       y += tm.tmHeight + tm.tmExternalLeading;
       pText = pEnd;
    }

    RestoreDC(hPrnDC, nPrnDC);
    RestoreDC(hOutDC, nOutDC);
    DeleteObject(hFont);
}
```

```
/****************************************************************************/
/*** GetErrorText                                                        ***/
/***                                                                     ***/
/*** Translates Print Manager error codes into error text.               ***/
/****************************************************************************/

LPSTR GetErrorText(int nErrorCode)
{
   static char *szErrText[] =
   {
      "General error",
      "Aborted by user",
      "Aborted by SPOOLER",
      "TMP directory full",
      "Not enough memory"
   };

   return (szErrText[~nErrorCode]);
}
```

JUSTIFY.C source code

```
/****************************************************************************/
/*** JUSTIFY.C                                                           ***/
/***                                                                     ***/
/*** Framework program for printed output.                               ***/
/*** Contains initialization, main loop and application window functions.***/
/***                                                                     ***/
/*** (c) 1991 by Abacus                                                  ***/
/*** Author: H. Huptasch                                                 ***/
/****************************************************************************/

#include <windows.h>
#include <string.h>

#include "justify.h"
#include "resource.h"

/****************************************************************************/
/*** Global variables                                                    ***/
/****************************************************************************/

/* To avoid changing the instance handle of an application, the handle    */
/* will frequently be declared as a global variable.                      */

HANDLE hInst;
```

```
/***************************************************************************/
/*** Prototypes                                                          ***/
/***************************************************************************/

int  PASCAL       WinMain(HANDLE, HANDLE, LPSTR, int);

/* Local functions for this module                                         */

static BOOL       InitClass(HANDLE);
static void       CallAbout(HWND);

/* Callback functions; must also be exported to .DEF files!                */

LONG FAR PASCAL   MainWndProc(HWND, WORD, WORD, DWORD);
BOOL FAR PASCAL   AboutProc(HWND, WORD, WORD, DWORD);

/***************************************************************************/
/*** WinMain                                                             ***/
/***************************************************************************/

int PASCAL WinMain(HANDLE hNewInst, HANDLE hPrevInst,
                   LPSTR lpCmdLine, int nCmdShow)
{
   HWND hWnd;
   MSG  msg;


   if (!hPrevInst)
      if (!InitClass(hNewInst))
         return (NULL);

   hInst = hNewInst;

   hWnd  = CreateWindow( CLASS_NAME,
                         APPL_NAME,
                         WS_OVERLAPPEDWINDOW,        /* window style      */
                         CW_USEDEFAULT,              /* x position        */
                         CW_USEDEFAULT,              /* y position        */
                         CW_USEDEFAULT,              /* width             */
                         CW_USEDEFAULT,              /* height            */
                         NULL,                       /* parent handle     */
                         NULL,                       /* menu or child ID  */
                         hNewInst,                   /* instance          */
                         NULL );                     /* additional info   */

   if (!hWnd)
      return (NULL);
```

```
   ShowWindow(hWnd, nCmdShow);
   UpdateWindow(hWnd);

   while (GetMessage(&msg, NULL, NULL, NULL))
   {
      TranslateMessage(&msg);
      DispatchMessage(&msg);
   }

   return (msg.wParam);
}

/****************************************************************************/
/*** InitClass:                                                          ***/
/****************************************************************************/

static BOOL InitClass(HANDLE hInstance)
{
   HANDLE     hMemory;
   PWNDCLASS pWndClass;
   BOOL       bSuccess;

   if ((hMemory = LocalAlloc(LPTR, sizeof(WNDCLASS))) != NULL)
   {
      pWndClass = (PWNDCLASS)LocalLock(hMemory);

      pWndClass->style          = NULL;
      pWndClass->lpfnWndProc    = MainWndProc;
      pWndClass->hInstance      = hInstance;
      pWndClass->hIcon          = LoadIcon(hInstance, ICON_NAME);
      pWndClass->hCursor        = LoadCursor(NULL, IDC_ARROW);
      pWndClass->hbrBackground = COLOR_WINDOW + 1;
      pWndClass->lpszMenuName  = MENU_NAME;
      pWndClass->lpszClassName = CLASS_NAME;

      bSuccess = RegisterClass(pWndClass);

      LocalUnlock(hMemory);
      LocalFree(hMemory);
   }
   else
      bSuccess = FALSE;

   return (bSuccess);
}
```

```
/**************************************************************************/
/*** MainWndProc                                                       ***/
/**************************************************************************/

LONG FAR PASCAL MainWndProc(HWND hWnd, WORD wMsg, WORD wParam, DWORD lParam)
{
   static WORD wFontSize = ID_FONT14;
   BOOL        bCallDefProc;

   bCallDefProc = FALSE;

   switch (wMsg)
   {
      case WM_CREATE :
         break;

      case WM_COMMAND :
         switch (wParam)
         {
            case ID_ABOUT :
               CallAbout(hWnd);
               break;

            case ID_QUIT :
               PostMessage(hWnd, WM_CLOSE, 0, 0L);
               break;

            case ID_WORK :
               DoPrint(hWnd, wFontSize);
               break;

            case ID_FONT08 :
            case ID_FONT10 :
            case ID_FONT12 :
            case ID_FONT14 :
            case ID_FONT16 :
               CheckMenuItem(GetMenu(hWnd), wFontSize, MF_UNCHECKED);
               CheckMenuItem(GetMenu(hWnd), wFontSize = wParam, MF_CHECKED);
               InvalidateRect(hWnd, NULL, TRUE);
               break;

            default:
               bCallDefProc = TRUE;
         }
         break;

      case WM_PAINT :
         {
```

```
            PAINTSTRUCT ps;
            HDC         hPrnDC;

            hPrnDC = GetPrinterDC();
            BeginPaint(hWnd, &ps);
            SetTextColor(ps.hdc, GetSysColor(COLOR_WINDOWTEXT));
            SetBkColor(ps.hdc, GetSysColor(COLOR_WINDOW));
            PrintPage(hPrnDC, ps.hdc, wFontSize);
            EndPaint(hWnd, &ps);
            DeleteDC(hPrnDC);
         }
         break;

      case WM_DESTROY :
         PostQuitMessage(0);
         break;

      default :
         bCallDefProc = TRUE;
   }

   return (bCallDefProc ? DefWindowProc(hWnd, wMsg, wParam, lParam) : NULL);
}

/**************************************************************************/
/*** CallAbout                                                         ***/
/**************************************************************************/

static void CallAbout(HWND hWnd)
{
   FARPROC lpProcAbout;

   lpProcAbout = MakeProcInstance(AboutProc, hInst);
   DialogBox(hInst, ABOUTBOX, hWnd, lpProcAbout);
   FreeProcInstance(lpProcAbout);
}

/**************************************************************************/
/*** AboutBox                                                          ***/
/**************************************************************************/

BOOL FAR PASCAL AboutProc(HWND hDlg, WORD wMsg, WORD wParam, DWORD lParam)
{
   switch (wMsg)
   {
      case WM_INITDIALOG :
         return (TRUE);
```

```
      case WM_COMMAND :
         if (wParam == IDOK)
         {
            EndDialog(hDlg, NULL);
            return (TRUE);
         }
         break;
   }
   return (FALSE);
}
```

14 The Serial Interface

This chapter discusses the the serial interface and how you can address this interface under Windows. The end of this chapter lists a demonstration program that encompasses information you read about earlier in this book. The CLPDEMO.EXE program implements the following Windows items:

- The clipboard (see Chapter 9)
- The timer (see Chapter 10)
- The serial interface (discussed in this chapter)

Note: This is not a tutorial on the serial interface. There are many reliable books about the basics of serial communication available at libraries and booksellers.

14.1 Interface Fundamentals

The subject of serial interfaces requires a great deal of adjustment for established MS-DOS programmers. Before we go into more detail about the differences between MS-DOS and Windows serial access, let's look at the basics of interface programming under MS-DOS.

We'll start with the serial interface hardware. Each serial interface has its own port module, called a UART (the acronym for Universal Asynchronous Receiver Transmitter).

When the UART receives a character, it triggers a signal to the 8259 interrupt controller using an interrupt request line. This interrupt controller has direct lines to all of the important components of the hardware, such as the timer, the keyboard, the parallel interface, floppy disk controller and hard disk controller. PCs from AT configuration on up have two of these interrupt controllers, since one eight-line unit is no longer enough. The components are connected in cascading (in a row) fashion.

The interrupt request of the slave (second) interrupt controller is passed to the third line (IRQ2) of the master (first) interrupt controller. The interrupt requests of the UARTS are also passed to the master, to IRQ3 (COM2) and IRQ4 (COM1).

If the bit for this entry in the interrupt mask register is set to 0, which means that this entry is allowed to register an event, then the interrupt controller passes the interrupt request to the CPU by setting the INT signal to logical 1. If the CPU allows the interruption, it causes the bus controller (module 8258) to set INT A (interrupt allowance) to logical 1. This allows the interrupt controller to give the interrupt number, which triggered the interrupt, to the data bus. The CPU reads the data bus, multiplies the interrupt number by 4 and then reads out the resulting memory address (32..64) of the interrupt vector table. The table contains the entry addresses of each interrupt handling routine. The CPU branches to this routine after backing up all of the status register contents on the stack.

This point takes us from hardware to software. Since MS-DOS no longer pays attention to whether the characters contiguous to the serial interface are received and backed up, until now you had to write your own interrupt service routines to implement this. Otherwise, you could lose characters at higher baud rates. A reference to this kind of function was entered at the place in the interrupt table that is read out during an interface interrupt.

Interrupt vector table

Address in dec.	Interrupt vector	Meaning
		Interrupts triggered by processor:
00 - 03	0	Divide by zero
04 - 07	1	Single step mode
08 - 11	2	Non-masked interrupt (NMI)
12 - 15	3	Breakpoint
16 - 19	4	Overflow
20 - 23	5	Print screen (hardcopy)
24 - 27	6	-
28 - 31	7	-
		Interrupts triggered by interrupt controller:
32 - 35	8 (IRQ 0)	Timer component (system clock)
36 - 39	9 (IRQ 1)	Keyboard
40 - 43	A (IRQ 2)	Slave controller output (on AT)
44 - 47	B (IRQ 3)	COM2: second serial interface
48 - 51	C (IRQ 4)	COM1: first serial interface
52 - 55	D (IRQ 5)	Hard drive controller
56 - 59	E (IRQ 6)	Floppy disk controller
60 - 63	F (IRQ 7)	Parallel interfaces (LPT)

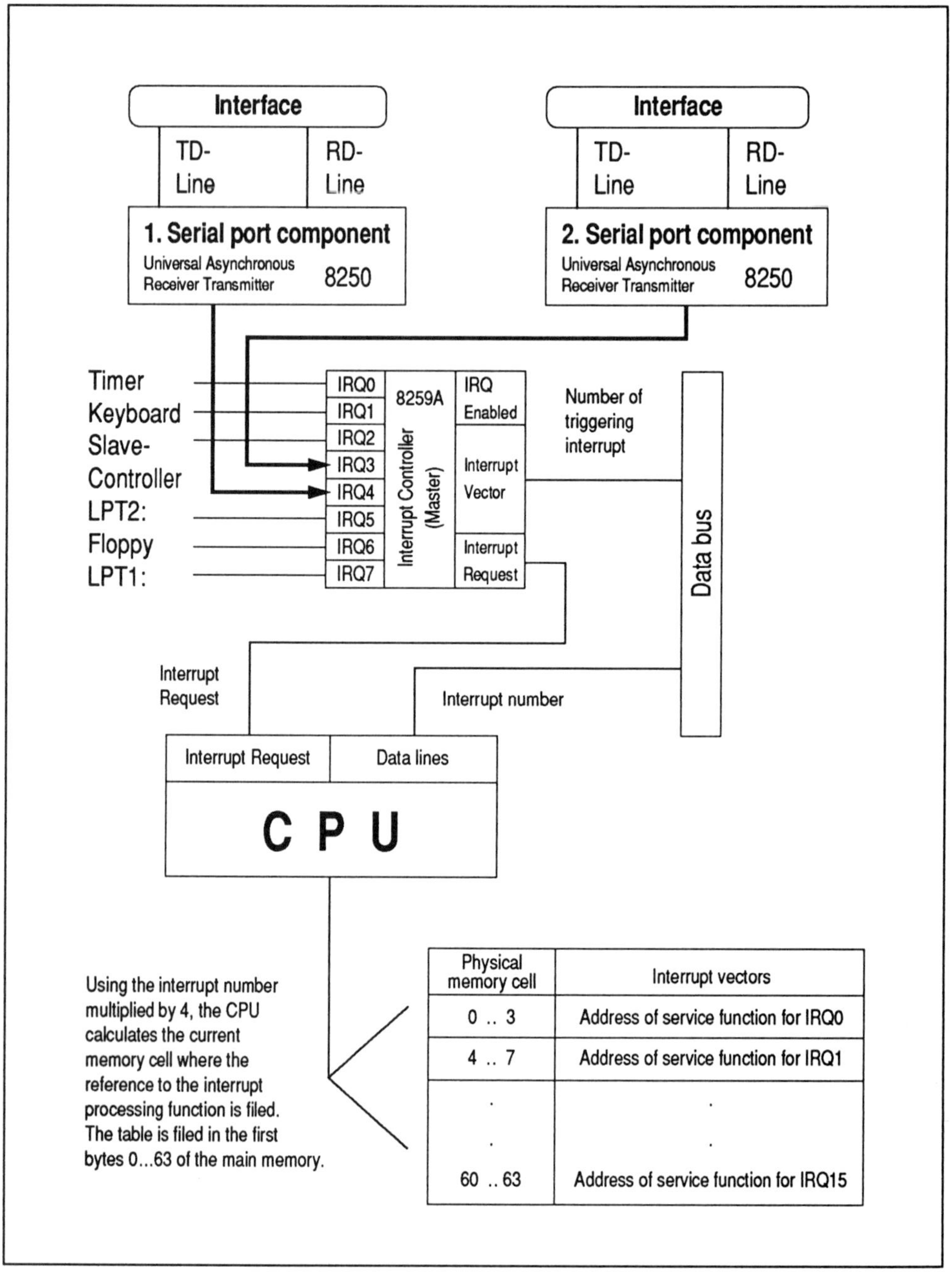

Interrupt processing on a PC

Interrupt processing runs very differently under Windows than it does under DOS. Windows no longer lets the programmer perform such far-reaching operations. A Windows device driver called COMM.DRV has replaced such routines. It's the only module allowed to work directly with the serial interface using interrupt vectors. It places all incoming data in the system message queue.

Drivers

Along with COMM.DRV, the device drivers for the mouse (MOUSE.DRV) and the keyboard (KEYBOARD.DRV) place their data in the system message queue. The system clock interrupts are an exception to this rule. The appropriate driver calls the SYSTEM.DRV driver directly by FAR call, a function within the USER.EXE module. See Chapter 10 for more information on timers.

The USER.EXE module empties the message queue and transmits the data to the appropriate application. USER.EXE does this by placing the data in a reception buffer, which is created by the application when the interface was opened. The data are sent in the reverse direction (i.e., from USER.EXE to COMM.DRV), and then from the send buffer to the interface.

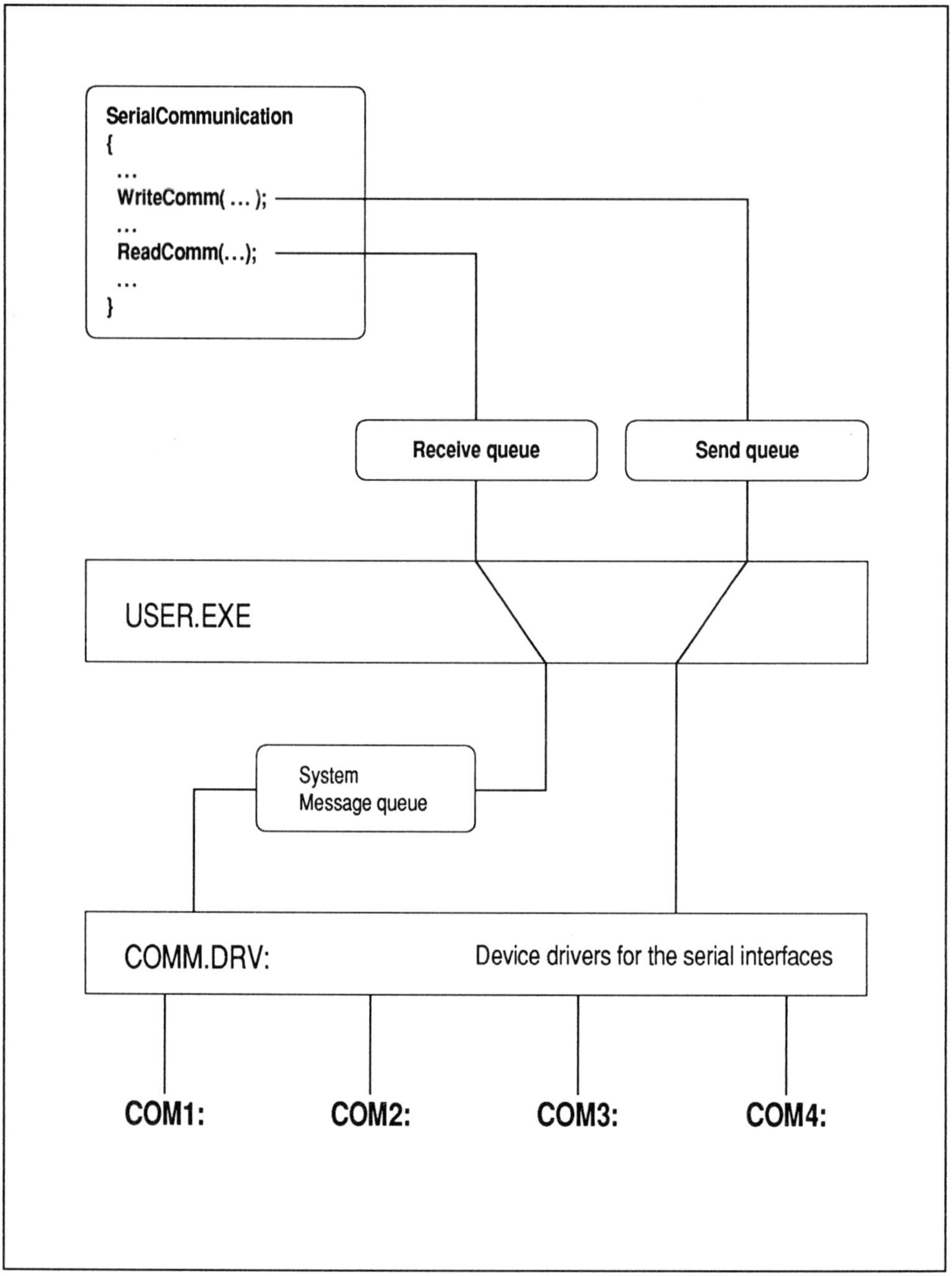

Communicating with serial interfaces

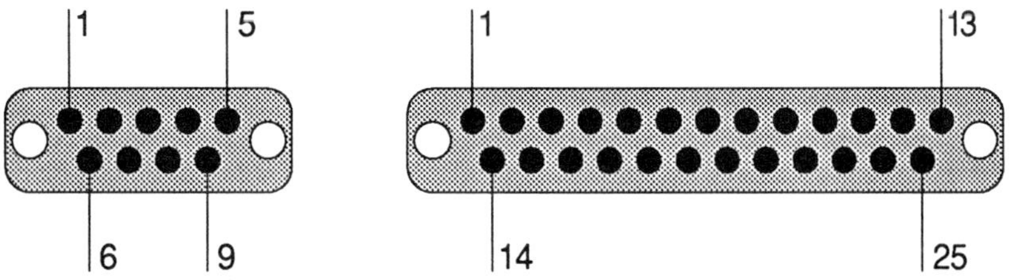

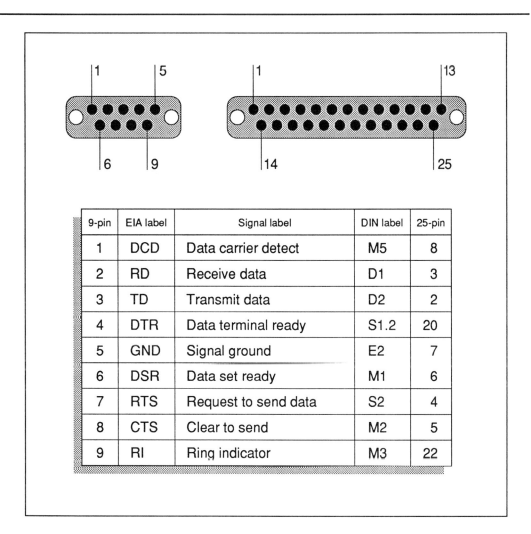

9-pin	EIA label	Signal label	DIN label	25-pin
1	DCD	Data carrier detect	M5	8
2	RD	Receive data	D1	3
3	TD	Transmit data	D2	2
4	DTR	Data terminal ready	S1.2	20
5	GND	Signal ground	E2	7
6	DSR	Data set ready	M1	6
7	RTS	Request to send data	S2	4
8	CTS	Clear to send	M2	5
9	RI	Ring indicator	M3	22

RS-232 interface pin layout

14.2 Programming the Serial Interface

Now that you know something about how the serial interface communicates with hardware and software, let's examine how Windows and the communication ports interact.

14.2.1 Initialization

You need a DeviceControlBlock to initialize a serial interface under Windows. The data structure DCB defines the device control block while the BuildCommDCB function initializes this block. You pass a string of characters to the interface in the first parameter. These characters specify the basic setting of the serial interface. The information is stored in the same order as in the MS-DOS MODE command.

Example: If you wanted to have the first serial interface work with a line speed of 9600 baud, 8 data bits, 2 stop bits and no parity, the MODE command would read:

```
MODE COM1:9600,n,8,2
```

This is the same string ("COM1:9600,n,8,2") that you have to pass to the BuildCommDCB function. There are different ways of generating this kind of initialization.

First, you could include such a default setting in the program code, as the example shows:

```
static char  szDefSetting[] =  "COM1:9600,n,8,2" ;
```

It's a lot smarter and more convenient to take the serial interface default values from the WIN.INI file. WIN.INI has its own range, called [ports], where you can find the defaults for all existing interfaces in the system. The Control Panel can be used to change these settings. Here's an excerpt from WIN.INI:

```
[ports]
COM1:=9600,n,8,1
COM2:=9600,n,8,1
COM3:=9600,n,8,1
COM4:=9600,n,8,1
```

For example, if you wish to access values, for the first serial interface, from within a program, call GetProfileString in the following manner:

```
GetProfileString((LPSTR) "[ports]",        // Range
                 (LPSTR) "COM1",           // Point
                 (LPSTR) szDefSetting,     // Own defaults
                 (LPSTR) szStdSetting );   // Default values
```

The function searches WIN.INI, in the [ports] range, for the point "COM1". If the function is successful, it places the default values in <szStdSetting> in WIN.INI. If the function doesn't find the point, it copies its own default settings to <szStdSetting>.

Next, the following command sequence creates the device control block:

```
if(BuildCommDCB(szSetting, &ComDCB) != 0)
{
     /*
       Error handling
 ...
       Could not create DCB
     */
}
```

14.2.2 Special settings

Now that we have covered the fundamentals, we can start working with the interface. Although we already set the fundamental parameters of the interface when we created the DCB, the function SetCommState still offers many other configuration options to hardware and Xon/Xoff flow controls. A glance at the DCB data structure shows that you can still set many serial parameters. The range goes a lot farther than what would be possible with a MODE command.

The DeviceControlBlock data structure DCB

BYTE Id	Communications port code digit CID
WORD BaudRate	Current baud rate
BYTE ByteSize	Number of data bits (4-8)
BYTE Parity	0-4=None, Odd, Even, Mark, Space
BYTE StopBits	0,1,2 equals: 1, 1.5, 2
WORD RlsTimeout	Set Timeout time to RLSD
WORD CtsTimeout	Set Timeout time to CTS
WORD DsrTimeout	Set Timeout time to DSR
	1st Bit field:
BYTE fBinary	Binary mode, an EOF test
BYTE fRtsDisable	Doesn't allow RTS signal
BYTE fParity	Turn on parity check
BYTE fOutxCtsFlow	CTS handshaking during transmission
BYTE fOutxDsrFlow	DSR handshaking during transmission
BYTE fDummy	Dummy that fills up the bit field
	2nd Bit field:
BYTE fDtrDisable	Doesn't allow DTR signal
BYTE fOutX	Release output X-ON/X-OFF
BYTE fInX	Release input X-ON/X-OFF
BYTE fPeChar	Release parity error replacement character
BYTE fNull	Release zero strippings
BYTE fChEvt	Release trans. character events
BYTE fDtrflow	DTR handshake during reception
BYTE fRtsflow	RTS handshake during reception
BYTE fDummy2	Dummy that fills up the bit field
char XonChar	Xon character for transm. and recept char
XoffChar	Xoff character for transm. and recep
WORD XonLim	Transmit X-ON threshold
WORD XoffLim	Transmit X-OFF threshold
char PeChar	Parity error replacement character
char EofChar	"End of File" character
char EvtChar	"Received Event" character
WORD TxDelay	Transmission delay between character

To set these parameters, you can update the device control block directly in program code, or through the user with the dialog box.

After adapting the device control block to special requirements, you can re-initialize by calling SetCommState:

```
if(SetCommState(&ComDCB) != 0)
{
    /*
       Initialization error
    */
}
```

To get an overview of the current interface setting, call SetCommState's counterpart:

```
GetCommState(&ComDCB);
```

Note: Remember that under Windows, the data structures are compressed. It is imperative that you use the compiler switch -Zp to transpose the application to ensure proper execution. If the switch is not set, accessing Windows structures, such as DCB in our example, will result in incorrect values.

14.2.3 Opening the serial interface

After initializing the interface according to our requirements, you must configure the send and receive buffers by opening the interface. Call OpenComm and pass the following parameters:

- The interface to be opened (e.g., "COM1:")
- The size of the send buffer in bytes
- The size of the receive buffer in bytes

These buffers comprise a visible interface to the serial communications port for the application programmer. USER.EXE, the Windows module, maintains them directly.

```
/*---< Open the serial interface >---*/
CID = OpenComm((LPSTR) szComName, nRxBufferSize,
                              nTxBufferSize);
```

If you opened the interface correctly, the OpenComm function delivers a single identification digit to the interface. Ordinarily it's a 0 for COM1:, a 1 for COM2:, a 2 for COM3: and a 3 for COM4:. These ID numbers applied to earlier versions of Windows, but may change in later versions. We recommend that you use the value returned by OpenComm.

From now on, this communication identification digit (CID for short) is the single-valued reference to the interface. All of the following write or read tasks use this CID to identify the interface from which they are reading or to which they are writing.

14.2.4 Reading and writing

Access to serial interface

There are two functions provided by the Windows API for placing data in the send buffer, or taking data from the receive buffer. They are called WriteComm and ReadComm.

The first of three parameters (nCid) is identical for both functions. A Long pointer to the data to be filed in the send buffer, as well as information about the length of the data, follows in WriteComm. One disadvantage to the WriteComm function is that it overwrites data in the send buffer when there is not enough room for the new data. To prevent this from happening, check how much data the buffer can accept before writing data. Call GetCommError, which gives you a current status overview of the interface. To do this, pass the nCid and a variable from COMSTAT.

The COMSTAT status information structure

BYTE fCtsHold	Send mode CTS hold
BYTE fDsrHold	Send mode DSR hold
BYTE fRlsdHold	Send mode RLSD hold
BYTE fXoffHold	Xoff signal received
BYTE fXoffSent	Xoff signal sent
BYTE fEof	"End of file" character found
BYTE fTxim	character to be sent
WORD cbInQue	No. characters in reception buffer
WORD cbOutQue	No. characters in send buffer

The following code fragment shows the essential steps you should address when you send data.

```
/*--------------< Place data in send buffer >----------*/
COMSTAT  CommStatus;                              // Interface status variable
GetCommError(nCid,(COMSTAT FAR*) &CommStatus); // Get status
nWritten = WriteComm(nCid,                        // Communications port
                     (LPSTR) lpData,              // Pointer to data
                      min( lstrlen(lpData),
                           TxQueSize - CommStatus.cbOutQue));
                                                  // Send only as many data as the
                                                  // send buffer can accommodate
if(nWritten < 0)
{
    // Determine cause
    GetCommError(nCid, (COMSTAT FAR *) &ComStatus); // Cause
      /*
```

```
        Error handling
      */
}
```

The nWrittenChars return value gives the WriteComm function information about the success of the write task. It indicates how many characters were actually written. It displays an error by returning negative values, whose absolute value also represents the number of written characters. A subsequent GetCommError call gives information about the cause of the error. Its return value clearly identifies the error (see list).

List of errors that can occur in serial communication

Constant	Value	Meaning
CE_RXOVER	0x0001	Receive buffer overrun
CE_OVERRUN	0x0002	Receive overrun error
CE_RXPARITY	0x0004	Receive parity error
CE_FRAME	0x0008	Receive frame error
CE_BREAK	0x0010	Break occurred
CE_CTSTO	0x0020	CTS timeout
CE_DSRTO	0x0040	DSR timeout
CE_RLSDTO	0x0080	RLSD timeout
CE_TXFULL	0x0100	Send buffer is full

Now that we know how data are output to the serial interface, it's time to learn about reading, or entering, characters. We mentioned the function in charge of this. Here, too, you use the first parameter to tell the function which interface to read from. The second parameter is a Long pointer to a string variable, into where the data are supposed to be copied. The last parameter specifies the maximum number of characters that can be copied.

Before trying to read characters from the receive buffer, you should first determine whether there are any data in there. Call GetCommError to get this information from the status variable.

Here's what a code fragment for reading characters would look like:

```
/*------------< Read data from the receive buffer >--------*/
COMSTAT   ComStatus;        // Status variable
GetCommError(nCid, (COMSTAT FAR *) &ComStatus);
if(ComStatus.cbInQue)
{
   // There are data in the receive buffer, begin reading...
```

```
    nRead = ReadComm(nCid, (LPSTR) szData, nMaxChars);
    if(nRead < 0)
    {
        // An error has occurred, determine cause..
        nError = GetCommError(CID, (COMSTAT FAR *) &ComStatus);
        /*
           Error handling
        */
    }
}
```

As we already know from the return value of the WriteComm function, ReadComm also displays how many characters it can actually read. If the number is negative, then the absolute value gives information about the number of characters read. In this case, call GetCommError to get more information about the error.

14.2.5 Closing the interface

Part of a proper connection release involves closing the communications port. Calling this function sends out all of the characters still in the send buffer, then releases the memory that was allocated for the send and receive buffers.

```
/*----------< Close the serial interface >---*/
CloseComm(nCid);
```

14.3 Programming Hints

Now that we've discussed handling serial interfaces under Windows, we'll give you some programming hints.

First, remember that multitasking under Windows was realized using the message polling principle. This also applies to Windows 3. True multitasking, based on the process known as time slicing, only takes place between the Windows session (Windows and all of the Windows applications that are running) and the standard MS-DOS applications running parallel to Windows applications.

In this environment, interface handling is a true break in style. After all, a Windows programmer is used to reacting to all kinds of information. But when errors occur in the serial interface, no messages are sent to Windows. So, it's up to the programmer to check the reception buffer regularly for newly arrived characters.

If the following construction resolved this, then multitasking under Windows would not exist:

```
do
{
  // we are waiting for incoming characters ...
  GetCommError(CID, (COMSTATUS FAR *) &ComStatus);
}
 while(!ComStatus.cbInQue);
```

Solving such a problem would require another powerful Windows component—the timer. See Chapter 10 of this book for more information about the timer.

For now, all you need to know is that the timer can check the receive buffer at specified intervals (e.g., one call per second). To do this, install a timer that calls a function that requests the reception buffer's status, removing characters if necessary.

The demonstration program in this chapter is an example of this. You'll find everything you need to install such a function in the CLPLINE.C module (look in the PollRxQueue routine of this module).

Finally, we'll present another alternative to the timer. If you replace the GetMessage function with a PeekMessage function within the message loop, you can create an ELSE branch. Whenever there aren't any messages in the applications message queue, the ELSE branch prompts for the interface status.

```
/*--------------------< Message loop >-------------------------*/
while (TRUE)
{
  bMsgAvail = PeekMessage((LPMSG)&msg, NULL, 0, 0, PM_REMOVE);
  if(bMsgAvail)                       // Message available
  {
    if (msg.message == WM_QUIT)       // Quit program
    {
      return (msg.wParam);            // wP of the last message
                                      // as return value
    }
    if (!(hDlgPipe != NULL && IsDialogMessage(hDlgPipe,
         (LPMSG)&msg)))
    {
      TranslateMessage((LPMSG)&msg); // Translate message
      DispatchMessage((LPMSG)&msg);  // Dispatch message
    }
  }
  else
    {
    /*-----------------------< Idle loop >------------------*/
    /*
      Check interface status, and if necessary, react.
    */
    }
}
```

14.4 Interface Layout and Null Modems

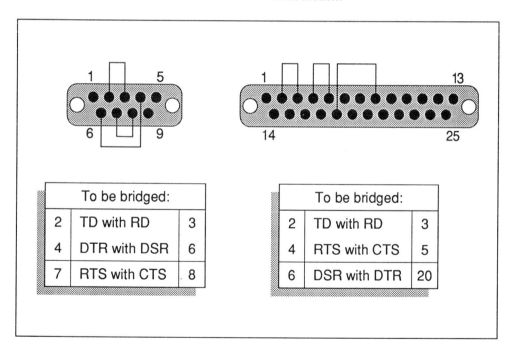

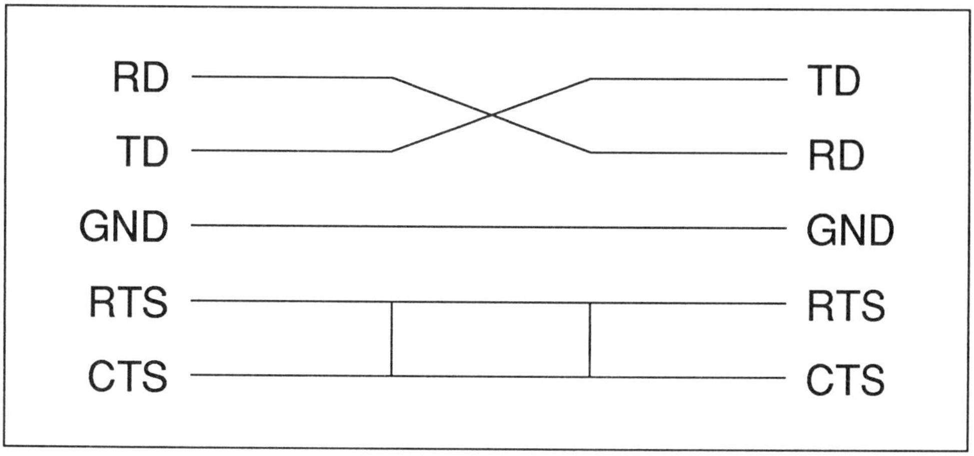

Null modem

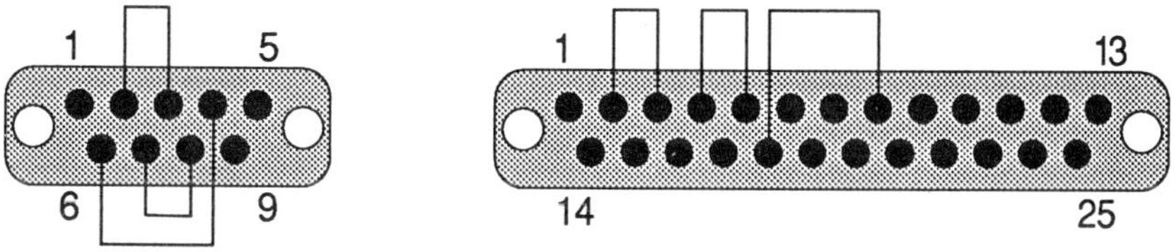

To be bridged:		
2	TD with RD	3
4	DTR with DSR	6
7	RTS with CTS	8

To be bridged:		
2	TD with RD	3
4	RTS with CTS	5
6	DSR with DTR	20

Pin layout

14.5 The Parallel Interface

Most users only associate serial interfaces with telecommunication. You can also use serial interfaces for directly processing the parallel interface.

Direct processing means triggering a device connected to the parallel port (usually a printer) by bypassing the GDI and all of the Windows printer drivers.

If you use communication functions on a parallel interface, remember that there are a few differences from working with the serial interface.

Unlike serial ports, parallel ports (LPTx) are not interrupt driven. This factor affects the OpenComm function. If you use OpenComm to open a parallel port, you don't need a receive or send buffer. The program doesn't pay any more attention to the parameters that define the sizes of these buffers. So, the following instruction is enough to correctly open the interface:

```
/*---------< Opening a parallel interface >------*/
LptId = OpenComm((LPSTR) "LPT1", 0, 0);
```

The ReadComm function also behaves differently in parallel access than it does in serial access. If you use this function to access the parallel interface, it will always give you a return value of NULL.

List of errors that could occur with the parallel interface

Constant	Value	Meaning
CE_PTO	0x0200	LPTx Timeout
CE_IOE	0x0400	LPTx I/O error
CE_DNS	0x0800	LPTx device is not Online
CE_OOP	0x1000	LPTx No paper error
CE_MODE	0x8000	Operation mode not supported

14.6 Communication Functions

`int BuildCommDCB(DCB FAR * lpDCB)`

Creates a device control block.

`ClearCommBreak(int nCid)`

Resets the interrupt status.

`int CloseComm(int nCid)`

Closing the communication interface.

`EscapeCommFunction(int nCid, int nEscape)`

Lets you send or delete RTS and DTS signals. You can also instruct the device to behave as though it had received an XON or XOFF character.

`int FlushComm(int nCid, int nQueue)`

Empties the specified send or reception buffer.

`int GetCommError(int nCid, COMSTAT FAR * lpCommState)`

Returns more exact information about any errors that might occur (fills a COMSTAT data structure).

`int GetCommEventMask(int nCid, int nEventMask)`

Returns information about recent events and deletes the event mask.

`int GetCommState(DCB FAR * lpDCB)`

Supplies extensive information, defined in the DCB data structure, about the current settings of the communications interface.

`int OpenComm(LPSTR lpCommName, int TxQueSize, int RxQueSize)`

Opens a communication interface (parallel and serial ports).

```
int ReadComm(int nCid, LPSTR lpBuffer, int nMaxChars)
```

Reads the received data from the installed receive buffer.

```
int SetCommBreak(int nCid)
```

Interrupts the sending process and transfers the device to interrupt status.

```
int SetCommState((DCB FAR *) lpDCB)
```

Sets communication interface with device control block default values.

```
int TransmitCommChar(int nCid, char cCharacter)
```

Places a character at the beginning of the send queue so that it is sent as the next character.

```
UngetCommChar(int nCid, char cCharacter)
```

Specifies which character is next to be read from the receive buffer.

```
int WriteCommChar(int nCid, LPSTR lpData, int nDataSize)
```

Places data in the send buffer, from where they pass to the interface.

14.7 Application: CLPDEMO.EXE

This application demonstrates clipboard, timer and serial access. Select and copy data from another application (e.g., Word for Windows) then call the CLPDEMO.EXE application. You can view the contents of the clipboard, specify serial port access and, provided that the selected data is text, transmit it over the serial interface.

CLPDEMO.EXE contains the following menus and menu items.

©
: Selecting this menu title displays a pair of animated About boxes, which describe the task of CLPDEMO.EXE.

File
: Allows clipboard text data to be transmitted over the serial interface (**Clipboard -> Line...**), and allows the user to exit the application (**Exit...**).

Edit
: Gives the user a choice of view modes (including a view of the owner), and provides the option of cutting all data from the clipboard.

Communication
: Offers items for configuring the serial interface (**Interface Setup...**), and controlling serial connection (**Connect...** and **Disconnect...**).

CLPFILE.H include file

```
/************************************************************************
 C L P F I L E . H     Header file for clipboard demo application
                       Defines data structures for a Clipboard file (.CLP)
                       into which clipboard contents can be stored.
************************************************************************/

typedef struct tagCLPHEADER
{
   WORD  wFileId,            // File ID: CLP_ID == 0xc350
         wFormatCount;       // Current number of formats in the file

} CLPHEADER;
```

```
typedef struct tagCLPITEMINFO
{
   WORD   wFormatId;          // Data format ID
   LONG   lDataLength;        // Length of data in bytes
   LONG   lDataOffset;        // 1st data byte's position relative to
                              // start of file
   char   szPrivateName[79]; // Name of generated private format
} CLPITEMINFO;
```

CLPPARAM.H include file

```
/************************************************************************
 ComSetup.H              Header file for ComSetup.C module
************************************************************************/
#define TXQUEUE          0
#define RXQUEUE          1

#define SI_BADID              (-1)     /* Invalid or unsupported ID   */
#define SI_OPEN               (-2)     /* Device Already Open         */
#define SI_NOPEN              (-3)     /* Device Not Open             */
#define SI_MEMORY             (-4)     /* Unable to allocate queues   */
#define SI_DEFAULT            (-5)     /* Error in default parameters */
#define SI_HARDWARE           (-10)    /* Hardware Not Present        */
#define SI_BYTESIZE           (-11)    /* Illegal Byte Size           */
#define SI_BAUDRATE           (-12)    /* Unsupported BaudRate        */

#define SI_RXOVER             0x1001   /* Receive Queue overflow      */
#define SI_OVERRUN            0x1002   /* Receive Overrun Error       */
#define SI_RXPARITY           0x1004   /* Receive Parity Error        */
#define SI_FRAME              0x1008   /* Receive Framing error       */
#define SI_BREAK              0x1010   /* Break Detected              */
#define SI_CTSTO              0x1020   /* CTS Timeout                 */
#define SI_DSRTO              0x1040   /* DSR Timeout                 */
#define SI_RLSDTO             0x1080   /* RLSD Timeout                */
#define SI_TXFULL             0x1100   /* TX Queue is full            */
#define SI_PTO                0x1200   /* LPTx Timeout                */
#define SI_IOE                0x1400   /* LPTx I/O Error              */
#define SI_DNS                0x1800   /* LPTx Device not selected    */
#define SI_OOP                0x2000   /* LPTx Out-Of-Paper           */
#define SI_MODE               0x9000   /* Requested mode unsupported  */

/*=============================< Data types >==========================*/
typedef struct
{
  WORD       wBaudRate;                /* Transfer rate               */
  BYTE       bByteSize,                /* Number of data bits         */
             bStopBits,                /* Number of stop bits         */
```

```
            bPortId,                 /* Interface number          */
            bParity;                 /* Type of parity check      */
  int       nRxQueSize,              /* Receive buffer size       */
            nTxQueSize,              /* Send buffer size          */
            nRxDelay;                /* Reading interval          */
}COMMPORTPARAM;
```

CLP_RC.H include file

```
/***************************************************************************
 WinAppRc.H      Resource definition file for clipboard demo application
***************************************************************************/

/*------------------------------< Defines >--------------------------------*/
#define FIRSTFORMATITEM     300   // First MenuItemId

#define MI_ABOUT            200
#define MI_QUIT             201
#define MI_SHOW             202
#define MI_WRITE            213
#define MI_DELETE           214
#define MI_OWNER            215
#define MI_SEPARAT          216
#define MI_CONNECT          217
#define MI_DISCONNECT       218
#define MI_COMSETUP         219

#define LB_FORMAT           120
#define EB_Owner            121
#define EB_Viewer           122
#define PB_SHOW             123

#define EB_FILE             500
#define EB_PATH             501
#define LB_FILES            600

#define PB_OK              1000
#define PB_ABB             1001

/********************************** Communication port parameters    */
#define CB_BAUD            200             /* Baud rate       */
#define CB_PORT            201             /* Interface       */
#define RB_7DB             210             /* 7 data bits     */
#define RB_8DB             211             /* 8 data bits     */
#define RB_1SB             212             /* 1 stop bit      */
#define RB_2SB             213             /* 1.5 stop bits   */
#define RB_3SB             214             /* 2 stop bits     */
```

```
#define RB_NONE            215                   /* NO parity        */
#define RB_ODD             216                   /* ODD parity       */
#define RB_EVEN            217                   /* EVEN parity      */
#define EB_TXSIZE          218                   /* TX buffer size   */
#define EB_RXSIZE          219                   /* RX buffer size   */
#define EB_RXDELAY         220                   /* RX read interval */


/*------------------------------------------------------------------------------*/
/*                 Global constant arrangement                                  */
/*------------------------------------------------------------------------------*/

#define    MAXPATHLEN              120
```

CLPDEMO.RC resource file

```
#include <windows.h>
#include "CLP_RC.H"
#include "CLPPARAM.H"
rcinclude CLPDEMO.DLG

OpenCut   BITMAP   OPENCUT.BMP
CloseCut BITMAP   CLOSECUT.BMP
OpenPin   BITMAP   OPENPIN.BMP
ClosePin BITMAP   CLOSEPIN.BMP
AppIcon   ICON     CLPDEMO.ICO

Menu  MENU
   Begin
       MENUITEM "",                          MI_ABOUT

       POPUP "&File"
       Begin
         MENUITEM "&Clipboard --> Line ...", MI_WRITE  GRAYED
         MENUITEM SEPARATOR
         MENUITEM "E&xit...",    MI_QUIT
       End

       POPUP "&Edit"
       Begin
         POPUP "&View"
         BEGIN
          MENUITEM "&Owner",         MI_OWNER
        END
         MENUITEM "C&ut",            MI_DELETE
       End
```

```
        POPUP "&Communication"
        Begin
          MENUITEM "&Connect...",        MI_CONNECT     GRAYED
          MENUITEM "&Disconnect...",         MI_DISCONNECT  GRAYED
          MENUITEM SEPARATOR
          MENUITEM "Interface &Setup..." , MI_COMSETUP
        End
    End

STRINGTABLE
BEGIN
    CF_TEXT,             "Text"
    CF_BITMAP,           "Bitmap"
    CF_METAFILEPICT,     "Metafile graphic"
    CF_SYLK,             "Microsoft Symbolic Link (SYLK)"
    CF_DIF,              "Software Arts' Data Interchange"
    CF_TIFF,             "Tag Image File"
    CF_OEMTEXT,          "OEM text"
    CF_DSPTEXT,          "Text in private format"
    CF_DSPBITMAP,        "Bitmap in private format"
    CF_DSPMETAFILEPICT,"Metafile graphic-priv. format"
    CF_PALETTE,          "log. color palette"
    SI_BADID,            "Bad or unsupported ID"
    SI_BAUDRATE,         "Unsupported baud rate"
    SI_BYTESIZE,         "Bad data bit size"
    SI_DEFAULT,          "Error in default parameters"
    SI_HARDWARE,         "Interface not connected"
    SI_MEMORY,           "Memory conflict: Send - receive buffers\nnot responding"
    SI_NOPEN,            "Interface could not be opened"
    SI_OPEN,             "Interface is already open"
    SI_MODE,             "Unsupported mode or port ID"
    SI_OVERRUN,          "Hardware-based data loss"
    SI_FRAME,            "LPTn: Feed error"
    SI_BREAK,            "Hardware BREAK registered"
    SI_CTSTO,            "CTS (Clear To Send) timeout"
    SI_DSRTO,            "DSR (Data Set Ready) timeout"
    SI_RLSDTO,           "CD  (Carrier Detection) timeout"
    SI_TXFULL,           "Send buffer full"
    SI_RXOVER,           "Receive buffer overflow"
    SI_RXPARITY,         "Parity error"
    SI_PTO,              "LPTn: Timeout"
    SI_IOE,              "LPTn: I/O error"
    SI_DNS,              "LPTn: Device not selected"
    SI_OOP,              "LPTn: Out of Paper"
END
```

CLPDEMO.DLG dialog box file

```
COMSETUP DIALOG LOADONCALL MOVEABLE DISCARDABLE 75, 29, 277, 134
CAPTION "Serial Interface"
FONT 8, "Helv"
STYLE WS_BORDER | WS_CAPTION | WS_DLGFRAME | WS_POPUP
BEGIN
    CONTROL "Data Bits", 101, "button", BS_GROUPBOX | WS_CHILD, 10, 81, 97, 27
    CONTROL "Buffer Size", 102, "button", BS_GROUPBOX | WS_CHILD, 118, 57, 151,
52
    CONTROL "Stop Bits", 103, "button", BS_GROUPBOX | WS_CHILD, 9, 52, 97, 26
    CONTROL "Parity check", 104, "button", BS_GROUPBOX | WS_CHILD, 117, 9, 152,
41
    CONTROL "OK", 1, "button", BS_DEFPUSHBUTTON | WS_TABSTOP | WS_CHILD, 19, 116,
41, 12
    CONTROL "Cancel", 2, "button", BS_PUSHBUTTON | WS_TABSTOP | WS_CHILD, 207,
116, 51, 12
    CONTROL "Baud Rate:", -1, "static", SS_LEFT | WS_CHILD, 11, 19, 40, 8
    CONTROL "Interface:", -1, "static", SS_LEFT | WS_CHILD, 10, 36, 46, 8
    CONTROL "", 200, "combobox", CBS_DROPDOWNLIST | WS_VSCROLL | WS_CHILD, 58,
17, 47, 62
    CONTROL "", 201, "combobox", CBS_DROPDOWNLIST | WS_VSCROLL | WS_CHILD, 59,
34, 46, 48
    CONTROL "1", 212, "button", BS_AUTORADIOBUTTON | WS_GROUP | WS_TABSTOP |
WS_CHILD, 15, 63, 26, 11
    CONTROL "1.5", 213, "button", BS_AUTORADIOBUTTON | WS_TABSTOP | WS_CHILD, 47,
63, 26, 11
    CONTROL "2", 214, "button", BS_AUTORADIOBUTTON | WS_TABSTOP | WS_CHILD, 80,
63, 21, 11
    CONTROL "7", 210, "button", BS_AUTORADIOBUTTON | WS_GROUP | WS_TABSTOP |
WS_CHILD, 48, 93, 26, 11
    CONTROL "8", 211, "button", BS_AUTORADIOBUTTON | WS_TABSTOP | WS_CHILD, 80,
93, 23, 12
    CONTROL "none", 215, "button", BS_AUTORADIOBUTTON | WS_GROUP | WS_TABSTOP |
WS_CHILD, 123, 33, 37, 12
    CONTROL "odd", 216, "button", BS_AUTORADIOBUTTON | WS_TABSTOP | WS_CHILD,
165, 33, 49, 12
    CONTROL "even", 217, "button", BS_AUTORADIOBUTTON | WS_TABSTOP | WS_CHILD,
219, 33, 41, 12
    CONTROL "Tx Buffer:", -1, "static", SS_LEFT | WS_CHILD, 124, 73, 36, 10
    CONTROL "Rx Buffer:", -1, "static", SS_LEFT | WS_CHILD, 200, 73, 39, 10
    CONTROL "Rx Reading Interval:", -1, "static", SS_LEFT | WS_CHILD, 124, 92,
78, 12
    CONTROL "ms", -1, "static", SS_LEFT | WS_CHILD, 238, 92, 16, 8
    CONTROL "", 218, "edit", ES_LEFT | WS_BORDER | WS_TABSTOP | WS_CHILD, 169,
71, 20, 12
```

```
    CONTROL "", 219, "edit", ES_LEFT | WS_BORDER | WS_TABSTOP | WS_CHILD, 243,
71, 20, 12
    CONTROL "", 220, "edit", ES_LEFT | WS_BORDER | WS_TABSTOP | WS_CHILD, 206,
91, 25, 12
END

FILESELECT DIALOG LOADONCALL MOVEABLE DISCARDABLE 11, 8, 153, 117
STYLE WS_DLGFRAME | WS_POPUP
BEGIN
    CONTROL "Filename:", 100, "static", SS_LEFT | WS_CHILD, 86, 26, 41, 12
    CONTROL "", 500, "edit", ES_LEFT | WS_BORDER | WS_TABSTOP | WS_CHILD, 86, 36,
60, 12
    CONTROL "Path:", 101, "static", SS_LEFT | WS_CHILD, 9, 8, 23, 12
    CONTROL "", 501, "edit", ES_LEFT | WS_BORDER | WS_TABSTOP | WS_CHILD, 35, 7,
112, 12
    CONTROL "", 600, "listbox", LBS_NOTIFY | LBS_SORT | LBS_STANDARD | WS_BORDER
| WS_VSCROLL | WS_TABSTOP | WS_CHILD, 6, 22, 70, 89
    CONTROL "OK", 1000, "button", BS_DEFPUSHBUTTON | WS_TABSTOP | WS_CHILD, 92,
75, 50, 13
    CONTROL "Cancel", 1001, "button", BS_PUSHBUTTON | WS_TABSTOP | WS_CHILD, 92,
97, 50, 13
END

INTROBOX DIALOG LOADONCALL MOVEABLE DISCARDABLE 90, 24, 189, 114
FONT 10, "Helv"
STYLE WS_DLGFRAME | WS_POPUP
BEGIN
    CONTROL "Clip && Connect", 101, "static", SS_CENTER | WS_CHILD, 1, 6, 187, 12
    CONTROL "Copyright  1990", 103, "static", SS_CENTER | WS_CHILD, 0, 70, 189,
10
    CONTROL "Abacus", 104, "static", SS_CENTER | WS_CHILD, 0, 80, 189, 11
    CONTROL "Authors: D.Honekamp && P.Wilken", 106, "static", SS_CENTER |
WS_CHILD, 0, 98, 188, 11
END
```

CLPDEMO.DEF module definition file

```
NAME            CLPDEMO
DESCRIPTION     'Clipboard application'
EXETYPE         WINDOWS
STUB            'winstub.exe'

CODE            PRELOAD MOVEABLE

DATA            PRELOAD MOVEABLE MULTIPLE

HEAPSIZE        0x2000
```

```
STACKSIZE        0x2000

EXPORTS          WndProc
                 MdfCommSetup
                 MdfIntroBox
                 PollRxQueue
```

CLPDEMO.MAK MAKE file

```
Mod  = S
Warn = 2

.c.obj:
   cl -W$(Warn) -c -Os -Zpe -Gsw -A$(Mod) $*.c

.rc.res:
   rc -r $*.rc

ALL: clpdemo.exe

clpboard.obj:  clpboard.c

clpparam.obj:  clpparam.c clpparam.h

clpline.obj:   clpline.c

clpintro.obj:  clpintro.c

clpdemo.obj:   clpdemo.c

clpdemo.res:   clpdemo.rc   clpdemo.dlg

clpdemo.exe:   clpdemo.obj clpboard.obj clpline.obj clpparam.obj clpintro.obj \
               clpdemo.res clpdemo.def
               link
clpdemo+clpboard+clpline+clpparam+clpintro,,,LIBW+$(Mod)LIBCEW/NOE/NOD,clpdemo.de
f;
               rc clpdemo.res
```

CLPBOARD.C source code

```
/****************************************************************************
 C L P B O A R D . C    Clipboard handling routines
****************************************************************************/

/*-----------------------------< Includes >------------------------------*/
```

```
#include        <windows.h>
#include        <string.h>
#include        <stdio.h>
#include        "CLP_RC.H"

/*--------------------------< Prototyping >-----------------------------*/
BOOL GetAllAvailableCfs(HWND hWnd);
void DisplayViewerAndOwner(HWND hWnd, HDC hDC);
void ServePrivateFormat(HWND hWnd, WORD wStatus, LONG lP);
BOOL ProcessWmPaint(HWND hWnd, WORD wP, LONG lP);
BOOL DisplayBitmap (HDC hDC, HBITMAP hBitmap, int x, int y);

/*------------------------< External variables >-------------------------*/
extern HANDLE      hInst;
extern HMENU       hwMenu;           // Main menu handle
extern HWND        hwMain;           // Main window handle
extern HWND        hClpViewer;       // Handle to first of a series of
                                     // clipboard viewers
extern HWND        hClpOwner;        // Current owner handle
extern int         LastFormatItem;   // ID for last format menu item
extern int         wSelFormat;       // Selected CF format
extern int         nSelectedItem;    // ID for selected CF format
extern BOOL        bOwnerInfo;

PAINTSTRUCT PaintStruct;

/**********************************************************************
 P r o c e s s W m P a i n t
 ===========================

 This function processes the WM_PAINT message for the main window.

 Parameters
 HWND          Window handle
 WORD          wParam parameter for WM_PAINT message
 LONG          lParam parameter for WM_PAINT message
**********************************************************************/
BOOL ProcessWmPaint(HWND hWnd, WORD wP, LONG lP)
{
   HANDLE      hClpData;  // Global memory block handle with clipboard
                          // contents
   LPSTR       lpClpData; // Pointer to global memory block
   RECT        Rect;
   HDC         hDC;

   /*--------------< Has a display format been selected? >------------*/
   if(!nSelectedItem)
   {
```

```
      // No: Pass WM_PAINT message to the default function
      return DefWindowProc(hWnd, WM_PAINT, wP, lP);
   }

   /*---------< Yes: Open clipboard >---------*/
   OpenClipboard(hWnd);

   /*---< Get device context and data from client area >---*/
   hDC  = BeginPaint(hWnd, (LPPAINTSTRUCT) &PaintStruct);

   /*---------< Depends on the selected display format >---------*/
   switch(wSelFormat)
   {
     case CF_BITMAP:
        hClpData = GetClipboardData(wSelFormat);
        DisplayBitmap(hDC, hClpData, 5, 5);
        GlobalUnlock(hClpData);
     break;

     case CF_TEXT:
     case CF_OEMTEXT:
        hClpData = GetClipboardData(wSelFormat);
        if(hClpData == NULL)
        {
           MessageBox(hWnd, "No access to\nclipboard contents","Error",
                MB_ICONEXCLAMATION | MB_OK);
           return FALSE;
        }
        lpClpData = GlobalLock(hClpData);
        GetClientRect(hWnd, (LPRECT) &Rect);
        DrawText(hDC, lpClpData, lstrlen(lpClpData), (LPRECT) &Rect,
                  DT_EXPANDTABS);
        GlobalUnlock(hClpData);
     break;

     case CF_OWNERDISPLAY:
        ServePrivateFormat(hWnd,2,0L);
     break;
   }
   if(bOwnerInfo)
      DisplayViewerAndOwner(hWnd, hDC);
   EndPaint(hWnd, (LPPAINTSTRUCT) &PaintStruct);
   CloseClipboard();
   return TRUE;
}

/**************************************************************************
 S e r v e P r i v a t e F o r m a t
```

```
====================================

This function prepares and sends WM_SIZECLIPBOARD and WM_PAINTCLIPBOARD
messages which change with the clipboard's ownership, when data in
CF_OWNERDISPLAY can be displayed in its own client area.

The functions are called as follows:

1. After CF_OWNERDISPLAY format is selected from the menu, parameters
   are window handles, wStatus == 1 and  lP == -1

2. If you want to display clipboard contents, pass all WM_SIZE messages
   to this function. Parameters are window handles, wStatus == 1
   and lP of WM_SIZE

3. For the duration of display, the WM_PAINT message for this function
   is passed. Parameters are window handles, wStatus == 2 (lP is unused)

***********************************************************************/
void ServePrivateFormat(HWND hWnd, WORD wStatus, LONG lP)
{
   HANDLE         hPsMem;     // Handle for PAINTSTRUCT data structure
   HANDLE         hRcMem;     // Handle for RECT data structure
   LPPAINTSTRUCT lpPaint;
   LPRECT         lpRect;
   HWND           hClpOwner;

   hClpOwner = GetClipboardOwner();

   switch(wStatus)
   {
      case 1:  // Pass a WM_SIZE message to the owner
         hRcMem    = GlobalAlloc(GHND, (DWORD) sizeof(RECT));
         lpRect    = (LPRECT) GlobalLock(hRcMem);
         if(lP == -1)
         {
            // Determine client area dimensions
            // This is only the case for the first owner.
            GetClientRect(hWnd, lpRect);
         }
         else
         {
            // Get client area dimensions from lP
            lpRect = (LPRECT) GlobalLock(hRcMem);
            lpRect->left   = 0;
            lpRect->top    = 0;
            lpRect->right  = LOWORD(lP);  // New width
            lpRect->bottom = HIWORD(lP);  // New height
```

```
        }
        SendMessage(hClpOwner, WM_SIZECLIPBOARD, hWnd,MAKELONG(hRcMem,0));
        if(lP == -1)
        {
           // First occurrence? Create WM_PAINT message
           InvalidateRect(hWnd, NULL, TRUE);
        }
        GlobalUnlock(hRcMem);
        GlobalFree(hRcMem);
     break;

     case 2:  // Pass a WM_PAINT message to the owner
        hPsMem   = GlobalAlloc(GHND, (DWORD) sizeof(PAINTSTRUCT));
        lpPaint  = (LPPAINTSTRUCT) GlobalLock(hPsMem);
        *lpPaint = PaintStruct;
        SendMessage(hClpOwner, WM_PAINTCLIPBOARD, hWnd, MAKELONG(hPsMem,0));
        GlobalUnlock(hPsMem);
        GlobalFree(hPsMem);
     break;
  }
}

/*************************************************************************
 D i s p l a y B i t m a p
 =========================

 Generate bitmap of clipboard and display in the client area

 Necessary global variables:
  hInstance   Handle for current instance of application

 Parameters:
  hWnd        Handle for window in which bitmap should be displayed
  hBitmap     Bitmap handle taken from clipboard
  x,y         Upper left coordinates of bitmap in target rectangle (window)

 Return values:
  TRUE,       If bitmap is correctly displayed. Otherwise, FALSE
*************************************************************************/
BOOL DisplayBitmap (HDC hDC, HBITMAP hBitmap, int x, int y)
{
   BITMAP    bm;
   HBITMAP   hOldBitmap;
   HDC       hMemDC;
   POINT     pt;

   hMemDC     = CreateCompatibleDC(hDC);
   hOldBitmap = SelectObject (hMemDC, hBitmap);
```

```
    SetMapMode(hMemDC, GetMapMode(hDC));
    GetObject(hBitmap, sizeof(BITMAP), (LPSTR) &bm);
    pt.x = bm.bmWidth ;
    pt.y = bm.bmHeight;
    DPtoLP(hDC, &pt,1);
    BitBlt(hDC, x, y, pt.x, pt.y, hMemDC, 0,0, SRCCOPY);
    DeleteDC(hMemDC);
    return TRUE;
}

/*************************************************************************
  G e t A l l A v a i l a b l e C f s
  ===================================

  This function determines if data can be placed in the clipboard and,
  if so, in what format. The format ID is changed into a string and placed
  in a second popup menu.

  Global variables
  hClpOwner
  LastFormatItem;
*************************************************************************/
int GetAllAvailableCfs(HWND hWnd)
{
  WORD  wFormat=0;
  WORD  fEnable;
  BOOL  bEmpty =TRUE;             // Clipboard status flag
  HMENU hSubMenu;                 // Handle for a POPUP menu
  int   nNewItemId=FIRSTFORMATITEM; // ID for first new menu item
  int   i;
  char  szFormat[80];
  char  szBuffer[90];

  if(!OpenClipboard(hWnd)) return 0;

  hSubMenu   = GetSubMenu(hwMenu, 2);

  /*---< Clear popup entries if already available >---*/
  if(LastFormatItem >= FIRSTFORMATITEM)
  {
     for(i=FIRSTFORMATITEM; i <= LastFormatItem; i++)
        DeleteMenu(hSubMenu, i, MF_BYCOMMAND);
  }

  /* Get list of valid formats and place in the popup menu */
  do
  {
     wFormat = EnumClipboardFormats(wFormat);
```

```
    if(bEmpty && wFormat)
       bEmpty=FALSE;

    switch(wFormat)
    {
       case 0:
          CloseClipboard();
          if(bEmpty)
          {
             EnableMenuItem(hwMenu, 2, MF_BYPOSITION | MF_DISABLED | MF_GRAYED);
             DrawMenuBar(hWnd);
             return 0;    // Clipboard empty
          }
          else
          {
             EnableMenuItem(hwMenu, 2, MF_BYPOSITION | MF_ENABLED);
             EnableMenuItem(hwMenu, MI_DELETE, MF_ENABLED);
             DrawMenuBar(hWnd);
             return nNewItemId-1;     // Clipboard contains data
          }
       break;

       case CF_BITMAP:          // Load standard name formats
       case CF_METAFILEPICT:
       case CF_SYLK:
       case CF_TEXT:
       case CF_DIF:
       case CF_TIFF:
       case CF_OEMTEXT:
       case CF_DSPTEXT:
       case CF_DSPBITMAP:
       case CF_DSPMETAFILEPICT:
       case CF_PALETTE:
          LoadString(hInst, wFormat, szFormat, 79);
       break;

       case CF_OWNERDISPLAY:     // Prompt for private data format names
          hClpOwner = GetClipboardOwner();
          SendMessage(hClpOwner,WM_ASKCBFORMATNAME, 79, (LONG) (LPSTR)
szFormat);
       break;

       default:
          GetClipboardFormatName(wFormat,(LPSTR) szFormat, 79);
       break;
    }
```

```
    wsprintf((LPSTR) szBuffer,"0x%4.4x %s",wFormat, (LPSTR) szFormat);
    /*---< Enter format in popup menu >---*/
    if(wFormat == CF_TEXT    ||
       wFormat == CF_OEMTEXT ||
       wFormat == CF_BITMAP  ||
       wFormat == CF_OWNERDISPLAY)
       fEnable = MF_ENABLED;
    else fEnable = MF_DISABLED | MF_GRAYED;
    InsertMenu(hSubMenu, MI_OWNER, MF_STRING | MF_BYCOMMAND | fEnable,
               nNewItemId++, (LPSTR) szBuffer);
  } while(wFormat);
} // End of GetAllAvailableCfs


/***************************************************************************
 D i s p l a y V i e w e r A n d O w n e r()
 ===========================================

 This function displays names and window handles for the current clipboard
 owners, as well as the number of viewers called. This information appears
 in the bottom line of the client area. This function begins when a
 WM_PAINT message is called

 Global variables
 hClpViewer
 hClpOwner

 Parameters
 HWND   hWnd    Handle for main window
 HDC    hDC     Handle for main window device context
***************************************************************************/
void DisplayViewerAndOwner(HWND hWnd, HDC hDC)
{
  char szOwner [35];
  char szViewer[35];
  char szBuffer[90];
  int  nBufLen;
  RECT rect;

  szOwner[0] = szViewer[0] = NULL;
  GetModuleFileName(GetWindowWord(hClpOwner, GWW_HINSTANCE), (LPSTR) szOwner,
34);
  GetModuleFileName(GetWindowWord(hClpViewer,GWW_HINSTANCE), (LPSTR)
szViewer,34);
  nBufLen = wsprintf(szBuffer,"[Owner: %s: %04x]    [Viewer: %s: %04x]",
             (LPSTR) szOwner, hClpOwner, (LPSTR) szViewer, hClpViewer);
  GetClientRect(hWnd, &rect);
  TextOut(hDC, 10, rect.bottom-30, (LPSTR) szBuffer, nBufLen);
```

```
}
```

CLPDEMO.C source code

```
/****************************************************************************

 C L P D E M O . C      Main module for clipboard application

****************************************************************************/

#include        <windows.h>
#include        <string.h>
#include        <stdio.h>
#include        "CLP_RC.H"
#include        "CLPPARAM.H"

#define     RXDELAY    1000     // Delay in milliseconds

/*---------------------------< Prototyping >----------------------------*/
// clpboard.c
int  GetAllAvailableCfs(HWND hWnd);
void DisplayViewerAndOwner(HWND hWnd, HDC hDC);
BOOL DisplayBitmap  (HDC hDC, HBITMAP hBitmap, int x, int y);
void ServePrivateFormat(HWND hWnd, WORD wStatus, LONG lP);
BOOL ProcessWmPaint(HWND hWnd, WORD wP, LONG lP);

// clpparam.c
BOOL FAR PASCAL MdfCommSetup(HWND hDlg, unsigned msg, WORD wP, LONG lP);
BOOL FAR PASCAL MdfIntroBox(HWND hDlg, unsigned msg, WORD wP, LONG lP);
BOOL ReadWinIniEntry(int CommPortId);
int  InitCommPort(COMMPORTPARAM *pCpp);

// clpline.c
int  TransmitClpData(void);
WORD FAR PASCAL PollRxQueue(HWND hWnd, WORD msg, WORD wP, LONG lP);
WORD InstallTimerFkt(void);

/*------------------------< Global variables >-------------------------*/
HANDLE      hInst;
HMENU       hwMenu;             // Handle for main menu
HWND        hwMain;             // Handle for main window
char        szAppName[] = "Clip & Connect";
BOOL        bOnline = FALSE;    // Set when serial communication
                                // is active.

// Variables for clipboard processing
```

```
HWND         hClpViewer;         // Handle for first viewer in viewer chain
HWND         hClpOwner;          // Handle for current clipboard owner
BOOL         bInitDone     = FALSE;
BOOL         bOwnerInfo    = FALSE;
int          wSelFormat    = 0; // Selected CF format
int          nSelectedItem = 0; // ID for selected CF format
int          LastFormatItem;     // Last Clipboard Format menu item from ID
                                 // based on GetAllAvailableCfs
BOOL         bPrivateFormatSelected = FALSE;
BOOL         bClpEmpty     = FALSE; // TRUE if clipboard is empty

// Variables for serial processing

BOOL         bCommInit = FALSE; // TRUE when interface is initialized
FARPROC      lpTmpProc;          // Temporary dialog box function
int          nCid,               // Current interface ID
             AktTimerId;         // Timer ID from Windows
HWND         hRxWnd;             // Child window handle
FARPROC      lpTimerFkt;         // Long pointer to the timer function
COMMPORTPARAM Cpp;               // Interface parameters

/**********************************************************************
 W n d P r o c       ### Callback - Function ###
 =============

 M a i n W i n d o w   -   F u n c t i o n
**********************************************************************/
long FAR PASCAL WndProc(HWND hWnd, unsigned msg, WORD wP, LONG lP)
{
   HMENU       hSubMenu;
   char        szBuffer[90];
   char        szFormat[80];
   int         action;

   switch (msg)
   {
      case WM_CREATE:
         hClpOwner      = GetClipboardOwner();
         hClpViewer     = SetClipboardViewer(hWnd);     // Setup
         LastFormatItem = GetAllAvailableCfs(hWnd);
         Cpp.nTxQueSize = Cpp.nRxQueSize = 256 ;
         Cpp.nRxDelay   = 220;
         SendMessage(hWnd, WM_COMMAND, MI_ABOUT, 0L);  // Start intro box...
         break;

      /*---< Messages which a clipboard viewer has during processing >---*/
      case WM_DRAWCLIPBOARD:
         if(hClpViewer)       // Does an additional clipboard viewer exist?
```

```
    {
       SendMessage(hClpViewer, msg, wP, lP); // Pass messages
    }
    wSelFormat      = 0;
    nSelectedItem   = 0;
    LastFormatItem = GetAllAvailableCfs(hwMain);
    hClpOwner       = GetClipboardOwner();
    bInitDone       = FALSE;
    bClpEmpty       = (LastFormatItem == 0);
 break;

 case WM_CHANGECBCHAIN:
    if(wP == hClpViewer)  // Is there another viewer?
    {
       hClpViewer = LOWORD(lP);  // Yes -- store that viewer
    }
    else if(hClpViewer)          // No -- pass message
       SendMessage(hClpViewer, msg, wP, lP);
 break;

 case WM_PAINT:
    return ProcessWmPaint(hWnd, wP, lP);
break;

 case WM_DESTROY:                /* End application */
    ChangeClipboardChain(hWnd, hClpViewer); // Disconnect viewer chain
    PostQuitMessage(NULL);
    break;

 /*---< For displaying CF_OWNERDISPLAY data >---*/

 case WM_VSCROLL:
    if(bPrivateFormatSelected)
       SendMessage(hClpOwner, WM_VSCROLLCLIPBOARD, hWnd,
                   MAKELONG(wP,LOWORD(lP)));
 break;

 case WM_HSCROLL:
    if(bPrivateFormatSelected)
       SendMessage(hClpOwner, WM_HSCROLLCLIPBOARD, hWnd,
                   MAKELONG(wP,LOWORD(lP)));
 break;

 case WM_SIZE:
    if(bPrivateFormatSelected)
       ServePrivateFormat(hWnd,1,lP);  // Send ==> WM_SIZECLIPBOARD
 break;
```

```
case WM_INITMENUPOPUP:
   if(HIWORD(lP) != 0) // System menu?
      break ;
   switch(LOWORD(lP))
   {
      case 1: // File menu
         // Adapt Clipboard --> Line...
         EnableMenuItem(hwMenu, MI_WRITE,
                        (bOnline && !bClpEmpty && (wSelFormat == CF_TEXT)
                         ? MF_ENABLED:MF_GRAYED));
         // Exit program only after interface shuts down
         EnableMenuItem(hwMenu, MI_QUIT,
                        (bOnline ? MF_GRAYED:MF_ENABLED));
      break ;

      case 2: // Edit menu
         // Cut clipboard adapted...
         EnableMenuItem(hwMenu, MI_DELETE,
                        (!bClpEmpty ? MF_ENABLED:MF_GRAYED));
      break;

      case 3: // Communication menu
         EnableMenuItem(hwMenu, MI_DISCONNECT,
                        (bOnline ? MF_ENABLED:MF_GRAYED));
         EnableMenuItem(hwMenu, MI_CONNECT,
                        (bCommInit && !bOnline ? MF_ENABLED:MF_GRAYED));
      break;
   }
break;

case WM_COMMAND:
{
  switch (wP)
  {
     case MI_QUIT:       // End program...
        if(MessageBox(hWnd, (LPSTR)"Do you really want to exit?",
                    (LPSTR)"Exit Program",
            MB_ICONQUESTION | MB_YESNO | MB_DEFBUTTON1 |
            MB_APPLMODAL) == IDYES)
        DestroyWindow(hWnd);
     break;

     case MI_ABOUT:
        lpTmpProc = MakeProcInstance((FARPROC)MdfIntroBox, hInst);
        action = DialogBox(hInst, "INTROBOX", hWnd, lpTmpProc);
        FreeProcInstance(lpTmpProc);
     break;
```

```
case MI_DELETE:
  if(MessageBox(hWnd, (LPSTR)"Clear clipboard contents?",
             (LPSTR)"Clipboard",
       MB_ICONQUESTION | MB_YESNO | MB_DEFBUTTON1 |
       MB_APPLMODAL) == IDYES)
  {
     OpenClipboard(hWnd);
     bClpEmpty = EmptyClipboard();
     CloseClipboard();
     InvalidateRect(hWnd, NULL, TRUE);
     UpdateWindow(hWnd);
  }
break;

case MI_OWNER:
   CheckMenuItem(hwMenu, MI_OWNER, bOwnerInfo == TRUE
                               ? MF_UNCHECKED : MF_CHECKED);
   bOwnerInfo = !bOwnerInfo;
   InvalidateRect(hWnd, NULL, TRUE);
   UpdateWindow(hWnd);
break;

case MI_WRITE:
   TransmitClpData();
break;

case MI_CONNECT:      /* Start session */
  if(nCid)
  {
     AktTimerId = InstallTimerFkt();    // Enable timer
     bOnline = TRUE;
  }
  break;

case MI_DISCONNECT:   /* Stop session */
   KillTimer(NULL, AktTimerId);    // Disable timer
   bOnline = FALSE;
   FreeProcInstance(lpTimerFkt);  // Release timer
   DestroyWindow(hRxWnd);
   CloseComm(nCid);
   break;

case MI_COMSETUP:     /* Serial parameters */
   lpTmpProc = MakeProcInstance((FARPROC)MdfCommSetup, hInst);
   action = DialogBox(hInst, "COMSETUP", hWnd, lpTmpProc);
   FreeProcInstance(lpTmpProc);
   if(nCid = InitCommPort(&Cpp) >= 0)
      bCommInit = TRUE;
```

```
              break;

           default:
              if((wP >= FIRSTFORMATITEM) && (wP <= LastFormatItem))
              {
                 nSelectedItem = wP;
                 hSubMenu      = GetSubMenu(hwMenu, 2);
                 GetMenuString(hSubMenu, nSelectedItem, (LPSTR)
szBuffer,79,MF_BYCOMMAND);
                 sscanf(szBuffer,"0x%x %s",&wSelFormat, szFormat);  // and
unpacked information
                 wsprintf((LPSTR) szBuffer,(LPSTR) "CF=%4x Name=%s MI=%d",
                          wSelFormat, (LPSTR) szFormat, nSelectedItem);

                 if(wSelFormat == CF_OWNERDISPLAY)
                 {
                    bPrivateFormatSelected = TRUE;
                    if(!bInitDone)
                    {
                       // WM_SIZECLIPBOARD with current client area size,
                       // then send WM_PAINT message
                       ServePrivateFormat(hWnd,1,-1L);
                       bInitDone = TRUE;
                    }
                 }
                 else
                 {
                    bPrivateFormatSelected = FALSE;
                    bInitDone = FALSE;
                 }
                 InvalidateRect(hWnd, NULL, TRUE);
              }
           break;
        }// switch wP
     }// case WM_COMMAND
     default:
         return(DefWindowProc(hWnd, msg, wP, lP));
   }
   return (NULL);
}

/***************************************************************************
 W i n M a i n
 =============

 Main function for Windows applications
***************************************************************************/
int PASCAL WinMain (HANDLE hInstance, HANDLE hPrevInstance, LPSTR lpszCmdLine,
```

```
                    int nCmdShow)
{
  MSG           msg ;
  WNDCLASS      wndclass ;

  if (!hPrevInstance)
  {
     wndclass.style          = CS_VREDRAW | CS_HREDRAW ;
     wndclass.lpfnWndProc    = WndProc ;
     wndclass.cbClsExtra     = 0 ;
     wndclass.cbWndExtra     = 0 ;
     wndclass.hInstance      = hInstance ;
     wndclass.hIcon          = LoadIcon (hInstance,(LPSTR) "AppIcon") ;
     wndclass.hCursor        = LoadCursor (NULL, IDC_ARROW);
     wndclass.hbrBackground = GetStockObject (WHITE_BRUSH) ;
     wndclass.lpszMenuName   = NULL;
     wndclass.lpszClassName = szAppName ;

     if (!RegisterClass (&wndclass))
         return FALSE;

     hInst  = hInstance;
     hwMenu = LoadMenu(hInst, "Menu");

     hwMain = CreateWindow (szAppName, szAppName,
                      WS_OVERLAPPEDWINDOW | WS_CLIPCHILDREN,
                      CW_USEDEFAULT, 0, CW_USEDEFAULT, 0, NULL,
                      hwMenu,
                      hInstance, NULL) ;

     ShowWindow(hwMain, SW_SHOWNORMAL);
     UpdateWindow (hwMain);
  }

  ReadWinIniEntry(1);    // Read WIN.INI values for COM2...

  if(hPrevInstance)
     return FALSE;

  /*--------------< Message loop >----------*/

  while(GetMessage (&msg, NULL, 0, 0))
  {
     TranslateMessage (&msg) ;
     DispatchMessage (&msg) ;
  }
  return msg.wParam;
}
```

CLPFILE.C source code

```
/************************************************************************

 C L P F I L E . C     This module contains all routines needed to store
                       or load clipboard contents to or from a *.CLP file

************************************************************************/

#include <windows.h>
#include <io.h>
#include <stdio.h>
#include <fcntl.h>
#include <io.h>
#include <stdlib.h>
#include <errno.h>
#include <sys\types.h>
#include <sys\stat.h>
#include <memory.h>

#include "CLPFILE.H"                              // Structure definitions

#define      CLP_ID         0xC350

/*************************************************************************
 C r e a t e C l p H e a d e r
 =============================

 Creates file header of type CLPHEADER.

 Return values:
 HANDLE  CreateClpHeader Handle for memory range in which CLPHEADER
                         is placed.
*************************************************************************/
HANDLE CreateClpHeader(void)
{
  HANDLE    hMem;
  CLPHEADER FAR *lpClp;

  hMem = GlobalAlloc(GMEM_MOVEABLE | GMEM_ZEROINIT, (DWORD) sizeof(CLPHEADER));
  if(hMem)
  {
     lpClp = (CLPHEADER FAR*)GlobalLock(hMem);
     lpClp->wFileId      = CLP_ID;
     lpClp->wFormatCount = 0;
     GlobalUnlock(hMem);
  }
```

```
  return hMem;
}

/**************************************************************************
 A p p e n d C l p I t e m I n f o
 =================================

 This function inserts a new structure block of type CLPITEMINFO at the end
 of the format descriptor block, and passes the given data.

 The first data byte's position in the data block (relative to the start of
 the data block) is passed, and entered in the current format descriptor
 block. The last valid address is the first stored in the data.

 Parameters:
 HANDLE   hClpHeader          File header handle
 HANDLE   hClpItemInfo        Handle for previous format descriptor blocks
 WORD     wFormatId           Format ID number
 LONG     lDataLength         Format data length in bytes
 char*    szPrivateName       Name, if private data exists

 Return values:
 HANDLE   Handle for format descriptor block to be re-allocated and expanded.
          NULL if error occurs.
**************************************************************************/
HANDLE AppendClpItemInfo(HANDLE hClpHeader,
                         HANDLE hClpItemInfo,
                         WORD   wFormatId,
                         LONG   lDataLength,
                         char*  szPrivateName)
{
   HANDLE           hNewMem;         // Handle for memory block to be
                                     // re-allocated
   CLPHEADER   FAR *lpClpHeader;     // Pointer to file header
   CLPITEMINFO FAR *lpClpItemInfo,   // Pointer to format descriptor blocks
               FAR *lpNewClpInfo;    // Pointer to new format descriptor block

   int              nNewSize;        // New memory block size

   lpClpHeader = (CLPHEADER FAR*) GlobalLock(hClpHeader);
   if (lpClpHeader == NULL)
   {
      MessageBox(GetFocus(), "hClpHeader could not be locked",
                 "AppendClpItemInfo", MB_ICONEXCLAMATION | MB_OK);
      return NULL;
   }
   nNewSize = (lpClpHeader->wFormatCount+1) * sizeof(CLPITEMINFO);
   if (hClpItemInfo == NULL)
```

```
    hNewMem = GlobalAlloc(GMEM_MOVEABLE, (DWORD)nNewSize);
  else
    hNewMem = GlobalReAlloc(hClpItemInfo, (DWORD)nNewSize, GMEM_MOVEABLE);
  if(hNewMem)
  {
     lpClpHeader->wFormatCount++;              // Increment format counter
     lpClpItemInfo = (CLPITEMINFO FAR*)GlobalLock(hNewMem);

     lpNewClpInfo = &lpClpItemInfo[lpClpHeader->wFormatCount-1];
     // Enter data
     lpNewClpInfo->wFormatId    = wFormatId;
     lpNewClpInfo->lDataLength = lDataLength;
     lpNewClpInfo->lDataOffset = ((lpClpHeader->wFormatCount>1) ?
                       lpClpItemInfo[lpClpHeader->wFormatCount-2].lDataOffset
                      +lpClpItemInfo[lpClpHeader->wFormatCount-2].lDataLength
                       : 0L );

     lstrcpy((LPSTR) lpNewClpInfo->szPrivateName, (LPSTR) szPrivateName);

     GlobalUnlock(hNewMem);
  }
  GlobalUnlock(hClpHeader);

  return hNewMem;
}


/***************************************************************************
 A p p e n d C l p D a t a
 =========================

 This function appends a clipboard data block.

 Parameters:
 HANDLE     hClpData     Handle for memory block containing clipboard data
 HANDLE     hData        Handle for data to be appended
 LONG*      lDataOffset  Parameter:     Offset within the memory block
                         Return value: New offset
                                   (1st byte of allocated memory)
 LONG*      lDataLength  Return value: Length of data to be appended

 Return values:
 HANDLE      Handle for re-allocated memory block.
             NULL if error occurs.
****************************************************************************/

HANDLE AppendClpData(HANDLE hClpData, HANDLE hData,
                     LONG* lDataOffset, LONG* lDataLength)
```

```
{
   HANDLE          hNewMem;      // Handle for memory block to be re-allocated
   LPSTR           pMem;         // Pointer to re-allocated memory block
   LPSTR           lpData;       // Pointer to fixed clipboard data
   int             i;
   char            szMBString[255];

   /* Determine data length */
   *lDataLength = GlobalSize(hData);

   if ((lpData = GlobalLock(hData)) == NULL)
   {
      MessageBox(GetFocus(), "hData could not be locked",
                 "AppendClpData", MB_ICONEXCLAMATION | MB_OK);
      return NULL;
   }
   if (hClpData == NULL)
     hNewMem = GlobalAlloc(GMEM_MOVEABLE, *lDataLength);
   else
     hNewMem = GlobalReAlloc(hClpData,
                             *lDataLength+(*lDataOffset)-1,
                             GMEM_MOVEABLE);
   if(hNewMem)
   {
      pMem = GlobalLock(hNewMem);

      for (i=0; i<(*lDataLength); i++)
        *(pMem+(*lDataOffset)+i) = *(lpData+i);

      *lDataOffset += (*lDataLength);
      GlobalUnlock(hNewMem);
   }

   GlobalUnlock(hData);

   return hNewMem;
}


/*****************************************************************************
 C l i p b o a r d T o F i l e
 ==============================

 This function writes clipboard contents to the specified file.

 Parameters:
 HWND       hWnd        Handle for window
 LPSTR      lpFileName  Name of file in which data should be saved
```

```
 Return values:
 int       1 if the function is successful.
           NULL if error occurs. The developer may wish to generate error
           messages based on these codes.
****************************************************************************/
int ClipboardToFile(HWND hWnd, LPSTR lpFileName)

{
  HANDLE   hClpBrd     = NULL,     // Handle for clipboard
           hClpHeader  = NULL,     // Handle for file header
           hClpItemInfo= NULL,     // Handle for format descriptor blocks
           hClpData    = NULL,     // Handle for data blocks
           hData,                  // Handle for clipboard data
           hNew;                   // Handle for range in which function
                                   // return values are stored

  WORD     wFormatId = 0;          // Format descriptor ID, initialized with
                                   // NULL, into which all file formats should
                                   // be stored

  LONG lDataLength;                // Data block length
  LONG lDataOffset = 0L;           // Data offset within the data block
                                   // First free byte

  CLPHEADER   FAR* lpClpHeader;   // Pointer to file header
  CLPITEMINFO FAR* lpClpItemInfo; // Pointer to format descriptor blocks
  LPSTR            lpData;        // Pointer to data used
  char             buffer[79];

  HANDLE      ClpFile;             // Handle for open file
  OFSTRUCT    of;
  int         n,i, len;
  char        szMBString[255];

 /*---< Set up CLP file header, ... >---*/
  if ((hClpHeader = CreateClpHeader()) == NULL)
  {
    MessageBox(GetFocus(), "CreateClpHeader failed",
               "ClipboardToFile", MB_ICONEXCLAMATION | MB_OK);
    return NULL;
  }

  /*---< Open clipboard >---*/
  if (!OpenClipboard(hWnd))
  {
     MessageBox(GetFocus(), "OpenClipboard failed",
                "ClipboardToFile", MB_ICONEXCLAMATION | MB_OK);
```

```
        return NULL;
    }

    /*---< Append an info structure for every clipboard format, ... >---*/
    while (wFormatId = EnumClipboardFormats(wFormatId))
    {
      switch(wFormatId)
      {
        case CF_BITMAP:
        case CF_METAFILEPICT:
        case CF_SYLK:
        case CF_DIF:
        case CF_TIFF:
        case CF_DSPTEXT:
        case CF_DSPBITMAP:
        case CF_DSPMETAFILEPICT:
        case CF_PALETTE:
        case CF_OEMTEXT:
        case CF_TEXT:
          /*  Default formats   */

          /* Get data ID from clipboard. */
          if(!(hData = GetClipboardData(wFormatId)))
          {
            MessageBox(GetFocus(), "GetClipboardData failed",
                   "ClipboardToFile", MB_ICONEXCLAMATION | MB_OK);

                          CloseClipboard();
            return NULL;
          }
          /* Copy data to reserved global memory range */
                    len = GlobalSize(hData);
                    wsprintf(szMBString, "GlobalSize(hData):<%ld>\nwFormatId:<%d>",
                  GlobalSize(hData), wFormatId);
                    MessageBox(GetFocus(), szMBString, "For AppendClpData", MB_OK);

          if((hNew = AppendClpData(hClpData, hData, &lDataOffset,
                                   &lDataLength)) == NULL)
          {
            MessageBox(GetFocus(), "AppendClpData failed",
                       "ClipboardToFile", MB_ICONEXCLAMATION | MB_OK);
            return NULL;
          }
          hClpData = hNew;

          /* Create format descriptor block and enter values.    */
          /* Format counter in file header will be incremented.  */
```

```
      GetClipboardFormatName(wFormatId, (LPSTR)buffer, 79);
      if ((hNew=AppendClpItemInfo(hClpHeader, hClpItemInfo, wFormatId,
                                  lDataLength, buffer)) == NULL)
      {
        MessageBox(GetFocus(), "hClpHeader could not be locked",
                   "ClipboardToFile", MB_ICONEXCLAMATION | MB_OK);
        return NULL;
      }
      hClpItemInfo = hNew;
      break;

    case CF_OWNERDISPLAY:
     /*
       Avoid writing data in this format, since the properties do not
       permit direct access. Instead, the clipboard receives a value of
       NULL other than the usual file handle.
     */
     break;

    default:
      /*
        private formats
      */
      break;
    }
}

CloseClipboard();

/*---< ... and finally, storage to a *.CLP file >---*/
if((ClpFile=OpenFile(lpFileName, (LPOFSTRUCT)&of, OF_CREATE))==-1)
{
   MessageBox(GetFocus(), "OpenFile failed",
              "ClipboardToFile", MB_ICONEXCLAMATION | MB_OK);

   return NULL;
}

/* Write file header to file. */
if((lpClpHeader = (CLPHEADER FAR*) GlobalLock(hClpHeader)) == NULL)
{
   MessaqeBox(GetFocus(), "hClpHeader could not be locked",
              "ClipboardToFile", MB_ICONEXCLAMATION | MB_OK);
   return NULL;
}

n = lpClpHeader->wFormatCount;
if(_lwrite(ClpFile, (LPSTR) lpClpHeader, (WORD) sizeof(CLPHEADER) )
```

```
        < sizeof(CLPHEADER))
{
   MessageBox(GetFocus(), "_lwrite: Error writing clipboard header",
              "ClipboardToFile", MB_ICONEXCLAMATION | MB_OK);
   return NULL;
}

GlobalUnlock (hClpHeader);
GlobalFree (hClpHeader);

/* Write format descriptor blocks to the file. The data offset must   */
/* be corrected after this, shifted relative to the beginning of the  */
/* data blocks.                                                        */

if((lpClpItemInfo = (CLPITEMINFO FAR*) GlobalLock(hClpItemInfo)) == NULL)
{
   MessageBox(GetFocus(), "hClpItemInfo could not be locked",
              "ClipboardToFile", MB_ICONEXCLAMATION | MB_OK);
   return NULL;
}
// Correct data offset
for(i=0; i<n; i++)
{
   (lpClpItemInfo[i]).lDataOffset += sizeof(CLPHEADER) +
                                     n*sizeof(CLPITEMINFO);
}

/* Write data in file                                                  */
if( _lwrite(ClpFile, (LPSTR) lpClpItemInfo, (WORD) n*sizeof(CLPITEMINFO) )
     < (int) n*sizeof(CLPITEMINFO))
{
   MessageBox(GetFocus(), "_lwrite: Error writing to CLPITEMINFO data",
              "ClipboardToFile", MB_ICONEXCLAMATION | MB_OK);
   return NULL;
}
GlobalUnlock (hClpItemInfo);
GlobalFree (hClpItemInfo);

/* Write data blocks to file. */
if((lpData = GlobalLock(hClpData)) == NULL)
   return NULL;

if( _lwrite(ClpFile, lpData, (WORD) lDataOffset)
        < (int) lDataOffset)
{
  MessageBox(GetFocus(), "_lwrite: Error writing to clipboard data",
             "ClipboardToFile", MB_ICONEXCLAMATION | MB_OK);
  return NULL;
```

```
  }
  GlobalUnlock (hClpData);
  GlobalFree (hClpData);

  close(ClpFile);

  return 1;
} // ClipboardToFile

/*************************************************************************
 F i l e T o C l i p b o a r d
 =============================

 This function places the selected file's contents in the clipboard.

 Parameters:
 HWND       hWnd         Handle for window
 LPSTR      lpFileName   Name of file whose contents should be placed
                         in clipboard.

 Return values:
 int        1 if the function is successful.
            NULL if error occurs. The developer may wish to generate error
            messages based on these codes.
*************************************************************************/
int FileToClipboard(HWND hWnd, LPSTR lpFileName)
{
  HANDLE    hClpData    = NULL; // Handle for data blocks


  CLPHEADER   ClpHeader;        // File header
  CLPITEMINFO ClpItemInfo;      // Current format descriptor block

  LPSTR       lpClpData;        // Pointer to data used

  HANDLE      ClpFile;          // Handle for open file
  OFSTRUCT    of;
  int         i;

  /*---< Open clipboard >---*/
  if(!OpenClipboard(hWnd))
  {
     MessageBox(GetFocus(), "OpenClipboard failed",
                "FileToClipboard", MB_ICONEXCLAMATION | MB_OK);
     return NULL;
  }
  EmptyClipboard();                          // Empty out clipboard
```

```
/*-----< Open file >-----*/
if((ClpFile=OpenFile(lpFileName, (LPOFSTRUCT) &of, OF_READ))==-1)
{
   MessageBox(GetFocus(), "OpenFile failed",
              "FileToClipboard", MB_ICONEXCLAMATION | MB_OK);
   return NULL;
}
/* Read file header from file. */
if(_lread(ClpFile, (LPSTR) &ClpHeader, (WORD) sizeof(CLPHEADER) )
        < sizeof(CLPHEADER))
{
   MessageBox(GetFocus(), "_lread: Error reading clipboard header",
              "FileToClipboard", MB_ICONEXCLAMATION | MB_OK);
   return NULL;
}

for(i=0; i < ClpHeader.wFormatCount; i++)
{
  /*------< Read format descriptor block >-------*/
  _llseek(ClpFile, (LONG) sizeof(CLPHEADER) + i*sizeof(CLPITEMINFO),
          SEEK_SET);

  if(_lread(ClpFile, (LPSTR) &ClpItemInfo, (WORD) sizeof(CLPITEMINFO))
     < sizeof(CLPITEMINFO))
  {
     MessageBox(GetFocus(), "_lread: Error reading CLPITEMINFO structures",
                "FileToClipboard", MB_ICONEXCLAMATION | MB_OK);
     return NULL;
  }
  /*----< Allocate memory and read data >----*/
  hClpData  = GlobalAlloc(GMEM_MOVEABLE, (DWORD) ClpItemInfo.lDataLength);
  lpClpData = GlobalLock(hClpData);
  _llseek(ClpFile, ClpItemInfo.lDataOffset, SEEK_SET);
  if(_lread(ClpFile, lpClpData, (WORD) ClpItemInfo.lDataLength)
      < (int) ClpItemInfo.lDataLength)
  {
    MessageBox(GetFocus(), "_lread: Error reading clipboard data",
               "FileToClipboard", MB_ICONEXCLAMATION | MB_OK);
    return NULL;
  }
  GlobalUnlock(hClpData);

  /*--------< Place data in clipboard >---------*/
  SetClipboardData(ClpItemInfo.wFormatId, hClpData);
}
close(ClpFile);
CloseClipboard();
```

```
  return 1;
} // FileToClipboard
```

CLPINTRO.C source code

```
/*************************************************************************
 C L P I N T R O . C    This module displays a "Parameters" dialog box for
                        installing and de-installing a timer, and for
                        displaying WM_TIMER messages.
*************************************************************************/

#include <WINDOWS.H>

/* External variables */
extern HANDLE hInst;

/* Function prototyping */
BOOL DisplayBitmap (HDC hDC, HBITMAP hBitmap, int x, int y);

/* Local variables */
RECT rect  = {10,50,350,130};  // Rectangle to be updated

/*************************************************************************
 M d f I n t r o B o x
 =====================

 This function demonstrates how a timer is added, and how the WM_TIMER
 messages react. These dialog functions are automatically called when the
 application starts; displays different bitmaps; and terminates
 automatically.
*************************************************************************/
BOOL FAR PASCAL MdfIntroBox(HWND hDlg, WORD msg, WORD wP, LONG lP)
{
  static int      nEvent;        // Event counter
  static int      nOffset;       // Bitmap array offset
  static WORD     wTimerId;      // Timer ID
  static HBITMAP  haBitmap[4];   // Array with 4 bitmap handles
  PAINTSTRUCT     PaintStruct;
  HDC             hDC;
  BOOL            bBeep;         // Beep-Flag 1:beep, 0: no beep

   switch(msg)
   {
      case WM_INITDIALOG:
         // Load the four display bitmaps ...
         haBitmap[0] = LoadBitmap(hInst, (LPSTR) "OpenCut"  );
         haBitmap[1] = LoadBitmap(hInst, (LPSTR) "CloseCut" );
```

```
        haBitmap[2] = LoadBitmap(hInst, (LPSTR) "ClosePin" );
        haBitmap[3] = LoadBitmap(hInst, (LPSTR) "OpenPin"  );

        // Set timer ...
        wTimerId = SetTimer(hDlg, 1, 300, NULL);
        if(!wTimerId)
        {
          /*
            Error message:
            No timers currently available in system...
          */
          EndDialog(hDlg, FALSE);
        }
        nEvent = nOffset = 0;
        return TRUE;
     break;

    case WM_PAINT:
       hDC = BeginPaint(hDlg, (LPPAINTSTRUCT) &PaintStruct);
       /*
          Display corresponding bitmap based on <nEvent>
       */
       bBeep = nEvent % 2 ? 1 : 0;
       DisplayBitmap(hDC, haBitmap[nOffset+bBeep], 155, 60);
       if(bBeep) MessageBeep(0);
       EndPaint(hDlg, (LPPAINTSTRUCT) &PaintStruct);
       return TRUE;
     break;

     case WM_TIMER:
     {
        nEvent++;           // Increment event counter...

        if(nEvent >= 11)    // End display of first bitmap pair
           nOffset = 2;

        if(nEvent >= 21)    // End display of second bitmap pair
        {
           int i;
           for(i=0; i<=3; i++, DeleteObject(haBitmap[i]));

           // Kill timer and end dialog box...
           KillTimer(hDlg,wTimerId);
           EndDialog(hDlg,TRUE);
        }
        else
        {
           InvalidateRect(hDlg,(LPRECT)&rect, FALSE);
```

```
            UpdateWindow(hDlg);
         }
         return TRUE;
      break;
      }
      default:
         return DefWindowProc(hDlg, msg, wP, lP);
   }
}
```

CLPLINE.C source code

```
/*************************************************************************
 C L P L I N E . C      Serial communication functions
 *************************************************************************/

#include <windows.h>
#include "CLPPARAM.H"

#define STX 0x2          // Start of a telegram
#define ETX 0x3          // End of a telegram

extern int      nCid;           // Serial interface ID
extern COMMPORTPARAM  Cpp;      // Current COM port parameters
extern FARPROC  lpTimerFkt;     // Instance address of PollRxQueue function
extern HWND     hRxWnd;         // Handle for child window, which displays
                                // received data
extern HANDLE   hInst;
extern HANDLE   hwMain;

HANDLE hData;
PSTR   pData;
int    ReceiveMode = 1;

void WriteChar (int ComNr, char SendChar);
BOOL WriteString (int Cid, LPSTR lpData, DWORD dwLength);
int  TransmitClpData(void);
WORD FAR PASCAL PollRxQueue(HWND hWnd, WORD msg, WORD wP, LONG lP);
WORD InstallTimerFkt(void);
LONG FAR PASCAL RxChildWndProc(HWND hWnd, WORD msg, WORD wP, LONG lP);

/*************************************************************************
  W r i t e C h a r ()
  ====================

  WriteChar sends a character to the serial interface.
```

```
  Parameters:

    unsigned int ComNr:         Serial interface (1-4).
    int          SendChar:      Character to be sent.

  Return values: None.
*****************************************************************************/
void WriteChar (int ComNr, char SendChar)
{
  char szData[2];

  szData[0] = SendChar;
  szData[1] = '\0';
  WriteComm(ComNr, (LPSTR)szData, 1);
} // WriteChar

/*****************************************************************************
  W r i t e S t r i n g ()
  ========================

  WriteString sends a string ended by '\0' to the serial interface.

  Parameters:

  unsigned int Cid:      Serial interface (1-4)
  LPSTR        lpData:   String to be sent

  Return values:         TRUE if the string can be sent. Otherwise, FALSE.
  ****************************************************************************/
BOOL WriteString (int Cid, LPSTR lpData, DWORD dwLength)
{
   COMSTAT          CommState;
   int              nOffset,
                    nWritten;
   DWORD            dwStopTime;
   MSG              myMsg;

   FlushComm(Cid, TXQUEUE);
   WriteChar(Cid,STX);
   nOffset  = 0;
   nWritten = 0;

   while (1)
   {
      nWritten = WriteComm(Cid, (LPSTR) &lpData[nOffset],
                           min( Cpp.nTxQueSize,
                           lstrlen((LPSTR) &lpData[nOffset])));
      if(nWritten < 0)
```

```
    {
    // Error while writing data ...
    GetCommEventMask(Cid,0xFFFF);    // Clear event mask
    return FALSE;
    }
    else
    {
     nOffset += nWritten;
     // Wait until all characters are sent
     do
     {
        GetCommError(Cid, &CommState);
     }while(CommState.cbOutQue);

     if(nOffset >= dwLength)
     {
        WriteChar(Cid,ETX);
        GetCommEventMask(Cid,0xFFFF);      // Clear event mask
        return TRUE;
     }
    }
           /*
    The following loop determines the status of the serial
    interface, which specifies whether the application will act
    as sender or receiver.

    This loop gets the system time and waits for about 4 timer
    clicks. During this time, the application releases the CPU for
    message processing, and for getting important WM_TIMER
    messages for PollRxQueue.
           */
          dwStopTime  = GetCurrentTime() + 200L;
    while(GetCurrentTime() < dwStopTime)
    {
    if(PeekMessage(&myMsg, NULL, NULL, NULL, PM_REMOVE))
    {
       TranslateMessage(&myMsg);
       DispatchMessage (&myMsg);
    }
    }

  } // while
} // WriteString

/**************************************************************************
 T r a n s m i t C l p D a t a ()
 ================================
 This function takes data in CF_TEXT format from the clipboard and
```

```
 places this data in the send buffer.
**************************************************************************/
BOOL TransmitClpData(void)
{
   HANDLE   hClpData;
   LPSTR    lpClpData;
   DWORD    dwLength;
   BOOL     bResult;

   if(OpenClipboard(hwMain))
   {
      hClpData = GetClipboardData(CF_TEXT);

      if(hClpData)
      {
      lpClpData = GlobalLock(hClpData);    // Get pointer to data
      dwLength  = lstrlen(lpClpData);      // Determine data length
      FlushComm(nCid, TXQUEUE);
      bResult = WriteString(nCid, lpClpData, (DWORD) dwLength);
      GlobalUnlock(hClpData);
      }
      CloseClipboard();
   }
   return bResult;
}

/**************************************************************************
 P o l l R x Q u e u e                          ### Callback function ###
 =====================

 This function will call all <nRxDelay> milliseconds from the timer. The
 parameter list from this function is passed by Windows.
 The global variable ReceiveMode controls function maintenance:
 Mode 1 - the function waits for start of telegram (STX).
 Mode 2 - On receipt of end of telegram (ETX) character, all data is
 copied to a buffer, and the edit window is closed.
**************************************************************************/
WORD FAR PASCAL PollRxQueue(HWND hWnd, WORD msg, WORD wP, LONG lP)
{
   COMSTAT  CommState;
   int      nRead,            // Number of characters read
            nSize;
   HANDLE   hMem;
   PSTR     pMem,
            pDes,
            pTmp,
            pMemTmp;
```

```
GetCommError(nCid,&CommState);     // Read interface status
nRead = CommState.cbInQue;         // Number of characters in
if(nRead <= 0)                     // receive buffer
{
   GetCommEventMask(nCid,0xFFFF); // Clear event mask
   return FALSE;
}

hMem = LocalAlloc(LMEM_MOVEABLE, nRead+1);
pMem = LocalLock(hMem);

nRead = ReadComm(nCid, (LPSTR) pMem, nRead);
if(nRead <= 0)
{
   GetCommError(nCid,&CommState);
   GetCommEventMask(nCid,0xFFFF); // Clear event mask
   return FALSE;
}

pMem[nRead] = '\0';         // Close buffer

switch (ReceiveMode)
{
  case 1:   // Wait for STX
   while((*pMem != '\0') && (*pMem != STX) )
   {
      pMem++;
   }

   switch (*pMem)
   {
     case '\0':                    // End of string
        LocalUnlock(hMem);            // Unlock data if no
        LocalFree(hMem);                      // STX can be found
        FlushComm(nCid, RXQUEUE);
        return FALSE;
     break;

     case STX:                     // Begin data telegram
        hData = LocalAlloc(LMEM_MOVEABLE, LocalSize(hMem));
        pData = LocalLock(hData);

        pTmp = pData;
                            pMemTmp = pMem;
        pMemTmp++;
        while((*pMemTmp != ETX) && (*pMemTmp))
        {
        *pTmp++ = *pMemTmp++;
```

```
      };
    *pTmp = '\0';                    // End string

         if(*pMemTmp == ETX)
         {
           SendMessage(hRxWnd, WM_SETTEXT, 0, (LONG)(LPSTR)pData);
           FlushComm(nCid, RXQUEUE);
           ReceiveMode = 1;
           LocalUnlock(hMem);
           LocalFree(hMem);
                    return TRUE;
           break;            // Receive complete telegram
         }
         ReceiveMode = 2;    // Wait for ETX (rest of telegram)
         LocalUnlock(hData);
         LocalUnlock(hMem);
         LocalFree(hMem);            return FALSE;
      break;
    }
   break;    // Wait for STX

   case 2:   // Wait for ETX
    pData = LocalLock(hData);
    nSize = lstrlen(pData);
    LocalUnlock(hData);

    hData = LocalReAlloc(hData, nSize+nRead, LMEM_MOVEABLE);
    pData = LocalLock (hData);
    pDes = &pData[nSize];
    pMemTmp = pMem;
    while((*pMemTmp != ETX) && (*pMemTmp))
    {
       *pDes++ = *pMemTmp++;
    }
            *pDes = '\0';

    if (*pMemTmp == ETX)        // Receive complete telegram
    {
                      SendMessage(hRxWnd, WM_SETTEXT, 0, (LONG)(LPSTR)pData);
        FlushComm(nCid, RXQUEUE);
        ReceiveMode = 1;
            LocalUnlock(hMem);
            LocalFree(hMem);
        return TRUE;
    }
    else
    {
       LocalUnlock(hData);
```

```
        ReceiveMode = 2;   // Wait for ETX (rest of telegram)
            LocalUnlock(hMem);
            LocalFree(hMem);
      }
     break;   // Wait for ETX
   }
}

/**********************************************************************
 I n s t a l l T i m e r F k t
 ==============================
 This function installs a timer function which calls all <Cpp.nRxDelay>
 milliseconds, and creates a child window from which all received data
 is displayed. This window is updated dynamically.
 The return value is NULL if no free system time is available, or the
 timer ID. This is provided by the de-installation of KillTimer.
 **********************************************************************/
WORD InstallTimerFkt(void)
{
   WORD     wTimerId;
   RECT     rRect;

   lpTimerFkt = MakeProcInstance(PollRxQueue, hInst);
   wTimerId   = SetTimer(NULL, 0, Cpp.nRxDelay, lpTimerFkt);
   if(wTimerId)
   {
      GetClientRect(hwMain,(LPRECT) &rRect);
      hRxWnd = CreateWindow ("EDIT", "",
                            WS_CHILD | WS_VISIBLE | WS_BORDER |
                            WS_HSCROLL | WS_VSCROLL |
                            ES_AUTOHSCROLL | ES_AUTOVSCROLL |
                            ES_MULTILINE | DS_LOCALEDIT,
                            rRect.right/2, rRect.bottom/2,
                            rRect.right/2, rRect.bottom/2,
                            hwMain,       // Main window
                            1,            // Child ID
                            hInst,        // Instance of application
                            NULL);        // No extra parameters
     ShowWindow(hRxWnd,SW_SHOWNORMAL);
   }
   else
   {
      // No timer available
   }
   return wTimerId;
}
```

CLPPARAM.C source code

```
/***********************************************************************

 C L P P A R A M . C    Module for adding serial interface parameters

***********************************************************************/

#include <WINDOWS.H>
#include <stdlib.h>
#include <sys\types.h>
#include <sys\stat.h>
#include <io.h>
#include <fcntl.h>
#include <string.h>
#include <stdio.h>
#include "CLPPARAM.H"
#include "CLP_RC.H"

/*==========================< External variables >=====================*/
extern char    szAppTitle;
extern int     nnCid;
extern HANDLE  hInst;

#define MAXBAUDRATE  5
#define MAXCOMPORTS  4


/*===========================< Local variables >=======================*/
DCB        CommDCB;
DCB FAR *  lpDCB;
COMSTAT    CommState;

char       szMsgBoxTitle[]= "COMx:-Status";     // Error box title

char       szDefSetting[] = "COM2:=48,n,8,1";   // Default values

char       szaCommPort[4][5]  = { {"com1"},
                                  {"com2"},
                                  {"com3"},
                                  {"com4"} };

char       szaBaudRate[5][6] = { {"1200"},
                                 {"2400"},
                                 {"4800"},
                                 {"9600"},
                                 {"19200"} };
```

```
WORD      waBaudRate[6]     = { 1200, 2400, 4800, 9600, 19200};
BYTE      waByteSize[2]     = { 7, 8 };
BYTE      waStopBits[3]     = { ONESTOPBIT, ONE5STOPBITS, TWOSTOPBITS };
BYTE      waParity[3]       = { NOPARITY,   ODDPARITY,    EVENPARITY };

char      szErrorMsg[80];

extern COMMPORTPARAM  Cpp;         /* Current line parameters */

/*****************************************************************************
 C l e a n P r o f i l e S t r i n g
 ====================================
 This function removes the equal sign (=) from the default string in WIN.INI so
 that the new string can be placed directly after the BuildCommDCB() function
*****************************************************************************/
void CleanProfileString(LPSTR lpTarget, LPSTR lpSource)
{
  while (*lpSource != '\0')
  {
    if(*lpSource != '=')
       *lpTarget++ = *lpSource;
    lpSource++;
  }
  *lpTarget = '\0';
}

/***************************************************************************
 R e a d W i n I n i E n t r y
 =============================

 This function searches WIN.INI for the parameter describing the interface
 (COM1:=0, ... COM4:=3), needed by <CommPortId>. If no such default is
 found in WIN.INI, then the entries given by <szDefSettings> are used. The
 function also generates a device control block for the appropriate
 interface.

 Parameters:
   CommPortId     Interface ID number

 Return values:
   BOOL          TRUE => DCB installed correctly, otherwise FALSE
***************************************************************************/
BOOL ReadWinIniEntry(int CommPortId)
{
   char  szStdSetting[30];
   char  szSetting[30];
   int   i;
```

```
   /*----< WIN.INI access >-----------------------------------------------*/
   GetProfileString((LPSTR) "[ports]", (LPSTR) szaCommPort[CommPortId],
                    (LPSTR) szDefSetting, (LPSTR) szStdSetting, 29 );

   /*---< Create DCB >-----------------------------------------------------*/

   CleanProfileString(szSetting,szStdSetting);  // Remove '=' character

   if(BuildCommDCB(szSetting,&CommDCB) != 0)
   {
     wsprintf((LPSTR) szErrorMsg,
             (LPSTR) "DCB could not be created for %s",
             szaCommPort[CommPortId]);
     MessageBox(GetFocus(), (LPSTR) szErrorMsg, (LPSTR) szMsgBoxTitle,
               MB_OK | MB_ICONEXCLAMATION);
     return FALSE;
   }

   i = 0;
   while(CommDCB.BaudRate != atoi(szaBaudRate[i])) i++;
   Cpp.wBaudRate = i;

   Cpp.bByteSize = CommDCB.ByteSize==8 ? 1 : 0;   // 7 or 8 data bits only
   Cpp.bStopBits = CommDCB.StopBits;
   Cpp.bPortId   = CommDCB.Id;
   Cpp.bParity   = CommDCB.Parity;
   return TRUE;
}

/*************************************************************************
 I n i t C o m m P o r t ()
 ==========================

 This function opens the serial interface specified by <CommPortId> and
 initializes the interface with the values given by the corresponding
 DCB structure <CommBCD[CommPortID]>.

 Parameters:
   int CommPortId     0=COM1:, ... 3=COM4:

 Return values:
   The return value appears whether the function was successful or not. If
   a positive value is returned, initialization was successful. Otherwise,
   -1 is returned. The CID is placed in the Id field of the appropriate DCB
   structure, and indicates the correct initialization.
*************************************************************************/
int InitCommPort(COMMPORTPARAM *pCpp)
```

```
{
   int  CID;
   int  PortId;    // 0 = COM1 ... 3 = COM4

   PortId = pCpp->bPortId;
   if((pCpp->nRxQueSize <= 0) || (pCpp->nTxQueSize <= 0))
   {
      wsprintf((LPSTR) szErrorMsg,
            (LPSTR) "Receive or Send buffer too small\n(RX Buffer: %d, TX
Buffer: %d",
               pCpp->nRxQueSize, pCpp->nTxQueSize);
      MessageBox(GetFocus(), (LPSTR) szErrorMsg, (LPSTR) szMsgBoxTitle,
               MB_OK | MB_ICONEXCLAMATION);
      return -1;
   }
   CID = OpenComm((LPSTR)szaCommPort[PortId], pCpp->nRxQueSize, pCpp-
>nTxQueSize);

   if(CID < 0)
   {
      LoadString(hInst, CID, (LPSTR) szErrorMsg, sizeof(szErrorMsg)-1);
      MessageBox(GetFocus(), (LPSTR) szErrorMsg, (LPSTR) szMsgBoxTitle,
               MB_OK | MB_ICONEXCLAMATION);
      CloseComm(PortId);
      return -1;       // Error during Open!
   }
   else
   {
      CommDCB.Id         = (BYTE) CID;
      CommDCB.BaudRate   = waBaudRate[pCpp->wBaudRate];
      CommDCB.ByteSize   = waByteSize[pCpp->bByteSize];
      CommDCB.Parity     = waParity  [pCpp->bParity];
      CommDCB.StopBits   = waStopBits[pCpp->bStopBits];

      FlushComm(CID,TXQUEUE);
      FlushComm(CID,RXQUEUE);

      if(SetCommState((DCB FAR *) &CommDCB) != 0)
      {
       wsprintf((LPSTR) szErrorMsg,
               (LPSTR)"Initialization error:\n%s
Baud=%d,Parity=%d,Byte=%d,Stops=%d",
               szaCommPort[PortId], CommDCB.BaudRate, CommDCB.Parity,
               CommDCB.ByteSize, CommDCB.StopBits);
       MessageBox(GetFocus(), (LPSTR) szErrorMsg, (LPSTR) szMsgBoxTitle,
                 MB_OK | MB_ICONEXCLAMATION);
       return -1; // Error during init!
      }
```

```
      /*-----< Control display of current parameters >-----------------*/
      GetCommState(CID, &CommDCB);
      wsprintf((LPSTR) szErrorMsg,(LPSTR) "COM: setup:\n%s %d,%d,%d,%d",
               (LPSTR) szaCommPort[PortId],
      CommDCB.BaudRate,CommDCB.Parity,CommDCB.ByteSize,CommDCB.StopBits);
      MessageBox(GetFocus(), (LPSTR) szErrorMsg, (LPSTR) szMsgBoxTitle,
                 MB_OK | MB_ICONEXCLAMATION);
   }
   return CID;       // Open and Init OK!
}

/*************************************************************************
  M d f C o m S e t u p ()
  ========================

  ### Dialog box function ### for line parameter options
*************************************************************************/
BOOL FAR PASCAL MdfCommSetup(HWND hDlg, unsigned msg, WORD wP, LONG lP)
{
   BYTE     i;

   switch(msg)
   {
      case WM_INITDIALOG:                          /* Initialization */
       for(i=0;i<MAXBAUDRATE;SendDlgItemMessage(hDlg, CB_BAUD, CB_ADDSTRING, 0,
(LONG)(LPSTR) szaBaudRate[i++]));
       for(i=0;i<MAXCOMPORTS;SendDlgItemMessage(hDlg, CB_PORT, CB_ADDSTRING, 0,
(LONG)(LPSTR) szaCommPort[i++]));
       SendDlgItemMessage(hDlg, CB_BAUD, CB_SETCURSEL, Cpp.wBaudRate, 0L);
       SendDlgItemMessage(hDlg, CB_PORT, CB_SETCURSEL, Cpp.bPortId, 0L);
       CheckRadioButton(hDlg, RB_7DB, RB_8DB,  RB_7DB + Cpp.bByteSize);
       CheckRadioButton(hDlg, RB_1SB, RB_3SB,  RB_1SB + Cpp.bStopBits);
       CheckRadioButton(hDlg, RB_NONE,RB_EVEN, RB_NONE+ Cpp.bParity);
       SetDlgItemInt(hDlg, EB_TXSIZE, Cpp.nTxQueSize, FALSE);
       SetDlgItemInt(hDlg, EB_RXSIZE, Cpp.nRxQueSize, FALSE);
       SetDlgItemInt(hDlg, EB_RXDELAY, Cpp.nRxDelay, FALSE);
       return(TRUE);
       break;

      case WM_COMMAND:                             /* Command received */
       switch(wP)
       {
          case IDOK:
             Cpp.wBaudRate  = (WORD) SendDlgItemMessage(hDlg,CB_BAUD,
CB_GETCURSEL, 0, 0L);
             Cpp.bPortId    = (BYTE) SendDlgItemMessage(hDlg,CB_PORT,
CB_GETCURSEL, 0, 0L);
```

```
            for(i = RB_7DB; i <= RB_8DB; i++)
            if(IsDlgButtonChecked(hDlg, i))
               Cpp.bByteSize = i - RB_7DB;

            for(i = RB_1SB; i <= RB_3SB; i++)
            if(IsDlgButtonChecked(hDlg, i))
               Cpp.bStopBits = i - RB_1SB;

            for(i = RB_NONE; i <= RB_EVEN; i++)
            if(IsDlgButtonChecked(hDlg, i))
               Cpp.bParity = i - RB_NONE;

            Cpp.nTxQueSize = GetDlgItemInt(hDlg, EB_TXSIZE, NULL, FALSE);
            Cpp.nRxQueSize = GetDlgItemInt(hDlg, EB_RXSIZE, NULL, FALSE);
            Cpp.nRxDelay   = GetDlgItemInt(hDlg, EB_RXDELAY, NULL, FALSE);

            EndDialog(hDlg, TRUE);        /* Close dialog box */
            break;

         case IDCANCEL:                   /* Cancel */
            EndDialog(hDlg, TRUE);
            break;

         default:
            return(FALSE);
            break;
      }
      return(TRUE);
      break;

     default:
      return(FALSE);
      break;
   }
}


/*************************************************************************
  C o m m E r r o r ()
  ====================

  Tests communication interface status, and displays any errors in a modal
  message box.
*************************************************************************/
short CommError(short Cid)
{
   short   nError, nStringId;
```

```
    nError = GetCommError(Cid, NULL);
    if(nError > 0) nStringId = nError + 0x1000;  // Create StringId
    else nStringId = nError;
    LoadString(hInst, nStringId, (LPSTR) szErrorMsg, sizeof(szErrorMsg)-1);
    MessageBox(GetFocus(), (LPSTR)szErrorMsg, (LPSTR)"Interface error",
               MB_ICONEXCLAMATION | MB_OK | MB_APPLMODAL);
    return(nError);
}
```

CLPSELEC.C source code

```
/***************************************************************************

 C L P S E L E C . C    Functions for realizing a file select box

***************************************************************************/

#include <windows.h>
#include <string.h>
#include <direct.h>
#include "CLP_RC.H"

extern HANDLE hInst;
extern char   szAppName[];

/* IO function prototyping */
int ClipboardToFile(HWND, LPSTR);
int FileToClipboard(HWND, LPSTR);

/*-----------------------------------------------------------------------*/
/*                        File select dialog box                          */
/*-----------------------------------------------------------------------*/

char FileName[MAXPATHLEN],
     CurName [MAXPATHLEN],
     LastName[MAXPATHLEN],
     DefFileExt[] = "CLP";



LoadFile(HWND hDlg)
{
  GetDlgItemText(hDlg, EB_FILE, (LPSTR)CurName, 15);

  if(DlgDirList(hDlg, (LPSTR)CurName, LB_FILES, EB_PATH, 0xC010))
  {
    /* EB_FILE contains drive or directory */
```

```
    GetDlgItemText(hDlg, EB_PATH, (LPSTR)FileName, MAXPATHLEN);

    if( FileName[ strlen(FileName)-1 ] != '\\')
      strcat(FileName,"\\");

    strcat(FileName, CurName);
    SetDlgItemText(hDlg, EB_PATH, (LPSTR)FileName);
    SetDlgItemText(hDlg, EB_FILE, (LPSTR)LastName);
    DlgDirList(hDlg, (LPSTR)CurName, LB_FILES, EB_PATH, 0x4010);
    return(FALSE);
  }

  GetDlgItemText(hDlg, EB_PATH, (LPSTR)FileName, MAXPATHLEN);
  if(FileName[ strlen(FileName)-1 ] != '\\')
     strcat(FileName,"\\");

  strcat(FileName, CurName);

  if(strchr(FileName,'.') == 0)            /* Add default extension */
  {
     strcat(FileName,".");
     strcat(FileName,DefFileExt);
  }
  return(TRUE);
}


/**************************************************************************
 M d f F i l e S e l e c t                         ### Callback function ###
 =========================

 This if the file select box's window function
*************************************************************************/
BOOL FAR PASCAL MdfFileSelect(HWND hDlg, unsigned msg, WORD wP, LONG lP)
{
  char  szBuffer[63];

  switch(msg)
  {
     case WM_INITDIALOG:   /* Initialize dialog box */
        getcwd(szBuffer, 62);
        EnableWindow(GetDlgItem(hDlg, EB_PATH), FALSE);
        SetDlgItemText(hDlg, EB_PATH, (LPSTR) szBuffer);
        strcpy(szBuffer, "*.");
        strcat(szBuffer, DefFileExt);
        SetDlgItemText(hDlg, EB_FILE, (LPSTR) szBuffer);
        DlgDirList(hDlg, (LPSTR) szBuffer, LB_FILES, EB_PATH, 0x4010);
        return(TRUE);
```

```
     break;

  case WM_COMMAND:
    switch (wP)
    {
      case PB_OK:
         if(IsWindowEnabled(GetDlgItem(hDlg, PB_OK)))
         {
           if(LoadFile(hDlg))
           {
              EndDialog(hDlg, TRUE);
           }
         }
         break;

      case PB_ABB:
         EndDialog(hDlg, FALSE);
         break;

      case EB_FILE:         /* Filename */
         if(HIWORD(lP) == EN_CHANGE)
         {
           EnableWindow(GetDlgItem(hDlg, PB_OK),
                        (BOOL)SendMessage(GetDlgItem(hDlg, EB_FILE),
                        WM_GETTEXTLENGTH, (WORD)0, 0L));
           GetDlgItemText(hDlg, EB_FILE, (LPSTR)CurName, 15);
           if ( strchr(CurName,'*') || strchr(CurName,'?'))
              strcpy(LastName,CurName);  /* Name as selection criterion */
         }
         break;

      case LB_FILES:        /* Directory */
         switch(HIWORD(lP))
         {
           case 1:
              DlgDirSelect(hDlg, (LPSTR)CurName, LB_FILES);
              SetDlgItemText(hDlg, EB_FILE, (LPSTR)CurName);
           break;

           case 2:
              if(LoadFile(hDlg))
              {
                 EndDialog(hDlg, TRUE);
              }
              break;
         }
         break;
```

```
       default:    return(FALSE);
     }
     break;

     default: return(FALSE);
  }
  return(TRUE);
}

/***************************************************************************
 G e t S e l e c t e d F i l e N a m e
 ======================================

 Returns the last selected filename in the lpFileName parameter. If the
 CANCEL button closes the file selection, the system defaults to the last
 filename selected.
***************************************************************************/
void GetSelectedFileName(LPSTR lpFileName)
{
  lstrcpy(lpFileName, (LPSTR) FileName);
}

/***************************************************************************
 P r o c e s s I o C o m m a n d
 ================================

 Process clipboard file read/write commands
***************************************************************************/
void ProcessIoCommand(HWND hWnd, unsigned msg, WORD wP, LONG lP)
{
  FARPROC     lpTmpProc;
  char        szFileName[MAXPATHLEN];
  char        szBuffer[80];
  BOOL        bSuccess;

  switch(wP)
  {
    case MI_LOAD:          /* Load clipboard file */
      lpTmpProc = MakeProcInstance((FARPROC) MdfFileSelect, hInst);
      bSuccess  = DialogBox(hInst, "FILESELECT", hWnd, lpTmpProc);
      FreeProcInstance(lpTmpProc);
      if(bSuccess)
      {
        GetSelectedFileName((LPSTR) szFileName);
        if(FileToClipboard(hWnd, (LPSTR) szFileName) == NULL)
        {
           wsprintf((LPSTR) szBuffer, "Error while loading:\n[%s]",
                    (LPSTR) szFileName);
```

```
          MessageBox(hWnd, (LPSTR) szBuffer, (LPSTR) szAppName,
              MB_ICONEXCLAMATION | MB_OK | MB_DEFBUTTON1 |
              MB_APPLMODAL);
        }
      }
      break;

    case MI_SAVE:          /* Save clipboard file */
      lpTmpProc = MakeProcInstance(MdfFileSelect, hInst);
      bSuccess  = DialogBox(hInst, "FILESELECT", hWnd, lpTmpProc);
      FreeProcInstance(lpTmpProc);
      if(bSuccess)
      {
        GetSelectedFileName((LPSTR) szFileName);
        if(ClipboardToFile(hWnd, (LPSTR) szFileName) == NULL)
        {
          wsprintf((LPSTR) szBuffer, "Error while saving:\n[%s]",
                  (LPSTR) szFileName);
          MessageBox(hWnd, (LPSTR) szBuffer,(LPSTR) szAppName,
              MB_ICONEXCLAMATION | MB_OK | MB_DEFBUTTON1 |
              MB_APPLMODAL);
        }
      }
      break;
  }
} // of ProcessCommand
```

15 Dynamic Link Libraries

DLL (acronym for Dynamic Link Library) are three letters discussed by anyone that works with Windows or OS/2. This chapter describes DLL and how it works. Let's begin with a better-known, related subject, static linking.

15.1 Static Linking

Let's begin with compiling, the process which changes most C source codes into executable programs. The compiler analyzes a preset C source text in passes, generating a machine code in the last step that the CPU can execute directly.

Note:

When we refer to a C compiler and linker, we refer to the Microsoft C system available from Microsoft Corporation.

Compiling

A compiled source code is also called a module. It doesn't always have to be a complete C program with a main() or WinMain() function. When using the c option, the C compiler (For simplicity's sake we refer to the Microsoft C compiler cl in the following sections) compiles source codes consisting of individual functions. The C compiler then generates .OBJ (object) files from these source codes. The .OBJ files are the starting point for the static linking process.

Linking

The linker needs the .OBJ files mentioned above as input to compile an .EXE (executable) program. This is where the libraries come into play. Almost all C programs use functions that are supplied by the compiler manufacturer. These functions (e.g., printf) are written with specific behavior in mind, and save the programmer the effort of coding these functions on his/her own.

A group of functions in one source code comprise a library. For example, the Windows SDK static runtime library, SLIBCEW.LIB, contains the object code of the Windows-compatible C runtime functions, designated for the SMALL memory model.

Anyone who wants to look at the range of function of this library can use the library management program, LIB.EXE. To do so, follow these steps:

1) Start LIB.EXE from MS-DOS.

2) After the copyright message, answer the defaults as follows:

```
Library name: slibcew <Enter>
Operations: <Enter>
List file: list <Enter>
```

The LIB program creates a text file named LIST, which is almost 2000 lines long. From this list you can read all the functions contained in the library, along with their names, and extra information such as offsets within the library, or the sizes of code and data areas.

During compilation, the C compiler usually first puts temporary entry and return addresses for all function references into machine code. It is then the task of the linker to resolve such function references. During the conventional static link process, the linker links the object code of the required functions from libraries it is familiar with, or additionally specified libraries, directly to the object code of the program to be created during the link process. Later, the linker replaces all of the function addresses, left open by the compiler, with the real function addresses it is familiar with at that moment.

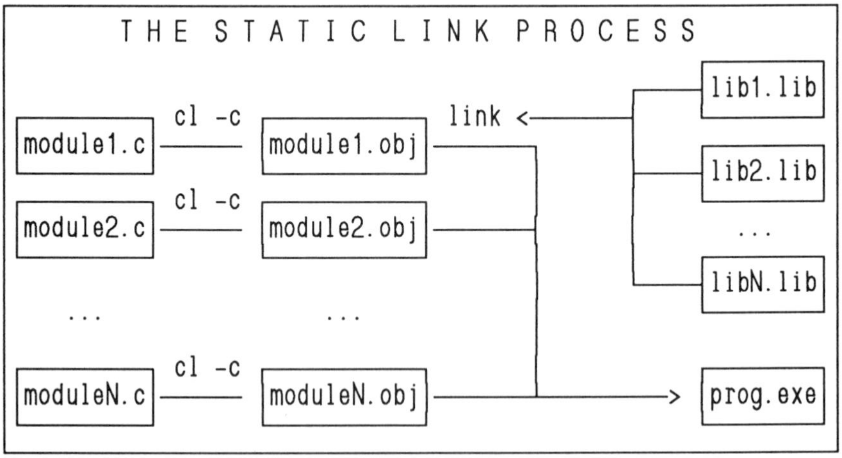

The linker is not only busy linking library functions. It must also resolve all of the external function references cited in the application's modules.

The linker is also responsible for providing the directly executable EXE file with a header, dependent on the operating system. In Windows programs, the EXETYPE WINDOWS instruction in the .DEF file of an application passes this header to the linker.

When a certain function is called several times in one program, the linker links the object code that corresponds to this function only once. On the other hand, if multiple programs use a certain library function, then the linker links the appropriate code to each of these programs. This results in multiple codes and higher memory demands.

15.2 Dynamic Linking

In a singletasking operating system such as MS-DOS, in which only one program runs at a time with perhaps a couple of interrupt-driven TSR programs in the background, this memory consumption doesn't matter. However, in a multitasking operating system such as Windows or OS/2, this same condition leads to a substantial waste of memory space.

That's why Windows and OS/2 support Dynamic Link Libraries (DLLs). These DLLs complement static libraries without replacing them. Dynamic Link Libraries are so versatile and practical that the Windows kernel is actually a collection of DLLs (i.e., KERNEL.EXE, GDI.EXE and USER.EXE).

Dynamic linker

The main difference between DLLs and static libraries is that several applications can use code sharing with DLLs. The code required for a certain function appears only once in the system, and all applications can then share that code. Also, the function code is loaded dynamically from the DLL during runtime, the first time an application calls that function. This dynamic load occurs if the function wasn't already loaded into memory by another application.

Let's take a closer look at the procedure the linker uses to create an .EXE file. When the linker resolves a function reference, it first checks the runtime library or any other specified static library (*.LIB) to see whether the function exists. If this is the case, it assumes the function code is available there and copies it to a specific location in the .EXE file.

If the linker encounters a function reference that belongs to a DLL function, it creates a relocation record instead of the DLL function. This relocation record consists of a data block containing all of the information needed to access and execute the function code at runtime. This information includes the DLL name, the function name or the ordinal number used to import a function from this DLL.

How does the linker know which functions are in DLLs? There are many ways to communicate this information to the linker. One possibility is to list all of the DLL functions used by an application in the IMPORTS section of the module definition file. The entries have to follow a certain pattern:

```
...
IMPORTS
    [Function_name Option] Module_name [Option]
                             ...
/* each additional entry in a separate line */
                             ...
```

[Function_name Option] is a character string of the form Functionname= and represents the names used by the application to call the function.

Module_name is a character string that indicates the name of the DLL file that contains the function to be imported. DLL files ordinarily have the .DLL extension under Windows 3. The module_name parameter is required.

Option is a character string of the form .DLL_Function name or .Ordinal_number. In the first form, the function is addressed within the module name DLL by its name, while in the second form it is addressed using a table index, the ordinal number. We have already seen ordinal numbers in the form @Number in the EXPORTS section of module definition files. Generally it's much quicker to access functions using ordinal numbers than it is using names. Ordinal numbers also save memory space. On the other hand, accessing by name is always clear cut to the programmer.

Here is a sample section of IMPORTS:

```
...
IMPORTS
   DrawGraph=GraphDLL.DrawProc
   GraphDLL.4
   GraphDLL.ShowDiagram
        ...
```

One alternative to the IMPORTS section is the use of import libraries. You declare an import library to the linker the same way you do with static libraries, either in the command line or in a separate link file. There is a special tool for creating an import library in SDK: IMPLIB. This program expects the module definition file of a DLL as its input. All of the functions that the DLL provides to other applications or DLLs are listed there in the EXPORTS section. IMPLIB evaluates this information and creates a special .LIB file for the linker. The linker can take all the relocation records for DLL functions from this file and insert the EXE file it is creating in the appropriate places. The LIBW.LIB file is an import library that we have used consistently in our make files. This contains all of the relocation records of the DLL modules KERNEL.EXE, GDI.EXE and USER.EXE.

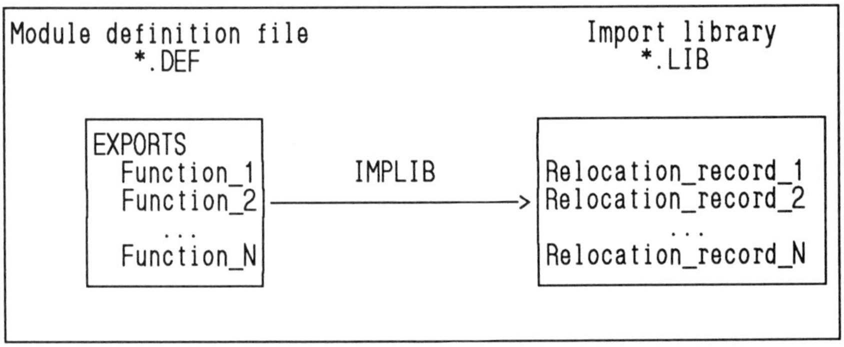

There is yet a third method for resolving a function reference that affects a DLL function. This method doesn't relate to the linker, however, but is performed by an application during runtime. In this method the application must know which DLL contains the function it is calling. It then loads the DLL using the LoadLibrary function, and receives a handle from the function. Each LoadLibrary function reference increases the reference counter of the DLL by one. The handle can pass the application along with the function name or an ordinal number as parameters of the GetProcAddress function, which returns a long pointer to the address of the function. This function pointer can be used in the form:

```
(* Function_Pointer) (...Parameter...)
```

as a function reference with parameters.

After the function reference, you call the FreeLibrary function using the handle returned from the LoadLibrary as a parameter. This lowers the DLL reference counter by one. If the reference counter reads zero, it means that none of the applications need the DLL and Windows can remove it from the memory again.

This method is mainly used when you load resources from a DLL at runtime, because you can also put certain resources (accelerators, bit maps, cursor, dialog box data structures, fonts, icons, menus and string tables) in DLLs. This prepares Windows for resource sharing.

Let's look a little deeper into what applications have in common with DLLs, and the differences between the two. They are both referred to as modules, which is where the term module definition file originates. DLLs and applications also have the same headers, which you can view with the help of the EXEHDR program. This helps you determine the functions that are exported and imported from a module. By using EXEHDR on the Windows DLLs KERNEL.EXE, GDI.EXE and USER.EXE you get a good overview of distribution of SDK functions to the individual modules.

The Windows device driver *.DRV is also a dynamic link library. One reason is that device drivers must always be addressable in the operating system. Having code in fixed DLL segments is the only way of guaranteeing this in EMS (Expanded Memory Specification) memory configurations. Code segments in memory can be faded in and out by the EMS driver unpredictably.

How do DLLs differ from applications? Unlike applications, DLLs don't have a WinMain() function which drives the entire program run of an application. DLLs also don't have a message loop. This means that DLLs are not subject to the polling multitasking mechanism of Windows. In other words, Windows does not view DLLs as independently executable programs. Another result of this is that when an application calls a function from a DLL, the scheduler in the Windows core doesn't perform a task change when it performs this function.

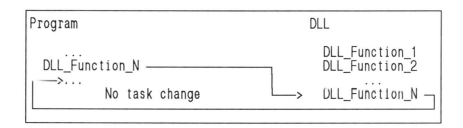

```
Program                                    DLL

     ...                                    DLL_Function_1
  DLL_Function_N ──────────────┐            DLL_Function_2
 ┌──>...                        │                 ...
 │          No task change      └──>        DLL_Function_N ─┐
 └──────────────────────────────────────────────────────────┘
```

Let's talk about the dynamic link process itself. This is how Windows handles the relocation records created by the linker during runtime, so that it can finally execute the function code. In order to accomplish this task, Windows must have some internal management tables. Among these are areas in the memory that are set up for each application to be executed. These areas have to remain available in the memory until the application is completed. We will refer to these memory areas as module management blocks, since Windows doesn't just create these blocks for applications, but also for DLLs.

The main purpose of a module management block is to provide the memory manager with minimal information for re-swapping segments removed from the memory with a certain module. The principle for this is similar to loading an operating system by diskette: In a certain area of the diskette (the boot block) is a code that ensures that all other parts of the operating system are downloaded in the correct sequence. The bootstrap loader, activated when you switch on the computer, only needs to know the address of this boot block. After that it no longer needs to download the operating system.

From the Windows memory manager's point of view, the module management blocks are like handles that have to be adapted to a new situation for each shift or delete operation, to guarantee access at all times to the required module. This brings us back to thunks, which we mentioned in connection with the MakeProcInstance function. You can divide a module management block into *thunks*.

Thunks

Thunks are pivots and hubs in the dynamic link process. When a function in an application calls a function located in a DLL, the linker inserts a relocation record which, in turn, causes a thunk in the module management area of the application to be called first. This is the first part of the dynamic link process.

The thunk of the application then does something remarkable: it modifies the relocation record in the application's function code. It modifies this code in such a way that the thunk in the module management block of the dynamic link library that is responsible for calling the function is called. This means that the thunk in the module management block of the application, called in the beginning, first performs its job.

After that, any time you call the DLL function within the application, it jumps directly to the appropriate DLL thunk. In turn, this has only the function of a go-between. It doesn't do anything else but jump to the address in the memory that contains the first command of the DLL function. If, however, this code is not in memory, the thunk first calls a routine that loads the required code from DLL into memory (DOS interrupt 3F is hidden behind the loading routine).

If the loading process was successful, the DLL thunk has to be adapted by Windows accordingly, in order to jump directly to the memory area where the function code was loaded during the next function reference.

If these processes seem quite complicated, keep the following in mind: By using module management blocks and thunks, you are greatly simplifying the task of the memory manager. When it shifts or deletes memory segments, all it has to do is make the proper adjustments in the appropriate module management blocks. It can then assume that the applications are able to access the required functions any time using the described mechanism.

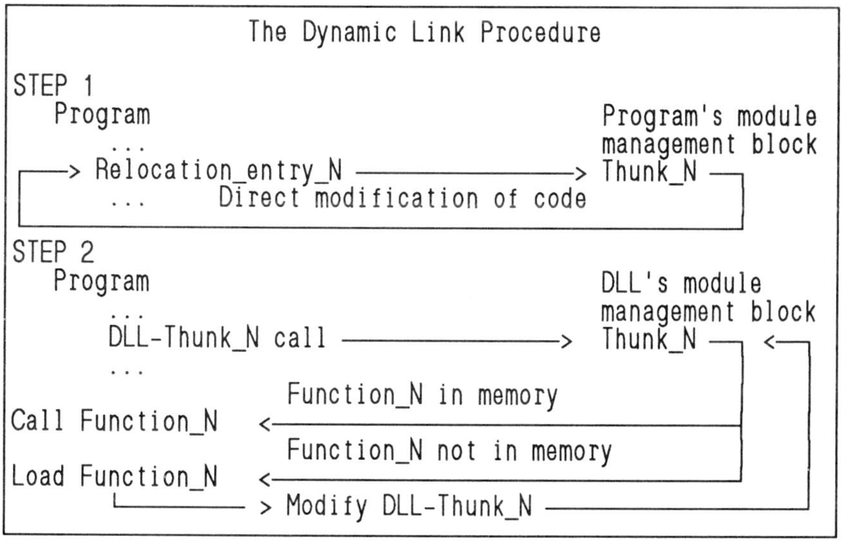

15.3 Programming DLLs

After describing the fundamental operation of the dynamic link process, we can finally turn our attention to creating DLLs.

Basically, the process for creating DLLs is very similar to the process for creating applications. Along with the source code containing functions, you also need a make file and a module definition file.

There are some special considerations to keep in mind when linking to DLLs. Although DLLs have their own data segment, they don't have their own stack. Instead, they use the stack of the application from which they were called. By itself, this fact is not a tragedy, but the problem is that many C runtime functions assume that when you call them, the stack segment register SS and the data segment register DS are on the same segment. When you call such functions with DLLs, you can get unexpected results under the right circumstances.

This circumstance can also lead to problems with functions written by users when the NEAR pointer placed in the data segment shows variables in the stack. To recognize such problems more easily, you should compile DLL modules with the -Aw option of the C compiler. When this option is turned on, the compiler pays attention to places, in source code, to which variables in the stack are referenced by NEAR pointers in the data segment. In such a case, the compiler gives you the following warning:

```
address of frame variable taken, DS != SS
```

and the programmer should then either use a FAR pointer or else declare the variable placed on the stack to be static. In this case, the compiler places this variable in the data segment and puts the pointer back in its proper place. Also remember that all of the parameters passed to a function are placed on the stack. Here is a small example:

```
// Example of a DLL function with stack and data segment variables
void FAR PASCAL DemoFunction (LPSTR lpszString)
{                       // lpszString lands on stack as parameter
  char * szString;      // Placed in data segment of the DLL
  char szBuffer[80]     // Placed in stack segment of calling application

/*****************************************************************
```

Using FAR pointers and functions that expect FAR pointers as parameters (e.g., lstrcpy) is not critical, since both segment and offset are used in the compiler's allocations.

```
*************************************************************/
lstrcpy(szBuffer, lpszString);
/*************************************************************
```

The following allocation is problematic since szString points to the data segment and szBuffer is in the stack segment. If you compiled with the -Aw option, the compiler would give you the warning "address of frame variable taken, DS!=SS". You can get more security by defining the preprocessor symbol _WINDLL. It's best if you do it right in the command line (with the switch -D_WINDLL). In this case unsuitable functions from the standard library are not declared in the corresponding Include files and the compiler (not the linker) gives the warning "no function prototype given", which indicates the illegal usage.

```
*************************************************************/
pString = szBuffer;
     ...
     ...
} // DemoFunction
```

Functions called by modules outside of the DLL have to be declared as FAR in DLLs. They also have to be exported to the module definition file of the DLL. Pointers that are passed as parameters from an application to a DLL function also have to be declared as FAR.

When functions are called in a DLL that uses the local heap (e.g., dynamic memory allocations with LocalAlloc), then the DLL has to be provided with a special initialization function. This is one of the few cases where the Windows programmer uses assembler functions. While this special function has to initialize the local heap of the DLL, it can also perform other tasks and is only executed once by Windows when the DLL is loaded into the main memory. This is not necessary for regular applications, since in this case Windows itself undertakes this task.

Why is it necessary to fall back on an assembler module for the initialization function? The reason for this is that, instead of getting its arguments in the stack, the initialization function of a DLL gets them in processor registers, which cannot be accessed from C. This doesn't mean that you have to steep yourself in assembler programming, however. You can use the assembler module LIBENTRY.ASM for initialization. LIBENTRY.ASM comes with SDK; it's in the SELECT directory of one of the sample program diskettes.

Basically, the following happens in this module: a routine, LibEntry is declared. Windows calls this routine each time a DLL is loaded into memory. The first task of this function is to back up values stored in certain CPU registers to the stack. When you call this function, certain values passed by Windows are in the following registers:

CX contains the heap size of the DLL, as specified in the module definition file that belongs to it. DI includes the instance handle of the DLL. DS contains the data segment (if the DLL has one—there are also DLLs that don't have a data segment) while the registers ES and SI together make up a long pointer to any passed command line character strings.

After placing the parameters above in the CPU stack, the LibEntry routine proceeds in the following manner: if there was no heap size specified in the module definition file, the LibMain function is immediately called as a subroutine. Otherwise the stack is prepared to call the LocalInit SDK function, that initializes a heap in a certain segment:

```
BOOL LocalInit; (WORD wSegment, PSTR pFirst, PSTR pLast);
```

The function creates a local heap, in wSegment, between the offsets pFirst and pLast. So the heap then has the size of pLast-pFirst+1 byte. If the heap was successfully installed, the function returns a value greater than zero; otherwise it returns zero.

The preparation for the stack within the LibEntry routine consists of placing the three parameters for the LocalInit function there. For wSegment, the data segment register DS is placed on the stack first, then the Start-Offset pFirst by assigning a zero to the AX registers. Then PUSH AX operation is defined at the beginning of the data segment. Finally, the CX register, which contains the size of the heap, goes on the stack for the parameter pLast.

After the call of the LocalInit function and if execution was successful, the LibMain function is also called. The LibMain function, now on the stack, contains the arguments of the initialization function. Otherwise zero is returned as a failure value and the LibEntry ends. Within the LibMain function, which can be recreated in C, the programmer can carry out some of his own initialization functions for the DLL. For example, you could register window classes or initialize global variables of the DLL. The LibMain function is expected to return 1 if execution was successful; otherwise it returns zero.

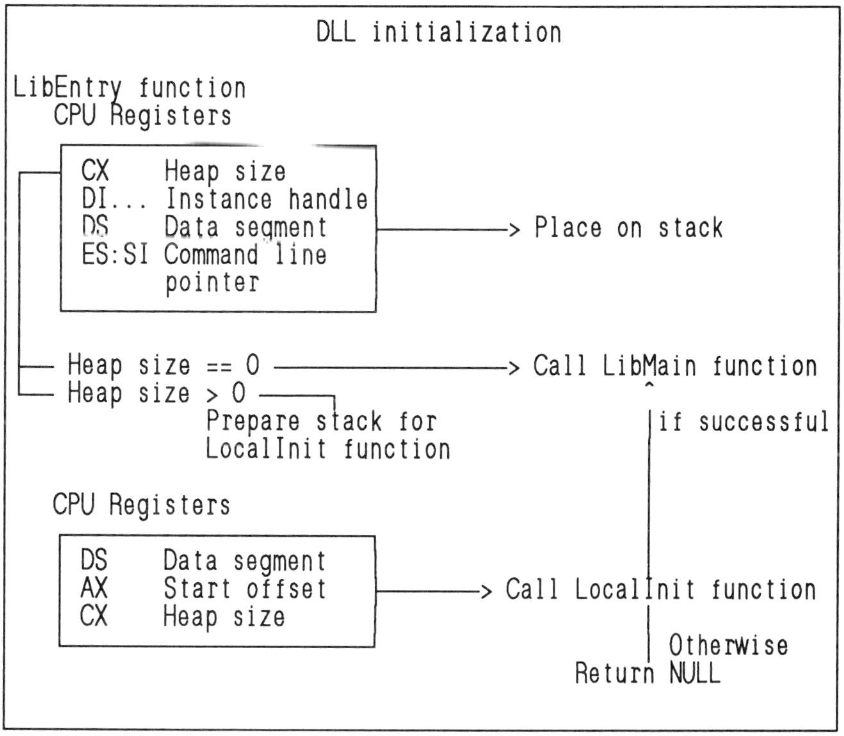

When you quit a Windows application, it can still close open files, release allocated resources, etc. by processing the WM_DESTROY message. Since Windows cannot send any messages to DLLs, you don't have these options here.

Instead, define a certain function within the DLL similar to the following:

```
int FAR PASCAL WEP (int nShutdownFlag)
{  switch (nShutdownFlag)
   {
     case WEP_SYSTEMEXIT:  // Exit Windows
       // Perform clean-up work
              ...
       return 1;
       break;
     case WEP_FREE_DLL:    // DLL is removed from memory
       // Perform clean-up work
              ...
       return 1;
       break;
     default:              // Should not happen
       return 1;
       break;
   }
} // WEP
```

Windows calls the WEP function (the name stands for Windows Exit Procedure) in two cases. Either Windows itself exits, or the memory manager removes DLL from the memory because the reference counter has reached the value of 0. The reference counter indicates how many applications are accessing a DLL at one time.

The WEP function can distinguish both cases on the basis of the nShutdownFlag parameters passed by Windows. In the first case, nShutdownFlag has the value WEP_SYSTEMEXIT and in the second case it has the value WEP_FREE_DLL. The return value of the function is always 1. As a Callback function for Windows, the WEP function has to be exported to the module definition file of the DLL. There is one task that doesn't need to be performed in the WEP function: the release of registered Windows classes with the help of the UnRegisterClass function. Windows automatically releases them.

15.4 Application: TRACEDLL.DLL

Let's look at a true application. The DLL, which we introduce in this section, can be useful during debugging or study of the runtime performance during program development. The module from which the DLL is created is TRACEDLL.C.

In TRACEDLL.C there are three other functions besides a WEP function. Since we don't need the local heap or the initialization arguments in this DLL, we don't use the LIBENTRY assembler module in connection with the LibMain function.

You use the OpenTraceFile function to open trace files. A trace file is a text file where formatted entries, with a date and time stamp from different processed functions, are written line by line during the runtime of an application.

```
int FAR PASCAL OpenTraceFile (LPSTR lpszTraceFile)
{
  int     nFileDescriptor;      // File handle
  static OFSTRUCT Of;           // Open File data structure

  nFileDescriptor = OpenFile(lpszTraceFile, (LPOFSTRUCT)&Of,
                             OF_CREATE | OF_READWRITE);
  if (nFileDescriptor == -1) // File could not be opened
  {
    MessageBox(GetFocus(), "Trace file could not be opened",
               "OpenTraceFile", MB_ICONEXCLAMATION | MB_OK);
  }
  return nFileDescriptor;
} // OpenTraceFile
```

The only parameter the function receives is a long pointer to the name of the trace file to be opened. Up until now we have been using the buffered f... I/O functions of the C runtime library for file operations in our examples, such as fopen, fread, fwrite, fclose. These functions are called buffered because the data do not go directly from the memory to the disk or vice versa during read/write operations. Instead, they are managed internally in buffers of a certain size. The file I/O from the program is usually managed optimally through buffered disk management, unnoticed by the program.

For program developers these functions are relatively convenient and have a variety of uses. Microsoft, however, does not recommend using these functions in Windows programs because the buffered file functions perform memory allocations internally, which run counter to the concept of memory management. This is similar to using the malloc runtime function for dynamic memory allocation in a Windows program. The request for memory is performed successfully, but the memory received cannot be moved as a block to a free call, which causes memory fragmentation.

The file system is, in general, the part of Windows where the programmer finds himself almost entirely at DOS level. Microsoft recommends using low-level file functions in applications. Among the standard low-level functions are open, read, write, close, fstat, lseek. They are referred to as low level because they run to the application unbuffered and are very strongly oriented to the operating system.

The Windows SDK offers some modifications of low-level file functions which make programming a little easier. By far the most extensive and powerful of these modifications is the OpenFile function, which we use in the OpenTraceFile function:

```
int OpenFile (LPSTR lpszFileName, LPOFSTRUCT lpOf, WORD wMode);
```

lpszFileName is a long pointer to a character string that comes from the ANSI character set. It states the name of the file to be opened. Windows converts the characters of this name to the OEM character set, used by DOS for file management.

lpOf is a type of long pointer to an OFSTRUCT data structure. Data structures like this are defined in the WINDOWS.H include file. Variables of this type contain information for each file opened with OpenFile. This information makes it possible to close and reopen the file more easily during the program run:

```
typedef struct tagOFSTRUCT
{
  BYTE cBytes;       // Number of bytes in the OFSTRUCT data structure
  BYTE fFixedDisk;   // Not equal to 0: File is on a hard drive
                     // Else: File is on a disk drive
  WORD nErrCode;     // With a return value of the OpenFile function of -1,
                     // contains DOS error code for more exact analysis
  BYTE reserved;     // Reserved by Windows
```

```
  BYTE szPathName[120]; // Character string (characters from OEM character set)
                        // Complete filename (may have been expanded by Windows)
                        // placed here. Expanded in this case, means
                        // that Windows completes the path of a relatively
                        // specified filename.
} OFSTRUCT;
```

As a general rule of file management under Windows, you should keep a file open only as long as is absolutely necessary. Microsoft's recommendation even goes so far as to say don't keep any files open past a call from GetMessage() or PeekMessage(). In other words don't keep it open past a potential task change. On the one hand, this is because the available FilePointers (Filehandles) for files are limited (usually 20). On the other hand, the principle of competition once again comes into play: As many of the running programs as possible want to use all of the available resources at the same time. Besides, serious errors all the way up to data loss can occur if an application makes changes in the file system during a task change (e.g., the user is prompted to change disks) while another program still has a file open there.

The solution: either increase the number (up to 255) of available FilePointers with the help of the SetHandleCount SDK function (of course, this procedure takes up some management buffer in the main memory) or even better, keep the currently opened file open for as short a time as possible.

OpenFile flags

Let's consider the third parameter of the OpenFile function. sMode is a combination of flags and indicates how the file should be opened. The most important flags are:

OF_READ	Open file only for reading.
OF_WRITE	Open file only for writing.
OF_READWRITE	Open file for reading and writing.
OF_CREATE	Create a file. An existing file is set at the beginning to zero bytes.
OF_REOPEN	Reopen a closed file. Windows doesn't use the lpszFileName parameter to open, but instead the

	szPathName filename of the OFSTRUCT structure.
OF_EXIST	Check whether file exists.
OF_PARSE	Fill OFSTRUCT variable with only information.
OF_PARSE	If specified file doesn't exist, have a dialog box appear, where the user can enter a new filename.
OF_DELETE	File is deleted.

The return value of the OpenFile function corresponds to the return value of the standard low-level open function. It is an integer value that shows a file pointer (or file handle) when the file has been opened successfully, and shows -1 when an error occurs.

We use the OpenFile function in the OpenTraceFile function to create a new file or overwrite an existing trace file. The OpenTraceFile function simply returns the file handle from the OpenFile function.

After the trace file has been successfully opened, we can use the RecordTrace function in our programs to make entries in important places in the file. At the end of the program we can use a text editor to look at them. These lines of entry state a combination of automatic date and time entries, and information strings preset by the programmer. Here's what they look like:

```
12/21/90 18:12:31 000043885 MainWndProc      MI_ADDRBOOK
12/21/90 18:12:36 000048279 MainWndProc      MI_ABOUT
12/21/90 18:12:37 000049542 MainWndProc      MI_QUIT receive
```

The first and second columns contain the current date and the current time. The third column has the recorded amount of time, in milliseconds, passed since Windows was started (the accuracy range of the system clock). This information is especially useful for analyzing the runtime performance of complex functions. The next column matches the character string passed to the lpszFunction parameter of RecordTrace function. This is where you specify the name of the function in which the RecordTrace function was called. The last column corresponds to the lpszInfo parameter of the RecordTrace function. The program developer can place a 40 character long character string with any information here. In the example above, the choice of certain menu items during a program run were recorded.

Let's look at the RecordTrace function more closely. Its first task is to determine the current date and time:

```
// How many seconds have elapsed since 1 Jan 1970, 00:00:00 GMT?
time(&lTime);
```

Calling the time function places the number of seconds passed since January 1, 1970 in the lTime variable. The localtime function then converts this value to a form that is easier to process:

```
// Convert this value to a tm data structure...
tmStruct = localtime(&lTime);
```

The information about the date and time are then packed in the tmStruct variable in separate fields, and we use an extensive wsprintf function reference to put all of the necessary information of the output line into the szFormat buffer variable:

```
wsprintf(szFormat,
        "%2.2d/%2.2d/%2.2d %2.2d:%2.2d:%2.2d %9.9lu %-15.15s %-.40s\r\n",
        tmStruct->tm_mon + 1,           // Month
        tmStruct->tm_mday,              // Day
        tmStruct->tm_year,              // Year
        tmStruct->tm_hour,              // Hour
        tmStruct->tm_min,               // Minute
        tmStruct->tm_sec,               // Seconds
        GetCurrentTime(),               // Windows system time
        (LPSTR)lpszFunction,            // Function name
        (LPSTR)lpszInfo);               // Information string
```

The only task that remains is to write this character string to the file. We use the _lwrite function:

```
nStringLength = lstrlen(szFormat);
// Write formatted string to trace file
nBytesWritten = _lwrite(nFileHandle, (LPSTR)szFormat, (WORD)nStringLength);
```

In principle, the _lwrite SDK function is identical to the write low-level function, which we could have used here also, except for the fact that _lwrite expects a long pointer as a data buffer parameter:

```
int _lwrite (int hFileHandle, LPSTR lpData, WORD wCount);
```

hFileHandle is the handle of the file to where wCount Bytes is to be written, beginning in the memory location where the lpData parameter points. The function returns the number of bytes actually written to the file.

The _lread function for reading data, which isn't used in the RecordTrace function, is the counterpart to _lwrite:

```
int _lread (int hFileHandle, LPSTR lpData, WORD wCount);
```

This time wCount Bytes is placed in the memory beginning in the memory location to where lpData is pointing. The return value is the number of bytes actually read (or zero, if the end of the file was reached at the start of reading and -1 for an error). The function used in the DLL for closing the trace file is CloseTraceFile:

```
int FAR PASCAL CloseTraceFile (int nFileHandle)
{
  return (_lclose(nFileHandle));
} // CloseTraceFile
```

Its only task is to call the _lclose-SDK function for closing a file. We also could have used the close runtime function. In that case, as with using the write and read function, it would have been necessary to include the <io.h> include file for function prototypes.

The WEP clean-up function in the TRACEDLL.C module doesn't have much to do. It simply returns the value 1:

```
int FAR PASCAL WEP (int nShutdownFlag)
{
  /***********************************************************************
   Since we don't have to perform any clean-up work, we return the value 1.
   ***********************************************************************/

  return 1;
} // WEP
```

That ends our discussion of DLL functions. Let's devote our attention to the MAKE file TRACEDLL.MAK, which contains all of the steps necessary for creating the DLL:

The object file TRACEDLL.OBJ from the source module TRACEDLL.C is compiled with the help of the:

```
cl -W$(Warn) -A$(Mod)w -c -Gsw -Zp -Os tracedll.c
```

instruction using the Aw option (the compiler should assume that the data and stack segments are different, i.e., DS !=SS).

After that, the linker comes into play. It creates the DLL TRACEDLL.DLL out of the object file TRACEDLL.OBJ:

```
tracedll.dll: tracedll.obj
$(Linker) /NOD /NOE /al:16 tracedll, tracedll.dll,, $(Mod)dllcew+libw,
tracedll.def
```

To perform this task it analyzes the specified module definition file TRACEDLL.DEF:

```
LIBRARY tracedll

EXETYPE WINDOWS

DESCRIPTION 'DLL Example'

CODE MOVEABLE DISCARDABLE

DATA PRELOAD MOVEABLE SINGLE

HEAPSIZE   0

EXPORTS
  WEP             @1 RESIDENTNAME
  OpenTraceFile   @2
  RecordTrace     @3
  CloseTraceFile  @4
```

We discover the first difference to the module definition file of an application in the LIBRARY instruction. Ordinarily the keyword NAME is here, instructing the linker to create an executable application, not a library. For DLLs the linker requires the keyword LIBRARY.

The instructions, EXETYPE and DESCRIPTION, correspond to prior use. The code segment of our DLL is defined as MOVEABLE DISCARDABLE, which means that it can be moved in memory and, if necessary, discarded. This is the most flexible solution for the memory manager. The data segment of the DLL is MOVEABLE SINGLE. You specify SINGLE for a DLL because it can have no more than one data segment (a DLL is not capable of multiple instances). If NONE is specified here, the DLL doesn't have a data segment at all.

We use the:

```
HEAPSIZE 0
```

instruction to announce that the DLL doesn't need the local heap.

One very important task of DLL module definition files is exporting functions to EXPORTS, because this is the only way that other modules can use the services of the functions available in the DLL. Of course you don't have to export functions used for internal purposes in the DLL. For exporting, we recommend specifying ordinal numbers after the name of the function for reasons of performance and memory space.

There is a special characteristic about exporting the WEP function. This function gets the keyword RESIDENTNAME as a comment. This keyword places the information for the memory manager connected to an exported function in memory, which makes it available at any time.

Using the information in the module definition file, the linker creates the DLL file, TRACEDLL.DLL. In addition to the libw.lib memory model-independent library, we also specified the DLL compatible, memory model-dependent mDLLCEW library. "m" stands for S, M, C or L. To prevent the linker from searching non-DLL compatible libraries when resolving function references, it is necessary to specify the /NOD linker option.

After creating the TRACEDLL.DLL file, we have the resource compiler process it:

```
rc tracedll.dll
```

In principle, the resource compiler should process all of the DLLs to be created, even if they don't contain any resources. The reason for this is that the resource compiler enters a kind of "Suitable for Windows 3" stamp in the header for DLLs.

The last step in the make file of the DLL consists of calling the implib program, which uses the module definition file to create an import library, tracedll.lib, for the DLL:

```
implib tracedll.lib tracedll.def
```

Modules that want to use functions from the DLL simply specify the import library as an extra library name in the linker command line of the make file. Then the module has to be relinked to insert the existing relocation entries of the import library into the executable module when DLL functions are called. We have already described this mechanism.

As soon as the relocation entries are in the executable module, the DLL can then be exchanged for a new version (provided the function names and their parameters are preserved) and the module doesn't need to be recompiled or relinked.

Among other things, this opens new perspectives to software manufacturers: For program updates the manufacturers can send a new DLL which supersedes the old DLL. When you reboot the program, the functions of the updated DLL are executed using the dynamic link process.

We should also point out that when you start an application that uses a DLL, the DLL has to be either in the current directory, in the Windows root directory, in the Windows system directory, in a directory defined in the PATH environment variable or in a network directory if you are using a network. Otherwise the program won't find the DLL and Windows will then prompt you, using a message box, to insert a diskette with the appropriate DLL into drive A:.

Let's look at adapting an existing application to TRACEDLL.DLL. On the companion diskette you'll find an application named ADDTRACE.EXE. This is a modified version of the ADDRBOOK.EXE (see Chapter 7). Make the following changes to make ADDTRACE.EXE access TRACEDLL.DLL:

- Add the following to the end of the global variable declarations:

```
int FdDebug;                    // File handle for trace file
```

- Add the following lines to the beginning of the function prototype declarations:

```
extern int FAR PASCAL OpenTraceFile (LPSTR);
extern int FAR PASCAL CloseTraceFile (int);
extern BOOL FAR PASCAL RecordTrace (int, LPSTR, LPSTR);
```

- Add these lines to the if (!InitFirstInstance...) loop:

```
{
  if (!InitFirstInstance(hInstance, hPrevInstance, nCmdShow))
    return NULL;

  // Open trace file - add these two lines to this loop
  if ((FdDebug = OpenTraceFile("trace.dat")) == -1) // NEW
    return NULL;                                    // NEW
}
```

- Modify the MainWindProc procedure as follows (notice that everything stays the same excepting the additions of RecordTrace and CloseTraceFile functions):

```
LONG FAR PASCAL MainWindProc (HWND hWnd, unsigned msg, WORD wP, LONG lP)
{
   int      nResult;             // Return value for DialogBox function

   switch (msg)
   {
     case WM_DESTROY:
       CloseTraceFile(FdDebug);  // NEW!!!!! Close trace file
       PostQuitMessage(0);       // Send WM_QUIT message
       break;

      case WM_COMMAND:           // Messages from menu bar
       switch (wP)
```

```
        {
          case MI_QUIT:              // Stop program
           RecordTrace(FdDebug, "MainWndProc", "MI_QUIT"); // NEW!!! Write record
           PostMessage(hwMain, WM_SYSCOMMAND, SC_CLOSE, 0L);
           break;

        case MI_ABOUT:              // "About address book" dialog box
          RecordTrace(FdDebug, "MainWndProc", "MI_ABOUT"); // NEW!!! Write record
...
```

- Change the MAKE file to add the DLL to the application (the companion diskette files are named ADDTRACE and ADDTUTIL, to differentiate them from the ADDRBOOK and ADDRUTIL files):

```
 Model = S
 Warn   = 2
 Linker = link

 all: addtrace.exe

 addtrace.res: addtrace.h addtrace.rc addtrace.dlg
   rc -r addtrace.rc

 addtrace.obj: addtrace.h addtrace.c
  cl -c -A$(Modell) -W$(Warn) -Gsw -Zpe -Os addtrace.c

addtutil.obj: addtrace.h addtutil.c
  cl -c -A$(Model) -W$(Warn) -Gsw -Zpe -Os addtutil.c

addtrace.exe: addtrace.obj addtutil.obj addtrace.def addtrace.res
  $(Linker) /NOD /al:16 addtrace+addtutil,addtrace.exe,,\
               libw+$(Modell)libcew+tracedll,addtrace.def
  rc addtrace.res
```

- Copy the DLL and its LIB file to the directory containing the application (the companion diskette will already have this available), and compile the application.

This application generates a trace file named TRACE.DAT, which can be viewed using a text editor, or typed using the DOS type command. TRACE.DAT lists the time, routine and function selected in ADDTRACE. See your companion diskette for the complete source listings.

15.5 Source Code: TRACEDLL.DLL

TRACEDLL.MAK MAKE file

```
Mod=S
Warn=3
Linker=link

all: tracedll.dll

tracedll.obj: tracedll.c
  cl -W$(Warn) -A$(Mod)w -c -Gsw -Zp -Os tracedll.c

tracedll.dll: tracedll.obj tracedll.def
  $(Linker) /NOD /NOE /al:16 tracedll, tracedll.dll,, $(Mod)dllcew+libw,
tracedll.def
  rc tracedll.dll
  implib tracedll.lib tracedll.def
```

TRACEDLL.DEF module definition file

```
LIBRARY tracedll

EXETYPE WINDOWS

DESCRIPTION 'DLL Example'

CODE MOVEABLE DISCARDABLE

DATA PRELOAD MOVEABLE SINGLE

HEAPSIZE   0

EXPORTS
  WEP             @1 RESIDENTNAME
  OpenTraceFile   @2
  RecordTrace     @3
  CloseTraceFile  @4
```

TRACEDLL.C

```
/************************************************************************
 T R A C E D L L . C
 ===================
```

```
 This module contains functions for opening and closing a trace file, and
 functions for writing formatted entries to this trace file. The functions
 use the Windows-specific OpenFile, _lwrite and _lclose, instead of the
 buffered f... C runtime functions.
 Entries written to a trace file are ASCII characters ended with a
 Carriage Return/Linefeed, so that the data can be edited by any standard
 editor or word processor.
 **************************************************************************/

#include <windows.h>
#include <time.h>

/*----------------------< Function prototypes >-------------------------*/

int  FAR PASCAL WEP (int);
int  FAR PASCAL OpenTraceFile (LPSTR);
int  FAR PASCAL CloseTraceFile (int);
BOOL FAR PASCAL RecordTrace (int, LPSTR, LPSTR);

/**************************************************************************
 W E P ()
 ========

 This function is used before removing the DLL from memory by Windows, or
 before exiting Windows.
 **************************************************************************/

int FAR PASCAL WEP (int nShutdownFlag)
{
  /*********************************************************************
   If no memory could be allocated, the value 1 is returned.
   *********************************************************************/

  return 1;
} // WEP

/**************************************************************************
 O p e n T r a c e F i l e ()
 ============================

 This function opens a trace file. Date and time stamps, and additional
 information about a file, is placed in the trace file by the RecordTrace
 function. An existing trace file with the same name will be overwritten.

 Parameters:

    LPSTR    lpszTraceFile  Long pointer to the trace filename (ended
                            with '0\')
```

```
 Return values:
    int                     Opened trace file's file handle.
                            -1 if opening was unsuccessful.
 ****************************************************************************/

int FAR PASCAL OpenTraceFile (LPSTR lpszTraceFile)
{
  int    nFileDescriptor;     // File handle
  static OFSTRUCT Of;         // Open File data structure

  nFileDescriptor = OpenFile(lpszTraceFile, (LPOFSTRUCT)&Of,
                             OF_CREATE | OF_READWRITE);
  if (nFileDescriptor == -1) // File could not be opened
  {
    MessageBox(GetFocus(), "Trace file could not be opened",
               "OpenTraceFile", MB_ICONEXCLAMATION | MB_OK);
  }
  return nFileDescriptor;
} // OpenTraceFile

/****************************************************************************
 R e c o r d T r a c e ()
 ========================

 This function is needed for storing formatted entries in a trace file.

 Parameters:

    int      nFileHandle    File handle of trace file previously opened by
                            OpenTraceFile
    LPSTR    lpszFunction   Long pointer to the function called by the
                            RecordTrace function (pointer ends with '\0')
    LPSTR    lpszInfo       Long pointer to a string containing trace
                            information (string ends with '\0')

 Return values:
    BOOL                    TRUE if the entry could be written successfully
                            to the trace file. Otherwise, FALSE.
 ****************************************************************************/

BOOL FAR PASCAL RecordTrace (int nFileHandle, LPSTR lpszFunction,
                             LPSTR lpszInfo)
{
  static time_t lTime;                   // Number of seconds since 1/1/1970
  struct tm * tmStruct;                  // Time format structure
  static char szFormat[255];             // Format string
  int    nStringLength,                  // Format string length
         nBytesWritten;                  // Number of bytes written
```

```
  // How many seconds have elapsed since 1 Jan 1970, 00:00:00 GMT?
  time(&lTime);

  // Convert this value to a tm data structure...
  tmStruct = localtime(&lTime);

  // ... and format the individual fields
  wsprintf(szFormat,
           "%2.2d.%2.2d.%2.2d %2.2d:%2.2d:%2.2d %9.9lu %-15.15s %-.40s\r\n",
           tmStruct->tm_mday,            // Day
           tmStruct->tm_mon + 1,         // Month
           tmStruct->tm_year,            // Year
           tmStruct->tm_hour,            // Hour
           tmStruct->tm_min,             // Minute
           tmStruct->tm_sec,             // Seconds
           GetCurrentTime(),             // Windows system time
           (LPSTR)lpszFunction,          // Function name
           (LPSTR)lpszInfo);             // Information string

  nStringLength = lstrlen(szFormat);

  // Write formatted string in the trace file
  nBytesWritten = _lwrite(nFileHandle, (LPSTR)szFormat, (WORD)nStringLength);

  if (nBytesWritten == nStringLength)
    return TRUE;
  else
    return FALSE;
} // RecordTrace

/****************************************************************************
 C l o s e T r a c e F i l e ()
 ==============================

 This function closes a trace file opened by the OpenTraceFile function.

 Parameters:

   int      nFileHandle   File handle of the trace file to be closed

 Return values:

   int      0 if file could be closed successfully. Otherwise, -1.
 ***************************************************************************/

int FAR PASCAL CloseTraceFile (int nFileHandle)
{
  return (_lclose(nFileHandle));
} // CloseTraceFile
```

16 Windows Memory Management

An operating system's performance depends greatly on how it uses system resources. Even in the age of the RAM is considered to be one of these limited resources, because of increases in the memory capacities of modules and programs.

It's no surprise that Microsoft's programmers concentrated on memory research when developing Windows. The result is a version of Windows for all kinds of processors used in PCs, from the 8088 to the 80486. Windows 3 automatically adapts to its hardware environment when you start the program. Internally Windows recognizes three operating modes: Real mode, standard mode and enhanced mode. Each operating mode takes advantage of different processor features. These operating modes use memory management and memory addressing efficiently. This chapter discusses these operating modes, and how each mode performs.

16.1 Real Mode

Let's start with real mode. Real mode places the fewest demands on the system, but also returns the lowest level of performance.

Processor: 8088 or 80x86

Main memory: minimum of 640K

Real mode's memory management concept is almost identical to the method of segmented addressing used by MS-DOS. We'll explain segmented addressing in more detail later in this chapter. For the moment, you must know this about real mode and segmented addressing:

- The address space has a maximum size of 1 Meg.
- 640K of this 1 Meg is available for MS-DOS applications.

This address space is divided into real mode in the following way:

FE00	ROM BIOS
F600	ROM BASIC
E000	
D000	
CC00	ROM extensions
C600	Hard drive operating system
B800	Color graphics adapter card
B000	Monochrome graphics card
A000	Video memory
	"Global heap": maximum memory space available
	Memory resident programs, MS-DOS device drivers
0060	Operating system — IO.SYS, MSDOS.SYS, resident COMMAND.COM, COMMAND.COM
0040	RAM-BIOS data
0000	Interrupt vector table

Memory division in real mode

As the illustration shows, the global heap represents a contiguous area in the basic real mode configuration. This heap is broken down into segments. These contain either code or data. You can assign attributes to these segments, which influence the way the memory manager uses these segments (more on this later). The memory manager recognizes FIXED, MOVEABLE and DISCARDABLE segments. In real mode, it places these segments in the global heap in the following way:

0x0A000	Upper limit of global heap in physical memory
	Discardable code segments (V) (^) Moveable code and data segments, discardable data segments Non-moveable code and data segments
	Lower limit of global heap in physical memory

Global memory division in real mode

Real mode lets you run applications written for earlier versions of Windows without memory conflict. However, since real mode severely limits performance, use other modes for newer applications.

16.2 Standard Mode

Your first alternative to real mode is standard mode. Windows 3 automatically changes to this operating mode when the following hardware requirements are given:

Processor: 80286, 80386, 80486

Main memory: 1 Meg RAM—2 Meg RAM

The basic difference from real mode is that Windows switches the processor to protected mode. You can determine the consequences of switching to protected mode by reading farther ahead, where we discuss the kinds of memory addressing used with different processor types. For now, let's just say that the programs, including Windows itself, use logical addresses for addressing memory in protected mode, rather than working directly with physical memory addresses.

In standard mode the global heap is divided into a maximum of three different blocks. The first block corresponds basically to the division from real mode, with which we are already familiar. The two other blocks are in different memory areas. First comes an area in *extended memory*, which refers to the area in the main memory above the 1 Meg limit. This area can ordinarily be accessed only when the CPU is in protected mode. Windows uses a special device driver called the extended memory driver (XMS). The memory manager executes all other accesses by going around the XMS driver. The exact location and size of this block depends on what was placed there before Windows was started.

The last block is an area in the high memory area (HMA). This refers to the first 64K segment in extended memory, right after the 1 Meg limit, between 0x10000 and 0x11000. A special device driver named HIMEM.SYS installs this block.

Note: If you ever have problems with Windows because it won't let you switch to standard or enhanced mode, although your PC fulfills all of the hardware requirements, check your CONFIG.SYS file. The HIMEM.SYS must be included in CONFIG.SYS.

These three non-contiguous memory blocks make up the global heap in standard mode. The following illustration shows how the memory manager uses the global heap.

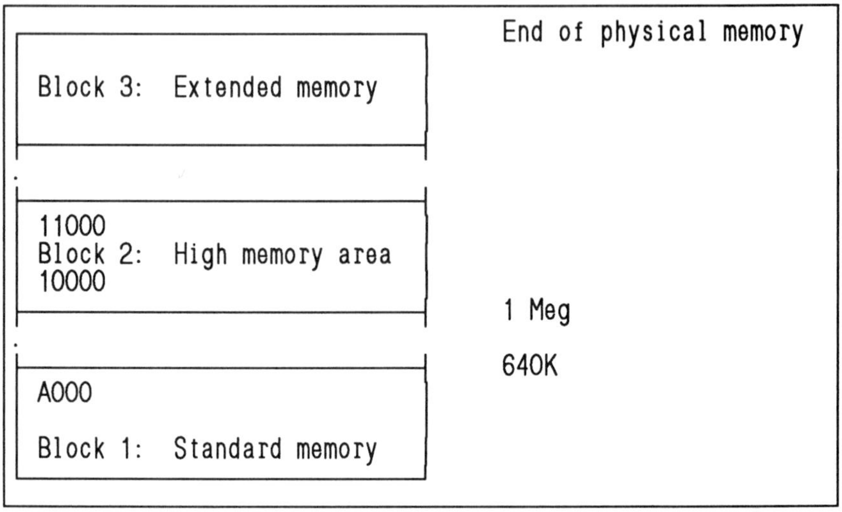

Global heap structure in standard mode

The illustration shows that the principal heap division is comparable to the division we are already familiar with from real mode. However, notice that this configuration, unlike real mode, is not a contiguous memory area.

End of Extended Memory	Upper limit of global heap
	| V Discardable code segments | V ^ Moveable code and data segments, discardable data segments Non-moveable code and data segments ^ | |
Standard Memory	Lower limit of global heap

Global heap division in standard mode

16.3 Enhanced Mode

A second alternative to real mode is enhanced mode. It places the greatest demands on the hardware:

Processor: 80386 SX minimum

Main memory: 2 Meg minimum

However, Windows also works the most effectively in extended 386 mode, and in some respects is viewed as a serious competitor of OS/2.

Note: The GetWinFlags function of the API supplies information about the hardware environment in which Windows operates.

Before we go into more detail about the kind of memory management, here is a short overview of the general performance of Windows in this operating mode:

- Takes advantage of the characteristics of the 80386, such as demand paging and virtual memory addressing. This type of memory management makes it possible to execute programs that are a lot larger than the available main memory in the system.

- Virtual MS-DOS machines. A multitasking mechanism was implemented in accordance with the time-slicing procedure, which utilizes the capabilities of an 80386 processor switched to protected mode, and starts a virtual 8088 CPU for each MS-DOS application. The user then has the opportunity to execute up to 16 standard MS-DOS applications in parallel, using time-slicing. Each application has its own address space of 680K, which is more than MS-DOS allocates for a single application. The user can also decide whether to have the MS-DOS application run as a full screen, or within a window.

- Data exchange using the clipboard. Windows users have been familiar with this kind of data exchange for the last three years. The clipboard is now also available to standard MS-DOS operations. This means that you can exchange data between two MS-DOS applications, as well as between Windows and MS-DOS applications.

Note: In view of the multitasking features of Windows 3, users often ask themselves what the difference between Windows 3 and OS/2. This is a rather complicated question that we cannot discuss in detail here. However, we would like to note the following. With the option of executing more than one standard MS-DOS application at the same time (parallel), Windows 3 has clearly become more efficient and powerful than the compatibility box of OS/2. Up until now, the OS/2 compatibility box switched the processor to real mode to execute a standard MS-DOS application, and then executed only this application.

As a result, all of the OS/2 applications stopped for the duration of the compatibility box. Unfortunately, however, when Windows 3 was developed, some corners were cut. For example, the compartmentalization of the individual MS-DOS applications was solved in an unsatisfactory manner. When an MS-DOS application crashes, it brings the entire system to a halt. Also, the multitasking, according to the time slicing method, is not consistent. All of the Windows applications continue running on a virtual 8086 processor, just as under Windows/386. The application continues to be responsible for releasing the CPU as soon as it is no longer required.

In other words, the method of multitasking used by earlier versions of Windows according to the principle of message polling has been retained. The multitasking behavior of OS/2 and the presentation manager is clearly more efficient and secure. In consideration of the evolutionary jump from Windows 2.xx to Windows 3, we can only hope that a new version of OS/2 will make the compatibility box a thing of the past.

But let's get back to the actual subject - memory management in extended 80386 mode.

Virtual memory management and demand paging

When the memory manager processes the memory requirements, it tries to make a contiguous area of the heap available to the application, in correspondence to the requirements. It proceeds in this manner until all of the physical memory resources have been distributed. Only then does the memory manager begin demand paging. For this purpose, the entire main memory is divided into pages 4K long. Using the "least recently used" (LRU) algorithm, Windows selects the page which hasn't been accessed for the longest time. The memory manager places this page into a swap file on the hard drive. You can define the maximum size of this file within the Windows configurations file, SYSTEM.INI. If there isn't any such entry there, the memory manager calculates the size depending on the amount of main memory physically available in the system. As an alternative, you could also create a permanent swapfile with the SWAPFILE.EXE utility program. Although such a swapfile requires hard drive capacity when Windows isn't even running, it allows the user faster access.

When an application tries to access code or data pages that the memory manager has placed in the swapfile, the 80386 processor triggers a "Page Fault" interrupt. This causes the memory manager to swap other pages and swap in the code or data pages the application needs in the free space created by the swap. If such pages have Long or Far pointers, they lose their validity when they are swapped, since it's not certain that they will be swapped back in the same place in the main memory.

In enhanced mode, Windows makes a maximum memory size of 4 Gigabytes available, which in reality, however, is determined by the size of the physical main memory and the swapfile. To conclude, we should mention that the global heap in extended 80386 mode is more comparable to the basic configuration of real mode than it is to the global heap of standard mode, which is split up into three different blocks. If the global heap in the basic configuration is a contiguous area in the physical main memory, in enhanced mode it is a large, homogeneous virtual address space.

End of Extended Memory	Upper limit of global heap in virtual address space
	Discardable code segments (|/ growing down) /|\ Moveable code and data segments, as well as discardable data segments /|\ Non-moveable code and data segments
	Lower limit of global heap in virtual address space

Global heap division in standard mode

16.4 Operating Mode Switching

After indicating the hardware requirements under which Windows automatically switches to a certain operating mode, we would also like to mention that you can make settings for this when you start Windows.

Use one of the switches described in the illustration below, when calling Windows from the DOS prompt. This runs Windows in the requested operating mode.

Windows can only switch to the mode preset by the switch when the necessary hardware is present.

Switch	Operating mode	System requirements
/r	Real mode	8088 up, 640K RAM
/s or /2	Standard mode	80x86 up, 1 Meg RAM
/3	Enhanced mode	80386 SX up, 2 Meg RAM

Switches for Windows operating modes

16.5 Local Heap

The local heap is a special memory area that, together with other application specific elements, forms the *automatic data segment* of an application. This private data segment can only be 64K in length (like other segments). It contains the following elements:

Offset	Element
	Local Heap
	Application-specific stack
0x10	Static data
0x00	Application task header (16 bytes)

max. 64K size

Automatic data segment

In contrast to the global heap, which is a system wide resource, the local heap is a private data area, which can be allocated to any Windows application. You can preset its minimum size of the local heap with the help of the keyword HEAPSIZE in the module definition file *.DEF. This default is a guaranteed minimum size, available to the application right after startup. During runtime of the application, this value can be exceeded. This means that if an application requires more space than HEAPSIZE reserved, the memory manager will comply with this until it reaches the maximum size of the automatic data segment.

Unlike this automatic dynamic increase of the local heap, releasing data objects doesn't automatically reduce memory size. This is the programmer's responsibility. With the LocalShrink function, Windows gives the programmer a tool for shrinking the local heap back to a compact size. The minimum size, defined by HEAPSIZE, is retained.

Refer to the following illustration for information on how the memory manager places data in the local heap:

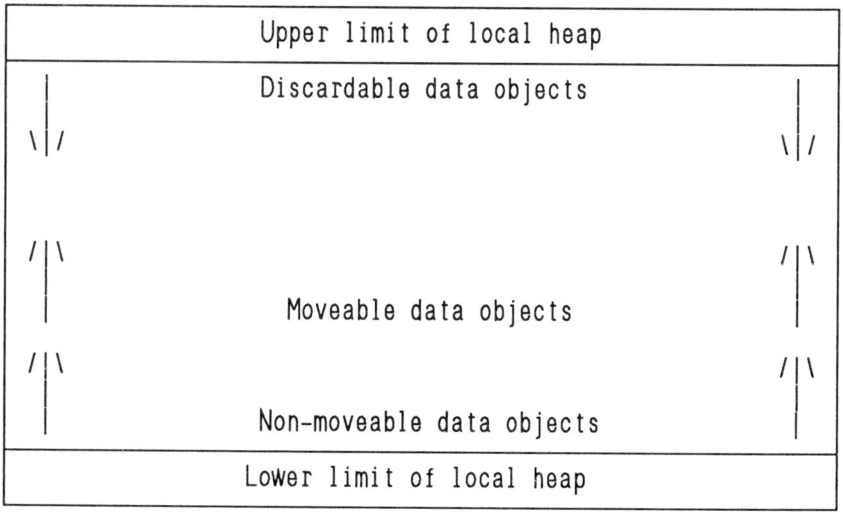

Division of the local heap

16.6 Data Classes

After introducing you to the global and the local heap, both of which give you the option of storing data, we should discuss the types of data existing under Windows. The following seven types of data can be differentiated:

Static data

All of the C variables are combined here that were defined with the keywords static, external or outside of function bodies.

Automatic data

These are all of the variables that are placed on the stack when you call a function.

Dynamic data

This requires the necessary memory space from the memory manager during the runtime of the application. Depending on their location, they are called:

Local dynamic data

This is created on the local heap of the appropriate application with the help of the LocalAlloc function.

Global dynamic data

This is placed on the global heap, a system wide resource, using GlobalAlloc.

Private data for windows of a class

If you want to carry different kinds of information to Windows, you can place the information in a private area that is then attached to the end of the Windows managed window data. To set up such an area, indicate the size of the extra area in bytes in the cbWndExtra field of the WNDCLASS structure.

The functions GetWindowWord/ SetWindowWord and GetWindowLong/SetWindowLong access this information. You address the data element by specifying an offset. The first element has the offset 0. After that, depending on the type of element, the offset is increased by 2 (with WORD) or else by 4 (with LONG).

Offset	Element	Element
0	1st WORD	1st LONG
2	2nd WORD	
4	3rd WORD	2nd LONG
6	4th WORD	
8	5th WORD	3rd LONG

Access to private Windows data

Private data for an entire class of windows

Just as you can allocate private data to windows of a class, you can also do the same with classes of windows. The WNDCLASS data structure also has a cbClassExtra field, similar to the cbWndExtra field, which specifies the size of the private window class data. This private data is appended directly to the WNDCLASS structure of the appropriate window class. Access to the data occurs in exactly the same way as described for window. The function pairs to use are GetClassWord/SetClassWord and GetClassLong/SetClassLong.

Resources

This is non-changeable data in the resource section of the *.EXE file of the appropriate application. When the program is being created, this data is linked to the actual program code after the link process with the help of the resource compiler (RC). One of the advanced kinds of Windows programming is defining any kind of private read-only data. You can also use the RC to link this data to the .EXE file.

16.7 Local Memory Allocation

To create a data block on the local heap, call the LocalAlloc function. You pass two parameters to this function. The first parameter specifies the type of data block - fixed or moveable. The second parameter specifies the size of the block in bytes.

If you reserve a fixed data block, LocalAlloc immediately returns a 16 bit address to the first byte of the data block. Since the memory manager doesn't carry a lock counter to fixed data blocks, you can do without the LocalLock and LocalUnlock calls, because Windows ignores them.

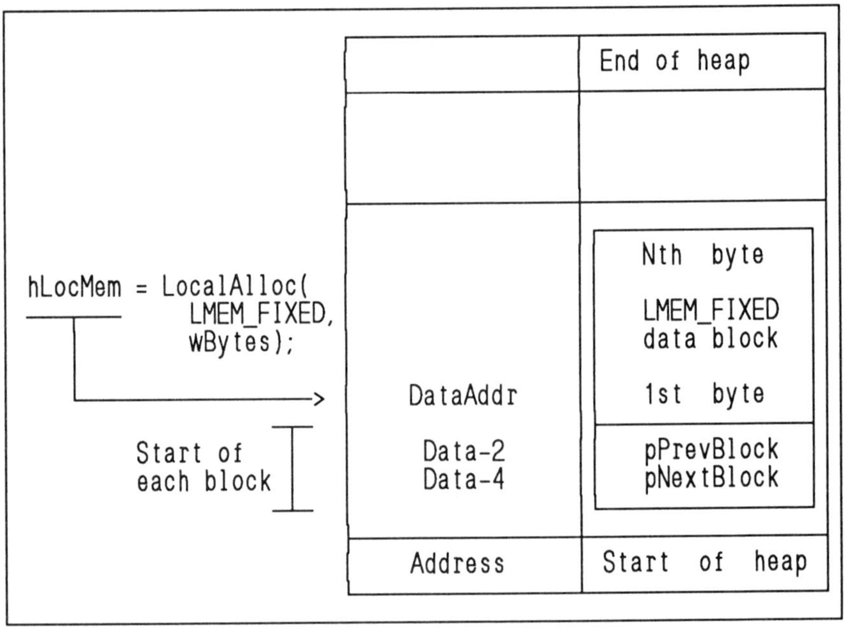

Allocating a fixed data block

Moveable data blocks are different. In addition to the actual data block, they also have a management head. With MOVEABLE data, the LocalAlloc function returns a 16 bit address to the management head. You must call the LocalLock function to get a valid pointer to the data block. The memory manager cannot move a data block when it is locked. It can only move the data block when the lock counter reads zero. Every time you call LocalLock, the counter is incremented, while calling LocalUnlock decrements the counter. A moveable data block should only be locked as long as is necessary to process the data.

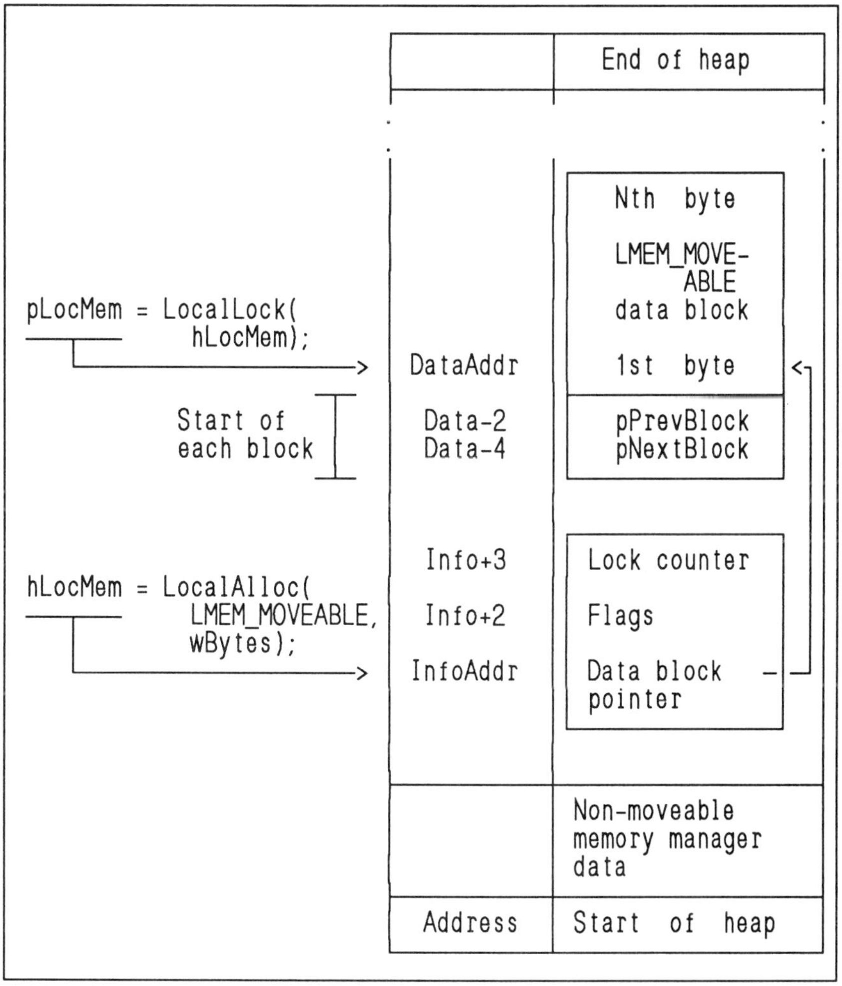

Allocating a moveable data block

When you work with dynamic, private data, there are some useful functions in the Windows API which you can use to influence the work of the memory manager. For example, there is the function pair LocalFreeze and LocalMelt. When you call LocalFreeze, it freezes the status of the local heap until you call LocalMelt. In the meantime, the location of the moveable or discardable data remains unchanged. This means that the memory manager cannot perform compacting.

```
LocalFreeze(0);                    /* Freeze local heap */
/*     Heap compacting locked ...
       location of the blocks is temporarily fixed...
*/
LocalMelt (0);                     /* Melt local heap */
```

This function pair is an alternative to the LMEM_NOCOMPACT Flag. When you call LocalAlloc, the LMEM_NOCOMPACT Flag instructs the memory manager to do without compacting when preparing new memory areas.

In our discussion about compacting, we should also mention the LocalCompact function. When you call this function with the NULL value, its return value gives information about the size of the remaining free memory area on the local heap.

The actual purpose of the LocalCompact function, however, consists of instructing the memory manager to prepare a contiguous memory area the size of the default. Here's how you might call it:

```
wLargestBlockSize = LocalCompact(wMinimalFreeBytes);
```

The memory manager responds by arranging all unlocked, moveable segments in such a way that any gaps between the blocks are removed. If the resulting free space still isn't large enough, the memory manager calculates how much space is taken up by unlocked, discardable segments and adds the obtained value to the free space. If this calculated space is not sufficient, the return value tells the function how much contiguous memory is still available on the heap.

You use the LocalFree function to delete a data block by passing the handle to the private data to the function:

```
LocalFree(hLocMem);
```

16.8 Global Memory Allocation

Along with putting data on the private heap, each application can also request global memory areas. Unlike the local heap, where you use a 16 bit NEAR pointer to access the data blocks, you now have to use a LONG pointer. Use the same procedure to get a pointer to the data block that we showed you for moveable local data. First, you call the GlobalAlloc function, specifying the kind and size of the block.

```
hGlobalMem = GlobalAlloc(GMEM_MOVEABLE, wBlockSize);
```

The handle returned by the function is an address within a data segment named BURGERMASTER. The memory manager creates a 4 byte piece of management information in this special segment for each global data block. The number of global memory handles that can exist simultaneously throughout the system is limited to 8192.

To be able to access the global data area, you have to use GlobalLock to protect it from being moved by the memory manager.

```
lpGlobalMem = GlobalLock(hGlobalMem);
```

Now you have a 32 bit pointer (lpGlobalMem) to the actual data region. This pointer remains valid until you use GlobalUnlock to release the data block again.

```
GlobalUnlock(hGlobalMem);
```

It's the reference to the data block, however, that remains valid. With the help of this reference and the use of the GlobalLock function, you can get a new pointer to the actual data block over and over again. The pointer can always point to different physical memory addresses.

Similar to private data, you release a global data block by calling:

```
GlobalFree(hGlobalMem);
```

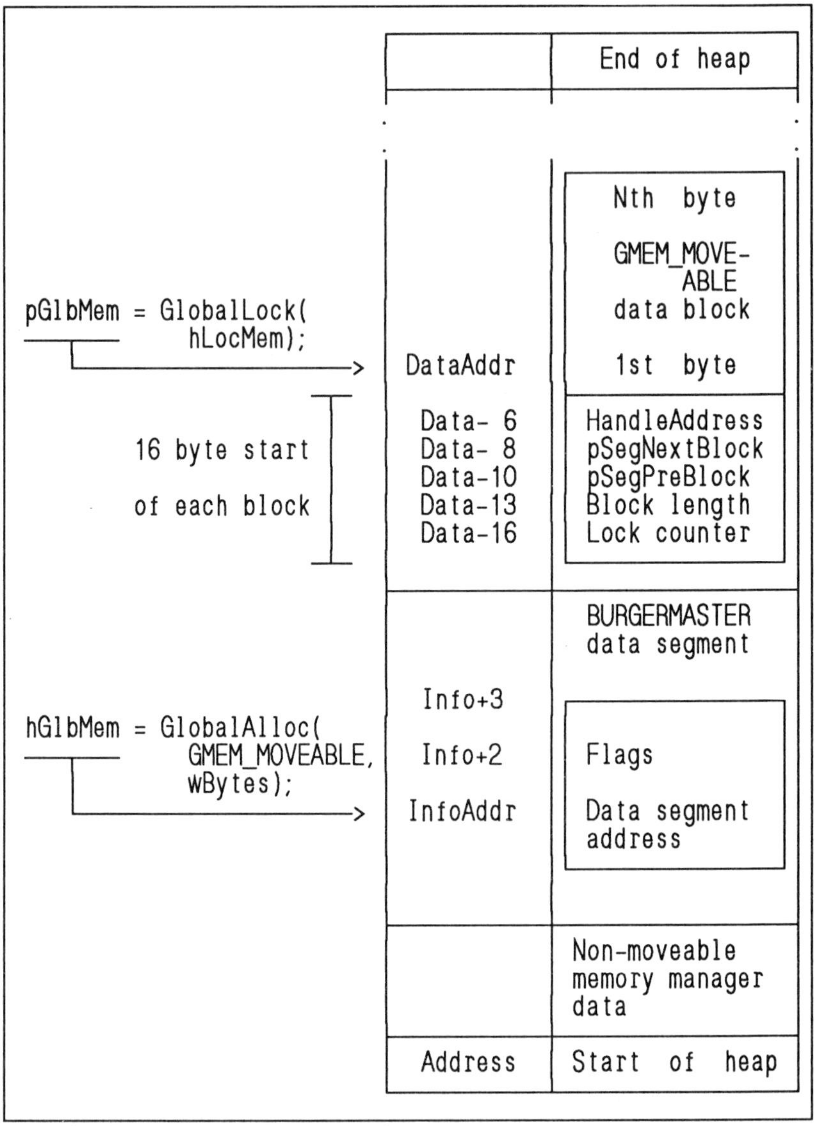

Allocating a moveable data block

16.9 Allocation Overhead

In this section we deal with the overhead produced by different allocation procedures.

The local heap consists of units of 32 bits each. These smallest units are also called the granulation or the granularity of an address space. Because of granularity, new data blocks have to begin with an address divisible by 4. Between the single blocks, unusable gaps develop, which can be up to 3 bytes long. The following examples demonstrate the kind of overhead that results when data is placed on the local heap.

Requested memory area	Management information	next number divisible by 4	Overhead absolute/pct.
5 bytes	4 bytes	12 (5+4+3)	4+3 = 7 bytes 140 %
256 bytes	4 bytes	260 (256+4)	4+0 = 4 bytes 1.56 %

Overhead of fixed local data

Requested memory area	Management information	next number divisible by 4	Overhead absolute/pct.
5 bytes	10 bytes	16 (5+10+1)	10+1=11 bytes 220 %
256 bytes	10 bytes	268 (256+10+2)	10+2=12 bytes 4.69 %

Overhead of moveable local data

Unlike the local heap, the global heap has a granularity of 32 bytes (i.e., the blocks of data always start at a 32 byte limit). At 16 bytes, the share of management information is considerably larger than the 4 or 10 bytes in the local heap. Along with that, you have to use either a FAR or a LONG pointer to access global memory areas. We have already indicated that such pointers have a special danger.

Requested memory area	Management information	next number divisible by 4	Overhead absolute/pct.
256 bytes	16 bytes	288=256+16+16	16+16=32 bytes 12.5 %
2048 bytes	16 bytes	2080=2048+16+16	16+16=32 bytes 1.53 %

Overhead of moveable global data

As the illustration shows, the amount of overhead for data blocks of 256 bytes is almost 13%. Compared to the 1.5% for reservations of larger areas (example 2K), this is rather high. But the high overhead ratio is not the only reason for creating a few large global data blocks instead of several small ones. The limit of 8192 global memory handles system wide is another reason. The application is free to logically subdivide this large block internally.

16.10 Processors

In this section we'll discuss the methods employed by different PC micro processors for memory addressing.

The 8088 processor

You are certainly aware of the fact that the good old 8088 - the heart of the first PC - can address a memory area of 1 megabyte, and that it doesn't even address it very well, as we shall see in a minute. The largest possible amount of contiguous information that the 8088 recognizes is two bytes large. With 16 bits, however, a maximum of 64K (=2 to the 16th power) can be addressed. To be able to address one megabyte of address space (a gigantic amount in those days), the developers at Intel—the firm that manufactured PC processors—used a trick that PC programmers are still suffering from. They invented *segmented addressing*. Segmented addressing is based on linking two 16 bit logical addresses. The address space was divided into single pieces, called segments. Within these segments, the memory cells were addressed by a second logical address, the offset.

Segment register	|ssss:ssss|ssss:ssss	16 bit
shifted left 4 times	ssss|ssss:ssss|ssss:0000	
+ Offset register	|0000:0000|0000:0000	16 bit
physical address	pppp|pppp:pppp|pppp:pppp	20 bit

s=Segment value, o=Offset value, p=physical address

Principle of segmented addressing

As you can see from the illustration, left shifting (= multiplication by 16, or adding four zeros) the segment address 4 times and adding up the offset register results in a physical address that is a maximum 20 bits wide. (2 to the twentieth power ==> 1 Meg). You also see that a segment can be up to 64K (2 to the power of 16) in size. Since the contents of the segment register are left shifted 4 times, the smallest segment division is 16 bytes. You also refer to these 16 byte progressions as paragraphs.

In order to access memory cells, the 8088 has various registers. We give you a short description of them here.

First, we have the code segment register (CS). When you load a program, the segment address of the code segment where the entry point is located is assigned to the code segment register. There is also the program counter (PC). This register, often referred to as an instruction pointer (IP), always carries the number of the next program instruction to be carried out. To find out where this machine instruction is located in the memory, add the contents of IP as offset to the segment address in the CS register according to the procedure we described before.

Addressing data

Addressing program data is like addressing program instructions. There is another register for this purpose, called the data segment register (DS). The DS register contains the start address of the area where all the necessary static data are located.

Along with instructions and data, there is another element, called the stack, which is necessary for program execution. Arguments to be passed to functions and all non-static data are placed on the stack, as well as return addresses of function references. There are three registers available for working with the stack. The stack segment (SS) register contains the segment start address, which is where the stack is located. The stack pointer (SP) serves as an offset to the SS. The base pointer (BP) can also be called to help the SS generate addresses.

One more thing about DS and SS registers is related to C programs. Most C compilers require that the static program data and the stack be in the same segment. You can address this data either using the DS or the SS register, since both contain the same segment address (DS == SS). By placing the stack and static data in one segment, you can use NEAR pointers as function parameters, with the result that the function doesn't have to distinguish between static data and stack data.

There are three other registers called the extra register (ES), the destination index (DI) and the source index (SI). We won't discuss them here, because they are not important to memory addressing. They are used in relocation operations, where either the DI or the SI register is added to the ES register.

The 80286 processor

This processor type introduced a new operating mode—protected mode. It was incompatible with its predecessors. In this operating mode, the programs no longer worked with direct, physical memory addressing. In their place came logical (also called virtual) memory addresses, which are represented by a descriptor. A descriptor is made up of a selector and an offset. With the help of the selector you can use a 16 bit long register to create a 24 bit address. This address specifies the physical base address of the corresponding segment. The offset is added then, similar to real mode.

Component	Length	Structure	Comment
Selector	16 bit	IIII:IIII|IIII:ITPP	I=Index (13 bits) 2^13 == > max. 8192 segments T=Table Indicator 0. GDT (global) 1: LDT (local) P=Privilege level
Offset	16 bit		2^16 ==> 64K

Structure of the selector

This selector represents a virtual memory address. The bits 3-15 are to be considered as an index value to a table, which defines the physical location of up to 8192 segments. The 80286 differentiates between a global and a local descriptor table. The table indicator specifies which one is called on to generate an address. If the table indicator is set to 0, the CPU accesses the GDT; otherwise it accesses the LDT. Through these tables, the programs have a logical address space with a maximum size of:

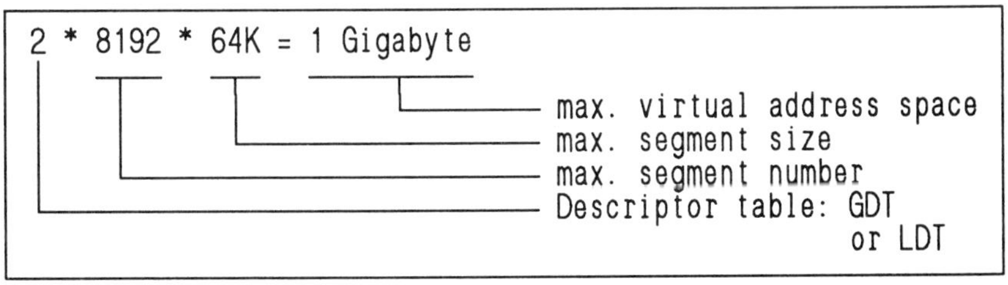

at their disposal. These virtual addresses are then reproduced on a real address space of up to 2^24 bytes (=16 Meg). The table entries achieve this. Each entry consists of 8 bytes, of which only bytes 1-6 are used, and are composed of the following components:

Component	Length	Position in entry	Comment
Physical segment base address "BASE"	16 bit	3+4: bits 0-15 5: bits 16-23	2^24 ==> max. 16 Meg
Segment upper limit "LIMITS"	16 bit	1+2: bits 0-15	2^16 ==> max. 64K
"ACCESS RIGHTS"	8 bit	6: bits 0- 7	

Structure of an entry in the descriptor table

The BASE components specify the physical base address of the segment. LIMITS identifies its length. As in real mode, a segment can be up to 64K. You use the 16 bit offset to address within the segment.

The 80386 processor

With the 80386, which was a further development of the 80286, the descriptor principle was refined. One of the most significant effects has to do with the final abolishment of the 64K sizes. As you will see a little later, it's possible to address segments up to 4 Gigabytes in size.

On the 80386 a virtual memory address is represented by a segment descriptor, which has the following structure.

Component	Length	Structure	Comment
Selector	16 bit	IIII:IIII|IIII:ITPP	I=Index (13 bits) 2^13 == > max. 8192 segments T=Table Indicator 0: GDT (global) 1: LDT (local) P=Privilege level
Offset	32 bit		2^32 ==> max. segment size 4 Gigabytes

Structure of the segment descriptor

In this way, a program can access a logical address space of 2^13 (Number Segments) multiplied by the maximum segment size of 2^32 (= 4Gb).

```
8192 * 4 GB = 64 Terabytes
 |      |          |
 |      |          └───── max. virtual address space
 |      └──────────────── max. segment size
 └─────────────────────── max. segment number
```

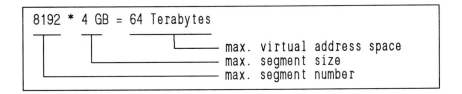

To reproduce the logical address space on to the real memory, you use a memory-resident descriptor table. Each entry within the descriptor table is 8 bytes large and consists of the following components:

Component	Length	Position in entry	Comment
Physical segment base addr "BASE"	32 bit	3+4: bits 0-15 5: bits 16-23 8: bits 24-32	2^32 ==> max. 4 Gigabytes
Segment upper limit "LIMITS"	20 bit	1+2: bits 0-15 7: bits 16-20 Bits 0-4 of byte 7 used only	2^20 ==> max. 1 Meg

Component	Length	Position in entry	Comment
Flags "FLAGS"	4 bit	Bit 7 of byte 7 contains G flag, Bit 6 gives the default segment size	Granularity bit: Bit=1:in bytes Bit=0:in 4K pages Segment size: Bit=0:32 bit Bit=1:16 bit
"ACCESS RIGHTS"	8 bit	6: bits 0- 7	

Structure of an entry in the descriptor table

The BASE components, which specify the physical start address, and the segment size, which is to be added, bring about the reproduction. This can be any value between 1 byte and 4 Gigabytes. It is preset by the LIMITS components. Since they can only address 1 Meg directly because of their length of 20 bits, the LIMITS component was linked with the granularity flag.

This flag indicates which base size of the LIMITS components, which value to multiply the contents by to get the final segment size. There are two different methods for calculating the definition of the current segment size:

```
     Granularity bit = 0 ==>  Segment size in 4K pages:
2^20   *   2^12   =   2^32
 |          |          |____ max. segment size 4 Gigabytes
 |          |_______________ 4096 bytes = one 4K page
 |__________________________ LIMITS value, size in pages
     Granularity bit = 1 ==>  Segment size in bytes:

2^20   *   1      =   2^20
 |          |          |____ max. segment size 1 Meg
 |          |_______________ Unit: byte
 |__________________________ LIMITS value, size in bytes
```

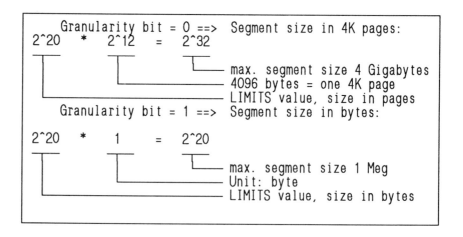

Windows programmers are confronted with granularity when overhead calculations determine whether to place dynamic data on the local or the global heap. We'll discuss this in more detail later.

There are several of these descriptor tables in protected mode. Since discussing them in detail would go beyond the limits of this chapter, we only provide a brief list of the most important ones:

GDT: Global Descriptor Table

Defines the location of up to 8192 segments, which constitutes the global address space of the system, which all of the applications can access.

LDT: Local Descriptor Table

This is the local, private address space of an application. This area is protected from access by other applications.

IDT: Interrupt Descriptor Table

This table houses 256 pointers to the start addresses of the interrupt service functions.

The table indicator, which is a component of the selector, specifies whether to use the GDT or the LDT to form the physical address.

16.11 Segmented Addressing Problems

Programmers must accept certain disadvantages resulting from the procedure of segmented addressing. In this section we discuss the consequences of these disadvantages for the programming language C. You're probably familiar with all the different pointer lengths that often drive programmers to despair.

For example, there are NEAR or SHORT pointers. These are 16 bit pointers that address a memory cell only by means of the offset address. They always work relative to the actual beginning of the segment. The opposite of these are called FAR or LONG pointers. They are 32 bits long and always address a memory cell completely, by means of both the segment and the offset address. The segment address is lower-order word and the offset address is higher-order word.

The various pointer lengths are significant in programming Windows. As we mentioned, there are segments under Windows that have the MOVEABLE attribute. The memory manager can move them so that the computer utilizes the main memory. It's not too hard for us to imagine that all FAR or LONG pointers addressing a certain segment lose their validity after the segments are shifted. Otherwise the segment address within the pointer would be pointing at the wrong segment. Unlike FAR or LONG pointers, NEAR or SHORT pointers retain their validity, since they address data only by means of the offset, relative to the beginning of the segment.

16.11.1 Memory models

Another product of segmented addressing are the different memory models. The C compiler prompts you to select a memory model adapted to the size of the program for translation. You can choose among the following:

The SMALL model: -AS

This memory model requires that the program consist of a code segment (maximum program length 64K) and a data segment (maximum size of static data 64K). This means that within this model you can address all data using NEAR pointers, by means of the offset. This is the basis for the high performance speed of such programs. Regarding Windows programming, this model allows you to move the data segment without having the NEAR pointers lose their validity.

The MEDIUM model: -AM

In this memory model a program can have more than one code segment, but only one data segment. The compiler generates FAR calls for all function references that aren't expressly defined as NEAR. This memory model is a little inconvenient for programmers, because they have to work with FAR and NEAR pointers. Although this provides a source of error and danger, Windows programmers have to get used to this, regardless of the memory model they selected.

The COMPACT, LARGE and HUGE models

All of the models above have one thing in common: They make it possible for a program to work with several data segments. However, we believe you shouldn't use them to create Windows applications, because the data segments are set to FIXED. This makes Windows extremely inefficient, and makes it almost impossible to run multiple applications. You can read more about this in the next subsection.

16.11.2 Segment attributes

The memory manager is familiar with three different classes of segments.

The main task of the memory manager consists of managing the resources of main memory as efficiently as possible. This makes programs, that are larger than the real memory area, executable. Since programs always run sequentially, it's not necessary to keep all of the instructions on reserve in the main memory at the same time. The same holds true for the program data. Assuming that you have this knowledge, they have now refined the program structure. They divided it into code segments and data segments. In addition, they defined three attributes which give the memory manager information about how it may treat the segments.

Fixed segments

If a segment is declared as fixed, it keeps its assigned position in main memory during the segment's entire life cycle. As the example shows, this is less than ideal. The illustration below shows the local heap of an application, after the application has created these five fixed data objects.

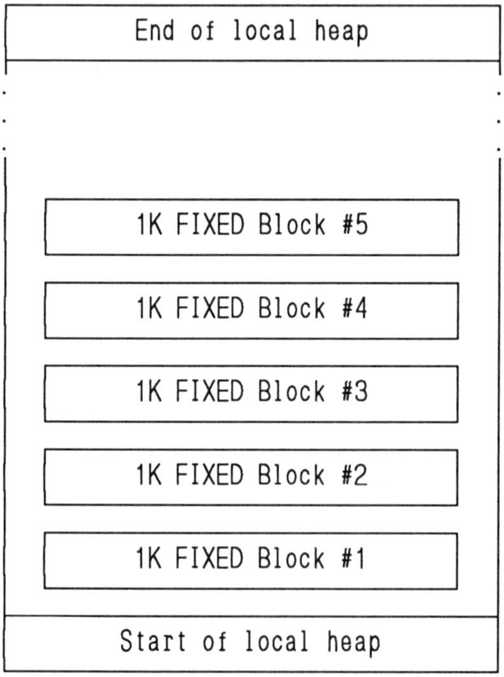

Local heap after allocating five fixed blocks

Now let's assume that blocks #2 and #4 are no longer needed, so you use LocalFree to remove them from the heap. The following illustration shows the local heap after freeing those two blocks.

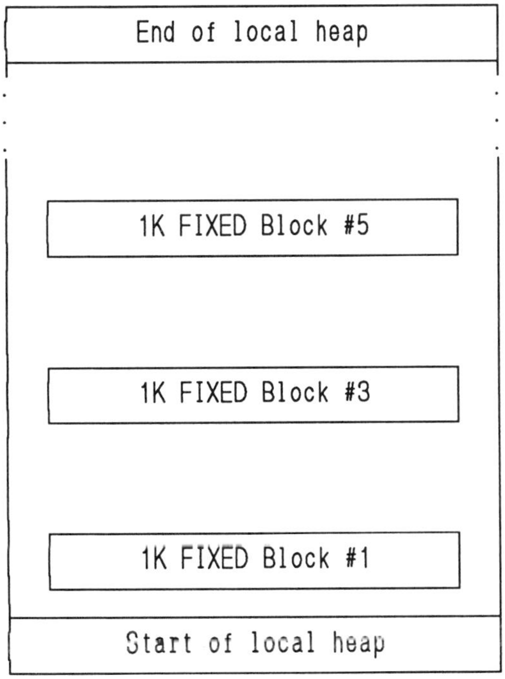

Local heap after freeing fixed blocks #2 and #4

Notice that the positions of blocks #1, #3 and #5 remain unchanged. This gives the programmer a few advantages, too. For example, long pointers to fixed data blocks retain their validity until the element is deleted. However, as the rest of the example shows, you should avoid fixed segments whenever possible.

Now you need another object that is 1.5K in size. Since it won't fit in one of the 1K spaces between block #1 and #3 or between #3 and #5, the memory manager places it above the last fixed block. If there are already moveable data objects, they have to be moved so that the fixed block has room. The following illustration shows what happens.

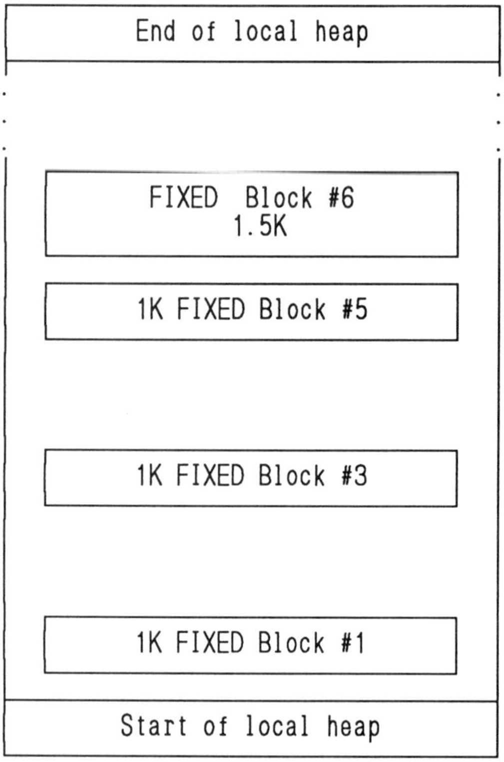

Local heap after allocating block #6

This example clearly shows that fixed segments have a hidden danger of fragmenting memory space, resulting in empty spaces that can no longer be used. In extreme cases it is impossible for the memory manager to create new segments, even though there would be enough free memory in the form of empty spaces. The next segment attribute shows how to counter this danger.

Moveable segments

The Windows memory manager can move these segments anywhere within the available system memory. We use the previous example to show what this means. We assume that blocks #1 to #6 have been allocated with the MOVEABLE attribute. As you can see from the following illustration, the memory manager used the request for a new, 1.5K block as a reason to compact the heap, in order to remove the gaps caused by freeing blocks #2 and #4. This makes room for the new element, without increasing the total requirements for heap space.

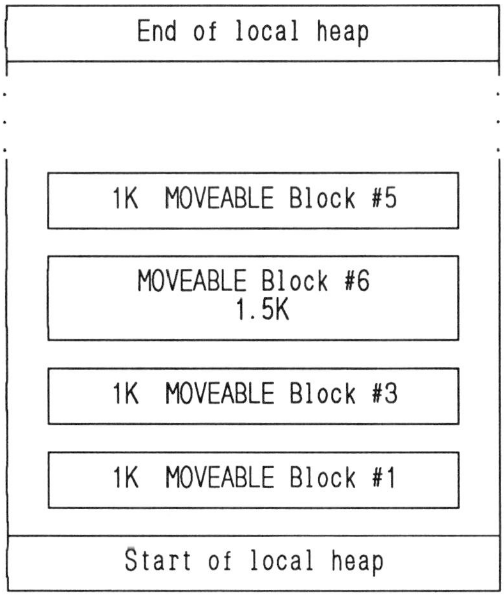

Local heap after allocating block #5

In such a move, all of the NEAR pointers related to this segment keep their validity, since their kind of addressing always refers to the current segment address. The pointer always contains only the offset value. In contrast to this, FAR pointers lose their validity when blocks are moved, since they contain the segment start address as well as the offset.

Discardable segments

Discardable segments are the third type of attribute. This attribute tells the memory manager that it is allowed to remove such a segment from the main memory if necessary for processing a memory requirement. This kind of memory optimization shouldn't be confused with swapping, where swapped files are backed up to one file - the swap file - and reloaded in the main memory when necessary.

In contrast to swapping, DISCARDABLE segments are actually thrown away. There is no data backup. As we will show you later, it's not necessary to back up. If the segment is a code segment, when you try to reaccess it, the memory manager reloads it directly from the *.EXE file of the appropriate application. Along with code segments, resources and segments that haven't been changed ("read only") after loading an application can also be designated as discardable.

When you declare a segment as DISCARDABLE, the memory manager assumes that the segment is also moveable, since there is no guarantee the memory manager will put it back in the same place where it got it. When the memory manager chooses which segment to swap, it uses the "Least Recently Used" algorithm (LRU). This algorithm always selects the segment that hasn't been accessed for the longest time.

16.12 Module Definition Files

There are defined attributes within the module definition file which can have a great influence on how an application runs and acts. We have already demonstrated the effects the three attributes, FIXED, MOVEABLE and DISCARDABLE can have on the memory area. We also covered the definition of heap and stack size, so that we only give a brief explanation here.

HEAPSIZE

HEAPSIZE defines the minimum size of the private data field, which Windows must make available to the application at the start of the program. However, Windows has the capacity to dynamically adapt the size of the local heap to the runtime requirements of an application, so the application can also request more space than specified in the module definition file.

STACKSIZE

This defined value specifies the size of the local stack. The stack should be at least 5K in size for Windows applications; 8K would be even better. In contrast to the size of the local heap, the defined stacksize is a fixed size that you cannot change for runtime.

Let's turn to the attributes that we haven't discussed yet. First let's talk about the loading behavior of an application. For example, you can have the entire program load into the main memory at once, or else have parts of the program download later. You use the following attribute to achieve this:

LOADONCALL

A segment with this attribute waits until you access it in the course of the program before loading to the main memory.

PRELOAD

Unlike the LOADONCALL segment, a segment with the PRELOAD attribute loads into the main memory the same time the application loads.

CODE

In principle, the attributes under CODE are valid for all code segments. The only exceptions are the segments that are listed by name under SEGMENTS. Here is an example: All segments except CodeSeg1 are supposed to be fixed and loaded during the startup phase of the application. CodeSeg1, on the other hand, should be moveable and discardable.

```
CODE   PRELOAD        ; Note: You don't have to specify FIXED
                      ; since it's the default setting
SEGMENTS
     CodeSeg1  MOVEABLE  DISCARDABLE  ; explicitly for CodeSeg1
```

DATA All the data segments not named under SEGMENTS are combined under DATA. Aside from the memory and load attributes of the CODE segment, these segments are different in another way.

Attributes for automatic data segments

MULTIPLE The MULTIPLE attribute, together with DATA, tells Windows to assign its own automatic data segment to every instance of an application. With the exception of dynamic link libraries (DLLs), that only occur in a single instance, all of the applications are defined with the DATA MULTIPLE attribute.

SINGLE Always define dynamic link libraries with this attribute. You should only designate other applications as SINGLE in exceptional cases, since this attribute causes all of the instances of the application to share one automatic data segment.

Note: The automatic data segment contains the task header, the stack, static data and the local heap of an application.

The following overview shows the default values of the resource compiler. Note that the default setting depends on whether or not the corresponding keyword in the resource file *.RC is executed.

Type	Memory flag	Load option	Comments
CODE	FIXED	LOADONCALL	Default setting with keyword
	MOVEABLE	PRELOAD	Default setting without keyword
	DISCARDABLE		Use only with MOVEABLE
DATA	FIXED	LOADONCALL	Default setting with keyword
	MOVEABLE	PRELOAD	Default setting without keyword
	DISCARDABLE		Use only with MOVEABLE

Segment types, their attributes and default settings

Data types	Automatic data segments	Comments
Standard application	MULTIPLE	Essential for giving each instance its own auto segment
Dynamic Link Library	SINGLE	DLLs have one instance only instead of multiples

Automatic data segments and their types

SEGMENTS You use this keyword to assign the attribute segments. This setting takes priority over the attributes set by CODE or DATA. Use the following syntax to assign an attribute:

```
<SegName> [CLASS <SegTyp>] [Memoryattribute] [Loadattribute]

    CODE or DATA
    MOVEABLE, FIXED
    PRELOAD, LOADONCALL
```

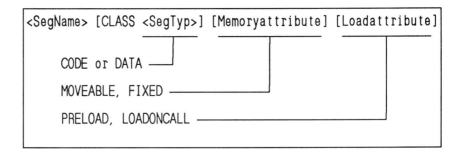

<SegName> represents the name of the segment, for which you are setting the attribute. Here's how to assign a name to a segment. As a rule the C compiler is in charge of this task. Ordinarily, it automatically gives the name "_TEXT" to C library functions and the start code in the code segment of the program. Also, it gives all of the functions within a source file their own code names. These code names are ordinarily made up of the name of the source file and "_TEXT".

However, if you would like to name the code segments yourself, use the switch "-NT <SegName>" during the compiling process.

Name of C source file	Standard segment name	Individual name using -NT
MAINPRG.C	MAINPRG_TEXT	cl .. -NT MainSeg ..
FCT_ONE.C	FCT_ONE_TEXT	cl .. -NT FctOneSeg ..
FCT_TWO.C	FCT_TWO_TEXT	cl .. -NT FctTwoSeg ..

Naming code segments

16.13 Windows Application Structure

Here are the elements of file structure necessary in designing a Windows application.

- Data and stack are in one segment, the automatic data segment.

- Compiler switches (e.g., -Gw for Microsoft C) create a Windows-specific prolog and epilog for all FAR functions. The frame, which is made of prolog and epilog, enables the functions to access parameters that are passed to them and place them on the stack. The functions also place their local variables on this stack. If you compile a short Windows program, using the -Fa switch, you can take a look at the ASSEMBLER listing prolog and epilog:

Windows Prolog	
NEAR functions	FAR functions

PUSH BP
MOV BP,SP
SUB SP,X
	PUSH DS
	POP AX
	NOP
	INC BP
	PUSH BP
	MOV BP,SP
	PUSH DS
	MOV DS,AX
	SUB SP

Windows Epilog	
NEAR functions	FAR functions

MOV SP,BP
POP BP
RET
	SUB BP,2
	MOV SP,BP
	POP DS
	POP BP
	DEC BP
	RET y

- Windows function references are always FAR calls, since these functions are in a different code segment than the application that calls them.

- Data transfer to Windows functions always by FAR pointer. The SMALL and MEDIUM models are best suited for creating Windows applications. In both models, you address all of the data in the data segment using NEAR pointers. This means, however, that such pointers, if they are to be passed to Windows functions (which are exclusively FAR functions), have to first be cast as FAR or LONG pointers.

```
LPSTR lPtr;           // Long-Pointer
PTR   nPtr;           // NEAR Pointer
lPtr = (LPSTR) nPtr; //
```

A CAST instruction causes the C compiler to add the segment address from the DS register to the contents of the NEAR pointer, and then pass this value to the Windows function. Here's what it looks like in assembler code:

```
MOV AX, WORD PTR _nPtr
MOV WORD PTR _lPtr, AX
MOV WORD PTR _lPtr+2, DS
```

Such castings are dangerous, because the long pointer loses its validity if the memory manager moves the segment. To be able to work correctly with such cast long pointers, we should try to determine when the memory manager moves segments (i.e., when long pointers can lose their validity).

Since Windows works in accordance with the message polling principle, long pointers are only in danger of losing their validity when users temporarily quit the function where such a casting occurred, making it possible for the memory manager to distinguish segments. However, this is only possible if you call such Windows functions as GetMessage, PeekMessage or WaitMessage. That means that the validity is preserved within the top down processing of a program fragment.

- If Windows calls Windows or other Callback functions, they are also always FAR calls.

16.14 Fine Tuning

Allocating fixed data

Avoid requesting room for a fixed data element if you have already created moveable elements. Since the memory manager is anxious to always place fixed objects as close as possible to the beginning of the local heap, the succeeding moveable objects must be reorganized to make room for the new element. These kinds of operations require a lot of computer time.

Dividing the code segments

While it is true that you should keep the size of the code segments small, when you think about dividing them, remember that there are also disadvantages to doing this. While you use NEAR calls to execute the function references within a code segment, you use a FAR call for a segment spanned call. As we already mentioned, every FAR call also results in an overhead using function prologs and epilogs.

Error messages for memory shortage

While you're using Windows, it's possible that you will reach the limit of available memory in the system. Although it is difficult to inform the user of this situation, it's not impossible if you keep the following points in mind.

1) Use a message box to display the message, since the code for creating such a box is always kept in the memory.

2) Set the MB_SYSTEMMODAL flag, so that the user can't activate another application.

3) Use the resource specified by IDI_HANDICON as a symbol, since it also always remains in the memory.

4) Since it's impossible to download resources (e.g., from Stringtable) when a memory shortage occurs, you should be prepared. It's wise to place a message text in the data segment as soon as possible, so that you can access it in emergencies.

Appendices

A The Companion Diskette

The companion diskette contains all of the sample programs in this book both in source text and in executable form. The file WINSYS.EXE is an archive file containing all of these files. The companion diskette also contains a short batch file named INSTALL.BAT, which unpacks the archived files onto your hard drive.

Use the following procedure to unpack:

- Use MKDIR or MD to create a subdirectory on your hard drive, if you wish to store the companion diskette files in a new directory, or use an existing directory.
- Copy WINSYS.EXE and INSTALL.BAT to the subdirectory on your hard drive. There should be at least 1 Meg of available memory space on the drive.
- Type INSTALL and press the <Enter> key to start unpacking.

INSTALL creates all of the necessary subdirectories automatically, and then copies the corresponding files from the archive to these subdirectories.

Companion diskette contents:

```
INSTALL.BAT     ;Batch file for unpacking the archive
WINSYS.EXE      ;Archive file
README.BAT      ;Current information, be sure to run it!
README1.TXT     ;First page of README information
README2.TXT     ;Second page of README information
```

The archive file, WINSYS.EXE, was created with the LHARC program (Copyright by Haruyasu Yoshizaki). If you have this program, you can also selectively extract only those sections of the program in which you are interested. The procedure for doing this is described in the guide to LHARC.

```
ADDRBOOK <DIR>              ;Address book application (Chapter 7)|
    ADDRBOOK.C
    ADDRBOOK.DEF
    ADDRBOOK.DLG
    ADDRBOOK.EXE
    ADDRBOOK.H
    ADDRBOOK.ICO
    ADDRBOOK.MAK
    ADDRBOOK.RC
    ADDRUTIL.C

CLPBOARD <DIR>              ;Clipboard/serial demonstration (Chapters 9, 10 and 14)
    CLOSECUT.BMP
    CLOSEPIN.BMP
    CLP_RC.H
    CLPBOARD.C
    CLPDEMO.C
    CLPDEMO.DEF
    CLPDEMO.DLG
    CLPDEMO.EXE
    CLPDEMO.ICO
    CLPDEMO.MAK
    CLPDEMO.RC
    CLPFILE.C
    CLPFILE.H
    CLPINTRO.C
    CLPLINE.C
    CLPPARAM.C
    CLPPARAM.H
    CLPSELEC.C
    OPENCUT.BMP
    OPENPIN.BMP

DDE <DIR>                   ;Program Manager remote control using DDE (Chapter 11)
    DDE.DLG
    DDE_DDE.C
    DDE_DLG.C
    DDE_EXE.C
    DDE_EXE.DEF
    DDE_EXE.DLG
    DDE_EXE.EXE
    DDE_EXE.H
    DDE_EXE.ICO
    DDE_EXE.MAK
    DDE_EXE.RC
```

```
DIALOG <DIR>                    ;Music database demonstrating dialog boxes (Chapter 4)
    DBOXDEMO.C
    DBOXDEMO.DEF
    DBOXDEMO.DLG
    DBOXDEMO.EXE
    DBOXDEMO.H
    DBOXDEMO.ICO
    DBOXDEMO.MAK
    DBOXDEMO.RC
    MUSIC.DAT

DIVERSE <DIR>                   ;Text output under Windows (Chapter 3)
    DIVERSE.C
    DIVERSE.DEF
    DIVERSE.EXE
    DIVERSE.H
    DIVERSE.MAK
    DIVERSE.RC

DLL <DIR>                       ;Sample DLL as trace utility (Chapter 15)
    ADDTRACE.C
    ADDTRACE.DEF
    ADDTRACE.DLG
    ADDTRACE.EXE
    ADDTRACE.H
    ADDTRACE.ICO
    ADDTRACE.MAK
    ADDTRACE.RC
    ADDTUTIL.C
    TRACEDLL.C
    TRACEDLL.DEF
    TRACEDLL.DLL
    TRACEDLL.LIB
    TRACEDLL.MAK

DYNDLG <DIR>                    ;Dynamic dialog box creation (Chapter 4)
    DYNDLG.C
    DYNDLG.H
    DYN_DEMO.C
    DYN_DEMO.DEF
    DYN_DEMO.EXE
    DYN_DEMO.H
    DYN_DEMO.MAK
    DYN_DEMO.RC
```

```
EYES <DIR>                    ;The EYES application (Chapter 6)
    EYES.C
    EYES.DEF
    EYES.DLG
    EYES.EXE
    EYES.H
    EYES.INI
    EYES.MAK
    EYES.RC

GRAPHICS <DIR>                ;GDI graphic functions (Chapter 5)
    GDIDEMO.C
    GDIDEMO.DEF
    GDIDEMO.DLG
    GDIDEMO.EXE
    GDIDEMO.H
    GDIDEMO.ICO
    GDIDEMO.MAK
    GDIDEMO.RC

HOOK <DIR>                    ;DDE hook monitoring using filters (Chapter 12)
    CPHOOK.C
    CPHOOK.DEF
    CPHOOK.DLG
    CPHOOK.EXE
    CPHOOK.ICO
    CPHOOK.MAK
    CPHOOK.RC
    CPHOOKRC.H
    HOOK.DLL
    HOOK.LIB
----- DLL <DIR>               ;DLL containing hook function
            HOOK.C
            HOOK.DEF
            HOOK.DLL
            HOOK.LIB
            HOOK.MAK

MDI <DIR>                     ;Multiple Document Interface demonstration (Chapter 8)
    MDICHILD.ICO
    MDIFRAME.ICO
    MDI_DEMO.C
    MDI_DEMO.DEF
    MDI_DEMO.DLG
    MDI_DEMO.EXE
    MDI_DEMO.H
    MDI_DEMO.ICO
    MDI_DEMO.MAK
```

```
    MDI_DEMO.RC
    MDI_INFO.C
    MDI_PROP.C
    MDI_RC.H

PRINTER <DIR>                ;Printed output (Chapter 13)
    ENUMFONT.C
    NDEVMODE.C
    ODEVMODE.C
----- JUSTIFY <DIR>          ;Text formatting and WYSIWYG
            DOPRINT.C
            JUSTIFY.C
            JUSTIFY.DEF
            JUSTIFY.EXE
            JUSTIFY.H
            JUSTIFY.ICO
            JUSTIFY.RC
            MAKEFILE
            RESOURCE.H
----- WINPRNT1 <DIR>         ;Minimum printing application
            DOPRINT.C
            MAKEFILE
            RESOURCE.H
            WINPRINT.C
            WINPRINT.DEF
            WINPRINT.EXE
            WINPRINT.H
            WINPRINT.ICO
            WINPRINT.RC
----- WINPRNT2 <DIR>         ;Improved printing application
            DOPRINT.C
            MAKEFILE
            RESOURCE.H
            WINPRINT.C
            WINPRINT.DEF
            WINPRINT.EXE
            WINPRINT.H
            WINPRINT.ICO
            WINPRINT.RC
----- WINPRNT3 <DIR>         ;Banding application
            DOPRINT.C
            MAKEFILE
            RESOURCE.H
            WINPRINT.C
            WINPRINT.DEF
            WINPRINT.EXE
            WINPRINT.H
```

```
            WINPRINT.ICO
            WINPRINT.RC

STRUCTUR <DIR>           ;Structure of a Windows application (Chapter 2)
    STRUCTUR.C
    STRUCTUR.DEF
    STRUCTUR.EXE
    STRUCTUR.H
    STRUCTUR.MAK
    STRUCTUR.RC

UNPACK.BAT               ;Batch file for unpacking the archive
WINSYS.EXE               ;Archive file
README.TXT               ;Current information, be sure to read it!
```

B The ASCII Table

Dec	Hex	Char	Dec	Hex	Char	Dec	Hex	Char	Dec	Hex	Char
0	00		32	20		64	40	@	96	60	`
1	01	☺	33	21	!	65	41	A	97	61	a
2	02	●	34	22	"	66	42	B	98	62	b
3	03	♥	35	23	#	67	43	C	99	63	c
4	04	♦	36	24	$	68	44	D	100	64	d
5	05	♣	37	25	%	69	45	E	101	65	e
6	06	♠	38	26	&	70	46	F	102	66	f
7	07	•	39	27	'	71	47	G	103	67	g
8	08	◘	40	28	(	72	48	H	104	68	h
9	09	o	41	29	)	73	49	I	105	69	i
10	0A	◙	42	2A	*	74	4A	J	106	6A	j
11	0B	k	43	2B	+	75	4B	K	107	6B	k
12	0C	♀	44	2C	,	76	4C	L	108	6C	l
13	0D	♪	45	2D	-	77	4D	M	109	6D	m
14	0E	♫	46	2E	.	78	4F	N	110	6E	n
15	0F	☼	47	2F	/	79	4F	O	111	6F	o
16	10	►	48	30	0	80	50	P	112	70	p
17	11	◄	49	31	1	81	51	Q	113	71	q
18	12	↕	50	32	2	82	52	R	114	72	r
19	13	‼	51	33	3	83	53	S	115	73	s
20	14	¶	52	34	4	84	54	T	116	74	t
21	15	§	53	35	5	85	55	U	117	75	u
22	16	▬	54	36	6	86	56	V	118	76	v
23	17	↨	55	37	7	87	57	W	119	77	w
24	18	↑	56	38	8	88	58	X	120	78	x
25	19	↓	57	39	9	89	59	Y	121	79	y
26	1A	→	58	3A	:	90	5A	Z	122	7A	z
27	1B	←	59	3B	;	91	5B	[	123	7B	{
28	1C	∟	60	3C	<	92	5C	\	124	7C	|
29	1D	↔	61	3D	=	93	5D	]	125	7D	}
30	1E	-	62	3E	>	94	5E	^	126	7E	~
31	1F		63	3F	?	95	5F	_	127	7F	Δ

Dec	Hex	Char	Dec	Hex	Char	Dec	Hex	Char	Dec	Hex	Char
128	80	Ç	160	A0	á	192	C0	└	224	E0	α
129	81	ü	161	A1	í	193	C1	┴	225	E1	β
130	82	é	162	A2	ó	194	C2	┬	226	E2	Γ
131	83	â	163	A3	ú	195	C3	├	227	E3	π
132	84	ä	164	A4	ñ	196	C4	─	228	E4	Σ
133	85	à	165	A5	Ñ	197	C5	┼	229	E5	σ
134	86	å	166	A6	ª	198	C6	╞	230	E6	µ
135	87	ç	167	A7	º	199	C7	╟	231	E7	τ
136	88	ê	168	A8	¿	200	C8	╚	232	E8	Φ
137	89	ë	169	A9	⌐	201	C9	╔	233	E9	Θ
138	8A	è	170	AA	¬	202	CA	╩	234	EA	Ω
139	8B	ï	171	AB	½	203	CB	╦	235	EB	δ
140	8C	î	172	AC	¼	204	CC	╠	236	EC	∞
141	8D	ì	173	AD	¡	205	CD	═	237	ED	Ø
142	8E	Ä	174	AE	«	206	CE	╬	238	EE	∈
143	8F	Å	175	AF	»	207	CF	╧	239	EF	∩
144	90	É	176	B0	░	208	D0	╨	240	F0	≡
145	91	æ	177	B1	▒	209	D1	╤	241	F1	±
146	92	Æ	178	B2	▓	210	D2	╥	242	F2	≥
147	93	ô	179	B3	│	211	D3	╙	243	F3	≤
148	94	ö	180	B4	┤	212	D4	╘	244	F4	⌠
149	95	ò	181	B5	╡	213	D5	╒	245	F5	⌡
150	96	û	182	B6	╢	214	D6	╓	246	F6	÷
151	97	ù	183	B7	╖	215	D7	╫	247	F7	≈
152	98	ÿ	184	B8	╕	216	D8	╪	248	F8	°
153	99	Ö	185	B9	╣	217	D9	┘	249	F9	•
154	9A	Ü	186	BA	║	218	DA	┌	250	FA	·
155	9B	¢	187	BB	╗	219	DB	█	251	FB	√
156	9C	£	188	BC	╝	220	DC	▄	252	FC	^{n}
157	9D	¥	189	BD	╜	221	DD	▌	253	FD	^{2}
158	9E	₧	190	BE	╛	222	DE	▐	254	FE	■
159	9F	ƒ	191	BF	┐	223	DF	▀	255	FF	

Index

Abacus pc catalog

Order Toll Free 1-800-451-4319

5370 52nd Street SE • Grand Rapids, MI 49512
Phone: (616) 698-0330 • Fax: (616) 698-0325

Beginners Books for new PC Users

Beginners Series books remove the confusing jargon and get you up and running quickly with your PC.

PC and Compatible Computers for Beginners - For the absolute newcomer to personal computers. Describes the PC and all of its components in a non-technical way. Introduces DOS commands.
ISBN 1-55755-060-3 $18.95
Canada: 52072 $22.95

MS-DOS for Beginners - Describes the most important DOS commands clearly and understandably. Teaches skills required to use your PC more effectively.
ISBN 1-55755-061-1 $18.95
Canada: 52071 $22.95

UNIX for Beginners - Clearly describes this popular operating system, Logon procedures, file concepts and commands using simple and clear examples.
ISBN 1-55755-065-4 $18.95
Canada: 52073 $22.95

Lotus 1-2-3 for Beginners - Presents the basics with examples, clearly, without using confusing 'computer jargon'. Includes Release 2.2 information.
ISBN 1-55755-066-2 $18.95
Canada: 52069 $22.9

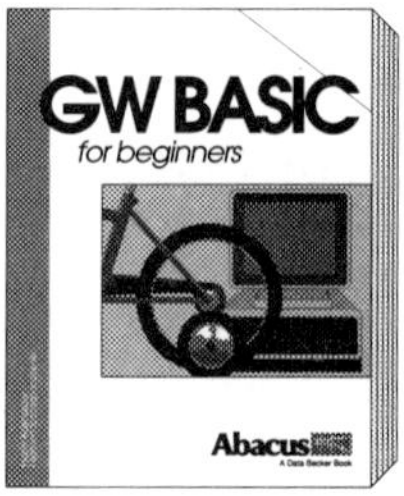

GW-BASIC Programming for Beginners* - A simple introduction to programming the PC using the BASIC language. Learn many of the commands writing sample programs and taking chapter quizzes.
ISBN 1-55755-062-X $18.95
Canada: 52068 $22.95

*Companion Disk available for $14.95 each ($19.95 CDN)

To order direct call Toll Free 1-800-451-4319

In US and Canada add $5.00 shipping and handling. Foreign orders add $13.00 per item.
Michigan residents add 4% sales tax.

Beginners Books for new PC Users

Beginners Series books remove the confusing jargon and get you up and running quickly with your PC.

COBOL for Beginners* - Teaches this popular language using MBP, MicroFocus and Microsoft COBOL. Includes quizzes, explanations and demonstrations.
ISBN 1-55755-070-0 $18.95
Canada: 53904 $22.95

dBASE IV for Beginners - Simply and easily explains the fundamentals of dBASE. Learn to operate this package quickly and use its powerful commands and functions.
ISBN 1-55755-069-7 $18.95
Canada: 52066 $22.95

QuickBASIC for Beginners - Learn QuickBASIC quickly and easily. Begins by teaching you to write small and simple applications to simplify your everyday tasks.Complete descriptions of all QuickBASIC commands.
ISBN 1-55755-111-1. $18.95
Canada: $22.95

DOS 5.0 for Beginners - Gets the new user up and running quickly using Microsoft's latest DOS 5.0. You'll find clear explanations and plenty of "hands on" examples here. Describes the most important DOS commands clearly and understandably.
ISBN 1-55755-112-X. $18.95
Canada: $22.95

WordPerfect for Beginners - Contains all the important information about WordPerfect.Learn the essentials of WordPerfect's command set through practical examples - from writing a letter to composing longer documents.
ISBN 1-55755-117-0. $18.95
Canada: $22.95

*Companion Disk available for $14.95 each ($19.95 CDN)

To order direct call Toll Free 1-800-451-4319

In US and Canada add $5.00 shipping and handling. Foreign orders add $13.00 per item. Michigan residents add 4% sales tax.

Developer's Series Books

Developers Series books are for the professional software developer that requires in-depth technical information and programming techniques.

PC System Programming is a literal encyclopedia of technical and programming knowledge. Features parallel working examples in Pascal, C, ML and BASIC. Explains memory layout, DOS operations and interrupts from ML and high level languages, using extended, expanded memory, device drivers, hard disks, PC ports, mouse driver programming, fundamentals of BIOS, graphics and sound programming, TSR programs and complete appendices. 930 page book and two disks with over 1MB of source code.
ISBN 1-55755-036-0. $59.95
Canada: 52444 $74.95

What readers are saying about
PC System Programming:

"The day I saw this book I bought it" F.R.

"Excellent work" G.O.

"This book is such a good reference and so complete and in-depth, I keep it next to my system reference manuals and my compiler manuals" J.K.

"Best written PC language book I've seen" AVR, Tulsa, OK.

Turbo Pascal System Programming gives you the *know how* to write better, faster, tighter and easier code using the popular Turbo Pascal system. Author Michael Tischer has written this book for other pros who need to understand the ins and outs of using Turbo for their programming projects.

Turbo Pascal System Programming details dozens of important subjects including writing Terminate and Stay Resident (TSR) programs using Turbo; building windows and menus; using expanded and extended memory; writing multi-tasking programs; understanding Turbo's memory management; combining assembly language with Turbo programs; using interrupts for system programming tasks; accessing the hardware directly and more.
750 page book includes two disks with more than 800K of source code.
ISBN 1-55755-124-3. $44.95 Available August.
Canada: 53910 $64.95

To order direct call Toll Free 1-800-451-4319

In US and Canada add $5.00 shipping and handling. Foreign orders add $13.00 per item.
Michigan residents add 4% sales tax.

Developer's Series Books

BASIC Programming: Inside & Out

The standard reference for all GW-BASIC, BASIC, QuickBASIC and Turbo BASIC programmers who want to be better programmers. Includes demo programs and routines you can easily adapt to your own programs. Describes sound and graphics, programming business presentation graphics, window management in PC-BASIC, using machine language, BASIC compilers, database management, create help screen editor, using pulldown menus, print multiple column and sideways and more. 600 page book with companion disk containing 360K of BASIC source code.
ISBN 1-55755-084-0. $34.95
Canada: 54384 $45.95

Computer Viruses & Data Protection

describes the relatively new phenomenon among personal computer users, one that has the potential to destroy large amounts of data stored in PC systems. Simply put, this book explains what a virus is, how it works and what can be done to protect your PC against destruction.
ISBN 1-55755-123-5. $19.95
Canada: 52089 $25.95

To order direct call Toll Free 1-800-451-4319

In US and Canada add $5.00 shipping and handling. Foreign orders add $13.00 per item. Michigan residents add 4% sales tax.

QuickBASIC Toolbox
is for all QuickBASIC programmers who want professional results with minimum effort. It's packed with powerful, ready-to-use programs and routines you can use in your own programs to get professional results quickly.

Some of the topics include:

- Complete routines for SAA, interfacing mouse support, pull-down menus, windows, dialog boxes and file requestors.
- Descriptions of QuickBASIC routines.
- A BASIC Scanner program for printing completed project listings and more.

This book/disk combination will teach you how to write even better QuickBASIC code.
330 page book with companion disk.
ISBN 1-55755-104-9 $34.95
Canada: 57911 $45.95

Assembly Language Step by Step
For lightning execution speed, no computer language beats assembly language. This book teaches you PC assembly and machine language the right way - one step at a time. The companion diskette contains a unique simulator which shows you how each instruction functions as the PC executes it. Includes companion diskette containing assembly language simulator.
ISBN 1-55755-096-4. $34.95
Canada: 53927 $45.95

To order direct call Toll Free 1-800-451-4319
In US and Canada add $5.00 shipping and handling. Foreign orders add $13.00 per item.
Michigan residents add 4% sales tax.

Productivity Series Books

Productivity Series books are for users who want to become more productive with their PC.

Tips & Tricks for your PC Printer
Describes how printers work, basic printer configurations using DIP switches, using MS-DOS commands for simple printer control. Includes utilities on a 5.25" companion diskette to demonstrate popular software commands. Useful printer accessories, font editor and printing tricks and tips. 400 pp. with companion disk containing essential printer utilities.
ISBN 1-55755-075-1. $34.95
Canada: 53903 $45.95

Laser Printer PowerTools
shows you how to harness all the capabilities built into your HP-compatible laser printer quickly and easily. You'll learn about both the built-in and add-on fonts, the whys and hows of printing graphics, understanding the Printer Control Language (PCL) and how to set up dozens of applications to get the most from your laser printer. The companion disk includes programs for printing ASCII files, initializing margins and fonts; printing soft fonts, using Word printer drivers, converting ASCII files to print characters. It also includes many sample files you can use to get the most out of your printer.

350 page book with companion disk.
ISBN 1-55755-095-6 $34.95
Canada: 53925 $45.95

To order direct call Toll Free 1-800-451-4319

In US and Canada add $5.00 shipping and handling. Foreign orders add $13.00 per item.
Michigan residents add 4% sales tax.

Upgrading & Maintaining your PC

Your PC represents a major investment. This book shows you how to turn your PC into a high performance computing machine. It describes what you'll see when you open the "hood" and how all of the parts work together. Whether you want to add a hard drive, increase your memory, upgrade to a higher resolution monitor, or turn your XT into a fast AT or 386 screamer, you'll see how to do it easily and economically, without having to be an electronics wizard.

ISBN 1-55755-092-1. $24.95

Canada: 53926 $33.95

Batch files make your computer sessions easier. **Batch File Powertools** shows you how to use powerful, easy-to-learn techniques for many DOS applications. You'll boost your computing productivity with these techniques for making truly powerful batch files. **Batch File Powertools** includes dozens of new batch commands for writing time-saving, easy-to-use "power" batch files.

Batch File Powertools includes BatchBASIC on the companion disk. BatchBASIC adds dozens of new commands to DOS to help increase your computing productivity. The companion disk also contains dozens of practical examples.

ISBN 1-55755-102-2. $34.95

Canada: $45.95

Stepping up to DR DOS 5.0

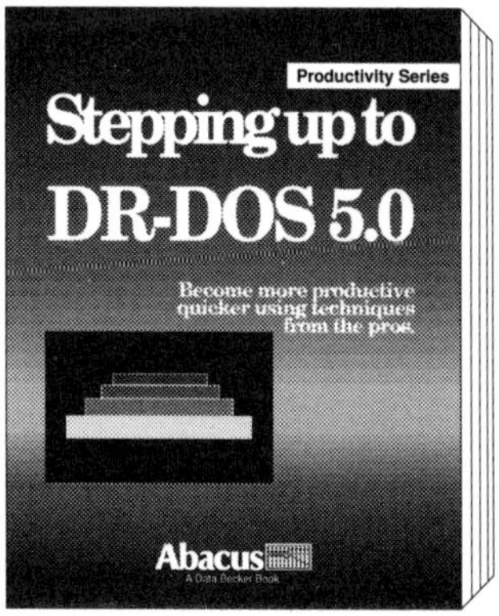

DR DOS 5.0 is a new alternative operating system to MS-DOS. Its many new features overcome some of the limitations that users find in MS-DOS.

This fast paced guide shows you the most important features of DR DOS 5.0. It presents practical examples to get you going quickly with DR DOS 5.0. It takes you step-by-step through the world of DR DOS 5.0. You'll find clear explanations and many "hands on" examples on using DR DOS. Learn the information you'll need to become more productive with DR DOS. 210 pages.

ISBN 1-55755-106-5. $14.95

Canada: 57913 $19.95

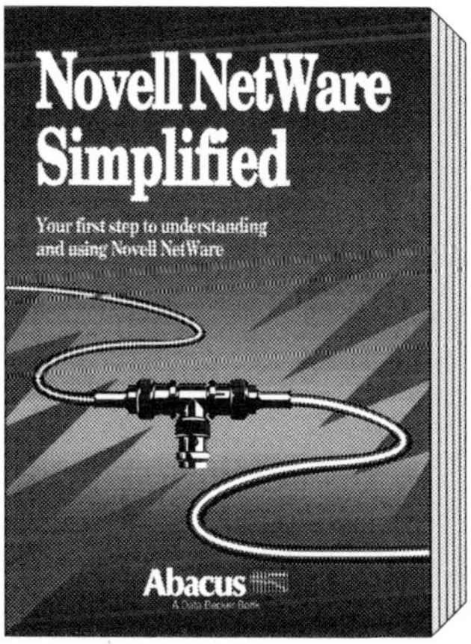

Novell NetWare Simplified answers many questions about file servers and workstations using the most popular LAN system. **Novell NetWare Simplified** is your first step to understanding and using Novell NetWare more effectively.

Some of the topics include:

- Installing extra printers and PC workstations.
- Memory requirements for each user.
- Sending messages through your systems.
- Developing a user-friendly menu system and more.

ISBN 1-55755-105-7. $24.95

Canada: 57910 $3395

To order direct call Toll Free 1-800-451-4319

In US and Canada add $5.00 shipping and handling. Foreign orders add $13.00 per item. Michigan residents add 4% sales tax.

Productivity Series Books

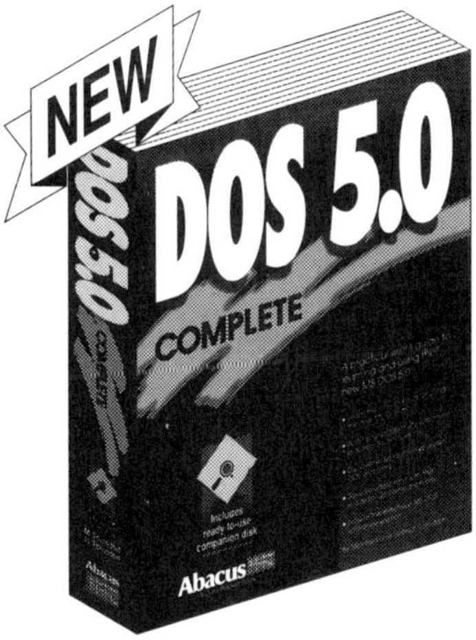

DOS 5.0 Complete

Not just another reference book - **DOS 5.0 Complete** is a practical user's guide to learning and using Microsoft's new DOS. It's an encyclopedia of DOS knowledge not only for the computer whiz but for the everyday user.

DOS 5.0 Complete is loaded with helpful hints for outfitting any computer with MS-DOS 5.0. From installing DOS 5.0 to using the new features for file, directory and storage maintenance you'll find techniques and hints here.

DOS 5.0 Complete has dozens of easy to follow examples. This book explains AUTOEXEC.BAT and CONFIG.SYS. The detailed explanations make this the most authoritative DOS book available. The friendly, easy to understand writing style insures that even beginners will grasp the fundamentals quickly and easily. And you'll find a complete DOS command reference.

Topics include:

- Learn the "ins and outs" of using the new MS-DOS 5.0
- Boost your productivity with these practical techniques
- Discover ways to solve your own DOS problems
- Save valuable time with the ready-to-run companion disk.
- Browse the extensive MS-DOS reference section
- Using DOS' new memory management features
- Using the improved SHELL ;for performing your computer housekeeping ;chores
- Using the new DOSKEY utility for faster command line editing and macro power.
- Using EDIT, the new full-screen editor
- Using QBASIC, DOS' new BASIC programming language
- Complete DOS command reference.

DOS 5.0 Complete includes a companion disk with example batch files, detailed explanations, and powerful tips and tricks to help you get the most out of MS-DOS 5.0. **DOS 5.0 Complete** will become THE source for reference information about DOS 5.0.

DOS 5.0 Complete
Authors: Michael Tornsdorf, Helmut Tornsdorf
ISBN 1-55755-109-X.
Suggested retail price $34.95 with companion disk.

To order direct call Toll Free 1-800-451-4319

In US and Canada add $5.00 shipping and handling. Foreign orders add $13.00 per item.
Michigan residents add 4% sales tax.

Productivity Series Books

Paradox 3.5 Now!
introduces you to this quality relational database without any ifs, ands or buts - from installation to actual operation. Three examples show you how easy it is to work directly with Paradox: an accounting database, a sales report and a library database. You'll learn how to create forms; enter data; edit, sort and search change database structures; generate and print reports; and a lot more. You'll also find tips for importing data, important information about PAL and the Engine.
Available August.
Author: M. Bohmer
ISBN 1-55755-121-9. $12.95

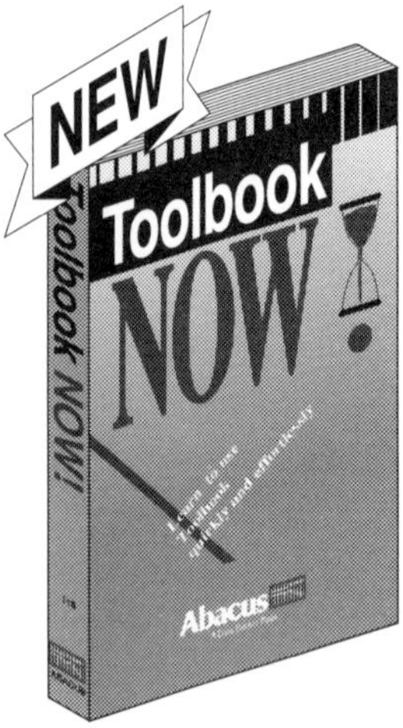

Toolbook Now!
is the effective and fast way to learn about Toolbook's environment and capabilities. Shows you how to manage data; get help through practical examples. You'll learn how to develop new applications and edit existing ones using the OpenScript system included in ToolBook. OpenScript makes it easier to create your own applications to run under Windows. You'll find development will take less time with this book. Includes helpful hints for installation, sample books (applications) like the Quick Tour, Buttons, Pages, Books, Fields, Graphics.
Available August.
Authors: V. Sasse and P. Shulz
ISBN 1-55755-119-7. $12.95

To order direct call Toll Free 1-800-451-4319

In US and Canada add $5.00 shipping and handling. Foreign orders add $13.00 per item.
Michigan residents add 4% sales tax.

Microsoft Windows 3.0 Software

Virus Secure for Windows

Eliminate potential valuable data loss and minimize your risks with Virus Secure.

Don't give viruses the chance to ruin your data when you're using Windows. Avoid virus infection and potential valuable data loss. **Virus Secure for Windows** provides complete data protection for your hard and/or floppy disks from computer virus infection. **Virus Secure** is written by virus authority Ralf Burger (author of Computer Viruses and Data Protection). This is security that will keep your data alive and your PC operations productive.

Virus Secure can be run by both beginning and experienced users. Beginners will like the clear user interface and detailed error system. Experts will like the numerous options offered by **Virus Secure.** Beginning and advanced users will learn how to protect their diskettes and hard drives from unwanted data loss caused by viruses.

Virus Secure can detect over 200 known viruses and has built-in power for recognizing new or unknown viruses. It can also distinguish "normal" changes from "unusual" changes that viruses can make. **Virus Secure** can also be expanded. You can easily expand the recognition of viruses using a standard word processor. **Virus Secure** allows you to stay up to date as new viruses appear in the PC community.

Item #S108, ISBN 1-55755-108-1. Retail price $95.00.
System requirements: PC AT, 386 or compatible, hard drive and Windows 3.0.
Windows not included.

Author Ralf Burger

Windows is a trademark of Microsoft Corporation.

MICROSOFT WINDOWS
Version 3.0 Compatible Product

To order direct call Toll Free 1-800-451-4319

In US and Canada add $5.00 shipping and handling. Foreign orders add $13.00 per item.
Michigan residents add 4% sales tax.

New BeckerTools 2.0 PLUS for Windows:
Indispensable utilities for every Windows user

If you're a Windows user, you'll appreciate **BeckerTools Version 2** for Windows. **BeckerTools** will dramatically speed-up your file and data management chores and increase your productivity. Where Windows' File Manager functions end, **BeckerTools** features begin by giving you powerful, yet flexible features you need to get the job done quickly. **BeckerTools** has the same consistent user interface found in Windows so there's no need to learn 'foreign' commands or functions. Manipulating your disks and files are as easy as pointing and clicking with the mouse. You'll breeze through flexible file and data functions and features that are friendly enough for a PC novice yet powerful enough for the advanced user. You won't find yourself 'dropping out' of Windows to perform powerful, essential DOS functions like undeleting a file or waiting for a diskette to be formatted. **BeckerTools** has the enhanced applications available at the click of a mouse button. Item #S110 ISBN 1-55755-110-3. With 3 1/2" and 5 1/4" diskettes. Suggested retail price $129.95.

Now includes–

BeckerTools Compress
Defragments and optimizes disk performance.
Optimizes your hard disk performance by defragmenting your files and/or disk. Multiple compress option lets you choose the type of optimization.

BeckerTools Recover
Rescues files and disks.
Checks and repairs common file and disk problems-corrupted FAT's, improperly chained clusters, bad files, etc. Could be a "Life-saver".

BeckerTools Backup
Fast, convenient file backup and restore.
File and disk backup/restore at the click of a button. Multiple select options, optional data compression, password protection and more.

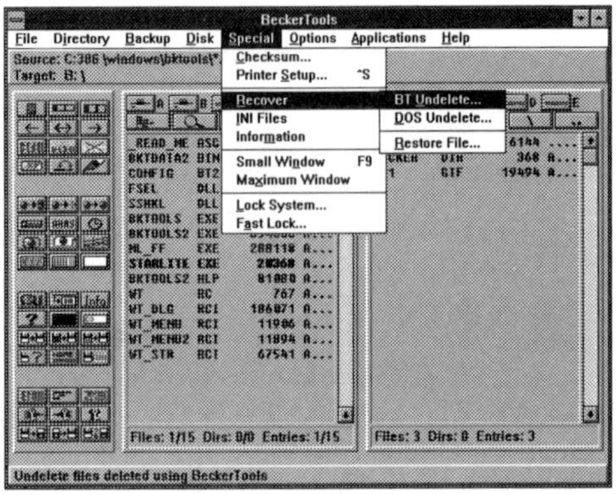

BeckerTools Version 2 Plus is as easy as pointing and clicking with the mouse. **BeckerTools** takes advantage of Windows' multitasking capabilities and **BeckerTools** keeps you informed of its progress as it works.

Here are some of the things that you can easily do with **BeckerTools Version 2:**

- Launch applications - directly from **BeckerTools**
- Associate files - logically connects applications with their file types
- Backup (pack files) hard disk - saves 50% to 80% disk space - with password protection
- User levels - 3 levels for beginning, intermediate and advanced users
- Undelete - recover deleted files
- Undelete directories - recover directories in addition to individual files
- Delete files - single, groups of files or directories, including read-only files
- Duplicate diskettes - read diskette once, make multiple copies
- Edit text - built-in editor with search and replace
- Format diskettes - in any capacity supported by your drive and disk type
- Compare diskettes - in a single pass
- Wipe diskette - for maximum security
- Screen blanker - prevent CRT "burn in"
- File grouping - perform operations on files as a group
- Create a bootable system diskette
- Reliability checking - check for physical errors on disk media
- Edit files - new hex editor to edit virtually and type of file
- Dozens of other indispensable features

To order direct call Toll Free 1-800-451-4319

In US and Canada add $5.00 shipping and handling. Foreign orders add $13.00 per item. Michigan residents add 4% sales tax.